ALSO BY ARTHUR HERTZBERG

The Zionist Idea
The Outbursts That Await Us (coauthor)
Judaism
The French Enlightenment and the Jews
Being Jewish in America

ARTHUR HERTZBERG

THE
JEWS
IN
AMERICA

Four Centuries of an

Uneasy Encounter:

A History

A TOUCHSTONE BOOK
Published by Simon & Schuster Inc.
New York   London   Toronto   Sydney   Tokyo   Singapore

Touchstone
Simon & Schuster Building
Rockefeller Center
1230 Avenue of the Americas
New York, New York 10020

1   3   5   7   9   10   8   6   4   2

1   3   5   7   9   10   8   6   4   2 (pbk.)

Library of Congress Cataloging in Publication Data

Hertzberg, Arthur.
The Jews in America : four centuries of an uneasy
encounter : a history / Arthur Hertzberg.
p.   cm.
1. Jews—United States—History.   2. United
States—Ethnic relations.   I. Title.
E184.J5H566   1989
973'.04924—dc20   89-36191
                                                                        CIP

ISBN 0-671-62709-0
0-671-72505-X (pbk.)

We gratefully acknowledge permission to reprint the following:
"To America," by H. Leyvik. Taken from *American Yiddish
Poetry: A Bilingual Anthology,* edited by Benjamin and Bar-
bara Harshav, the University of California Press. Copy-
right © 1986 The Regents of the University of California.
Used by permission.

"Israel and American Jewry," by Arthur Hertzberg. Reprinted from *Commentary,* August 1967, by permission; all
rights reserved.

Acknowledgments

The most pleasant task of all in writing a book is to remember and thank the many people who have helped. The greatest debt of all, I owe to my father, Harav Zvi Elimelech Herzberg, who was leader of the Chasidic community in Baltimore until his death in 1971. He said many times that American Jews were drawn overwhelmingly from one class of the Jews of Europe, the poor. Testing this remark against the evidence that I collected in research, I concluded that he had understood American Jewish experience better than almost anyone else of the last generation.

Until his untimely death in the fall of 1988, my greatest companion was Shmuel Ettinger, professor at the Hebrew University and the central figure in Jewish historical studies in Israel. In many hours of discussion in Jerusalem or Englewood, New Jersey, we often disagreed, but always agreeably. The Hebrew edition of this book will be dedicated to the memory of this great scholar and beloved friend. Much of this book was first drafted in 1982 in Jerusalem at the Institute of Advanced Studies of the Hebrew University, where I spent most of the year as Fellow. That environment reflected the generosity of spirit and high intellectual standards of the director, Professor Aryeh Dvoretsky. Henry Graff, friend and colleague in the History Department of Columbia University since 1961, helped greatly and generously with puting the specifics of the American Jewish experience in the context of American history as a whole. My colleagues and friends in the Middle East Institute at Columbia, Professors Richard Bulliet, Lisa Anderson, and Gregory Gause, have sustained me in my work.

Since the spring of 1985, I have spent most of the academic year at Dartmouth College in the Department of Religion. The chairmen under whom I have served, Ronald Green and Robert Oden, and all my colleagues in the department, have

ACKNOWLEDGMENTS

helped me to think my way through aspects of this text. Sandra Curtis, the academic assistant of the department, has been extraordinarily supportive. Timothy Duggan and Bernard Gert, of the Philosophy Department at Dartmouth, have been generous with their time and their counsel. On literary matters, the novelist, Alan Lelchuk, has let me impose on his knowledge and his time. Deans Hans Penner and Dwight Lahr, Associate Deans Richard Sheldon and Gregory Prince, and the executive officers Foster Blough and Robert Griesemer have provided student assistants and other forms of support. David McLaughlin and James O. Freedman, his successor as president of Dartmouth, have done everything within their power to help me; I am deeply grateful for their friendship.

This book could not have been written from the study of documents alone. I am indebted to the congregations for what I learned in more than four decades as a rabbi, ten years in Nashville, Tennessee, at the West End Synagogue, and the next twenty-nine years in Englewood, New Jersey, at Temple Emanu-El. Much of what I know about organized Jewish life I learned by being involved since my teens, and especially in the 1970s when I served as president of the American Jewish Congress, and, concurrently, as a member of the executive of the World Zionist Organization.

Many younger people helped at various stages in the research of this book. Thanks are due to Noam Marans, who worked hard with me on the question of who came to America, and Mark Friedman, who helped devotedly and intelligently on the final chapters and the "Notes on Sources." Several of my students at Dartmouth labored at producing the manuscript. Special thanks are given to Edward Nelson, Jevin Eagle, Jamie Heller, Gary Katz, Andrew Klein, and Michele Dogin. In earlier stages of the work I was helped by a number of my students at Columbia: Rena Hozore, Jay Lefkowith, Mark Segall, Steven Farber, Noah Schonfield, and Andrew Hyman. In June 1989, in Paris, Françoise Pistre volunteered to help me rewrite the last chapter, and Nancy Shore helped especially with the "Notes on Sources." William Ober, physician, historian, and friend of many years, read proof with exacting care. My greatest debt of all is to two people who worked with me through the years in Englewood, Reby Evans and Carol Ivanovski. Their devotion was extraordinary. I am deeply grateful.

Books are nurtured by other books, often very obscure ones. Scholars depend on two lifelines. One is the goodwill of librarians, and those who work in the libraries of Dartmouth, Columbia, the Jewish Theological Seminary of America, and the Hebrew University have been helpful, indulgent, and unfailingly sympathetic. The other lifeline is the support of people who care about ideas. This book exists in large part because of their generosity. I am grateful to Edgar Bronfman, to Joseph and Arlene Taub, and to Harry Starr and William Frost of the Littauer Foundation for their friendship, and for the spirited discussions with each of them which helped me formulate some of the thinking in this book.

Don Cutler has been friend and confidant through a long campaign. In the last two years, as this book was finished and rewritten, Alice Mayhew and her associate David Shipley, at Simon and Schuster, have contributed, as great editors do, to making an author do better than he set out to do. I would also like to thank Mary Solak for her fine copy editing.

The one who has given most to this book is my wife, Phyllis. She has collaborated in every sentence, and she has borne with grace all the personal deprivations that are inevitable when "a work in progress" is inside the tent. This book is dedicated to her, to our daughters, their husbands, and our first grandchild.

Arthur Hertzberg

For Phyllis,
Linda and David,
Susan and Stephen,
Rachel and Michelle,
and the other grandchildren, d.v., yet to come
that the tradition may continue

Contents

CONTENTS

Introduction

In 1782 St. John de Crèvecoeur, a minor French nobleman who had come to New York to farm, described America as the land of "the poor of Europe who are settled here." American history is the tale of the society that the poor, unrestrained by the "classes," created in the new land. American Jewish history is also the story of the poor: the Jewish poor of Europe, of their unique success in America, and of the new Jewishness that they fashioned in the place that they called, by turns, the "golden land" and "America, the thief," in which the dreams of many came to naught.

The Jewish community, like the rest of America, was never a random sample of all of European Jewry. Poverty and anti-Semitism pushed mostly the poor out of Europe. The better off and the better educated could, until the Nazi era, stay put and survive even in difficult times. This assertion about the class origins of Jewish migration is central to this book. Two striking facts make the point.

First, in 1906, the year when some two-hundred-thousand Jews, more than ever before or since, came to the United States, only fifty listed themselves as professionals (at that time, between five and ten percent of the Jews in the various countries of Eastern Europe, including Czarist Russia, were in the professions). The intellectual and religious traditions of American Jewry thus have shallow roots.

Second, there was in almost all the immigrants to America a conscious anti-European streak. This was especially true among the immigrant Jews who felt betrayed by the societies, the governments,

13

the rabbis, and the rich Jewish leaders who had cast them out, or, at the very least, had failed to find room for them. Such immigrants were not predisposed to construct in North America a replica of their unhappy European past. They would not allow the very people who had betrayed them in Europe to exercise authority in America. The immigrants wanted to give to their Jewishness the aroma of the religious tradition and of folk memory, but on the condition that they could decide on what they wanted to keep and remember. Their Jewishness was essentially ethnic culture.

It is a major contention of this book that this American Jewishness reached its zenith in the 1960s and the years immediately thereafter— but that this era is now over. Most American Jews are now three or even four generations removed from their immigrant origins. They are now living in a society which is more open to Jews than any before in the long history of the Diaspora; immigrant memories and ingrained fears of anti-Semitism are fading.

Why is America suddenly so open? Historians continue to argue about anti-Semitism in America. Some think it was of little account before the Civil War, but no one doubts that from the 1860s to the 1950s the prejudice was serious. It is, therefore, too convenient to maintain that America is different because it had no medieval past— no structure of systematic exclusion of Jews. Though France had a very medieval past, which included elaborate anti-Jewish legislation, the French Revolution gave Jews, and everyone else, equal citizenship. But America, by the nature of its society, was different. In France, and almost everywhere else in Europe, the state represented a majority culture which demanded that minorities assimilate. Such demands were made in America as well, even though an expanding economy needed workers from everywhere. The Puritans wanted no aliens in their Commonwealth; some of the founders of the Republic wanted to impose conformity to republican virtue; in the 1890s aristocrats and nativists joined in the fight to protect the predominance in America of the descendants of the oldest settlers.

The United States was not by its nature more virtuous than Europe. America supported slavery and, for almost a century after the Civil War, condoned Jim Crow laws. America imported Chinese coolies to help build the railroads and then refused to allow them to stay, interned Japanese Americans in 1942, and kept Catholics and Jews on the fringes of society.

INTRODUCTION

Those who fought to limit mass migration to the United States won their battle only in 1924, too late to save the dominant role in America for descendants of the older settlers. Though Jews were only about eight percent of the newcomers to the United States between 1880 and 1924, Henry Adams, the New England Brahmin, was not entirely wrong in his fulminations that the open door to America was giving Jews the chance to challenge his class. Of all the battles that American Jews fought for themselves and their brethren abroad, this was the most fateful. The victories before 1924 were the seed of a radical and permanent change in the nature of America; the defeat, which barred hundreds of thousands more from coming to America, was a preamble to the Holocaust, and even to the creation of the State of Israel.

John F. Kennedy was elected president by the excluded minorities: Catholics, blacks, Jews, and blue-collar workers, who represented various ethnic groups. The descendants of the older America voted against him. Kennedy's election was as profound a turning in American history as the end of the frontier had been in the 1890s. Even so liberal and humane a spirit as Reinhold Niebuhr, the most famous Protestant thinker of the day, asserted in 1960 that the presidency was not entirely a secular office; it represented the spirit of America, and the dominant element in the American spirit was Protestant Christianity.

The recent history of anti-Semitism in America is particularly revealing. Jews had fought for centuries for their total equality in America, and they had failed. Despite the war with the Nazis, the murder of six million Jews in Europe, and America's postwar affluence, anti-Semitism did not lessen in the late 1940s—it actually increased. Only in the 1960s did anti-semitism begin to fade. Two decades later, by the mid-1980s, Jews had become an important element in almost all of America's elite.

Very early in the story of Jews in America, those who wanted to exclude them had kept saying that admitting Jews meant opening the doors to such outlandish people as Turks and Muslims. The objectors were correct. Jews succeeded only when America became an untidy jumble of ethnic identities, ideological factions, and economic interests. The fight of Jews for total equality could not be won in confrontation with a solid majority; the victory could occur only when power was widely dispersed among many, very different "factions."

15

INTRODUCTION

It is not an accident that the reputation of James Madison has risen in recent years. In *Federalist Paper Number Ten* Madison, defending the proposed new Constitution of the United States in 1788, described a loosely textured society of factions. He insisted that the thirteen colonies, by then independent states, were marked by numerous divisions, in religious opinion, region, and economic class. He did not imagine for a moment that any of these identities or associations would be made to conform to each other. He argued for "representative government" because he thought those elected to office would be men who would stand beyond any particular interest and would adjudicate among them for the public good. Madison denied that any particular American virtue inhered in the culture or values of any of the "factions."

Madison's vision of the Constitution fits the new American society. The "factions" are now numerous, and none will concede to any other group the right to question its Americanism. Jews have been among the major architects of this new society. They were critical to the election of Kennedy in 1960, and their support of Israel in June 1967, before and during the Six-Day War, was an unabashed expression of Jewish solidarity in an America in which Jews had never talked up quite so boldly in their own interest. In their new boldness, Jews had really become "just like everybody else." They fought for their interests and made alliances with other groups. The difference from the past was clear and striking. In the 1860s, Judah P. Benjamin, who served as secretary of state of the Confederacy, was constantly attacked as a Jew. In the 1970s Henry Kissinger, national security adviser and secretary of state in the Nixon and Ford administrations, was a figure of controversy, but not as a Jew.

In the course of nearly four centuries, American Jews have realized their emancipation. Only in America, of all their settlements among the Gentiles, do Jews have significant power. But is this untidy American society viable? What can the "factions," including the Jews, do to ensure stability? What, for that matter, are the Jews to do with themselves? In a supremely open society, they can no longer define themselves by fear and exclusion. The era of ethnicity is ending and the question is now open: How will American Jews affirm their Jewishness? To imagine this future, we must first search the past.

1.

New Amsterdam:

The Last Stop

I

No one knows when the first Jew arrived in North America. That question cannot be answered. "New Christians," Jews who had converted to Christianity under force, were among the first Spaniards to come to Mexico. They arrived with the conquistador, Hernando Cortes, in 1519. By 1521 there were so many "New Christians" in Mexico that the Spanish closed the territory to all those who could not show four generations of Catholic ancestors. Immediately, false documents which described such ancestors were sold on the black market in Spain and Portugal. Soon it was widely rumored that in Mexico there were more "New Christians" of Jewish origin than Catholics. The Inquisition was formally established in Mexico City, as an independent tribunal of the Holy Office, in 1571, but the extirpation of heresy had begun earlier. The Church discovered a "Judaizer" in 1528; he was soon burned as a heretic in the first auto-da-fé in America.

There were probably some Judaizers among the Spaniards who crossed the Rio Grande a few years later into what is now the south-

western United States. A friar or two among the founders of the
first Christian missions in the American Southwest were rumored
to be "Marranos," that is, crypto-Jews, who practiced Judaism in
secret, but these Marranos were isolated individuals.

Many of those who were persecuted as Judaizers in Spain and
Portugal, and later, in Mexico, were not guilty. They had already
abandoned the Judaism from which they sprang. The "New Christians" who came to America were from the middle class or even the
nobility; they did not come to find bread, but, rather, to escape
persecution. They had been falsely made into "Jews" by enemies
jealous of their positions in government and society. Some, those
who did practice Judaism in secret, were actually guilty of the
"crime" of which they were charged. In 1599 Luis de Carvajal was
burned at the stake in Mexico City, and he remained a defiant,
believing Jew to the very end: "This is the path to the glory of
Paradise. . . . I would give away a thousand [lives], if I had them,
for the faith of each of His holy commandments." Half a century
later Tomás Treviño de Sobremonte was the host of a secret synagogue which met in his home in Mexico City. He was condemned
to the auto-da-fé, but not only because he Judaized. He knew, as he
said to the Inquisitors, that economic jealousies had played a role: "I
have been of service to the residents of the cities where I have lived
since I came to this country, because I have supplied them with goods
at lower prices than the other traders, my motto being small profits
and quick returns."

The situation on the Atlantic coast of North America was different.
The scattering of individual Jews who arrived in the 1600s were not
fleeing the threat of being burned at the stake; they were looking for
the chance to make a living. In the seventeenth century, even in the
most tolerant European lands, Jews were still restricted to peddling
and moneylending and to a few trades. On the new frontier a Jew,
if he did not trumpet his Jewishness, might be left alone to do anything to which he might turn his hand. Antiquarians have found
rumors, some of which represent probable facts, that there were
settlers of Jewish origin among the founders or near founders of most
of the thirteen colonies. These individuals could not have been very
devoted to their Jewishness, for they knew in advance of their coming
that there would be no way for them to practice Judaism on the
frontier. Without exception, these stray Jews soon disappeared into

the majority community, mostly by intermarriage. The reecho of their presence in America is to be found in the history of some of the oldest American families. One reads or hears stories (some families tell them with pride and others whisper at them as a deep secret) that a Jewish peddler passed through some early outpost on the frontier and that he remained to marry a daughter of the house. Such happenings have, of course, not been limited to the encounter between Jews and Gentiles. The ongoing assimilation of individuals—few or many—into the majority is part of all immigrant history, but the prime subject of minority history is the community which affirms its identity. For the Jews, that history began in North America in 1654.

In early September of that year twenty-three Jewish refugees—recent research suggests that there may have been fewer—landed in New Amsterdam. Their original destination had been the islands of the Caribbean, but when their ship, *Ste. Catherine,* had made port in Jamaica and in Cuba, the Spanish had not allowed them to remain. By the time their ship reached harbor in North America, the group had run out of money. Only their furniture remained, and it could not be sold for enough to pay the exorbitant fare the captain demanded. The very moment that the gangplank was down, the captain went to the local court to sue his passengers. He may have thought that the authorities in this farthest outpost of the Dutch West India Company would pay the bill for these Dutch Jews. At very least, he was informing the governor of New Amsterdam, Peter Stuyvesant, in the strongest terms that he would take these refugees no farther. A group of Jews had thus arrived on American shores for whom New Amsterdam was not the port of choice, but their last hope. Peter Stuyvesant was confronted with a problem that he did not want: the Jews were too numerous to ignore; they would not disappear quickly as individuals among the thousand souls who then inhabited New Amsterdam. If they remained, Jews as a community would have their first outpost in North America.

This band on board the *Ste. Catherine* were running from Recife (it was called Pernambuco in those days), Brazil, the easternmost point of South America, which the Dutch had conquered from the Portuguese in 1630 and had held until it was surrendered back to the Portuguese in January 1654. Jews had come from Europe to Recife in large numbers. According to their own minute book, in 1645 there were 1,450 Jewish souls in Recife. There they had founded a large, European-style community, the first in the New World. There was a synagogue in Recife and two schools. More significantly, in 1641 Isaac Aboab da Fonseca arrived to be their rabbi, bringing along Moses Raphael Aguilar as his deputy. Orthodox religious authority of the classic kind thus existed in Recife. Isaac Aboab wrote a hymn in Hebrew (published) and a volume on theology (unpublished) during his tenure in Recife; these were, of course, the first such works to be produced in the New World. Earlier, Aboab had been a teacher in Amsterdam in the yeshivah, the school of Talmudic studies, where the young philosopher Baruch de Spinoza had been his student. When Aboab returned to Amsterdam, in 1654, he was added to the rabbinate of the community and joined in excommunicating Spinoza for the heresy of denying the divine origin of the Bible. The Jewish community of Recife had, thus, been a place where the inherited Jewish religious values had reigned. It had been a European Jewish community, a little Jewish Amsterdam, which had been transplanted with all its institutions to the Americas.

After Recife fell, its Jews scattered. The pattern of their dispersal was not new. In the last years of Dutch rule, the economy of embattled Recife was disintegrating. It was the port for the export of sugar from the plantations in the backcountry, and this territory was increasingly reconquered by the Portuguese. A majority of the Jews had gone home to Holland to rejoin the established Jewish community from which they had come. When Recife surrendered, there were still 650 Jews in town. Some, especially a few plantation owners of great wealth, chose to remain under the Portuguese in order to protect their property. Inevitably, they had to become Christians, but a number remained crypto-Jews. The twenty-three refugees who came to New Amsterdam could make neither choice. They were affirming Jews with no intention of becoming Marranos, and they were too poor to have any hope of reestablishing themselves in Holland. Their sole alternative was to push themselves into a place where they were not wanted.

The governor of New Amsterdam, Peter Stuyvesant, did not like Jews. Though he did use such terms as "Christ killers" or "Christ rejecters," as he fought against letting them stay in town, his quarrel with them was primarily economic. The animosity had started in Curaçao, on the northern shore of South America, where Stuyvesant had served as the principal agent of the Dutch West India Company, before his headquarters was moved to New Amsterdam. The company needed farmers. Grain had to be sent to the American colonies from Holland, because the get-rich-quick types who were going out to these far places on the edge of civilization had no patience for clearing the land and plowing the soil. The gold of El Dorado beckoned, or, at very least, the hope of making a quick fortune by trading with the Indians. The authorities in Amsterdam had allowed themselves to be persuaded by Jo'ao de Illan, a Jew who had been born as a Christian in Portugal, to establish a Jewish farming colony of some sixty families in Curaçao. The Dutch West India Company was grateful for this promise of help. De Illan received a large grant of land—but he did not farm. He preferred to raise horses and smuggle them to Spanish possessions in the Caribbean and even to New England (thus, incidentally, establishing the first commercial contact between the Puritans and the Jews). Peter Stuyvesant was furious. The Dutch West India Company was upset by his reports, but it did not chase de Illan off the land. He had friends among the company's powerful Jewish stockholders, and the company did not want to annoy these interests. Stuyvesant had thus lost his first battle with Jews.

He was to lose again in New Amsterdam. To be sure, in an earlier instance, in the summer of 1654, when two Jews, Solomon Pietersen and Jacob Barsimson, arrived from Holland with some capital and with passports giving them full permission to land and to trade in the colony, their Jewishness was not an issue to Stuyvesant. But the twenty-three on the *Ste. Catherine* presented a far different problem. Two weeks after they landed, Stuyvesant heard the complaint from the local merchants and from the Church that "the Jews who had arrived would nearly all like to remain here." Stuyvesant decided to chase them out. Using the usual formulas of religious invective—he called the Jews "repugnant," "deceitful," and "enemies and blasphemers of Christ"—Stuyvesant recommended to his directors that "Owing to their present indigence they [the Jews] might become a charge in the coming winter, we have for the benefit of this weak and newly-developing place, and the land in general, deemed it useful to require them in a friendly way to depart."

To be sure, Stuyvesant and his allies were not believers in religious toleration, for this idea had barely appeared in the middle of the seventeenth century. In the 1650s decent men still knew what the truth was, especially in religion, but Stuyvesant had not decided to expel the Jews because he detested rejecters of Christ. The governor of New Amsterdam was an employee of the Dutch West India Company, and the purpose of this firm was not to foster Christianity among the Indians; it existed to make money for its stockholders—and the company was not doing very well. It had made a real profit only once, in 1629, when its ships cornered and pillaged the "silver fleet," the Spanish galleons carrying that year's silver yield from the mines of Peru to Spain. This onetime act of piracy had paid handsomely, but the mundane business of the trading outposts in the Western Hemisphere was barely breaking even, in the best years. New Amsterdam was losing money: Curaçao and Suriname were showing small profits; Recife had just fallen. If the Dutch burghers who had put their money in the West India Company were to see a return, they needed the investment of new capital. It made good sense, then, to oblige the rich Jews of Amsterdam. And so, in the winter of 1654–55, Peter Stuyvesant's bosses in Amsterdam were reluctant to uphold their representative in a squalid little quarrel in their outpost at the mouth of the Hudson. The leaders of the Dutch West India Company had no patience with the local merchants, who were arguing that the advent of these Jews would hurt the profits of the company; this contention seemed hollow to the directors in Amsterdam. The local merchants in the colony were, indeed, supposed to operate for the benefit of the company, but, without exception, they had for years been trading for their own account and stealing from the owners. Peter Stuyvesant himself was, in fact, as guilty as the rest, and the company knew it.

When Stuyvesant's letter arrived in Amsterdam, the Jewish investors in the West India Company were consulted. Their response was frank and pointed: "There are many of the nation [i.e., Jews] who have lost their possessions at Pernambuco [Recife]. They have arrived from there in great poverty, and part of them have been dispersed here and there. Your petitioners had to expend large sums of money for their necessaries of life, and through lack of opportunity all cannot remain here to live." There was free farmland in New Amsterdam. This outpost imported grain from Holland, and it was crying out for hands to work the fields. Why not get the right for poor Jews to stay there by pushing them into becoming farmers, or, at least, by suggesting that they might do so? In this same memorandum the Jewish leaders wrote: "Yonder land is extensive and spacious . . . The Company has by a general resolution consented that those who wish to populate the Colony shall enjoy certain districts of land gratis. Why should now certain subjects of this State not be allowed to travel thither and live there?"

But the directors in Amsterdam of the West India Company did not believe the suggestion that the men among these twenty-three Jews, who had not been very successful at trade in Recife, were now eager to farm in the semiwilderness. The officers of the company also knew that at that very time Jo'ao de Illan was failing, willfully, in the project which they had blessed, to create a Jewish farming settlement in Curaçao. The decision by the West India Company was given in a letter they wrote to Stuyvesant on April 25, 1655: "These people may travel and trade in New Netherland and live and remain there, provided the poor among them shall not become a burden to the Company or to the community, but be supported by their own nation." They added, repeating arguments that had been made in the Jewish brief, that this had to be done out of consideration for the losses of Jews in Brazil and "because of the large amount of capital which they still have invested in the shares of this Company."

In this letter the authorities informed Stuyvesant that they had given passports to five Jews of means, several of whom had just arrived in Amsterdam from Recife. The West India Company had opened New Amsterdam to Jews. Poor Jews were already in place. Five rich families were now being allowed into New Amsterdam [one, Abraham de Lucena, was already there] to add to its trade and, incidentally, "to take care of their own poor."

Despite all this, the local interests refused to give in. They did not like Jews, and they did not want more competitors in a place where trade was languishing. Every kind of harassment was tried. The Council in New Amsterdam made difficulties about a cemetery for Jews, and it tried to stop private worship in individual homes. In such bigotry the Calvinists in New Amsterdam were not singling out the Jews, for they were doing the same, or worse, to dissenting Protestants and, of course, to Catholics. Stuyvesant made the connection in one of his letters to the company: "Giving them [the Jews] liberty, we cannot refuse the Lutherans and Papists." Consequently, on March 13, 1656, the authorities in Holland confirmed that Jewish worship would be forbidden in New Amsterdam, even in private, so "that the wolves may be warded off from the tender lamb of Christ." The Jewish leaders in Amsterdam, of course, intervened, citing the obvious precedent that there were open synagogues in Amsterdam itself. The order was reversed. The directors of the company soon wrote to Stuyvesant that Jews might "exercise in all quietness their religion within their houses, for which end they must without doubt endeavor to build their houses close together in a convenient place on one or the other side of New Amsterdam—at their choice—as they have done here."

The houses that these Jews built or, more probably, rented in New Amsterdam were exactly the same as all the other houses in town, with one marked exception, the food in their kitchen. The twenty-three in New Amsterdam were almost certainly the first Jews in America to observe the rituals of kosher cuisine. It was usual practice in those days that heads of families learned how to slaughter fowl according to the prescribed rituals. Despite the clear intention of the order by the company, that Jews establish themselves in an enclave of their own, they scattered among the Gentiles on several streets. Still, these were within a short walk of one another. Jews had to be able to gather for prayer, and on the Sabbath and on festivals, travel by any conveyance, even by horseback, was forbidden by religious law. The Jews who came to New Amsterdam had not been constrained to establish a ghetto, but where they lived was the first Jewish neighborhood in America.

The wrangle about the freedom of religion had, in essence, been an irrelevance. Jews had come to New Amsterdam to trade. If they succeeded in remaining, they would one way or another conduct their own worship services. Stuyvesant knew it, even as he fought against "their abominable religion." The real question was economic; how much pressure could Jews mount in Amsterdam to counter the continued stonewalling of all the local interests against them? Stuyvesant had ruefully become a realist. He knew that the Jews would prevail. In the very letter in which he thanked his superiors for prohibiting the public exercise of Jewish religion in his town, he added, "What they may be able to obtain from your honors, time will tell."

Stuyvesant's problem was not even with the West India Company alone. In the 1650s the Dutch Republic was more nervous about its commercial future than it had been for decades. The Dutch had invented the doctrine of mercantilism, the notion that the state existed not to save souls but to increase wealth. For such purpose, Jews or Turks—all who brought money and commercial connections—were welcome. Spanish and Portuguese "New Christians" had begun arriving in Holland before 1600, and they were allowed to drop their Christian disguise and to live as Jews. Some had been admitted to the Amsterdam mercantile exchange at its very beginning in 1611; the Jews were seated in a good place, together with the sugar refiners and the securities dealers. The next year, there were ten "Jew brokers" among the three hundred sworn members of the exchange. A few years later, in 1618, the French envoy in Holland wrote to Paris about "the cleverness, commercial energy, and communal solidarity of the Jews." They kept in touch with other Jews all over the world, even with secret communities in England and France, so that "the Jews in Amsterdam are the best informed about foreign commerce and news of all people in the world"; therefore, "they are needed by the city."

The Jewish leaders in Amsterdam thus knew that they had the power to cajole or even to intimidate the West India Company—but these rich Jews were also afraid. Even in Amsterdam, the most liberal of European cities, no one knew how many poor Jews would be tolerated by the civic authorities. The Jewish population of Amsterdam had been growing through the century with little problem, but the 1650s were a turbulent time. The leaders of the Jewish community had to conduct frequent fund-raising campaigns to pay for the relief of their poor, who kept drifting into the community from all over Europe. Such a collection was again made in the summer of 1654, to help those who had fled from Recife. It is an interesting detail that Baruch de Spinoza, who was then still a member of the Jewish community, is recorded as dutifully giving five florins to this drive on September 13, 1654. In the next year the pressures increased. The Jews in Eastern Europe were being slaughtered by the Ukrainians in a series of murders that had begun in 1648. A shipload of refugees escaped through the Baltic Sea, but the Jews of Amsterdam were afraid to let them stay. There was always room in mercantilist Amsterdam for Jewish capitalists, but the elders of the city were becoming restless at the sight of poor Jews who kept insinuating themselves into the city. They were trying to make a living as peddlers and as petty traders in competition with the local retailers. These tensions made Amsterdam's rich Jews nervous. They reflected this discomfort in their letter to the West India Company: "through lack of opportunity all cannot remain here to live." They were far too nervous to want their twenty-three wandering compatriots back. It was better that these refugees from Recife remain in a distant colony.

American Jewish history thus began with no ringing debates about religious freedom or about the rights of individuals. The twenty-three remained in New Amsterdam, and began the first avowed Jewish community in North America, because money talked. The Dutch West India Company needed the Jews, even as many restrictions against Jewish trade persisted in Amsterdam itself, and religious prejudices based on Calvinism remained strong there. On the frontier in the New World, the company was much more open and obliging—and yet there was continuing struggle in the colony about the rights of Jews and especially about the open practice of Judaism.

II

The five wealthy merchants who arrived in New Amsterdam in 1655 belonged to the international network of Jewish men of affairs who descended from the "aristocratic" Jews of Spain and Portugal, the Sephardim. They carried a big stick; they could threaten to move elsewhere, taking their money and commerce with them. As befitted their power and station, these five families immediately demanded the right to own houses in New Amsterdam. David Ferara and Salvador Dandrada fought this issue out with the local authorities. It took them only a few months to win, but they never exercised this right. They had come to New Amsterdam to try out the place as a base for large commercial enterprises, and they would not commit themselves to remain until they saw the possibility of success. Even after winning the quarrel over owning houses, these Jews were still harassed with a minor, troubling restriction; they were denied the right to employ Christian servants. This annoyance reflected a larger policy. Having been forced to accept Jews in New Amsterdam, Peter Stuyvesant continued to try to hem them in with all the restrictions that still existed on the books in Amsterdam. In Amsterdam, Jews could engage in large enterprises, in wholesale commerce of all kinds, but not in retail trade, for it competed with local merchants. This prohibition was passed, but it was simply ignored in New Amsterdam.

The crucial quarrel was about the fur and tobacco trade, the colony's most lucrative pursuits. The rich Jews who had come in 1655 wanted to enter this business; they kept moving upriver, and angering their competitors. Albany (then called Fort Orange) was the major trading post to the north. Jews were soon there, competing with those who had been trading with the Indians. In September of 1655 the Dutch moved south and captured the Swedish colonies on the Delaware River (it was then called the South River). Three of the Jewish merchants immediately shipped goods there, but Stuyvesant and the Council of New Netherland would not let them do business. In late November, an exchange between the Council and these merchants—Abraham de Lucena, Salvador Dandrada, and Jacob Cohen—resulted in a temporary compromise. The Jewish shippers were permitted "to send one or two persons to the South River in order to dispose of the same [i.e., the goods shipped], which being done, they are to return hither." The inevitable appeal to Holland brought back a decision in March 1656 that Jews had the right to trade on the Delaware. They were soon back on the river, exchanging cloth and liquor for furs and tobacco. David Ferara even traded for tobacco in the English colony of Maryland.

By April 1657, the battle of the five merchant families for economic rights had succeeded. Four of them—all except David Ferara, who seems then to have been away trading for tobacco in Maryland—joined in a petition to Stuyvesant and the Council in which they asked for the right to be enrolled as burghers of New Amsterdam. Notably, they did not ask for the "great burgher right," which carried with it full political equality, to which the Jews did not aspire. They wanted the right to engage in retail trade, which could be exercised by possessors of the "small burgher right." The petitioners argued that they, too, paid taxes, and that they were entitled to "the same freedom as other inhabitants of New Netherland enjoy." This time the authorities did not respond with delaying tactics. Perhaps the local interests now needed these Jews, for they were among the largest taxpayers. More probably, the colony as a whole was becoming less and less governable. That spring, English settlers on Long Island rebelled against Dutch rule in the "Flushing Remonstrance," in which they protested the persecution of Quakers and pleaded for toleration of all settlers without regard to their religion; the remonstrants specifically included the Jews among those to be permitted in the colony. Stuyvesant, the son and son-in-law of Calvinist ministers, could not persist in religious oppression; Stuyvesant, the surreptitious partner of a number of local merchants, could no longer protect these interests.

Neither the Jews nor the company were, however, permanently wedded to New Amsterdam. For the company it soon became clear that this was the least interesting of its remaining possessions. Great and immediate profits were likelier in the Caribbean, in the sugar trade. Dandrada, Ferara, and the rest had come to New Amsterdam to get much richer quickly, and this was not happening. They began to leave, most probably to go back to Holland. By the time the English fleet came, during the Dutch-English War, not a single one of these Sephardi hidalgos was left in town. The Scroll of the Law, which they had brought with them from Amsterdam when they arrived in 1655, had been returned to the mother congregation in 1663. Most of the twenty-three who had come on the *Ste. Catherine* had also taken off for other places. Of the two who had "met the ship," one, Solomon Pietersen, seems to have remained: he is not identical with Solomon Pietersen La Chair, a notary public, a position one could acquire only by taking the oath "on the true faith of a Christian." The other, Jacob Barsimson, had simply disappeared; he was perhaps the husband of a lady who was recorded in 1680 in Barbados as a widow.

Only one Jew who had been visible in Dutch New Amsterdam, Asser Levy, was prominent in English New York. He was one of the refounders of the Jewish community in the 1670s. Levy was different from those who left as the Dutch colony was failing. They were Sephardim, bearers of the Jewish culture that had been created in Spain and Portugal before the total expulsions of Jews in 1492 and 1497; he was an Ashkenazi, that is, he came from the Yiddish-speaking communities of Central and Eastern Europe, which the Sephardim regarded as lower caste. The Sephardi hidalgos belonged to a network of international traders; Levy was a self-made businessman, who had arrived poor, and not among those who had come from Recife. In fact, the first battle that he personally fought with the local authorities was caused by his poverty. In that era, standing guard was not anywhere regarded as an honor, or a mark of political equality. On the contrary, well-off people, even those on the frontier, bought out from military duty.

The Jewish attitudes to such duty were different. In Europe Jews had rarely been asked or allowed to bear arms, because they were excluded from society. This had broken down in the New World. When Recife was besieged, Jews had fought beside the rest. One ex-Marrano who had helped defend Recife had been executed after its fall, as a traitor to Portugal. In New Amsterdam the five Sephardi entrepreneurs paid a tax in lieu of military service in the "trainbands" (the local home guard) without giving the matter a second thought, but Asser Levy and Jacob Barsimson could not afford even the measly sum of sixty-five stivers. On November 5, 1655, they petitioned "to keep guard with other burghers, or be free from the tax which others of their nation pay, as they must earn their living by manual labor." Levy and Barsimson were refused, and they were told that they could leave the colony if they wished. Levy kept pushing, and within two years he had won the right to serve in the militia. For that matter, it was Levy, and not the Sephardim, who had initiated the battle for "small burgher rights"; he needed the right to petty retail trade more than they, and he intended to stay in New Amsterdam.

The commerce of the well-to-do Sephardim had not gone well; they were already contemplating leaving New Amsterdam, and so they had remained in rented quarters. In 1661, Levy bought a house in New Amsterdam, perhaps the first one that a Jew owned there or anywhere in North America. In seven years he had become a middleman, selling finished goods imported from Amsterdam and trading even in Fort Orange (Albany). He was perhaps involved directly in the fur trade; more probably, he sold supplies to the traders. When the British were on the attack in 1664, Levy was taxed a hundred guilders as his share of the fund for strengthening the fortifications. This was as much money as each of the five rich Sephardim had been assessed in taxes on their arrival in 1655. Levy had become well-to-do. In the course of his first ten years in the colony, despite resistance from unfriendly Dutch authorities, he had spread out in many directions. He had become a representative of Dutch merchants in New Amsterdam and a moneylender. He even sold liquor. In 1660 he was given license to be a butcher. Levy did not open a slaughterhouse until 1678 after the Dutch left. He had a

Christian partner in this business; it is of some interest that this abattoir was located on the very site of present-day Wall Street.

Levy was also spreading out in public life. Since 1657 he had been marching with the militia. It is likely that Levy was excused from his duties in the militia on Sabbaths and Jewish holidays, for such exceptions continued to be made in colonial New York, and elsewhere in the English colonies, until the American Revolution. In 1671, under the British, he sat on a jury, the very first Jew in America to be allowed to hold such office. One of the cases that was tried that term involved his old enemy, Peter Stuyvesant, who had remained in New York after the surrender. Levy seems to have been completely fair, because Stuyvesant won the case. Levy lent money that year to the Lutherans to help them build a church. That same year, a Jewish peddler was given a reduced fine by a court in New England as "a token of their respect to . . . Mr. Assur [sic] Levy."

Levy had to be an aggressive person who fought for his rights. New Amsterdam was a rough town. A visitor reported that eighteen languages were spoken in this outpost of only a thousand souls, that all the streets were mud ruts, and that every third building was a grogshop. It was definitely not safe to walk around at night. Such an environment inevitably bred disputes. Jews were no different from all the rest of the inhabitants. There is record of a suit that Levy brought against a butcher who had accused him of associating with thieves. Mrs. Abraham de Lucena called someone a rogue; he responded by calling her a whore. This quarrel was patched up in court with mutual apologies. An even more interesting case never came to trial. Elias Silva was accused of having "carnal conversation" with the Negro slave of another man. He was arrested, but there is no record of any action by the court.

So long as the community existed under Dutch rule, Levy was part of it, but what happened to his Jewish piety in 1663, when almost all of the other Jews were gone? In the spring of 1664, did Levy bake his own unleavened bread, the matzoth, for Passover? Did he keep the room in which the now departed community had said its prayers, as his private, personal synagogue? When no other Jews were looking, did he perhaps work on the Sabbath—or did he insist on being odd, even when he and his family were the only Jews in town? Asser Levy had to redecide everything in his Jewish life that the inherited tradition had decided for all of his ancestors. It is clear from Levy's estate that he remained to the very end an affirming Jew. According to the official inventory, his possessions included pistols, a gun and two swords—but also a Sabbath light, goblets which were undoubtedly used for saying the Friday night blessing over the wine, and a spice box which was used for the ceremony marking the end of the Sabbath.

Levy's religious problems were not new. They had been experienced for centuries by isolated European Jews who made their living by peddling from wagons, without any fixed habitation. His chance to get rich in less than ten years was much more "American." Levy had risen and prospered because New Amsterdam, and almost all of the other North American colonies, had been created without any pretense of a religious purpose. They were economic entities, which needed population, and thus they were essentially hospitable to Jews, or to anyone else who wanted to work and make something of himself. Those who had money, and expected large immediate returns, like the five Sephardi families who had come in 1655, had other places to go, even if they were Jews. For the rising poor, like Asser Levy, New Amsterdam had put fewer obstacles in their way than any other place in the world—and so it was to remain in New York for generations to come.

2.

Puritans and Jews:

Truth vs Error

I

Asser Levy was fortunate that he lived in New York, to which people had come to make money, and not in Boston, which was founded as a godly commonwealth. In the middle of the seventeenth century these ungodly views prevailed in Amsterdam, and therefore in New Amsterdam, but Boston was dedicated to making God's kingdom on earth. The Puritans were obsessed by the Jewish Bible—but they were not hospitable to Jews, or to Judaism. They had left Europe, which was their "Egypt," the place of their enslavement, and had gone out into the American wilderness on a messianic journey, to found the New Jerusalem. In the famous sermon on the *Arbella,* the ship which had brought the second group of Puritans to Massachusetts Bay in 1630, John Winthrop had compared the passengers on board his ship both to Noah's Ark and to the dry bones in the vision of Ezekiel. These were to be the ancestors of a new mankind, after Europe was destroyed for its sins. Soon, Samuel Wakeman, one of the New England divines at the heyday of Puritanism, preached an election day sermon in which he asserted that "Jerusalem was, New England is; they were, you are God's own, God's covenant people; put but New England's name instead of Jerusalem."

The Puritans were convinced that they were the true Jews, the ultimate and total heirs of the promises that God had made in the Hebrew Bible. The errors of the biological Jews had to be excluded.

Essays without number have been written to argue that the Puritan theocracy, which was so self-consciously modeled on biblical Judaism, created a pro-Jewish core to the American intellectual and political tradition. This reading is wrong. Because the Puritans knew that they had the truth, they were intolerant of all other believers. One of the founders of New England, Nathaniel Ward, wrote in 1645 that anyone who "is willing to tolerate any religion . . . besides his own . . . either doubts his own or is not sincere in it." An even more important figure, John Cotton, had denied, emphatically, that "God did ever ordain [democracy] as a fit government for either church or a commonwealth." Edward Winslow, who had been governor of New Plymouth, was even more emphatic in a letter that he wrote to his friend, John Winthrop, the former governor of Massachusetts Bay. Winslow said that he "utterly abhorred" universal tolerance, for that "would make us odious to all Christian commonweales . . . to allow and maintaine full and free tollerance of religion to all men . . . Turke, Jew, Papist . . . or any other." A generation later, in 1681, another divine, Samuel Willard, looked back on the Puritan beginnings of Massachusetts and flatly asserted that the first to come were "professed enemies of toleration." No other version of Christianity could be tolerated. This Puritan intolerance is remembered to this day primarily because witches were hanged in Salem, to protect the faithful from those who were consorting with the devil. It has been more than half forgotten that Quakers were being hanged in Boston, because Christians who were not Puritans were "vipers in the garden of the Lord."

Jews, however, had never been Christian. Even at the height of Puritan power in New England, they were never in danger of their lives. Yet, they were never welcome. The first test of the attitude of the Puritans toward Jews in their midst came in 1649. Solomon Franco arrived from Holland, in charge of goods consigned to the major general of the Boston militia, Edward Gibbons. Franco may have jumped ship or he may have been left behind. It is not known whether he wanted to remain in Boston, but the local authorities gave him no choice. He was a Jew who had no intention of converting to Christianity in its Puritan version. On May 3, 1649, they decreed to "allow the said Solomon Franco six shillings per week out of the Treasury for ten weeks, for subsistence, till he can get his passage into Holland," and they commanded him to leave before the ten weeks of grace ran out. In 1675, when Rowland Gideon, one of the first Jews to do business in Boston, had to appear before a court, he had known that he was an alien, for he begged the court to be kind by acting as "fathers of this scattered nation." But Gideon did have a text to quote at these Puritans; he reminded them of the biblical injunction that "God commands our fathers that the same law should be for the strangers and sorjouners as for the Israelites." Gideon won the suit, but he did not remain in Boston.

On the other hand, at the very beginning of their settlement in North America, some Puritans had allowed a family of Jewish extraction to remain in their midst. In 1621, Moses Simonson and family, reputed to be "from the Jewish settlement in Amsterdam," landed in Plymouth harbor one year after the *Mayflower*. They had no trouble remaining because the Simonsons had probably already turned Christian in Holland before joining the Pilgrims, or, at very least, they converted in Plymouth. One of their daughters is known to have married a grandson of Miles Standish and John Alden.

Thus, at the very beginning of their settlements in New England, the Pilgrims had let a convert remain in Plymouth, and the Massachusetts Bay Colony had chased professing Jews out of Boston. Three generations after the beginning of these colonies, Samuel Willard summarized Puritan attitudes in a sermon that he preached in 1700: the Jews were a "scorn and reproach to the world"; it was best to keep them out, for only "the happy day of their conversion could improve their condition." This was standard Christian doctrine, but there was a particular twist—and a unique intensity—to this attitude. The conversion of the Jews was necessary, and not primarily for their own good, or to avoid the infection of society through their presence as Jews. Every Jew who converted to Puritanism assured the Puritans that they were right: they were the true Israel. There was an even more pressing reason for converting the Jews: the end of days was coming, and one could not wait patiently for the Jews to see the light; had it not been foretold that Jesus would appear again, but only if the obdurate Jews acknowledged him as Savior?

The Puritans were faced with a quandary. The Second Coming could not happen unless most Jews were converted, but the bulk of this obdurate people would remain in Europe, unavailable to the light of Puritan truth. Fortunately, for the Puritans, the answer to this problem lay in America's sizable Indian population. Some of the founding fathers of New England concluded that the Indians should be Jews. And it was therefore "proven" through a "discovery" made by a rabbi (what greater expert!) that this was so. The man who made this discovery was Manasseh Ben Israel of Amsterdam. An able, though not outstanding, scholar of the Talmud and a Kabbalist who wanted to help effect "the end of days," a Latinist, a man whose friend Rembrandt made an etching of him, Manasseh was unusual even in Amsterdam, the most open society of the day. When he suggested that the Indians of the Western Hemisphere were descendants of the Lost Ten Tribes of Israel, this "finding" speedily reached New England.

Manasseh Ben Israel did not, of course, invent the idea. This myth had begun a century earlier in South America, when the Spanish and Portuguese were conquering the continent. But in 1649 Manasseh revived the story with a very clear purpose of his own. During the convulsions of the late 1640s in England, as Charles I was being tried and beheaded and Oliver Cromwell was coming to power, Manasseh began to think that he could persuade the new rulers of the British Isles that the time had come to allow the Jews to return to the land from which they had been banished by Edward I in 1290. By claiming that the Indians were Jews, Manasseh's first line of argument was to appeal to the Puritan hope for the "end of days." In a pamphlet entitled *The Hope of Israel,* Manasseh maintained that the messianic era was about to begin. The Jews would, first, have to spread out to the four corners of the earth; therefore, they had to be allowed into England immediately. As for America, the farthest corner of the world, Manasseh asserted that the Indians were Jews. He told a strange story: Antonio de Montezinos, who was also known as Aaron Levi, had come to Amsterdam in September 1644 and had testified before its rabbinic court that he had met Indians in Ecuador who were Jews. Montezinos said that he had taken a long and adventurous journey to a riverbank, on the other side of which a goodly throng of Indians assembled in his honor (they would not let Montezinos cross over). They gave ample evidence of being Jewish by reciting the "Here O Israel" in Hebrew.

It is questionable that Manasseh and his colleagues in Amsterdam believed this story. If they did, it makes no sense that they kept such good tidings secret for five whole years. Manasseh Ben Israel seems to have put the tale told by Montezinos out of his mind until 1649. That year, strange tales seemed more likely, because revolutionaries in England were shocking Europe in 1649 by daring to execute their lawful king, Charles I. In any event, Manasseh found this story useful in his effort to persuade Christian believers in England to readmit the Jews. Several of them did accept this tale with great enthusiasm; they spread it abroad, even before Manasseh's pamphlet was printed in 1650. It was through these enthusiasts that the story traveled almost immediately to New England, where it had an interesting life of its own. Manasseh seems to have first told the story in Amsterdam to an English Puritan, John Durie, who was chaplain to Mary, princess of Orange. Durie repeated it to a friend in London, Thomas Thorowgood, who was involved in supporting John Eliot, the first and most famous Puritan missionary. Thorowgood instantly imagined that the Indians whom Eliot was trying to convert were the same as those whom Montezinos had encountered, and so he published a pamphlet under the sensational title of *Jews in America*. A few months later John Durie published a pamphlet of his own in which he fully supported Thorowgood's views on the Indians in North America. In order to make his point totally convincing, he told the Montezinos story as he had received it from Manasseh Ben Israel.

The only person who seems to have kept his head, at least for a while, was John Eliot, the missionary and apostle to the Indians in New England. Eliot had begun his mission in 1646; a year later, in 1647, he wrote the first printed account of the Indians whom he was trying to convert. This was a sober production in which Eliot guessed that the Indians of North America were most probably "Tartars passing out of Asia into America." There was not the slightest suggestion of any possible Jewish origin. Eliot even included a down-to-earth forecast that not many Indians were likely to convert at any time soon, for mass conversion of those who had not yet accepted

Christianity was likely to happen only when "the Jews come in." It was only after Thorowgood, his chief financial supporter in England, had made the suggestion that these Indians were Jews, that Eliot allowed himself to be half-persuaded that this might be true. Eliot then argued, without much conviction, that he "saw some ground to conceive that some of the Ten Tribes might be scattered even thus far." It is nearly certain that Eliot said this to humor Thorowgood. Eliot was always broke; he needed the money that Thorowgood was collecting in England.

Roger Williams, the radical theologian who most troubled the early Puritans, seems to have believed the notion that the Indians were of Jewish origin, and so did a number of more orthodox Puritan divines. But the idea was abandoned, as the Puritans got to know the Indians better. What did remain at the center of Puritan concern was messianic speculation, which had been at its height in the 1640s and 1650s when the myth of the Jewish origin of the Indians had been floated. The spiritual leaders of New England remained particularly attentive to any rumor of messianic expectations, and especially when such hopes appeared among the Jews. In the 1660s there was a major convulsion in world Jewry. Shabtai Zvi, a Kabbalist from Smyrna, proclaimed himself the messiah. He appeared immediately after the mass murder of Jews in the Ukraine from 1648 into the mid-1650s, and at a time when the Inquisition was persecuting crypto-Jews in Spain and Portugal and their possessions with unabating vigor. Jews wanted a miracle, and so most of world Jewry believed him. In many places sober people sold their goods and awaited the new age in which they would return to Zion. These strange events were widely noticed, everywhere, and even in New England. As early as 1669 Increase Mather, the second generation of the most important Puritan divines, had preached sermons in which he had maintained that "some great revolution of affairs" is widely expected, "not only by Protestants but also by Papists, Jews, Turks, Mohammedans and other idolators." Both the Turks and the pope were about to fall, leaving the field clear for the true Christianity of the Protestants; they would lead the way toward the Second Coming. Jews would join with the Gentiles in one universal society. The Jews would return to Judea "to repossess their own land." In a preface to these sermons by Mather, another Puritan divine, John Davenport, wrote that

Mather was maintaining something "reasonable," because there were constant reports from various places in the world that "the Israelites were upon their journey towards Jerusalem," and that they were being carried in great multitudes in that direction by miraculous means "to the admiration and astonishment of all who had heard it." Davenport added that the Jews had written to "others of their nation in Europe and America to encourage and invite them to hasten to them." No communications from the followers of Shabtai Zvi to Jews in America have yet been found, but it is conceivable that such letters were sent. By 1669, the date forecast for the restoration of the Jews (the year 1666) had passed, and the "messiah" himself had converted to Islam, but the messianic convulsion had not yet ended.

A more immediate encounter with contemporary Jewish reality by a Puritan leader occurred in 1689, when William Sewell of Boston was in London as a representative of the Massachusetts Bay Company to try to renegotiate the terms of the royal charter that had been forced on the Puritans five years earlier. Sewell took occasion to see the synagogue and cemetery of the Sephardim. His account of his visit to the cemetery was quite fair. Sewell was interested in the Jewish burial practices; as he left, he told the keeper that he wished that they might meet in heaven. This was a most tolerant encounter, but theological ideas about converting the Jews were not foreign even to the worldly William Sewell. Two years earlier Sewell had recorded hearing a sermon by Samuel Lee, a preacher from Bristol, Massachusetts, who was also visiting in London, in which Lee had asserted that the end of days was near, the conversion of the Jews was imminent, and that "the Jews were called and would inhabit Judea and Old Jerusalem."

Thus, in the great days of Puritanism in New England a consensus had been reached about Jews. Even the most tolerant Roger Williams remained deeply committed to converting them. He insisted that he "did profess a spiritual war against Judaism and the Turks." What separated him from the rest was his belief that Jews, along with all other dissenting faiths, could best be persuaded of the truth of Puritan Christianity only at close range, if they were allowed into the civil society. In one of his pamphlets Williams denounced the Christian world for persecuting the Jews, "for whose hard measure the nations and England have yet a score to pay." When Williams was banished from Massachusetts for heresy, he established a commonwealth in

Rhode Island on the principles of complete civic equality. This settlement was the first to allow the Jewish community to be established
in New England, in Newport.

II

The Puritan founders of the Massachusetts Bay Colony had arrived
in 1630 with a charter which gave them unparalleled power. They
were not governed from England; they governed themselves. Since
their purpose was the creation of a godly community, the church
and the state were essentially one. This endeavor began to founder
after half a century. In 1684, Charles II withdrew the original charter,
and he thus weakened Puritan control over Massachusetts. When his
successor, James II, came to the throne in the next year, he soon
instructed the royal governor to permit "liberty of conscience in
matters of religion to all persons." This decree was issued for the
benefit of Anglicans and Catholics, but, in effect, it also included the
very few Jews who were then to be found anywhere in New England.
Nonetheless, despite these defeats in London, the Puritans continued,
in the last days of the seventeenth century, to hope for God's final
victory in New England. The greatest of all their scholars, Cotton
Mather, took to wearing a skullcap in his study and to calling himself
a rabbi. Mather was no eccentric on the fringes of New England.
True, he was moody and imperious. He was twice denied the post
which he wanted all his life, the presidency of Harvard College, but
even his enemies acknowledged that Mather was the moral leader of
Boston and the greatest scholar in North America. He also bore the
right names. His grandfathers, John Cotton and Richard Mather,
had been leading figures among the Puritan divines who had put
their stamp on the Massachusetts Bay Colony.

At the moment at which Mather donned the skullcap, probably
in 1696, and took to calling himself "rabbi," he was completing his
most important book, the *Magnalia Christi Americana,* a huge account
of the founding of the Massachusetts Bay Colony. In this book
Mather defined and summed up the meaning of the Puritan venture
into the American wilderness. In this account, he "invented" New
England as a redemptive society. Mather retold Puritan history in
biblical, mythic accents. In Mather's tale, the generation of his grand-

parents had left the slavery of Europe not simply to escape persecution. They had come on a messianic journey to bring about the
Second Coming of Christ. John Winthrop, the founding governor
of Massachusetts, was the new Moses; the essential meaning of his
enterprise was to establish the new Zion. Among the Puritans, some
thought that the "City on the Hill" was a refuge for a saving remnant,
which would remain as God's kingdom on earth after Europe and
the rest of the sinful world were destroyed in the conflagration of
Armageddon. Others held that the Puritan theocracy was redemptive.

All the opinions among the Puritans agreed that they, and not the
Jews, were the chosen people. In the late 1690s when Cotton Mather
was finishing the *Magnalia Christi,* he was also writing a textbook
for the conversion of the Jews. It was a set of "proofs" from their
own Bible, using verses from the Old Testament alone, to establish
the incontrovertible truth of Christianity. Mather hoped that this
book would, in the first instance, convert the Frazon brothers, who
were the only avowed Jews then trading in Boston. Mather was
disappointed, for the Frazons remained Jews. When one of them died
a few years later, his body was transported to the Jewish cemetery
in Newport, Rhode Island. Mather had failed with the Frazons, but
he was encouraged by the news that his book brought a Jew in South
Carolina to conversion. Mather must have patted his skullcap with
approval—and in renewed hope—when the news came from South
Carolina, but there were no more such encouraging stories. The Jews
ignored Mather's book.

The question of the Jews had occupied Mather from the very
beginning of his spiritual journey. At twenty-one, he went through
the crisis that all Puritans were supposed to experience, that of struggle with his "lusts" in order to become spiritually reborn, and thus
to offer "proof" of having joined the "elect," that is, those who had
been chosen by God to be His people. Mather wrote about this in
his diary. The rhetoric is biblical: he had resolved to "circumcise all
lusts of the flesh." Mather had found a place in his spiritual world
for the biblical commandment of circumcision, but it no longer
meant, as the "literalist Jews would have it," something mundane
and even vile. At twenty-one, Mather had found a way of giving
the commandment a Puritan interpretation: he would be "active in
the execution of all these evil inclinations as the Jews were in the

execution of my dearest Redeemer." Thirteen years later, as he was completing the *Magnalia Christi,* Mather had another experience of inner illumination. This divine light assured him of his own central role in the world. He wrote in his diary that he would not be the one who bears witness "unto the Lord for no less than all the nations and kingdoms." He was now both a rabbi and a prophet; he was donning the skullcap to define a program by which the kingdom of Christ would be realized. At the top of the list, Mather assigned himself the task of the "conversion of the Jewish nation." Mather then turned to such minor matters as the fate of France and of the British dominions, and the well-being of his own province, all of which had to fit into the divine scheme.

Mather kept hoping for the ultimate triumph of Puritanism, but it did not come. He had to live with his disappointments, and not only about the Jews. His father, Increase Mather, had already been troubled half a century earlier, while some of the founding fathers of Puritanism were still alive, by the growing tendency of men of affairs to put their own interests first, thereby changing New England from "a religious to a worldly interest." When Increase Mather spoke, around 1650, New England had already grown to a population of perhaps thirty thousand, and most of those who had come were not, like the earliest founders, godly people. Nonetheless, the elect, those few who were admitted to membership in the Puritan congregations, continued to govern the Massachusetts Bay Colony as a theocracy for half a century until the original charter was revoked.

The response in New England to this fundamental change, which took civil rule away from the Puritans and put it in the hands of a royal governor, was a religious revival called the New Piety. The Puritans consciously turned inward, away from public affairs, which they could no longer dominate. Cotton Mather became a leading exponent of this New Piety. He even began to believe, in the last decade of his life, that prophecy had begun again. Cotton Mather gave up on the notion that there would be large-scale conversion of the Jews, or that this was a necessary part of the drama of the end of days. He consoled himself by holding all the harder to the hope that the end of days was at hand, that Christ would soon rise again— and the elect, the chosen, would be given the glory they deserved.

Despite this change of mind, Cotton Mather rejoiced in any convert. In Mather's last years there was one such case in Boston. Judah

Monis, a Jew from Italy who was probably originally from Algiers, had arrived in Boston from New York in 1720. Two years later Monis converted to Christianity before a large crowd in College Hall at Harvard. He was soon appointed to teach Hebrew there, and he was the author of the first grammar of that language, and the first book which used Hebrew type, to be published in America. Mather was not the clergyman who officiated at Monis's conversion, but he was deeply moved by this event. In 1724 Mather observed in his diary that he ought to go and talk to Monis about passages in the Old Testament which were unclear to Mather, but which Monis might understand better, for "a Jew rarely comes over to us that he brings treasures with him." Monis had indeed brought "treasures" for Puritan believers. At his public baptism, he published "three discourses written by Mr. Monis himself, the Truth, the Whole Truth and, Nothing but the Truth." Monis even delivered one of these "discourses" as a speech at this great occasion. What he had to say uplifted the elite of Boston. This learned Jew defended Christianity, and especially the Doctrine of the Trinity, on the basis of "the Old Testament with the Authority of the Cabalistical Rabbies, Ancient and Modern." Christianity thus stood confirmed in Boston, out of the mouth of a Jew who even sometimes claimed to have been a rabbi.

Monis seems to have been sincere in his conversion, even though Cotton Mather's father, Increase, was guardedly dubious in the introduction that he wrote to the printed version of Monis's *Three Discourses*. Increase Mather's doubts were disproved by Monis's later life. When he retired from Harvard in 1760, after thirty-eight years of teaching, Monis went to live with relatives of his late wife (they had married after Monis's conversion) in Worcester County, Massachusetts. Monis was a leading figure in the local church, and he even presented the congregation with two silver communion cups, which might possibly have been the kiddush cups that he had used in his earlier, Jewish life. In his will Monis left money for the relief of poor widows of Massachusetts clergymen. The fund still exists and is administered by the American Unitarian Association which Monis's church joined some time after his death. In any event, on the day of Monis's conversion, Cotton Mather had reason to remember that he had written a book more than twenty years before to prove Christianity from the Jewish Bible, the Old Testament.

Mather left College Hall that day in the sure and certain faith that the Second Coming was near, and that the few Jews in the colonies would join Monis before long and would thus help bring about the "end of days."

But these hopes were vain. When Monis converted in 1722, organized Jewish communities were functioning in New York and in Charleston, South Carolina. Decade by decade other Jewish communities were being established in port towns all along the seaboard, as far south as Georgia. Nearer at hand, in the middle of the century, the Jewish community in Newport, Rhode Island, which had existed in the 1680s and had evaporated after 1700 for unknown reasons, was refounded in the 1750s by a group of Jewish sea traders and merchants. In the course of the eighteenth century, Jewish merchants did settle in Boston and in other places in New England, but they had no more rights than Anglicans, Quakers, and Baptists, who continued to be taxed for the support of the Congregational Church, and, even after these taxes were abolished in 1727–28, these Christian minorities were still harassed. But, in 1740 the British Parliament passed the Plantation Act which allowed all the immigrants of the colonies, except Catholics but including Jews, to be naturalized. The Puritans had to bow to this law. Individuals were allowed to trade in New England, and sometimes even admired, but they were nonetheless held at arm's length. The older attitudes, that Judaism was a false religion and that Jews could be accepted in society only if they converted, remained firm, even though the Puritans were losing ground in New England to secular, commercial interests.

Ezra Stiles was the Puritan divine (he later lost much of his orthodoxy) who was the most involved with Jews. He had come to Newport in 1755 as a Congregational minister, and remained there for twenty-three years, until he became president of Yale College in 1778. There were then some fifteen Jewish families in this port city, and several were important in the sea trade and in the civic community. Stiles became very interested in their synagogue. In 1767 he began to study Hebrew under the guidance of Isaac Touro, who was the religious functionary of the congregation. Newport's Jews were the hosts to a succession of rabbinic visitors from abroad, who came to collect alms for the Holy Land. The most striking figure among these emissaries was Isaac Carigal. Stiles went far out of his way to become friends with this rabbi, and a portrait of Carigal, painted for

Stiles, still exists. Carigal is depicted with piercing eyes and a long, thin, black beard, dressed in Oriental clothing. The relations between Stiles and Carigal were so friendly that there were exchanges of letters, in Hebrew, after Carigal left Newport for Barbados in 1774.

Stiles admired the public-spiritedness of some of the leading figures in the Newport Jewish community, and yet, when he first encountered these Jews, he wrote in his diary in 1762 that the dispersal of the Jews was a dire punishment which they merited for having rejected the Lord, and that it was inconceivable that a community of Jews could exist permanently in America. Stiles wrote this before he began to study Hebrew seriously or had met Carigal, but, even as he came to know the Jews of Newport better, he never changed his mind. In 1781, during the American Revolution, Stiles gave a speech to inaugurate a new academic year at Yale in which he insisted that the Jews did not understand their own Bible correctly. They were wrong to deny that the Old Testament taught the basic Christian doctrine of a "suffering Messiah." Hillel, the greatest figure of rabbinic Judaism, had misled the Jews. He had willfully corrupted biblical teaching in the years immediately before the appearance of Jesus.

The Puritans had begun, in the seventeenth century, by excluding all other Christians from their city of God. By the end of the eighteenth century, when the Republic was being founded, they had moved to accepting other Protestants—but not Catholics—as part of their America. The attitude toward Jews was ambivalent. Catholics and even other Protestants had nothing to teach Puritans. Jews, however, might help them understand the Hebrew Bible. Still, one had to be on guard against the Jews' cleverness and perversity. Judah Monis had not been liked, even though he was valued as a Hebraist. The students at Harvard complained that he was a bad teacher and, more pointedly, that he demanded too much money as payment for his grammar book, which was the required text in his class. A copy of the grammar that was owned by one of Monis's students still survives. This student amended the title page so that it no longer read "composed and accurately corrected by Judah Monis, M.A." The student wrote, instead, "confuted and accurately corrupted by Judah Monis, Maker of Asses." And Stiles, who prided himself on writing letters to Rabbi Carigal in Hebrew (it was very bad Hebrew), wrote continually in his diary that the rabbi was a rabbi and thus the representative of bad doctrine. Jews, no matter how intriguing they might be as individuals, remained outsiders. They could become part of America only if they ceased being Jewish.

A great question had been joined in colonial times: Was America to become the land of Asser Levy—a land of equal opportunity for any immigrant—or was it to be the land of the Puritans—a society which demanded conformity?

3.

Colonial Jews:

Almost Free

I

The Jews who came to colonial America were specks of dust, individuals picked up by some wind in Europe and blown across the Atlantic. Jewish poverty was increasing during the eighteenth century. Hordes of Jewish vagabonds were walking from town to town all over Europe looking for handouts; Jewish petty traders, the backbone of European Jewry, were increasingly in trouble throughout Europe. But only a very few Jews came to America. Many more might have come but the New World was remote and the journey dangerous. More important, the mass of those in trouble could not imagine living outside the established traditional Jewish community. They knew that it would be hard to be a Jew on the edge of the wilderness. Thus, those who crossed the Atlantic represented the few among European Jews who were least bound by tradition.

Colonial Jews were not very different from colonial Christians. The Americans, these "new men," were an unruly lot, even in religion. On the frontier all religion was remade by laymen. In colonial times both the Episcopalians and the Roman Catholics had no bishops in the colonies; these new settlements were treated as missionary territories. After the Revolution, in 1784, Samuel Seabury, the Episcopalian priest in New York, found his way to Scotland, after the authorities in London had put him off for many months; he was consecrated in Aberdeen as the first Episcopalian bishop in the United States. Six years later John Carroll was raised in London to be the first Roman Catholic bishop of a newly established diocese in Baltimore.

During the next half-century both these centrally organized churches established their network of authority throughout the United States, but the bishops of both churches were often defied. Under American conditions individual congregations were in law, from colonial times, independent bodies. Their properties were owned by individual trustees, and the laity chose their clergy. In Virginia, the most "English" of the colonies, the pattern was established very early; the clergy were the hired men of the congregation. This distemper with authority did not abate after bishops appeared in the United States. The Episcopalian bishops in America would never acquire the power of their English counterparts. The congregations remained the owners of the church buildings; they were never transferred to a central authority. Among the Roman Catholics the battles became especially bitter. Some congregations preferred to remain independent so that they could elect their own priests, even though they were excommunicated as schismatics.

Even in New England, where Puritanism was dominant, there was more disorder than uniformity. The very heart of Puritanism was the assertion that religious authority flowed from the individual congregation. It alone could consecrate a minister as its spiritual leader. It was an archheresy for a Puritan minister to be ordained by bishops of the Church of England or by Presbyterian elders. The flight of the founding fathers of the Massachusetts Bay Colony into the wilderness had represented a profound and very self-conscious act of breaking with Europe. The Puritans came to the New World to establish there a purer Christianity, to free the true faith of the corruption that had disfigured it in the old country. Puritanism was a shaping influence on all the other expressions of religion in early America. It did not succeed in teaching the lesson of Calvinist obedience to the awesome will of God, but all the sects learned from the Puritans what they wanted to hear, that no human authority stood above them.

In colonial America, the synagogues were like the churches; they were free associations. Individuals could choose to ignore the synagogue or to use it for whatever Jewish purposes they might wish. Many abandoned their Jewishness in North America during the seventeenth and eighteenth centuries. Where such individuals were prominent, their Jewish origins are widely remembered, very often to the discomfiture of their descendants. The Monsantos in New Orleans are an example of such immigrants. Upon arrival in America, this family was involved in the slave trade in New Orleans. They intermarried early and their Jewishness soon ceased to matter to them or to those around them. There were also some formal conversions to Christianity by adult Jews. Ezra Stiles told in his diary of meeting two Jews from London who had become Christians in Europe. In 1728, the pastor Henry Caner baptized Mordecai Marks in Fairfield, Connecticut; it is possible that Marks agreed to this step because he was about to marry a Christian. Michael Hayes, of a well-known New York family, joined the Baptist Church in Philadelphia around 1770. He was perhaps angry with his father for having cut him out of his will; the reason that the father gave was because of his "disobedience and general conduct." It is impossible to estimate the numbers of those Jews who left the Jewish community in colonial and early republican times, or to measure their influence on American life. The proportion was high, perhaps one in four of all the Jewish immigrants.

The Jews who cared established institutions which seemed to be exact copies of those that they had left behind in Europe. They had no other models. They therefore created synagogues in which the ritual was Orthodox, along with cemeteries, facilities for the slaughter of animals for food according to the kosher ritual, and mikvaot (ritual baths). The lay leaders of the earliest colonial synagogues behaved like their peers in Europe; they tried to enforce obedience to the ancient ways by all their members—but they failed, for, unlike the authorities of the Jewish communities in the European ghettos, the Americans had not the power to coerce. In the 1760s, New York's only synagogue fined members of the congregation who did not attend Sabbath services, but this practice was abandoned within twenty years because it was unenforceable. The earliest statutes had ruled that no one who was intermarried could be buried on the grounds of the synagogue's cemetery. Such offenders were eventually allowed to rest with other Jews, though the congregation stood fast on the rule that non-Jewish members of the family could not be accorded that privilege. Jewish shops in New York were closed on the Sabbath in the last half of the eighteenth century, but some Jews began to break ranks and open their stores on the holy day.

Even earlier, in the 1740s, Lutheran Pastor Henry Melchior Mühlenberg asserted that the Jews in Philadelphia were "practicing atheists." This was no doubt an overstatement, but we do know that several decades later, in the revolutionary era, the congregation in Philadelphia was troubled by members of the synagogue who desecrated the Sabbath. It was even more troublesome that some known Jews were entirely indifferent. According to a statement in a draft constitution of the synagogue, in the 1770s, sanctions were recommended against "people in the community who do not want to make any contribution and separate themselves from the group and do not want help to support the community."

The population of avowed Jews was some 250 in the year 1700 and perhaps 2,000 at the time of the Revolution. By the middle of the century, synagogues existed in five cities; in Charleston, New York, and Philadelphia, Jews numbered in the several hundreds. In these three centers, the communities were large enough and rich enough to invite a rabbi to be their religious leader, but they did not. This was a matter of choice. Many a poorer and smaller town in contemporary Europe was then supporting a fully structured Jewish community, with a rabbi at its head. It is not true that rabbis were hard to persuade to come to the New World. In the years of the American Revolution there were rabbis in Suriname, Curaçao, and Jamaica. In Jamaica, the learned rabbi of Kingston, Isaac Córdoba, was busy writing a defense of the Bible against the godlessness of the greatest paladin of the Enlightenment, Voltaire. The rabbi feared the inroads of Voltaire's thinking on the young of his congregation. His volume was first published anonymously in Jamaica in 1788 but there were soon two editions in the United States, in Philadelphia in 1791 and in Richmond in 1804.

The dangers to the faith seem to have been at least as serious among the Jews of the United States as among those of Jamaica. Otherwise, what need was there of two printings of Córdoba's book in the

United States? The work was actually read by American-educated children of immigrants to colonial America; it is listed among the goods in several estates. Nonetheless, despite the presence of some troubled, questioning younger people, the authorities of the various synagogues felt no need to persuade a rabbi such as Córdoba to come to New York or Philadelphia. The Jews in the American colonies employed only functionaries, such as cantors and ritual slaughterers. A resident rabbi or two might have insisted on exercising authority over the laity and on cultivating the study of the sacred texts.

This estimate of American Jews in the last half of the eighteenth century, that they did not care about Jewish learning, is confirmed by two stories from Rhode Island. The Jewish community of Newport was at the height of its prestige in the 1770s. Led by Aaron Lopez, the leading Jewish shipowner in America, these were among the most acculturated and elegant Jewish merchants. They thought of themselves, and were regarded by others, as belonging to the Jewish hidalgos of North America—and they were not lacking in generosity. After Lopez died by drowning, he was praised by a newspaper in Newport for representing "the most amiable perfections and cardinal virtues that can adorn the human soul." Ezra Stiles wrote: "His beneficence to his family connections, to his [Jewish] nation and to all the world is almost without parallel." Lopez supported numerous widows and orphans, and so did the rest of the Newport community. But these charitable men were indifferent to an offer that was made in the early 1770s by the founders of Rhode Island College, the ancestor of the present Brown University. The college opened its doors to Jewish students, and it extended an invitation to Jews to "have a tutor of their own religion." The founders of the college went even further; they would be glad to establish a chair in "Hebrew and Oriental languages" if Jews would contribute the money. The Jewish merchants declined. They were raising their children to succeed in business, not to go to college or to become Hebrew scholars.

Lopez and his friends were not totally indifferent to Jewish learning; they simply believed its proper place was in Europe or the Holy Land. The subject of Jewish learning was raised almost inevitably by Rabbi Isaac Carigal during his visit to Newport in 1773. Carigal had come to America to collect money for the academy of rabbinic studies (yeshivah) in the holy city, Hebron. The state occasion of

Carigal's visit was a sermon that he gave for the Shevuot (Pentecost) Festival. Carigal pleaded for "the frequentation of sacred colleges and synagogues where we daily hear the word of the Lord." He went on to insist that study of the Bible and of the rabbinic literature which flowed from it were the surest antidote to sin; it was the source of all the Jewish virtues. His listeners were moved by this plea. Carigal was sent on his way with a handsome donation for Hebron, but no school of Jewish studies was established in Newport. On the contrary, the leaders of this community were then spending their evenings playing cards together in a social club they had established; it was a cardinal rule of this establishment that the business of the synagogue should never be discussed. After Carigal's visit, as before, the sons of the merchants in Newport and elsewhere in the colonies were given sufficient instruction to celebrate their bar mitzvahs and to participate in the ritual of the synagogue, but only a handful of native-born Jews in all of colonial America were ever taught enough of the tradition to be able to conduct the service of the synagogue.

A letter from Haym Salomon, a man of business who maintained close relations with the leaders of the Continental Congress, confirms this picture of the inner life of early Jews in very graphic terms. He wrote in 1783 from Philadelphia, one of the three most established Jewish communities of colonial times, that "there is very little *Yiddishkeit* [Jewishness] here." This is all the more striking since Haym Salomon himself was hardly a paragon of Jewish piety. Haym Salomon himself seems to have known just enough Hebrew to read the prayer book mechanically, and to dictate letters in bad Yiddish, but beyond that he had no Jewish education. He had no doubt that America was not the place for learned Jews. In the last days of the Revolution, he passed a message back to his father in Europe: "Should any of my brothers' children have a good head to learn Hebrew, I would contribute towards his being instructed." The implication was clear that such a nephew should stay in Europe, and not come to America. Salomon told an uncle that Jewish learning meant nothing in America, and that it was better that this uncle not come to join him in Philadelphia. Another correspondent from Philadelphia wrote to relatives in Amsterdam two years later that "most of the sons of this province are not devoted to Torah and do not understand our tongue." An unsigned letter exists from the days of the Revolution in which a Jew announced that he was going back to Europe because America was no place for a man of piety; religion was weak and only money was well respected. Such discouragements would be written back home to Europe from all the future waves of immigration. They would act, as they did in the eighteenth century, to reduce severely the number of learned Jews who came to America.

Lopez and Salomon reflected the flatness of two functioning Jewish communities, Newport and Philadelphia. Elsewhere, on the frontier, where Jews were but a small, unorganized handful, or, even more difficult, lived as isolated individuals, the religious problems were far worse. Some immigrants wrote pained letters in Yiddish back to their families in Poland, in which the writers spoke of the Sabbath as a memory and of their inability to keep the dietary laws. Male children were often circumcised several at a time when a circuit-riding mohel appeared. But the picture was not all negative, even in outlying places. In 1754, a number of Jews from Philadelphia were engaged in land purchase and speculation in Lancaster, Pennsylvania; a congregation was formed there in 1776, and a synagogue was built in 1789. In Newport and New York, preserved kosher meat (salted beef) was imported on a regular basis from Jamaica, where it was prepared under the auspices of the local rabbinate. Great care was taken to make sure that these preserves arrived suitably labeled. Early in the nineteenth century this traffic was reversed; kosher meat was exported from New York to the islands.

Non-Jewish observers and travelers were struck by the hard struggle of some Jews to cling to their religion and by the complete indifference to the tradition of others. They reported on Jews who went to great lengths not to eat pork and to observe the Jewish Holy Days, but they told of others who did eat pork and who worked on the Sabbath. A Swedish scientist, Peter Kalm, observed as early as 1748 that "many of them (especially the young) when travelling did not make the least difficulty about eating this or any other meat." On the other hand, one can cite Hart Jacobs, who asked the authorities in Philadelphia in January 1776 to be exempt "from doing military duty on the city watch on Friday nights, which is part of his Sabbath." This wish was granted, provided the citizen performed "his full tour of duty on other nights." Aaron Lopez kept his business closed on the Sabbath and he refused to see anyone on business affairs, even at home, on any of the Jewish Holy Days. Occasionally, as in the case of two Jewish bankers, pious Jews let their businesses be run for them on the Sabbath by a trusted Christian employee.

Inevitably, technical problems in the Jewish religion arose which were beyond the competence of the local people. Marriages could be performed according to Jewish ritual by semilearned laymen, but conversions and religious divorces were more technical matters, requiring rabbinic learning and specific skills. Such learning was rarely to be found in America before the 1840s. Conversions to Judaism were often defective in form. One such case involved the second wife of Abraham Alexander, who was the cantor of Beth Elohim in Charleston, South Carolina, until he resigned in 1784. That same year he was married to a Huguenot lady. She lived as a faithful and observant Jew all her life, and yet she was denied burial in the Jewish cemetery because her conversion had not been carried out according to the prescription of Jewish ceremonial law.

And yet, American Jewry of colonial times was not totally Philistine and bereft of knowledge of the tradition. Several learned laymen did turn up, possibly because they were fleeing creditors in Europe. One such figure was Jonas Phillips, who arrived in Charleston, in 1756, at the age of twenty, as an indentured servant. After three years of such servitude, Phillips moved to Albany, where he opened a store, but the business that he hoped to do with the British garrison, which was then fighting the French and Indian War, was not sufficient to keep him from bankruptcy. Jonas Phillips soon moved to New York. He was employed for four years, in the 1760s, by the local congregation as the *shohet,* the ritual slaughterer of animals for kosher meat. To perform this task required some learning in Jewish religious law, which Phillips had evidently proved to the rabbis who had granted him qualification in Europe. He wrote rabbinic Hebrew well enough so that he could correspond with the rabbis in London. Manuel Josephson, of German birth, was probably even more of a scholar. Josephson made his living as a merchant in New York, but he was often consulted on matters of Jewish law. He wrote excellent rabbinic Hebrew, and he owned the best library of rabbinic texts in colonial America. It is clear from his will that he did not believe that there was a future in America for knowledge of the rabbinic texts. He specified that his volumes in Western languages be sold at auction, but that his books in Hebrew be packed up and sent back to Europe.

Rabbi Córdoba's refutation of Voltaire was the only original work by a Jew on Judaism that was published in early America, and this book had not been written in the United States. Nonetheless, colonial Jews did produce the first translation of the prayer book into English. The first volume appeared anonymously in 1761 in New York; it contained the evening service for the High Holy Days. Five years later, a much larger volume appeared; it included all of the Sabbath prayers and all of the High Holy Day liturgies. The name of the translator, Isaac Pinto, was given on the title page. Pinto was probably also the anonymous translator of the earlier volume. In the introduction to the second book, Pinto wrote that translation of the liturgy in English was required, because Hebrew is "imperfectly understood by many" and "by some, not at all." Pinto's translations were accurate, reflecting substantial knowledge of biblical and rabbinic Hebrew.

II

By mid-eighteenth century a few Jewish families had already lived in North America for two and some for even three or four generations. The most prominent were several branches of the Franks family. They had come to New York and Philadelphia from England as merchants and army purveyors. Everyone knew them to be Jews, but, even though some of its members belonged to synagogues, the Franks clan was already in the process of evaporating from the Jewish community. David Franks, who lived in Philadelphia, was the most prominent of them all. He remained part of the family business, and he seemed to have maintained good personal relations with his relatives, but he married a Gentile and all his children were baptized at birth. David Franks himself had been born and educated in New York City. His father, Jacob Franks, was president of the Jewish congregation for seven terms, and he was a man of some learning in rabbinic texts. David's bar mitzvah was, of course, celebrated in the synagogue. After David's father died, he observed the traditional period of mourning, and he even continued for a while to contribute to the synagogue in New York, but he never joined the congregation in Philadelphia, where he lived. David Franks owned one of the most elegant homes in Philadelphia; he was one of the few men of business there who had his own carriage. He remained in touch with Jews because he did business with them, especially with members of his own family, but he did not move socially in Jewish circles. David Franks was too elegant for that; he found his friends among the descendants of William Penn, who had founded the colony, and the rest of that circle. And yet, David Franks remained a Jew. To the end of his life he insisted on swearing oaths not "on the true faith of the Christian" but with his hand resting on the Hebrew Bible.

David Franks was not the only American Jew who remained Jewish despite intermarriage, and despite the social distance that he kept from other Jews. Unlike Franks, his cousin, Benjamin Levy, was even married to a Jew, but the family drifted out of the Jewish community. Levy did so well socially in Philadelphia that he was among the elite who were invited to contribute to the Pennsylvania Hospital, and he was among the signers, in 1767, of a formal address to welcome Lieutenant Governor John Penn. Benjamin Levy and his family moved to Baltimore. When his wife, Rachel, died, she was buried there in an Episcopalian cemetery. It is likely that this was decided by her children, who had intermarried and become Christians.

By the end of the colonial era, the handful of Jews on the Eastern Seaboard of North America had already defined three types. Some were like the second and third generation of the Franks family; they were rapidly assimilating, because success and social acceptance were their dominant concern. Others, a minority, followed after Jonas Phillips, who fought very hard for the preservation of Orthodox Judaism in the New World. The majority were assimilating into Gentile America, while maintaining considerable Jewish feeling. Haym Salomon represents this mainstream of early American Jews. He was the largest contributor to the Mikveh Israel Congregation in Philadelphia, but he was hardly its most pious member. Like so many Jews in the generations that were to follow, he paid his respects to the Lord by coming occasionally to services and by writing the synagogue generous checks.

Colonial America was different from Europe. In Europe in those days, assimilation usually meant the assumption of a new identity through religious conversion, or remaining Orthodox. A third option had begun to appear in Europe in those days: a few had ceased believing in the Orthodox tradition, and yet they chose to stay within the Jewish community. Such men were very busy inventing new definitions of Judaism to justify their changes in belief and practice. In the 1770s and 1780s, the philosopher Moses Mendelssohn and a whole circle of friends and disciples in Berlin were trying to define how one could be both a man of the world and a Jew. In America, there was no contemporary echo of the writings of Moses Mendelssohn. Partial or very nearly total nonobservance of the commandments of the religious tradition became the norm very early without any attempt at an intellectual defense. In America, those who wanted to leave Judaism did not need to convert or to explain themselves to themselves. If they wished, they could live on the border, as some did, between leaving and remaining. American Judaism was becoming in practice almost as many "Judaisms" as there were individuals. A new version of a Jewish persona was defined in America as early as the eighteenth century: it was an individual who lived like everyone else, and yet "felt Jewish."

In eighteenth-century America such Jewishness did not last beyond a generation or two. There is little doubt that before 1800 less than half of the grandchildren of the early Jewish settlers remained Jews. We know from precise genealogical tables that one-third of the grandchildren of those who remained Jews in the time of the Revolution had left the community by 1840. The rate of assimilation had decreased, no doubt because by then there were already more Jews in the United States, at least three times as many as the two thousand of the 1780s. There was thus a greater possibility of marrying within the fold. In generations to come, the rate of assimilation of the grandchildren of immigrants would remain fixed at one-third. "German Jews" and "Russian Jews" would, in turn, define their Jewishness in America in the same terms as the handful of colonial Jews: to be a Jew meant to "feel Jewish," rather than to be learned or pious.

III

Biblical Jews were ever present in the minds of the Puritans, but there were almost no living Jews in Massachusetts or elsewhere in New England except in the port city of Newport, Rhode Island. The existing Jews were in the middle and the southern colonies, from

New York to Georgia and South Carolina. Jews were discussed and sometimes they were harassed, but the tensions were of marginal importance. True, Jews had no political equality in any of the colonies before the Revolution; officials had to swear their oaths "on the true faith of a Christian," or by affirming their belief in the divinity of both the Old and the New Testaments. The situation varied from colony to colony. The charter for South Carolina, written by the philosopher John Locke, allowed any seven people to assemble and to constitute a church, including "Jews, heathens and other disenters." Maryland, on the other hand, even though founded by Catholics, had specified in its charter that only Christians would be allowed to live in the colony, even though stray Jews who came to trade or even to settle were not overtly molested.

Nowhere, not even in the most tolerant places, did Jews have secure rights to vote in elections for representatives to colonial legislatures. Jews did vote in New York in 1737 in a bitterly contested election, but their votes were thrown out. The argument against them was that Jews had no such rights in England, and that they remained guilty of the Crucifixion. In Rhode Island in 1762 the lower house of the legislature held that Jews did not have the right to hold office or to vote in elections. Nonetheless, Jews seem to have voted in local elections in several of the colonies, because nobody bothered to stop them. Peter Kalm had remarked as early as 1748 that "Jews enjoyed all the privileges common to other inhabitants." What they lacked in equality seemed insignificant or irrelevant to a foreign observer.

The vital issue for Jews in the eighteenth century was economic rights. Here, the Jews in the American colonies were, both in law and in practice, free and equal at least half a century before this was true even in England itself. Despite some laws on the books, the rights that Jews had fought out very early in New Amsterdam, to trade in local commerce like all other burghers, were never seriously contested either there or in any other colony. Their right to engage in sea trade was denied by the English, as part of their ongoing attempt under the Navigation Act of 1660 to limit the import and export trade of all English colonies to English ships, which were manned by Englishmen. Individual Jews managed to win exceptions to this rule. Rabba Couti, a Jewish burgher from New York, won a case in 1672 before the Council for Trade and Plantations, which held that he was not an alien. The Navigation Act of 1696, as originally drafted, would have excluded from international trade anyone who was not a native of one of the colonies, or born in England. This provision was dropped under pressure from Jews and Huguenots in London, who appeared on behalf of their brethren in the American colonies. The Jewish petition argued that Jews were the enemies of the Inquisition, and that they regarded the land which gave them refuge as "their native country." These problems ended when the Naturalization Act of 1740 was passed; it allowed all Protestants, Jews, and Quakers to be naturalized in the English colonies. After that, the difficulties that Jews had were not different from those of all other American sea traders. The pattern had thus been set a generation before the Revolution: in America, as nowhere else, Jews could make their living without constraint, as they pleased.

Nonetheless, many of the Jews who came to the colonies in North America did not remain. They did not do as well in the New Land as they had hoped. We know of a Jewish merchant community of some twenty families in Newport in the 1680s, but this community was not the ancestor of the famous and more important one which existed in the middle of the next century. In a number of cemeteries in the Caribbean—in Barbados, Jamaica, Curaçao, Suriname, and St. Eustatius—there are gravestones of people who lived a good part of their active lives in the American colonies, and even in the nascent Republic, and then went elsewhere. Some left in search of a more Jewish life, but most were looking for a better living.

As early as colonial times, the economic profile of the Jew was radically different from that of the rest of the country. In earliest America, more than four out of five people made their livings working the land, but not the Jews. They were the only denomination which consisted, in its large majority, of city people. The country needed middlemen and artisans, and those were the skills that Jews had acquired in Europe where for many centuries very few had been permitted to farm. In the next two centuries Jews would enter many new occupations, but the identification of Jews with the cities, and with the urban economy and culture, has remained fixed as a fact of American and of American Jewish life.

Attempts would be made in the future, some of them successful, to limit Jewish immigration to America, but there was never any serious discussion by non-Jews (as there was often in Europe in the eighteenth century and thereafter) that Jews ought to be restratified economically by sending them off to "healthy" occupations on the land. This dream, or fantasy, would be harbored by some Jewish immigrants to America toward the end of the nineteenth century and the beginning of the twentieth, but it never penetrated the consciousness of American anti-Semites (perhaps, in part, because these Jew haters were often themselves farmers, and they had no desire to have Jews in the farm across the road).

In the North American colonies Jews were totally absent from the one heavy industry of those days, the making of iron. They were of no consequence in the trade of grain and tobacco, the two most important agricultural exports of the era. These products were raised on farms and plantations in Maryland and Virginia, where there were hardly any Jews. Jews did figure very early, even before 1800, as middlemen in the sale of copper, but they were not principals in the few small mines that were being worked in the eastern United States. On the eve of the Revolution, most Jews were artisans or petty merchants. Only a very few were well-off, and even they did not have the capital with which to launch themselves toward the highest reaches of the American economy. There were only two marked exceptions to the rule that colonial and early American Jews were artisans or middlemen. There were some farmers in Georgia. Aaron Lopez manufactured candles in Newport from the spermaceti of whales; this was the only economic endeavor in which in the eighteenth century Jews were important, producing about thirty percent of the total output. Jewish financiers were of little consequence, because North America was then no great financial center. The Franks family of army purveyors (this pursuit involved advancing large credit to military authorities) had branches in New York, Philadelphia, and Montreal at various times, but the center of the enterprise was in London.

There was some anti-Semitism, even in the colonies which were hospitable to Jews. Even in supposedly tolerant Charleston, South Carolina, a Jewish funeral procession was attacked in May 1743, probably because of some economic quarrel between the family of the deceased and Gentile competitors. In almost every quarrel between Jew and Gentile, somebody managed to throw in the slur that the Jews had crucified the Lord, and that they were therefore untrustworthy, even in business. At the very beginnings of Jewish settlement in America, the Reverend John Megapolensis had asked the authorities in New Amsterdam to expel them, not only because he hated their religion, but because the Jews had no other God "than the unrighteous Mammon, and no other aim than to get possession of Christian property, and to win all other merchants by drawing all trade towards themselves." Right before the Revolution, in 1770, Ezra Stiles confided to his diary without a breath of doubt that in London, Jews headed a spy operation in the colonies on behalf of the government and that all their agents were local Jews. On the other hand, colonial Jewish businessmen were often complimented for their honor and uprightness. On the whole, the language about Jews was no more hostile—indeed, less so—than the rhetoric that was often directed against Catholics.

Almost everyone who mentioned the Jews in colonial America suggested or at least implied that they ought to convert to Christianity, but there were no missions to the Jews anywhere. American society was, then, in the process of becoming. A colony might exclude people it did not like, but those who were admitted were by and large not troubled in the exercise of their religion. Colonial society was too fragmented and untidy for persecution to work. The persecuted could, like Roger Williams, move into the wilderness and start their own settlement, or they could avoid places like Boston and do business in places like the more tolerant Philadelphia. Contrary to the later, nativist myth, the population of colonial America was not overwhelmingly Protestant, of English origins. Some forty percent of the earliest Americans came from all over Europe, and they belonged to an enormous variety of religious sects, such as Quakers, Mennonites, and Seventh-Day Baptists. In this complex early America, Jewish religious rites were not entirely strange or unique.

Sometimes the sects even helped each other. Jews made the first "interfaith" gesture as early as 1711, when seven contributed to the building of Trinity Church in New York. After the middle of the eighteenth century, Jews and Christians had worked together in organizing several Masonic lodges. When the new synagogue building in Newport was dedicated in 1763, the governor of the colony and other civic dignitaries were present. The symbolic high point of this Jewish-Christian amity was probably the sermon that Rabbi Carigal delivered in that synagogue in the spring of 1773. The congregation, that day, included the governor of Rhode Island, judges and other civic officials, and, of course, Ezra Stiles. The sermon was given in Spanish, but it was soon translated into English and offered for sale to the general community. Carigal impressed his audience, according to Stiles's diary, with his elocution, and even more with his garments: "a fur cap, scarlet robe, green silk damask vest, and a chintz under-vest—girt with a sash or Turkish girdle—beside the alb [prayer shawl] with tzitzith [ritual fringes]."

Before and after this great occasion, Carigal had engaged in many conversations which involved comparisons of Jewish and Christian theological doctrines. His Christian interlocutors, led by Stiles, did not accept Carigal's Jewish views, but they had great respect for his learning and intelligence. Carigal proved that Jews could be more than successful merchants: they had ties to the Holy Land, and they belonged to a tradition of learning—like the Puritans. Carigal's visit gave Newport's Jews vicarious dignity. The honor and the money that the Jews of Newport gave to Carigal, in all his Oriental Jewish splendor, acted to make the community into a "normal" American denomination.

But Jews were the only settlers in the colonies who were not Christian. They were therefore, inevitably, the most exotic. At the state occasion at which Carigal had preached, the governor had come out of respect for the importance of the Jewish merchants of Newport, and Stiles attended because he was fascinated by the Oriental Jewish sage who preached the sermon, but the governor stood at the head of a colony which had refused to naturalize Lopez (he had had to appeal to Massachusetts, of all places), and Stiles kept confiding to his diary that he admired Lopez and Carigal, but he wanted them to turn Christian. There is no written record of what Lopez and Carigal thought that day, but they must have marveled at the presence of the Christian dignitaries, even as they knew that the visitors to the synagogue were half hiding some ambivalences about Jews. Lopez had been born a Marrano in Portugal, and he and his wife had fled to America in 1752 in fear of the Inquisition. Carigal came from Hebron, where Jews were *dhimmi,* a tolerated, sometimes persecuted, minority of inferior status. Lopez and Carigal knew that even in America Christians did not regard Jews as their equal—and yet, America was different.

4.

Revolutionaries—and Some Tories

I

The American Republic would have been founded exactly as it was if there had not been a single Jew in the thirteen colonies. There were simply too few of them for their efforts to make a serious difference during the Revolution. True, the great majority of the two thousand Jews who dwelt in America were Whigs, supporters of the revolt. Even by the most unsentimental estimate, they did contribute far more to the American cause than anyone could have expected from so small a community. Almost a hundred Jews have been identified as soldiers in the revolutionary armies. The first patriot to lose his life in Georgia was Francis Salvador. In July 1776, he accompanied William Tennent, a Presbyterian evangelist, to North Carolina to try to persuade some Tories to join the Revolution. On August 1, Salvador was ambushed and shot and scalped by Tories and their Indian allies. In Charleston, South Carolina, almost every adult male Jew served in the military. Captain Lushington's company, which was half Jewish, became known as the "Jew Company." One of its braver soldiers, Jacob I. Cohen, some years after the war, was the owner of land in Kentucky, and he hired Daniel Boone to survey his property. There was one area of military action in which Jews took a notable part. About six percent of the American privateers, the warships that were outfitted and sent to sea by individual owners or companies, were financed by Jews, with Aaron Lopez of Newport in the lead.

The contribution of Jews for the conduct of the war was even greater among the civilians. Mordecai Sheftall, the leader of the Jewish community in Savannah, was also a central figure among the rebels in Georgia. When the British occupied Savannah in December 1778, Sheftall was jailed on a prison ship. The British governor of Georgia, James Wright, was so enraged at the Jewish Whigs that he wanted to bar those who had fled from ever returning to the colony. He wrote home to London that "These people, my Lord, were found to a man to be violent rebels and pursecuters [sic] of the King's loyal subjects." One hundred men bearing arms, even with an outsized proportion of heroes, were not the hinge of the Revolution—but Jews played a more than honorable role in achieving independence.

Jews also helped to keep the Continental Congress from going bankrupt. The most important figure in this tale was Haym Salomon, who had arrived in New York by 1775 and had opened a business as merchant on commission, securities dealer, and ship broker. Salomon joined the rebels very early. In 1776, he was arrested by the British in New York, but he was released from jail at the request of the Hessian mercenaries, who needed a purveyor who spoke German. Salomon quickly became rich, but was betrayed in August 1778 as a Whig sympathizer and he fled to Philadelphia. Soon Salomon was lending money to the Continental Congress. In the last days of the war, after his friend, Robert Morris, became superintendent of finance, Salomon advanced the American government over two hundred thousand dollars in hard currency to help provision the armies. What he got in security was paper which was never redeemed. Salomon died bankrupt in New York in 1785, and his family, despite half a century of effort, never succeeded in collecting the debt.

Most of the Jews were partisans of the Revolution, but a pronounced minority were Loyalists. Jewish artisans and small merchants almost all rallied to the cause of the rebels. The Jewish Tories were mostly shipowners who were involved in the direct import of finished goods from England. There were, indeed, more Jewish Loyalists than the first, "patriotic" historians of colonial Jewry wanted to find. The Hart family were Tories. They rivaled Aaron Lopez among the Jewish merchants and international traders in Newport, Rhode Island. On July 1, 1780, the Assembly of Rhode Island formally deprived three members of the family of their rights and property. Soon thereafter, Isaac Hart was brutally murdered because of his support of the British. Nevertheless, some of the international Jewish traders were partisans of the Revolution. Isaac Lopez, of Newport, was the most prominent. He had long flaunted the British by dealing directly with the islands in the Caribbean. Lopez was even praised by local authorities in Rhode Island for his attainments as a smuggler, and he continued during the Revolution to run ships which evaded the blockade by the British navy.

Jewish opinion was split in New York, as well. In 1776, when the British occupied the city, a "loyal address" was presented to General Sir William Howe; among its signers were fifteen Jews. A number of Jewish partisans of the Revolution did flee to Philadelphia, along with their cantor, Gershom Mendes Seixas; he was the first Jew who was born and trained in America to become the religious leader of a congregation. The Jewish Tories of New York did not, however, remain without a clergyman. Isaac Touro, the cantor of the congregation in Newport, Rhode Island, left that city when the rebels were in control, and found his way to New York. In 1783, when peace was made, Touro left for Jamaica, where he could live under the British crown. He soon died and his family, including his son Judah, who was later to become famous as a philanthropist, returned to the United States.

Jews were also divided in Philadelphia. Haym Salomon fled to New York to escape British occupation, but David Franks did not. The Franks family changed sides a few times. They were, by turn, purveyors to the army, whether Patriot or British. When General Sir William Howe occupied Philadelphia in 1778, Rebecca Franks, a celebrated beauty and charmer, the daughter of David Franks, was the belle of the ball in the social circle of British officers. In 1782, she married one of Howe's officers, Lieutenant Colonel Henry Johnson. After the war, Rebecca went to England with her husband. Colonel Johnson was eventually made a baronet; the Johnsons ended their days in Ross Castle in Ireland.

The Patriot majority of American Jews, represented by Haym

Salomon of Philadelphia, Aaron Lopez of Newport, and Mordecai Sheftall of Savannah, were not crucial to the American Revolution. Their importance to Jewish and American history lies not in what they did, but simply because they were there. The decisions by the Constitutional Convention to create absolute equality in the United States among all kinds of believers and nonbelievers was made in awareness that there were Jews in America, and in the expressed intention that they, too, should benefit from the new Constitution.

This document defined the rights of citizens in the federal government, but the individual states lagged behind. By law, Jews did not have full rights in any of the colonies, and the situation did not change all at once during and after the Revolution. By 1777, only one state, New York, had given complete political equality to men of all faiths, or none. In 1790, Virginia, Georgia, South Carolina, and Pennsylvania followed suit. It took many decades for the last obstacles to be removed from all of the state constitutions. Some of these documents retained the provision that oaths for public office had to be taken on the "true faith of a Christian," but the federal Constitution was evermore the dominant political arrangement. The vestiges of exclusion in colonial times eventually faded from all the state constitutions. The last to fall was New Hampshire, which waited until 1868 to delete a Christian oath as a requirement for office.

When the Constitutional Convention assembled in Philadelphia in 1787, there were some fears that Jews might be limited by the national government to the rights that they already had in the colonies, and that they would thus be excluded from voting and from holding office. Jonas Phillips addressed a petition to the assembled delegates. He begged them not to require officeholders to be sworn in on "the true faith of a Christian." Phillips was particularly worried about the deliberation at the Constitutional Convention, because the Jews had lost a battle in the state assembly of Pennsylvania eleven years earlier. In December 1783, a group which included Haym Salomon and Gershom Mendes Seixas had petitioned in protest against the state constitution which required that members of the assembly had to "acknowledge the Scriptures of the Old and New Testament to be given by divine inspiration." This declaration effectively excluded Jews from office. The writers of the petition called this act "a stigma upon their nation and their religion." It is revealing and important that the writers of the petition more than gently threatened the authorities in Pennsylvania. They themselves had no great passion for public office, but, so they argued, maintaining such exclusions would harm Pennsylvania: Jews in Europe or elsewhere who might want to come to America might prefer to go to places like New York "where there is no such like restraint laid upon the nation and religion of the Jews." This protest by Jews in Philadelphia was the very first time in American history that Jews demanded equality, citing their services as patriots as the undeniable argument. This petition was ignored, but the religious test was removed six years later, when a new state constitution was written.

Phillips's petition to the Constitutional Convention was unnecessary, though he could not have known it, because the deliberations of that body were taking place in total secrecy. Two weeks before he wrote, the Constitutional Convention had passed, on August 20, the sixth article of the new national Constitution: no religious test would be required of officeholders. Two years later, the First Amendment to the Constitution strengthened this foundation of the new American Republic by decreeing the separation of church and state. In federal law, Jews, the smallest of all recognizable minorities, now had totally unrestricted freedom and equality in the United States.

II

Like everyone else in America in the era of the Revolution, Jews, of course, knew that they were living in the midst of great events, and yet they reacted as Jews: they were not quite ready to believe their good fortune. Even after they had read the new Constitution, they needed reassurance that their place in America was secure.

Popular anti-Semitism had always existed. The uneducated and unreflective mass of the immigrants to the New Land, of whatever origin, had brought with them the age-old stereotypes that Jews were alien and bad. The more specific charge, that Jews did harm to the economy, was very seldom made in colonial America, but it was hurled during the Revolution. When the British invaded Georgia in 1778, a number of the Jews in Savannah sent their families to Charleston for safety, while they remained to fight. A letter in the

Charlestown Gazette on December 1, 1778, accused the Jews of disloyalty. The anonymous writer charged that the Jews, "after taking every advantage in trade the times admitted of in the state of Georgia, as soon as it was attacked by an enemy, fled here for asylum for their ill-got wealth, dastardly turning their backs on the country, which gave them bread and protection." Equally anonymously, "a real American and true-hearted Israelite" answered the next day that the attack was a lie because only women and children had been evacuated, while all the men had remained for their patriotic duty.

The economic charge against Jews was made once again in Philadelphia in 1784. Miers Fisher, a former Tory, returned to Philadelphia at the end of the war and tried to obtain a charter to open a bank. He argued that his bank would serve the public by reducing the rate of interest; the citizens of Pennsylvania would thus be protected against the usury of the Jews. An anonymous "Jew Broker" (he was probably Haym Salomon) answered in the press. The writer was outraged that Fisher had defamed the Jews of Philadelphia. How dare he say such things against people who had been "second to none" in their "patriotism" and their "attachment" to the American cause. Salomon did suggest that there might have been a few Jews who had behaved badly in business, but were the many to be punished for the sins of the few? How could Miers Fisher suggest that Jews as a whole behaved less well than all other Americans, when the truth was that they were to be found among the best patriots of all?

The first direct attack on Jews, after the declaration of the United States, was made in the early 1790s. Jews seem to have been criticized (we do not know by whom) for their supposed clannishness. Dr. David Nassy, who was in medical practice in Philadelphia in the 1790s, seems to have been the first polemicist in America to defend Jews against the charge of clannishness. He listed a number of Jews in Philadelphia who were "lawfully married to Christian women, who go to their own churches, the men going to their synagogues, and who, when together, frequent the best society." Such Jews could not be accused of self-segregation, so Dr. Nassy argued. Nassy was evidently not an opponent of assimilation.

A more serious incident took place in 1800. A leading figure in the Philadelphia Jewish community, Benjamin Nones, was attacked in the *Gazette of the United States*, a publication of the Federalist party, for being a Jew and a Republican (i.e., a supporter of what is today the Democratic party). Nones did not flinch. He affirmed his loyalty to the revolutions in the United States, in France, and in Holland, because these were the only regimes which had yet given equality to Jews. Nones's answer to the *Gazette* was a passionate expression of Jewish anger at centuries of persecution:

> *I am a Jew.* I glory in belonging to that persuasion, which even in its opponents, whether Christian, or Mahomedan, allow to be of divine origin—of that persuasion on which Christianity itself was originally founded and must ultimately rest—which has preserved its faith secure and undefiled, for near three thousand years—whose votaries have never murdered each other in religious wars, or cherished the theological hatred so general, so unextinguishable among those who revile them. . . .

> But I am a Jew. I am so—and so were Abraham, and Isaac, and Moses and the prophets, and so too were Christ and his apostles. I feel no disgrace in ranking with such society, however it may be subject to the illiberal buffoonery of such men as your correspondents. . . .

> I am a *Republican!* . . . Among the nations of Europe we are inhabitants everywhere—but Citizens of nowhere *unless in Republics. Here, in France, and in the Batavian Republic alone, we are treated as men and as brethren. In republics we have rights,* in monarchies we live but to experience *wrongs.* . . .

> How then can a Jew but be a Republican? In America particularly. Unfeeling & ungrateful would he be, if he were callous to the glorious and benevolent cause of the difference between his situation in this land of freedom, and among the proud and privileged law-givers of Europe.

Thus, in the earliest days of the United States, society was largely open to Jews, but some ambivalence about them did persist. Their enemies, who were fortunately not many, insisted the Jews were obnoxious. Jews answered that they had as much right to be in America as anyone else. The "Jew Broker" had even defended their right to have a few unlovely characters among them; Jews had earned such total equality by their superior services to America. Dr. Nassy had answered critics by assuring America that Jews were becoming just like everybody else, and by more than hinting that they would soon blend totally into the majority through intermarriage. Benjamin Nones gloried in being both a political liberal, an enemy of privilege everywhere, and a totally devoted Jew. All these types would recur in future generations.

III

At the time of the American Revolution the vast majority of the Jews of Europe lived in Poland, a country that was being divided and redivided by the emperor of Austria, the king of Prussia, and the czar of Russia. Despite their troubles, the Jewish masses in Poland were as inert in the 1770s and 1780s as the rest of the population. Some heard rumors of the revolt in America, but what they heard left them puzzled. Rebellion against the state had not been an option for Jews for sixteen centuries, after the last revolt against Rome had been crushed in Judea in the year 135. In the Diaspora, even under very bad conditions, Jews had always tried to make accommodations with authority; they had not imagined the possibility that they might be among the armed rebels, who were helping to make a new political order that would include them as equals.

Western and Central Europe were much more aware of the American Revolution. Because the war that the Americans and the English were fighting in America affected the balance of power in Europe, Frederick the Great of Prussia was a close observer of the events in America. France, hoping the American revolt would weaken Great Britain, was much more involved. The financial subsidies provided by France and its direct military intervention on behalf of the rebels were critical to the survival of Washington's forces and to the eventual success of the Revolution. Even so, there was remarkably little echo of the American Revolution and of the founding of the Republic among the Jews of France and Germany. What was said—and what was not said—prefigured the reactions future generations of European Jews would have to America.

The Jews of France were almost totally uninvolved in the American Revolution. In 1782, after the British defeated the French fleet under de Grasse in the Caribbean, an appeal was made in Bordeaux to purchase another ship. The vessel cost 1.5 million livres. The amount was quickly raised among the grand bourgeois of the city; Jews contributed a little more than 60,000 livres to this subscription. This was an act of loyalty to the policy of France; it did not represent any special identification of the Jews of Bordeaux with the Americans. Indeed, the first and only serious discussion in French by a Jew of the revolt in America had been negative. Isaac de Pinto, the first Jew to be a figure of some consequence in French letters, had published a pamphlet in 1776 denouncing the American rebels. He had argued that it was to the interest of the major powers to guarantee peace and order in the world; therefore they should join in obstructing the independence of the American colonies. The Americans were leading to "the overthrow of order and true liberty . . . it is the temper of Oliver Cromwell." Great Britain was not simply enforcing a tax on tea, so Pinto argued; it was defending the basic principles of political order and legitimacy.

Pinto's reaction to the American Revolution was not as strange as it seems. He was a man of the Enlightenment who wanted to think of himself as belonging to the European intelligentsia. In 1762, he had written a famous open letter to Voltaire, in which he had argued against Voltaire's contempt for the Jews. Pinto pleaded for equality at least for the Sephardim; they had become Westernized men of affairs and they were thus different from all other Jews. Pinto did include some Ashkenazim: "The rich among them are devoted to learning, elegance, and manners to the same degree as the other peoples of Europe, from whom they differ only in religion." Pinto more than hinted that his candidates for acceptance in society had ceased believing in the Jewish religion, but they would not leave the fold "because of the delicacy of their emotions," and because they had "the greatness of soul" to continue to be identified with "a religion which is proscribed and held in contempt."

Years before the American and French revolutions, Pinto used the language of the Enlightenment to redefine the age-old position of the Jewish upper class. They wanted no political overturns. Pinto presented his "clients," the "enlightened Jews," as already belonging to the economic and intellectual world of the high bourgeois of Europe. Pinto painted the Jewish men of business as the most clear-headed among the partisans of mercantilist economic interests. Such

Jews deserved permanent admission to the club of the powerful.

Reacting to the beginnings of the American Revolution, Isaac de Pinto had thus become the archetype of modern Jewish political conservatism. He was soon imitated even in America. After the Republic was established, Jews were among the first to put the spirit of rebellion behind them. As groups fought each other in those early years of the United States, Jews tried to be as inconspicuous as possible in public. They reserved their otherness for the intimacy of the synagogue. In politics they pronounced themselves to be the best and most devoted upholders of order in America. A few were so eager to identify with established America that they were even to be found among the earliest nativists.

Pinto, writing in French, had not written for Jews; he had addressed himself to the learned world. Among Jews, only a small minority, to be found among the Sephardim of Bordeaux and Bayonne, could read him in French. The bulk of the Jews in France, some thirty thousand, lived in the border region between France and Germany in the two provinces of Alsace and Lorraine. Their lives had remained unchanged for centuries. Except for a few rich army purveyors and horse traders, most made poor livings by lending small sums to the peasants or selling them goods on credit. In 1777–78 the peasants were incited against the Jews. This unrest in eastern France brought the discussion of "the Jewish question" to a head. The enemies of Jews had been saying for decades, even in the language of the Enlightenment, that the misery of the Jews was their own fault: supposedly, they preferred the unlovely, "Jewish" occupations of petty moneylending or peddling. Therefore, society had no choice but to defend itself by walling off the Jews in a separate enclave. Reformist opinion held that the Jews had no preference for these pursuits; they had been condemned to such degradation because most Jews had not been allowed to do anything else. In this fateful debate, the favorable situation of American Jewry played an important role.

The first pleading for the Jews was published by Christian Wilhelm Dohm in 1781. The work, entitled *Concerning the Political Reform of the Jews,* appeared first in German and the next year in French. Dohm was an official of the court of Frederick the Great, the king of Prussia, where the events in America were closely watched. Moses Mendelssohn, who was the first Jew to acquire a reputation in German literature and thought, had asked Dohm to write in defense of the Jews. The money to pay Dohm for his trouble came from the leader of the Jews in eastern France, Cerf Berr. In his book, Dohm maintained that the Jews would give up moneylending and peddling, if the state and majority society would only let them. As convincing proof that this could happen, Dohm cited the Jews in America. They were engaged in productive occupations. They were so grateful to the societies which had given them freedom that they now supported the Revolution against Great Britain. If these Jews in North America were capable of such transformation of themselves, so were all other Jews who were still living in misery in Europe.

There were other reverberations in Germany of the unique good fortune of the handful of American Jews. In 1783, as the peace treaty between the rebellious colonies and the mother country was being signed, an anonymous Jew wrote a letter in German to the president of the Continental Congress. The author asked for a definition of the conditions under which a group of families, perhaps as many as two thousand, would be allowed "to settle into the desert in America and convert it into a fertile land." The writer described the misery of the Jews of Germany in the darkest colors. He knew that reformers like Dohm wanted to help the Jews, but the anonymous petitioner doubted that such efforts would do any good. Europe was not going to change for the better. America was the place where Jews could start over again. Nothing came of this letter, but the suggestion that European Jews might establish an enclave of their own in America had been made for the first time.

But America was far away and strange; it set no immediate precedent for Europe, where monarchs still reigned everywhere, except in Switzerland. All Europe knew by 1789 that Jews, too, had been included as equal citizens by the Constitution of the United States, but this was no precedent for the Jews in France. On the eve of the French Revolution they prepared requests *(cahiers)* for the Estates General, which Louis XVI convoked in 1789. In these documents, the Jews asked for the right to trade and to be artisans "on a plane of equality with the rest of His Majesty's subjects," but not for any change in their political status. In the debates in France about Jews between 1789 and 1791, their unparalleled status in America was barely mentioned, but it did not have to be. The new American

Republic of virtue and equality was the immediate model for the French revolutionaries.

The American Revolution was a much gentler and more modest affair than the one in France, but it can be argued that the events in America were ultimately more important for the history of mankind. The American Revolution was certainly more important for Jews. The emancipation of the Jews in France was granted grudgingly, between 1790 and 1791. Other countries in Western and Central Europe granted Jews political equality in the course of the nineteenth century, but everywhere after a bitter fight. When these laws were blown away by Adolf Hitler, few resisted. The results of the American Revolution have lasted.

Despite the attacks on Jews in the age of the Revolution and of the founding of the Republic, they had many more friends than enemies—and the Constitution was profoundly in their favor. But the Jews themselves were not quite sure what the new Republic represented for them. Was it a total transformation of their history in exile? Or was the American Revolution a sign of profound stirrings in heaven itself that the end of days and the restoration of the Jews to Zion were near? And the Christians were not at all sure what they wanted the Jews to become in the new America.

5.

James Madison's America

During the era of the Revolution and of the founding of the Republic, there was almost no debate about Jews, but the views of the Enlightenment in Europe, and of the heirs to the Puritan tradition in America, and of the Whigs who wrote the Constitution were all stated, if only by inference.

Thomas Paine, the most radical intellectual among the makers of the American Revolution, transplanted to America the open bitter criticism of the Bible that was current among the "enlightened" of Europe. One of the first essays that he wrote in America, a few weeks after he arrived in 1774, was an attack on the enslavement of the Negroes. Some of those who defended this practice had said that slavery had been permitted to the Jews in the Bible. Paine replied that "the example of the Jews, in many things, may not be imitated by us"; he went on to quote passages from the Bible in which Jews had been ordered utterly to destroy several nations. On the other hand, in his most famous pamphlet, *Common Sense,* Paine quoted biblical history as authority for attacking the principle of monarchy.

74

The prophet Samuel had been opposed to establishing a monarchy, as contrary to the will of God. "In the early ages of the world, according to scripture chronology, there were no kings; the consequence of which was, there were no wars."

But Paine's basic teaching was undisguised contempt for the Bible. He wrote *The Age of Reason* in 1793, after he had left America for France. This tract, which was widely read in the Republic Paine had helped found, centered around the notion that

> Whenever we read the obscene stories, the voluptuous debaucheries, the cruel and torturous executions, the unrelenting vindictiveness, with which more than half the Bible is filled, it would be more consistent that we called it the word of a demon, than the Word of God. It is history of wickedness, that has served to corrupt and brutalize mankind; and, for my own part, I sincerely detest it, as I detest everything that is cruel.

Paine was as contemptuous of Christianity as he was of Judaism:

> But when, according to the Christian Trinitarian scheme, one part of God is represented by a dying man, and another part, called the Holy Ghost, by a flying pigeon, it is impossible that belief can attach itself to such wild conceits.

There was, however, a half-explicit difference between Paine's attacks on Christianity and his distemper with Judaism. For Paine, Christianity was a false religion which ought to be abandoned. Those who would free themselves of such superstitions would then be able to move on to the God of Reason. Judaism was the religion of the Jews; as was self-evident, the Jews of that time were the biological descendants of those of ancient times. His calling Moses "that chief assassin and imposter" was more than an attack on the religion of the Jews; it was a slur on their character. This was all the clearer in *The Age of Reason,* where Paine maintained that the ancient heathens "were a just and moral people, and not addicted, like the Jews, to cruelty and revenge." This "ancient Gentile world," according to Paine, respected virtue and distanced itself from vice; they had been defamed by "the Jews, whose practice has been to calumniate and blacken the character of all other nations."

In *The Age of Reason,* Paine injected into America a distinction between Christians and Jews that had been made by Voltaire: Christians were Gentiles who needed to unlearn the religion that some sectarian Jews had once foisted on them; the Gentiles would then return to their roots in ancient, pagan philosophy. Jews, however, needed to be cured of their very character—and who knows whether such a character is curable. Paine himself never asked this question explicitly, but those who read him had to conclude that practicing Jews were a danger to enlightened society, and that only those who would assimilate completely might be acceptable.

This "enlightened" idea, that Jews should assimilate into the majority, was acceptable to believing Christians, the very Americans who were the most outraged by Paine's attack on the Bible. In their view, the new American society was to be a Protestant commonwealth. The most interesting exponent of this vision was Ezra Stiles. Even as he expressed the new patriotism, Stiles remained an heir of the Puritans. He kept repeating that the Jews were perverse outsiders. As we have seen, Stiles had inaugurated a new academic year at Yale in September 1781 by insisting, as he had before, that the Jews did not understand their own Bible correctly. Those who were still devoted to rabbinic Judaism might be equal citizens, but their religion was an affront to the truth. Stiles did not expect the Jews, or the Catholics, for that matter, to become Calvinist Christians, but he did identify America with Protestantism. The new American society was, for Stiles, the realization of the dream that the Puritans had had of founding a new Zion in the wilderness. Writing about America during the Revolution and immediately thereafter, Stiles asserted that the founding of America was the climax of human history; the new Republic was to be the example, and salvation, for all of humanity. America as a whole had now replaced the theocratic Massachusetts Bay Colony which had been founded by the Puritans as "the City on the Hill." Those who chose to come to the United States would become part of this new glory. Stiles implied strongly that the alien who came in any other spirit had better stay home, for what he brought with him was out of keeping with the meaning of America. The Americans were the new "chosen people," and their history was the realization of sacred drama.

Stiles was not tenderhearted about those who did not fit into the new order. Like his Puritan forebears, he knew that some people had to be excluded, or held as second-class citizens, lest they contaminate the New Jerusalem. He was fierce enough in his last years to become not only a partisan of the French Revolution but also a defender of regicide, of the execution of kings by revolutionaries. Such acts were necessary in order to make an end of the old order and to usher in the new. Stiles died too soon, in May 1795, to have the time to take full account of the French Revolution. His fervent appreciation of the new, republican America, therefore, remained the capstone of his spiritual career. He expressed it in the sermon that he gave in Connecticut on election day in 1783. He foresaw an America that would extend its population all over the continent and that would be the center of international trade. Stiles was certain that a representative democracy, where the government was not imposed from above by a monarch, would guarantee the happiness of all its citizens. In such a democracy the people would elect leaders of stature and merit, and they would have the chance periodically to reverse any errors that they might have made. This glorious new American society would extend liberty of religion to all Protestant denominations. Jews, and Catholics, would exist largely on sufferance until they assimilated and disappeared. Stiles, the Hebraist and the friend of the Jews of Newport, and of its rabbinic visitors, defined an Anglo-Saxon, Protestant republic.

One deep truth was reflected by the dissimilar visions of Paine and Stiles: the American Revolution was a break with the past; it was a fresh beginning. The victory of a bunch of colonial irregulars against the might of the British Empire was improbable and near miraculous. The sound of the music that the British band had played at Yorktown, Virginia, in 1781 reechoed among the revolutionaries. Lord Cornwallis, the most experienced British general, had surrendered in a formal ceremony to the tune of the song, "When the world turned upside down." The three million inhabitants of the new state in North America, who had withstood the might of Great Britain and astonished the world by establishing a republic, were the obvious candidate for the role of that perfected society which the thinkers of the Enlightenment, or the patriotic Christians, were imagining. The American settlement was relatively new, no more than 150 years old in the 1780s, and its inhabitants, by the very fact of their emigration to the New World, had come to America to make a fresh beginning. But the dreamers of a new America did not speak with one voice.

77

Most opinion agreed that society needed to be made better, but, in their majority, Americans were willing to wait for the blessings of liberty to transform the unworthy into true citizens, and to leave the worthy untroubled. The only test was obedience to the political arrangement of the new Constitution.

The visions of Tom Paine and Ezra Stiles were not enshrined in the Constitution. On the contrary, the defense of untidiness was the basic and undoubtable meaning of the American Constitution. The motto on the Great Seal of the United States, *novus ordo saeclorum* (a new order of the ages) did not mean, despite Tom Paine and Ezra Stiles and those who thought like them, that the United States was being defined as a redemptive society. The authors of *The Federalist Papers,* and especially James Madison, were absolutely clear that they meant the contrary: the American Constitution spelled out a form of government which would enable many utterly dissimilar "factions" to be themselves; that many such "factions" and "interests" existed in the United States was the guarantee that a political majority could not be formed to suppress any minority. Thus, the new American Constitution was not a program for creating a harmonious society of the like-minded. On the contrary, social disharmony, the continuing warfare between many, often dissimilar subgroups, was the surest guarantee of liberty.

James Madison was the most eloquent, and the clearest-headed exponent of this definition of the new United States. Madison was consistent and absolutely clear in making the distinction between loyalty to the new political arrangements and pressure toward conformity of any kind. In 1776 and again in 1785 he fought very hard to forbid the establishment of religion in Virginia. Because there were few Jews or Catholics in the state, this action meant that the Episcopal Church was being put on a plane of equality with all other denominations. In 1789 Madison was the principal author of the First Amendment of the Constitution in which it was decreed that the Congress could make no law establishing any religion or prohibiting its "free exercise." Here, Madison still seems to have been thinking mostly about equality among the Protestant sects. He wrote that he wanted "to disestablish individual Protestant churches in the several colonies (such as the Episcopalians in Virginia and the Congregationalists in Massachusetts and Connecticut) and to keep peace among them."

The separation of church and state in America had much wider meaning; it made faith, any faith, into a private, personal matter. It gave equality to all believers and unbelievers. But it was still possible to imagine that all other behavior, both public and private, could, and perhaps should, be governed by a new culture of republican virtue. In a very few years, that attitude would become the explicit doctrine of those who made the French Revolution. They guillotined people for lack of *civisme* (civic virtue), for not belonging to the new revolutionary culture. Jews were told explicitly, in the debates at the very beginning of the French Revolution, that they would be granted equality only if they gave up their Jewish specificness.

In *The Federalist Papers,* Madison made it unmistakably clear that no such conformity was demanded of anyone by the American Constitution:

> If a majority be united by a common interest, the rights of the minority will be insecure. There are but two methods of providing against this evil: the one by creating a will in the community independent of the majority—this is, of the society itself; the other, by comprehending in the society so many separate descriptions of citizens as will render an unjust combination of a majority of the whole very improbable, if not impracticable. The first method prevails in all governments possessing an hereditary or self-appointed authority. This, at best, is but a precarious security; because a power independent of the society might as well espouse the unjust views of the major, as the rightful interests of the minor party, and may possibly be turned against both parties. The second method will be exemplified in the federal republic of the United States. Whilst all authority in it will be derived from and dependent on the society, the society itself will be broken into so many parts, interests, and classes of citizens, that the rights of individuals, or of the minority, will be in little danger from interested combinations of the majority. In a free government the security for civil rights must be the same as that for religious rights. It consists in the one case in the multiplicity of interests, and in the other in the multiplicity of sects.

This was no casual utterance in *Federalist Paper,* Number 51. Madison knew exactly what he was saying, for he had referred in an earlier essay (Number 39) to the political teachings of Montesquieu. As Madison understood him, Montesquieu had taught the impor-

tance of the confederation of small groups: in such a political structure, there would be so many interests that no majority could be
mustered to oppress a minority. Madison knew that the various
minorities were not necessarily pure and virtuous. On the contrary,
they "are united and actuated by some common impulse of passion,
or of interest, adverse to the rights of other citizens or to the permanent or aggregate interests of the community." But one dare not
remove faction, either by destroying liberty or by "giving to every
citizen the same opinions, the same passions and the same interests."
In *Federalist Paper,* Number 10, Madison, after defining the problem,
insisted that human nature is various in all its parts, and that "the
protection of these faculties is the first object of government."

Madison never entertained the thought that the various "factions"
that he was discussing would resemble one another. His America
was not going to be some tidy arrangement of ethnic subgroups, or
of religious sects, or of economic interests. The word "faction," as
he used it, meant the turbulence of all kinds of groups, which cohered
for often totally dissimilar purposes:

> A religious sect may degenerate into a political faction in a part of
> the Confederacy; but the variety of sects dispersed over the entire
> face of it must secure the national councils against any danger from
> that source. A rage for paper money, for an abolition of debts, for
> an equal division of property or for any other improper or wicked
> project, will be less apt to pervade the whole body of the Union
> than a particular member of it; in the same proportion as such a
> malady is more likely to taint a particular county or district, than
> an entire State.

Madison was thus listing all of the special interests that came to
his mind, for they were present in his America. It was still possible
to imagine, as even he did sometimes in his later years, that such
complexity needed to be countered by some devotion to national
unity, but Madison always returned to defining national unity as the
devotion to all the political institutions which had been created by
the Constitution. Madison's writing in *The Federalist Papers* presumed
without question that the various "factions" in America existed because each had some power; they did not survive on each other's
goodwill.

It was, of course, possible, then and later, not to want any more "factions" in America, but this was not what Madison taught. He defined America as a place to which people had come—and obviously more would come in the future—to associate in any way that they wished. The only restriction was that they could not band together to destroy the Constitution. New groups would matter in America to the degree to which they succeeded, under that Constitution, in acquiring the power which flowed from their achievements.

In its first encounter with Jews, the new government of the United States spoke not in the accents of Paine or Stiles, but in those of Madison. In 1790, the six congregations which then existed in the United States decided to write a letter of congratulation to George Washington on his inauguration as the first President. As was to happen again and again in the next two centuries, all of the Jewish bodies could not agree to act together. In the end, four of the congregations wrote one letter and the other two, the synagogues in Richmond, Virginia, and Newport, Rhode Island, wrote separately, but in the same spirit. The rhetoric of these letters is instructive. These congregations did not describe themselves as Jews or as Israelites; they used the phrase "children of the stock of Abraham," no doubt to suggest that they belonged to the same tradition as the Christians, who often called themselves descendants of Abraham. Those who drafted those letters wanted to sound as little separatist as possible. The operative plea, in the words of the Jews of Newport, was to ask of the new President that his government give "to bigotry no sanction, to persecution no assistance." Washington echoed the sentiment in his response, in which he affirmed that "the children of the stock of Abraham" were indeed equal within the new Republic, in which "all possess alike liberty of conscience and immunities of citizenship."

Unlike some of his most important colleagues in the making of the Revolution, Washington was not a reflective man. There is no evidence that he ever thought about the relation of Jews to society in any theoretical way. He did know that there had been some dramatic scenes of Jewish-Christian amity and cooperation in those earliest years of the Republic. Gershom Mendes Seixas, the cantor of the congregation in New York, had participated in Washington's inaugural on April 30, 1789. Some months earlier, so Benjamin Rush reported, "the rabbi of the Jews, locked in the arms of the ministers of the gospel, was a most delightful sight" at Philadelphia's great parade to celebrate the acceptance by Pennsylvania of the United States Constitution. There had even been a kosher table at that mammoth party. The year before, in 1788, the Jews of Philadelphia had turned to Gentiles for help in building their synagogue. Benjamin Franklin was among the contributors. None of this was entirely new, for, as we have seen, such interfaith occasions had occurred in colonial days. Washington was responding in the spirit of this tradition and of the recent interfaith events. He was, in fact, saying to the Jews exactly what he was declaring to the Catholics in those very days. George Washington wrote to the New Church in Baltimore: "In the enlightened age and in this land of equal liberty . . . a man's religious tenance [sic] will not . . . deprive him of the right of attaining and holding the highest Offices that are known to the United States."

II

Jews responded to the founding of the Republic in several ways. Their participation in the Revolution as equals had predisposed some to enter public office, even before Washington had made it clear to both Jews and Catholics that they had the right, and even the duty, to participate in the staffing and management of the new government.

Toward the end of the Revolutionary War, David Salisbury Franks was sent abroad twice as courier of diplomatic documents. In 1784, he was appointed vice-consul in Marseilles, and the next year he went to Morocco as part of an American delegation which negotiated a treaty to end piracy directed against American vessels. Franks was thus the first Jew to be appointed to a post in the diplomatic service of the United States. A young Jew, Simon M. Levy, was a member of the first class to graduate from West Point in 1802. In the early decades of the nineteenth century, two grandsons of Jonas Phillips, Mordecai Manuel Noah and Uriah Phillips Levy, became prominent in American life, Noah as politician and writer and Levy as naval officer. Both Noah and Phillips were attacked by anti-Semites; their enemies said that as Jews they were unworthy of offices of trust in the public service. But Franks, Levy, Phillips, and Noah were the first avowing Jews to hold office in government.

The immediate religious response to the American Revolution reflected older ideas about the "exile of the Jews," but here, too, there was a shift in response to the new age. The man who thought most about these issues was Gershom Mendes Seixas. He wasAmerican-born, and more fully integrated into New York society than any Jewish clergyman was ever to be until the twentieth century. Seixas was for many years a trustee of King's College (which later became Columbia University). The sermon that he preached in his synagogue in New York on November 26, 1789, as part of the day of thanks-giving and prayer to celebrate the ratification of the Constitution, is particularly interesting and instructive. Seixas took pains to empha-size that the children of Israel still needed to return to their earliest estate, when they dwelt in their own land which God had promised to their ancestors. He would "cause us to be again established under our own government, as we were formerly." Seixas was grateful that "we are, through Divine goodness, made equal partakers of the benefits of the government . . . with the rest of the inhabitants"; nonetheless, he did not allow himself or his listeners to forget that "still we cannot but view ourselves as captives in comparison to what we were formerly, and what we expect to be hereafter when the outcasts of Israel shall be gathered."

Seixas returned to the messianic theme in a sermon that he preached in his synagogue nine years later, on May 9, 1798. He asserted that "the depravity and corrupt state of human nature that prevails almost throughout the world" assured him that "the glorious period of redemption is near at hand" and that God would soon be "again collecting the scattered remnant of Israel and establishing them ac-cording to His Divine promise."

There had been earlier echoes within the small American Jewish community of the hope for the Redemption. Ezra Stiles reported in his diary that the Jews in New York had expected the Messiah to come in 1768. There was another prediction that the miraculous year was to be 1783; this speculation was reported by both Stiles and Gershom Mendes Seixas. A vague story exists that someone came to New York in 1788 and told its Jews of "proofs" of the continued existence of the Lost Ten Tribes of Israel. In 1795 a ship captain docked in New York and told of a Jewish community in Pien-ching, now K'ai-feng, China. The leaders of the synagogue hastened to write a letter in Hebrew to these far-off brethren. They inquired whether the Jews of China were descended from those who had been exiled after the destruction of the Second Temple, or whether they were remnants of the Ten Tribes who had been scattered in Asia after the destruction of the First Temple. No answer was ever received to this missive, perhaps because by then the remnants of Chinese Jewry knew little Hebrew. However, in the very act of sending it, the leaders of the synagogue in New York signified that they continued to believe in the messianic redemption of the Jews and in their ingathering from the exile.

By 1807, in response to Napoleon's calling together a "Sanhedrin" in Paris to get the Jews to adjust their religion to the new circumstances of political equality in his empire, Seixas had become more guarded and ambivalent. He no longer was certain, in a sermon that he preached on January 11, 1807, that God "means to accomplish our re-establishment . . . as a nation in our former territory." Seixas thought that at the very least Jews would be "a particular society" in the Gentile world, equal in rights to all other religious groups. Nonetheless, he remained enough of a messianic mystic to cling to the belief that the Jewish people in exile could now expect that "the third time is nearly and rapidly approaching when we shall be established forever."

These messianic dreams of Gershom Mendes Seixas seemed to be repeating, in American English, the kind of visions that he had learned from pious books in Hebrew. Raphael Mahler, the contemporary Israeli scholar who has studied these sermons and writings, has pronounced Seixas a proto-Zionist, the first in the United States. This is not so. American Zionism has never thought that the Jews of America themselves were or should be on their way to the Holy Land. From Zionism's beginnings in the late 1880s, Zionists in America have imagined that they, secure in the land of liberty, would help their less fortunate brethren in Europe establish the Jewish homeland. As a "Zionist," Seixas belongs not among modern, activist nationalists, but rather among Orthodox Jewish believers in the Messiah, who would come to restore the Jews to ancient glory. But there was an "American" element in his messianic sermons. Some of the Protestant preachers agreed in those years with Ezra Stiles that the new United States was itself the redemptive society. Christian revivalists saw the creation of the Republic as a strange and wonderful event, which gave them hope that the Second Coming was at hand. Seixas was saying to his congregants that the "end of days" was near, but that it would happen as the Jews, and not as Christians, had predicted. Messianic times were on the way but they would not begin with the Second Coming of Christ.

The pronouncements by Seixas were heard in the synagogue, but there is no reason to believe that his congregants paid sermons much attention. Even if they did, the notion that the Messiah might come had no practical effect on what they were doing with their lives. In the here and now, the Jews of New York and Philadelphia, and of all of the other places in which Jews lived, were establishing themselves in business. Some were even becoming part of high society. They were settling in to live in America, like everyone else, as equal citizens.

The news of the freedom for Jews in America made an increasing difference in Europe. In 1819 an American Christian, W. D. Robinson, published a pamphlet in which he urged Jews to form a company to buy land in the upper reaches of what is now Mississippi and Missouri, to resettle some of the poor Jews of Europe. Such suggestions remained schemes on paper only. European Jews were city and village people. Excluded from the land by feudalism, many Jews lived in the villages and bought and sold cattle and grain, but they had not farmed in Europe for many centuries. There was no reason to come to the United States to do what they did not know. But, even though Robinson's pamphlet as such had little echo in Europe, it reflected an atmosphere of acceptance of Jews as Jews in the early United States. They were being invited to the New World and not told that they were unwelcome. This was heartening knowledge to European Jews—and soon there was a reaction.

After the fall of Napoleon in 1815, the rights that the French Revolution had extended to Jews remained secure only in France and in Holland. In Germany, this freedom was reversed, and medieval anti-Jewish restrictions were reintroduced. The young Jews who had taken advantage of their emancipation under French rule in the Rhineland were now trapped. One such, Karl Marx's father Heinrich, saved his career as a lawyer by converting to Christianity in 1817. Others of that generation remained in the fold and fought for the emancipation of the Jews. Several such intellectuals organized a society in Berlin to raise the respect for Judaism and thus to help persuade the state to grant Jews equality, but they were not very hopeful of success. These men looked over their shoulders to America. In 1822, one year after the society had been founded, they wrote to Mordecai Manuel Noah, asking him to become associated with their body and to be their link with the United States. The three signers of the letter (Eduard Gans, Leopold Zunz, and M. Moser) did not conceal their objective from Noah. They wrote "the better part of European Jewry are looking with eager countenance of hope to the United States of North America." They dreamed of immigration because they wanted "to exchange the miseries of their native soil for public freedom," and they invited Noah and his friends to "establish a perpetual correspondence with us about the means of transplanting a vast portion of European Jews to the United States." Nothing came of this effort. There is no record of a response by Noah, who was probably less than enthusiastic about the scheme. Large migration was not yet possible, at very least because sailing ships were still the only mode of crossing the Atlantic.

III

In the United States, the discussion about Jews continued, even as their equality under the Constitution was never questioned by anyone. Social critics of various kinds continued to suggest that Jews still needed to reform themselves to some degree.

John Adams, the second president of the United States, had been influenced by the Enlightenment, even as he distanced himself from the most extreme "enlightened" views about Jews. He was well read in the works of Lord Bolingbroke and Voltaire, who were the sources of Tom Paine's distemper with the Bible, but Adams rejected the charge made by all three of these thinkers that the Bible had been a negative moral influence. In 1809, Adams wrote that "the Hebrews have done more to civilize men than any other nation." Without the Jews, so Adams asserted, mankind would not have "a doctrine of the Supreme, Intelligent, Wise and Almighty Sovereign of the universe, which I believe to be the essential principle of morality and consequently of all civilization." While John Adams did not pretend that he loved the Jews, he insisted that one had to try, even though "it is very hard work to love most of them." Adams even believed in the restoration of the Jews to their own land, to Judea. His reason was the hope that such an event "would soon wear away some of the asperities and peculiarities of their character, possibly in time [for them] to become liberal Unitarian Christians." In 1818, Adams, responding to a letter from Mordecai Manuel Noah, was totally positive. He voiced the hope that Jews might be "admitted to all privileges of citizenship in every country of the world." It was the duty and glory of the United States to take the lead in making an end of "every narrow idea in religion, government, and commerce."

Noah sent this same letter to several others among the still-surviving Founding Fathers of the United States. He included, for each of them, a copy of his discourses on the consecration of the new synagogue building on Mill Street in New York. James Madison responded that freedom of religion and opinion belonged equally to everyone, but not, interestingly enough, because this freedom was, of itself, an absolute value. Madison saw this basic rule of the American Constitution as "the best human provision for bringing all either into the same way of thinking or into that mutual charity which is the only proper substitute." Madison would not have been more comfortable with the first option, that of assimilating all America into one opinion. On the contrary, he had always believed in untidiness, in the right of various identities to be themselves in America. In his own personal behavior, Madison had not acted as an ideologue, who was so firmly persuaded of his principles that they admitted no exceptions. Despite his passion for the separation of church and state, Madison had, as a leader in the House of Representatives, created the office of chaplain and he had hired a Protestant divine. As president, Madison had appointed Noah in 1813 to be American consul in Tunis, but Madison had allowed his secretary of state, James Monroe, to withdraw the appointment in the next year on the avowed ground that Noah's Jewishness was a liability in dealing with the local rulers. Madison's practice was, in this case, worse than his theory in *The Federalist Papers*.

Thomas Jefferson, too, harbored some ambivalence about Jews. He responded to Noah's letter by asserting that Jews have "a particular need, evidently greater than that of any others, to pay more careful attention to education." They should labor to achieve equality in science, that is, in secular learning, so that "they will become equal objects of respect and favor." Jefferson was thus expressing the view of the mainstream of the Enlightenment, that all men could attain equal place in society, but the "entrance fee" was that they should adopt the ways and the outlook of the "enlightened." Jefferson apparently did not consider that a Yiddish-speaking Jew who knew the Talmud was equal in usefulness to society with a classically trained thinker like himself.

The most forceful expression of early American ambivalence toward Jews is to be found in the writings of Hannah Adams. A descendant of Henry Adams of Braintree, Massachusetts, and thus a distant cousin of John Adams, Adams published in 1812 a volume on the history of the Jews which was based in part on the work of the Abbé Henri Grégoire, a leader during the French Revolution in the battle for the emancipation of the Jews. In addition to her literary and personal connections with Grégoire (who thought that kindness, and not persecution, was the best approach to converting the Jews), Hannah Adams was also associated with the earliest efforts of the London-based Society for the Promotion of Christianity among the Jews in America. In her history, Hannah Adams wrote that the suffering of the Jews was due to their rejection of Christ. She did, however, note that during the Christian Middle Ages, "while Christendom was involved in darkness and ignorance," the Jews had learned from the Muslims to be in the forefront of learning. In her continuing quarrel with the Jewish religion, Hannah Adams judged Jewish rituals as too rigid. She accused Jews of continuing to regard themselves as "the chosen people, superior to all others," and she asserted that they still "look down on all nations." Hannah Adams did not make any political suggestions. She certainly accepted the equality of the Jews under the American Constitution, but she believed, like Ezra Stiles a generation earlier, that American freedom was simply an opportunity for Jews to be converted to an enlightened Christianity.

There was, however, one new note in Hannah Adams's work. She was aware that the solvents of the Enlightenment had worked on a number of Jews, and that many had "imbibed the principles of infidelity and no longer believed in the divine inspiration of the Bible and the coming of the Messiah." For Hannah Adams, this development was entirely negative; nonbelieving Jews were not candidates for conversion. Indeed, she feared that Jewish faithlessness increased the danger of such "infidelity" in Christian circles. The first hint was thus expressed in America by an enlightened Christian that the secularization of the Jews might be a subversion of American culture.

Another form of ambivalence about Jews appeared in the most important journal of early national days, the *Niles' Weekly Register,* which was edited in its greatest days by Hezekiah Niles. Niles fought hard for total equality everywhere in America, including such states as Maryland, which continued to exclude Jews from public office, but Niles, too, thought that Jews were different. He said several times in his journal that "Jews are consumers, not producers." Perhaps the best definition of the early republican attitude toward the Jews is to be found in several of Niles's comments in 1820. He asserted that while "this is the most preferrable country for the Jews, they will not cultivate the earth nor work at mechanical trades, preferring to live by their wit in dealing and acting as if they had a home nowhere." Nonetheless, Niles asserted that "all this has nothing to do with their rights of men." It is not clear whether Niles was being critical of the potential immigrants from Europe, or whether he included also the already-assimilated Jewish residents of the United States. Perhaps he did not know himself.

American Jewry, then and later, has remained nervous about this lack of clarity. Jews have kept insisting that they have become a "normal" American group, even though they have remained city people in a country in which farmers and ranchers are the mythic Americans, and non-Christians in a country of many religious sects. The basic mold was set early: while the Jews were accepted as a part of America under the Constitution, everyone knew that they were different. In the earliest days of American history, Gentiles and even Jews pretended less often than in some later times that they thought that Jews were "just like everybody else." A certain unique nervousness began early in the relationship between this minority and the rest of the country. It would remain.

6.

Patriots in the New Nation

In the early nineteenth century, most American Jews were native-born. This changed in the 1830s, when the "German Jews" began to arrive, for they came in such numbers that they soon constituted a majority of the Jews in America. During the next century, successive waves of immigration ensured that every census until 1940 would continue to show a majority of foreign-born. The critical difference between the community these days and the one that existed in the early years of the Republic is size: there were perhaps six thousand Jewish souls in the United States in the 1820s; in the 1940s, and after, there were over five million. Nonetheless, the early, small community acted in ways which seem remarkably contemporary.

In those early days, Jews had little trouble in entering the American economy. The country was growing. Despite losses to commerce which were caused by the War of 1812, and the economic panic of 1819, the first three decades of the nineteenth century were heady days. This was the era of the Louisiana Purchase of 1803, when the United States more than doubled in size, and of the creation of new towns and cities on the frontier in the West, beyond the Appalachian Mountains. New York, Philadelphia, and almost all the other port cities were growing; they had become cities with a past, with established societies and institutions. Jews were part of this growing economy, both on the frontier and in the major cities. No American Jew then possessed a great fortune on par with the Astors in America or, among Jews, the Rothschilds in Europe, but American Jews were almost all part of the urban middle class.

After 1800, Jews, for the most part, had remained in their accustomed pursuits as merchants and middlemen. Most were and remained moderately well-off storekeepers. Some, such as the parents of Judah Benjamin, the future secretary of state of the Confederacy, did not do well (his mother kept a fruit shop), but they were helped by relatives. Others found their way into the very center of the social and economic establishment. In New York, Daniel Peixotto was a physician of high professional reputation and social acceptability. John Moss, a Jew who came to Philadelphia from England in 1796, had quickly integrated into the economic oligarchy of the city; he sat on the boards of the Lehigh Coal and Navigation Company and of the Commercial Bank of Pennsylvania. Despite the persistence of some anti-Semitism, the social position of some Jews was strong. In Philadelphia, the Gratz family, which had become a clan of leading merchants, remained socially acceptable even though Simon and Hyman Gratz went bankrupt in 1826. A daughter of the house, Rebecca Gratz, conducted a salon attended by many of the best American writers. Through her friend Washington Irving, Rebecca Gratz was sufficiently well-known in Europe so that it was reputed that Sir Walter Scott had modeled Rebecca, the Jewish heroine of his novel, *Ivanhoe,* after her.

Rebecca Gratz was devoted to Jewish causes, and especially to teaching young people about their religion in classes that she organized on Sundays, but the Jewishness of most was evaporating. A contemporary Jewish observer, Jacob Lyons of Savannah, Georgia, wrote in 1820 that "a synagogue, as it exists in the present organization, will not be found in the United States fifty years hence." This was not a wild guess. By 1837, when the descendants of colonial Jewry were into their third generation, the rate of intermarriage was one in three. The old synagogues remained, but individual members

rarely came to worship services. The congregations were burial societies. A shrinking minority was still Orthodox, but the majority
was passive and largely indifferent. A few did care enough to want
to make changes. This happened for the first time in America in
Charleston, South Carolina, in the mid-1820s. The Beth Elohim
Congregation in that city was, then, still undeviatingly Orthodox.
In fact, in the synagogue's new constitution which was promulgated
in 1820, it had even been decreed that those who were "publicly
violating the Sabbath or other sacred days shall be deprived of every
privilege of the synagogue." The reigning Orthodoxy was, however,
that of the older generation.

In 1824 perhaps two-fifths of the entire community, over forty
adults, petitioned the synagogue for a revision of the rituals. These
members asked that some of the prayers, all of which were said in
Hebrew, be repeated in English. They wanted to remove "everything
superfluous" from the service, and to add a sermon to the Sabbath
service. When these requests were ignored, Isaac N. Cardozo, David
N. Carvalho, and Abraham Moise, businessmen, and Isaac Harby,
a writer, took the lead in forming a Reformed Society of Israelites.
On January 16, 1825, this body was formally organized; within a
year it had fifty members, almost half of all the families who had
previously belonged to Beth Elohim. The reformers established their
own Sabbath service, almost entirely in English, and they worshiped
with uncovered heads. But Harby and his friends were breaking with
Orthodox beliefs even more than with Orthodox rituals. These
younger Jews in Charleston belonged to a time and place in America
when it was possible for Thomas Cooper, then president of South
Carolina College, and a major figure in town, to deny to successive
senior classes "the authenticity of the Pentateuch"—and to pro-
nounce Holy Writ to be a tissue of errors.

These views were reflected in the prayer book of the Reformed
Society of Israelites. It was based on the assertion that only the moral
law, not the ritual prescriptions, was divinely revealed. The editors
of this volume added that they were acting "for themselves and for
their children and for all those who think the period has arrived when
the Jew should break in pieces the sceptre of Rabbinical power." The
messianic hope for the return of the Holy Land was never mentioned
in the new prayer book, except very obliquely in the marriage service.
The ten articles of faith which were put at the front of the volume

were a Deistic document addressed to all mankind; the Jews and the Jewish religion, as such, did not figure.

The society of religious reformers in Charleston did not last long. It began to fall apart soon after Isaac Harby left for New York in 1828 in search of his fortune as a writer and teacher (he died there within the year). By May 2, 1833, the society was formally disbanded, and the moneys that had been collected toward building its own synagogue were returned. The stirrings that this group represented were not even important, as precedent, in the bitter battle that was to begin two decades later over transforming the parent congregation, Beth Elohim, into the first Reform synagogue in America. By then, that synagogue was largely in the hands of newer immigrants. Nonetheless, Isaac Harby is a significant figure in the history of Jews in America. He was the very first Jew in America who made his career as a writer. Harby had nothing original to say, either in his essays or his plays, but he did reflect the intellectual and religious outlook that dominated, then, among cultivated young men and women—and he was bold enough, together with Cardozo, Carvalho, and Moise, to refashion Judaism to be American.

Mordecai Manuel Noah was much more picturesque, gutsier, and more successful than Isaac Harby. At least formally he remained an Orthodox Jew, even though he observed the rituals of the tradition in a most eclectic way. Noah was a curious mix. Upwardly mobile, a patriotic American and self-dramatizing, Noah tried to act heroically on the stages of both American and Jewish history. He was a disciple of Jonas Phillips, his maternal grandfather who had raised him in Philadelphia, and of Gershom Mendes Seixas, to whose New York synagogue Noah belonged. Noah was born in 1785. His father was a bankrupt who seems to have faded out of the family. He grew up in the home of his grandfather. He was apprenticed to learn the trade of gilding and carving, but he spent all of his spare time reading in the Philadelphia public library. In 1808, Noah was one of the founders of the Democratic Young Men in Philadelphia, who advocated Madison's candidacy for president. He had begun to write even before he took a hand in politics, for a play of his was put on the boards while he was still in his teens. In 1809 Noah moved to Charleston, South Carolina, to edit the *City Gazette*. The paper supported the reelection of James Madison as president. Madison was under attack from his opponent, Governor DeWitt Clinton of New

York, for having entered the War of 1812 with Great Britain. Noah defended Madison. After the election, which Madison had won with the help of South Carolina's electoral votes, Noah traveled to Washington to ask for political reward. As we know, the President appointed him American consul in Tunis, a post for which Noah had been campaigning since 1811.

On his return from Tunis, Noah moved to New York and established himself as a journalist, playwright, and political figure. His uncle, Naphtali Phillips, published a newspaper in New York, the *National Advocate,* and Noah became its editor in 1817. This paper supported the Democratic party, which meant Tammany Hall. This organization, which had begun in politics in 1789 as a group of middle-class opponents of the Federalists, had become coextensive with the Democratic party in New York. In fact, in the very year in which Noah assumed the editorship of the *National Advocate,* Tammany was both strengthened and changed by Irish immigrants who forced their way into the organization. Until the *National Advocate* was sold in 1824, Noah was near the very center of Tammany politics. He derived political advantage from this connection. In 1821, Noah was given an interim appointment to the office of high sheriff of New York by a Tammany-controlled Council of Appointments. When he ran for election the next year, it was alleged by his enemies that one of the tasks of the sheriff was to supervise hangings, and that it was against Christian sentiment for a Jew to be an instrument in the execution of true believers. These were anti-Semitic remarks, but the attacks on Noah as a Jew were no more vicious, and perhaps even less so, than the calumnies which were the usual rhetoric of politics in those days. Worse things were being said then by Protestants and by Catholics about each other.

Noah broke with Tammany in 1825, when he supported its enemy, DeWitt Clinton, for governor. The next year he established a newspaper of his own, the *New York Enquirer,* in opposition to Tammany Hall. In 1829, Andrew Jackson, whom he had supported for president, named Noah "surveyor and inspector of the New York Port." This was a substantial piece of patronage: Noah's salary was $5,000 a year, plus fees for various services, and he was able to continue editing the *Enquirer.* Twelve years later, in 1841, Noah was made a judge of the Court of Sessions. Without ever reaching high office, Noah had a middling career in politics. He might have done better had he not been a Jew, but that is unlikely. Journalism has seldom been the launching pad for major political careers in America.

As a Jew, Noah had apparently paid attention to the sermons of Seixas. In 1825, he staged and acted the principal role in the most theatrical event of the first two centuries of American Jewish history. As a supposed preamble to the ultimate ingathering of all the exiles to the Holy Land, Noah made himself the center of an effort to found a self-governing Jewish entity in the United States. Noah issued a proclamation to announce that he had helped purchase a tract of land on Grand Island in the Niagara River, which he renamed Ararat. This place was to be an ark of refuge for all the Jews of the world. Noah styled himself "high sheriff of the Jews," among other magniloquent titles, and he even presumed to instruct the leaders of the Jewish communities in Europe (who had no advance knowledge of what Noah was doing) to make regular collections in support of his enterprise and to report to him on their activities. Noah proclaimed that in God's name "do I revive, renew, and re-establish the government of the Jewish nation, under the auspices and protection of the Constitution and laws of the United States of America." This refuge was to be a "temporary home" for the Jews. In Ararat, "an asylum is prepared and hereby offered to them [the Jews] where they can enjoy that peace, comfort, and happiness which have been denied them through the intolerance and misgovernment of former ages." Noah even knew of the seventeenth-century notion that the Indians were the remnants of the Ten Tribes; he proposed in Ararat to begin the effort to reunite these American aborigines with their long-lost Jewish brethren.

The inauguration of Ararat took place in the early fall of 1825 in a ceremony in St. Paul's Episcopal Church in Buffalo, New York. Noah himself marched in between two rows of brightly uniformed local militia. An enormous crowd gathered to behold this spectacle, but these were almost all curious Gentiles. A leading American paper, *The Weekly Register,* mocked Noah as a land speculator who had invested in land on the island and now wanted to get rich quick by selling parcels to Jewish settlers. A Jewish journal in Vienna refused to take such theater seriously, especially since the gaudy inauguration had taken place in a church. Noah's colorful first act had no continuation; no one bought land, and no spade was ever turned in Ararat. All that remains of Ararat today is the memory of its founder's bombast, and, remarkably enough, the cornerstone that he dedicated that day, which turned up some years ago and now rests in the museum of Buffalo's Historical Society.

Ararat failed, but Noah had conceived it as a stopgap on the way to the ultimate, classic Jewish dream of the ingathering of the exiles. He returned to this theme, on which his minister Seixas had preached a quarter of a century earlier, in a speech which he gave in New York in 1837. Noah stated the traditional view that it was forbidden to try to compute the exact date of the Restoration. Nonetheless, he asserted that "faith does not rest wholly on miracles" and that "the Jewish people must now do something for themselves" to prepare for the Restoration. He proposed that a sum of twelve to thirteen million dollars, "a sum of no consideration to the Jews," be found with which to buy Syria (it then included Palestine) from the pasha of Egypt.

The restoration of the Jews to the Holy Land was the "last cause" of Noah's life. Noah even tried to enlist Christian support. In 1845 he spoke before two large and distinguished audiences in New York, which included the Roman Catholic bishop of the city and several leading Protestant ministers. Noah argued that the return of the Jews to the Holy Land was a necessary preamble in Christian theology to the miracle of the "end of days," and, therefore, it was to the Christian interest to help the Jews regain Zion. This approach was angrily rejected by Jewish critics both in New York and in London. They thundered that Noah was dangerously clever in trying to use those Christians, who wanted to convert the Jews, as his allies in an effort to reestablish a Jewish kingdom in Judea. In fact, Jewish opinion in Europe was dominated in those days by the drive for equal citizenship. A suggestion of reestablishing the Jews in Zion, especially if made to Christians, was feared, because it opened the door to the argument that Jews were aliens who should be sent back to Palestine. Noah had essentially agreed with these enemies of the Jews in Europe. He had accepted the idea that Jews remained alien in all of these lands, and that, except for America, their only hope was to return to Zion.

In this speech, Noah rose to his most eloquent climax in praising the United States as "the only country which has given [Jews] civil and religious rights equal to that of all other sects." The United States had therefore "been selected and pointedly distinguished in prophecy as *the* nation, which at the proper time, shall present to the Lord his chosen and trodden-down people and pave the way for their restoration to Zion." Noah did not expect the Jews of America to go to Palestine ("we may repose where we are free and happy"), but he was sure that almost all the rest of the Jews in the world, who are "bowed to the earth by oppression," would gladly leave their places of bondage and reestablish themselves as "a nation, a people, a sect."

Noah was a superpatriot and even a nativist. As early as 1817, he had urged Columbia College to appoint only Americans to teaching positions; he did not want to permit "the minds of our children to be warped by foreign prejudices." It is perhaps not an accident that Noah acted out the role of belonging to the older America, and even to the elite which set norms for college education, in the very year in which the Irish first fought their way onto the political scene by breaching Tammany Hall. Noah's attitude toward immigrants was that it took at least a generation for them to become passably American, and this could happen only through great educational effort. His attitude toward the Irish did not become more accepting after he broke with Tammany Hall, in which they were an increasing power. In 1835, he was an avowed supporter of the newly formed Native American party, the forerunner of the Know-Nothings of the next two decades. But Noah could not try to exclude the Irish and other immigrants without having to face the question of the Jews. As late as the 1830s, Noah was clearly not eager to welcome uncouth foreign Jews to New York or Philadelphia, because Jews like himself might find their own integration into America called into question. He preferred that they go to Ararat on the American frontier or directly to Palestine. Occasionally, he suggested that Jewish immigrants were a better element, easier to integrate into America than any of the other new arrivals. Inevitably, and correctly, Noah was attacked for these views by James Gordon Bennett, the leading figure among New York editors and journalists, who wondered how someone who belonged to a tribe that "had been aliens and renegades throughout the world" would dare foster the principle of social exclusion.

But Noah moved with the times. At the end of his life Noah allied himself with the Central European Jews who had begun to arrive in some numbers in his last years. He needed these newcomers, because

his own contemporaries and their children had become largely uninterested in their Jewishness. Noah found his Jewish continuity in
the immigrants.

Noah was universally regarded as the premier public figure among
American Jews of that day. He made a career both in politics and as
the leading spokesman of American Jews—and his self-assumed role
as leader of the Jews made him more newsworthy and important
than his modest successes in politics. Noah was often ridiculed by
his enemies as a publicity seeker and sensationalist, but that was a
very American thing to be. In those very days, P. T. Barnum began
his career, in 1835, by parading an aged lady around the country as
supposedly 161 years old and the nurse of George Washington. Revivalists were traveling from town to town making national repu-
tations by use of exaggerated rhetoric. Among the more educated,
attending lectures was the prime form of entertainment, and lecturers
increased the demand for their services by being colorful. It was,
therefore, not unusual that the most striking figure among the Jews,
who were still regarded as an exotic minority, might be a bit of a
mountebank.

The supreme example of American Jewish success was Judah
Touro, the son of Isaac Touro, who had been the cantor in Newport,
Rhode Island, before the Revolution. Touro, in life, was a much
more sedate and drab figure than Noah. In 1801, at the age of twenty-
six, Judah Touro left New England for New Orleans. Though he
never became one of the major powers in the business world of New
Orleans, he did accumulate a substantial fortune. For most of his life
Touro had little to do with the attempts to found a Jewish community. In New Orleans, though, he did provide the money with
which to purchase an Episcopal Church building for a synagogue.
Touro died in 1854. Touro, who seems never to have worshiped
together with his fellow Jews in New Orleans, continued to contribute to the upkeep of the grounds of his father's old synagogue.
That congregation had vanished in the early 1800s, leaving behind
only a building and a cemetery. At Touro's death, his body was
brought from New Orleans and interred in Newport. Touro then
became famous. In his will, he had given away the largest amount
of money, many hundreds of thousands of dollars, that anyone in
America had yet donated to charity. His benefactions included non-
Jewish and Jewish causes in New Orleans. He left money for Jewish

institutions in seventeen cities throughout the United States, and for the relief of the poor in the Holy Land. Touro's will had enormous resonance throughout the Jewish world. Those who were thinking about coming to the United States in the 1850s imagined that they might ultimately find their fortune in some town or city, as Touro had found his in New Orleans.

Touro's life, death, and apotheosis into charity were an appropriate epitaph for colonial and early republican Jewry. Touro's Jewishness belonged to the past. He remembered the synagogue in Newport, in which he had been the son of the poorest Jew in town, the cantor. When he became rich, his benefactions extended to Jews and Gentiles alike, as had the benefactions of Aaron Lopez, the richest member of the synagogue in Newport in the 1770s and 1780s, when Touro was a child. But there was a generational difference between Touro and Lopez. The earlier figure lived within a functioning Jewish community; Touro kept very personal memories of his childhood, and he returned to his family in death, but Touro spent his active years with little connection to his Jewishness. Such biographies would recur again and again among future generations of American Jews. For that matter, the careers of Isaac Harby and Mordecai Manuel Noah would also be reinvented, when future waves of Jewish immigration to the United States reached their second and third generation. Adjustments to America would evoke and reevoke the desire of Harby to fashion Judaism into a "respectable" American denomination. Public figures would arise again and again in generations to come to repeat Noah's attempt to range the Jews within the American elite.

All of these figures—Harby, Noah, and Touro—essentially accepted the notion that there was an American society which set norms of conduct, and that they would find ways of being accepted into this society. They wanted to be liked and included. The striking exception in that generation was Uriah Phillips Levy, first cousin of Mordecai Manuel Noah. Levy had the most "American" of all careers, for he was a professional navy officer. Levy had run away to sea in 1802 at the age of ten. He rose in fifteen years through the ranks to be commissioned in March 1817 as lieutenant in the navy. He spent the next forty some years in and out of the navy. He was court-martialed six times. Some of the woes he brought upon himself by a volatile temperament, but most of his problems were caused by his opposition to the dominant orthodoxies of the service. Levy was opposed on principle to the practice of punishing seamen by flogging, and he violated the code of the naval establishment by going to Congress. The officer corps never forgave him. Levy remained defiant. He was kept as an outsider, and he was often accused of derelictions of duty. In 1857, he was finally vindicated of all charges against him and given command of the USS *Macedonian,* of the Mediterranean Squadron. Later that year, he was made commodore of the squadron, and held that rank for some months before he was ordered home in May of 1860. Even in this exalted rank, Levy remembered his religious obligations. He spent the Day of Atonement that fall with the Italian Rothschilds. When he sailed home, he brought along a wagonload of earth from the Holy Land to New York, and he was thanked by the Spanish-Portuguese congregation to which he belonged, for such earth was used in funeral rituals to pillow the heads of the dead.

From the very beginning of his navy career, in 1812, Levy was doubly in trouble. He had arrived in the service not as a midshipman, through the Naval Academy, but from the ranks, by being given a warrant as a sailing master—and he was a Jew. On both counts he repeatedly had difficulty with officers in the wardrooms of the ships on which he sailed. The eminent American historian, George Bancroft, had been secretary of the navy in 1845–46, and he had refused to give him a command. Bancroft testified in the proceedings in November and December of 1857, in which Levy was vindicated and recalled to active duty, that he "never doubted Captain Levy's competence," but that he kept him out of the service in large part because of "a strong prejudice in the service against Capt. Levy, which seemed to me, in a considerable part attributable to his being of the Jewish persuasion." Bancroft added that he held the same liberal views as the President and the Senate, who had given him the rank of captain, but that, as secretary of the navy, he had to take account of "the need for harmonious cooperation which is essential to the highest effectiveness."

Levy pursued his cause vigorously in the proceedings in late 1857. Dozens upon dozens of American figures of the highest reputation spoke up for him, including thirteen officers who were still on active duty in the navy, and six others who had been previously connected with the service. Against Levy there stood the insistence of some of

his old enemies that charges which had once been dismissed or regarded as minor should still be invoked as proof of his incompetence.
Levy himself knew that he was being attacked as a Jew. Testifying
in his own behalf, he warned American Christians against "the persecution of the Jew":

> And think not, if you once enter on this career, that it can be
> limited to the Jew. What is my case today, if you yield to this
> injustice, may tomorrow be that of the Roman Catholic or the
> Unitarian; the Presbyterian or the Methodist; the Episcopalian or
> the Baptist. There is but one safeguard; that is to be found in an
> honest, whole hearted, inflexible support of the wise, the just, the
> impartial guarantee of the Constitution.

Levy's travail prefigured exactly the much more important battle
two generations later, in 1916, over the confirmation of Louis Dembitz Brandeis to the Supreme Court. Then, too, the issue was that
Brandeis was regarded as an outsider by the American legal establishment and that he was a Jew. Then, too, the American aristocracy
split between the nativists and those who defined America as a society
that was open to all talent that was lawfully employed.

Levy won in 1857, because he appealed to the America of the
Founding Fathers. He invoked them, not merely because it served
his cause, but as one who was deeply devoted to their memory. Levy
had bought Jefferson's home, Monticello, in 1836, and he kept it as
a kind of private shrine to the memory of the author of the Declaration of Independence. From the very beginning of his career to its
end, Levy had refused to accept the notion that he had to make
himself agreeable to his peers in the navy. The American tradition
which he revered, and from which he claimed protection, was not
the goodwill of society but the laws of the Constitution.

7.

The German Jews
Arrive

I

    Western and Central Europe were convulsed in 1848 by revolutions against the reigning monarchs. Most of these insurrections failed, and those who made them, if they were fortunate enough to remain alive and out of jail, fled to safer places. Some of these political refugees came to the United States, where the most prominent among them, such as Louis Kossuth, the leader of the revolt in Hungary, were feted and lionized. These rebels were heroes who reminded Americans of the great age of their own country, sixty or seventy years before. It was an honor at the time for an immigrant to claim to be a "Forty-eighter"; their supposed numbers inevitably grew in later memory, when families were adorning their history with an honorific past.

A few decades after their arrival, the "German Jews" were cultivating the myth that large numbers among them had been revolutionaries in Europe, but the claim had no basis in reality. The most assiduous antiquarian research has turned up fewer than twenty names of Jewish immigrants to the United States who had anything to do with the liberal revolutions. The typical migrant of those days came from the family of a Bavarian cattle-dealer or peddler. He was usually a younger son who could find nothing to do in an impoverished region which was becoming overpopulated. Moreover, in the middle years of the nineteenth century, the better-off European Jews were not leaving the small towns and villages in which they had lived for generations to emigrate to America. Enterprising people with some little capital at their disposal could move closer to home, to Berlin, Prague, or Vienna, to make their fortunes. As before, in colonial times, the Jews who left for North America in the middle of the nineteenth century were the poorest, and the least educated.

It was equally mythic that these "German Jews" were all from Germany. Many came from other places in Central Europe such as Bohemia and Moravia: some came from Posen, the easternmost province of Prussia, which had been Polish until the late eighteenth century. And yet, even though America was enormously attractive in the years before the Civil War—it was the country of cheap land and new cities—it did not evoke mass migration from all over Jewish Europe. There was little emigration from Prussia because the Industrial Revolution had already begun there, and the economy was making room for a growing population. Anti-Semitism had never really abated in the towns and villages of Alsace and Lorraine, where the bulk of the Jewish population of France lived, but these Jews did not migrate in any numbers to the United States; many went, instead, to Paris. The largest Jewish population was, of course, in Russia, but in the middle of the nineteenth century, most Jews still lived there in a traditional society. The thought of emigrating and breaking ties with the community simply did not occur to them. Transportation was still primitive, and America seemed far away.

Perhaps half of all the immigrants were from Bavaria. This migration from Bavaria was a special case. It began in the 1830s and 1840s because economic doors were closed to a specific part of the Jewish community, the younger children of the petty traders and cattle dealers, the pursuits which were permitted to Jews in that region. The villages in Bavaria continued to do what they had done for centuries: they would not allow a Jew to establish a new family unless a "place" was made for him through the death or removal of someone else. Younger sons of local families who wanted to marry thus had to leave. They could not go to the cities of Bavaria. These were stagnant, for Bavaria had not even begun to experience any stirrings toward manufacture and industry. Emigration was thus the obvious choice—and in the 1840s transportation from Central Europe was ever easier and cheaper, as the railroads were built and the steamships began their regular, competing services on the North Atlantic.

These Jewish immigrants were as poor as the millions of Gentiles from Germany and Ireland, who were then coming to America, but the Jews were different. They were better prepared in advance to rise quickly in America. Many of the German Gentiles and the majority of the Irish were farmers. The Jews were peddlers and middlemen. The Germans and the Irish were mostly illiterate; even the poorest of the Jewish men could usually read, for they had been taught to read the Hebrew prayer book. Such literacy could—and was—transferred to German, and soon to English. Consequently, many of the Jews were ahead, on arrival, in the race for success in the New Land.

It was a time for success. America was booming and there was need for more population. The country was following its "manifest destiny," to extend American rule and settlement all the way to the Pacific. In the 1830s, when the first great surge of immigration began, some six hundred thousand people came to the United States. In the next decade the number was one and a half million, and in the one thereafter, the last before the Civil War, the immigration almost doubled to nearly three million. America was changing during those years from an almost entirely agricultural society to one in which almost half of all the citizens lived in cities. The figures are startling: in 1820, four out of five Americans made their livings on farms; by 1860 this number was down to a bit more than half. New cities were being founded, and almost all the older ones were growing rapidly, as trading posts and manufacturing centers. A market was being created in America itself to exchange what the farmers produced for what the cities manufactured. Never again in American history were middlemen to be so much in demand. The Jews who were then arriving from Central Europe brought with them long experience in buying and selling. There would never again be the opportunity for the majority of a wave of Jewish migrants to get rich in their own lifetimes.

Many began by selling from pushcarts, and soon from stores, in the already existing major cities. As early as the 1830s, Jews were selling old clothes on Chatham Street on the Lower East Side of New York. This was a lucrative business because, until the Civil War, selling old clothes was a more important trade in America than making new garments. Buyers and sellers bargained; inevitably, the buyers often resented the price they were persuaded to pay. As early as 1833, a British traveler described Chatham Street as a place which was inhabited mostly by "the Tribe of Judah," as anyone could see who went to shop there, because of "their long beards, which reached to the bottom of their waists." These merchants were not the children or grandchildren of Judah Lopez or of Haym Salomon, for the Jews who were present in America in colonial times had taken off their beards years before. Fifteen years later the neighborhood was already entirely Jewish, or so a contemporary visitor from the South maintained: "a Yankee (cute as they are) shopkeeper in Chatham Street could not exist." Later still, in 1853, Cornelius Matthews, a dramatist and journalist, wrote a sharp, ironic account of Chatham Street. He asserted that in ancient times, when Manhattan belonged to the Indians, the street had been one of their warpaths. It remained so even in these supposedly civilized times: "The old Redmen scalped their enemies; the Chatham clothes-men skinned theirs." It should be remembered that these were "German Jews," many of whom would forget how they had begun in America and would be maintaining several decades later that only "Russian Jews" were capable of sharp business practices. By the late 1840s, this area of Jewish shops in New York extended to the major streets which were to be the heart of the Jewish Lower East Side for the next hundred years: Houston, Division, Grand, and the Bowery. There are vivid accounts of comparable "Lower East Sides" in those days in Baltimore, Cincinnati, and Philadelphia. In Baltimore, several blocks of Lombard Street were then a market for dry goods and old clothes, but its specialties were such items as prayer shawls and kosher food of all varieties.

There were, of course, some tragedies and failures. On May 7, 1849, the *New York Sun* carried a story that "the body of a German named Marcus Cohen was found on Friday last. On account of pecuniary embarrassment he terminated his existence." There were other business failures, which did not end so tragically—but most of the immigrants succeeded. In Easton, Pennsylvania, twenty-four Jews out of seventy in town were peddlers in 1850, but the numbers kept dropping year by year. The pattern is the same in Richmond, Virginia, in Syracuse, New York, and in a host of other communities in the eastern half of the country. It was different in Minnesota and in the western states in general, including California. Those Jews who came there in the years before the Civil War had often already done their stint as peddlers in the East. They usually came to the place of their second settlement with enough capital to become merchants immediately on arrival. It is significant that in the Gold Rush of 1849, as towns and trading posts sprang up everywhere in the Far West, there were Jewish storekeepers in every one of them, but there were very few Jews among the prospectors for gold. Such prospectors might get rich quickly in one fantastic strike, but storekeepers were fairly sure of a stable living, and more. Even in these unusual conditions, most Jews stuck to what they knew. Trade was an almost certain avenue to wealth.

In this great, first tide of immigration, there were some 100,000 Jews; between 1820 and 1860, their numbers in the United States increased from perhaps 6,000 to 150,000. On the eve of the Civil War, Jews were no longer a handful scattered in the port cities on the Eastern Seaboard. They were to be found everywhere, in dozens upon dozens of American towns and cities. The normal pattern of the Jewish immigrant to America was to peddle for a few years and then to settle down and open a store. He also tended to send for other members of his family, and even for a wife, from back home. Thus, various nascent Jewish communities in midwestern or southern towns soon represented interrelated families with ties to the same places in Germany. Most of these immigrants became, in less than twenty years, substantial merchants on the main streets of dozens of cities.

A few Jewish capitalists came to the United States before the Civil War; they were men such as Philipp and Gustav Speyer from Frankfurt and Adolph Ladenburg from Mannheim. These were members of established banking families, and they went immediately into the trade in the United States. Oddly enough, despite an early start, these never became the most important Jewish firms, though Ladenburg, Thalmann and Co. was prominent in the financing of American railroads. The overwhelming majority of the great Jewish fortunes were amassed by more recent immigrants who began very poor. Marcus Goldman, the founder of Goldman, Sachs and Co., the famous and still extant Wall Street firm, arrived in Philadelphia in 1848 where he peddled for two years; he then opened a men's clothing store in which he made his basic capital. Around 1850, Abraham Kuhn and Solomon Loeb, founders of Kuhn, Loeb & Co., were partners in general commerce in Lafayette, Indiana, before they moved to Cincinnati, to open a general store. Henry Lehman arrived in 1844 and peddled in Alabama. Within a year he opened a store in Montgomery and, together with his brothers Emanuel and Mayer, went into cotton brokerage. Perhaps the most striking success story of those days was that of Joseph Seligman, who arrived in 1837 and worked for a year in a store in Mauch Chunk (now Jim Thorpe), Pennsylvania. He then peddled among the backcountry farmers with a pack on his back. By 1841, together with three of his brothers, he had opened a store in Selma, Alabama, which they also used as a base for peddling. A few years later they already owned a number of such stores in small towns in the South. In 1846 they broadened their horizon and established a dry goods importing house in New York; four years later, two of the brothers were to be found in San Francisco, selling clothing to the many who were coming west in the Gold Rush. By the time the Civil War began, the Seligmans were established in New York as a financial firm. They were the very first Jewish immigrants to make the leap from merchant to financier. The Seligmans became really wealthy only during and after the Civil War. Before 1861, the Jewish peddlers who became merchants had become well-off, but they were not yet rich enough to be envied.

II

Jews were too few to become the prime target of American nativism. This was reserved for the Irish and the Germans. In the four decades between 1820 and the Civil War, 1.7 million Irish and 1.3 million Germans arrived in the United States. Almost all the Irish were Catholic, and so were the majority of the Germans. American nativism began to take notice of these migrations very early, after the War of 1812, when the first trickle started to arrive. The Irish were supposedly bringing the pope and his minions, the priests and bishops who were then appearing in America in substantial numbers, to burrow under and to destroy the purportedly clean, simple, and decent values that American Protestantism had taught. One of the journalists who promoted the notion that the Irish "could not understand or appreciate the excellence of this [the American] form of government" was Mordecai Manuel Noah. The German immigrants were attacked because they had the enraging notion that their culture was superior to what was to be found in America. Obviously right-thinking Americans could not stand for such ideas. In 1854, the Native American party, the "Know-Nothings," became a full-fledged national movement. In the next year it renamed itself the American party. This nativism barely mentioned the Jews. There were a few stray Jews among its members, including one named Lewis Levin, who was married to a Catholic. Indeed, Lewis was elected to Congress for three successive terms (1845–51) as the candidate of the American party.

The Jewish immigrants, at least those who lived in the northeastern cities, were mostly Democrats. This was the party of Andrew Jackson, of the "new men," of the outsiders who were making something of themselves on the frontier, and, for that matter, in the cities. They could not find a home among the Whigs, the party which retained much more of the flavor and the prejudices of the older America. Jews held political office in remarkable numbers. For half a century, Emanuel Hart was a power in New York's Tammany Hall. Hart became the leader of the Jewish forces in the Democratic party in New York after Noah broke with Tammany in the mid-1820s. He was even chairman of the Central Committee for some years. Hart won election to one term in Congress. In Philadelphia, Henry Phillips was elected to Congress in 1856 as a Democrat. In the South, the Jews were, with few exceptions, proslavery Democrats. In Richmond, Gustavus Meyers was the only Jewish member of the city council for almost thirty years (1827–55). Henry Hyans was elected lieutenant governor in Louisiana in 1856. Most of these figures (like Senators Judah P. Benjamin and David Yulee) were from the older Jewish settlement, but there were also local officeholders who were generally newer immigrants.

But the Jews of those years were not all racing for a place in the existing political machines. Some took risks. When the new Republican party was organized in the 1850s, with opposition to slavery as its central plank, there was a high proportion of Jews among its founders. In Chicago, four of the five founders of a German-language wing of the Republicans were Jews. Jewish leaders of the party were especially important in the West, the region from which Lincoln came. These included an old friend of Lincoln's, Abraham Jonas of Quincy, Illinois, and newer ones such as Henry Greenbaum, a Democratic alderman from Chicago who, in 1855, changed parties to support Lincoln. Perhaps the most striking Jewish Republican was Louisville's Lewis N. Dembitz. In 1860 Dembitz made one of the three speeches nominating Lincoln at the Republican Convention. Dembitz was the uncle of Louis Brandeis, a future justice of the Supreme Court. In Philadelphia, Rabbi Sabato Morais, the minister (i.e., the cantor and preacher) of the Sephardi congregation, defied his lay leadership and helped organize the Republican party in Pennsylvania. Morais was Orthodox, and his faith, as he understood it, commanded him to be an abolitionist. Almost all of these Jews in politics were newcomers, and some of them were very recent arrivals, but that was not unusual at a time when the political institutions, especially those on the frontier, had been formed just a few years earlier.

III

On three occasions before the Civil War, American Jews took public action in "foreign affairs." The first was in 1840. In February of that year a Capuchin monk, Father Tomas, and his Muslim servant had disappeared in Damascus. The French consul, Ratti-Menon, encouraged the local officials to charge that Jews had murdered them in order to use their blood for the baking of matzoth. This libel had recurred frequently since the Middle Ages in Christian Europe; it had now made its first appearance in the Middle East. A number of Jews, children among them, were jailed. Some died under torture. The Jewish communities in France and England took action as soon as they heard of this outrage. The protest meeting held in London in July 1840 came to the attention of President Martin Van Buren. Van Buren wrote immediately, through his consular agent in Damascus, to the Egyptian authorities to express "surprise and pain that in this advanced age such unnatural practices should be ascribed to any portion of the religious world." Still unprompted, Van Buren sent a comparable message to the American minister in Turkey.

For their part, the Jews protested not only in the old established communities such as Charleston, Savannah, Richmond, and Philadelphia, but also in the new community of Cincinnati. The most interesting meeting was held in New York on August 19, 1840, in Congregation B'nai Jeshurun, the first Ashkenazi congregation in the city. Its creation had predated the large-scale migrations of the Jews from Germany, for it had been founded in 1825 by some of the first arrivals from England and the Continent. The meeting was to be held there, and not in the more aristocratic and "American" surroundings of the Sephardi congregation, Shearith Israel, because most of its leaders wanted to avoid "foreign entanglements." But the most striking public figure among the Sephardim, Mordecai Manuel Noah, delivered the speech of the occasion. It represented, at the very dawn of Jewish "foreign policy" in America, a summary of its future content. Noah denied that American Jews, who were "exempt from such outrages," have the right to ignore the problems of other Jews. On the contrary, they have the obligation, "in proportion to the great blessings that we enjoy," to defend less fortunate Jews, and to help with money and public support. The reasons that he gave were history, religion, and, above all, group feeling. Though scattered all over the world, "we are still one people, bound by the same religious ties, worshipping the same God, governed by the same sacred awe, and bound together by the same destiny. The cause of one is the cause of all." That was the view of the majority of American Jews. The fearful older settlers were outvoted by some in their own ranks, together with the bulk of the newer immigrants.

On this first occasion when American Jews acted on behalf of their brethren abroad, pressure in Washington had not been necessary, because President Van Buren had intervened on his own, but his example was not followed by his immediate successors. In the 1850s the United States, under two administrations, negotiated a commercial treaty with Switzerland. Almost all the cantons in the Swiss Confederation then excluded Jews from residence; the United States had agreed that they would have the right not to grant visas to Jews who were American citizens. A delegation went to see President James Buchanan, but he refused to renegotiate the agreement. In 1858, American Jewry was even more seriously angered by the tragic case of Edgardo Mortara. This six-year-old Italian Jewish child was seized by papal police in Bologna and taken from his parents because the maid in the Mortara household said that she had secretly baptized him. The Church therefore insisted that in canon law Edgardo Mortara was irretrievably Catholic. Despite an international outcry, there was no retreat. Edgardo Mortara was hidden and educated in a Catholic institution; he eventually became a priest. American Jews asked Washington to intercede, but such help was refused. The secretary of state wrote that "it is the settled policy of the United States to abstain from all intervention in the internal affairs of another country." The Mortara case did add to tensions in the United States between Jews and Irish, for the Catholics in America supported the pope. This confrontation probably helped move some Jews into the Republican party on the eve of the fateful election of 1860. An angry Jewish journalist commented on Buchanan's action by saying that Van Buren had been willing to intervene in 1840, because Muslims had no votes in the United States; Buchanan had done nothing in 1858, because Catholics made a difference in an American election.

Before 1840, American Jews had never intervened on behalf of their brethren abroad. There had been a few such efforts earlier in Europe, but the Jews in America had been too remote and unimportant to be asked to join. Now, in the middle years of the nineteenth century, the situation was different. European Jewish leaders in Europe, led by Sir Moses Montefiore who was helped by the Rothschilds, asked the Americans to join in protests against assaults on the rights of Jews in Russia or the Near East. In America these efforts brought together, for the first time, the native and the immigrant communities. In these actions, American Jews had taken a step beyond worrying about their immediate families, and more distant relatives, whom they had left behind in the old country. Those who joined together to help endangered Jews in Damascus or Bologna, or to rap the knuckles of the Swiss, were acting not for cousins but for strangers.

American Jews had adopted the misery of other Jews as their cause. This caring was their principle of unity. American Jews were not one society, for the older settlers regarded the newcomers as uncouth and embarrassing. Religion was not a unifying force, because the new immigrants were generally unwelcome in the existing congregations, and they were, themselves, more comfortable in synagogues of their own creation. Old settlers and immigrants could unite only in good works on behalf of other Jews.

In the middle of the nineteenth century, American Jews, in their large majority, made another fateful decision. They entered the arena of American politics to help their brethren all over the world, and they were willing to face whatever problems in America such actions might cause them. In the 1850s, it was already of some discomfort to be refused help by two presidents.

By 1861 Jews had been arriving in America for two and a half centuries. Like almost all other immigrants, they had been coming to succeed, and many had been willing to travel as light as possible on the way to that success by abandoning much or even all of their religious and cultural distinctiveness. Direct help and political effort on behalf of other Jews had become the common denominator of being Jewish in America as early as the 1840s and 1850s. This would remain the dominant "theology" of American Jews for the next century or so, even to present days.

8.

Worshiping America

I

      In the 1840s and 1850s, American Jews of all persuasions agreed on "foreign affairs," but such concerns were not at the center of their Jewish agenda. The American Jewish community was still too small and too poor to make a difference in the politics of world Jewry. More important, America itself was still a minor player on the international stage. World politics were dominated then by England and France. Sir Moses Montefiore, from England, and Adolphe Crémieux, the foremost Jew in politics in France, were the delegation who went to Damascus in 1841 and saved the Jews who were still alive in jail. Montefiore and Crémieux succeeded because they were backed by governments which were then the dominant powers in the Middle East.

  The tens of thousands of immigrants to the United States in those years had, first, to find ways of surviving in a strange country. Like all other new arrivals, their first support was each other. From New York to California, the Jewish immigrants of the 1840s and 1850s banded together in two hundred new synagogues—but this represented no religious revival. These congregations did, of course, provide religious services, but their prime function was to make immigrant Jews less lonely. There was no "great awakening" of piety, of commitment to ritual and tradition. Such observances had more than half-evaporated among the older settlers, and they were lessening rapidly among the new immigrants. A pious minority did exist, and many others belonged to the synagogues, even if they seldom attended. But numerous immigrant Jews chose not to belong. The religious institutions and the functionaries that the caring minority sustained did act to make the rest more comfortable. In San Francisco, the male children of Jews who were not associated with the nascent synagogue were circumcised as early as 1849; bodies of individuals who had not been known as Jews until their death were sometimes brought in from mining camps to be buried on consecrated ground. There were many such stories everywhere in those turbulent years.

The most common sentiment was family feeling, the sense of belonging as Jews to each other. The new immigrants sustained each other not only by meeting together in the synagogues, they founded numerous clubs and self-help societies. In such organizations, believers, semibelievers, and nonbelievers could all gather together— to affirm their togetherness. "Service organizations," which lasted and gained in power and importance in the next several decades, were founded in America in the 1840s and 1850s. These were associations of individuals and not confederations of synagogues. From their beginnings these bodies were created with no religious program; they were an extended family. The immigrant Jews were part of a very American pattern. Alexis de Tocqueville, the French visitor who wrote *Democracy in America,* his classic account of what the United States was like around 1830, was amazed by the energy that Americans put into "joining." Self-help organizations, of people who were comfortable with each other, became even more important in the next several decades. All the new immigrants, and especially those who came without families, needed such companionship. The typical Jewish immigrant to America in those days was most often a young man who came alone. Many Jews tried very hard, as soon as they knew some English, to join existing American organizations. For a short while, they succeeded. Since colonial times, a handful of Jews had belonged to the Masons. The Masonic lodges remained open to the larger numbers who applied in the 1840s and 1850s, but this did not last. There was soon a "ghetto" among the Masons. "Jewish" lodges were organized, and some "mixed" lodges became Jewish by the attrition of their Gentile membership.

But American society was not as open as the Jewish immigrants hoped. There was social anti-Semitism, as Mordecai Manuel Noah and Uriah Phillips Levy, of the older settlers, could have told them. Immigrant Jews were told very early that they were not wanted, and that they had no option but to organize their own social and self-help organizations. A dozen young men applied in 1843 to the Odd Fellows Lodge, but they were refused membership. These young Jewish immigrants then met together and organized a comparable body of their own, the Independent Order of B'nai B'rith. In the preamble to their constitution the founders proposed to do everything from "uniting Israelites in the work of promoting their highest causes and those of humanity," to visiting the sick and providing for widows and orphans. The emphasis on "humanity," by the founders of B'nai B'rith, was a way of saying that they, the Jews who had been forced into an organization of their own, were truer representatives of the cause of a united mankind than the Gentiles of the Odd Fellows, who had excluded them. This assertion would recur over and over again for the next century or so, as the quintessential response by Jews to anti-Semitism.

Like the Odd Fellows and the Masons, B'nai B'rith began as a "secret order" with all the paraphernalia of such a body: passwords and bombastic secret rituals. The new organization grew very rapidly. By 1851 its membership in New York City alone was seven hundred; there was comparable growth in other centers of Jewish population. It soon spread throughout the country. By 1860, three imitating organizations had been created. These "orders," as they all were called, served as extended families, and as such they had important self-help purposes. The dues and fees bought some personal insurance. B'nai B'rith, for example, gave a widow thirty dollars to help pay for her husband's funeral, along with some continuing payments to her and to her children until they reached thirteen. In an age when government relief did not exist, and when the Jewish rich were too few to help, such insurance was critical.

By 1849, there were already some fifty Jewish organizations—charitable, social, and fraternal—in New York, and their combined membership was far greater than that of the synagogues. Henry Jonas, one of the founders of B'nai B'rith, wrote in 1852: "These associations address themselves to the demoralized condition and low intellectual status of the Jews." What this remark meant in context was that B'nai B'rith worked hard to Americanize its members, to help them forget their humble origins in Europe, and to feel themselves to be as good as any other American. This was an immediate and important need. It was far more urgent than the need to say daily prayers, or keeping kosher, which had become more and more difficult within the turmoil of lives which were being spent peddling on the road or keeping stores open for fifteen hours a day. The synagogues thus became places in which to celebrate the major festivals and the rites of passages, such as bar mitzvahs, confirmations, marriages, and deaths. The "societies" were becoming the major home of organized Jewish life.

In mid-nineteenth-century America social barriers were not yet as high as they were to become later in the century, but it was clear, even in the 1840s and 1850s, that a Jew was regarded as different. It was noted over and over again, by friends as well as critics, that Jewish merchants drove themselves harder than anyone else, and that they seemed to do well more quickly. The Gentile majority knew very little about Jewish beliefs and practices, but everyone knew that all Jews denied the basic teaching of all the other religions in America, faith in Jesus. This issue was often painful, especially in the smaller towns of the Middle West and South. Christian revivalists came to these towns again and again to preach the Gospel. Almost invariably, they confronted and tried to convert the owner of the general store who was often the only Jew in town. The Jews usually refused to be converted, but inevitably, the pressure of Christianity on their lives was very heavy. Their children were attending schools where they were usually the only dissenters from the Protestantism which pervaded the atmosphere. There were prayers in the morning, stories about Jesus in history lessons during the day, and hymns, at very least during the Christmas season.

When the newcomers became numerous enough to form a community, in towns such as Nashville, Tennessee, or Grand Rapids, Michigan, the synagogue which they established was at first a carbon copy of those that they had left behind in the town or village from which they had come. Some Jewish laymen, perhaps even most, clung to these forms, and not merely or even primarily out of piety. The Orthodox synagogue was a reminder, on the frontier, of the home of their childhood. But these Jews had come to that frontier to be different than they had been in Europe. Their children were growing up in an American world. Even more than their parents, this younger generation needed a synagogue which was not "foreign."

Everywhere, the religious institutions themselves were rapidly being adjusted to the American scene. With one exception, Temple Emanu-El in New York, every synagogue that these newcomers established had begun as Orthodox. In roughly twenty years the vast majority had been transformed into "Reformed" congregations. Almost everywhere sexes were no longer separated; there were organs, and prayers in German, and soon in English. As was to be expected, these changes were deplored by the Orthodox, who were ever weaker and more on the defensive, but the dominant tide in mid-century favored the "moderate reformers," who were creating a "respectable" American Judaism. The tone was set by laymen who were refurbishing their synagogues so that they would be acceptable to the Gentile majority. These changes were made by laymen on no authority except their own—not rabbis, but rather storekeepers in Memphis and clothing manufacturers in Rochester, New York, and their peers all over Jewish America. These are the principal ancestors of the most "American" version of Judaism: that Jewish religion—and everything else that Jews believe or do—must not act to keep Jews apart in America; Judaism and the Jewish community must be reshaped and used as instruments of the success of Jews in American life. There was no ideological content to these reforms. The immigrant reformers were not Deists, like Isaac Harby in Charleston in the 1820s. They were tinkering with synagogue ritual and with their religious practices for pragmatic reasons—to become "American" as rapidly as possible.

Who were these laymen? The minutes and other documents of the nascent congregations of the 1840s and 1850s were not recorded by educated men. The most interesting of these texts is the account book of a messenger who came to America in 1849 to collect money for support of Jews in the Holy Land. The givers entered their contributions in their own hand; thus the institution to which they were donating had a way of checking up on their emissary's accounts without being totally dependent on his honesty. Some of the well-known figures of that period, including Mordecai Manuel Noah, were among the donors. The most interesting signatures were from Syracuse and Utica, in upstate New York. These modest contributors signed their names in Hebrew and in Yiddish, and several even added a few lines of text, to describe their origins. A few appear to have been men of some Jewish learning, but the educated (they were most likely to be stray individuals from Eastern Europe) were exceptions. Most of the immigrants of the 1840s and 1850s knew no language except Yiddish, as it was still spoken then among German Jews, and street German.

Despite rebuffs from Gentiles, and feeling most at home with each other, these immigrants wanted to become part of the larger society. They had left Central Europe at a time when the battles for equality for Jews were being fought, but they had not yet been won anywhere east of France. America was different. Here Jews were equal, in law, upon arrival, and they refused to believe that social exclusion of Jews, to the degree to which it existed in the New Land, was anything more than a vestige of outworn attitudes. In America, so they thought, anti-Semitism was in process of vanishing. This optimism was the faith of the "German Jews" from their immigrant beginnings.

The Gentiles whom they approached first were the German immigrants, with whom they shared a language. This union with Germans was sought because it could happen "only in America." Jews were still being excluded from all such bodies back home in Germany. Friendship between German-speaking Jews and Gentiles did exist, but only for a while, in such centers of German immigration as New York, Cincinnati, and Milwaukee. In New York, the Arion Glee Club had Jewish members among its founders. By the late 1860s, however, the club had barred Jews and even added anti-Semitic songs to its repertoire. In the earliest years after their arrival in the United States, Jews were a majority in the audiences of the German theater in New York. Many of the Germans did not like it. Theodore Griesinger, writing from Stuttgart in 1856 about his stay in America, talked sarcastically about the newly rich Jewish wives who showed off their finery by "bend[ing] over the railing of the first gallery." This involvement in German culture was essentially a brief phase. For a generation these immigrants still spoke German with each other, and for a decade or two it was the language of the sermons in their synagogues. There was even among some a conscious identification with the glories of German *Kultur,* which was then claiming to be the most important intellectual tradition of the Western world.

Almost without exception, however, these immigrants wanted to become American as quickly as possible. B'nai B'rith began in German, but it moved to English by 1855. The minute book of Temple Emanu-El, which was on the way to becoming the leading congregation of the "German Jews" in New York, changed languages, from German to English, as early as 1856.

II

The leader and the symbolic figure of this generation was Isaac Mayer Wise. His life is the central story of the "German Jews" in America, from their arrival until the immigrant generation was totally gone around 1900, the year of Wise's death. Wise was not much different from the flock he led. At the zenith of his career, he was very proud of his intimate social intercourse with the laity. He ate and drank with them gladly, though he did draw the line at playing cards with his parishioners. These Jews had come to America to succeed, and to leave their lower-class status in Europe behind. They did not want to be encumbered by memory and by guilt—and neither did Wise. Wise held to this view self-consciously, with remarkable consistency, throughout his long and often stormy life. He was thinking such "American" thoughts even before he left Bohemia for the United States.

In the mid-1840s, Isaac Mayer Wise was religious functionary and schoolmaster in Radnitz, a small town in Bohemia. He was not very learned in the Talmud, and there is even some doubt to this day whether he had actually ever been ordained. He took some courses at the Prague University, but he received no degree. Nonetheless, he took to calling himself "Rabbi" immediately after his arrival in the United States, and he added "Doctor" some years later. America offered ambitious men like him the chance to be big fish in a new and growing pond. In 1846, when Wise came off the sailing boat, together with his wife and a two-year-old daughter, after a harrowing journey of sixty-three days, there was no one in New York to challenge his definition of himself as a Jewish spiritual leader. Wise hated the old-school lay leaders, the *parnassim,* who continued to direct the Jewish communities in Europe with their accustomed autocracy. He thanked God that "in America, there were no petty tyrants, like the chief rabbis of England and Germany," to rule over less well-placed Jewish clerics. Wise had come to the New Land to leave these older authorities behind.

Wise arrived with only two dollars in his pocket. The journey of the Wise family from dockside to the Lower East Side was not without incident. A porter of German origin tried to overcharge him. When Wise refused to pay, the porter reviled him as a dirty Jew. But, despite such incidents, in America even anti-Semitism was different. Jews were still exotics, at least in the recently founded cities of the Middle West. In 1817, when the first Jew had arrived in Cincinnati, a farm woman who heard the news journeyed two days in a horse and wagon to see the horns and tail which a Jew was supposed to possess—but she came to Cincinnati much more out of curiosity than out of unkindness. On the advancing frontier Jews were excluded from nothing in the economy which they really wanted. The remaining discomforts of being Jews in a Gentile society were little in comparison to the European anti-Semitism which they had left behind.

Wise's character was vigorous, and pugnacious. He picked some fights which brought immediate discomfort to his laity. His admiring biographers have, therefore, praised him as a leader who fashioned American Reform Judaism according to his will. This estimate of Wise does not survive critical examination. The battles that he chose to fight were all related to his one consuming passion, to make the Jews absolutely at home as equals in America. Only a year after he became the rabbi of the Plum Street Temple in Cincinnati, he published an attack on the Board of Education for its decision that a portion of the Bible was to be read as part of the opening exercise of all schools. Fourteen years later the Board reversed itself. Wise joined with Roman Catholics in supporting the Board against strident Protestant opinion. A lawsuit was brought. The Board was reversed in the Superior Court, but finally won in the Supreme Court of the State of Ohio. Laymen in Wise's congregation complained of Wise's boldness in confronting the Protestant majority because such a policy aroused anti-Semitism—but such arguments were tactical. These laymen wanted the result of Wise's actions, an American public life that was religiously neutral, but they did not want to bear the pain of the fight.

In the 1850s, Jews were far better off than Catholics. Some Jews thought that they would be accepted by the Protestant majority if they kept their heads down, for the Catholics were then the prime object of exclusion. This was undoubtedly in the mind of some of those who were angry with Wise, when he joined the Catholics in going to court against prayers in American public schools. Wise was the first Jewish leader to create such an alliance. This was an important choice. Jews were on the border between being considered exotics and being tolerated. Catholics were severely embattled; there were several murderous riots against them in the 1850s in New York. In 1855 Wise made a decision: he would not accept toleration at the cost of living under the pressure of Protestantism which pervaded public life. He insisted that the majority had to be forced to accept the notion, even if only grudgingly, that the sensibilities of Jews, and of Catholics, should not be offended in America.

Wise was particularly sensitive to Christian teachings which blamed Jews for the Crucifixion. Over and over again, he protested Thanksgiving proclamations which contained Christian references. Wise challenged every slur on Jews, and he advocated the boycott of anti-Semites. He fought very hard against Christian missionaries who were trying to convert the Jews. He joined in all the interventions in Washington against foreign governments which discriminated against Jews. This is the record of a man who was often ahead of his flock—but Wise was running ahead in the direction in which his congregants wanted to go. He was doing battle for the deepest desires of his contemporaries. They wanted to be at home in an America in which the dominant Protestantism would have no special status.

Wise was even more the representative figure of his generation as religious reformer. He was never ideologically consistent. At various times, he accepted and then rejected the religious authority of the Talmud and other rabbinic writings; he maintained that he subscribed to the divine origin of the Bible, without being particularly obedient to its culinary injunctions. Like the laity, his central objective was to rearrange Judaism to be at home in America. In the late 1840s, near the beginning of his years in the United States, Wise began to work toward defining a *Minhag America,* a liturgy and set of practices which would belong uniquely to the New World. The older Judaism in which he and the other immigrants had been raised was full of the sorrow of being Jewish in an unfriendly world. Here in America, so Wise insisted, the time had come for Judaism without tears.

But as religious leader, Wise here, too, sometimes ran ahead of his flock, especially in the early years, but he was pulling them in the direction in which the majority wanted to go. Wise ran into trouble in his very first pulpit in Albany, New York. He had come there in 1846 to be the rabbi of the existing congregation, which was then still Orthodox. It split in the next year, because the bulk of the laity would not accept Wise's program of religious reform. There was even a fistfight on the pulpit on the Day of Atonement, in 1849, between the newly arrived Rabbi Wise and the president of the congregation. A minority followed Wise, but the Reform congregation which they created was not religiously radical enough for him; it did not provide him with a platform for his ambitions. He gladly accepted election in 1854 as the spiritual leader of a congregation in Cincinnati that had been founded twelve years earlier by Jews from Central Europe. Its building was situated in what was becoming an undesirable neighborhood, and so a new building was begun in 1863. This was to become Wise's cathedral.

On August 24, 1865, the B'nai Yeshurun Congregation dedicated this splendid structure. Since there was no tradition of synagogue architecture, for few such buildings had survived destruction in Europe through the centuries, a style had to be invented. The new building in Cincinnati was decidedly Moorish, but its towers were shaped like pomegranates rather than minarets, and there was a great and imposing dome. In his dedicatory address, Isaac Mayer Wise announced with pride that he had named the new house of worship a temple, and not a synagogue, because divine service would be held there in the spirit of "gladness and not in perpetual mourning, as in the synagogue." Some months earlier, in preparation for this event, Wise had published an account of the first years of the congregation. He had introduced a choir to accompany the service, and a new prayer book, *Minhag America,* "the American rite," which he had edited. This was the one tangible result of his labors for the last fifteen years to create an American-Jewish code of ritual practice. The essential theology of this new prayer book was that "doctrines inconsistent with reason are no longer tenable." The Jews were politically equal in the United States and were on the way to such equality, so Wise believed, all over the world. Therefore, they have a home and "cannot feel homesick." Jews no longer "wish to return to Palestine, nor do we pray for the coming of the Messiah." One can almost feel Wise pulling himself erect to full height as he wrote the climactic sentence: "We are American citizens and Israelites by religion."

His congregants more than shared in this glorying in America. On the day of dedication, Wise pronounced that "Judaism welcomes the light of day, and decks itself with becoming pride." In Cincinnati in those days, this was very true. On the Sunday before the dedication, $90,000 was raised to help pay the remaining cost of the building. Whatever else the congregation owed was realized by the sale of pews; the first two were bought for $4,600 each. These amounts represent at least ten times the present value of the dollar; very large amounts of money, in real value, were thus being given by men who had been peddlers less than twenty years before.

Wise gloried in exchanging pulpits with the fashionable Protestant ministers whose churches were literally across the street from his Plum Street Temple, but Wise knew that the major protection of the equality of Jews in America came not from such goodwill but from the Constitution. In 1855, he had decided not to be quiet but to join with the much more hated Catholics to try to push the Protestant majority away from dominance in civic life. This was Wise's most shining hour.

III

In the 1850s most people in America hoped that the issue of slavery could be avoided; so did most Jews. In the Southern states Jews almost unanimously supported the proslavery interests. In the Midwest and in the border states, Jewish wholesale houses had many customers in the South. These merchants knew that slavery was a moral issue, but they hoped it would be resolved "gradually." And yet, some voices were raised powerfully against slavery.

The issue came to a head in the winter of 1860, as the Civil War was breaking out. As was to be expected, the Jewish clergy in the South, without exception, endorsed the Confederacy. These preachers, most of whom were quite recent immigrants from Germany, summoned up great passion in their defense of states' rights. They repeated the conventional Southern platitudes of that day, that the black race was incapable of taking care of itself, that slavery was a way of discharging the responsibility of whites toward their childlike inferiors, and (to quote J. M. Michelbacher of Richmond) that the North was inciting the slaves "to assassinate and slay men, women, and children." So loyal were some of these Southern rabbis to the Confederacy that one of them, James Gutheim of New Orleans, went into exile in 1863, after the Union troops had conquered the city, rather than take an oath of allegiance to the Union.

In 1860, the most important Jewish intervention in the public debates was by Morris Raphall of New York, the best-known Orthodox American rabbi. Raphall had recently been the first Jewish clergyman to act as chaplain of the day in Congress. Raphall preached and printed a sermon in which he maintained that Judaism did not forbid slavery, though he carefully added that he was speaking only of the days of the Bible. Why had he chosen that moment for such a supposedly scholarly exercise? Raphall wanted to preserve the Union, and he seems to have thought that slavery, deplorable though it was, had best be allowed to wither. It is at least conceivable that Raphall, who had come to New York from Manchester, England, had some concern for the cotton interests in the South, which were providing the mills of Manchester with the raw material for their production of textiles. This sermon was widely, and correctly, understood as support for the South. Raphall's sermon raised a storm. The antislavery forces hastened to print the English translation of a doctoral dissertation that had been written in Germany by Rabbi Moses Mielziner. He had come to the United States to a still Orthodox congregation in Philadelphia and later went to the "Reformed" pulpit of Temple Emanu-El in New York. In his dissertation, Mielziner had established that Jewish slavery had been well-nigh abolished in ancient times by Talmudic legislation. The clear implication of his work was that slavery in the United States was morally unacceptable.

Isaac Mayer Wise had been an antiabolitionist before the war. After it broke out, he was a moderate loyalist. Some years later, he managed to "remember" that he had been a great and passionate proponent of Lincoln. The truth is that as late as 1863 he had been a

Democrat and a frequent critic of the war. Indeed, he was ready to run in that year as a "Copperhead" (i.e., antiwar) Democrat candidate for senator from Ohio, but his congregation vetoed this plan. What Wise was actually doing, as the Civil War broke out, was straddling the fence. He joined the debate over Raphall's sermon. Wise did not like Raphall; he had an old score to settle with him from 1849, when they first debated each other in Charleston. Wise's ringing declaration, then, that he did not believe in either the resurrection of the dead, or in a personal messiah, had caused him trouble in his congregation in Albany. Wise therefore relished disagreeing with Raphall on slavery. Wise argued in his journal, *The Israelite,* that Moses had been opposed to slavery, and that he had legislated on this issue in order to make "the acquisition and retention of bondsmen contrary to their will" an impossibility.

Having mocked Raphall's scholarship, Wise then proceeded, quite astonishingly, to reverse himself. As he contemplated the contemporary South, Wise said that "we are not prepared, nobody is, to maintain that it is absolutely unjust to purchase savages, or rather their labor, place them under the protection of the law, and secure them the benefit of civilized society and their sustenance for their labor." One suspects that such sentiments did not make him enemies in 1860 in his congregation, which included many merchants in the Southern trade. In Baltimore, the Orthodox rabbi, Bernard Illowy, agreed totally with Raphall. He invoked the Bible to insist that "these are irrefutable proofs that we have no right to exercise violence . . . against institutions, even if religious feelings and philanthropic sentiments bid us disapprove of them." These reverend gentlemen were not indifferent to human suffering. Wise wanted peace between North and South because there were Jews on both sides of the conflict. Most of the congregations which accepted his leadership were, in fact, in the South. Jewish organizations such as B'nai B'rith, which had chapters by 1861 in both the North and the South, simply avoided taking any public position. These laymen, and Rabbis Wise, Illowy, and Raphall, were behaving no differently than a number of Protestant leaders who were "Copperheads" because they were trying to protect the unity of their communities. This was not Wise's shining hour.

The only truly devastating criticism of Raphall was written by the

best lay Jewish scholar of those days, Michael Heilperin, a Polish
Jewish intellectual who had taken part in the Hungarian revolution
of 1848. Heilperin had made a career in America as an editor in a
magazine of general circulation, but he retained connection with the
Jewish community. He responded to Raphall's sermon by calling it
a "divine sanction of falsehood and barbarism." Heilperin pronounced himself to be "outraged by the religious words of the rabbi."

Two rabbis did take substantial personal risks in joining Heilperin.
In Philadelphia, Sabato Morais, the spiritual leader of Mikveh Israel
Congregation, which had been founded in colonial times, was an
uncompromising abolitionist. These views were resented by many
in the congregation; he survived in this pulpit only because Moses
Aaron Dropsie, the richest individual in the synagogue, defended
him. In Baltimore, David Einhorn, the rabbi of the "Reformed" Har
Sinai Congregation, had much more trouble. Baltimore was more
Southern than Northern: the state of Maryland almost seceded on
the eve of the Civil War. Abraham Lincoln had to be sneaked through
Baltimore in the dead of night on his way to Washington for his
inauguration. By denouncing slavery in the most vigorous terms,
Einhorn upset the Jews, many of whom were in trade with the South,
and angered the Gentiles. His life was not safe. He had to leave
Baltimore in 1861 and find himself another pulpit. On the eve of the
Civil War the issue of slavery had thus cut across denominational
lines in American Jewry. Morais was Orthodox, and Einhorn was
the most radical "reformer" of all American rabbis. They agreed on
very little, except that both found slavery morally repugnant; both
were certain that Jews could not avoid the greatest moral issue before
America.

IV

Wise never completely won the leadership of American Jewry, not
even at the height of his influence in mid-century. The Orthodox
were, of course, opposed to him. A few representatives of the "old
school," the first transplants to the United States from the European
yeshivoth, the Talmud academies of the Old World, had already
come to America. They were simply heartsick at what they saw.
Abraham Rice was the first rabbi who had been trained in a yeshivah

to settle in the United States. He came to Baltimore in 1840, where he lived unhappily ever after. Before his eyes, and in utter disregard of his pleading, the Baltimore Hebrew Congregation began to institute "reforms," such as the use of an organ to accompany the Sabbath service, the abolition of the separation of sexes at prayer, and even a revision of the Orthodox prayer book, the text of which had been sacrosanct for many centuries. Rice's face, in the only portrait of him that remains, is wan and sad. His eyes seem to be looking across the Atlantic to the vibrant academy of Talmudic learning in Pressburg (Bratislava), in Slovakia, where he had studied under Moses Schreiber, one of the great rabbinic authorities of that generation. Rice resigned his position as rabbi in 1849. He wrote in utter despair to a friend in Germany: "I dwell in darkness without a teacher or companion. . . . The religious life in this land is on the lowest level; most people eat forbidden food and desecrate the Sabbath in public. . . . Under these circumstances my mind is perplexed and I wonder whether it is even permissible for a Jew to live in this land." For the next thirteen years Abraham Rice, ill and broken, tried to support himself and his family by keeping a store. When he died in 1862, his colleague, Bernard Illowy, preached the eulogy in the blackest accents: "We must acknowledge to our own shame that since the downfall of the Jewish monarchy there has been no age and no country in which the Israelites were more degenerated and more indifferent towards their religion than in our own age and in our country."

These outcries reflected a decline in Jewish piety which seemed almost inevitable. In 1853, Leo Merzbacher, then the rabbi of Congregation Anshe Chesed in New York, wrote that "in reality, there is no one here who has not changed greatly in the observance of ancient regulations." Nonetheless, these new immigrants had begun by founding their congregations as exact replicas of those they had left behind in Europe. The first congregation in Chicago, which was named in Hebrew "Congregation of the Men of the West," was established in 1846 on so Orthodox a basis that its members scrupulously observed the Sabbath by keeping their businesses closed. Before the Civil War, the overwhelming majority of the newly formed congregations had on the surface moved but a little away from the principles and practices on which they had been founded. I. J. Benjamin, a European Jewish scholar who traveled through the

United States in the 1850s, gave a very optimistic report of Judaism in America. He saw the situation as "full of hope" and as advancing toward an "exalted and prosperous future." He found, then, more than two hundred Orthodox congregations, and only eight Reform ones. The situation was to be exactly reversed in twenty years. In 1880, the United States census reported that there were some two hundred Reform congregations and only six Orthodox ones.

And yet, Reform never triumphed completely in America. Wise was opposed throughout his career by an American "enlightened" Orthodoxy. Isaac Leeser was the spokesman for this view. Leeser had even fewer pretensions than Wise to Jewish learning. He had come to Richmond, Virginia, from his native Prussia in 1824, at the age of eighteen. Leeser claimed no rabbinic degree, and he actually spent his first five years in the United States working in his uncle's general store. In 1829, he became the minister of the Spanish-Portuguese synagogue in Philadelphia; Leeser was retired, unwillingly, in 1850, and he remained in that city until his death in 1868. Leeser was a moderate who wanted American Jews to adopt a dignified, English-speaking, "Western" form of the Orthodox Jewish faith. In religion, he tried to cooperate with the reformers, so long as they did not go very far in breaking with tradition. As communal leader, he worked harder than anyone else to create national Jewish associations which would allow for some religious diversity. As scholar, he produced, among other works, the first translation of the Bible into English done by an American Jew (1845).

Leeser was not a man of forceful character; he was a thoroughly decent person who seemed easy to push around—and yet he, and the far more pugnacious David Einhorn, kept Wise from taking over all of American Jewry. They did not allow him to create his cherished *Minhag America,* the American religious rite—with himself as the high rabbi, of course. Both Leeser and Einhorn would not countenance the idea that American Jews were a new religious phenomenon. American Jews were living under unprecedented conditions, but that did not make them a new tribe in world Jewry. For both Leeser and Einhorn, the Jewish religion remained a worldwide phenomenon. All Jews, everywhere, were part of the same religious people.

The battle between Orthodoxy and Reform first came to a head in America on a national level in 1855. Isaac Mayer Wise called a conference of rabbis in Cleveland. He proposed to define American

Judaism and to organize a central religious body. Wise wanted this meeting to succeed, that is, to include everybody in American Jewry. He took the lead in pronouncing the Bible to be divine, and in specifying that Scripture was to be "expounded and practiced according to the comments of the Talmud." Wise himself did not believe this declaration, for he had already frequently denied the authority over modern Jews of biblical and Talmudic commandments. Leeser soon left the meeting, because he could not trust a body led by Wise to be even mildly Orthodox. Einhorn, who was not there, attacked the meeting from the religious left. In the next year, in 1856, Einhorn published a Reform prayer book of his own, entitled *Olat Tamid* ("a perpetual offering"), with a translation into German, which was far more radical in its theology and practice than Wise's "American Rite." For his part, Leeser kept a weekly journal, *The Occident and American Jewish Advocate,* alive from 1843 to the end of his life in 1868. Despite enormous difficulties, Leeser persisted in publishing this weekly, in which he continued to challenge "reform." Near the end of his life, in 1867, Leeser founded Maimonides College, the first seminary to train rabbis to be established in America. The effort soon collapsed, but Leeser had at least flown the flag of moderate traditionalism against Wise's well-known hope to establish a rabbinic seminary of his own, to train rabbis for his "American" Judaism.

In the middle years of the nineteenth century, Wise was the acknowledged religious leader of the Jews in the Midwest and the South, but Leeser and Einhorn had some followers even there. They were much stronger on the Eastern Seaboard, which was nearer to Europe than Wise's bastions west of the Appalachians.

In 1860, fighting over slavery, Einhorn, Heilperin, and Morais, who disagreed about many things, had together asserted that being Jewish meant that one had moral responsibility for the pain of the friendless. Einhorn, Heilperin, Morais, and Leeser kept asserting, in their various ways, that being Jewish meant belonging to an ancient, worldwide, tradition, which Jews had no right to reform into American respectability. Leeser died in 1868, but the others lived on into the next era. Einhorn died in 1879, living long enough to exercise a major influence on the ideological self-definition of Reform Judaism in America. Morais and Heilperin were alive when the newest wave of immigrants, the East Europeans, began to come in large numbers in the 1880s. Heilperin was at pains to encourage the Jewish scholars and Hebraists among them. Morais took the lead in 1887 in founding a traditionalist (i.e., anti-Reform) rabbinic school, the Jewish Theological Seminary of America. These men were only a few, but they did not allow American Jewry to be swept away entirely by the doctrine of adjustment to America in the name of success.

9.

Getting Rich Quick

I

     In 1860 thousands of Jews were still peddling, but more thousands had settled down to keep store in cities and towns in both the North and the South. One of the distribution networks for the South radiated from Baltimore, a city on the border which was then a seaport equal in importance to New York. Cincinnati was another major commercial center; it looked down the Ohio River to the entire middle South. In both these cities important Jewish communities had already formed; they traded with Jewish merchants in the smaller towns. It was not easy to get goods from one place to another. Despite the thirty thousand miles of railroad track that were laid by 1860, an integrated system of transportation did not yet exist. Most of these lines were small and local, and their gauges were often mismatched so that railroad cars could not be moved from one line to another. Nonetheless, goods were distributed, and profits, often large ones, were made by middlemen, especially in the agricultural South.

     The story of the economic rise of Jews during and after the Civil

War cannot be told without some attention to the question of smuggling across the military lines between the Union and the Confederacy. Smuggling was a well-established, even major, economic enterprise during the four years of the war. There were many scandals on the Union side involving people in very high places. By its very clandestine nature, there are no reliable estimates of the significance of smuggling in the economic history of the Civil War. Jews were involved. In 1862, their participation in smuggling led to the issuance of an order by Ulysses S. Grant, then commander in the Department of the Tennessee, in which he unfairly named Jews as the worst offenders and then expelled them from all the territory under his jurisdiction. This Order Number 11 is the one overtly anti-Jewish decree in all of American military history. The question of the role of the Jews in smuggling has, therefore, become clouded by apologetics, then, and to this day. The story needs to be retold without the prior presumption that Jews were always saints without blemish.

The tale is briefly told: Grant was then in command of the Department of the Tennessee, having conquered the state from the Confederacy. During the war, smuggling across the battle lines was more often than not tacitly condoned by both governments. That was how the North got some of the cotton it needed, and the South got some coffee and some manufactured goods. The trade was widespread, and it even involved army officers who offered protection in return for payoffs. At the end of 1862, General Grant's command had lost patience with the amount of smuggling in the area. An order was issued which was directed by name against the Jews. They were "hereby expelled from the Department within twenty-four hours of the receipt of this order." As soon as this document was published, it caused a storm. Jewish delegations began to organize to protest to President Lincoln. However, before the formal protests could be made, an individual, Cesar Kaskel from Paducah, Kentucky, who was a friend and supporter of Lincoln, simply went to Washington and made the President aware of the order. It was promptly revoked. By the time the formal delegations arrived, they simply thanked the President for what he had done. Most unfortunately, a resolution to revoke the order had meanwhile been introduced in Congress, and it lost in both Houses. Congress was willing to believe that the Jews were indeed unusually prominent among the smugglers and speculators.

Though a military order directed specifically at Jews and not, in more general terms, at all those engaged in smuggling, was indefensible, the question does have to be asked: Did Jews play a role of special prominence in the smuggling trade? The records of trials by civil and military courts for these crimes show that Jews amounted at most to some six percent among all of those who were convicted for economic offenses of any kind. There is no reason to believe that Jews were specially singled out for prosecution. But these figures are suspect, as perhaps too low, on the evidence of what various rabbis were saying at the time. A few months before General Grant's Order Number 11, Rabbi Jacob Peres wrote from Memphis to Isaac Leeser, that more than twenty Jews had been in prison in Memphis for smuggling. The rabbi called such activity a "profanation of the name of God." His colleague in Memphis, Rabbi Simon Tuska, was equally upset with the practices of Jewish traders from the North who had followed the Union Army. Leeser himself responded to the order in an article in which he deplored "the crowd of needy adventurers who travel, or glide through the highways and byways of the land in quest of gain, often we fear unlawful." Leeser added that some of these adventurers pretended to be good Jews when they were not. David Einhorn insisted the Jews were no worse than others, but that it was the duty of the Jews to uproot such crimes which brought disgrace to the whole Jewish community. The most interesting point in Einhorn's passionate sermon was his remark that "little rogues are brought to punishment, whereas big ones are allowed to escape." The rabbis of that time seem to have felt that Jews were "overrepresented" in smuggling, but that they were not the major figures in this trade.

There is reason to believe that some of the staff officers who composed Order Number 11, which Grant signed, were involved in protecting large-scale smuggling endeavors by Gentiles. During that period an order was issued in Memphis declaring fifteen clothing firms off-limits for various infractions, while allowing only two to continue to furnish uniforms to the troops. It was not accidental that all fifteen of the firms were Jewish-owned, and that the two which were declared acceptable were not. It takes no great stretch of imagination to conclude that those who tried to create this monopoly, by military order, stood to benefit from the action. Jews were certainly not the only smugglers and illegal traders, but only apologetic fervor would insist that they were unimportant. They seemed to have been comparatively petty smugglers; they were, therefore, not the best protected among these illegal traders. Nonetheless, it is beyond doubt that some Jewish fortunes and many more Gentile ones have roots in profits that were made in smuggling during the Civil War.

Jews were singled out in Grant's Order Number 11 because anti-Semitism, which had been almost nonexistent in the United States, had been aroused by the turmoil of the war. The financier August Belmont was widely attacked in the Northern press as a "Jew-banker" who was a crypto-supporter of the South. The charges were totally false, on two counts. Belmont was hardly a Jew because he had effectively left the Jewish community long before the Civil War. In 1837, when he arrived in New York as representative of the Rothschild banking interests, he was known as a Jew, but he soon abandoned his Jewish identity. Belmont found his way to the top of American society, marrying the daughter of a national hero, Commodore Matthew Perry. It was even less true that Belmont was a secret supporter of the South. Though Belmont was a leading Democrat, the chairman of the national committee of the party, and therefore leader of the political opposition to Lincoln, he was totally committed to the cause of the Union. He even organized and equipped, at his own expense, the first regiment of soldiers who were German-born. But these facts did not deter the anti-Semites.

Belmont's loyalty and the active patriotism of the overwhelming majority of Northern Jews did not stop the press across the country from repeating the charge that Jews dominated the speculation in gold and that they were "engaged in destroying the national credit in running up the price of gold." The New York Dispatch said that on the corner of William Street and Exchange Place one saw only the "descendants of Shylock." The Jewish journals in New York countered by asking those who made such remarks to walk through the gold exchange and count Jews. Obviously, those anti-Semitic outbursts were false, as a minority of the newspapers knew and said, but they were part of the "evidence," together with Order Number 11, for the restatement in America of a classic anti-Semitic theme: the Jews are doing too well; therefore all those who are doing too well in business or finance are Jews.

Grant's order was revoked because of the constitutional guarantees

against singling out any group, and because of the towering personality of Abraham Lincoln. But overt anti-Semitism of the economic
variety, which had made its debut in the New World in Peter Stuyvesant's New Amsterdam, had now reappeared in America to trouble
a much larger community.

There was some vocal anti-Semitism in the Confederacy during
the war years. Here, too, the prime targets were two Jews who, like
Belmont, had abandoned their Jewishness. Judah P. Benjamin and
David Yulee, two former United States senators, were under constant attack as being untrustworthy because they were Jews. Benjamin was under the worse fire, because he was the closest friend
and adviser of Jefferson Davis, the president of the Confederacy. It
was convenient to attack Davis through him, and to attack Benjamin
as a Jew. After the defeat, Benjamin was the only major leader of
the Confederacy who went into exile rather than make his peace with
the Union; he ended his life as a barrister in London. Despite Benjamin's obvious passion for the Southern cause, several of his critics
in the Confederate Congress even introduced a resolution, which
Davis ignored, in which they asked for the resignation of Secretary
of State Benjamin, as an act which would be "subservient to the
public interests."

Economic anti-Semitism was less pronounced in the South than
in the North. The blockade of the Confederacy by Union ships meant
that very little was getting through from Europe or from the Caribbean. As prices went out of reach, the people who were buying
from middlemen became even angrier. The slurs on unpatriotic merchants included snide remarks about Jews. Jews, however, were not
major targets of this anger—the blockade-runners had the worst
reputation for price gouging, and there were almost no Jews among
them.

The more serious anti-Semitism was in the North, and not only
for economic reasons. The charge that Jews were slackers, that they
avoided army service, appeared for the first time in American history.
In 1863, the Irish went on a rampage in New York against the
proposal to impose a military draft. This would have made them
fight for the Union, a cause they regarded as a Protestant one. The
Irish rioted in Jewish neighborhoods, as well, and they looted Jewish
stores. The outcry was that Jewish middlemen were taking unfair

advantage as they sold scarce consumer goods. This was class anger. The Irish in New York were poor, mostly laborers, while the Jews had already risen into the middle class. Such tension between the two groups would continue for many decades.

There was a more pervasive canard that Jews were not pulling their weight in the army. This particular anti-Semitic charge, that Jews had not fought in the Civil War, was to be repeated quite often to the very end of the century, as the generation which had been young in the 1860s came to maturity and took over the leadership of America. What lent substance to the charge was the fact that in the Civil War it was possible to avoid the army. In the North, payment of three hundred dollars bought an exemption; in the South, one could get out of military service by providing a substitute. In both regions people who were well-off were much more likely to avoid the army than poor people, and many immigrant Jews could already afford to buy their way out of service. The charge of slacking was not true, but it persisted, and it was not answered adequately until it arose again in the 1890s. In 1891, Simon Wolf, a Washington lawyer who had been the American Jewish lobbyist and representative in the capital for a number of decades, felt it necessary to collect the evidence for Jewish participation in the Civil War. He published a book entitled *The American Jew as Soldier, Patriot and Citizen,* in which he listed eight thousand men who had served in the Union and Confederate armies, and the list was obviously incomplete. The task of "antidefamation," of "proving" in the face of hostile attack that Jews were "good Americans," did not begin with Wolf's book. A century earlier, Haym Salomon had made the same argument when he had replied to an attack on Jews: he proclaimed that the Jews had served beyond their numbers in the armies of the Revolution.

In the immediate years after the Civil War, most Jews remained in retail trade. The business directories of the cities are instructive. Between 1865 and 1875 the number of Jewish business firms in Baltimore more than doubled. In Cincinnati there were three times as many Jewish businesses in 1880 as there had been in 1860; in those two decades the number had multiplied by four in Cleveland. The increases in New York, Philadelphia, Chicago, Milwaukee, and St. Louis were of a similar order. We have no way of knowing how well-off the owners of these firms were, but it is obvious that new businesses are not established if older ones are doing badly. In the economic depression of 1879, some fifty-two thousand American businesses failed, but there seemed to have been very few Jews among them. By 1880, about half of the Jewish business firms in the country were in clothing and allied occupations, both in manufacturing and in retail sales. Three-quarters of all the clothing businesses of all kinds were controlled by Jews. They owned an even higher proportion of the department stores that were then being opened on the "main street" of almost every city in the country. There were, of course, unsuccessful Jews who remained artisans or employees. These were to be found in the larger cities where two-thirds of the Jews in the labor force worked for other people. On the other hand, by the 1870s nine out of ten Jews in the smaller towns were self-employed businessmen.

The several Jewish firms which were established on Wall Street in the 1860s were being attacked by American anti-Semites who insisted that Jews dominated the stock market, but in actual fact none was at the front rank until near the turn of the century. Even as late as 1880, only two percent of the gainfully employed Jews were in finance, and almost all of these were employees and not principals.

Despite General Grant's Order Number 11 (which he deeply regretted for the rest of his life), anti-Semitism in America did not inflict substantial damage during and after the Civil War. Essentially Jews were not in competition with other economic interests. The strength of the "German Jews" was that they had created an enclave of their own in the American economy; they had concentrated in a few middlemen occupations which they dominated. In the mind of America, by the 1870s and 1880s, there was a "Jewish economy" of clothing manufacturers, storekeepers, department-store owners, and some financiers. This concentration in a very few pursuits acted to define Jews as different. The families which owned the major clothing firms, department stores, and financial houses were heavily inter-related. In a highly competitive world only members of the family could be trusted. Thus, the "German Jews" had repeated in America an age-old pattern of the ghetto. In the medieval ghetto in Europe, Jews had been forced into a very few pursuits, and they were a trading network in which everyone knew everyone else. In America, Jews largely remained in these pursuits in the first two generations after their arrival in the 1840s and 1850s, and they remained an extended family, from New York to San Francisco.

Social anti-Semitism reinforced this separateness. In 1877, there was a famous incident when Joseph Seligman, then a leading banker in America, arrived in his own railroad car at Saratoga Springs, New York, to spend a vacation in what was then the summer capital of the socially aspiring new rich. The owner of the hotel in which Seligman wanted to stay refused to have Jews on the premises. Such exclusion of Jews was to remain very common for at least the next half-century in American resorts of all classes. All over urban America, in those years, when well-to-do Jews moved into posh neighborhoods, the Gentiles soon moved out; they left the Jewish new rich in what amounted to a gilded ghetto. Thus, the "German Jews" cohered as a group, in part by exclusion. Their Gentile peers in business might have lunch with them, but they stoutly refused to introduce these Jews to their wives. The newly rich Jews had no choice but to create social institutions which were parallel to those of the Gentile upper middle class. When they were immigrants and poor peddlers, these Jews had imagined that they would be accepted by "society" when they came to wealth. The newly rich "German Jews" discovered in the 1870s and 1880s, during America's Gilded Age, that this was not so. The Gentiles who had just come to money were themselves fighting to enter "society," and they were even less hospitable to the Jews than the older aristocrats. A seal was thus set on a peculiarly American formulation of what makes a Jewish community: clannishness by Jews and exclusion by Gentiles, reinforcing each other. The affirmation of Judaism played a much lesser role. In the new circumstances of wealth, the situation of these Jews was no different than it had been in the 1840s, in poverty, when the Odd Fellows had rejected them and forced them to found B'nai B'rith.

But, even as Jews were being annoyed by social exclusion, the national government was remarkably hospitable. Within months after Joseph Seligman had been insulted in Saratoga Springs, General Grant, the new President of the United States, offered him a seat in his cabinet, which Seligman refused because he did not want to leave his business as banker. Had Seligman accepted, he would have been the first Jew to serve in so high an office in the federal government. The most prominent "German Jew" of his time, Joseph Seligman, was repeating the experience of Uriah Phillips Levy, of the older settlement, a decade earlier: he was an American not because society was willing to forgive him for being a Jew, but because the Constitution guaranteed equality.

In the decades after the Civil War the "German Jews" built elaborate temples in every major and middle-sized city in America. Like Isaac Mayer Wise and his laymen in Cincinnati, their peers everywhere wanted to announce, and to claim, their status among the American upper middle class. The great occasions of the life cycle, such as marriage and death, were celebrated in these buildings. The major Jewish festivals were occasions for large gatherings. But their social clubs were at least as elaborate and even more central to their lives. The network of Jewish social organizations which, as we have seen, had been started in the 1840s and 1850s, grew in members and in the quality of their amenities. In Philadelphia, for example, a group of "German Jews" had founded the Mercantile Club in 1853. It contained among its members such figures as Marcus Goldman and Charles Bloomingdale, the progenitor of the Bloomingdale's department store clan. In the first years of the club's existence, it moved to several ever-posher rented quarters. Finally, in 1880, the club occupied "a handsome and well-furnished house" of its own. In Atlanta, the Concordia Club, which was founded in 1877, had an elegant building which was much admired and commented upon. In Rochester, New York, several clubs were created in those years. They were finally united into a grand and elegant place which was "well-considered by the general community." In 1881, this club was disbanded and a new club called the Eureka was founded. The club members bought a mansion and refitted it at great expense. By 1893 the property of this club was worth the then princely sum of a hundred thousand dollars. In San Francisco in the 1870s, the wealth of ten of the leading members of its Reform congregation was estimated at the combined total of forty-five million dollars. When Isaac Mayer Wise visited the city in 1877, he was, of course, taken to the mansion of the Concordia Club (this was a favorite name for such establishments in various cities), which he described as "an elegant place."

Within these clubs an intense social life was lived, balls were held, and marriages were arranged. These clubs even attempted to suggest that they were the arbiters of taste and elegance for the entire community. Such claims ran into difficulty with Gentile critics, who regarded such a notion as a presumption on the part of any nouveaux riches, and certainly on the part of Jews. So, in San Francisco a Mr. Greenway, of the Jewish elite, declared that there were only four hundred persons in town who were fit to go into good society. He was mocked in a newspaper as representing the "parvenu advertising society" trying to hand down "a new set of commandments to take the place of the old, reliable ten that Moses broke."

Those who had arrived at the economic status which enabled them to live within the society of the clubs obviously did not have working wives. On the contrary in this Gilded Age, well-to-do women were overdressed and affected airs, thus establishing, as the contemporary sociologist Thorstein Veblen soon observed, that people of wealth engaged in "conspicuous consumption" and "conspicuous display." Rich men were announcing their success through what they could give their women to wear, and by freeing them from work. Some of these wives took frequent trips back to the old country, to Germany, to display their wealth. They did not always succeed in being accepted in what they thought was their new dignity. The older, more structured European society was not easily impressed, even by success in America.

For all the glitter and success of this German Jewish immigration, some of the immigrants remained poor, and problematic. The charitable organizations which had been created in the 1840s and 1850s existed for self-help for the newly arrived. In their extension and growth after 1865 these organizations acquired the character of the rich taking care less of their own poor than, more and more, of the East Europeans. In Rochester, New York, for example, a group of men and women met in October of 1877 to form a Jewish orphan asylum. Two years later this endeavor was consolidated with comparable bodies in Syracuse and Buffalo. These were not self-help agencies, as B'nai B'rith and its competitors had been in the immigrant days of the 1840s and 1850s. The widows and the orphans of the "German Jews" usually had rich relatives who took them in. The new social agencies which were created in the 1870s, and thereafter, expressed the concern of the "German Jews" for the newest immigrants, the very "Russian Jews" whom they regarded as socially and culturally inferior. Most of these orphans were of East European origin, for by the 1870s there were substantial numbers of Jews from Russia and Austria-Hungary in these upstate communities.

After the Civil War, the Jews of Syracuse organized both a society for visiting the sick and a much more elaborate one for taking care of the poor, and especially for burying the dead of poor families who could not afford funerals. In New York, a great network of such charitable bodies kept growing in the post–Civil War period. In 1867 Edmond Pelz, a German who had visited the United States, published a book in Hamburg about New York; he complained that the German Gentiles had been attempting to establish a hospital but had managed to raise only thirty thousand dollars, one-tenth of the sum that was needed, while the Jews had already built their hospital long before. (Mount Sinai Hospital had been established by the oldest American Jews, the Sephardim, in 1855; it was rebuilt at great expense and renamed in 1869 by the "German Jews.")

In the 1870s and 1880s, the "German Jews" built Jewish hospitals and established a variety of social service organizations in all the major cities of the United States. Creating these agencies cost large amounts of money, but the affluent "German Jews" were generous. They were imitating the behavior of generations of Jewish rich, that it was the responsibility of those who had money to take care of their poor brethren. So it had been in America, at least most of the time; the first Jewish settlement in New Amsterdam had taken care of its own poor; Haym Salomon had praised his own generation for doing the same. Always, from the beginning, there had been another reason: such charities were necessary as self-protection for the Jewish rich. The Jewish poor had to be kept from becoming a problem to America as a whole. By the 1870s, even before the migration from Eastern Europe became massive, the growing number of socially dependent cases was creating a threat of anti-Semitism. In such arguments there was a large element of the thesis that was becoming ever more widespread among the "German Jews," that all would be well in America, and that anti-Semitism simply would not have appeared, had the mass migration from Eastern Europe not arrived.

This assertion could not be further from the truth. On the contrary, when the great immigration of "Russian Jews" was at its height in the 1890s, Populist anti-Semitism attacked the Jews on Wall Street, and not this mass which was then largely laboring in sweatshops.

The farmers in the Midwest and the South had no quarrel with industrial labor in the East. They were at war with those who determined interest rates and the value of money. To the degree to which they unfairly centered their attack on Jews, who were, as we have seen, not really important on Wall Street, they were attacking not the newest arrivals, but the successful Jews who had been in America for a generation or so.

But this was not how the "German Jews" perceived their situation. They did feel threatened; in their view these new arrivals were underscoring the foreignness of Jews in America. Their very first concern was thus to try to limit immigration, but, if not, at least to "Americanize" the new immigrants as quickly as possible. On the surface this meant to teach them English and Western manners, but much more than that was soon attempted. The German Jewish rich wanted to disperse these Jewish masses around the country and not have them crowd into several of the major cities, and especially not into New York. They wanted also to effect economic restratification, that is, for the East European Jews to engage in a whole host of occupations other than commerce, to which they were all aspiring. There was particular emphasis on the need to farm, and much money and effort were expended in promoting such settlements. This criticism of Jewish economic abnormality was never directed by "German Jews" at themselves, for they had no doubt that they ought to remain near their businesses. They wanted these new arrivals to furnish them with the rest of the economic pyramid of farmers and workers, in "healthy" occupations spread all over the country, which would allow their German Jewish patrons to be the two or three percent at the top. The Americanization of the immigrants would validate the older settlers as representatives of a "normal" Jewish economy, existing side by side with the economy of the country as a whole.

The older settlers thus accepted responsibility for the new migration, in part in order to protect themselves, but the concern of the "German Jews" for the newly arrived Yiddish-speaking masses was not entirely self-serving. There was much compassion for, and even identification with, these poor "coreligionists," as the new immigrants were then called in the circles of "our crowd." And yet both the involvement in the newest arrivals and the recoil from them reflected the fears and needs of the "German Jews" in those days.

To gain acceptance for themselves in America was the central issue of their agenda; it colored everything that they felt and did.

II

The desire of the "German Jews" for equality in America continued to involve them in the fight against the notion that America was a Protestant, Christian country. On this issue, the very Jews who wanted society to accept them as nice, inoffensive people were increasingly eager to do battle. During the Civil War, there might have been some reason for Jews to want to avoid raising any seemingly divisive issue, but a notable and largely unsuccessful battle was waged over religious discrimination against Jews in the military. Congressional legislation had provided that for a clergyman to be appointed a chaplain in the military establishment, he needed to be a minister of some Christian denomination. Jewish representation did succeed in removing this qualification from the law, but no rabbi was admitted to the army. Several Jews, not all of them ordained rabbis, did serve on the fringes of the chaplaincy, especially in hospitals, but nowhere, not even in one or two largely Jewish companies from northeastern cities, was there a Jewish chaplain in the field.

In the 1860s, Jews continued the fight that Isaac Mayer Wise had begun a decade earlier against the notion that America was a "Christian country." Jews opposed the Sunday blue laws, which prohibited keeping businesses open on the Lord's Day, but usually to no avail. Christian prayers and Bible reading in the public schools remained a perennial issue, and here, too, the Jewish counterattack met with only qualified success. Having failed in the 1850s, Isaac Mayer Wise did succeed in having such readings eliminated from the schools of Cincinnati, where the number of Jews among the students was quite substantial. The case was appealed and reappealed by both sides, until the Supreme Court of Ohio finally held that such Bible reading was an infringement on the separation of church and state. In 1869, Wise explained why he was willing to confront Christian opinion: "We want secular schools or nothing else, nor has any state a shadow of a right to support any other." In another connection Wise had said: "We stand or fall with the liberal phalanx of this country, come what may." Wise had wrapped himself in the Constitution. In a religiously neutral America, Reform Judaism, the religion of the successful middle class, would be one of the many American religious denominations, and it would be fully equal to all of them.

But these Jews wanted, desperately, to be liked. During their first twenty years in America, the German-Jewish immigrants had made relatively minor changes in their synagogue ritual. It was in the era immediately after the Civil War that the reformers in the United States became the most radically untraditional sect in all of world Jewry. The new rich formally jettisoned almost all of the Jewish rituals. In Europe at that time, religious reform had become less radical as the years went by, both because the inherited tradition still largely dominated the organized Jewish community and because the dominant forms of Christianity in Europe were Catholic, Orthodox, or highly structured Protestant. In Europe, except for the temple in Hamburg, there was never a single synagogue anywhere in which worship was conducted bareheaded. By the 1870s, this was becoming the majority form of American Reform congregations. These synagogues almost all abolished the dietary laws and removed head coverings from the men at prayer; some even observed the Sabbath on Sunday. Most of the laity was, of course, given comfort by a Judaism which had dispensed with all of the ritual restrictions on Jewish conduct and had thus encouraged individual Jews to mix freely with their Gentile neighbors. Such temples, with their impeccable decorum and their churchiness, could act as calling cards for those who had now become rich enough to move to Fifth Avenue in New York and to its equivalent all over America. The Christian patterns which these temples chose to follow were the same as those affected then by many of the descendants of the old Puritan elite. Their churches had all begun as Congregationalist, holding fast to Calvinist theology, but many of them had turned Unitarian or Universalist in the nineteenth century.

Everywhere, the Jewish temples cultivated formal interfaith activities. Such theologically liberal Protestant churches were the ones which were most immediately available for relations with Jews. For example, as early as 1870, Berith Kodesh, Rochester's Reform congregation, was host to a lecture given by Newton Mann, the minister of the First Unitarian Church. Three years later this clergyman was invited to preach from the pulpit. In 1874, Berith Kodesh, together with both the Unitarian and the Universalist churches in town, gave a joint Thanksgiving service. This was a great occasion for the Reform Jews of Rochester, and it continued annually until nearly the turn of the century. The event grew by the accession in the 1890s of the Plymouth Congregational Church. The trustees of that institution were so pleased that they congratulated their minister, William T. Brown, who had also been exchanging pulpits with the rabbi, for this display of "the tolerant and enlightened spirit which is the chief glory of our country." Unfortunately for this seemingly idyllic scene, the Reverend Mr. Brown became increasingly radical in his social and political views. The clothing industry, which was the major employer in Rochester, was in turmoil because a boycott had been declared by the American Federation of Labor against the manufacturers, who were Jews, and who were the leaders of the Berith Kodesh Congregation. Mr. Brown's flock stood by him in his identification with the cause of labor, but the trustees of Berith Kodesh considered him to be "subversive of existing social organization." They instructed their rabbi, Dr. Max Landsberg, not to join in any religious services together with the Reverend Mr. Brown. This action took place in 1901. It is useful to cite it here, in a discussion of a somewhat earlier time, to make the point that interfaith activity was not an end in itself, for spiritual reasons, for these German Jews. It was, rather, a way of drawing closer to their Gentile peers. When interfaith sometimes clashed actively with class interest, it was economic interest that usually prevailed—but, as we shall soon see, it was not always so.

In the 1870s Isaac Mayer Wise finally succeeded in realizing his dream to create the forms of national Jewish religious organization. His model was the major Protestant denominations, which met regularly in national and church conferences and in clerical associations. Such bodies existed even among those denominations which were not hierarchical, such as the Congregationalists, where the central body had not the power to legislate ritual forms or conformity of belief for individual congregations. All these Christian denominations had long before established seminaries to train their own clergy; they had ceased being dependent on Europe. This example had become especially important to the American Reform synagogues, because rabbis of European origin then occupied all of the pulpits. Most such men remained foreign; many never became truly comfortable in English. Some took theology "too seriously." There were those among them who believed in the "un-American," old-fashioned idea that rabbis had authority over their congregations. Such a notion was harbored, as we have seen, not only by Orthodox figures such as Sabato Morais but even by an ultrareformer, such as David Einhorn, who was far more religiously radical than Isaac Mayer Wise. In the 1870s, the American synagogues of the comfortably rich could thus be persuaded that they needed a new generation of rabbis, American-born and trained, who would minister to them rather than attempt to command them. The earlier stirrings before the Civil War toward creating national synagogue and rabbinic organizations and a rabbinic seminary in America had failed. They were opposed or ignored because they were understood as attempts to impose older Jewish discipline in the New Land. Now, after the Civil War, a generation who had come to wealth and power was willing to pay for such bodies, because it did not fear them.

The first organization that Isaac Mayer Wise put together was the Union of American Hebrew Congregations, which he created in Cincinnati in 1873. The twenty-eight synagogues which came to the meeting were those of the South and the West. There was no one from the East at this founding conference, but within two years the eastern congregations of Reform persuasion joined the union. The conference that Wise had called in 1855 in Cleveland, to found a national body of all the synagogues in America, had failed because most of the congregations were then in the uneasy opening stages of turning reformed. He succeeded in 1873, because Reform then dominated the scene. The central task of this new body was to create a seminary for the training of young Jews, to give them, in Wise's formulation, an "enlightened education" in the Jewish religion, to prepare them for the rabbinate. The Hebrew Union College was opened in 1875, in the building of Wise's temple in Cincinnati, and so Cincinnati had laid claim to being the religious center of American Jewry. Some years later, in 1889, the organizational structure of Reform Judaism in America was completed by the creation of the Central Conference of American Rabbis.

The word "reform" was not mentioned in the names that were devised for these three bodies. The rhetoric meant to suggest that they represented not a part, or a faction, but all of American Judaism. Almost all of the two hundred congregations which were rich enough to own buildings were identified with the Union of American Hebrew Congregations, but Wise and his colleagues knew very well that there were, by the 1870s, a growing number of Orthodox synagogues with buildings of their own, and many Orthodox prayer conventicles, in every city of the country. A few were older congregations, which had remained Orthodox despite the trend to Reform. Most were being created by Yiddish-speaking Jews from Russia and Austria-Hungary, who had begun to arrive in some numbers in the 1870s. The creators of the self-styled "Union of American Hebrew Congregations," "Hebrew Union College," and "Central Conference of American Rabbis" were consciously asserting that the "Polish forms of the Jewish religion" were marginal and alien in America. At the very least, the Reform Jews suggested that they were aristocratically distant from such backward people—as the older Jewish settlers, who claimed to be Sephardim, had suggested in the 1840s when the "German Jews" had first arrived.

And yet Wise and his supporters began to fail in the 1870s, at the very height of their success, and not merely because Jews from Eastern Europe were beginning to arrive and create their own way of Jewish life and Jewish worship. Within the "reformed" camp itself, major figures existed who rejected harping on Americanization and on social acceptance as the central themes of Jewish religious life. These opponents of Wise controlled the meeting which took place in Pittsburgh in 1885, at which the official platform of Reform Judaism was formulated. The central figure in this endeavor was Kaufmann Kohler, who was then the rabbi of one of the reformed congregations in New York. Wise and Kohler detested each other. Kohler, the son-in-law of Wise's old enemy, David Einhorn, was also a substantial scholar and theologian, whose learning made Wise feel inferior. Kohler invited a number of Reform rabbis to Pittsburgh in November 1885 to consult together and to adopt a joint statement of their views. Wise had little choice but to attend. He accepted the eight-point program for Reform Judaism that was written there, though he would have preferred a less challenging statement.

The more radical, ideologically-minded people who wrote the Pittsburgh platform were dealing with a problem other than the social acceptance of Jews. They faced squarely the basic theological question: What was left of "Mosaic legislation," after these reformers had announced that "they accept as binding only the moral laws of Judaism" and that they reject all the ceremonies that "are not adapted to the views and habits of modern civilization"? In the light of these assertions, why cling to Judaism? Those who framed the Pittsburgh Platform answered that Judaism needed to continue to exist as a prime agent in the bringing about of universal morality. This was the "mission of Israel." The authors of this document added that "the spirit of the broad humanity of our age is our ally in the fulfillment of our mission." The question still remained: What was the content of that "mission"? These rabbis answered in the eighth, and concluding, section of the Pittsburgh Platform: "We deem it our duty to participate in the great task of modern times, to solve on the basis of justice and righteousness the problems presented by the contrast and evils of the present organization of society." Judaism in America had thus been defined as the "conscience of the rich," as a call to the Jewish rich to concern themselves with the poor.

In one of its meanings, the doctrine of the Pittsburgh Platform was a very bold bid indeed for the complete social acceptance of Jews in America. Isaac Mayer Wise had been contenting himself all his life with the dream of leading respectable rich Jews to be welcomed by respectable rich Christians, to their class. Those who framed the Pittsburgh Platform went far beyond Wise even in their social aspirations. In the 1880s, the most advanced Protestant theology in America was the "Social Gospel"; Christianity was then being translated into concern for all those who were suffering in this world. Through the Pittsburgh Platform, Reform Judaism had asserted that the Jews were now ready to join with other well-to-do Americans in worrying about the poor. The "German Jews" had announced, unilaterally, that they no longer thought of themselves as being on approval in any sense in America. They were not a problem even to themselves, so they said; they had now declared themselves to being among the problem solvers. In effect, social anti-Semitism was ignored. It was assessed to be marginal, on the way to disappearing in the new world of enlightened humanity.

Most of those who have commented on the Pittsburgh Platform have remembered its anti-Zionism, its firm declaration that Jews did not regard themselves as a nation in exile—but this assertion was hardly new and original. It was simply a restatement of what reformers had already said at the synods in Germany in the 1840s. Such views then dominated among the Jewish bourgeoisie everywhere, in Central and Western Europe and, of course, in America.

What was really new in the Pittsburgh Platform was the assertion that Jews as a religious group had an obligation to take risks for the creation of a more just society. The convenor of the Conference who agreed to the inclusion of these lines on social justice in this document was Kaufmann Kohler; he had married into the family of David Einhorn, the flaming abolitionist of 1860. Einhorn had been a minority then, in part because the "German Jews" still felt themselves to be too weak and foreign to do battle for social justice in America. In 1885, a quarter of a century later, these very Jews were now affluent and powerful, and some of them felt impelled by conscience to fight for all the poor, as Uriah Phillips Levy had fought, a generation earlier, to stop the flogging of sailors.

Statements about social justice were being made occasionally by Jewish religious reformers in the Old World in those years. In an ever more anti-Semitic, and more ideological, Europe such statements were not much more than verbiage. Those Jews in Europe who were taking risks for the cause of a more just society were not in the Reform synagogues; they were, instead, in the movements which were trying to make political revolutions. There were few liberal rabbis in Europe among these revolutionaries. America was different. Here there was room, even in the midst of social anti-Semitism, for some of the Jewish well-to-do from the temples, and especially for some of their rabbis, to join the cause of social reform. The most immediate result of the Pittsburgh Platform was that a generation of Reform rabbis soon arose who took its call for social action seriously. The young Stephen S. Wise (he was not related to Isaac Mayer Wise) began his public career as rabbi in Portland, Oregon, in 1900, where he fought successfully for a law limiting child labor. Judah Leon Magnes went to the length of being a pacifist in the First World War. Both had stormy careers from their beginnings, but both were legitimate leaders in Reform Judaism because the Pittsburgh Platform had justified intervention on behalf of the poor.

Some rabbis made themselves unpopular with their overwhelmingly capitalist congregants by supporting the organization of labor unions. As the East Europeans kept arriving in their tens and hundreds of thousands, several Reform rabbis joined to help found the Jewish Agricultural Society, which created farming settlements for immigrants. The young Henrietta Szold, daughter of a Reform rabbi in Baltimore, took to teaching newcomers the English language and

American ways. Even more remote figures who felt most threatened by the new arrivals, such as the aging Isaac Mayer Wise, could not stand aside and pretend that they were uninvolved or unmoved. In the 1890s, Wise spoke for the Reform effort to help the new immigrants.

Felix Adler and Lillian Wald were perhaps even more interesting examples of these social concerns, precisely because both Adler and Wald were by choice on the fringes of the Jewish community. Felix Adler, the son and chosen successor of Samuel Adler, the rabbi of Temple Emanu-El in New York, really believed the universalist ideas of Reform Judaism. He took these values to demand that he abandon all traces of ethnic Jewishness. In the 1870s, Adler left the organized Jewish community and founded the Ethical Culture movement, to express a high-minded concern for all the underprivileged. Adler took with him some of the younger elements within Reform Judaism in New York. He founded a body that was in theory free of ethnic loyalty, even though the Society for Ethical Culture consisted overwhelmingly of Jews. Nevertheless, despite this break, Adler continued to harbor marked components of Jewish feeling. He had a deep and abiding concern for the miseries of the Jewish masses who were arriving from Eastern Europe. Adler was once even accused by a Rochester Jewish newspaper of suggesting that the Jews vote as a bloc in national elections, in order to further their interests. The charge was basically true. Adler did give such advice to the Jews on the Lower East Side of New York in several elections; he urged them to vote their interests as poor people.

Lillian Wald came from a rich German Jewish family in Rochester. She could, therefore, have spent her life in the comfortable society of "our crowd," but she decided to become a nurse. Wald worked among the immigrants of New York's Lower East Side. In 1895, she founded the Henry Street Settlement, to provide health, educational, and recreational services to those who were living in tenements. As the years went by, Wald fought for every cause of social reform in her day, including, especially, the support of trade unionism. Like Rabbi Judah Leon Magnes, she opposed the entry of the United States into the First World War; Wald remained a pacifist during the conflict. The "Social Gospel" was Lillian Wald's faith. She was a believer in the universal brotherhood of man, and, despite her involvement with the Lower East Side, she was no partisan of "the things that make men different."

Adler and Wald were not willing to affirm that they had a special commitment to the Jewish people; as each worried about Jews, they insisted that they were acting on the stage of American society as a whole. The majority of their contemporaries remained within Judaism. For some, their Jewish ties represented inertia, or, as has been said above, they were based on family feeling. For others, it was a deep commitment to be in the forefront, as Jews, of the battles for social justice in all the world, and especially in American society. There were laymen, and not only rabbis, among the second generation of the "German Jews" who believed that Jews had a "mission," that they had been set apart by God Himself to take risks for justice. Joel Elias Springarn, the founder of the National Association for the Advancement of Colored People, was one among many such people.

These Jews of the second generation were not content simply to disappear, or to pretend to themselves that they were disappearing, among the successful in America. These reformed Jewish idealists wanted to be different, and to make a difference, as Jews. They answered anti-Semitism by trying to remake America. They knew in their bones that they had special responsibilities because they were Jews. These men and women were not "adjusting" to the existing America, and, least of all, to the life of their own enclave of rich, respectable Jews. The classic doctrine of Jewish theology, "chosenness" had reappeared among them, in America, in the guise of their special vocation to fight for social justice.

10.

The Russian Jews
Arrive

I

In the half century after the end of the Civil War,
no less than thirty-five million people came to America. This was,
by far, the largest wave of immigration in American history. These
masses came to the United States because Europe was becoming
overpopulated, especially with the poor. Modern medicine had cut
the death rate of infants, but the birthrate still remained high. The
problem was especially acute in southern Italy and in Czarist Russia.
The Industrial Revolution had barely come to these countries. There
were too few new jobs to provide work for the ever-larger numbers
of the poor. This was the "push" factor: the lack of hope in Europe
was making mass migration necessary. The "pull" factor was the
attraction of America: the still-existing frontier offered land for those
who wanted to farm, and the industrialization of America was creating millions of jobs in the cities. "Pull" was so important that any
falling off in the American economy resulted within a year in a
slackening of immigration from Europe.

More than two million of these newcomers were Jews. These

masses represented at least fifteen percent of all of European Jewry and nearly eight percent of all the immigrants to America. This migration, so it has often been argued, was caused by a third factor that was specific to Jews, the flight from anti-Semitic violence. In fact, pogroms (physical attacks on Jews) played a minor role as a cause of the emigration of Jews from Eastern Europe. The dominant cause of mass migration was poverty. Almost all middle-class Jews managed to find ways of reestablishing themselves elsewhere in Russia; it was the peddlers and the tailors who left for America. America gave the "Russian Jews" the chance to rise from the class in which they originated, but it is much better to imagine that one's grandparents were already part of the "better people" in Russia, and that America was the haven of refuge from anti-Semitism. This myth suggests by implication that those who arrived were the bearers of a high intellectual and cultural tradition. The truth is starker, and more heroic. The Jews from Russia arrived in the United States penniless and largely uneducated even in Judaism; they rose, in less than two generations, to the very apex of American life.

Immediately after the pogroms of 1881–82, in which hundreds of Jews were killed or injured all over Czarist Russia, there was some flight to America, but the numbers did not increase radically until late in the decade. Even as czarist persecution of Jews was increasing in those years, especially through the expulsion of many thousands of Jews from Russia's villages and towns, more Jews moved to the cities in Russia than fled abroad. Those who had some money, or family connections, tended to remain. The poorest left for America. It is striking that there had been no pogroms in Austria-Hungary or Romania, and yet a larger proportion of the Jewish population of these countries emigrated westward in the late nineteenth century than came from Czarist Russia. In the Austro-Hungarian Empire, Franz Joseph I protected Jews against violence; in Romania, anti-Semitic outbreaks were checked to some degree by the guarantees of equality for all that Romania had given in 1879, when it was granted independence in the Treaty of Berlin. Anti-Semitism did indeed limit the economic possibilities for Jews in all three countries, but the middle class found ways of surviving. It was the poor who were most affected by the lack of opportunity; they were the people who emigrated.

The Jews who arrived in the United States before the First World

War were, thus, not a random sample of all East European Jewry; they were the masses without the classes. The evidence for this assertion is overwhelming. It is to be found in literature of the era, in the languages that Jews wrote, and in the many contemporary statistical studies of East European Jews, both in Europe and later in America. There was, indeed, a long tradition, of at least a century and a half, of rabbinic and intellectual distaste for the New World. It was most pronounced during the very years of the largest Jewish mass migration to the United States. This European literature has not been read in any connected fashion, until now, by students of American Jewish history. There has, perhaps, been a certain unwillingness to confront this tradition of contempt for America. The reading of such literature suggests that the "better people" were kept from coming to the United States. The truth is that few of the "better people" wanted to come to America. Contemporary essays and later memoirs support this thesis; it is proved beyond doubt by the immigration statistics of those years.

A few modern Hebrew poets and a novelist or two had been cast up on American shores in the years when hundreds of thousands were on the move. Most of them were teaching in Jewish afternoon schools, which supplemented the public schools with some instruction of religion and Hebrew as a language. Almost without exception the theme of these writers was their personal alienation in Jewish America, which they depicted as uncouth, money-mad, and destructive to the spirit. Israel Efros, one of the Hebrew writers of that generation, expressed this distance, and this sorrow, in a striking epic poem entitled *The Wigwams Are Silent*. Efros published the poem in 1932, but it was written earlier, and reflected the mood of his first experiences in the United States as a young immigrant in the first years of the century. On the surface this was a poem about Indians, the noble savages, the purity of whose culture had been destroyed by American greed. But, on another level, the author was his own "Indian," an East European Jewish intellectual, caught among his contemporaries whose souls were being destroyed, so he thought, in the sweatshops. It did not matter whether they succeeded in business or whether they failed to rise into the beginnings of affluence. The result in spiritual impoverishment, so Efros and all the other Hebraists insisted, was the same. The shtetl, idealized by nostalgia, had been the home of Jewish purity, the "wigwam" which was now increasingly silent because it had been abandoned by those who had come to America. Eventually a number of the Hebrew writers in the United States found their way to the renascent Jewish settlement in the Land of Israel. Few of those who remained in "exile" ever really made peace with America.

The most important Jewish writer to come to America was Sholem Aleichem (pen name for Sholem Rabinovitz), who came to New York for the first time in 1906. He hoped to stay, but he could not bear the place (he shared the dominant view of European Jewish intellectuals that American Jews were raw and uncouth), and he returned to Russia after a few months. When the First World War broke out, Sholem Aleichem had no choice but to gather his family and leave for New York. In these last two years of his life he tried to adjust to America, but he remained a fish out of water. His last major work, *Mottel Peise, the Cantor's Son,* was a tale about a young man who came to America impoverished, but from a family of some learning and of European Jewish middle-class values. Sholem Aleichem died in 1916 before the second, "American" part of the novel (it was running in installments in one of the Yiddish dailies) could be finished, but the clear message of the tale was that America was not a comfortable place for the likes of Mottel Peise.

Like almost every immigrant, Mottel Peise, on arrival, went looking for *landsleite,* that is, other immigrants from the same hometown in the old country. The Lower East Side of New York was then brimming with many hundreds of such associations. There *greene* ("greens"), that is, newly arrived immigrants, met people they had known who were *gelle* ("yellows"), who had been in America for some time and could offer the "greens" guidance. Mottel Peise followed the pattern; he went to find his "extended family" from back home, but he discovered that it was a world turned upside down. The earliest arrivals from his shtetl had been, back home, the most ignorant and socially unacceptable. They were now the leaders of the association of his compatriots. A learned man, a ritual slaughterer back home, had been reduced to helplessness and total poverty. He lived off the occasional good graces of the masters of the association.

The most famous of Sholem Aleichem's characters, Tevye, had dreamed in Europe, in a line that has been given international currency in the musical *Fiddler on the Roof,* of what he would do "if I were a rich man." His most immediate fantasy was that, as a rich man, he would sit at the east wall of the synagogue, in the most honorific place; the rabbi would then listen to him, rather than to those to whom he usually paid attention. Mottel Peise, the cantor's son, found that Tevye's dream had been realized on the Lower East Side. There, unlearned people of the lower classes in Europe were sitting at an eastern wall in a synagogue of their own devising. They were appointing religious functionaries who would listen to them. In America, among his fellow townsmen Mottel Peise was not the cantor's son. In New York, so those who had come earlier insisted, such a self-image was irrelevant, and even obnoxious. In America a man was judged only by how successfully he made his way in the New World. "Better people" like Mottel Peise, or his creator, Sholem Aleichem, had to accept this truth. They could not impose the older order of respect on the immigrant masses.

A significant number of Jewish literary and intellectual figures did arrive in the United States between 1905 (the year when the First Russian Revolution was suppressed) and 1914, but, in their majority, like Sholem Aleichem, they recoiled from the immigrant masses which had arrived earlier. This was inevitable, not least because the learned Jews of Europe had helped create the very reality which now made them heartsick. The European rabbis had always, even before the 1880s, been especially harsh in forbidding their class to go to the New Land. In 1826 the rabbis of London had refused to recognize conversions to Judaism performed in America. The despondent accounts of the earliest American rabbis acted to confirm the view in Europe that America was no place for a learned and pious Jew.

Equally pained descriptions were sent back home from America in the 1880s and thereafter. Among the many reporters the most interesting was, perhaps, Zvi Falk Widawer. A scholar and Hebraist who came to America in the hopes of settling in the New Land, Widawer traveled to most of the major cities in the country, but he felt so totally alien in the United States that he soon went back home to Russia. Widawer summed up his assessment of American Jewry in a striking paragraph. Writing from San Francisco for a Hebrew journal published in Russia, Widawer asserted that "the Jews who live in this land did not endure long journeys and untold hardships in order to slake their thirst for the word of God and to busy themselves in the Torah in a free and untroubled place. Jews came here only to achieve the purpose which occupied their entire attention in the land of their birth. That purpose *was* money." A few years later, in 1889, an unsigned reportage to an Orthodox journal published in Galicia, the southern part of Poland which then belonged to the Austro-Hungarian Empire, echoed this opinion. The correspondent wrote from New York that "there is no faith and no knowledge of the Lord among most of our brethren who dwell in this land." He added that "the younger generation has inherited nothing from their parents except what they need to make their way in the world; every spiritual teaching is foreign to them." He then went on to plead with his readers to remain in their native land rather than come to the new country of "lies and vain dreams, which promise gain only to those who transgress the laws of the faith." Such accounts were coming back to Europe, then, from many sources. They inevitably acted to "prove" that the rabbis who opposed immigration to America had been right.

In 1893 the most distinguished moralist among the rabbis of Europe, Israel Meir Ha-Kohen, who was universally known by the title of his most important book, *Hafetz Haim* ("the seeker of life"), went beyond exhortation; he ruled against the mass migration to America. He knew that this emigration could no longer be stopped, but he pleaded with those who would heed the views of rabbis to prefer persecution in Russia to economic success in the United States. What was new in the pronouncement of the *Hafetz Haim* was an injunction that those who must go to far-off lands beyond the sea should at least leave their children behind, and they should return to Eastern Europe after making their fortune. In another passage, written in the same year, the *Hafetz Haim* ruled: "A man must move away from any place which causes turning away from the way of the Lord, even if he knows for certain that he will have great economic success there." This authority insisted that even those who know that they will retain their piety should not go to such far-off lands; the Lord's punishment upon such an uncaring population will not distinguish between the pious and unfaithful. The *Hafetz Haim* had heard that there were destructive tornadoes, floods, and temperatures of sixty degrees (centigrade) in these lands beyond the sea. Such natural disasters represented the wrath of the Lord.

These opinions became so fixed that they would remain firm among the major leaders of European Orthodoxy even in the interwar period, as the situation of European Jewry was radically worsening for all Jews, of all socioeconomic classes. In Poland, Hungary, and Romania, Jews were, then, under unrelenting attack, and there was often physical violence, but the rabbis did not urge immigration. On the contrary, the most prominent figures stood firm in urging the faithful to avoid America. Writing in the 1920s and 1930s, in his book *Divrei Torah* ("the Words of the Bible") Elazar Shapira, the rebbe (Chasidic leader) of Munkacs, insisted that there were three gates to hell: the faithlessness of some elements in European Jewry, the absolute commitment to money in America, and the secularist Zionism rampant in Jerusalem. The worst of all the options for a pious Jew was to go to the United States, for there even repentance was not possible.

To be fair, such absolute negation of America was not the only opinion among rabbinic leaders. Chaim Halberstam, the rebbe of Zanz in southern Poland, who died in 1876, is recorded as saying that the days of *galut America* ("the American exile") have now begun, but (so he "knew" as kabbalist) that this is the last "exile," after which the Messiah would come. His younger contemporary, Joshua of Belz (who died in 1894), was ambivalent about America. There is an oral tradition that was recounted by his grandson, Aaron, the fourth rebbe, that when some refugees from the pogroms in Russia arrived in Belz in 1881, Joshua advised them to go to the Holy Land and not to America. Later, many communities in the United States asked Joshua to visit, or even to stay, but he would not. There is even a story, not otherwise confirmed, that a delegation of two men came from the United States to invite him to come to the New Land for a one-year trial period, because of the grave danger to the souls of American Jews. Joshua deliberated and then answered a few days later: the world is full of evil spirits; in Europe many generations of the pious have exorcised such spirits and purified the atmosphere, but in America no one has yet done this. He could not, therefore, leave for America, but he advised the delegation to go to Lithuania, where the rabbinic leaders were less sensitive in the matter of evil spirits. The delegation went to Lithuania, so the tale goes, and persuaded Rabbi Jacob Joseph to come to New York as chief rabbi. The two delegates also went to the Chasidic leader, Ezekiel of Shinova, who was on the verge of agreeing to a visit to the United States but was dissuaded by Joshua of Belz. Ezekiel wanted the two of them to go together to "fix" America. Joshua preferred to do this by reciting one of the Psalms each day, in prayer for America's Jews.

Joshua of Belz and Ezekiel of Shinova were confused about America. They were torn between their certainty that it was the domain of evil spirits and their concern for the Jews who had gone and were going there. But, as the tide of emigration grew ever higher, even the rabbis could no longer simply write off the Jews of America, especially since some of the accounts from America had, indeed, given reason to believe that all was not hopeless. In 1887 Moshe Weinberger wrote the first book-length account in Hebrew on *Jews and Judaism in New York.* In large part his description was negative. He claimed there was no Jewish education, religious observance was very low, and peddling a disastrous occupation. He also wrote that the American reformers were too powerful, and that the Orthodox rabbis and other clergy were irresponsible and for sale. For Weinberger, there were, however, bright spots. There were neighborhoods in New York where everything was closed on the Sabbath and where more *sukkot* (outdoor booths) had been built to celebrate that festival than had been erected by the same people in anti-Semitic Russia.

Even Abraham Cahan, the editor of the *Jewish Daily Forward* and, as such, the leading voice of Jewish socialist secularism in America, gave testimony to the existence of Orthodox observance among the majority of the immigrants. Looking back upon the 1880s in the memoirs that he wrote forty years later, Cahan recounted that the majority of the Jewish workers, whom the labor unions were trying to organize, were Sabbath observers. Indeed, in his first post as editor of a Yiddish newspaper, even before he came to the *Forward,* Cahan wrote a much-admired column under the title "The Proletarian Preacher." In that role, Cahan derived socialist lessons from the portion of the Torah (the Five Books of Moses) which was the biblical lesson of that week in the synagogue. According to Cahan, Moses was the original example of a strike organizer: did he not lead the Jews to refuse to meet the piecework quota set by the pharaoh? The majority of the immigrants were not ideologues and they tried, upon arrival, to maintain many of the accustomed ways. Cahan could lead them to the labor unions only by using the rhetoric of religion.

To be sure, during those years the anarchists were organizing antireligious festivals on Yom Kippur—and a striking amount of other forms of ideological antireligion did exist. In the struggle to make a living, tens of thousands of these conventionally pious workers and petty bourgeois from Eastern Europe did work on the Sabbath, but they did so reluctantly, and with pain. Those who were joyfully abandoning the older ways in the name of socialism or anarchism were a minority. In the immigrant days, most of the homes on the Lower East Side continued to keep kosher.

Thus, the majority of immigrant Jews and their children, who were neither completely Orthodox nor ideologically secularists, could no longer be defined by the standards of the inherited Jewish law. But how could one simply write off so many hundreds of thousands as bad Jews? A change in outlook was signaled by Rabbi David Zvi Hoffman, the leading rabbinic authority in Central Europe. Hoffman was willing to accept as valid a writ of religious divorce that was written in America, even though it was likely that the witnesses to this document were unacceptable as participants in a proceeding in Orthodox religious law, because they did not observe the Sabbath. In Hoffman's opinion, those who desecrated the Sabbath in America were not heretics who had rejected the authority of the tradition. On the contrary, they were trapped in negative conditions, "like children made captive by non-Jews." Therefore, they were acceptable witnesses in a religious proceeding. America was a sad fact for which allowances had to be made.

Even as most of the immigrant Orthodox rabbis in America continued to lament their fate, some rabbinic countervoices began to be heard. The most prominent and forthright was Chaim Hirshenson, who served as a rabbi in Hoboken and Union City, New Jersey, in the 1920s. Hirshenson had been born in the Holy Land and was descended from a very distinguished family of rabbinic scholars. And he himself was a sufficiently learned Talmudist to be accepted as an equal by the leading Orthodox authorities in Europe and Palestine. But Hirshenson did not regard the American Jewish community as beyond the Jewish pale. Despite his awareness of mass defection from Jewish observance, Hirshenson hailed the American Jews for their "holy passion" for helping to rebuild the Land of Israel. On several matters he tried to find reasons for lightening the burden of Jewish law, so that the many in America who did not observe these rituals would not be guilty of defying tradition. Hirshenson, while using Orthodox rhetoric, was doing for the "Russian Jews" what Isaac Mayer Wise had done two generations earlier for the "German Jews."

Hirshenson was describing what the Jews of America had made of their Judaism—deeds of charity, concern for Jews abroad, and especially those in Palestine, and selective observance of the rituals of the tradition—and finding this to be pleasing in the eyes of the Lord. God might make other demands of the communities of Europe or the Holy Land—so Hirshenson suggested—but He was willing to accept and even to be pleased with what He found among the Jews in America. Hirshenson responded with passion to one of his bitterest critics, a rabbi from Buffalo who repeated every one of the standard Orthodox charges against American Jewish life. In a sharp exchange of letters, Hirshenson asked his critic why he persisted in remaining in Buffalo: "Why don't you leave this land, in which you evidently remain for a mess of pottage, and go to the Land of Israel?" Hirshenson added that America should be judged with charity, because this was the community through which the bulk of the Jews in Europe and in Palestine were rescued during the years of trouble of the First World War and thereafter.

Even the protective and forgiving Hirshenson did not maintain that American Jews, except for a very small minority, were, by the older standards, learned or pious. The statistical accounts of those who arrived in the United States prove that only the poor, and the not very learned, came. This was clear as early as 1905, in the very midst of the mass migration. In that year, Isaac M. Rubinow wrote an essay entitled *The Russian Jew in the United States,* in which he stated that "it is evident that business and professional classes make up only a small percentage of the Russian Jewish population of New York City—much smaller, indeed, than that of the German Jews. The vast majority of the Russians are on a much lower economic level. They belong to the masses, as against the classes. The cause will be easily understood if we remember that the average Russian Jewish immigrant brought the magnificent capital of eight dollars into this country, while the average non-Jewish immigrant was the happy possessor of double that fortune." In a recent review (in 1975) of the immigrant statistics, Simon Kuznets, an economic historian, remarked that among the immigrants from Russia after 1897 and from Austria in 1900, "the commerce and professional groups are underrepresented." In both countries more than thirty percent of the Jews made their living from commerce, and five to seven percent were in the professions. Among the immigrants only five percent listed themselves as business people and only one and a third percent were professionals.

To be sure, many petty traders in Europe told the authorities at Ellis Island that they were laborers. These immigrants presumed that "laborers" were less likely to be excluded on arrival in the port of New York. The lowest economic group to come to America may thus have included more petty bourgeois than Kuznets or Rubinow asserted, but it is beyond doubt that the elite was definitely under-represented in the mass migration. The most revealing and incontrovertible figure in Kuznets' statistics concerns professionals. A doctor or a rabbi in Europe was hardly likely to claim to being a laborer; professional occupations were both honorific and in demand in America. More important still, the years after the failure of the First Russian Revolution in 1905 was the period when intellectuals and professionals from Eastern Europe did begin to arrive in some numbers. Even then, these elite elements were few in number. On average about six percent of the Jews of Eastern Europe were in the professions; even after 1905 less than one percent of the newcomers were professionals.

American Jewish history is thus, demonstrably, the tale of the transplantation to America of one part of European Jewry, the least educated. Some of these immigrants soon turned into dress manufacturers or movie moguls, and some of their children and grandchildren became writers and professors, while remembering that the literacy of most of their parents had not extended beyond reading the *Jewish Daily Forward*. Few remembered even in passing that they had not been exposed to the classic texts of Judaism, which, through the centuries, had been written in Hebrew. The folk culture of the Jewish poor was what the descendants of the immigrants accepted as Jewishness—and rebelled against.

II

Like the rest of American immigrant history, the painful and heroic saga of American Jewry is class history—but with a fateful and fundamental difference. The move of Jews to America was not only a flight from poverty; for many it was an act of rebellion or at least of defiance. The Irish and the Italians also arrived poor, but they were not angry with the Church. They soon brought over their priests and bishops, whom they venerated in America even more than they had back home. Jews, in contrast, could not wait to free themselves of the authority of their rabbis.

The angers did not begin in America. For two generations deep and unparalleled hatred had been growing among the Jewish poor in Czarist Russia against the Jewish elite. This was caused by a tragedy which took place in the middle of the nineteenth century, when the leaders of the Jewish community sold out the children of the poor in order to protect their own. In 1827, the czar decreed that young Jewish men of eighteen (much younger children were often taken) would be forced into the army for at least twenty-five years. None were stationed near their homes, for the clear intention of the czar was to convert their young people to Christianity. Each Jewish community was assigned a quota of how many such children it had to provide. It was all too human for members of the communal elite to protect their own children and to send the children of the poor. Since the quota had to be met, even as mothers and fathers hid their children, the authorities of the Jewish communities employed *chappers* ("grabbers"), people who roamed the streets and grabbed any teenage boy they could find to give him to the Russian military.

Before this episode ended in 1856, at least forty thousand—and by some estimates nearly one hundred thousand—Jewish children had been forced into this slavery. Many of these recruits were the uncles of those who, twenty years later, were to leave for America. Such immigrants had been raised on heartrending tales of communal leaders who refused to relent and return children who had been seized by the *chappers*. They had sung bitter folk songs about the selfishness of the rich and of the alliance of many (though not of all) of the rabbis with the powerful. Here is an early, inelegant translation in America of one such song:

> The streets are flooded with tears,
> Our hearts are torn by fears.
> Alas!—how great is our dismay;
> Will never dawn a brighter day?
>
> Tots from school they tear away
> And dress them up in soldier's gray.

And our leaders, and our rabbis
Do naught but deepen the abyss.

Rich Mr. Rockover has seven sons,
Not a one a uniform dons;
But poor widow Leah has an only child,
And they hunt him down as if he were wild.

It is right to draft the hard-working masses;
Shoemakers or tailors—they're only asses!
But the children of the idle rich
Must carry on, without a hitch.

America was the place where those who had been most deeply
wounded could go to escape the authority which had betrayed them.

The battle of the poor against the rich was being waged in Eastern
Europe throughout the nineteenth century over the issue of how the
Jewish community was to be financed, and this battle was transferred
as early as the 1880s to the United States. When attempts were made
to establish European-style chief rabbinates in New York and in
Chicago, these efforts foundered almost immediately over the issue
of who was to supervise the supply of kosher meat. Everywhere in
Russia this was done under the control of the official Jewish community, which derived large parts of its income from a tax levied
on each kosher chicken, or on each pound of meat that was sold in
the supervised butcher shops. In the United States the supplying of
kosher meat was a matter for "free enterprise." Individual producers
each hired a rabbi, or often someone without credentials who claimed
rabbinic authority, to certify that their provisions were kosher. In
both New York and Chicago the attempt to end this liberty, bordering on license, met with bitter opposition by most of the meat
suppliers and by the rabbis who worked for and with them. The
battles became so venomous that in New York the spirit and health
of Rabbi Jacob Joseph, who had been called in 1888 by five congregations to be "chief rabbi," was broken. In Chicago in the first years
of the twentieth century, an even greater rabbinic figure, Jacob David
Willowski, left the city, and the office of "chief rabbi." After eighteen
months he returned to Europe in bitter disgust. In both cities the
anti-chief-rabbi forces won the day, because they tapped deep sources
of resentment against authority. The placards which festooned both

cities were full of hatred for those who had paid their way in Europe by "sucking the blood of the poor" and who were now trying to come to America to repeat the pattern.

A different Jewish culture arose among the lower class, Yiddish-speaking, immigrant Jews of the United States than was to be found among their contemporaries in Europe. By 1900 there were major Jewish settlements in Vienna, Warsaw, and Odessa, with populations of roughly two hundred thousand each. These cities were centers of intellectual and cultural ferment. Before and after the turn of the century, a bewildering variety of modern Jewish movements, both political and cultural, were arising or reaching their height. Zionism, as ideology, was created mostly in Vienna and Odessa; Warsaw, Lodz, and Vilno were the principal homes of the several varieties of Jewish socialism: Odessa and Warsaw were the main centers of modern literature in Hebrew and Yiddish. Branches of all the contemporary movements in Europe existed among the immigrants to America, but none derived its major energies from its members in the New World. The vast majority of the newcomers were looking not for ideologies, secular or religious, but for rest from hard work. The East European Jewish ghettos in the United States in those years were very different from their counterparts in Europe. They provided mass audiences for the Yiddish theater, especially for the performances on Friday night and Saturday matinee. Virtuoso cantors entertained in the synagogues on Sabbath morning. Yiddish newspapers fought circulation wars by publishing the most lurid and tear-jerking serialized novels. Here are some of the titles from the 1890s: *The Kidnapped Child, or the Hangman of Berlin; Among Cannibals; The White Slaver; Innocent in the Lunatic Asylum; Crime of Passion, or the Intrigues of a London Lunatic Asylum; Suffering in Innocence;* and *The Vampire.* The author of these particular works was Isaac Rabinowitz, a Hebrew poet who had come to the United States in 1893; he had no choice but to eke out a miserable living working sixteen hours a day at such writing.

In the last decade before the First World War and during the war years themselves, New York did become the home for some of the important ideologues of Zionism and socialism, and for some of the most distinguished writers in Yiddish. The young David Ben-Gurion, who was the first prime minister of Israel, was in New York during the First World War. He had fled from Palestine, where he was under the suspicion of the Turks, who had guessed correctly that he was no supporter of their continued rule in the Holy Land. Ben-Gurion was then, as always, imperious and utterly devoted to his one consuming passion, the creation of a Jewish state. In New York he did participate in the immediate work of local Zionist groups which were sympathetic to his political views, but it never occurred to him for an instant that New York might become his home. While in New York, he courted and married a nurse, Paula Munweis, in 1917. Characteristically, he bolted from City Hall immediately after the wedding ceremony to speak at a Zionist meeting. Ben-Gurion's chief preoccupation in those years was with organizing Jewish volunteers to fight in the Middle East for the Allied cause. When such a body was organized, he enlisted and found himself in Egypt in August of 1918. At the end of the war, Ben-Gurion returned, of course, to Palestine.

During those years two of the preeminent ideologues of socialist Zionism, Nachman Syrkin and Ber Borochov, were in New York. In 1888, Syrkin was a Russian émigré in Germany. Ten years later he was the first to propose the possibility of a marriage between Zionist nationalism and socialist internationalism. After a few years in Russia, Syrkin emigrated to the United States in 1906. In New York he wrote much in Yiddish, and he changed his mind and his politics often enough to upset his most devoted disciples. Syrkin kept dreaming, most of the time and especially in his last years, of a socialist Zion, which would be a "light to the world," but he never went to Palestine. Syrkin died in New York in 1924. Ber Borochov spent the war years in New York as a refugee from Czarist Russia, where he was wanted by the police. Borochov was a more radical and revolutionary ideologue and politician than Syrkin. He was one of a handful of important young Marxists who found a way in the early 1900s to harmonize revolutionary socialism with nationalism and, in his case, with Jewish nationalism in its Zionist forms. Borochov's true homeland was the laboring Jewish masses in Russia. When the revolution came in 1917, he hurried back. He died in Kiev a few months later of pneumonia.

Overall, the Jews had the lowest rate of reemigration from the United States of any group that came in the era of mass migration. Those who did return were people with ideological reasons for not remaining, like Widawer, or Rabbi Willowski, or Ben-Gurion, or

Leon Trotsky (who spent some months in New York). Small as the
rate of Jewish reemigration was, those who left represented an outsized proportion of the religious and secular Jewish intelligentsia who
had come to America. Those intellectuals who remained were, quite
often, bent and fashioned by the Jewish masses for their purposes.
As we have seen, Rabbi Hirshenson forgave the masses for their lack
of interest in Jewish learning and praised them for their charitable
hearts and their passion for the defense of world Jewry. A comparable
process transformed B. C. Vladeck, who arrived in the United States
in 1908. A revolutionary who had labored for armed insurrection
against the czar and who believed in class struggle, Vladeck, under
American conditions, where, unlike Russia, the government could
be called to account at the polls or in courts of law, quickly became
much more moderate. In New York he soon realized that capitalism
was there to stay. Very few of the immigrants, even as they sighed
in the sweatshops, thought that they would be better off if they
devoted themselves to tearing the system down. On the contrary,
these workers—even those who remained workers all their lives—
thought of themselves as temporary proletarians. They all wanted
to become capitalists, if only by buying a candy store, as quickly as
possible, and they did not raise their children to be proletarians.
Vladeck, the labor leader, followed after his followers; he was transformed in America from a revolutionary socialist into a social reformist.

Vladeck also changed his views as a Jew. He arrived in New York
a convinced anti-Zionist. Within a decade the *Jewish Daily Forward,*
which he managed, was participating in relief efforts for the Jews of
Palestine, and it was encouraging political activities to support Jewish
claims on the land of the ancestors. The mass of the immigrants,
even many who professed to be socialists and internationalists, were
emotionally committed to every expression of Jewish creativity, and
particularly to the renascent settlement in Palestine—and Vladeck
went with them.

This rapid transformation of a revolutionary socialist and anti-
Zionist is enormously revealing. What Vladeck encountered in
America among the immigrant masses was their lasting concern for
Jews all over the world. In order to lead these masses, Vladeck had
to surrender any theoretical ideology which separated him from these
sentiments. To be effective in New York, he had to accept American

capitalism, and he bowed with ever greater warmth toward the Zionist communes, the kibbutzim, in the Galilee and the labor unions
in Tel Aviv and Haifa. Vladeck and Hirshenson were both talking
about the same phenomenon, immigrant American Jewry as it had
defined its Jewish consciousness, in its own way—but what was this
self-definition?

III

At least on the surface, the folk religion of the immigrant Jewish
masses from Eastern Europe was an amalgam of group feeling, some
religious observance, and the cumulative anger of the poor at the
European Jewish elite. This description could have been applied a
half-century earlier to the "German Jews." They, too, had arrived
as immigrants with group feeling for each other; they had brought
with them large elements of Orthodox Jewish religion and they
harbored envy, and even some anger, at the more successful Jews
back home. Nonetheless, there were critical differences between these
two waves of immigration.

The "German Jews" had felt displaced, but they had not hated
their country of origin. On the contrary, the "German Jews" had
regarded their identification with Germany as so much a mark of
honor that many were pro-German through the early years of the
First World War, until the United States entered the conflict. Among
the East Europeans who came late in the nineteenth century, the
immigrants from Austria-Hungary were not angry with Emperor
Franz Joseph I; on the contrary, they admired and even loved him
as the friend and protector of the Jews. But these Jews from Franz
Joseph's empire were a minority of perhaps one-tenth of the immigrants. The large majority of the newcomers came from Russia
and Romania, and they had no attachment to their former homes.
So long as the czar ruled Russia, everyone who left for America
remained worried every day about the well-being and even the safety
of his relatives. As these immigrants looked back to the lands of their
birth, they hoped every day that the governments of Russia and
Romania would fall.

The "German Jews" had never been so intensely troubled by the
fate of their relatives in Europe. The Jews of Central Europe were

still not free and equal in the middle years of the nineteenth century, but they were in no immediate danger. By 1870 Jews had been granted equal rights by a newly united Germany; the last discriminations against them had been removed by the Austro-Hungarian Empire three years earlier. The "German Jews" in America had had nothing to do with bringing about these decrees of equality; these actions were the results of the domestic political processes in Europe. It was less and less possible for modern, capitalist states to grant everyone equality and still discriminate, by law, against the Jews. In those liberal years, the Jews in Germany and in Austria-Hungary were on the rise. Some were getting rich and many were entering the professions. "German Jews" in America had come from these countries, and so they had no immediate involvement in Jewish misery. The problem of Jews meant the sufferings of a different tribe, of those in Eastern Europe.

The hundreds of thousands who came from Eastern Europe were much more immediately involved, every day, with the relatives whom they had left behind. The system of anti-Jewish legislation remained in place until the czar was overthrown by the democratic revolution in February 1917. There were pogroms and other outrages throughout the years before the czar fell, and there was vast suffering in the border wars which raged murderously for several years after the Russian Revolution in October 1917. From the day of their arrival in the United States, these immigrants followed the events back home with pain and passionate involvement. Some among them found ways of supporting reformist or revolutionary parties in Russia; most banded together in *landsmanshaften,* societies of expatriates from the same town or region, to help the Jewish communities from which they came. For the Jews from Eastern Europe the woes of European Jewry were thus very personal. One might lose religious faith on the way to America or soon after arrival, and thus abandon the Jewish God—but abandoning one's family, which was in endless danger, was an unforgivable act of betrayal.

The "German Jews" had had the opportunity, so long as they could ignore anti-Semitism in America, or look upon it as marginal and vanishing, to imagine that they were becoming Americans of the Jewish persuasion who harbored some social conscience about the problems of the Jews in remote Russia. The immigrants from Eastern Europe never had the luxury of such detachment. From their beginnings in America, they were a disunited, brawling group. They disagreed vehemently about politics, religion, sexual mores, but all the immigrants were closely connected with the Jews whom they left behind. This caring was the emotion that all shared. It was their common bond. The immigrants from Eastern Europe became a community as they wept over the millions of Jews who remained behind, or as they tried to help them. As we shall see, they and the "German Jews" formally joined in this effort in 1915, when they pooled their resources for relief of those in the war zones. These concerns united most Jews then, as they had once before in the 1840s and 1850s, when Mordecai Manuel Noah had led many of the older settlers into uniting with the immigrants of that era, the "German Jews" who had just arrived, in trying to help those who were being persecuted in Europe and in Syria.

There were other differences between the new and the earlier waves of immigration. The "German Jews" were always more at home with Gentiles than the East Europeans. In Europe, the "German Jewish" immigrants had still spoken some combination of West European Yiddish and the dialect of their region. The language in their mouth was not High German, but they spoke very nearly the same language as the German Gentile majority among whom they lived. Gentile farmers and Jewish cattle-dealers were not vastly different in culture. The differences between Jews and Gentiles in the villages of Bavaria in the 1830s were mostly to be found in religion. Even in America, these were the premises on which the distance of "German Jews" from non-Jews was based. What the "German Jews" did not bring with them was a fixation on the culture of their Jewish in-group as superior to that of the Gentiles. On the contrary, these "German Jews" regarded themselves as "better" because they thought they represented the virtues of Germany in America.

The East Europeans had a radically different mind-set about their relationship to the non-Jewish culture from which they came. They had been living in Russia in the towns where the mob might explode into anti-Jewish violence, or in the countryside as artisans among largely illiterate peasants. The folk memory of the "German Jews" deplored the peasants as being capable of *rishus,* that is, of Jew hating, but there were no other criticisms. The folk tales of the Eastern Europeans kept emphasizing the prevalence of drunkenness and irresponsibility among the peasants, and the superiority of Jewish family life and of Jewish culture. To be a Jew meant to preserve this supposed edge.

The Yiddish-speaking immigrants were not only different from the "German Jews" who had come earlier; they were also different from the other immigrant groups of that era of mass migration. They were the most intensely involved of all in maintaining their separateness in America. Almost all the immigrants, of whatever origin, regretted the loss of their "island within," of the ethnic and family ties which had sustained them in Europe. There were some variations: the Irish and the Italians were much more devoted to maintaining their ethnic identity than were most of the other groups. But the Irish and the Italians knew that the values of the Irish or Italian countryside, transplanted to America, were obstacles to reaching the highest levels of American life. In order to rise in America, Irish and Italian immigrants knew they had to unlearn the mind-set that had been bred into them by their past. To the degree to which they clung to the older mentality, these immigrants remained vegetable farmers and blue-collar workers, garbagemen and policemen, into the second generation. The immigrant Jews of those days had a different attitude. They knew that they had to learn American manners, and that the observances of the Jewish religion, and especially of the Sabbath, were obstacles to success. (In the 1920s the children of the immigrants were studied by Louis Wirth, who wrote a famous book, *Children of the Ghetto,* and by other sociologists; those who had remained completely Orthodox in their devotion to Jewish religion were less successful than those who had given up at least some of the religious regimen.) And yet, Jews continued to believe, into the second generation and beyond, that "Jewish values," the specific heritage that the immigrants had brought with them from Eastern Europe, had to be preserved. Their Jewishness—the "Jewish head"—was the critical element in their success in America. This "Jewish head" was the heritage of siege mentality, of centuries of being an embattled bastion in a hostile "exile," and of having only one tool for survival, the use of one's wits. Even in a much less hostile America, Jews believed that they could advance only if their "Jewish" virtues provided them with the energies to excel.

This attitude did not prevail among all the immigrant Jews, and certainly not among all of their children. Some felt confined by the Jewish world in which they had been raised; it was too at odds with the New World they wanted to enter. Among the children of the immigrants, such writers as Mary Antin and Henry Roth, at least by implication (and they were far from alone), spoke for this attitude. Mary Antin had herself been born in Poland; she came to the United States, to Boston, in her early teens. At a time when intermarriage was very unusual, she fell in love with a Gentile, one of her teachers at Columbia University, and married him. Soon, in 1912, an auto-biographical novel appeared entitled *The Promised Land.* Mary Antin accepted assimilation; she insisted that to become part of America Jews had to get rid of every trace of their European past. Henry Roth was more ambivalent than Mary Antin. His novel *Call It Sleep* de-scribed immigrant life on New York's Lower East Side right before the First World War, when that ghetto was at its most vibrant and most congested. Roth depicted that society, as seen through the eyes of a child, in all its dirt and intensity. The world outside, beyond its boundaries, is at once threatening and enticing. The children, who are the major protagonists of Roth's novel, are mostly on their way out of the culture and the pieties of the immigrant ghetto. They want to embrace other, more "American," sensibilities. Though there is more than a hint in Roth's novel that this turning away causes a sense of loss and guilt, it also offers a more powerful sense of lib-eration, of moving from physical and spiritual congestion to the open space of America.

A vast literature has been written to describe the immigrant "Lower East Side," in New York and its equivalents in all the other large cities to which Jews came in the years before 1914. On the surface, the culture and practices of the Jewish small towns in Eastern Europe were transplanted unchanged to these American ghettos—but this was not so. The critical difference was America itself. Those who lived the culture of the "Lower East Side" had not come to the United States to establish such centers of ethnic intensity; they had come to succeed and to move away. A small, intense minority was committed, for less than a generation, to several varieties of social-ism. This was the only doctrine which proposed the immigrant ghetto as a major base for effecting radical change of American society as a whole, but even in its heyday, in the second decade of the twentieth century, when the socialists won some victories at the polls in the Lower East Side of New York, socialism never approached being the dominant force among the immigrants. For most of its inhabitants, the "Lower East Side" was never more than a temporary dwelling of convenience.

It is even more true that the immigrant ghetto was not created as a bastion of Judaism. The inherited values of the Jewish religion had, indeed, been brought along to America. Their abandonment, in part or total, did trouble the majority of the immigrants and most of their children, but this was the pain of losing one's past much more than any assertion about the present or the future. This clash between the older values and "America" is the central theme of the most famous of the immigrant novels, Abraham Cahan's *The Rise of David Levinsky*. In Cahan's tale, Levinsky, a young Talmudic scholar, comes to the United States. There, he abandons the older ways and achieves worldly success. But, by the end of his life, Levinsky is in despair. Belonging neither to the world into which he had been born nor to any contemporary ideal, he is lost. Finally, he turns to the socialism of the workers in his factory. They, at least, had values for which they were fighting, and a sense of community. Levinsky was still too "Jewish" to believe that success is enough.

Antin, Cahan, and Roth all defined the same alternatives for the newly arrived Jews: assimilation into conventional American life or life in a separate immigrant Jewish world. Antin and Roth knew only that one or the other choice had to be made, but Cahan proposed a different answer. Cahan suggested that Levinsky would have been better off if he had used his energies to further the cause of socialism. In Cahan's description, Levinsky knew that those of his contemporaries who had organized labor unions were crusaders in the battle for social justice. Levinsky was aware that their particular fervor for social justice owed something to their Jewishness. Jews were not poorer than all the other immigrants, but they had had unique, age-old experience in doing battle with the hostile authorities, with resisting the powerful who controlled society. This energy could be used to help make a new America.

The bulk of the immigrant generation, and of their children, accepted none of the alternatives that the novelists offered. They were not busy abandoning their Jewishness, like Mary Antin, or becoming socialists, as Cahan suggested. They organized numerous synagogues, first in the immigrant ghettos and soon in Harlem in New York City, the "second settlement" where the more affluent moved a decade or two after their arrival. Hundreds upon hundreds of self-help organizations, cemetery associations, and "friendly societies" were established. As early as the 1880s, the Catskills began to become the summer home for the Jews of New York, though some of the more affluent and better educated among the East Europeans went to the Poconos, in Pennsylvania. Most of these Jews could do nothing else but invest their energies in creating a discrete American Jewish community of their own. These East Europeans did not want to vanish into some undifferentiated majority.

Most knew that they could not assimilate, even if they wanted to. They might try, like David Levinsky, to ape the clothes, the cigars, and the manners of the Christian business friends with whom he lunched at the Waldorf, but Levinsky knew that he remained an outsider. The Gentile majority did not forgive him for his Jewish origins, even as they beheld an individual who had worked to forget the memories of his youth and to learn to behave like any other successful American businessman. The non-Jews, especially the old-line Protestants, were no longer as religious as they used to be, but they knew that they were Christian, at least in relation to Jews. Unlike Mary Antin, who believed that the non-Jews were ready to assimilate the Jews, most immigrant Jews knew that even at their most assimilated they would remain "amateur Gentiles." This barrier did not necessarily force Jews to define their Jewishness in ways comparable to those by which Christians defined their Christianity. Christians tended to think of themselves as belonging to a religion; the mass of immigrant Jews spoke of being part of the Jewish people. Still, Jews and Christians agreed on one fundamental assertion: a person was either one or the other, either a Jew or a Gentile. The Jew/Gentile barrier was erected jointly, by anti-Semitism among the Gentiles and by group feeling among the Jews.

The immigrants from Eastern Europe had known in advance that New York was not the New Jerusalem. Very few of them had any illusion about their own future. They knew that they were likely to struggle and to remain poor for the rest of their lives. They themselves would never see the promised land, for they would never get beyond the ghetto and the sweatshops. But their children would enter America. The immigrant generation lived *far die kinder,* for the children. The young were supposed to enter businesses and professions which were closed to the children of the poor Jews in Eastern

Europe. A significant minority among the children of the immigrants became physicists, like Isidore Rabi, or novelists, like Saul Bellow, but their immigrant parents did not understand them. The opportunity for education in America meant, in the minds of parents, that the children could rise from the pushcarts and the clothing factories to working in offices. They would be doctors or lawyers or men of business.

The immigrants knew in advance that distaste for Jews had not disappeared in the New World. The Yiddish papers in Europe told many stories of discrimination. Despite Emma Lazarus's poem on the base of the Statue of Liberty, inviting the tired, huddled masses of the world to America, the immigrants harbored no fantasy that welcoming committees of the Gentile majority would be waiting in New York harbor to enfold them in loving arms. East European Jews knew that American Gentiles were not virulent Jew haters, like many of their enemies in Russia and Romania, but Gentiles remained Gentiles, everywhere. Sometimes they were less hostile and, on some happy days, they might even be friendly, but the Gentile majority remained everywhere and, at best, largely unaccepting of Jews. This was the mind-set of the immigrants, as they sang, even in America, folk songs about the differences between Jews and Gentiles.

The happiest knowledge of the immigrants about America was that here, unlike Czarist Russia, the law was not their enemy. Almost immediately after landing, immigrants did two things: they went to find a job, and they enrolled in Americanization classes. Everyone, almost without exception, wanted to become a citizen. This required passing an examination to prove that the newcomer understood the Constitution of the United States. When citizenship was granted, the ritual required the candidate to swear allegiance to the Constitution and, of course, to foreswear all other political loyalties. The new citizen now had rights equal to everyone else's, but the ritual had not admitted him to American society. On the way home from the ceremony which made him an American, he would still pass signs in shop windows, advertising for sales help, saying "no Jews wanted," or he would read the somewhat politer formula "Christians only" in the want ads of the newspaper that he would buy in the subway on the way home.

The "German Jews" had been few, and they had defined themselves in an open, expanding America and, to a very great degree, on its frontier. It was easy for them to think of themselves as different from other Americans only in religion. The "Russian Jews" came to the cities, when America needed hands for the factories, and they came in large masses. These Jews, and their children, would have far more trouble finding their way into America.

11.

"This Is Our Country"

In the mid-nineteenth century, American anti-Semitism had been mildly endemic, but it was not immediately threatening to American Jews. Religious antipathy continued to exist, but Jews had been accustomed for centuries to slighting remarks from Christians. Social barriers had increased after the Civil War, but they were of little consequence. Jews might be kept out of resorts and clubs, and old canards about their supposed sharp practices might be repeated, but few believed that Jewish businessmen were really different from Gentiles. The "German Jews" had succeeded in persuading themselves, and most Americans, that, even at their supposed worst, the few Jewish Wall Street bankers were no more obnoxious or un-American than such plungers and speculators of the Gilded Age as Jay Gould and Diamond Jim Brady.

Only with the advent of the "Russian Jews" did serious anti-Semitism appear in the United States. The main target of the Jew haters were the foreign, Yiddish-speaking immigrants. The "German

Jews" wanted to believe that the attacks were not directed toward them at all; they were suffering only because they were "coreligionists" of the benighted "Russian Jews." This was not true. The attacks were not limited to "Russian Jews." The "German Jews" were under direct fire; they were accused, frontally, of lacking legitimacy in America. They were told that they had no right to the wealth and the place in America that they had earned so quickly.

In December 1891, Henry Rogers, a well-known essayist and journalist, published a letter in a leading magazine, in which he attacked the record of Jews during the Civil War: "I had served in the field about eighteen months before being permanently disabled in action, and was quite familiar with several regiments; was then transferred to two different recruiting stations, but I cannot remember meeting one Jew in uniform, or hearing of any Jewish soldier."

This charge had to be answered. Jews had to prove that they had done their share, or even more, as citizens. In immediate response to Rogers's broadside, the "German Jews" became devotees of the study of American Jewish history. In December 1892, the American Jewish Historical Society published its first quarterly. The central personalities in this endeavor were men such as Cyrus Adler, Simon Wolf, and Max Kohler, all American-born children of immigrants from Central Europe. These men had no relationship to the Jews who had come to the colonies, but that did not deter them from writing with special relish, and in great antiquarian detail, about Spanish-Portuguese Jews in colonial America. Every soldier who served in the Revolution was described at length. It was established that there had been perhaps fifty Jewish-American Revolutionary soldiers (further research has since found fifty more), and that this number was far higher, in proportion, than that of any other group in the American population. Simon Wolf, as we have seen, the semi-official Jewish lobbyist in Washington at the turn of the century, summed up this argument for the rights of Jews in a book entitled *The American Jew as Soldier and Patriot* (1895). Wolf compiled long lists of Jews who had been in uniform in the various wars in the United States, and he took particular pride in those who had died for the country. Jewish blood, too, had helped water the tree of liberty. There had been Jews at Valley Forge and Yorktown, and at Gettysburg and Appomattox. Gentiles had no right to question the legitimate place of Jews in an America which they had helped create and defend.

Without quite saying so, the successful "German Jews" of the 1890s were laying claim to colonial Jewry; they were making ancestors out of Haym Salomon; of Gershom Mendes Seixas, the Jewish clergyman in New York in the time of the Revolution and the early years of the Republic; of Aaron Lopez, the sea trader from Newport, Rhode Island, and all the Jewish soldiers of the Revolution. This was exaggerated. There had been some intermarriage between the descendants of the older settlers and the immigrants from Central Europe who came in the mid-nineteenth century, but this biological continuity was of little consequence. The "German Jews" had essentially founded a new American Jewish community, but this Jewish claim to older legitimacy in America was in keeping with the spirit of the times. The Irish, the Italians, and a whole host of other minorities were then founding "historical societies" to argue that men and women of their kind, and not the Protestant settlers alone, had helped fashion America.

What the "German Jews" found harder to face was the question of the foreignness of the newly arriving Jewish masses. Here the Jewish situation was unique. All of the other ethnic groups which had come to the United States in large numbers after the middle of the nineteenth century did not find well-established predecessors who were expected to take responsibility for the newcomers. The descendants in Pennsylvania of the Hessian mercenaries of German stock who had remained in America after the Revolutionary War had been too poor and isolated to become the responsible elite of the millions of German immigrants who came to the United States in the next century. Others, like the handful of English Roman Catholics in Maryland, were too few, and too different from the Irish, to become the leaders of the millions who fled to America during the Potato Famine and thereafter.

The Jewish situation differed because the earlier and largely successful immigrants lived "uptown" in the very same cities where the newly arrived East Europeans were working "downtown," in sweatshops. Many of the newest Jewish arrivals worked, first, for German Jewish employers. Even if the older arrivals would have wanted to disclaim connection, as some did, it would have made no difference.

Gentiles, both friends and foes—and most Jews—persisted in regarding Jews of all provenances as belonging to one community.
The "German Jews" were thus trapped: they were inevitably involved with the "Russian Jews," but they wanted to keep their distance. They told themselves that they were "better people," and they
told it to anti-Semites. Let the critics of the Jews be aware that their
distemper was caused by the uncouth newcomers and that it should
not extend to the proper, older arrivals.

As early as 1881, the year of the great wave of pogroms in Russia,
spokesmen for the "German Jews" were saying such things in public.
The *North American Review* was then the leading organ of opinion.
A German Jewish writer argued that "no people . . . is willing to
be judged by its immigration." He exhorted the American majority
to stop social discrimination against Jews of his class, who were
respectable Americans, because the "unfavorable impression of the
Jew" they harbor was formed by their observing the immigrants.
Another writer suggested that year that the best way to protect
existing American Jewry against the problems that would come with
the arrival of many immigrants from Russia would be "to send
American Jewish missionaries to Russia to civilize them there rather
than give them an opportunity to russianize us in the event of . . . a
colossal emigration." This suggestion was, on the face of it, empty
rhetoric. There were hardly enough "missionaries" available among
a Jewish community of perhaps a quarter of a million in 1880 to go
to Russia to teach six million Jews middle-class table manners, Amer-
ican-style, and Tevye, and his children, were hardly waiting for such
instruction. To learn to copy "German Jews" was not their most
pressing concern. This suggestion about a mission to Russia was an
outburst of pique—and of a sense of trap. The resident American
Jews knew that they were landed with a problem they could not
escape.

In those painful, earliest years, the committees in Germany and
France that were helping the Russian Jews had essentially one solution, to send the runaways from Russia forward to America. The
Americans soon ran out of resources with which to help the new
arrivals. Even the most charitable were afraid of the bad impressions
the newcomers were making on the Gentiles. As early as October
1881, M. A. Kursheedt, the secretary of the Russian Emigrant Relief

Fund, wrote from New York to the Alliance Israelite Universelle, in Paris, that many of the Jewish refugees had become peddlers, thus representing a "great source of annoyance to us as they have settled in this city and crowd the filthy tenements in a certain section of the East Side." Kursheedt had evidently forgotten that the "German Jews," for whom he spoke, had begun as peddlers less than forty years before, and that some of them had lived, in the 1840s and 1850s, in the very streets that now housed the poor Russians.

Though Kursheedt and his colleagues were ever more upset by the tide of immigrants, they would not, and could not, abandon them. The next month, in November 1881, a group of prominent Jews established the Hebrew Emigrant Aid Society to help the newcomers. A few weeks later, these very circles, acting under another organizational label, wrote a formal letter to the alliance announcing that American Jews would accept no more refugees. By the spring of the next year, as more Jews came in flight from renewed pogroms in Russia, frantic appeals for money appeared in the Jewish press; if the newcomers were left to their own devices, "an element of Jewish tramps and paupers . . . will disgrace the name Israelite through the land."

The Hebrew Emigrant Aid Society disbanded early in 1883, probably out of the fear that if it continued to do such good work, it would attract more immigrants. Augustus A. Levey, the secretary of the aid society, resigned, saying that "only disgrace and a lowering of opinion in which American Israelites are held . . . can result from the continued residence among us of such wretches." A few years later, in 1890, Oscar Straus, a leading figure among the Jews of America, asked the Belgian-Jewish philanthropist Baron Maurice de Hirsch not to "foster, encourage or stimulate emigration to America." Straus feared that further increase in the numbers of Russian Jews in America "would be a calamity and a misfortune, not only for the immigrants, but for all American Jews." And yet in the very midst of their ambivalences about the refugees, the established American Jewish community actually did extraordinary service in the difficult crisis years of 1881–82. Some nineteen thousand Jews arrived during those two years, and fourteen thousand of them were helped with money, until they could find jobs, by the Hebrew Emigrant Aid Society alone.

II

Though the "German Jews" were almost unanimous in regarding themselves to be a different breed, they were also very nearly of one mind in accepting responsibility for the "Russian Jews." This concern was only in part a form of self-defense against the anti-Semites, as a way of keeping these "Russian Jews" from being too embarrassing. There was an element of wanting to behave, and to be seen to behave, in the way expected of "better people" in the America of the last decades of the nineteenth century.

On the surface, the proper "German Jews" were behaving like their Gentile peers. The turn of the century was the era of the "Social Gospel." The "best people" among the Protestants were translating their Christianity into a set of obligations to help the poor. A wide variety of institutions, from charity hospitals to soup kitchens, were established all over America. The "German Jews" soon did exactly that for their poor "coreligionists." But there was one essential difference between the Christian and the Jewish endeavors. The Jewish philanthropists were very much more involved in the Jewish masses than the Christian "best people" were in the Christian poor. It was not only that the behavior of the Jewish masses would reflect on the older settlers. It was more than that: if the leadership of the Jewish elite was not accepted by the newer masses, then the "German Jews" had no real role in American society. The "German Jews" were expected by everyone, especially by Gentiles, to lead their own kind. If they did not, they could be attacked as an overprivileged, small group of still semiforeign rich people.

In the 1880s and 1890s, the "German Jews" created a network of charity organizations to take care of the "Russian Jews." In every major city, they founded free medical clinics, relief agencies, and an increasing variety of social services, including classes in Americanization, to teach immigrants English, and American ways of behavior, and to prepare them to pass the test for citizenship. In New York, the United Hebrew Charities had been created in 1874, when the first trickle of immigration from Eastern Europe had begun. By the 1890s, this organization was raising and spending a million dollars each year, a very large sum for those days. In Boston, a federation of all the various philanthropic bodies was created in 1895, and by the next decade, such federations existed in Chicago, Philadelphia, St. Louis, Milwaukee, and Cleveland. The newest Jewish arrivals were glad to use these facilities, but for the most part the "Russian Jews" resisted the idea that they should obey the wishes of the philanthropists. These two communities had different agendas. The older settlers wanted Jews to be quiet; the newer arrivals had not yet made their way in America, and so they could hardly avoid the noise of social and economic conflict. The older settlers were, at least in theory, Jews by religion ("Americans of the Jewish faith," in Isaac Mayer Wise's formulation), while the newer arrivals thought of themselves as a people, a national minority, not all of whose members were religious believers, not even in theory.

Social class was equally important. The poor have never liked the rich, and the immigrants on the Lower East Side were a prime example of this rule. The East Europeans had brought substantial class angers with them to the new land. The overwhelming majority of these immigrants had scores to settle with the communal leadership of their former homes. Many were to transfer these angers to America, especially to the "Germans," the rich Jews they found in America. Here effective revolt against those who claimed authority in the community could be mounted more easily than in Europe.

Yet, despite these early skirmishes, the "German Jews" needed the immigrants—the poverty of the newcomers guaranteed the class status of their benefactors. Still, it is too shallow to think that the "German Jews" helped the poor simply to ward off anti-Semitism or to guarantee their class status in America. Their passion for such good works had deep roots in a very old Jewish tradition which had been transplanted unimpaired from Europe. The commandment of the Jewish religion to be charitable to the poor had been reinforced through the centuries by the insistence of a hostile world that it wanted, least of all, to be troubled by Jews with problems. For many centuries, the *parnassim,* the leaders of the ghetto, had accepted responsibility for the poor, even when the rich did not feel charitable, as an act of conscience. In the open society of the New World, observing all of the other commandments of the Jewish tradition had become matters of personal choice, but concern for poor Jews was the one *mitzvah* (religious injunction) which anti-Semites enjoined. When the first group of Jews came to New York in 1654, they were allowed to remain because the leaders of the Jews in Amsterdam promised the hostile governor of New Amsterdam, Peter Stuyvesant, that they would provide for those who might become indigent in America. In the 1780s, Haym Salomon reminded hostile critics that Jews continued to take care of their own; so did Mordecai Manuel Noah and Uriah Phillips Levy in the 1830s, and Jewish leaders after them in all succeeding generations. Throughout the ages, the well-to-do Jews have often complained about these obligations to the poor. Some even tried to avoid them, but religion and custom—and anti-Semitism—were firm in teaching that the poor were, unavoidably, the responsibility of the rich.

Jacob Schiff, the leader of the "German Jews," was very self-consciously a *parnas* in the European mold. Schiff was different from most other German immigrants. In 1865, at the age of eighteen, he had come to the United States from Frankfurt, Germany. Schiff did not come from the poor, but descended from a very distinguished family. Eminent rabbis were among his ancestors, and his father had been associated with the Rothschilds in the banking business. Upon arrival in New York, Schiff did not peddle or open a store; instead, he went to work in a brokerage firm. In 1875, after marrying Solomon Loeb's daughter, he moved to the Wall Street firm Kuhn, Loeb and Co. Ten years later, Schiff was made head of the firm. Under his leadership, Kuhn, Loeb and Co. was particularly important in financing several of the major American railroads and in floating loans for both the American and for foreign governments.

Schiff used his wealth like a *parnas,* in the grand manner. He gave princely gifts to such causes as the American Red Cross, Barnard College, and Harvard University, and to almost every charitable and religious institution, of whatever shade of opinion and belief, among American Jews. The dominant passion of his life was to exercise the responsibility that he felt for the Jews of Russia. Schiff took the lead in underwriting a Japanese bond issue of two hundred million dollars in the winter of 1904-5, when Japan was fighting its war against Russia. He fought hard against any American financial support for the czarist government. More quickly than any other leading "German Jew," Schiff understood that the tide of immigration could not be stopped. He felt the moral responsibility to help more Jews escape from oppression and to help the masses who were arriving. His towering personality helped sweep away the initial desire among a few "German Jews" to pretend that the Russian immigrants were a different tribe.

When the 1903–5 wave of pogroms occurred in Russia, the "German Jews" reacted almost as one. They were outraged, and they hastened to help both the victims who were still in Russia and the many immigrants who were fleeing to the United States. Schiff and his colleagues fought hard against any restriction of immigration, and especially against the attempt to impose quotas based on national origins.

All of these attitudes were expressed in a very high moment, the celebration that was held on Thanksgiving Day, 1905, in Carnegie Hall to celebrate "the two hundred and fiftieth anniversary of the settlement of the Jews in the United States." This was a date of convenience, for the first boatload of Jews had arrived in New Amsterdam in September 1654. The organizers of the celebration chose to commemorate the formal decision by the Dutch West India Company, on April 26, 1655, that gave the Jews the right to remain. Carnegie Hall was crowded on this festive occasion. There was an address by Grover Cleveland, a former president of the United States, as well as speeches by the governor of New York and the mayor of the city. President Theodore Roosevelt sent a letter, and Vice President Charles W. Fairbanks sent a telegram. Dr. David H. Greer, the Episcopal bishop coadjutor of New York, spoke in the accents of a liberal Christian, and the rabbi of Temple Emanu-El, Joseph Silverman, prayed for the well-being of American democracy. These dignitaries, together, were declaring Jews to be part of the very essence of America, past and present. Theodore Roosevelt wrote what this assemblage wanted to hear, that "even in our colonial period, the Jews participated in the upbuilding of this country" and that "they have become indissolubly incorporated in the great army of American citizenship." He went on to confront the critics of the new immigrants squarely: "This is true not only of the descendants of the early settlers and those of American birth, but of a great and constantly increasing proportion of those who have come to our shores within the last twenty-five years as refugees reduced to the direst straits of penury and misery."

Roosevelt's letter echoed the themes that were stated in the opening speech of that celebration by Jacob Schiff who chaired the gathering. Jews have been part of "the developement of the New World" and, therefore, they "believe that we are justified in the claim that this is our country." Schiff made no claim that "the Jewish citizen has done more than his civic duty," but he felt the need to emphasize the significant role of the Jews in the making of America, to counter "the attempts so frequently made to consider us a foreign element." Jews everywhere are ardent admirers of America, and everywhere they set their faces "longingly and hopefully toward these shores."

Perhaps the most interesting speech of this celebration was made by Oscar Straus, not in New York, but in a parallel celebration the day before in Boston's historic Faneuil Hall. Straus had long repented for his letter in 1890 to Baron de Hirsch which expressed deep fear of further Jewish immigration. On the contrary, he talked with pain and passion about the "massacre of thousands of helpless men, women and children in Odessa, Kief, Kishineff, and a hundred cities, towns and hamlets throughout Russia." Speaking in Boston, Straus appealed to the tradition of the Pilgrims who, so he asserted, had come to "our continent, that it shall ever be a shelter for the poor and persecuted." Therefore, he concluded, America must remain open to those who need its freedom and hospitality:

> To bar out these refugees from political oppression or religious intolerance, who bring a love of liberty hallowed by sacrifices made upon the altar of an enlightened conscience, though their pockets be empty, is a grievous wrong, and in violation of the spirit of our origin and development as a free people, for they, too, have God's right to tread upon American soil, which the Pilgrims have sanctified as the home of the refugee.

The leaders of the "German Jews" had a vision of America: immigrants came, bringing with them foreign ways, but they soon unlearned them and became Americans. The one distinction among its citizens that America permitted was religion, so Jews were Americans of the Jewish faith. They, the "German Jews," were proud of their achievement in becoming such Americans, and they fully expected the "Russian Jews" to remake themselves in this long-existing pattern. Had not the Jews of colonial and revolutionary times regarded themselves as Americans of the Jewish religious persuasion? This assertion about the past was not true. Colonial and revolutionary America had been untidy societies where identities were not clear-cut. The separation of church and state in the Constitution did not mean that religion was the only difference among its citizens that the United States would tolerate. As James Madison noted in *The Federalist Papers,* that clause in the Constitution meant simply that the government was barred from legislating for or against religion, as it was forbidden to curtail freedom of speech. The law did not enjoin the supremacy of Anglo-Saxon culture.

In 1905, the "German Jews" could advance no such interpretation of the earliest definition of America. This was the heyday of nativism, and of other forms of distaste for foreigners. It was simplest to agree with the superpatriots that America was a social club, while insisting that the whole history of the New World was one of receiving immigrants and quickly transforming them into members.

This doctrine about America was expressed most clearly by the speech that Louis Marshall, a brilliant lawyer closely associated in Jewish affairs with Jacob Schiff, made at another celebration in Albany. Marshall said frankly that these meetings had been organized across the country for a reason:

> It is . . . to prove that the Jew is not a parasite, an exploiter of the country, or a newcomer within its gates, that we are celebrating on this occasion. It is not to call attention to the Jew as a religious factor, but as a civic element in the grand composite of American citizenship. He is an American of the Americans—a Jew by faith and religion, an American in all that that term can betoken.

The immigrants from Russia, so Marshall insisted, "when transplanted to American soil in a few years, become dignified, industrious, patriotic, self-respecting and productive citizens." In the climactic paragraphs of Marshall's oration, he referred back to the promise the Jews had made in 1655 to the Dutch West India Company, "that the poor among us should not become a burden to the community but should be supported by us." Marshall stood tall as he proclaimed that this promise had been kept for two and a half centuries. The burden has been heavy and it will probably remain so, but "to me it is a source of pride and exaltation that, although we are citizens of a common country, the religious duty of caring for our own . . . had been especially imposed upon us." Fulfilling this obligation was his generation's continuity with the first Jewish settlers, who had made such a covenant with America, expressing "the gratitude that we owe to the God of our Fathers Who has led us out of Egypt to this land of freedom."

The response of the "German Jews" to the anti-Semites and to those who would stop immigration had thus been made. Schiff, Strauss, and Marshall defined America in 1905 as a country of immigrants, all of whom, regardless of when they came, both contributed to America and were remade by it. In these celebrations, the "German Jews" were promising to do their utmost to hasten such transformation of the "Russian Jews" into "America." As one could have expected, the organizers of these grand celebrations convinced themselves, and their existing friends in the majority society, that Jews were cofounders of America and that America would be enriched by the energies of the newest Jewish immigrants. However, the enemies of the Jews remained unconvinced.

III

Henry Adams, grandson of John Quincy Adams and great-grandson of John Adams, thought himself a "rather superior person," but he thought that his sister, Louise Catherine, was far brighter. She married a Jew, Charles Kuhn of Philadelphia, and some of the earliest references to Jews in Adams's writing seem to have been influenced by the presence of a Jew in the family. In 1864, he had written that "fashion was not fashionable in London until the Americans and the Jews were let loose." Adams depicted Jewish figures in his novel, *Democracy,* without rancor and even as allies in the fight for political reform. Nonetheless, in 1879, the year before he published the novel, Adams wrote from Spain: "I have now seen enough of Jews and Moors to entertain more liberal views in regard to the Inquisition." Adams remained ambivalent about the kind of Jew who tried to enter society. He was wary but interested in such people as the young art critic Bernard Berenson, or Sir Francis Palgrave, the historian of early England who had been born "Cohen." He disliked Vienna because its cultural life was dominated by Jews. Adams was hostile to Westernized Jews, though he was not totally on the warpath against them, but he hated the East Europeans. He, and other aristocrats like his brother, Brooks Adams, and his friend, Henry Cabot

Lodge, became vehement, often to the point of hysteria, at the sight of beards and caftans.

In 1901, Henry Adams visited Russia. The first sight that he saw after crossing the border, was "a Polish Jew . . . in all his weird horror." The sight of such figures, so he wrote in a letter from Warsaw, "makes me creep." In his most famous book, *The Education of Henry Adams,* published in 1918, Adams contemplated the flood of such immigrants to the United States, who numbered by then more than two million. Adams lamented the death of his America; the future belonged to the unwashed: "Not a Polish Jew fresh from Warsaw or Cracow—not a furtive Jacoob or Ysaac still reeking of the Ghetto, snarling a weird Yiddish to the officers of the customs— but had a keener instinct, an intenser energy, and a freer hand than he—American of Americans."

But Henry Adams was, indeed, a descendant of Puritan ancestors. It had been bred into him that Jews were heirs to those who had written the Hebrew Bible, and in that role they were dangerous, because they were counterclaimants to being the true scriptural elite. Adams's description of himself on the very first page of his auto- biography, as an alienated aristocrat, reached back to the Puritan encounter with the Jews of the Bible: "Had he been born in Jerusalem under the shadow of the Temple and circumcised in the Synagogue by his uncle and high priest, under the name of Israel Cohen, he would scarcely have been more distinctly branded, and not much more handicapped in the races of the coming century, in running for such stakes as the century was to offer." Two ancient stereotypes about Jews were thus alive in Henry Adams: Jews are an all-too- talented, wrongheaded competing elite, and they are, at the same time, dirty and disease-bearing, the heirs to the "synagogue of Satan." On both counts, Jews had to be kept at bay. In 1894, several of Adams's friends joined other young Boston aristocrats in organiz- ing the Immigration Restriction League. They wanted to limit the admission of "unhealthy elements," which meant Jews, Slavs, and Italians.

In those days it was not even necessary to be an overt hater to claim that the health of the United States was based on the "men of the sturdy stocks of the north of Europe" and that "the more sordid and hopeless elements" which came from southern Europe had to be kept out, because they had "neither skill nor energy nor quick intelligence." These anti-Italian remarks were made as self-evident and beyond need of any proof by Woodrow Wilson in his professorial *History of the American People.* But there were countervoices among American intellectual and social aristocrats. Thomas Wentworth Higginson, a Brahmin peer of Adams and Lodge, wrote in 1897 that there was no such thing as pure-blooded English, for the ancestors of the majority of the American colonists represent "a race so mingled and combined . . . that it can claim no purity of strain, but only the strength of composite structure." Higginson was bold enough to say that America had not been made great, at least in its economy, by the original settlers, but rather by the immigrants. Everybody, including the patricians of that day, were descended from immigrants who came poor, just like the millions who were arriving these days. To be sure, there were more criminals among the immigrants than among the older settlers, but crime is always more present among the poor and "the eminent scoundrels, who are rich and shrewd enough to keep out of prison, are rarely foreigners."

Those who wanted to restrict immigration found allies among the nativists, the Populists, and in the labor organizations. Tom Watson, the Populist leader from Georgia, incited his followers against the immigrants. He wrote in the 1890s: "The scum of creation has been dumped on us. Some of our principal cities are more foreign than American. The most dangerous and corrupting hordes of the Old World have invaded us. The vice and crime which they have planted in our midst is terrifying." Watson blamed "the manufacturers and bankers" who then "wanted cheap labor and did not care how much harm to our future might be a consequence of their heartless policy."

These attacks were directed against all foreigners, not primarily against Jews, but Populism did have its anti-Semitic element. Ignatius Donnelly, a former congressman from Minnesota, published a novel in 1891 called *Caesar's Column,* in which he warned against "Jewish bankers" who were helping "to turn the farmers into serfs." Other Populists were even more violent. Those who demanded freedom from Wall Street bankers very often identified these bankers as Jews. Even the very Gentile firm of investment bankers, J. P. Morgan and Company, which had no Jew on its staff even as an office boy, was slurred as a Jewish house. The poor immigrants arriving from Eastern Europe could be imagined, in anti-Jewish fantasy, as recruits for ever more powerful and more dangerous Jewish forces. Yet, despite the anti-Semitic fringe among the Populists, and the specific attacks on Jews by some of the nativists, Jewish immigrants were not the sole target, or even the principal one, in the era of mass migration.

The Italians, who were by far the largest group of newcomers, were under the fiercest attack. In 1891 in New Orleans, eleven Italian immigrants were lynched, in a riot led by patricians, after they had been acquitted of a charge of murder. This lynching was the only such outbreak in those years. It was an American pogrom, but it was directed against Italians, not Jews. Even though they were Catholic, the Irish took little interest in the Italians and essentially wished that they would stop coming. Cyrus Adler, the president of Dropsie College in Philadelphia, complained in 1912 that there was no interest among the Irish in that city in joining a coalition with other minorities to oppose restrictions on immigrations.

The essence of the battle against immigration was the repeated attempt to enact legislation requiring that newcomers prove their literacy. The proponents of such a law presumed that their favorite stock, the Aryans from Northern and Western Europe, could read; "inferior people" from other regions were much less literate, and so nearly half of those who arrived at American ports would be sent back. American business and industry generally opposed such a law. In good times, more labor was needed; in bad times, as the Knights of Labor charged repeatedly, cheap immigrant labor was useful in lowering wage rates and in breaking strikes. Enlightened opinion, for which Higginson had spoken, continued to believe that immigrants of any provenance were a useful addition to America. No matter what the immigrants might seem to be, their children would become, as many had already proved, upstanding Americans. Moreover, the immigrants mattered increasingly as voters, and so those who would push restrictions had to contend with their displeasure. President Theodore Roosevelt was himself ambivalent about the new immigrants, but, in a bid for the Jewish vote, he chose Oscar Straus, the first Jew to serve in a United States cabinet, to be secretary of commerce and labor, and thus the chief immigration officer of the United States in 1906. Roosevelt wanted the votes of the Jews for Charles Evans Hughes, the Republican candidate who was running for governor of New York against William Randolph Hearst.

In the course of the battle over immigration, there was a growing majority in Congress for restriction, while presidents stood firm for twenty years, from 1897 to 1917. Legislation requiring the immigrants to prove literacy passed four times in Congress, and it was vetoed by four presidents, two Democrats, Grover Cleveland and Woodrow Wilson, and two Republicans, William Howard Taft and Theodore Roosevelt. The difference between the presidents and Congress was in the nature of their constituencies. The White House was sensitive, even under Democrats, to the needs of big business, which wanted large immigration to provide workers for industry, but also to the growing numbers of recent immigrants who were becoming citizens and voters. Jews had already become, by 1910, a political factor in such major states as New York, Illinois, Pennsylvania, and Ohio, because they were roughly ten percent of the population of Chicago, Cleveland, and Philadelphia, and more than a quarter of the inhabitants of New York City. Most congressmen, on the other hand, came from districts with few Jews, or other recent immigrants, or they represented sections of the big cities which felt threatened by the expanding immigrant ghettos. The presidential vetoes of restrictions on immigration were a first instance of the growing importance of the "Jewish vote." All of the four presidents were men of goodwill, though only Grover Cleveland was entirely free of personal ambivalence about immigrants in general and Jews in particular. The vetoes were proof that power counted—the power of the National Association of Manufacturers in unusual alliance with Jewish immigrants who were beginning to matter in American politics.

Despite the restrictive majority, a strong minority in Congress, enough to sustain these vetoes, held to the ideal of generosity and openness. Joseph G. "Uncle Joe" Cannon, the legendary Speaker of the House, began on the side of the restrictionists, but by 1906 he had changed his mind. Cannon snorted that if illiterate immigrants had been excluded from the United States in the past, his ancestors would have been rejected. The implication was clear: the partisans of literacy tests had fraudulent memories of their own forebears.

Senator Henry Cabot Lodge did try, during the first attempt to enact literacy restrictions, to sneak in a clause aimed directly at Jews. In 1896, during a Senate-House conference on the first such bill, Lodge framed the clause to permit entry to the United States only to those who were literate "in the English language or the language of their native or resident country"; he had the phrase "or in some other language" deleted. The chief sufferers would have been the Jews, for most of those who were fleeing Russia were literate in Yiddish but not in Russian. The Jewish lobbyist in Washington, Simon Wolf, challenged Lodge; he denied that he had any anti-Jewish intentions, but Wolf did not believe him, then or later. The outcry against the proposed law sent the bill back to the conference committee, and the second session restored the pro-Jewish formula: "or in some other language." President Cleveland nonetheless vetoed the law, because, so he said, he did not believe that the "new immigrants" were an inferior breed.

Lodge's assault on the "Russian Jews" united the "German Jews" in total resistance. Isaac Mayer Wise, who despised Yiddish, nonetheless wrote with contempt of the action Congress was contemplating. The literacy test had almost been accepted by Jewish opinion when it was first proposed, but Lodge's anti-Jewish version convinced the "German Jews," in the language of an editorial in the *Jewish Messenger,* that the "test of illiteracy is an unworthy standard for the American public." Other groups joined the fight. In 1906 the National Liberal Immigration League was formed, including Poles, Italians, and Germans, along with some Protestants from the older America, such as Charles Eliot, the president of Harvard, and Woodrow Wilson, the president of Princeton (who had moved away from his earlier near nativism). Jews were the effective leaders and most active members of this association. The continuing fight for an "open door" was widely understood to be a matchup at the very top between Jews and Boston patrician anti-Semites.

The end of the battle over literacy tests came in February 1917, when Congress overrode President Wilson's veto. The bill that was sustained had exempted from the literacy test those aliens who could prove that they were "seeking admission to the United States to avoid religious persecution—whether such persecution be evidenced by overt acts, or by laws, or governmental regulations." Illiterate Jews from Czarist Russia thus had precedence over illiterate Italians from Sicily. But this "victory" was temporary. The tide had been running toward the limitation of immigration as the older American stock was feeling increasingly threatened. Frightening statistics were being published to prove that a few more years of unrestricted immigration would make the older stock a minority in the land.

In 1911, after years of study, Congress had issued the Dillingham

Report, in forty-two volumes, on the whole question of immigration. The underlying premise of this study was to set up the older America as the preferred America and to cast doubt on the abilities of the new immigration. One of the more seemingly objective attacks was the proposition that the new arrivals were bad for the economy. The American Jewish Committee, which had been organized in 1905 to protect the rights of Jews, commissioned an answer. In 1914, Isaac Hourwich argued, in a book entitled *Immigration and Labor,* that the newer immigrants were adjusting to America and rising in the economy as quickly and as constructively as the older waves of immigration. He denounced the Dillingham Commission for writing "upon the supposition that immigrant races represent separate zoological species." In those very years, Franz Boas, a professor of anthropology at Columbia University who was a "German Jew," was busy measuring hundreds of immigrant crania to prove that there was as much physical room for brains in the skulls of these unwanted newcomers as in the supposedly "better heads" of the Aryans—but, unfortunately, nobody except those who agreed with him before he began his labors paid much attention to these "scientific" results.

So long as Jews were under attack together with Slavs and Italians, they were not the worst off of the three. The decent mainstream of American opinion, which might be prepared to believe bad things about all the new immigrants, was persuaded (as the vote in 1917 proved) that Jews were owed special consideration, because they were the object of persecution. The rise in a very few years of the first group of Jewish immigrants to come to affluence—by the early 1900s, some sixty thousand had moved out of the Lower East Side to the middle-class environs of Brooklyn and Queens—made it hard to doubt that the "Russian Jews" had brains and talent. The continuing, intense concern of the "German Jews" provided the "Russians" with charitable and political protectors of the kind that no other group in America enjoyed.

This era ended in the immediate aftermath of the First World War, after the Russian Revolution. Jews like Leon Trotsky were prominent in the making of that revolution. The "Red Scare" identified the "Russian Jews" in America with the threat of Communism. The continuing fight to restrict immigration was, then, directed at Jews more than at any other group. The "German Jews" still fought beside the recent immigrants and their children, but there was a note of tiredness and even of embarrassment among some. The battle had become primarily that of the "Russians."

The "Russian Jews" would soon stand alone for internal reasons as well. There had been continuing tensions even when the "German Jews" were the undisputed leaders of the community. Only in 1902, after a furious fight, did the United Hebrew Charities in New York admit a very few newly well-to-do immigrants to its board. The leadership of the American Jewish Committee remained entirely in the hands of the "German Jews" until well after the First World War. Socially, in the Reform temples, and especially in the clubs that had been established by the older Jewish settlers, the barriers had remained nearly impenetrable. Some "German Jews" did identify with the "Russians" very personally. In Baltimore, Henrietta Szold taught English to immigrants in the 1890s, and she soon very nearly became one of them. In New York, Judah Leon Magnes, the rabbi of Temple Emanu-El, led in the founding of the Kehillah, the overarching Jewish community organization, and he kept moving ever closer to the East Europeans.

Despite these exceptions, "German Jews" and "Russian Jews" remained separate communities. The "Germans" continued to hope that the "Russians" would follow after them and become, or at least talk as if they had become, "Americans of the Jewish religious persuasion." But this rhetoric was irrelevant to the mass of the "Russian" immigrants and to their children. They were trapped by prejudice, in an essentially narrow enclave in America, and they had to fight their way out. They could not wait to be accepted, first, by the "German Jews" and then by Gentile America. For the children of the ghetto, there was no profit, or balm, in respectability.

12.

The Invention of the Jewish Mother

I

The children of the immigrants had no role models. They resented the traps into which they had been born, and they were angry with the powerless fathers who could not liberate them. They had no choice but to invent themselves, as Jews and as Americans.

The most serious and symbolically most important breaks between the generations occurred at the doors of the synagogue. The young refused to follow their parents to regular prayers in the hundreds of conventicles that the immigrants had established. The religion of the father was destroyed in America, but it was replaced by the religion of the mother. This was the fateful shift in the New Land.

The evidence of the destruction of the role of the father is overwhelming. As is well known, the Lower East Side of New York attracted the attention in the 1890s and early 1900s of some of the most incisive observers of American society, men such as Hutchins Hapgood, Jacob Riis, and Lincoln Steffens. What struck all three with particular force was the break in religion between fathers and sons. Steffens described it in his autobiography as a "tragic struggle." "We would pass a synagogue where a score or more boys were sitting hatless in their old clothes, smoking cigarettes on the steps outside, and their fathers, all dressed in black, with their high hats, uncut beards and temple curls, were going into the synagogue, tearing their hair and rending their garments. . . . Their sons were rebels against the law of Moses; they were lost souls, lost to God, the family, and to Israel of old."

Sholem Asch, one of the most famous of the Yiddish writers, confirmed these observations. He did not settle in America until after the First World War, but in 1910 he paid a visit of five months. Asch found that Jewish parents from the Old World and their Americanized children were more alien to each other than Jews anywhere else in the world. Asch made these points, both directly and with very transparent symbolism, in a short novel called *America 1918*. "In the children there awoke a yearning for unshackled liberty" and "their fathers' piety became a matter of jest." Children made a point of not going to synagogue with their parents on the Sabbath but of running off to football matches: "Father, mother, and son were mourning a home that had been and was no more." The one son who did remain true to the old religious and family traditions died after a few months in America.

The revolt of the young against the inherited religion represented the destruction of the authority of the father within the immigrant family, and not only in the realm of religion. Upon arrival in the United States, fathers accepted upon themselves the burden of making a living for their family, but many failed. In the early 1900s among working-class families, less than one-in-five could support themselves on the father's earnings. The immigrant Jewish family was, if anything, a bit worse off than the average of the working class, both native and immigrant, as a whole. In innumerable families wives and children had to do piecework at home. More often, to make ends meet, children had to take to the streets very early to shine shoes, sell papers, or do anything that might come along. To survive economically, many fathers abandoned the Sabbath and disregarded other traditions. Fathers who could neither protect the family nor hold themselves up as a model of values often felt that they had no choice but to withdraw into themselves in silent despair. That helpless father recurs again and again in the many memoirs that were written by the children of the immigrants.

With the destruction of the father, the "Jewish mother" was invented in America. Contrary to popular mythology, the Jewish-American immigrant mother was not a transplant from Europe; she never existed in the traditional Jewish culture. This figure made her appearance in this time of dislocation, the era of mass migration. The immigrant mother became the source of family loyalty for her children because she was their protector. Her labor helped eke out the family budget and made survival and schooling possible. Her own anger with the schlemiel, the father, helped to feed the rebellion of the children. She raised her sons to achieve for her what her husband had failed to do. But this Jewish mother was not simply a goad to success. She had Jewish purposes of her own. They included, at very least, that the children not intermarry, and that some decent formal respect be paid to the Jewish proprieties, and that they succeed. This was the folk religion of the mothers.

These immigrant mothers brought much less knowledge of the religious traditions to America than even their unlearned husbands. In the nineteenth century the majority of East European Jewish women, certainly among the poor, were illiterate. Nearly half of the women who came to America could not read or write in any language. To be sure, some of the immigrant mothers betrayed their families. One of the staple plots of the Yiddish popular stage was the love affair between the married immigrant woman and one of her "boarders." Men, by the tens of thousands, had come ahead of their families, to accumulate some money so that they could bring their wives and children to join them in America. These "boarders" took rooms with established immigrant families who needed the extra income. Young women were thus in close contact with men away from their wives. Some complications and tragedies ensued, but such love triangles in the home affected only a few, and the children did not always know what was happening. The image of the Jewish mother was barely dented by such incidents.

The shift of children's loyalties from father to mother was not the only strain on the family. The most pervasive problem was desertion. As men arrived, leaving families behind, some simply broke connections with their wives and children in Europe. Many others brought their families over, or got married in America, but ran away when they failed in the task of fending for their wives and children. The Jewish charities in the major cities spent so much money to help deserted wives and children that they united in 1911 to found a National Desertion Bureau. This agency existed into the 1930s, until roughly twenty years after the end of the mass migration. Cumulatively it, and other charitable organizations, dealt with a hundred thousand cases. In many of the situations, they located the runaways and got them at least to contribute to the support of their families.

In human terms, the National Desertion Bureau made an enormous contribution, but this agency has been the least noticed among all the bodies that served the mass migration. The problem that it addressed is discomforting even in memory. One hundred thousand cases of desertion during the era of the mass migration means that at some point nearly one-quarter of the Jewish fathers in America deserted their families, either the ones they had left behind in Europe or the ones they had established in the New World. Because the subject is so painful, there is little oral tradition in American Jewish families about desertion. The proof that it was a serious problem is incontrovertible. The evidence of these traumas is not to be limited solely to the files of the National Desertion Bureau. Rabbinic literature of the first decades of this century, both in Eastern Europe and in the United States, contains a flood of references to the problems of abandoned wives, who were appealing to the rabbis to find ways of freeing them from the bonds of marriage by securing a religious divorce (which could not be issued, in Orthodox Jewish law, without the active consent of the husband).

Contrary to the established cliché, the Jewish family was not largely intact in the time of mass migration. Many Jewish mothers, in fact, raised their children alone. One suspects that the insistent emphasis on the intact Jewish family as part of the explanation of Jewish success is self-serving: it underlines a difference between the Jewish ghettos of the Lower East Side two generations ago and the impoverished African-American ghettos of today, where the majority of families are headed by women. The situation was never that grim among the East European immigrants. Most families were headed by men, but, between desertions and early deaths, a large number, perhaps on the order of one in five or, at the very least, one in six of the immigrant young were raised by their mothers.

Poverty and desertion were not the only assaults on the immigrant family; there was also disease. "Consumption," or tuberculosis, was the great scourge of the workers in sweatshops. The cure in those days was to leave the city for the cleaner and purer air of the mountains. The beginnings of Jewish settlement in the Catskill Mountains near New York were often boardinghouses that were created for sufferers from consumption. The need for such facilities soon spread to the Rocky Mountains, where the National Hospital for Consumptives was established in Denver in the 1890s.

Not all of the immigrants from Eastern Europe remained poor, or ill. Some succeeded with astonishing speed. By the mid-1880s, rich "Russian Jews" were moving to New York's Upper East Side, the very citadel of the "German Jews." As early as 1886, they founded an Orthodox synagogue, Kehilath Jeshurun, in that neighborhood. Recent immigrants were the initial guarantors of the salary of the chief rabbi of the Orthodox community in New York, Rabbi Jacob Joseph, who was brought to the city from Vilno in 1888. Abraham Cahan's *The Rise of David Levinsky* is, in part, about the economic success of such an immigrant. The children of these parents did not have to attend the public colleges. Some simply entered the family business; others were among the first Russian Jews to enter the elite American colleges.

All of the families, rich or poor, were deeply and inevitably divided by the Americanization of their children. The most obvious attacks on the integrity of the family were the dance halls and the street culture, including Jewish gangs. But the educated minority were also very much a problem to their parents. Merit examinations had been instituted in New York in 1901, and Jews immediately began to find their way into the school system. By 1905, Jewish students were already a majority in the City College of New York; they were nearly half of the student body at the Normal School, the teachers' college for women that was the predecessor of Hunter College. The men and women followed different paths. The men were struggling through college in order to make careers in honorific professions; by 1910 Jews were already roughly one-quarter of all the students in American medical schools. Very few of the women were raised with such ambitions. Those who went to college were preparing themselves for secure "feminine" jobs as teachers. In the early years, these were mostly women graduates of the Normal School. Here, too,

Marie Antin's autobiographical writing is most instructive. She tells that parents "in their bewilderment and uncertainty, had to address their children to learn from such models as the tenements afforded. Parents had to take the law from their children's mouths because they had no other means of finding out what was good American form." The result was "an inversion of normal relations" which strained and often broke up the family.

The role models that young Jews could not find at home, they inevitably looked for elsewhere. In the immigrant ghetto itself, the revolutionary movements, socialism and anarchism, offered alternatives to the helpless fathers. There was a role to be had in society for those who were heroic enough to dare to remake the world. Revolutionary ideology was never, not even in its heyday at the turn of the century, as dominant among the immigrants as many observers maintained both then and later. On the contrary, the large majority of the immigrants adhered to the traditional religious forms as best they could, and they worked toward leaving the proletariat as quickly as possible. But socialist and anarchist agitation did play a role in the destruction of the Jewish father, of nullifying whatever authority he might have brought with him from Europe, and of replacing him. The revolution demanded new role models. A new society could best be made by the young; a new dispensation required defiance of fathers rather than deference to whatever authority they might still represent.

In reading the writings of antireligious Jews of the 1890s and of the early 1900s, one is impressed by their sense of themselves as being part of a worldwide battle to release men from the bonds of the past. These atheists and anarchists thought of themselves as doing among Jews what leading American agnostics such as Robert Ingersoll and, soon, Clarence Darrow, were doing among Christians. Left-wing Jews regarded all eight of the Haymarket martyrs in Chicago, the four who were hanged, the one suicide, and the three who went to jail in 1886 for the throwing of a bomb during a strike rally which killed policemen, as heroes to be revered. These revolutionary immigrants were imparting freedom to their children—not the freedom to open a shoe store, but the hope of making in America the revolution that had not yet happened in Russia—and which seemed hopeless before it did happen in 1917.

Almost all of the earliest Yiddish poets and novelists were socialists or anarchists who wrote from the sweatshops. Such writing was usually lurid, but it did reflect, in a heightened, declamatory way, the lives of its readers. One of the favorite themes was the oppression of the workers by the Jewish bosses. This class struggle within the ghetto was understood, as a matter of course, to reflect the inequities of capitalist society as a whole. Hope was to be found only in the possibility that an end would be made of capitalism. The immigrants knew that they could not make the revolution because they were too foreign. They could not lead in America, but their "American" children were sworn to the task.

Morris Rosenfeld, the first of these proletarian poets to be translated into English, railed at the meaninglessness of a life spent tending and feeding the sewing machine. The message was clear: there had to be a world that was better than this oppression. The novelists took this theme of social protest further. Leon Kobrin was perhaps the most prolific of all the Yiddish writers in America. In one of his stories, entitled "A Common Language," which was written in the 1920s, the hero is a night watchman who catches a thief and begins to beat him. "Suddenly it struck me. Maybe he had no home for himself and his child? Who knows what kind of place this Ameritchke is? Maybe that's why he went out to steal on a night like this? Maybe he had done it for the sake of his child." The thief was an Italian. "We talked, he in his language, and I in mine." In the end, the hero gets fired for helping the thief.

Moshe Nadir was much more self-consciously political. It was inevitably so, for he wrote for the Yiddish Communist daily, the *Morgen Freiheit*. In one of his stories from the 1920s, Nadir told about a workers' strike. The story, entitled "Thoughts About Forty Cents," was written, ironically, from the perspective of a capitalist. "With the fish course my wife also served me a bit of news about a town called Roosevelt where they had shot into a crowd of strikers without any rhyme or reason. I felt my blood begin to boil." As Nadir's capitalist "hero" eats on, through the various courses of a sumptuous meal, his sympathies gradually shift against the workers and toward the employers. He lights up a Havana cigar and makes himself comfortable in an easy chair. "And at this point I saw how trivial those workers are, to risk their necks for a measly forty cents a day." Even in the writings of the socialist novelists, the workers failed more than they succeeded.

But the socialist novelists and essayists wanted the immigrants to fight back. Revolutionary consciousness meant that Jews should not be passive as they had been throughout the centuries in Europe. They should stand up against the bosses for the rights of labor, as the workers had done in Nadir's story, but above all, Jews were enjoined not to cower before anti-Semites, as they had in Europe, but to confront their tormentors. In one of the numerous stories that revolve around this theme, Joseph Opatashu described the ambivalent response of Jews to anti-Semitism in America: they tried to ignore it, to pretend that it was not there, until on occasion the provocation became too great to be avoided. In "How the Fight Began," a gang of children is teasing an old Jewish peddler, and only one young Jew among the onlookers has the courage to get up to defend him. "The few Jews in the car buried their heads deeper in their newspapers, looking up nervously at the scene, trembling in fear and angry agitation. But fear was strong enough to keep them frozen in their places." Then this gang of young hooligans began to tease a young Jewish woman. At that point, "the Jews behind their newspapers threw them away and clenched their fists, and that is how the fight began." America, the "golden land," was thus an arena of struggle, of pain, and even of defeat. In the sweatshops the bosses were "bloodsuckers," and on the streets the Jew-haters were always mocking and harassing "kikes" and "sheenies." The passivity of the immigrant fathers was irrelevant, or worse, in the New Land. Their children had to find their own courage to fight back, and, in fighting back, they taught at least a few of the fathers to be "Americans."

II

Riis, Steffens, and Asch had observed that the children belonged much more to the culture of the streets than to that of their families. David Nasaw, in his book *Children of the City,* has recently confirmed Riis's contemporary accounts: "The early twentieth-century city was a city of strangers. Most of its inhabitants had been born or raised elsewhere. Only the children were native to the city—with no memory, no longing, no historic commitment to another land, another way of life. . . . Work, money, and the fun that money bought were located on the streets of the city."

The streets have never taught immigrants to America primary lessons in virtue. On the contrary, some of those who were raised on the streets, without strong role models at home, have turned, generation after generation in America, to crime. Young Jews, children of immigrants, followed the pattern. Almost always, except perhaps in Puritan New England, crime has been a major avenue for quick material success in America. There has usually been no generational succession in crime, for western gunslingers who consistently outdrew their enemies sometimes ended their careers as sheriffs, and some of their children became governors. Jews were not exempt from this rule. In the era of the mass migration, the Irish had at first dominated the criminal scene in the big cities. So it was with the Jews. Large-scale prostitution had not existed in pre-emancipation Jewry, though there were, of course, many individual examples of sexual misconduct. In the late nineteenth century, with Jews moving into the big cities of Eastern Europe, and away from the constraints of their native smaller towns and villages, prostitution began to appear in Europe. There was Jewish prostitution in Warsaw and in Odessa. In Moscow and St. Petersburg there was both real prostitution as a trade and the pretense of it: some respectable Jewish women accepted internal passports as prostitutes, because that "trade" was one of those which conferred special permission on Jews to reside in areas from which they were excluded.

But Jewish prostitution, and several other kinds of crime, were prevalent in the New World. At least one-third, perhaps half, of the known prostitutes of New York, then, in the early 1900s, were Jews. The French, Irish, Germans, and Italians were next in order, but the Jewish proportion seems very nearly to have equaled the total number of all the rest put together. The explanation for this anomaly is probably to be found in a demographic fact; unlike all the rest, Jewish immigrants were coming to the half-dozen largest cities, led by New York, where perhaps seventy percent of these immigrants were settling. Big cities are the locus of crime, as small villages, towns, and farms, where many of the other ethnics were settling, are not. The most striking aspect of these statistics is that more of the Jewish prostitutes seem to have been native than foreign-born. The native-born seem to have had the initial skills of language, at-homeness, and streetwiseness, which their parents, as immigrant newcomers, did not have.

THE INVENTION OF THE JEWISH MOTHER

How much crime was there really on the Lower East Side of New York? This was a painful issue in the years of mass migration, and it has been debated since by historians. In September 1908, the police commissioner of New York, Theodore A. Bingham, published an article in *Harper's,* under the title "Foreign Criminals in New York." Bingham argued that in New York, the Jews and the Italians, two of the largest communities, were the source of numerous gangs and that these "criminal organizations" needed to be watched by specially trained police details. He went on to say that with a million Jews now in New York, perhaps a quarter of the population, "it is not astonishing that half the criminals should be of that race." He attributed this supposed propensity to crime to the foreignness of those Jews, and he went on to assert that "Jewish criminals tend not to attack people but rather to commit crimes against property." He was particularly sulfuric about Jewish juveniles under sixteen: he asserted that they were especially prominent among the offenders.

This article aroused a storm. The Jews of the Lower East Side reacted to it as a portent of American anti-Semitism, parallel to the kind that they had been experiencing in Europe. They protested with fury. The leadership of the older Jewish settlers, including Jacob Schiff, who was by then the universally acknowledged "king of the Jews," joined the outcry against the assertion that Jews were the main source of criminality in New York. In a few days, Bingham withdrew the remarks "without reservation," but the question remained alive. At the time Bingham spoke, he was probably telling the truth. There was quite a large amount of petty juvenile crime, such as stealing from pushcarts and picking pockets, but the overwhelming bulk of the young people who engaged in such endeavors did not graduate into careers in crime. The young Eddie Cantor, who was later to become a famous entertainer, was a leading member in a gang called, of all things, "Pork-faced Sams." One of the principal tricks of this group was to steal from stores and then sell the owners their own stock.

Gambling was a pervasive Lower East Side recreation. The numerous regular games in homes or other gathering places were largely innocent, but the ghetto did breed professional gamblers. The flashiest of New York's big-time gamblers, Arnold Rothstein, had been born in Philadelphia in 1892 to a respectable, pious family of Jewish immigrants from Eastern Europe. Rothstein could have followed after his father, and become a moderately successful businessman, but he chose instead to be a high roller and casino gambler. Rothstein bribed police officers and judges, he helped support the Tammany machine, and he hobnobbed with the titans of American industry, if only to gamble with them in his own establishment. One famous night, Percival H. Hill, the head of the American Tobacco Company, lost a quarter of a million dollars to Rothstein. This was not the only occasion when the upstart gambler took the leaders of American industry to the cleaners. For that matter, Rothstein was also a famous pool player, and he became even more of a "name" when he defeated a professional from Philadelphia in a game which lasted thirty-four hours. The most famous sports scandal in American history, fixing the World Series of baseball in 1919, was a gamblers' coup engineered by Arnold Rothstein. He arranged to bribe a number of key players on the Chicago White Sox to throw the series. This "feat" earned Rothstein a fortune in bets. In his personal habits, Rothstein had learned from his big-business clients to act the swell. No less an authority than Lucky Luciano, one of the leading criminals of the 1920s and 1930s, paid Rothstein a tribute in his memoirs. Luciano reported that Rothstein had taught him "how to dress, how not to wear loud things, and how to have good taste."

Is is even true, contrary to Jewish apologists then and later, that the immigrants were indulgent to certain kinds of crime. Violence was universally deplored, but clever fraud was for some a way of survival. A little arson to collect insurance was acknowledged as something which occurred with some frequency; the perpetrators were not universally condemned by the community. A contemporary joke told of a petty businessman who had committed arson several times. When he could no longer get fire insurance, he turned inquiringly to one of his friends and asked, "How do you make a flood?" Arson got to be so much of a nuisance and danger that in the early 1890s eighteen of New York's worst arsonists were sent to jail, some for life. The attitude among the immigrants toward such crimes was rooted in centuries of Jewish experience in the Diaspora. The law had always been the enemy of the Jews; to circumvent it was often the only way to survive, and, therefore, to outfox authority was a praiseworthy act. Such an attitude was, of course, to be found among other immigrant groups. Poor peasants everywhere had survived through the centuries by poaching on the estates of the rich.

Criminality was not limited to New York's Lower East Side. There were comparable, though smaller, groups of offenders in Chicago and in Philadelphia, as well as in Cleveland, Boston, Detroit, and Newark. Surprisingly, Minneapolis, which had a comparatively small Jewish community, produced an outsize number of youth gangs and criminals. There may have been as much crime in New York as Bingham had charged, but something was happening that he could not predict: crime was a half-generation occupation for almost all of the young who engaged in it. It created no model for the next generation.

The more socially respectable avenue to quick fame and fortune was sports. The Jewish immigrants had no tradition in sports activities. In Europe, sports had belonged to the Gentiles, and even among them, not to the poor. The children of the immigrants, however, became almost immediately avid participants in sports, especially in those that required little space and equipment, both of which were in short supply in the Lower East Side. The sports in which Jews excelled early were those in which the individual engaged in a kind of "free enterprise," and which might lead quickly to large rewards. Thus, there were no Jewish tennis players or golfers, for these sports were, then, entirely amateur. Those sports were doubly alien to the children of the immigrants because they required courts, or many acres of ground, and this much room could not be found among the tenements. Tennis and golf would later be picked up avidly by many of these second-generation immigrants as one of the marks of their arrival in America.

Despite the strong and ingrained religious tradition against doing physical harm to others, many of the young in the ghetto took to boxing. Training space was minimal: all that was needed was a ring and a place for a punching bag. Such room could be made in any decrepit building. For at least two decades, the Lower East Side was the breeding ground of great Jewish fighters, such as Abe Attell, Benny Leonard, Ruby Goldstein, and Barney Ross, all of whom were children of immigrants. At one point in the 1920s, seven of the nine boxing championships were held by Jews. The striking exception was the heavyweight championship, simply because the Jews did not produce many physical specimens in that weight range. Even so, one of the leading champions of the 1930s, Max Baer, pretended to be a Jew, because Jews were so prominent among the fight fans.

It was an advantage for a fighter like Baer to say that he belonged to "this well-known line of Jewish champions and hopes."

Sports are very often on the border of criminality, because they have always been the object of betting and of fixing. Entertainment was on a higher level of legitimacy, but, like crime and sports, it, too, offered the possibility of success in one's own lifetime. To be sure, there had been a tradition of entertainment in Eastern Europe. Klezmer musicians had performed, especially at weddings, and there was usually a *Badchen,* a composer of impromptu verses, who both praised and mocked the assemblage. These are, perhaps, the cultural ancestors of America's Jewish music-makers and stand-up comedians. The immediate models for the young Jews who tried to sing and dance their ways to fortune were the Irish entertainers, who dominated the vaudeville stages at the turn of the century. The great wave of Jewish immigration came when the main forms of entertainment were theater and vaudeville. Live entertainment was a mass industry, which the older Protestant America had left to the Irish. Jews moved very rapidly into vaudeville. The new Jewish entertainers even brought with them a new audience, their contemporaries from the Jewish ghetto. "Pat and Mike," who made jokes about the rubes and the camaraderie between Jews and Irish, became a favorite team on the circuit. At the turn of the century, "Jewish" figures were widely expected to be part of every program on the vaudeville stage.

Some of the song and dance men and women and the comedians became stars. There is no way of estimating the proportion of Jews among the performers on the vaudeville circuit after the turn of the century. We do know, however, that by around 1910 something on the order of sixty percent of vaudeville houses in the ten largest cities were owned by Jews. Most of these owners were not new immigrants. They descended from the older "German Jews," who had come to the United States before or immediately after the Civil War. But these older Jewish settlers held no monopoly. Soon, by 1900, such people as the Balabans, more recent immigrants who had begun as children of the ghetto, had made their way into this expanding business.

Jews were much more important in the newest entertainment enterprise, the movies. At the beginnings of the movie industry, during the Silent Era, Jews figured prominently as characters in the short films. These early movies were largely directed at the immigrant market in the cities. As the movies spread throughout the country, Jews disappeared from the screen. Smalltown and rural American life was, then, overwhelmingly white and Protestant. It took very nearly a generation for Jewish actors and directors to play a role of significance in Hollywood, and, even then, the vast majority of these figures anglicized their names and their total demeanor. Even Paul Muni, who was the superstar among the serious actors in the early days of talking pictures, worked hard not to mention that he had come to Hollywood from the Yiddish stage on Second Avenue in New York.

During the earliest years of Hollywood, Jews rapidly became the large majority of the entrepreneurs. The business of moviemaking was dominated by such men as Louis B. Mayer, Samuel Goldwyn, Adolph Zukor, David O. Selznick, Harry Cohn, the Fox Brothers and the Warner Brothers—to mention only the most prominent. They built the major studios, and they presided over Hollywood at its most flamboyant. What these men put on the screen was very smoothly American, but what they spoke among themselves was an English accented by the Yiddish that had been the first language for most of them, including those who had been born in America.

At the inception of the movie industry, it was Jewish entrepreneurs more than anybody else who seized the opportunities of the new invention and took the risks. Some became glitteringly wealthy, if only for a while. These men were themselves the incarnation of the very Horatio Alger myth which Hollywood often celebrated. Yet, even as they told the story of poor farm children rising from the log cabin to the presidency, or to a Fifth Avenue mansion, they were not yet ready to tell their own story, of rising from the streets of the ghetto to sit beside the swimming pools of Beverly Hills. Some of these men failed, or they destroyed each other. Ultimately, all of the major studios would be controlled, directly or indirectly, by the bankers who provided them with capital. The story of the rise and fall of the Hollywood moguls would eventually be told by some of their children in memoirs or in novels, often with bitterness, as the recurrent tale of unslakable hunger for success.

Recently, the early days of Hollywood have been examined again, with new respect for the astonishing creativity of those who invented the first and still dominant form of worldwide mass entertainment. There is even increasing reference to the yearning of some of the Hollywood moguls for artistic respectability. From Jewish perspectives the movies have been seen as another example of how the Jews, when society was intent on excluding them from established businesses, found their way into the American economy. Jews had to take the risks of beginning new pursuits. The movies were exempt from the endemic anti-Semitism which kept Jews out of white-collar jobs in the banks, the insurance companies, the railroads, steel making and coal mining.

What did the entry of many of these children into largely unprecedented pursuits mean for the shaping of American Jewish experience? The point has already been made that religiously traditional lives were inconceivable in any of these endeavors, even though there is an account of at least one Jewish gangster from Cleveland who wore a skullcap at all times, and who was totally observant of Jewish rituals, as he plied his violent trade as "enforcer." This interesting gangster may have had a parallel or two among Jewish entertainers or Hollywood moguls, but, altogether, such "orthodox" Jews were the merest handful. Those who ventured out farthest from the immigrant ghetto, to Hollywood or into the boxing ring, had to invent a new persona for themselves. There were no models in the Jewish past for the behavior of fighters, gangsters, or movie moguls. All of these new Jews (so they have told in their many autobiographies) had ineffectual fathers; they were their own ancestors.

They also imagined America, for they did not know it. The movie czars, the entertainers, the boxers, and the criminals were usually school dropouts. These were the people who had taken to the streets rather than finish high school and go on to college. They had thus not been reached by American middle-class norms, which the schools imparted. Some of them rose to finance movies about the American gentility they had never encountered. They imagined an America that never was, and hoped that this mythic America would accept them.

III

F. Scott Fitzgerald's famous novel of the 1920s, *The Great Gatsby,* considers this problem. The hero of the novel is supposed to have been fashioned after Arnold Rothstein. In Fitzgerald's story, the Rothstein figure is called Jay Gatsby. He came to Long Island, a precinct of established American society, to win acceptance through his wealth and his manners. Gatsby failed, for, in a moment of crisis, he was brutally reminded that he remained an outsider. The story of Gatsby is thus the tale of an assimilationist who has abandoned his past and who has nothing left to live for when he is rejected. This may have been true of Arnold Rothstein, that he wanted to be accepted by the swells whom he aped, and from whom he won money gambling, but it is not likely. No matter what his surface manners might have been, Rothstein, the gambler, was twice an outsider, and his gambling coups had about them an air of defiance and a suggestion that the America which was fascinated by him, and held him in contempt, was not as righteous as it pretended: the titans of industry came to his casino, and baseball idols were for sale. One cannot know whether Rothstein harbored within himself some Jewish "island within" of defiance and pride, but it is possible. Such feelings were present in most of his generation, even among those who tried to assimilate.

Jewish pride—and guilt—were imparted by almost all of the Jewish mothers, and not only by them. In theory, socialism was a universalist ideology which taught the abandonment of all ethnic distinctions, but most of the spokesmen of socialism among the Jewish immigrants insisted on the importance of maintaining Jewish group feeling, and even of holding onto some respect for the religious heritage. There are many exchanges on the subject of Jewish continuity in the famous letter-column, the "bintel brief," of the *Jewish Daily Forward*. A son of unbelieving parents discovered that his parents, who had always treated even the Day of Atonement as just another day, were upset that he wanted to marry a non-Jewish young woman. He wrote to the *Forward* on the presumption that he would find sympathy and support, only to discover that the socialist and freethinking editors of the paper insisted, with the same seeming illogic that the letter-writer attributed to his parents, that it was imperative that he marry a Jew and that he continue to identify with the Jewish community. This was no isolated exchange, for the *Forward* took a comparable attitude even in its earliest years, when it was most ideologically socialist and secularist. In response to numerous questions about proper behavior for secular nonbelievers, in order not to offend the sensitivities of the vast mass of Jews on Yom Kippur, the *Forward* insisted that nonbelievers should be enormously discreet in their refusal to fast and to attend synagogue on that day.

The editors of the *Forward* did not doubt that the children of the immigrants would move from Yiddish to English as their primary language; they actively encouraged such Americanization. This newspaper preached to the largely Jewish labor unions and to the Jewish socialists (most of whom were organized into a party of their own, apart from the main body of American socialists) that they were not a separate enclave; they were part of all the forces that were fighting for a just society. And yet, those who read the *Forward* knew that the commitment of Jews to remain Jewish was beyond question and discussion.

Even the pleasures that Jews enjoyed in the immigrant ghetto helped maintain some feeling of continuity between the generations. In the 1880s, near the very beginnings of the mass migration, Jacob Riis reported that "the young people in Jewtown are inordinately fond of dancing." By 1900, when the Jewish population of the Lower East Side was some four hundred thousand, there were so many dance halls in the neighborhood that one or two of them could be found on every block. These were frequented by the young. The parents objected, at very least because spending time and money on such endeavors was regarded as wasteful. But all the objections were of little avail. A rage was exploding in America, among the immigrants themselves and especially among their children, for whatever pleasures could be enjoyed in the present. This passion emerged from a desire that had been pent up among the European Jewish poor for many generations; they had been double barred for centuries from "this world," both as poor people and as Jews. Now, in America, the passion for enjoyment had at last found the opportunity to express itself, because here no one was limited to making do with devotion to the spirit. In the dance halls, the young sought to learn how to enjoy pleasure in an "American" way, but they were moved by a hunger for this world that they shared with their parents.

The men and women of the older generation expressed this desire, in part, through their passion for the Yiddish stage, and especially for those sentimental productions, such as plays about the sweatshops or about the clashes between parents and their "Yankee" children, that mirrored their own lives. The big occasions, not only in New York but also in Chicago, Philadelphia, and Boston, were Friday nights and Saturday matinees, when such performances were being held in contravention of the religious injunctions which prescribed the observance of the Sabbath. In the synagogues, the immigrant years before 1914 were the high point of the era of the virtuoso cantors; tickets were sold for the services that they conducted. Those who mobbed such services by superstar cantors, such as Yossele Rosenblatt and Zanvel Kwartin, came to pray, and to be entertained and moved by the talents of these men, who were called "sweet singers of Zion." Giant ads appeared in the Yiddish press inviting people to buy tickets for the services that these cantors conducted. There were often policemen at the doors of the synagogue to make sure that those without tickets were not admitted.

The parents who went to the Yiddish theaters or to the synagogues, and the children who went to dance halls and Broadway shows, did meet in the catering establishments. Weddings, bar mitzvahs, and other family occasions were celebrated with ever greater elaboration. In his memoirs, Dore Schary, of movie fame, tells of his parents' catering business, which opened in the Jewish ghetto in Newark just before the outbreak of the First World War. Schary Manor was a roaring, stormy success from the very beginning. Jewish families flocked to it for their sons' bar mitzvahs, their daughters' weddings, their own anniversaries, or for charity banquets. Business grew so that within a few months, the Manor had to be moved to a large mansion.

Schary's grandfather was a Jew of the old school, and the move away from the older life began when the grandfather died. Schary's father lived an "American" life: "Papa believed in full and generous living. His wardrobe was huge and chosen with great taste. Though he didn't drink and smoked few cigars, he was an avid and reckless pinochle player and a ravenous eater. He was courteous and particularly gallant to women, who were as attracted to him as he to them. On those holidays or for family celebrations when he took us to New York, he arranged for orchestra seats in the theater and the best table at Delmonico's or Lorber's, ordered the finest food and champagne, and tipped the waiters lavishly."

Jews who had had little to eat in Europe had thus created the caterers' culture with its outstanding characteristic of eating too much at every family occasion. The stuffed derma, the knishes, and the "sweet tables" became the assurance that the world was now different. In the language of Yiddish theater ditties of that era, "stuffed geese is no longer a delicacy for the rich; in the golden land everyone can enjoy this dish." Overeating was the revenge, and the apotheosis, of the poor. Among heaping platters of Jewish foods (some of which had never existed in Europe), two or even three generations of post-immigrant Jews could meet on a mutual ground of feeding their bodies, and thus giving assurance to their souls. Here a view of America was asserted that both generations held in common: in the old country poor Jews could only dream of joy in the world to come; the New Land was the place in which the Jew could attain pleasure in this world.

These pleasures of the catering halls could not be divorced entirely from the synagogue. To be sure, political radicals and secularists of several varieties avoided religion and devised forms of their own for celebrating marriages and conducting funerals, but this was not the practice of the overwhelming majority of the immigrants and their children. On the great occasions in the personal lives of individuals, and of families, even the children whom Jacob Riis had seen sitting on the steps defiantly smoking cigarettes on Sabbath morning were in the congregation. The young came with their parents to worship services on the High Holy Days, they attended the Passover Seder at the family table, they were married by Jewish clergy, and they observed the rituals of mourning as prescribed by the tradition. These rituals were practiced out of family feeling. The Jewish God was not entirely absent, for those who observed this regimen felt that they were giving Him the minimum that He was due. Even those who had no faith were in synagogue to appease the father, to be less guilty toward the mother for having inflicted the pain of abandoning her for the wider world, and to demonstrate how far the child of the ghetto had gone in conquering America.

All of these themes came together in the famous first talking picture, *The Jazz Singer*. It was produced in 1927 and premiered in New York in February 1928. Al Jolson, the best-known Jewish entertainer of the day, played the son of a cantor who abandoned his father's calling to sing on the American stage. The theme of *The Jazz Singer,* the pain of loss, and of longing for the Jewish certainties of childhood, had been a major subject of American Jewish writers in the three languages—Yiddish, English, and Hebrew—in which they wrote. And yet, the appearance of *The Jazz Singer* marked a turning point in American Jewish life. For the first time, the Jews who dominated

Hollywood came out of the closet as Jews. This self-revelation of the children of the immigrants was possible because 1928 was the high point of the economic "boom." Jews were well-off: they were, at that moment, less afraid of anti-Semites than ever before, or than they were to be again in two years, after the Crash.

Al Jolson was, himself, the son of a cantor in Washington, D.C. Like the hero of the movie, Jolson had begun as a performer by singing in a synagogue choir, but he had reached the height of his stage career as a minstrel, singing "Mammy" in blackface. Suddenly, in 1928, Al Jolson told the essence of his Jewish autobiography on the screen for all America to see. Being Jewish, especially as it expressed itself in the inner torment of what was lost when the Jewish past was forgotten, had become a subject that could be discussed in front of Gentile America. In the movie the son of the cantor returns home from his "American" life, at least for the Day of Atonement, to replace his dying father in the synagogue, while the mother looks on with tearful blessing from the ladies' gallery. The mother approved of the son, as the father could not, both because he had succeeded in America, and because he returned home for the Day of Atonement. The silent, weeping mother in the ladies' gallery is thus archetypal: it is her Jewishness that *The Jazz Singer* represented.

In 1928, the very year in which *The Jazz Singer* was being screened all over America, Ludwig Lewisohn, who was then one of the best-known figures in American letters, published a call to return to Jewish identity under the title *The Island Within*. Lewisohn was not an East European, for he came of German Jewish stock. As a young man in the early years of the twentieth century, Lewisohn had made a career as the most important interpreter in America of modern German literature. He was involved in political and social causes, and he even served for a short while after the First World War as literary editor of *The Nation,* which was then the most important liberal journal in the United States. In midlife, Lewisohn suddenly returned to Jewishness. *The Island Within* was a plea for the return of the Jew from the inhospitable Gentile world to the inner life of the Jewish community (the hero was, like Lewisohn himself, unhappily intermarried). In a few years the result of Lewisohn's own turning was that he became a Zionist and that he grew ever closer to East European culture in Yiddish. Lewisohn soon became an editor of Zionist journals, and he kept attacking the Jews among the Marxist and Freudian intelligentsia for their alienation from Jewishness. But Lewisohn's career was of concern only to small coteries, even among Jews. The assimilating Jewish intelligentsia, whom he attacked, essentially ignored him, and the organized Jewish community which became his home was, to use his own term, an "island within." It was then a private preserve in which some Jews asked and debated questions about themselves, in substantial isolation from all of America.

By their very nature, intellectuals and ideologues leave a paper trail, for a large part of their trade is to write. The documentary record of the immigrant generation is full of the writings of socialists, anarchists, and of an infinite variety of other movements and cliques. The mass and the passion of this writing have seduced some historians of the immigrant past into believing that new ideologies dominated the ghetto, and that the bulk of the children of the immigrants were raised in left-wing, secularist, Yiddish-speaking families. Some were, but most were not. *The Jazz Singer* offers a much truer picture of the mainstream. The Jewish masses were to be found in the congregation of the old cantor, the father of the "jazz singer." The young Jews who attended sometimes wished that they had other options. Some were proud of what they had made of themselves in America. Whatever their inner feelings about their Jewishness, most knew that they could be neither "German Jews" nor Gentiles. The children of the immigrants had only one option, to be exactly that, children of the Jewish ghetto in the New World. They could make their way into America only by force, by acquiring power.

13.

The Russians Defeat the Germans

I

Between 1914 and 1918 the "German Jews" lost control of American Jewry. The "Russian Jews" rebelled, and won, in the name of Zionism. This fight involved the most serious of all issues: how should Jews behave before the eyes of the American majority? Did they have to play the game by some supposedly "American" rules? Did they always have to appeal to the majority in the name of "freedom and justice for all" like the "German Jews"? Did they have to agitate for the freeing of Jews from the sweatshops in the name of the universal rights of labor? Or could they press, forthrightly and avowedly, for the Jewish interest?

Before 1914, the Zionists were a negligible force in America. When war broke out, the Zionists persuaded Louis Dembitz Brandeis to place himself at their head, and thus a new chapter began in the history of American Jewry. Brandeis, a famous lawyer and a friend of President Wilson, gave Zionists instant respectability. Under his leadership, Zionism was transformed from a movement of small, overwhelmingly "Russian" immigrant groups, who were not even on the margin of American politics, into a viable public force.

On the surface Brandeis was a strange kind of leader for the Zionists. Born in Louisville, Kentucky, in 1856 to recent immigrants from Bohemia, who were not much involved in Jewish life, Brandeis had a brilliant career at Harvard Law School, and by the late 1880s had become a successful Boston lawyer. True, many of his initial clients were "German Jews" to whose social set he inevitably belonged, but he was even more peripheral to the Jewish community than the most assimilated among them. There was some memory in his family of its origins in Prague in a circle that still harbored loyalty to the memory of Jacob Frank, the false messiah who had appeared in Poland in the latter half of the eighteenth century. Brandeis's mother was very opposed to Jewish particularism. In his earliest Boston years, he was to be found, at least once, on the list of contributors to the First Unitarian Church. On the other hand, he had been deeply influenced in his earliest years by an uncle, Louis Dembitz (whose family name he adopted as his own middle name), a learned, Orthodox Jew.

After 1900 Brandeis began to get involved somewhat tentatively in Jewish affairs. The turning point came in 1910, when a bitter garment workers strike, involving both Jewish workers and Jewish employers, was being fought out in New York. Brandeis was known as a leading Progressive, and as an eminent lawyer who had represented capitalists. He was approached to help resolve the conflict. Brandeis succeeded in negotiating an agreement that was a first in labor/management relations in America. The workers and the bosses signed a contract to standardize working conditions throughout the industry, and they agreed to refer all disputes to binding arbitration.

Brandeis was transformed by this encounter. He had come to know the recent immigrants, and he "was impressed, deeply impressed, that these Jews with whom I dealt showed in a striking degree the qualities which, to my mind, make for the best American citizenship, that within them there was a true democratic feeling and a deep appreciation of the elements of social justice." Brandeis was particularly moved by the fact that even the employers were not totally obdurate, "that each side had a great capacity for placing themselves in the other fellow's shoes . . . That set these people apart in my experience in labor disputes."

At the same time, Brandeis started to become alienated politically from the bulk of the "German" Jews; they were overwhelmingly conservative in their politics, and he was an ever more passionately convinced Progressive. As he was settling the garment workers' strike, Brandeis began to believe that the East Europeans were better Americans than the impeccably "American" Jewish bourgeoisie into which he had been born. These new and, on the surface, very foreign immigrants represented "the age-old ideals of the Jews," which were identical with "the twentieth century ideals of America."

In 1913 Brandeis surprised everyone, including his own family, by joining the Zionist movement. There was some evidence that he found in Zionism a way of expressing his own alienation, and even anger, with the German Jewish leaders. That year he had all the more reason to be angry. Brandeis had worked very hard in the election campaign of Woodrow Wilson. The president-elect was known to be contemplating appointing Brandeis to the cabinet as secretary of the interior. Jacob Schiff, the acknowledged leader of the "German Jews," was rumored to have informed Wilson that the leadership of American Jewry did not regard Brandeis as a representative Jew. Schiff supposedly even hinted that such an appointment would cause trouble, because of Brandeis's supposedly pronounced "leftist" views, and that the possible fallout in anti-Semitism would be an unwarranted and unnecessary problem for American Jews.

There is no proof beyond rumor that such representations were made, but the leading figures among the "German Jews" were known to hold such views. The overt opposition to Brandeis's being offered a cabinet post at the beginning of the Wilson administration came from the Democratic party establishment, which vetoed him as a Progressive and a radical. Brandeis did not react to this defeat by becoming angry with Woodrow Wilson, who had made the decision to exclude him. Brandeis was in and out of the White House within days of the beginning of the new administration. It is, however, not entirely fanciful to suppose that he displaced his anger at the defeat in 1912 on those to whom Wilson had listened, and especially the Jews among them. To lead the East European immigrant masses against the German Jewish classes was a conceivable counterattack.

The private representations against Brandeis in 1913 had not been the first time that the Jewish establishment had sided against him. In 1906, when the "German Jews" had organized the American Jewish Committee, Cyrus Adler had suggested Brandeis's name as a founding member, but the nomination was rejected. This internal rift became public in 1916 when President Wilson nominated Brandeis to the Supreme Court. Brandeis was the first Jew to be named to the high tribunal. His enemies saw in Brandeis a radical, a role model of disrespect for authority, and subversion of established order. Brandeis knew very well why his opponents hated him. Writing in the third person during the battle, he said, "The dominant reasons for the opposition to the confirmation of Mr. Brandeis are that he is considered a radical and is a Jew."

Jacob Schiff and Louis Marshall did not dislike Brandeis because he was a Jew, though they kept complaining to both Jews and Gentiles that Brandeis had been a marginal, uninvolved Jew until he turned Zionist. The clear implication was that such a Jew should not be usurping leadership from them, the legitimate leaders of "Americans of the Jewish faith." Schiff and Marshall privately asked President Wilson to withdraw the nomination. As the controversy heated up, they remained silent in public. They did not testify against Brandeis in the confirmation hearings or send negative letters to the Senate committee. Nonetheless, the opinions of this circle were expressed for all to read in a May 26, 1916, editorial in *The New York Times*. The editorial reflected the views of its German Jewish publisher, Adolph Ochs: "Mr. Brandeis is essentially a contender, a striver after changes and reforms. The Supreme Court by its very nature is the conservator of our institutions." There were "German Jews," such as Henry Morgenthau, Sr., who were Democrats and supporters of Brandeis, but the establishment had made its view clear. It wanted to be perceived as completely "American," and it was distancing itself from Jews who were shaking up past custom and privilege. In the mind of America, and not only of anti-Semites, Brandeis was cementing the identification of Jews with "radicalism." The line of cleavage had been reached in American politics, between the "German Jews" and the leader of the "Russians."

The bitter, public, Gentile opposition to his nomination came from Boston. Brandeis was not some decorous, conservative lawyer who had supported the privileged classes in return for their approval. Though he had been no consistent white knight—he had taken cases in which he defended corporations against their workers—Brandeis had risen to national fame in fighting for restrictions on child labor, in battling for civil service reform, and by befriending the unions. He had fought against the New Haven Railroad, in which many Boston patricians had stakes. The president of Harvard, A. Lawrence Lowell, circulated a petition against Brandeis, and a large number of Brahmins signed with him. On the other hand, the president emeritus of Harvard, Charles Eliot, wrote the Senate committee in favor of Brandeis, and so did nine of the eleven professors at the Harvard Law School. A. A. Berle, who was then serving as a Congregationalist minister in Boston, offered the best and oft-quoted summary of the attitude of the enemies of Brandeis:

> Long and unchallenged control of everything in the Commonwealth has given many of these gentlemen the perfectly natural feeling that whoever is not approved by them is ipso facto a person who is either "dangerous" or lacking in "judicial temperament" . . . They simply cannot realize, and do not, that a long New England ancestry is not prima facie a trusteeship for everything in New England. That is in my judgement the real spring of most of the opposition.

Hillel Rogoff said the same that spring in the *Zukunft*, the monthly of the Jewish socialists: Brandeis was opposed by those who refused to accept that a Jew who wanted to change society belonged in that ultimate temple of America, the Supreme Court. Seats on that bench were reserved, so they insisted, for people like themselves. Walter Lippmann, defending and supporting Brandeis, expressed this opinion in *The New Republic*: Brandeis was feared and distrusted only by "the powerful but limited community that dominated the business and social life of Boston. He was untrustworthy because he was troublesome." The Brahmins of Boston had thus split in public over Brandeis's nomination. President Lowell of Harvard wanted only respectable Jews, and not too many of them, on America's public premises. Ex-President Eliot saw America, past and present, as constantly refreshing itself from new, even sometimes untamed, energies.

On June 1, 1916, after a bitter and bruising fight, Brandeis was confirmed. The battle that preceded the vote in the Senate was even more of a watershed than it appeared to be at the time. For years, the Jews of "downtown" had been railing against the paternalism of the "uptown" Jews, but there had been little criticism of their political attitudes. The "German Jews" had led the "Russians" in their fight against the czar, and against home-grown anti-Semitism. Now the Yiddish press was full of attacks on "Sha-sha Jews," that is, on those who wanted the Jews to be inconspicuous and to make no waves. This attitude continued to harden following Brandeis's confirmation. After he had been elevated to the Court, Brandeis had resigned all his other public positions, but he remained the undoubted, active leader and role model of the "Russian Jews."

II

In providing political legitimacy for the East European immigrants and for their children, Brandeis was far more important in the critical second decade of the twentieth century than much more "Jewish" figures, such as Stephen Wise and Judah Leon Magnes. Both of these men were Reform rabbis who had begun their careers in leading congregations of "German Jews," but they had moved away, very quickly, to identify with the East Europeans. Wise was one of the earliest American Zionists; he had joined the movement for the creation of a Jewish national home in Palestine before the turn of the century, and he was present in Basel as a delegate from America at the Second Zionist Congress in 1898. Wise came back to New York in 1907, after more than six years in Portland, Oregon. A few months earlier, he had been the leading candidate for the pulpit of Temple Emanu-El in New York, but he refused to agree that the lay board could censor his sermons. Wise made a public scandal of this altercation and he proceeded to create a platform of his own, the "Free Synagogue." Wise was a major figure in the fight for the American Jewish Congress, but the leader was Brandeis. Magnes had begun his public career as one of the rabbis of Temple Emanu-El in New York, the "cathedral" of Reform Judaism. In 1910, he had left that pulpit because he was ever more uncomfortable with the anti-Zionism and anti-Orthodoxy that pervaded the congregation. Magnes identified ever more with the new immigrants. For the next years, until he became embattled and marginal as a pacifist opponent of America's entry into the First World War, Magnes, the well-connected and well-established "American" Jew, was one of the preeminent leaders of the Yiddish-speaking ghetto.

Nonetheless, neither of these figures could stare down such powerful representatives of the "German Jews" as Jacob Schiff or Magnes's brother-in-law, Louis Marshall. Brandeis was the only American Jew who could challenge them from the left and in the name of the masses. He was the type of alienated aristocrat about whom Karl Marx had once talked when he explained the role of the Marquis de Lafayette in helping the dispossessed make the French Revolution. Jacob Schiff was Brandeis's major target. Schiff was a man of enormous presence and of princely charity. Though he was personally the leading member of Temple Emanu-El, Schiff helped in 1900 to reorganize the traditionalist Jewish Theological Seminary. Schiff had been born in Germany in an Orthodox family, and he retained much of the religious outlook of his youth. Schiff never did business on the Sabbath, even as he made it a practice to take a ride, grandly, in his carriage through Central Park on Sabbath afternoons. He went frequently to the Lower East Side, where he supported many social services and cultural institutions, to visit with his poorer brethren, and even to debate with them.

On one fabled occasion Schiff announced at the Educational Alliance, in the very heart of the Lower East Side, that he could not possibly be a Zionist because his sensibility was divided into thirds: one part American, one part Jewish, and one part German (that of the *Kultur* of his origins). A distinguished Zionist figure who was then living in America, Shmarya Levine, is reputed to have heckled him by asking: which third is which? Levine is supposed to have added, with vulgarity as well as irreverence: are the thirds divided horizontally or vertically? Reminiscing at Columbia University in 1968, near the end of his life, David Dubinsky, leader of the International Ladies Garment Workers Union, told of clashes with the police, when he led demonstrations against the capitalist bosses in his radical youth. Often, he and his comrades were jailed—but they were soon bailed out by Jacob Schiff, the archcapitalist Wall Street banker. These stories are worth telling because they help to bring to life the figure of an imperious hidalgo who did not avoid the immigrants by barricading himself in his Fifth Avenue mansion. Even his critics and enemies knew that Jacob Schiff was the towering figure in American Jewry and by near total consent the greatest lay figure in all its history.

Schiff had unbounded and very personal concern for all kinds of

Jews, even for those with whom he vehemently disagreed, but he drew the line at the nationalist theories of Zionism. Schiff supported the Jewish Theological Seminary generously until 1906, when he fell out with its president, Solomon Schechter, over Zionism. He then cut off support, and he ceased coming on Sunday mornings to board and committee meetings. Instead he used that time to go to the Montefiore Hospital in the Bronx, making a point of letting it be known that he was helping to count the linen in the laundry. He soon relented and came back to active involvement in the seminary, but his opinions did not change. An American Jew could not be a Zionist, so Schiff argued, because that would call into question his loyalty to the United States; one could not be, as the Zionists would have it, part of the Jewish nation and an American patriot at the same time. In 1916, at the height of the fight with the Zionists over "the war aims" of the Jewish people, Schiff pronounced:

> It is quite evident that there is a serious break coming between those who wish to force the formation of a distinct Hebraic element in the United States, as distinct from those of us who desire to be American in attachment, thought and action and Jews because of our religion as well as cultural attainments of our people. I am quite convinced of it that the American people will not willingly permit the formation of a large separate Hebraic group with national aspirations, and that if not we, our posterity are to become sufferers in consequence.

Schiff and his peers were, of course, responding to the outcry at the turn of the century against "hyphenated" Americans. They feared that Zionism would help "prove" the nativist case, that Jews had a different agenda than that of the American majority, as defined by the nativists. Schiff did push, sometimes even imperiously, to get the American government to help Jews in distress, but he and his colleagues spoke always in the name of such general American values as freedom and equality for all. He never demanded of America that it change its own self-definition in any respect.

Schiff was the "king of the Jews" until his authority was challenged by Louis Dembitz Brandeis. That Schiff would lose was inevitable, for by 1914 the "Russians" outnumbered the "Germans" by ten to one. Some of the East Europeans had quickly prospered in America. The more affluent had already established "second settlements" in

Brooklyn and Harlem. Nevertheless, August 1914 was a turning point, and not merely because the events of the next three years hastened the process of this "ethnic succession." What happened during the war years was no mere change of leaders; it was a revolution in the very content of American Jewish politics. The "Germans" had labored to achieve acceptance in America; the "Russians" pushed their angularities on the American majority.

III

The heightened vulnerability of the Jews in Eastern Europe after the outbreak of the First World War brought on the shift to Zionism in America. The front of hostilities between the Central Powers (Germany and Austria-Hungary) and the czarist empire ran through Poland and the Ukraine. This was the major center of Jewish population in the world, for it included the Russian "Pale of Settlement," the part of the czar's domain in which Jews were permitted to live; it also included Galicia, the southern part of Poland, which had been acquired by the Austrian Empire in the Partition of Poland at the end of the eighteenth century. Most of the hundreds of thousands of recent Jewish immigrants to the United States had come from this region. Every family had immediate relatives in the path of war. The situation of Jews in the war zone was particularly bad because the czarist regime had not relented in its anti-Semitic policies. It was all the worse for Jews because the advancing German armies were received as liberators; as the tide of battle changed and the Germans and Austrians retreated, Jews were attacked by the returning czarist authorities as spies and traitors. Even where there was no direct persecution, the Jews lacked food, shelter, and medical attention. Hundreds of thousands of underemployed Jewish poor had had all too little of the necessities of life in peacetime. In war, when there was no work, the situation was simply disastrous—and it was all the more so because the disruption of communications largely stopped the normal remittances from relatives in America.

The immediate reaction of American Jews to the war was to organize several relief organizations. The German Jewish leaders, Jacob Schiff, Louis Marshall, and Felix Warburg, Schiff's son-in-law and banking partner, convoked a meeting in October 1914 to establish the American Jewish Relief Committee. At the same time, the Orthodox community founded its own body, the Central Relief Committee. Within a month these two groups agreed to create the Joint Distribution Committee of American Funds for the Relief of Jewish War Sufferers. The Jewish unions remained aloof for a year; they supported their own People's Relief Committee. By 1915, they, too, agreed to work through the Joint Distribution Committee. All three of these groups which constituted the "Joint" (as it was popularly called) raised money separately, but their representatives sat together on the board of the operating agency. The lion's share of the money (more than two-thirds of the thirty-eight million dollars that was raised and spent between 1914 and 1920) came, of course, from the rich, who were the "German Jews." The other groups deferred to them—but the creation of the "Joint" was a turning point. It was the first major step forward for the East Europeans. The "monopoly" of the "German Jews" in the field of Jewish foreign policy had ended. The "Germans" and the "Russians" had sat together in the New York Kehillah, but the "Joint" marked the first time that the "Russian Jews" were admitted as equals in an endeavor on behalf of the Jews of the world.

Most of the "German Jews" remained opposed to Zionism, but one cause involving the Yishuv, the settlement in Palestine, did unite all elements of American Jewry. In 1915, after the Turks entered the war, they became highly suspicious of the Jews of Palestine, on the correct assumption that the new Zionist settlers favored the Allies. The Turkish military governor ordered all the Jews out of Palestine, and eighteen thousand were actually forced to leave. The majority went to Egypt. This expulsion was ended by the intervention of Turkey's principal ally, the German government; it did not want the Jews of America to be alienated. The ambassador of the United States in Constantinople (now Istanbul), Henry Morgenthau, Sr., spoke forcefully to the Turkish government but, even more important, he helped to organize relief for the Yishuv. A neutral, American ship, the *Vulcan,* came through the Mediterranean in 1915 with food and medical supplies. The bill was paid by the Joint Distribution Committee, the organization in which German and Russian Jews collaborated. Indeed, the "Joint" spent almost fifteen million dollars in support of the Yishuv during the war years. The rationale for this action was that those who were not Zionists—that is, those who did not share the state-building purposes of the Zionist settlers—would not, on that ground, discriminate against these pioneers when they were in need of humanitarian assistance. Some of the "German Jews" saw beyond the rhetoric of "humanitarian aid" to recognize that the "Russian Jews" had won yet another battle. The Zionist efforts in Palestine were now on everyone's budget.

A pattern was set for the future: financial aid would be extended to the Yishuv by a united American Jewish community as long as humanitarian concerns would be used as the explanation. On this basis, the Zionists could tap the resources of those who opposed nationalist ideology, and the non-Zionists could express their belonging to the extended family of all Jews while talking about the universal value of kindness to the downtrodden. This pragmatic alliance, to cooperate in relief efforts, worked well, then and later, but the Zionists and their opponents could not help but engage in raucous public battle with each other.

The big question was political, the future of East European Jewry: Could their lives be restored and even improved after the war in the places in which they lived? Was it more likely that many Jews would not be able to find a place for themselves when the hostilities ended? Should the Zionist solution, of establishing a Jewish homeland in Palestine, be embraced even by those who were not in ideological sympathy with Jewish nationalism, because such a homeland would offer a place for many Jews who would have to leave the countries of their birth? Should one, indeed, agree with the Zionists that the only permanent solution to anti-Semitism, and to the homelessness of the Jews, was in a Jewish state?

The preliminary skirmishes on these issues occurred almost immediately, in the fall of 1914. The "German Jews" had fought hard in America against restrictive immigration bills, and they were to continue the fight during and after the war. This battle was a matter of honor; they really did not want more immigrants. The existing East Sides were problem enough. The consensus in German Jewish circles was that Jews in danger in the war zones should not be encouraged to emigrate; they needed to be supported until a better time would come in their own countries. The old-line American Jews were not merely afraid of another wave of mass immigration to the United States. They refused to abandon the battle for a worldwide democratic order, for that would imply a lack of faith in the future of democracy even in America. One simply could not surrender on the insistence that Jews had as much right as anyone else to a future in their native lands.

This was not simply or even primarily an ideological debate about what direction American Jews would give their "unfortunate brethren" in Europe. In practice, both sides soon agreed to help both those in need in Europe and the emigrants regardless of destination; few doubted that there ought to be special concern for the settlers in Palestine. But, unlike the "German Jews," the immigrant masses were using their allegiance to Zionism to say something about themselves. They felt themselves to be an ethnic group, an extended family, a "peculiar people" in America. They would not pretend, as the "German Jews" more than half believed, that they were a religious denomination or a bunch of believers in universal abstractions about justice and democracy. Their chosen leader, Brandeis, might talk in such rhetoric, as he defined Zionism as a variation on the ideals of Progressivism in American politics. But the mass of East Europeans knew better. Zionism was for them a way of asserting folk feeling. American Zionism was an emotion and not an ideology. Zionism, in theory, insisted that the Jews were everywhere in exile, even in America. The recent immigrants, and their children, who were beginning to edge their way into American life, believed that proposition no more than they believed the rhetoric of the "German Jews." Despite their problems with sweatshop owners and with anti-Semites, the immigrants believed that America was different from all the previous habitations of the Jews.

Before 1914, Zionism in America had thus already defined itself as fundamentally different from Zionism in Europe. For the Europeans, Zionism meant that its adherents had banged the door shut on the surrounding culture, and that they looked to the possibility of emigrating to a new life in Palestine. In America, the bulk of the Zionists were immigrants who had made the decision not long before in Europe to leave for the United States and not for Palestine. They could hardly be asserting that their coming to the New World had been a mistake, and that Zionism required of them that they repack their bags and leave for Palestine. American Zionism existed to help the pioneers and to take pride in them.

Those who were constructing this sentimental, unideological program knew that theirs was a different brand of Zionism, and they were capable of self-mockery. The remark was going around in American Zionist circles as early as the 1890s that an American Zionist was someone who gives someone else a five-dollar contribution to send a European Jew to Palestine. But after 1914, those five dollars meant much more than the gibe implied. The donors were now bonding together to throw off the yoke of the "German Jews" and to enter the American political process.

The late summer of 1914 brought with it a further and decisive turning point in the self-understanding of American Zionism. The issue was power—and powerlessness. For twenty centuries, Jews in the Diaspora had been dependent on the goodwill of others. They were a people without a country of their own and without an army; they could only implore aggressors to be kind. Even after the Jews were made, by law, into equal citizens, their powerlessness remained a problem. The laws might proclaim the right of Jews to absolute equality, but these laws were not obeyed, or ignored and flouted. The modern Zionist movement arose out of a tragic assessment; wherever the majority society was heavily influenced by anti-Semitism, laws that proclaimed equality would not be heeded. Jews had to acquire some power which was securely in their own hands.

The identification of the "Russian Jews" with Zionism was deeply rooted in anger at their powerlessness. They were being told repeatedly that they were inferior both by the "German Jews" and by Gentiles. By acting as Zionists, these immigrants ceased being silent protégés of the "German Jews." By demanding power in the American Jewish community, and by refusing to let the "German Jews" speak for them to the Gentiles, the immigrants had taken the first major step toward refusing to remain "on approval" in America.

IV

On August 30, 1914, there was a Zionist meeting in New York to face the new problems that had been brought on by the outbreak of the war. The headquarters of the World Zionist Organization were in Berlin, and the members of its executive were scattered on both sides of the war fronts. The American Zionist movement, because it was situated in the greatest of the neutral countries, was asked to take over many of the responsibilities of the World Zionist Organization, especially the concern for the nascent Zionist settlements in Palestine. At this meeting Brandeis was elected chairman of the Provisional Executive Committee for General Zionist Affairs. In effect this meant that he had become the leader of American Zionism. In his acceptance speech, Brandeis spoke with total frankness. He admitted that he had been "to a great extent separated from Jews" and that he was "very ignorant in things Jewish." He had become identified with Jews because of their "deep moral feeling" and he cared about "the young Jewish Renaissance in the Holy Land." Brandeis warned that this "child of pain and sacrifice faces death from starvation." He accepted the office because he had come to "feel that the Jewish people have something which should be saved for the world; that the Jewish people should be preserved; and that it is our duty to pursue that method of saving which most promises success." Until that day in August 1914, Brandeis's East European followers were the poor relatives of the World Zionist movement. They had provided little money and no political or intellectual distinction. Suddenly they were the custodians of the whole of the Zionist future. Brandeis, a great name in America, one of the "German Jews," a kind of Moses who had grown up in the court of pharaoh, and then returned to them, had come to lead them.

That August day held another critical turning point. By his own confession, Brandeis was ignorant of things Jewish, but he felt no need to study Talmud or learn Hebrew as a prerequisite to Zionist leadership. It was more than enough, in his mind, that he identified Jews and Judaism with a passion for morality and intelligence, and that he set before himself, and American Jews as a whole, the labor for Zion as their common task. In effect, Brandeis had presented Zionism in America not as an outgrowth of Jewish history and tradition, which he did not know, but as their total replacement. Brandeis defined Zionism as a set of high-minded political and economic labors for Zion.

Thus, while Brandeis provided prestige to the masses, he was even more important to them because he helped them define themselves. It was Brandeis who made legitimate in American Jewry the severing of Jewishness from Judaism, including even the new Judaism of the Zionist settlers in Palestine—in the name of Zionism. The founder of the modern Zionist movement, Theodor Herzl, who was almost totally removed from the religious and cultural aspects of Jewish life, had done this before, but the bulk of his followers had opposed him on these issues. The European Zionist movement had identified itself ever more closely with the building of national Hebraic culture. Zionism without culture, a movement that had fund-raising and the mounting of political pressure as its content, existed only in America.

The American environment as a whole played a shaping role in defining this local brand of Zionism. European Zionists lived in countries where ideologies were taken seriously; the New World has very seldom been the home of deep ideological ferment, for Americans have usually been doers rather than thinkers. Even recent immigrants, such as the first generation of American Zionists, responded to the majority culture by fashioning their Zionism into a set of tangible acts instead of a national ideology. Deeds were, of course, more accessible to the mass of Jews than ideas. These predispositions were accentuated, and very nearly cast in concrete, by the events of the war years. This was not the time for publication of a grammar of modern Hebrew, or for engaging in deep reflections on the meaning of Jewish history. The Yishuv, the Jewish settlement in Palestine, was under the hostile rule of the Turks, and it had to be safeguarded. The time demanded that American Jews come to the rescue by exerting political pressure and sending money and supplies.

In the early months of 1915 agitation began first in England and then in the United States for the Zionist movement to identify with the cause of the Allies. The British government was pressured to accept an all Jewish detachment into its armed forces. If Jews fought in the war as a national unit, so the argument went, then the Jewish people would be recognized as a cobelligerent with a right to make claims at the peace table. The men available for such a unit were Russian immigrants to England (until late in the war, the British army was all volunteer) and their cousins in the United States, before it entered the war in 1917. Young Jews who had been born in Czarist Russia were not eager to go fight for the Allies. A Jewish formation was therefore proposed; the Jews as a people could point to their share in the victory and they would have the right to ask at war's end for a homeland in Palestine. The Zion Mule Corps was organized in 1915 among the Russian Jewish immigrants to Great Britain. This supply unit took part in the Gallipoli campaign, the abortive attempt by Britain to force the Dardanelles Straits. Because the Zion Mule

Corps was in action against Turkey, which possessed Palestine, Jews had at least shared in a battle for the liberation of their homeland. Jews had fought under a battalion flag of their own on a war front that included the ancestral home of the Jews.

After the failure of the action at Gallipoli, Great Britain disbanded the Zion Mule Corps. Its volunteers went back to England, but the notion of helping the military liberation of Palestine was not dead. Quite on the contrary, two young men who were then already leading figures in the Yishuv, Yitzhak Ben-Zvi and David Ben-Gurion, arrived in New York from Palestine in 1915. They came to organize a Jewish unit to fight as part of the British army on the battle line between the British and Turks on the very borders of Palestine. It took more than two years of effort to persuade the British to accept such a unit, but the result was two battalions which were attached to the Royal Fusiliers. Ben-Zvi and Ben-Gurion, and a number of men whom they had enlisted while America was still neutral, found their way through Canada to the recruiting offices for these two battalions; one of the two units consisted mainly of volunteers from America. In the spring of 1918, these two battalions were sent to Egypt. These Jewish units actually fought on the front in the campaign to conquer Palestine, and they were in the country by the end of the war. The Balfour Declaration had already been issued on November 2, 1917. Great Britain had declared, through its foreign secretary, that it favored the establishment of a Jewish national home in Palestine. Thus the presence of a Jewish military formation under its own flag was of great symbolic and emotional significance to the Jews. Here was the kernel of a Jewish army in the Jewish Palestine.

The number of Jews who actually went to fight in Palestine was not large. There were some eight hundred, of whom about two hundred came from the United States, but hearts were lifted in America by high-flown words about "the first Jewish army since Bar-Kochba" (he had been the commander of the last revolt against Rome in the years 132–35). There were meetings all over the country in praise of the soldiers of the Jewish people. The American Jews had helped out with money. They had saved the Jewish settlement from hunger and expulsion by the Turks, and they had supported the cause of the Jewish fighting battalions. In return, American Jews received a glorious sense of their own power and of their participation in the renaissance of Jewish power in the land of the ancestors.

V

The skirmishes, the guerrilla warfare, and the pitched battles between the "German Jews" and the "Russians" culminated in one titanic fight: whether to organize a countrywide, representative body, the American Jewish Congress. Of their own free will, American Jews had created many organizations, both large and small, but there was no structure that encompassed all American Jews. Therefore, no orderly way existed to create a consensus about the "war aims" of the American Jewish community. This situation was essentially comfortable for the "German Jews," who had created the American Jewish Committee in 1906 to represent their political views. The members of this body were a small, self-chosen elite of the rich and "American" Jews, and they preferred to continue to make policy without interference from the Jewish masses. The only way in which Brandeis and his associates could challenge this plutocracy was by insisting on the pernicious doctrine of "one man, one vote" in Jewish affairs. This meant that those who had money would be expected to continue to pay the bills for Jewish needs while being denied control of Jewish political policy.

The Zionists had the upper hand almost from the beginning. Emotions were running high at the sight of European Jews in trouble, but, more important, it was difficult to argue in a democratic America against democracy in Jewish life. There was much infighting and intrigue, but within two years, the "German Jews" had lost the battle. In the end, the "Germans" had to agree to the calling of elections throughout the United States for an American Jewish Congress, in which the delegates would vote on the "war aims" of American Jewry.

A preparatory session of the American Jewish Congress took place in Philadelphia in 1916, where Stephen Wise spoke for the Zionists; they wanted, "not relief but redress, not palliation but prevention, not charity but justice." Thus the Zionists, who were at the head of the vast majority of the East Europeans, announced their independence from the German Jewish philanthropists. Internal Jewish politics made it difficult to proceed to immediate elections for the American Jewish Congress. President Wilson intervened in this internal affair of the Jews (this was the first such act in American history). Wilson suggested to Brandeis that such a Jewish demonstration would be inopportune at that stage of the war. The elections were postponed until the spring of 1918. One element in immigrant Jewry, the left-wing socialists, boycotted the election because it was, then, still opposed to the Zionists, who were in control of the movement for the American Jewish Congress. The masses refused to follow this socialist splinter among the immigrants. Hundreds of thousands of votes were cast, and it was a nearly complete victory for the Zionists. In an imperfect world, it could not be doubted that the results were largely representative.

When the meeting finally took place in December 1918, the American Jewish Congress agreed by overwhelming majority to push for a Jewish national homeland in Palestine. The representatives of the American Jewish Committee, who were present under the leadership of Louis Marshall, succeeded in softening the resolution so that it was not an outright insistence on a Jewish state. On this basis, they were able to agree to a united American Jewish delegation to lobby at the future peace conference. There were, however, some people in this group, most notably Cyrus Adler (speaking, so everyone presumed, for Jacob Schiff), who remained in opposition. In Adler's view, if Zionist aspirations were a cause of any prominence at the peace conference, the anti-Semites in the new successor states to the Austro-Hungarian and Russian empires would simply be able to say to Jews: "Get out to your own homeland."

On March 2, 1919, a delegation from the American Jewish Congress presented a memorial to President Wilson asking him to support the Balfour Declaration. The anti-Zionists in the American Jewish Committee, including Adolph Ochs, the publisher of *The New York Times,* refused to go along with their own more moderate leaders, who had participated in the American Jewish Congress. On March 5, 1919, they published their own memorial of "warning and protest." They were opposed to the "demands of the Zionists for the reorganization of the Jews into a self-governing, ethnic entity in America and to the creation of Jewish territorial sovereignty in Palestine."

The American Jewish Congress had been envisioned as a continuing body, a voluntary parliament of American Jewry. This did not happen, because after the war almost all the groups, except the Zionists, preferred to go their own ways. Nevertheless, the victory of the Zionists in forcing even this one meeting in Philadelphia was a great turning point in American Jewish life. The East European immigrants had used the only weapon that they really possessed, their numbers and their passion, in the only forum in which these assets mattered, in the first election that American Jews had ever held on a nationwide basis. The moderate majority among the "German Jews" did not simply walk away, not then, during the fight for the American Jewish Congress, or later. They led in supporting relief efforts which helped Jews in need everywhere and especially the Zionist settlements in Palestine.

Numbers mattered. The Zionists had acquired mass support. In 1914 the enrolled strength of the American Zionist movement had been less than 12,000; within four years there were 176,000 members in the American Zionist Federation, and more belonged to a variety of smaller Zionist bodies. In the next several years, Zionist strength grew some. Membership then dropped dramatically. But, despite ups and downs in the Zionist rolls, the feelings of the East European majority of American Jews remained consistent: the Jews were a worldwide people, and Jews in trouble were safest and best off in their own land.

At times of upset and danger like the First World War (or, later, in the Hitler years), this emotion translated itself into rising Zionist membership. Whether organized or unorganized, the masses of the East Europeans had made an irrevocable choice: they thought of themselves not as "Americans of the Jewish faith," but as members of a people. The mainstream of the German Jewish establishment moved toward the "Russian Jews," for they would not abandon or alienate themselves from their larger family. The self-definition of "Americans of the Jewish faith" remained in force in theory, but in real life it was displaced by the label, non-Zionist—not an opponent of Zionism, but a fellow traveler, who cared about the Jews in Palestine, but who did not adhere to a nationalist definition of the Jewish people.

Some years earlier, before the rift over the calling of the American Jewish Congress, Louis Marshall had even learned Yiddish in order to be able to communicate with the immigrants; his influence in the American Jewish Committee was toward moderate, nonconfrontationist policies. Felix Warburg, Jacob Schiff's son-in-law, continued to cooperate with the Zionists in nonpolitical concerns, including the physical and cultural renaissance in Jewish Palestine. Men like Louis

Marshall and Felix Warburg were religious believers; they knew that helping people (and especially Jews) had been commanded by God. But they also wanted to belong to the Jewish people—and the masses of that people, the immigrants, had moved in a few short years from being a protectorate of the "German Jews" to the very center of Jewish and American life. The total opponents of Zionism among the "German Jews," the old believers of Reform Judaism, had been pushed to the margin.

Virtually all the "Russian Jews" would remain poor, and all would be semi-alien, for another generation, but by the early 1920s, they had become the dominant force in American Jewry.

14.

Closing the Gates

I

The children of the immigrants had to fight for power in America, not least because Congress kept telling them that they were really not wanted. The Constitution of the United States guaranteed equality for all citizens, but even in law that promise was not kept until 1965. For more than forty years the immigration law had been biased, overtly and without apology, against Jews, Slavs, and Italians. They were admitted to the United States in small numbers to ensure that the population of the country would continue to be dominated by the descendants of immigrants from Northern and Western Europe. Congress had implicitly declared that some people were better than others; America wanted more tall, blond, blue-eyed immigrants, and fewer short, dark-skinned brunettes.

During the war over American immigration policy which had begun in the 1890s, two propositions had been advanced by those who wanted to close the doors of America. The first was a basic premise, thought to be so self-evident that it needed no proof: the American population must continue to consist, in its majority, of descendants of the earliest, prerevolutionary white Anglo-Saxon Protestants. Statistics were produced, with supposedly impressive scholarly authority behind them, to "prove" that American society was barely in its majority of such composition, and that further immigration of Slavs, Italians, and Jews would tip the balance in an "un-American" direction. It was argued, further, that the original American stock would be flawed by the introduction of more such immigrants, because Slavs, Italians, and Jews were of a lower intellectual and moral stature—and statistics were invoked to "prove" that Slavs, Italians, and Jews were unintelligent, indeed that they were the least bright of all the groups in America except for the Native Americans.

In the war years, immigration became a more important issue. Most of the Jews of Europe lived in the borderlands where the Russians fought the Austro-Hungarians and the Germans. By 1917, at least one million on both sides were refugees. Jewish relief efforts, which emphasized the great suffering of these refugees, could only suggest, both to friends and enemies, that there would be large-scale emigration as soon as the war was over. This became even more certain after the armistice in November 1918. The Bolshevik Revolution was at that time a year old. Several counterrevolutionary armies were trying to overthrow the Reds, and the newly created Polish army was attempting to advance into Russia. Between 1919 and 1921, at least sixty thousand Jews were slaughtered in this region, some by the Poles and most by the Ukrainians, often under the pretense that Jews were supporters of the Bolsheviks.

Both Zionists and "German Jews" were eager to help the sufferers, but in radically different ways. The Zionists maintained that Jews in trouble in Europe should go to the nascent national home in Palestine. Zionists and non-Zionists joined in fighting hard and successfully for guarantees of equality before the law in all the states, including Poland, which had been created by the peace treaty of 1919. These men sincerely believed that Eastern Europe would settle down after the war into a culture of parliamentary democracy. Many even added the hope that the Bolshevik regime, which they did not like because it was Communist, would in its own way treat Jews with fairness and equality. For a very short while, a wish bordering on fantasy existed among those who opposed the pessimism of the Zionists about the future of the Jews in Europe that many who had already come to the United States would want to return to their original homes.

The reverse was true. Jews in Eastern Europe were undergoing no renaissance; they were being murdered by the thousands. The Joint Distribution Committee acted courageously, sending relief wherever possible during the fighting between the Bolsheviks and White Russians, and during the Polish-Russian War. The Jewish effort was "legitimate," because the American government itself, much as it detested Bolshevism, had allowed a commission under Herbert Hoover to raise and spend millions between 1919 and 1921 in revolutionary Russia to alleviate suffering. Jewish relief continued even after the Hoover Commission ceased to function. These humanitarian endeavors were not attacked in the United States, even at the height of the Red Scare of 1919–21. The leaders of the Joint Distribution Committee were "German Jews" who were beyond suspicion of Communism.

The sight of the horrors in Eastern Europe moved the chairman of the House Immigration Committee, Albert Johnson, to propose a two-year suspension of immigration, as an emergency measure until a permanent policy could be worked out. Early in 1921, Johnson reported to the House that East European Jews had come through Ellis Island in great numbers in the previous few months. He quoted an unnamed officer of the Hebrew Immigrant Aid Society as saying, "If there was in existence a ship that would hold three million human beings, the three million Jews of Poland would board it to escape to America." More damaging still to the cause of the Jews, Johnson quoted Wilbur S. Carr, the head of the United States Consular Service. Carr had surveyed the conditions at a number of ports in Europe, and found that the Polish Jews were the worst of all the potential immigrants. They were "filthy, un-American and often dangerous in their habits . . . lacking any conception of patriotism or national spirit." As we have seen, something like this had been said almost a century earlier, in the 1830s, by a British traveler—and repeated by American observers—about the "German Jews," who were then trading on Chatham Street in New York.

Though the forces pushing for immigration restrictions had not forgotten their distaste for Slavs and Italians, Jews were still their main target. When hearings were held in the Senate on the proposed legislation, Jewish representatives testified, chiefly to deny that there was any probability of large-scale immigration from Poland. Some of the Jewish leaders, even among the "Russian Jews," were admitting in private that such immigration would be difficult to digest, but they opposed quotas on Polish Jews as an affront to the Jews already in America. The Senate committee heard comparable opinions from representatives of American business, and it therefore agreed that there was no immediate emergency. The Senate substituted its own proposal for an immigration law—it decided to limit the numbers of new arrivals to three percent of the foreign-born of each national group who were present in the United States according to the census of 1910. The House concurred in the Senate version. This bill was signed by Warren Harding in May 1921. For the first time in all of American history, immigration restrictions based on national origins had become law. The editorial writers of the Yiddish press knew exactly what had happened. In the words of the *Morgen Journal:* "Our kin is fleeing from persecution both individual and governmental, and the question of emigration is to most of our brethren one of life or death, not merely of economic betterment. We are more hopeful than others that in the end the portals of our country will remain open for victims of political and religious persecution."

This hope would not be realized. On the contrary, the pressure kept mounting for an even more restrictive immigration policy. There were two new notes in the antiforeign outcry: the fear of the Bolsheviks, that more radicals would come from Russia to join the deplorable number who were already present in the United States, and the supposed certainties of eugenics as a way of controlling the quality of human population.

In 1919, A. Mitchell Palmer, the red-baiting attorney general of the United States, went looking for the Bolsheviks in America. He used the Justice Department's Bureau of Investigation (forerunner of the Federal Bureau of Investigation) to help in the tracking down of Communists. Palmer had no particular bias against the Jews, but his campaign against Communism lent itself to such uses. Jews were prominent among Communists, both in Russia and in the United States. A forgery of a generation earlier, the *Protocols of the Elders of Zion,* was published in the United States in 1919. The document asserted that Jews were all part of a conspiracy to dominate the world, and that this conspiracy was directed by a central body of influential Jews. The *Protocols of the Elders of Zion* had most probably been concocted twenty years earlier by the secret police of the Russian czar to justify his anti-Semitic policies. Henry Ford, the most famous industrialist in America, financed a daily newspaper in his hometown of Dearborn, Michigan, *The Dearborn Independent,* which had this fantasy reprinted in hundreds of thousands of copies. The *Protocols* made it possible to believe that Jewish capitalists like the Rothschilds and Communists like Leon Trotsky were all part of the same power directorate, and that these known leaders were controlled by even more mysterious and remote figures. This theory of Jewish world conspiracy would thus "explain" the success of the Bolshevik Revolution—and it could act as a warning against allowing the Jews to extend their wealth and power in any society, including the United States. On the basis of this forgery, Ford's paper became the chief trumpet of anti-Semitism in America in the 1920s.

The trouble with the accusation of Jewish Communism was that it had just sufficient truth in it to make the tale plausible to Jew-haters. Though Communism was never a strong force in America, not even in its salad days before and during the Russian Revolution, Jews were very prominent in the movement. In the 1920s, there were approximately fifteen thousand enrolled members of the Communist party of the United States; the Yiddish-speaking section represented about one-tenth of the membership, but Jews were also very important in the English-speaking section which numbered, by 1925, 2,282 of the total membership of 16,325. This rising membership was motivated by domestic exclusions in America, but it reflected, as well, the large initial sympathy within the Jewish community for the Bolshevik Revolution. In the earliest years of the new regime, both Jewish religion and Jewish nationalism were persecuted, and their institutions were essentially outlawed, but the Soviet Union did allow and encourage secular Jewish culture in Yiddish. In the 1920s there was substantial sympathy for the Soviet Union among many Jews who abhorred Communism and were outraged by the persecution of religion. The Bolshevik regime was perceived, then, as the one government in the world which actively fought anti-Semitism and fostered Yiddish culture. Jews were thus a striking, obvious, easy-to-find element in American Communism, and the "defense" of the country against subversion could, and was, easily translated into lessening the numbers and the power of Jews in America.

The old outcry against Jews, Slavs, and Italians was given additional respectability by the supposed science of eugenics. In 1911, the American Breeders Association had commissioned a study to find "the practical means for cutting off the defective germ-plasm in the American population." The conclusions of the study were published three years later. The authors were supremely confident that they could point out scientifically the bearers of defective genes, such as "the feeble-minded class" and the "pauper class," as well as the bearers of epilepsy and insanity. Sterilization was the defensive measure of choice to protect the population. Such thoughts were sufficiently respectable so that Louis Marshall, a longtime leader in the fight for open immigration, was a member of the expert advisory committee. He clearly did not foresee that theories about eugenics would be used in a very few years to help curtail the immigration of "undesirables" from Europe.

The secretary of the committee, Harry H. Laughlin, was the scholar who would reassure the House Immigration Committee in 1924 that it did well by the Republic when it passed the new immigration law in the spring of that year. Under this bill, quotas were now based on figures from 1890, when the foreign-born from Southern and Eastern Europe were much fewer. The result was that less than 6,000 Jews could be admitted in any year from Poland, about 2,000 from Russia, and 600 from Romania. These were the countries from which almost all Jews had come in the past. Italians were no better off; less than 4,000 would be allowed to come to America in any one year. In contrast, the quota for Germany was 51,000, for Great Britain and Northern Ireland, 34,000, and more than 28,000 for the Irish Free State. Switzerland was allocated almost as many places as Russia; Norway had more than 6,000 and Sweden had more than 9,000.

The bias of the law was clear. Hearings were held in November 1924, when the committee already had in front of it the figures on arriving immigrants in the fiscal year which had ended June 30. More than 60,000 Italian immigrants and 50,000 Jews had arrived. Henry Laughlin told the committee the truth when he defined the basis of the new law as the assertion that "immigration into the United

States . . . is primarily a biological problem, and secondarily a problem in economics and charity." The committee had adopted an immigration policy on "the biological basis."

Lest the committee have any second thoughts about the "biological basis" of the quota law, Laughlin used very recent "scientific" evidence from army experts which "proved" that people from Southern and Eastern Europe were intellectually and morally inferior. He paraded the results of standardized intelligence tests which had been given to a random group of about a hundred thousand draftees into the American army after the United States entered the war. The categories of analysis ranged from the "very superior," persons who were "capable of high-class creative work," to "very inferior," that is, the kind of person in whose case it was "doubtful if the value of labor equals cost of supervision." In five elaborate tables Laughlin reiterated the same message: of all the recent immigrants, the English were the most intelligent, and Russians, Greeks, Italians, Belgians, and Poles were almost totally stupid. American Negroes, though much less intelligent than native-born whites, were three times as bright as the Belgians, seven times as intelligent as the Poles, and fifty percent brighter than the Russians. It did not seem to have occurred either to the army psychologists or to Dr. Laughlin that the intelligence tests were based on schooling in, and comprehension of, standard English, and that Negroes and recent immigrants, even the Einsteins among them, were at a marked disadvantage. One suspects that the authors of this study, and those who used it against the people whom they regarded as "undesirable," were not motivated by pure, self-critical zeal for scientific truth. There was more than a breath of the doctrine of Aryan supremacy in the air.

Congress overwhelmingly supported this law, while the opposition to it was divided. Though the National Catholic Welfare Conference had called the Johnson Act of 1921 racist, and the Federal Council of Churches, of the Protestants, asked for restrictions on immigration not based on race, neither group testified at the congressional hearings in 1924. Even Jewish congressmen, such as Emanuel Celler of New York, were willing to accept immigration quotas if the base year were kept at 1910, and not the much more restrictive 1890. On the surface, all Jews, "German" and "Russian" alike, were united in opposing the law, but the "German Jews" were visibly upset by the Red Scare. In January 1919, the *American Hebrew* had published an editorial in which it warned that "the immigrants from Russia and Austria will be coming from countries infected with Bolshevism and it will require more than a superficial effort to make good citizens out of them." Two years later, in September 1921, this same journal was busy trumpeting the one hundred percent Americanism of the Jews. Louis Marshall, who remained firm in opposing any attempt to restrict immigration, wrote in 1921 to Israel Zangwill, the Anglo-Jewish man of letters and politics, that a large number of Jews who disliked the new immigrants were actually on the side of restriction.

In the mid-1920s, the second generation, the children of the immigrants, was still young and largely inarticulate. Its spokesmen did not participate in the debate about immigration, but the passage of the law taught these children of immigrants a bitter lesson. They were second-class citizens in America. They were, at best, on approval. To be sure, Henry Ford was forced in 1927 to recant his anti-Semitism. It was bad for business. Ford cars were being boycotted by Jews and by some liberal Christians. Ford wrote a letter to Louis Marshall withdrawing his anti-Semitic allegations, and he closed down *The Dearborn Independent*. This was a victory of sorts, but fundamental damage had been done. Red-baiting and nativism set the seal on a conviction that was widely held in the 1920s by people who did not consider themselves Jew-haters. Jews were not seen as individuals; they were attacked as a group for being different and clannish, with a tendency toward political radicalism. But the Jews learned something. Jews read the victory as a result not of a change of heart by Ford but as his bowing to the power that they had marshaled against him. This incident was an important lesson in a truth about America: it is better to depend on power than on goodwill.

In the face of attacks by the anti-Semites, the Jewish leadership of the 1920s was back where their predecessors had been in the 1890s. They were again forced to "prove" their patriotism and their contribution to the making of America. The American Jewish publications of those years were full of lists of Jews who had achieved honorific positions in politics and in law and medicine. These lists were sad reading, and not only because such apologetics could never convince anti-Semites that they were wrong. The numbers that could be found were small, far less than the proportion of the Jews in the

American population as a whole (it was then three and a half percent).

Three centuries earlier the Puritans had created their common-wealth to include only the elect. Jews were particularly alien, because only the Puritans understood the truth of the Bible; unconverted Jews were subversive. In the 1920s, these notions, in up-to-date versions, now dominated immigration policy and much of American social thought. There were inferior races who had to be kept out, and kept at a distance even after they arrived. Jews were particularly problematic, because they had a marked propensity to radical or revolutionary ideology. Before the onset of the Second World War, almost no Jew could make a free, personal decision about his edu-cation and career. At every turn, the fact of his Jewishness meant that many, if not most, options were simply not available to him. There was a fence around Jews.

II

In the 1920s and 1930s, American-born Jews in New York and Chi-cago were almost as much in the ghetto as Polish-speaking Jews in Warsaw or Romanian-speaking Jews in Bucharest. To be sure, there were no pogroms in America and little physical violence, but many occupations excluded Jews entirely. Despite the protests of their ene-mies that the Jews controlled banking and finance, the opposite was true. Jews had remained a minority on Wall Street, even as America was experiencing its stock-market fever in the years before the Crash of October 1929. There was an effective ban on allowing the Jews into the banking business. Banks could be created only through state or national charter. Only one such charter had ever been issued to Jewish owners, to a New York concern called the Bank of the United States. After the crash of 1929, this bank was actually among the most solvent. It was forced into bankruptcy because none of the larger banks would give the Jewish-owned bank any help in weath-ering the crisis. The few Jews who held jobs in banking, even at the lowest rungs of management, were usually those who hid their origins. In the insurance industry, almost no Jews could be found in the central management of the various firms. Thousands of Jews were independent agents. Such endeavors were white-collar versions of pushcart peddling; the insurance companies were willing to make a profit on whatever policies these petty Jewish businessmen would sell. The situation was the same in heavy industry; the management of the steel and the coal companies, and the auto manufacturers, were simply closed to Jews.

The barriers in education were equally formidable. Before the early 1920s, Jews who applied were admitted quite freely to Ivy League schools. The Jewish proportion at Yale rose from two percent in 1901 to thirteen percent in 1925. At Harvard the proportion was seven percent in 1900 and twenty-one and a half percent in 1922. In 1922, it leaked from Harvard that a Jewish quota was being imposed. Jews had become so prominent that they were changing the character of the colleges and challenging Gentile supremacy. President A. Lawrence Lowell of Harvard, who had led the attack against Brandeis, defended the idea of a quota by suggesting that if "every college in the country would take a limited proportion of Jews, we should go a long way toward eliminating race feeling among the students." Lowell was forced to retract his view because of public outrage, but in actual fact the proportion of Jews in the Harvard student body went down after this incident. At Yale, a decision was made that students should henceforth be admitted on the basis of "character" rather than strictly on scholarship. Dean Frederick Jones had found that "every single scholarship of any value is won by a Jew" and "that we could not allow that to go on, we must put a ban on the Jews." He agreed that "in terms of scholarship and intelligence, Jewish students lead the class, but their personal characteristics make them markedly inferior." At Columbia a Jewish proportion of forty percent in 1920 was cut in half within two years.

The quotas in the medical schools forced many hundreds of young Jews to go abroad, to schools in various countries in Europe, especially to Italy, for their medical education. Even after they graduated, Jewish doctors were still in trouble; the Gentile-controlled hospitals allowed very few Jews to join their staffs. In the 1920s and 1930s, Jewish hospitals existed not so much to take care of Jewish patients as to provide places in which Jewish doctors could practice. There were so few Jewish professors in the American medical schools that medical education and research were essentially closed to Jews. Jewish doctors had little choice but to enter private practice. This was equally true of the Jewish lawyers, for there were very few Jewish firms—and the non-Jewish firms simply did not hire Jews.

A Jewish lawyer could only hang up a shingle and hope to build a personal practice.

These increasingly severe quotas in the colleges and universities were a lesser part of the problem. At least in theory, the administrators who had enacted these exclusions had tried to "explain" that Jews could be assimilated only in small, dispersed numbers. There was no such pretense at the top of American intellectual life. The most modern American writers, Ernest Hemingway and F. Scott Fitzgerald, mentioned Jews only to insist that they were irretrievably outsiders. The English departments of the universities allowed very few Jewish teachers on the premises. By anti-Semitic definition, no matter what he knew or thought, a Jew was simply incapable of entering into the spirit of Anglo-Saxon literature, or, for that matter, of American history. Lionel Trilling worked at his alma mater, Columbia University, as an instructor in English between 1932 and 1936, but was not reappointed. The spokesman of the department explained to him that he would not be happy there "as a Freudian, a Marxist, and [a] Jew." It took the personal intervention three years later of Columbia's formidable president, Nicholas Murray Butler, to force Trilling's appointment as assistant professor in Columbia's English Department. Even so, Trilling's painful victory was rare. The existing American intellectual establishment of the 1920s and 1930s never made room for Jews. Some American intellectuals had found Jews interesting, in early immigrant days, as exotics who wrote in Yiddish and lived in a pulsating ghetto. Their children were no longer exotic. They were American-born and educated, brilliantly so, but their very achievement in becoming "Americans" stood against them. They had become potential competitors of their Gentile fellow students—and even of their teachers. Almost without exception these young Jews were kept out of America.

But academically trained Jews who were trying to enter the professions were a minority. The majority of the children of the immigrants, and of their parents, were going into business in the 1920s. In the years before the Crash of October 1929, many were getting rich. This contradicts one of the accepted "truths" about the history of the Jews in America, that the "German Jews," who arrived in the middle of the nineteenth century, became rich in their own lifetimes, but that the East Europeans did not achieve wealth until the next generation. Supposedly, they had to wait because there were so many of them. This construction offers a partial explanation of the differences between the "Germans" and the "Russians," but it leaves out a significant and little remembered part of the story. It skips from the sweatshops of the 1910s to the mass unemployment of the 1930s, without paying attention to the 1920s. In that decade, the Roaring Twenties, as the stock market rose steadily from 1924 until the famous Crash in October 1929, a considerable number of the East European immigrants were becoming wealthy all over America. These new rich were the immigrants themselves and not their children, who were then still too young to be making fortunes. It was not until 1940 that a bare majority of all American Jews were native-born.

Those who devised the questionnaires for self-studies of Jewish communities almost never asked questions about income and wealth: don't let anti-Semites know that the Jews are doing "too well." The several studies that were done by outsiders were no more informative, for Jews were even less likely to tell Gentiles the truth about their earnings. Consequently there is no direct evidence to support the assertion that a considerable minority of the East European immigrants were becoming rich in the 1920s. But rising gifts to Jewish charities make this assertion highly probable. Between 1918 and 1926, the donations to domestic Jewish charities nearly doubled. In 1918 the Jewish federations (community chests) of the four largest Jewish communities—New York, Chicago, Philadelphia, and Boston—disbursed a bit over $4.8 million to the local agencies they supported; in 1926 the disbursements had reached $8.5 million. These figures, which came from a set of tables published each year in the American Jewish Yearbook, appeared for the last time in 1926: they were growing at a rate which the yearbook's editors, always concerned about anti-Semitism, did not want used by enemies of Jews and "Wall-Street bankers."

It can be argued that these contributions to domestic charity came in those years primarily from the rich "German Jews" (there is no breakdown by origin of the contributors). However, the formation of new congregations and especially the erection of new synagogue buildings in that decade point to an increased wealth among the "Russian Jews." In 1908 there were only seventeen hundred permanently organized Jewish congregations in the United States; ten years later, at the end of the war, there were two hundred more. In the years 1917–19 a building boom began; seventy-three new synagogues were dedicated in those years, and no more than ten were Reform. By 1928, the number of organized congregations had jumped to three thousand. These new synagogues were not being organized by "German Jews," who had more than enough space in their existing temples. Over a thousand new congregations, with the budgets that they required, were funded in the 1920s by recent immigrants who suddenly had the necessary money.

The boom in synagogue building was even more striking. A number of Reform congregations built new buildings in that decade, moving with their congregants to more elegant surroundings, but the new synagogue buildings, in their vast majority, were paid for by recent immigrants. A large number of imposing synagogues were built in the 1920s in the neighborhoods of "second settlement" into which East European Jews were moving. Whether on the Grand Concourse in the Bronx or on Park Heights Avenue and Forest Park Avenue in Baltimore, the newly affluent "Russian Jews," by placing their synagogue buildings on the most public thoroughfares, were announcing their presence on the American scene, just as the "German Jews" had done in the 1860s and 1870s.

The pitched battles of the early 1920s over the exclusion of Jews from the "best" colleges is another oblique proof of the rise of the East Europeans to affluence. Two decades earlier their children had been going to the city colleges; by the early 1920s many were still poor, and their children made their way to the Ivy League schools by winning the competition for scholarships. However, there was not enough such aid to poor, bright Jews to explain the Harvard class of 1922, in which very nearly one out of every four students was a Jew. Most were paying tuition, there and elsewhere among the Ivies, because their parents could now afford the bills. The economic profile of immigrant Jews as a whole had been transformed in twenty years. In 1900, the immigrants were two-thirds workers and one-third in white-collar pursuits. By 1920 two-thirds were in business or white-collar jobs and only one-third were still workers. When the best private colleges more than half-closed their doors to Jews in the early 1920s, this was a blow not only to poor Jews but also to newly affluent immigrants and their children.

Many immigrant Jews participated in the bull market of the mid-1920s. In the era of speculation, poor Jews of yesteryear had a particularly passionate need to believe that the future was unbounded. But, of course, the immigrants who became rich in the 1920s did not all engage in speculating on the stock market. In a buoyant economy hundreds upon hundreds entered the risky business of manufacturing clothing, and they did very well until the Crash came and consumers had no money with which to buy new clothes. Numerous other kinds of small businesses and retail stores prospered before 1929. The massive move of Jews to new neighborhoods provided large opportunities in real estate. New buildings were going up in the Bronx and on the Upper West Side of New York, and in equivalent places in all the other cities in which there was large Jewish population. The builders of these high-rise apartment houses, or of row houses in Brooklyn, were almost all Jews. So long as the economic situation was on the upswing, apartments were in demand, rent was paid on time, and the assets of the entrepreneurs kept growing. After the Crash, many of those who had built these buildings were very soon bankrupt. Their tenants could not pay rent, and soon the landlords could not meet obligations to the banks which held the mortgages. The Jewish labor unions, which had felt powerful and rich in the 1920s, could not keep up with the payment of benefits to members out of work. Jewish charities had much less money to pay for social services for the poor, and their money now came mostly from the "German Jews," who, being better established, were weathering the Depression.

The Crash of 1929 aborted the dash of a significant minority of East European immigrants to affluence in their own lifetime. They, the parents, were bankrupt, and they would not be able to pass on functioning businesses and fortunes to their children. Many of the American-born young who had been enjoying the pleasures of the Jazz Age had to find jobs in the America of the Depression years, in which anti-Semitism was rising. They were suddenly poor and defenseless Jews, even in America.

III

In discussing anti-Semitism in America before the Second World War, too quick a jump has often been made to 1933, the year in which Hitler came to power in Germany. The story of anti-Semitism in the United States between the two wars has thus tended to become an account of the effect in America of reechoes first of Bolshevism and then of the Nazis. It is, of course, undeniable that anti-Semitic propaganda played a large role in whipping up sentiment, for the propagandists provided a rationale for excluding Jews. The anti-Semites were in agreement on one central point: the Jew is alien, subversive, and dangerous; he cannot be allowed the freedom of unfettered competition to achieve a place in society. The American economic pie had shrunk, and Jews were cast for the role of aliens who were eating an undeserved share of the scarce food.

After 1929, American anti-Semitism arose not in the areas where Nazi propaganda was the most virulent, in big cities such as New York and Baltimore, but in the Farm Belt and the Far West. The editors of *Fortune* magazine, who in 1935 conducted a survey of American anti-Semitism, devised an indirect question: Do you think that Germany is being helped or hurt by the Nazi exclusion of Jews? Across the country, the results were much less encouraging than the editors of *Fortune* tried to make them out to be. Over half the respondents answered that Germany had been hurt by its policies. About a third were indifferent to the question, and some fifteen percent nationwide answered that Germany had been helped. In the Farm Belt and Far West the indifferent and the antagonistic added together to more than half of those who answered the questions.

The 1930s were the time of massive disaster in the Farm Belt, both because prices had fallen drastically and because of the drought which had reduced the farmland to dust. Hundreds of thousands of dispossessed farmers, the Okies, took to their Model Ts and drove west to California. It was easy to suggest to these pained and bankrupt farmers that the Jews were somehow behind their downfall. George Winrod and Gerald L. K. Smith, the most extreme voices of anti-Semitism in the Midwest, used the rhetoric of Populism. Winrod and Smith were not, however, the most prominent preachers of anti-Semitism in America in the 1930s. That role was seized by a Catholic priest, Charles Coughlin. His prime audience was not the farmers, but rather the industrial workers. Coughlin was the pastor of the Shrine of the Little Flower in Royal Oak, Michigan. He had taken to the radio as an advocate of the New Deal, but he soon turned to preaching anti-Semitism. His message was popular in Detroit, where the auto industry was in ever-greater trouble, and among the industrial unemployed throughout the country, for until the Second World War most had little hope of returning to their jobs.

To be sure, other factors were important in the growth of anti-Semitism in the 1930s. Much of the population of the Midwest was of German extraction and preferred to think well of the mother country, even under the Nazis. The blue-collar workers to whom Coughlin appealed were predisposed to think in terms of race, because many, both white and black, had their roots in the South. Those who were striking in Detroit against the auto manufacturers risked being injured or sometimes even being killed on the picket lines of the 1930s. Jews were prominent among union officials and strike organizers, but that did not endear them to the workers. Here were "New York Jews" with white-collar jobs in the union bureaucracies, trying to tell blue-collar workers who had been fired how to fight the bosses. Many were predisposed to make Jews the scapegoat for their woes, because it was safer and more emotionally satisfying. As always, anti-Semitism was rising in America among the masses during times of economic dislocation.

As the recovery from the Great Depression began, Jews were visibly better off than most other groups. Toward the end of Franklin Delano Roosevelt's first term, the depression in production had not yet ended, but white-collar jobs were beginning to increase, if only in the staffing of the New Deal bureaucracies. The steelworker in Pittsburgh who had not had a job in six or seven years was usually interviewed for home relief by a newly employed caseworker, who very often was a Jew. Indeed, social work began to flourish as an "industry" under the New Deal. Before the advent of Roosevelt, caseworkers had been employed in very small numbers by private charity agencies. The new governmental bureaucracies for administering relief required thousands of such functionaries. Inevitably, a large number of Jews sought these new jobs. All of the New Deal agencies were staffed by a notable number of Jews, for Roosevelt had opened these newer bureaucracies to the "merit system." Roosevelt was thus the major employer in America who did not discriminate against Jews, and he was, inevitably, their hero. An age-old drama repeated itself; Jews were being hired in a new "industry," the government agencies which had just been created, because the older pursuits were keeping them out. These new jobs were insecure, but the Jews who held them were resented by those who had no jobs at all.

The net result of the Jewish experience in the decade during the Great Depression was the conviction among Jews that they remained outsiders in the American economy. Their security could come only if the government itself consciously tried to include them in the promises it had made to all Americans. Jews could not afford a laissez-faire government. They required a share in political power; they had to be indispensable to the coalition which elected the government, and that government had to act to widen the field of possibility for Jews. Otherwise, no matter what the children of the immigrants might do, their successes could be taken away from them. The way to fight the systematic exclusion of Jews was politics.

In the mid-1930s the respectable representatives of American Jewry were still trying to finesse the difference between Jews and all other Americans by insisting that there was no difference. The "German Jews" kept repeating the doctrine that being a Jew was like being a Methodist, that is, it meant belonging to one of the many religious denominations in America. But the mass of the East Europeans and their children knew that none of this was true—and so did the most perceptive Gentiles. In America the Jews were a sui generis minority; for them, and for all those who related to them, whether friend or foe, this was not a multireligious or multiethnic country; it was a Jew/Gentile country. But in their need to "arrive" in America, Jews kept hoping that this was not so, or, at the very least, that Jews could persuade the Gentile majority of some definition of American society that would obscure this line of cleavage.

15.

Children of the Ghetto

I

Jews never had an alternative to America. They could not go "home," because they had none in Russia, Poland, and Romania, which remained hostile to Jews. Therefore, Jews needed acceptance in America more than any other minority.

Many Gentiles, of all the ethnic groups, could, and did, go home when times were bad and they could find no work. Others returned after they had succeeded in making enough money to buy a farm or a business. But not the Jews, neither the poor nor the successful. The most telling proof of this difference is to be found in the statistics for the last year of mass migration to the United States, the fiscal year which ended on June 30, 1924. The restrictions of the new quota law hit the Italians as hard as the Jews. Those who returned to Europe from both groups knew that they would have great difficulty being readmitted. Nonetheless, while 23,000 Italians went back home that year, only 260 Jews returned to their place of origin. Even the Irish, few of whom had ever gone back, had a higher rate of reemigration; more than 1,500 returned to the home country in 1924.

Jews not only needed acceptance in America more than any other ethnic group, they also needed it more quickly. The Irish, Slavs, and Italians came from the farms, and most were willing to remain farmers or laborers for at least a generation after they arrived in America. Jews had lived for centuries in the cities and small towns of Europe, on the margin of the economy and society. The New World meant, for them, the chance to achieve in New York what they could not reach in the Moscow of the czars: to become professors, merchants, and white-collar bureaucrats. In the early 1920s, Harvard, Yale, and Columbia did not feel constrained to impose quotas on Slavs, Irish, and Italians, because few of their children were then applying to universities. Jews were the first ethnic group to try to breach the American Establishment. They were the first to be told that they were not true Americans. Inevitably, they were the first of all the ethnic groups to counter this attack by trying to remake themselves, and to redefine America, so that they would be "just like everybody else."

Their German Jewish predecessors had solved the problem of self-definition by insisting that Jewishness had no cultural or ethnic content; they were Jews by religion. This formula was borrowed from Europe, where Jews had tried to present themselves in the nineteenth century as Frenchmen or Germans of the Jewish religious persuasion, just like other Frenchmen or Germans, who were Christians. The Gentile majorities in Europe were not convinced. They continued to feel that being French or German meant that the individual had age-old roots in the culture and religion of the majority. In America, opinion was not quite as firm, but even the friends of the Jews did not contest the proposition that America was, culturally and historically, largely Christian.

Theodore Roosevelt was not an enemy of the Jews; he had even vetoed a bill restricting immigration, and as we have seen, he had written a warm greeting to the 'celebration in Carnegie Hall of 250 years of Jewish settlement in the United States. But Roosevelt thundered, again and again, against "hyphenated Americans," by which he meant anyone who did not quickly sever ties with his past and assimilate into American society. Roosevelt did not specify that this American society was determined by Protestant Christian norms, though he probably felt that it was at the essence of true Americanism. Roosevelt would have felt at home with Ezra Stiles. That ex-

Puritan divine had proposed in the earliest years of the Republic that America was a redemptive society to which all newcomers would have to conform.

The repeated demand, by the Puritans, by Ezra Stiles, and by Theodore Roosevelt, that newcomers assimilate, was demeaning. It suggested that nothing that an immigrant might bring with him was of value to the existing society, except, perhaps, as an exotic curiosity. The older, "German Jews" had made no such total concession to the majority, for they had insisted that their Judaism, even as they reformed it into American respectability, was the equal of Christianity. The "Russian Jews" had to preserve a comparable dignity. Some rejoiced in getting rid of their Jewish past, but most could not accept the thought that they should be ashamed of everything they were before landing on Ellis Island. Even assimilation could not be allowed to mean total self-abasement.

But how does one retain some pride in being Jewish and become an American? The first formal attempt by some "Russian Jews" to answer this question was the theory of the "melting pot." This notion was invented in the early 1900s at the height of mass emigration. The United States was imagined as a big pot seething with various nationalities, both old and new. As new elements were tossed into this pot, the stew kept changing in flavor and composition. The "American" was, therefore, not a fixed, existing type; he was always still in the process of becoming. This formula was a bold attempt to make Pilgrim Fathers and sweatshop workers into equally important actors in the making of the "American." The theory of the melting pot accepted the premise of the nativists about society: to be an "American" meant not merely to obey the law; one had to belong to American society. But there was a basic difference between the nativists and the proponents of the melting pot. The nativists said that American society had been defined permanently by the older America; the supporters of the melting pot argued that American society was constantly evolving.

Very little has been said about the other implications, at least for Jews, of the notion of the melting pot. All the other immigrants bore no responsibility for the future of the culture from which they came. Germany, Russia, Italy, and all the other European countries would continue to safeguard their various languages and traditions even if everyone who went to America transmuted his origins into knock-wurst, vodka, or marinara sauces. Jews had a "homeland" in Eastern Europe, but they were everywhere an embattled minority. Indeed, all of the Jewish ideologies of that day, from revolutionary socialism to Zionism, began with the premise that the existing Jewish life in Eastern Europe was not viable and that in its present form it was not worth preserving. The suggestion that the Jews in America should assimilate was therefore based only in part on any certainty that Jewishness was safe in its older centers in Russia and Poland.

The idea of the melting pot was not conceived in America. This new definition of America was constructed in England by Israel Zangwill, from the same intellectual material which Theodor Herzl had used when he designed his version of Zionism. When he published *The Jewish State,* in 1896, Herzl had posed these alternatives: Jews should choose either national existence in Palestine or assimilation; they should finally reorganize themselves, "normalize," and become "like everyone else." In 1914, Zangwill said exactly this in an afterword that he wrote to his drama, *The Melting Pot,* which had been produced six years earlier. The point of the play had been its advocacy of intermarriage between Jew and Christian as a way of dissolving even the greatest of differences among Americans. In the last lines of the play, the Jewish hero addresses his Christian wife. He regards the New World as far more glorious than even Rome or Jerusalem because America is the place where "all races and nations come to labor and look forward." Zangwill remained convinced of this idea; he defended it again in 1914, in the afterword to the new edition, by insisting "that the conditions offered to the Jew in America are without parallel in the world." In the New World, the Jew is a "citizen of a republic without a state religion." All of those who were speaking for maintaining some form of Jewish apartness were missing the meaning of this messianic moment: "In America . . . the Jew, by a roundabout journey from Zion has come into his own again." The rabbis who had denounced Zangwill for proposing the "solution of the Jewish problem by dissolution" were wrong, because Zangwill did not believe that assimilation is "universally applicable." In the play itself, its hero had asked his uncle, "Why, if he objects to the dissolving process, did he not work for a separate Jewish land?" Throughout this essay, there is a presumption about the mass of Jews in Eastern Europe: they are kept separate by anti-Semitism; they should be saved by being given the choice between national life in Jerusalem or "the melting pot" in New York.

The concept of the "melting pot" established a premise which would be the basis for all the other Jewish theories about the nature of America: the New World was not merely a place to make a living or to be free from persecution; becoming part of America was to participate in the drama of redeeming the Jews in this world. Jews could no longer be hectored by the older America as latecomers who were bringing their supposedly uncouth and pushy ways to an existing and defined America which they had not helped to run. This was heady stuff for some Jews; they could assimilate into America in good conscience, and even in glory. But his formula of the melting pot did not persuade many leaders of the old American Establishment, not even liberals such as Theodore Roosevelt.

The concept of the melting pot was rejected by Jews as well. The existing Jewish life in America was in trouble; it was threatened by its foreignness and its shallowness, but most Jews were not going to abandon their Jewishness for assimilation. Some were at war with themselves and with the world about their Jewishness, but most accepted it as a fact of nature.

Horace Kallen and Mordecai Kaplan, the first intellectuals among the children of the immigrants to think about America, began with the presumption that Jews were in America to stay—as affirming Jews. Kaplan had been brought to New York in 1887, at the age of eight, by his father, who was a distinguished rabbinic scholar of the old school. Kaplan himself was raised on the Lower East Side of New York on the Talmud, and he was ordained as a rabbi in 1902 at the Jewish Theological Seminary, but he also studied at Columbia under John Dewey, whose philosophy of pragmatism Kaplan embraced. Kaplan was unshakably a Jew, but he wanted to enter the mainstream of American life. Along with Horace Kallen (who had studied at Harvard under William James, another important American philosopher of pragmatism), Kaplan proposed a theory of "cultural pluralism." Kaplan and Kallen defined America as a creation of all the various ethnic groups which came to the New World. They denied the melting pot because they insisted that each of these groups had the right to cultivate its links to its origins. The force of this assertion was to dethrone the Protestant Anglo-Saxons, who were the earliest arrivals, from their self-assumed position of being the only true Americans. The Talmudic learning of Kaplan's father was thus pronounced to be as much a part of the American heritage as the Puritans' Calvinist theology. Kaplan imagined an America in which both traditions lasted, side by side, as equals.

Writing in *The Nation* in February of 1915, Horace Kallen defied the older America, and those who were decrying "hyphenated Americans." He conceded (in my view, wrongly) that "the writers of the American Declaration of Independence and of the Constitution of the United States were not confronted by the practical fact of ethnic dissimilarity among the whites of the country." The situation was different now: "Their descendants are confronted by it." Kallen refused to back down and accede to the doctrine of assimilation in any form, including the melting pot. He insisted, passionately and vehemently, that inherited identities are inalienable:

Men may change their clothes, their politics, their wives, their religions, their philosophies, to a greater or lesser extent: they cannot change their grandfathers. Jews or Poles or Anglo-Saxons, in order to cease being Jews or Poles or Anglo-Saxons, would have to cease to be, while they could cease to be citizens or church members or carpenters or lawyers without ceasing to be. The selfhood which is inalienable in them, and for the realization of which they require "inalienable" liberty is ancestrally determined, and the happiness which they pursue has its form implied in ancestral endowment. This is what, actually, democracy in operation assumes. There are human capacities which it is the function of the state to liberate and to protect in growth; and the failure of the state as a government to accomplish this automatically makes for its abolition. Government, the state, under the democratic conception is, it cannot be too often repeated, merely an instrument, not an end.

As the model for the new America, Kallen proposed Switzerland, with its three languages and cultures. There was, however, one critical difference: "The common language of the commonwealth, the language of its great tradition, would be English, but each nationality would have for its emotional and involuntary life its own peculiar dialect or speech, its own individual and inevitable esthetic and intellectual forms." Kallen knew, clearly and unmistakably, that he was proposing an unprecedented structure of society, a new "symphony of civilization" that would be composed of differing nationalities. He did not pretend for a moment that he was affirming a process that had been in motion since the beginnings of America. Kallen was clear and forthright in presenting cultural pluralism as a new idea. It was the contemporary way to assure everyone his full human rights in a democracy, for each American would be encouraged to have a direct and respected relationship to his ethnic group. Kallen knew that the older America would resist: "The question is, do the dominant classes in America want such a society?"

Kallen addressed this question to the Gentile Establishment, but that was not the only question that he and Kaplan had to answer. They had to explain what it meant to be a Jew in this culturally plural American democracy. How could one demand equality, and the role of a cocreator of America, and yet continue to insist on the classic Jewish faith in the "chosen people"? How could one accept this doctrine, even in the attenuated version of the immigrant family, that Jews were, somehow, unique? Kallen had no problem. As a completely secular person, Kallen distinguished between "Judaism," which he used as a name for inherited religion, and "Hebraism," which meant for Kallen the cultural expressions of Jews as a community. Kallen was persuaded that all American identities were rapidly becoming secular. In the New Land, Jews would behave like the Irish, the Italians, and all the other ethnic groups by using only those elements of their past which spoke to their present needs in America.

Kaplan, the rabbi, insisted that Jewishness had religion as its central element, but his definition of religion was unprecedented. Having become a philosophical pragmatist, Kaplan had ceased believing in a transcendent God, the Person who had spoken at Sinai to His creatures and who had revealed His will to them. Kaplan's God was "natural," which meant that He was conceived as a word which summed up the highest values of a community. All of the ethnic minorities in America, Kaplan argued, shared the basic values of American democracy, but each subgroup expressed these values through a different set of symbols derived from its history. Kaplan had thus ruled out the most striking of all Jewish doctrines, the faith of Jews that they were the "chosen people." In practice, he conceded even more. Kaplan wanted no segregation from the cultural life of the majority. He asserted that "Jews have no intention of following the example of the Catholics in contesting the prior right of the State to the education of the child." He thus refused to use private education to preserve Jewish culture. He was too busy entering America, by differentiating himself from Catholic separatism, to ask an obvious question: What about boarding schools such as Groton and Andover, which continued to be the training schools of the Protestant elite?

Both Kallen and Kaplan were thus eager to present the Jews as the model for all other ethnic minority identities in America. Kaplan and Kallen had produced a set of definitions of America, and of the Jews, which seemed to solve the question of how one can be both a Jew and an American.

Kallen helped Brandeis win the fight for the American Jewish Congress (in which, in effect, Jews had declared themselves to be an ethnic minority with its own political agenda), but, overall, his impact on the organized activities of the community was not large. Kaplan did have at least one important success in shaping American Jewish institutional life. Right after the First World War, he founded the movement for the creation of "Jewish centers," and he continued to be the inspiration for the many dozens that were being created in the next several decades. These "centers" were different from the Americanization agencies that the "German Jews" had put up at the turn of the century. The purpose of the new Jewish centers was to provide a place of Jewish assembly, where ethnic and family loyalties could be cultivated through recreation and cultural endeavor. In Kaplan's earliest formulations, these centers were to exist as extensions, and even transformations, of the synagogue; religion played the most prominent role, but even so, it was only one of many elements in the "reconstructed" synagogue. Many centers were not, however, affiliated with synagogues. They were created as secular expressions of Jewish ethnicity. In both sets of institutions, there was large emphasis on providing programs which would attract people to the building, with the implicit assumption that the old Jewish learning and piety were too forbidding, and too identified with guilt, to be, now in America, the cement which held Jews together. The pervasive contemporary jibe at Kaplan's synagogue-center was to call it "The Shul [synagogue] with a Pool."

Kaplan knew that he was creating the Reform Judaism of his own day for the East Europeans, and that he was, thus, reenacting what Isaac Mayer Wise had done two generations earlier for the German Jews. Like Wise, Kaplan insisted that his version of Judaism affirmed American democracy, and that he had redefined Judaism in America as an active, forward-looking, and optimistic faith. Kaplan was less clear, even to himself (and in this, too, he repeated Isaac Mayer Wise), that he was essentially acceding to the nullification of rabbinic authority. Kaplan was constructing a new model of American Jewish life which, because it was not bound by the past, had no need for those who had been its guardians. In his own, "reconstructionist" synagogue, Kaplan even abandoned the title "Rabbi." For a number of years, in the 1930s, he followed the example of the Ethical Culture Societies in which the clergy were called "Leaders." In theory, Kaplan kept insisting that decision making in his "synagogue-centers" was a democratic enterprise and that rabbis could, at most, offer some informed opinion, but that theirs was never the deciding vote.

Kaplan never really believed these theories, for his own heritage and temperament stood against them. He was the descendant of many generations of rabbis, and he was personally a commanding, often intolerant presence. More importantly, even as he asserted democracy in religion, Kaplan was a deep traditionalist. He fervently believed that his very modern formulations would lead his American Jewish contemporaries to accept the major forms of their inherited tradition, not as divine commandments but as "folkways." Jews would no longer look at Judaism and feel guilty because they were disobedient. Kaplan's reconstructed Judaism would supposedly be so attractive that Jews would affirm it with joy. Here, too, he was repeating Isaac Mayer Wise, who had announced eighty years earlier that the American Jewish "temple," with which he was replacing the synagogue of old, would represent a new Judaism, without tears, rejoicing in democracy. Jews would no longer be compelled to come to synagogue out of guilt, or fear, or even the compulsion of Orthodox fundamentalism; they would come to Wise's temple rejoicing in its beauty and in the uplifting quality of the music and decorum of the service. Kaplan, eighty years later, was offering the joys of togetherness and the warmth of selective memory of the Jewish past.

Kaplan's most difficult problem of self-definition in America was that he was a Zionist. Indeed, by the 1920s he had been adopted by the mainstream Zionist organizations, the men's Zionist Organization of America, and the women's group, Hadassah, as their official thinker. These organizations invited him repeatedly to their platforms, to provide the intellectual rationale for Zionism in America. He talked away the stark assertion of the European and Palestinian Zionist ideologies that Jews were irretrievably different from Gentiles. Kaplan refused to accept the fundamental Zionist assertion that it was better for a Jew to live in his own homeland, in a majority culture which was his, than to live in a minority, even if it was a democracy. This might be true of European lands, but America was different. Indeed the nascent Jewish majority in the ancestral land had much to learn from those Jews who were, like himself, being refashioned by their unique experience of American democracy. But, above all, Kaplan used Zionism as a "task" to preserve Judaism in America. It did not matter, for Kaplan, whether a Jewish majority and state were ever achieved in Palestine—and before the 1940s, that hope did seem distant. Judaism was to be a pragmatic, "American," problem-solving faith; its major continuing Jewish preoccupation, one that would last and keep Jews busy for generations, was the Zionist endeavor.

The theories of cultural pluralism, defined by Kallen and Kaplan, served to "legitimize" Jews in America, and to make them comfortable with themselves: they sanctified what the mainstream of the Jewish community wanted to feel. Jews were just as good Americans as everyone else; Jews had the right to think of themselves as a group, with a past. Still, the theoretical formulations by Kallen and Kaplan were never really believed. Most Jews never accepted the all-too-logical assertions by Kallen and Kaplan that the price of equality in democracy was, at the very least, the abandonment of any thought of "chosenness." The mainstream of American Jews never doubted that they were special, and different, from all the other minorities. Why suffer from anti-Semitism, which one could avoid by assimilation or, if need be, religious conversion, just for the sake of asserting an ethnic identity that was as important, and as unimportant, as that of the Sicilians, the Slovaks, or the Albanians?

The rhetoric of cultural pluralism did have its uses. It was convenient when demanding equality from an unfriendly majority, and it helped in forgiving oneself for straying away from the older religious norms. Nevertheless, it was never dominant among American Jews, because the evidence of their own lives was against it. American society was not becoming more plural and more open. On the contrary, it was keeping Jews at arm's length, even as they were increasingly the most educated, culturally creative element in America.

II

Most of the young Jewish intellectuals could not understand America as a melting pot, for it kept refusing to melt them in. Cultural pluralism was irrelevant, not least because most of the younger intellectuals were refusing to adhere to any discrete ethnic culture. This intelligentsia had no other option but to make its alienation into a form of heroism.

Before the Second World War, ideologues, from anarchists and Communists to psychoanalysts, were proposing to fashion a reborn world in America, a new Garden of Eden, each according to his own doctrine. Almost all of the Jews among them knew that they were "other," and that this otherness was linked to their Jewish origins. In theory, these dreamers dealt with their Jewishness by preaching its abandonment; the Messianic Era could come, as Paul of Tarsus had once said nineteen centuries earlier, only to a world in which there was "neither Jew nor Greek." But Paul in his day had continued to insist that this new age for all mankind could happen only if the Jews exercised special leadership in bringing about the new dispensation. A comparable notion about the special role of Jews existed, though it was sometimes disguised even from themselves, among Jewish Marxists, Freudians, or modernists in art and literature. They thought of themselves as the prophets of the new in politics and culture. They needed this grandiose self-image, for this was a generation which was without fathers, either Jewish or Gentile; these intellectuals stood alone. As Isaac Rosenfeld wrote in those days: "A Jewish writer feels that he may at any time be called to account not for his art, nor even for his life, but for his Jewishness." But this Jewishness was no continuing commitment to a separate Jewish identity and tradition. It meant standing over against society for a while to exhort it to create a new age in which there would be neither Jew nor Gentile.

As both friends and enemies knew, Communism was especially attractive to this dispossessed Jewish intelligentsia. Karl Marx was a formidable "ancestor," and Joseph Stalin was already, in the Communist clichés of the 1930s, the "father of all the peoples." Though the mid-1930s were a high-water mark for adherence to Communism among the children of the immigrants, they also signaled the beginning of retreat and falling away. The Great Depression had caused growth in the influence, and numbers of domestic radicalism. The call from the Soviet Union for a "popular front" against Nazism reechoed even in non-Communist circles. But there were also the purge trials in Russia in the late 1930s. Stalin was consolidating his personal power by accusing those whom he did not trust of spying for the Nazis. Fabled figures in the making of the Bolshevik Revolution were tried and shot; tens of thousands were sent to jail. In Arthur Koestler's phrase, there was "darkness at noon." (This was the title of a novel that he published in 1937 in Europe, but the book was read, widely and immediately, in America.) Koestler himself had been a Communist; he left the movement in outraged disbelief at the purge trials.

In the United States, many of the Jews who followed Communism were motivated by immediate "Jewish" concerns; the Soviet Union was supposedly free of anti-Semitism. This faith was shaken by the purge trials, because some of the major makers of the Bolshevik Revolution who were Jews, such as Lev Kamenev and General Jan Gomarnik, were shot as traitors who had supposedly conspired with Hitler. Even the Communist Yiddish daily in New York, the *Morgen Freiheit,* which had been siding with Arabs against Jews in Palestine, was shaken by controversy. The paper followed the Stalinist line, but some of its contributors resigned, and more left after the signing of the Stalin-Hitler pact in August 1939. Nonetheless, the majority of Jewish Communists remained in the party into the next decade. Aging immigrants could not give up a lifetime of psychological investment: many lived together in housing which had been built in the Bronx by Communist-dominated unions. Adults and children spent time together in Yiddish-speaking summer camps, which were creations of the party. Those who abandoned this immigrant, Communist subculture were shunned by the friends whom they had known best and longest.

The second generation, the American-born, were less concerned about the status of Jews in Russia. They were concerned about themselves. Many Jewish teachers, doctors, and lawyers joined the party in anger at their great difficulty in finding a place in America. Jewish teachers, who were entering the profession in the Depression years, were the first to be fired when budgets were cut. Doctors and lawyers had difficulty gaining appointments to hospitals or law firms. These young professionals thought they needed the revolution in America, or they would spend their lives out on the street, looking through the window at America. Many such young Jews, who were given their first jobs by the New Deal, moved to support Franklin Delano Roosevelt, but a significant number continued to believe that they would have an equal chance only in an American equivalent of Russian Communism. A significant minority of bright Jews thought that they would rise by merit, and unencumbered by anti-Semitism, to high places in society only after a revolution in America.

A small but intellectually significant group of these left-wingers were not Stalinists but Trotskyites. Some had recoiled early from Stalin, recognizing him to be a Communist Russian czar, and not the leader of a universal ideology. A handful of Jewish intellectuals identified passionately with Trotsky, who was like them, or like what they wanted to be: an intellectual of Jewish origin, a revolutionary thinker who could be mentioned in the same breath with Karl Marx, and a fighting Jew, unprecedented for many centuries, who had been the commander of all the Bolshevik armies. This Trotskyite handful condemned both the Soviet Union, under Stalin, and the democracies, which were dominated by appeasers in Europe and isolationists in America. One could only hope for a new age when both rotten structures, Stalin's Soviet Union and the capitalist West, would be replaced by a decent, worldwide revolutionary order.

In all their clashing varieties, these intellectuals and professionals were all alienated from America. There was no home-grown revolutionary tradition into which they could fit, not even American Populism. In the Depression years the Populist impulses were tainted with antiforeignism and anti-Semitism. These Populists were mostly midwestern radicals, and they were not imagining an America in which they would be led by the Jewish intelligentsia. Even within the Communist party, which was based in the cities, mostly on the East and West coasts, some Gentiles, blacks among them, refused to accept the dominance in the party of white-collar Jews. Radical Jews in America, therefore, did not derive their radicalism from older American left-wing traditions or constituencies. The Jewish radicals were "cosmopolitans"; they could not really feel that they were the unquestioned leaders of the American radicalisms. The Communist party made a great point of having a Gentile, Earl Browder, as its head, and the leader of the socialists was a former Christian minister, Norman Thomas. Jews were very nearly forced to look toward Europe for inspiration and legitimacy. Moscow was the capital for the Communists. American Jewish Trotskyites were emotionally "in exile," together with their leader, who was chased from country to country by pressure from Stalin after he expelled Trotsky from Russia in 1926. The Jewish socialists in the Bund looked to Poland, where the party was strong and creative even in the bad times for Jews in the 1930s. The believers in modernism in art and literature looked to Paris, Berlin, and Vienna for inspiration, for the center of these movements was there and not in America.

The advent of Hitler was, therefore, not so paradoxically, a spiritual milestone for all these "post-Jewish Jews." More than two hundred thousand Jewish refugees were admitted to the United States between Hitler's ascent to power in 1933 and America's entry into World War II at the end of 1941. Those who came were largely middle-class people from Central Europe. An extraordinarily significant minority among these refugees were scholars and artists who were the very glory of European culture. These newcomers were different from all the earlier immigrants. There were ranking scientists, artists, and social thinkers among them, such as Albert Einstein, Marc Chagall, Theodor Adorno, Max Horckheimer, and Hannah Arendt. These people were not only incredibly learned. They were perceived by young American-born Jewish intellectuals as light bearers of modernity. In the 1930s and the 1940s, they provided legitimacy for the American Jewish intelligentsia.

They were teachers who could be adopted as fathers. Growing up in Europe, these Jewish intellectuals had already faced the question of where to situate themselves in a hostile culture; they had solved the problem by extolling their "marginality," and by inventing the "international style." It was painful to be on the margin, but it was also ennobling. Franz Kafka, who had become the most read and quoted writer of the displaced European Jewish intelligentsia in the 1930s, had lived on the margin of both the German and the Czech communities. These Europeans brought Kafka with them to America. They did not read him as a Jew who moved from the margin in search of community but rather as the archetype of an alienated man who was condemned to sit forever outside the majority culture. In his novel *The Trial,* he wrote of the individual who waits endlessly outside the door of a judgment chamber, hoping to be admitted to face the judges and, at least, to be told the name of the crime for which he is accused. Even though the word "Jew" is not once mentioned, this was a very "Jewish" tale. It could, and was, read as a parable about a Jew waiting for the Gentiles to tell him on what terms they might accept him—but the answer never came. The story cried out for some resolution. One could not live forever in limbo with Kafka's antihero. Perhaps he could discover his "crime," if some skilled physician would sit with him and help him look into his soul. Perhaps this unfortunate sufferer would then be welcomed by the nameless judges as one of their own, when he would have become, like them, untormented and cheerful.

"Marginality" helped the native-born Jewish intellectuals to explain their own situation in America: Jews were excluded by the capitalists, who dominated the society (and Jews even had some trouble with the poor), but Jews were the people who were most attuned to the newest, most cosmopolitan currents in culture and thought. In America in the 1930s, Jewish intellectuals who did not believe in the Jewish God were thus asserting that they were the true prophets of Western culture, the breakers of the existing idols, and that they were being persecuted by anti-Semites for their prophetic role. Here, under fairly transparent cover, the un-Jewish Jews among the children of the immigrants were replaying the classic themes of Jewish history: exclusion and chosenness.

This self-definition as "alienated prophets" was especially strong in the 1930s among the Jewish disciples of Leon Trotsky, who were editing and writing for the *Partisan Review.* Sidney Hook, Irving Howe, and a number of others who were a part of that circle as young men have attested to a pervasive alienation from America. Hook has written that the editors of the journal were "almost exclusively European in their cultural orientation," and that "they were largely ignorant of and indifferent to American traditions. . . ." Howe has told that the editor of the *Partisan Review,* Philip Rahv, was among those in the circle who "took an acute private pleasure, through jokes and asides, in those aspects of intellectualism that mark Jewishness: quickness, skepticism, questioning." However, on the pages of the journal in its heyday, Jewish issues were never discussed directly. Rahv himself made one glancing reference, in all of his writings, to the "cleverness" of Jews, and that remark was not meant entirely as a compliment. These young intellectuals, in Howe's words, "refused to acknowledge ourselves as part of a Jewish community encompassing all classes and opinions." They had chosen to belong to the "straggling phalanx" of the international Stalinist Left. And their heroes were such "non-Jewish Jews" as Rosa Luxemburg and Leon Trotsky.

This Trotskyite splinter group of the intelligentsia was surer that it was bringing the light of the revolution to the world in the 1930s and into the 1940s than the much more numerous Stalinists. The rightness of their politics was confirmed in their minds by the treason trials of the late 1930s, when Stalin shot almost all of the surviving leaders of the Bolshevik Revolution, and even by the murder of Trotsky by Stalinist agents in Mexico in 1940. But America was not moving toward the revolution. The New Deal and the onset of the Second World War gave American capitalism another chance, even as Jews were still semioutsiders in America. The question had to be posed: Is marginality, in and of itself, a light-bearing mission?

Ultimately it is not. As Jewish intellectuals found out from some of their European teachers, a passion for the revolution can be sustaining, but the sheer loneliness of being outside of society is unbearable. Abraham, the ultimate ancestor of all Jews, including these brilliant young writers, had known some thirty-five centuries earlier that to represent a minority opinion against the reigning idolaters is a dangerous role, but Abraham had been sustained by faith in the one God. As world revolution tarried, what sustained "marginal" intellectuals, both the European "fathers" and their new American "children," for whom the Jewish God was an outworn myth and for whom Communism was becoming a failed faith? The door was now open for psychoanalysis.

In 1938 Sigmund Freud had fled from Vienna to London. In 1939 he published *Moses and Monotheism,* a book in which he tried to "cure" the Jews of their "illness," as Freud diagnosed it. Moses, so Freud asserted, had been an Egyptian, and not a Jew, and the doctrine of monotheism was not Jewish. It had been proclaimed first by a young revolutionary pharaoh, Akhenaton, and had been brought to the Jews by Moses. Jewish tribalists had murdered the bearer of this universalism. The hidden trauma of the Jewish people was the "suppressed memory" of this murder. The only way for Jews to return to health was to admit the crime, and to abandon their ethnic separatism. Freud's fanciful, and totally unsupported, "historical" reconstruction of the biblical drama of Moses and the Jews was a plea for assimilation, with the clear implication that "cured," that is, de-Judaized, Jews would stem the tide of Nazi anti-Semitism. This assumption was obviously wildly wrong, for the Nazis hated assimilated Jews even more than affirming ones. Assimilated Jews were more likely to occupy central positions in contemporary culture and politics.

Nonetheless, despite the illogic of Freud's argument in *Moses and Monotheism,* psychoanalysis became the "religion" of elements of America's Jewish intelligentsia. The psychoanalysts were not only an alternative to the agents of Stalin; they seemed to have an answer to the most pervasive, personal problem among many younger Jews, the question of their relationships with their parents. This pain lent itself to analysis in terms of one of Freud's basic insights, the supposed desire of the child to destroy his father and to possess his mother. As the revolution tarried, it seemed ever less likely that a classless America, according to Karl Marx, would free these children of immigrants from the woe of their Jewishness. Some hoped that Freud might purge them of their pain by freeing their inner selves of their ancestors. "Analyzed" young Jews would finally be able to realize Mary Antin's dream of walking into the warm sunlight of a joyous America. But the analysts, and their Jewish analysands, could never shake off Freud's own bitter knowledge, that psychoanalysis was an overwhelmingly Jewish cult.

Psychoanalysis as theory promised a universalist salvation; it suggested that it might achieve the Enlightenment's world of reason, now renamed superego. Psychoanalysis as cult reinforced a feeling, deeply embedded in the psyche of its believers, most of whom were Jewish, that they were at war with society, and that they had only their Promethean "chosenness," as the bearers of the truth, to sustain themselves. The Freudians, too, were sectarians, very much on the margin of society, and certainly "foreign" in the eyes of even the most literate Americans. Jewish intellectuals of the 1930s did, as Trilling's enemies at Columbia had told him, belong to Marx and Freud, and not to established America. They were in the same situation as their brothers and cousins in business; they were enraged by their exclusion from the promises of America, and they were sustained by feeling (no matter what its rationalization) that they were special.

But what were their Jewish roots? Looking back on those years, Irving Howe has written that he thought of himself, then, as descending from such archetypes as Solomon Maimon, the Lithuanian Jew who had come to Germany in the last years of the eighteenth century and transformed himself into a serious philosopher. Maimon had lived a picaresque and miserable life, outside both the Jewish and the German communities. Howe asserted that Maimon prefigured those in America who, though they wrote about politics and culture, had left the Jews, and were disregarded by the Gentiles. This assertion of intellectual affiliation was basically false. Solomon Maimon, and the far greater figure of Baruch Spinoza a century earlier, had both been educated, first, in a classic yeshivah, where they had learned the sacred texts in Hebrew. Both Spinoza and Maimon are intelligible only if one takes into account the tension between the religious and intellectual culture of Judaism, which they actually knew, and the new thinking and forms of living to which they found their way. In class terms, for that matter, Spinoza and Maimon—and such contemporary European figures as Ahad Ha-Am (pseudonym for Asher Ginzberg), the founder of cultural Zionism, and David Ben-Gurion, the first prime minister of Israel—came from the middle class, while the parents of the new American Jewish intelligentsia were almost without exception from the less-educated poor.

In the 1920s and 1930s, there were already some such classical scholars, and even a few writers in modern Hebrew, in America, but they were an ignored handful. Few among the immigrants, and even fewer of their children, knew Hebrew, except to say prayers by rote. The overwhelming preoccupation in the New Land was to survive and to succeed, and Jewish learning was not a useful tool in these endeavors. Secular learning, the kind that one acquired in college, was clearly useful; there was hope that it would lead to a career; it was a way to "America." But Jewish learning was held to be irrelevant. The secular intelligentsia simply ignored the bearers of Hebrew as museum pieces. No one adopted them as "fathers" to be emulated. They could have taught the intelligentsia the classic culture of Judaism, but no one came to listen, except some candidates for the rabbinate and a small handful of intellectual oddballs. Thus, the children of the immigrants learned to be intellectuals, either from books or from Gentile professors. Their own Jewishness was constructed out of ideological slogans and pronouncements about Jews by often unfriendly outsiders, in tension with childhood ghetto memories of fear, shame, pride, and defiance.

Most Jewish intellectuals of the 1920s and 1930s knew no Jewish world before the arrival of their parents on Ellis Island, or their own entry into City College. They did not rebel against the world of the Talmud, for they never knew it. The young Jewish writers were, almost without exception, children of parents who had brought very little formal Jewish education with them to the New World. A few of the fathers did know the Hebrew texts, but generally they did not transmit the learning that they had once acquired; most knew very little. Irving Howe's father ran a grocery store in the Bronx, and the Jewish culture that he imbibed was Yiddish; it was the world for which the *Jewish Daily Forward* spoke. Nathan Glazer has given a comparable account of his own parents. Even Alfred Kazin, who had a somewhat different personal history, is a case in point. He told, in his autobiographical memoir, *A Walker in the City,* that his father was a house painter who was almost totally silent. The son did not discover until near the end of the father's life that the older man had had some rabbinic education in his youth in Russia, and that he had buried that secret during his son's formative years because he wanted his son to be an "American." Those of the immigrant parents who were different from the majority, like Kazin's father, most often accepted the notion that their heritage was useless in the New World. They wanted their sons to find new "fathers" in Gentile America.

Kazin went to school in a very tough neighborhood in Brooklyn. His parents kept reminding him that if he did not do well in class, there "yawned the great abyss of a criminal career"; school was for him, therefore, "the stage for a trial." Immigrant parents—silent fathers and dreaming mothers—drove their children to succeed because, as Kazin observed, these children were their "America."

> I worked on a hairline between triumph and catastrophe. Why the
> odds should always have felt so narrow I understood only when
> I realized how little my parents thought of their own lives. It was

not for myself alone that I was expected to shine, but for them—
to redeem the constant anxiety of their existence. I was the first
American child, their offering to the strange new God; I was to
be the monument of their liberation from the shame of being what
they were. And that there was shame in this was a fact that everyone
seemed to believe as a matter of course. It was in the gleeful dis-
counting of themselves—what do we know?—with which our
parents greeted every fresh victory in our savage competition for
high averages, for prizes, for a few condescending words of official
praise from the principal at assembly.

Such parents did want their children to remain Jews, but the Jewish
education that almost all the immigrants gave their children, including the intellectuals-to-be, was only sufficient to teach them to mouth
the rituals at bar mitzvah or, at most, to say some of the liturgies in
Hebrew without understanding the words. The rest of their exposure
consisted of folk religion and family memory. Thus, in their flight
from the "Lower East Side," such American-born intellectuals carried with them the pain of their immigrant Jewish beginnings, but
very little of the dignity that the yeshivah conferred even on those
who rebelled against and abandoned it.

The new, young, Jewish intelligentsia believed neither in the melting pot nor in cultural pluralism. Whether left-wingers or not, the
dominant mood among them in the 1930s was assimilation. Jews in
arts and letters almost always wrote and composed as "general Americans"; they were at great pains to avoid any reference to Jews in the
characters that they depicted. George Gershwin, for example, talked
occasionally about composing an opera on biblical themes, but that
work was never begun. The opera that he did compose was *Porgy
and Bess,* which was set in Charleston, South Carolina; it was about
the agony, the blasted hopes, the dreams of plenty, and the ultimately
triumphant courage of at least one heroic figure among the Negroes
in Catfish Row. The libretto for the opera was written by a white
Gentile, DuBose Heyward, and his subject had been Negroes. It is
no surprise that Gershwin found this tale suitable for his first opera,
for Jewish artists and performers had a particular affinity in those
days for expressing their Jewish angst through Negro characters.
Gershwin composed *Porgy and Bess* in the very years in which Al
Jolson and Eddie Cantor were appearing on vaudeville stages all over
America in blackface. In Cantor's most famous movie, *Whoopee,* he

alternated between blackface and Indian red, while throwing in an aside or two in Yiddish.

George Gershwin was a Jew from the Bronx, the child of Yiddish-speaking immigrants—and the Negroes in *Porgy and Bess* seemed to be Jews in blackface. Gershwin had rarely seen any of the tormented Negro characters whom he described so eloquently; it was in the Bronx ghetto of his childhood that the composer had seen picturesque criminals like the villain, Sportin' Life, and tragic men of principle, many of whom had been stunted by poverty and exclusion, like his crippled hero, Porgy. In the Bronx there were many women like Bess, the heroine of the opera, who was torn between the fast-talking Sportin' Life and the good and faithful Porgy. It was on their journey from the Bronx that invisible "cripples," the children of immigrant Jews, had traveled the hard road, on their knees, to Manhattan and to America.

This process of avoidance, of masking the Jewish origins of his characters, is nearer the surface in the work of a younger contemporary, Clifford Odets: "I have a serious artistic problem. I don't feel I write completely American characters; they always come out a little Jewish." Odets knew enough about himself to admit that he "was really trying to disavow being a Jew. If the truth must be told, I yearn for acceptance like a youth of eighteen." What he ultimately hoped for, as he often said, was the Anglo-Saxon Protestant respectability of a Sidney Howard, a Maxwell Anderson, a Robert Sherwood. This passionate desire to annihilate the Jewish self was expressed in the names that he gave some of his characters. The protagonist of his play *Golden Boy* (1937) is named Joe Bonaparte, but in his notes for the play, Odets wrote, "Papa Bonaparte is sort of a Jacob character." The family in *Paradise Lost* (1935) is called Gordon, as an antidote to having identified the family in his first play, *Awake and Sing!* as Jews named Berger.

The Odets of the 1930s did write some plays which were overtly about Jews of his generation trapped in the Bronx, but his solution to their problem was assimilationist. In *Waiting for Lefty* (1935), the workers, who are Jews, were asked to rally against the bosses. When the Gentile Dr. Barnes fires the Jewish Dr. Benjamin from the staff of the hospital, Benjamin knows that he is meeting "an old disease, malignant, tumescent," and that he had met this disease before. He is losing his job, despite his seniority, because Jews are let go first—but Odets cannot let it go at that. Dr. Benjamin is surprised that there is "such discrimination, with all those wealthy brother Jews on the Board." Barnes replies that there "doesn't seem to be much difference between wealthy Jews and rich Gentiles. Cut from the same cloth." In two lines Odets, who was then a Communist, thus summarized the doctrine that Karl Marx had propounded a century before in his essay, "On the Jewish Question"—there really are no Jews or Gentiles, there are only capitalists and workers. Jews will solve their problem, anti-Semitism, only through social revolution. They can bring that revolution closer by giving up on any notions of Jewish group solidarity.

By the end of the 1930s, American Jews of the second generation were intellectually in an ever more untenable position. Their fathers had failed them. The path to America, through education, remained blocked. The revolution had, at very least, not yet succeeded; its tarrying was the cause of desperation in the very midst of rhetorical bravado about the dialectic certainty that capitalism would soon collapse. To be sure, the intellectuals were really better off than they were saying. They had not arrived at the center of American thought and literature, but many had jobs. They were working for New Deal agencies and so they were not starving. The most striking problem of this intelligentsia was its alienation from the Jewish community, but that was a problem that most refused to recognize. The active involvement in any separate Jewish existence was left to the "backward."

III

Almost all the neighborhoods, even the newer ones, in which Jews lived in the 1930s were still overwhelmingly Jewish. This living together was the major form of personal association. People met each other on the stoops in front of their houses, and in the candy stores. There were organizations of many kinds, from "friendly societies" to political groups. The synagogues did not seem, then, to be the dominant expression of Jewish identity. The formal memberships—as opposed to those who "bought tickets" or congregated outside on the street during the High Holy Days—were small. Nonetheless, the changing nature of religious life was the most accurate indicator of the future shape of life of the mainstream American Jews.

In the 1920s and 1930s, the Reform temples still seemed powerful, but they were increasingly becoming relics. The Reform movement had denounced Zionism when it first appeared, and the majority of the rabbis had remained hostile, even as the major lay leaders were becoming moderates. The Central Conference of American Rabbis, the organization of Reform rabbis, had made anti-Zionism into an article of faith. At their annual conventions the rabbis resolved again and again that Judaism was a "religion of universal significance" and that ethnic loyalties were both regressive and un-American. Many of the Reform temples were reluctant to admit the East Europeans, but they could not keep the doors tightly closed. Their memberships were dropping. The grandchildren of the original "German Jews" were intermarrying with non-Jews at the rate of one in three. The "German Jews" had fewer children, and they generally cared less about their Jewish identity than their parents or grandparents. The Reform temples were attractive to some of the nouveaux riches among the children of the immigrants. These "Russian Jews" did not accept the anti-Zionism that still pervaded many of the temples, and they were not comfortable with being snubbed. Yet, they fought to be admitted as members, or at least to send their daughters to the Reform Sunday schools, so their children might arrive among the "better Jews." In the 1920s and 1930s the social clubs which the "German Jews" had created a generation or so earlier, because they were excluded by the Gentiles, still stood firm in refusing to admit East European Jews. One might pray beside the "Russians" on the High Holidays, but it was still not conceivable that one would play golf with them on weekends. The story was told in those days of the "German Jew" who blackballed an affluent recent immigrant from membership in his country club, saying that "a man who speaks with an accent cannot possibly play golf."

But the 1920s and the 1930s were the last hurrah of old-line Reform Judaism. The Zionist minority among the Reform rabbis was increasing. In 1922, Stephen Wise established a new rabbinical school called the Jewish Institute of Religion which proposed to train rabbis for all the shades of Jewish belief, on the basis of an overarching commitment to the "unity of the Jewish People." Obviously, no one in the Orthodox community regarded rabbinic ordination from a liberal seminary as valid; in practice, this school was oriented toward a Zionist Reform Judaism. Its library never rivaled the great collections at the Hebrew Union College or of the Jewish Theological Seminary of America, but it was the preeminent place in America for books of modern Hebrew literature. The students at the Jewish Institute of Religion were themselves children of East Europeans; so were most of the congregants in the newer Reform congregations which they led.

Change was remaking even the older establishments of Reform Judaism. Very early, even before 1900, the Hebrew Union College had been forced to recruit its students not from the Reform laity but from the various immigrant East Sides. Though many of these men would play it safe for years, and preach "universalism" from their pulpits, their ingrained particularist feelings about the Jewish community could not be silenced forever, and especially after Hitler appeared in 1933. The formal reversal took place at a meeting of the Central Conference of American Rabbis in 1937 in Columbus, Ohio. There was a hard and bitter fight whether to have any platform at all; the tiebreaking vote was cast by the president, Felix Levy. The resolution avoided the issue of a Jewish State, but the creation of a Jewish national and cultural center in Palestine was declared to be one of the aims of Reform Judaism. Even more bitter and divisive battles would yet come, but the antinationalist upholders of "classic Reform Judaism" had become a shrinking minority in their own house. Henceforth, Reform Judaism took greater pride in Jewish ethnic feeling, and pretended less that it stood for prophetic "ethical monotheism."

In the 1920s and the 1930s American Conservative Judaism also defined itself. The Jewish Theological Seminary had been founded in 1886 by a handful of rabbis and laymen of the older America settlement, the few who refused to go along with the then triumphant Reform Judaism. Their purpose was to create a Westernized, English-speaking Orthodox rabbinate to serve congregations in America. Very few such synagogues had resisted the tide to Reform, but it was hoped that their numbers would increase. By 1900, the seminary had very nearly evaporated. It was then revived by the leaders of the Reform "cathedral" synagogue, Temple Emanu-El, and soon moved from midtown to the neighborhood of Columbia University. Solomon Schechter, a distinguished rabbinic scholar and historian (in religious practice he was a liberal traditionalist), was called from Cambridge University in England to New York to head the revived seminary. At its new beginnings, in 1902, it was not imagined that a new denomination was arising, for avowed Orthodox Jews, some of whom were even among the founders of the Union of Orthodox Jewish Congregations, taught on its faculty.

The new seminary began, at least in the minds of the laymen who refounded it, on an ill-defined premise. Jacob Schiff, Louis Marshall, and their friends wanted to produce Westernized rabbis who would help in the grand task of Americanizing the East European Jewish masses. Such English-speaking traditionalist rabbis already existed then in England, Germany, and France. They had defined decorous, mildly Orthodox congregations which were not socially embarrassing. Schiff and Marshall did not imagine that the American version of such synagogues would be centers of Jewish nationalist feeling, but the Conservative synagogues were soon out of control. The faculty and the students of the Jewish Theological Seminary were almost all from Eastern Europe; most were themselves recent immigrants. They had brought to America a Jewish identity which had been fashioned in the Austro-Hungarian and Russian empires, where Jews were still treated not as a religious denomination but as a national minority. On the immediate level of religious practice and observance, the Conservative synagogue was particularly comfortable for the children of the immigrants. The traditions and the rituals of Orthodox Judaism were upheld there, with one striking change— the separation of sexes at worship was abolished almost everywhere. The individual laymen were also subject to very little pressure about their personal religious conduct. But there was more to the Conservative synagogues than religious adjustment. The essence of the faith of Conservative Judaism was passion about the intense, and unique, history of the Jews. The effort for Zionism came naturally to such believers. Many of the members and sympathizers of the Zionist Organization of America, and Hadassah, belonged to Conservative synagogues. The home for a Zionist meeting, especially when a visiting emissary from Palestine was on tour, was most often the local Conservative synagogue.

Throughout the 1920s and the 1930s membership in the Conservative congregations kept rising, both in absolute numbers and in relation to the Orthodox and the Reform. In 1935 a reasonably reliable estimate showed a million Jews who identified themselves as Orthodox. The Conservative synagogues, the newest denomination, claimed three hundred thousand members, and Reform had only two hundred thousand.

Group emotion was, of course, powerful among the small minority of the American-born who had remained Orthodox in religion. A yeshivah had been established in New York as early as 1886; another was founded in 1897. These two institutions merged in 1915. This school encouraged its students to acquire a secular education. Its president, Bernard Revel, was not content to send his students to City College for their academic degrees; he wanted a college as part of his Talmudic school. By 1928 Revel had succeeded. The Yeshiva College, the first such school in all of Jewish history, accepted its first students. The motto on the seal of this new institution indicated that knowledge of the sacred literature and meticulous observance of every ritual of the Jewish tradition would be combined with secular learning. But there was suspicion regarding this new institution among the immigrant rabbis who ministered to Yiddish-speaking congregations. The new, "modern Orthodox" rabbis were competitors, and they were less learned in the Talmud. Most of the older men refused to accept these college-educated rabbis as true representatives of the Orthodox faith.

All of the religious communities, of all the clashing persuasions, had been transformed in America. In none of them, not even the Orthodox, was there any serious expectation that the laity would be trained in Jewish learning. The differing religious groups represented degrees of intensity of immigrant memory. The Orthodox congregations housed the immigrants, while the Conservative synagogues were becoming the religious home of their American-born children.

IV

The morale of Jews was lower in the 1930s than at any time ever. The Depression seemed endless for everybody, but Jews had a unique problem: anti-Semitism was more threatening than ever before in American history. Jews had withstood poverty and exclusion many times before, but the threats in America were especially upsetting.

If not here, where could Jews ever hope to attain equality among the Gentiles?

Looking inward, Jews felt more fear than hope about the future of Jewish culture. The 1930s were the tipping point for the population of American Jewry. The census of 1940 was the first to show a preponderance of native-born Jews. The institutions that the immigrants founded were still flourishing but they were clearly past their peak. The circulations of the Yiddish dailies kept dropping, as the immigrant subscribers died. The theaters on Second Avenue were closing one by one. By 1940, no more than four or five were open at any time, as compared to the roughly twenty that had existed in the heyday of the Yiddish stage. The immigrant culture was dying, and there was little sign in the 1930s of the rise of an American Jewish culture in English of comparable viability.

The news from abroad was even bleaker. To be sure, tens of thousands of Jews from Germany were arriving in the United States, but these were not the immediate relatives of the East Europeans. Their own brothers and cousins were mostly in Poland or Romania. These immigration quotas were oversubscribed, or blocked by instructions from Washington. Applicants from Poland, where homegrown anti-Semitism was as hurtful in those years as that of the Nazis, were told to wait for twelve to fifteen years before the American consulate in Warsaw could consent even to interview them. Jews could do little about their immediate relatives in Europe except send them a few dollars.

There was also growing fear about the new Zionist settlement in Palestine. Murderous riots had taken place in 1929. Arabs had killed Jews, most notably in Hebron. The tensions kept getting worse. The essential response of the British, who held the mandate for Palestine, was to appease the Arabs by trying to limit the growth of Jewish numbers in the land. Right before the war began in 1939, this process reached its climax when the government issued a White Paper in which Jews were given seventy-five thousand more places in Palestine during the next five years, after which the door to Palestine would be closed to Jews. The Yishuv, the Zionist settlement, was endangered and friendless. The declarations in favor of Zionism that were made by American politicians, especially at election time, were ritual rather than serious politics. The Middle East was remote from the United States; it was in Great Britain's sphere of influence. In the decade between 1929 and 1939, even the most Zionist American Jews had few illusions about their power to help the Jews in Palestine with anything more than money. Such funds were very short during those years of the lingering Great Depression.

The most searing heartache of the 1930s was the gulf between parents and children. The parents had come to America "for the children," but most of the children were not succeeding. The immigrants had wanted some kind of continuity with their own Jewishness, but the most intellectual of their children were alienated, on radical principle of one kind or another. Parents wanted *naches* (joy and continuity) from their children, but there was very little *naches* to be had. Never mind all the theories about the melting pot, cultural pluralism, or world revolution, which promised to confer equality on Jews. The Gentiles were not listening, American Jews felt powerless, and they were afraid.

At this worst of times Franklin Delano Roosevelt was the source of hope.

16.

FDR:

The Benevolent King of the Jews

I

The Jews loved Franklin Delano Roosevelt with singular and unparalleled passion. Most Americans admired Roosevelt for leading the country out of the Great Depression, and they gave him an unprecedented landslide victory in 1936, but the Jews felt that he was their special protector. No president of the United States had ever surrounded himself with so many Jews. Benjamin V. Cohen and Samuel Rosenman were among his most trusted lieutenants. His friend and neighbor in Dutchess County, New York, Henry Morgenthau, Jr., was secretary of the treasury. Felix Frankfurter, the famous professor of law at Harvard, commuted regularly to the White House. Jews were thus very visible, almost defiantly so, in the upper reaches of the Roosevelt administration. These men were not always heeded by Roosevelt, for he was a master of playing off his advisers against each other, or of eliciting from them the kind of advice that he wanted to hear. The Jews fared no differently from all the rest in his inner councils, but their presence in the President's entourage was a signal of hope to the masses of Jews, when they felt endangered by anti-Semitism at home and by the Nazis abroad.

It was at least equally important to Jews that Roosevelt broadened the Civil Service. Members of minorities who could pass examinations had a chance at many jobs in government and in education from which they had previously been excluded. Jews were especially delighted, because they were, in the 1930s, the single largest pool of underemployed college graduates. A host of young lawyers was hired by government agencies, especially by the new ones that were created by the New Deal. To be sure, Roosevelt pushed very few Jews into the older, existing bureaucracies. The Departments of State and War remained bastions of older establishments, but that was barely noticed by anyone. Roosevelt's coming to power represented the first entry of Jews in numbers into the government. The overwhelming majority of these "new men" were the children of recent immigrants; they were ever more grateful to Roosevelt.

So were their parents. Their culture, in Yiddish, had been regarded as exotic, and as their own private business. Valid American culture was not in the language of the immigrants; it was in American English. Roosevelt, the patrician from Groton and Harvard, of impeccable old American pedigree, acted in disregard of this prejudice. One of his most decisive acts in combating the Depression was to create the Works Progress Administration (WPA) soon after he came to power. This agency paid for numerous endeavors which put people to work at government expense. The WPA even financed theaters and writers, and not only in English. Unemployed Yiddish writers worked together in a study of the many hundreds of *Landsmanshaften,* the associations of immigrants from the same town or area, which existed in New York in the 1930s. The result of the study was published, under the imprimatur of the WPA, in a volume in Yiddish. The experience and the language of the Jewish immigrant ghetto had thus been pronounced by the United States government itself, for the very first time, to be part of the expression of American life. The Yiddish writers project of the WPA was moral recompense for the discrimination against Jews in the immigration laws.

Thus, during his first term, Roosevelt was perceived by Jews to be surrounded by Jewish courtiers, to be the protector of the Jews against their enemies, and even to have respect for their culture.

Roosevelt was the special shield of the Jews—or so they thought.

Even as he was doing little for the Jews of Europe, the Jews of America continued to believe in his "special" love for them. The root of the attitude toward Roosevelt was deep in many centuries of Jewish experience. As an endangered and often reviled minority, Jews had depended on "benevolent kings" to protect them. In many societies, both in Christian Europe and the Muslim Middle East, Jews had been the king's financiers, businessmen, physicians, and advisers, men who depended on the king's favor. They were on his side against noblemen, merchant guilds, and peasants, who generally did not want to pay taxes or to support the king's wars. To be sure, the king was often not as well disposed to the Jews as they wanted to believe. On occasion, he simply milked them for money and then expelled them from his domain. But the Jews wanted to believe— indeed, had to believe—that the king really respected them, and that he had been misled by wicked advisers. So, for example, when King Ferdinand and Queen Isabella expelled the Jews from Spain in 1492, Jews blamed the royal court and the Church for having given the royal family bad advice. This half-truth, half-fantasy about "benevolent kings" was enshrined in the prayer for kings, emperors, and even czars in the synagogues of Europe. The formula was a prayer that the ministers and the advisers of the kings might be enlightened by God to give the ruler, who is, by definition, benevolent, the kind of advice which would make him look kindly on Jews.

During Roosevelt's first term, as he became their "protector" in America, the Jews reenacted this ancient psychodrama. They believed, on the evidence of all the good things that Roosevelt did do for them, in the "good king Roosevelt." They hoped that he would eventually save their brethren in Europe. Jews attributed Roosevelt's inaction to the cabals of bureaucrats in the State Department, the present-day "successors" of the king's unfeeling, or anti-Jewish advisers. They preferred not to see him as a politician who balanced his political need of the Jews against the interests and the prejudices of all his other constituencies. They preferred, instead, to rejoice in the New Deal as their own, almost messianic deliverance in America.

The special passion of the Jews for Roosevelt was strikingly clear in the election of 1936. In 1932, when Roosevelt had run against Herbert Hoover, he had supposedly won over seventy percent of the Jewish vote, but they were not then his greatest supporters. The Italians were even more enthusiastically on his side; nearly eighty percent voted for Roosevelt. In 1936, the Jews were in the lead among his supporters. They gave him ninety percent of their votes, a bit more than he got from the nearly as enthusiastic Irish and Italians. Roosevelt received an unprecedented number of endorsements that year, across the entire Jewish political spectrum.

The mainstream of the Jewish community was almost entirely for him, but even many of the Communists, most of the Socialists— and almost all the rabbis—joined the chorus of those who praised him. Although the *Morgen Freiheit,* the Communist daily, railed against Roosevelt as an instrument of American capitalism, many of its subscribers voted for Roosevelt and not Earl Browder, the party candidate. Among the Socialists, the split of opinion was open and pronounced. In 1932 at least one-fourth of the 900,000 who voted for Norman Thomas, the Socialist candidate for president, had been Jews. Four years later, almost all had abandoned Thomas. In April 1936, the *Zukunft,* the Socialist monthly journal in Yiddish, endorsed Roosevelt, writing that he "has no fixed philosophy or fixed convictions concerning all of the difficult problems which confront the country. But, he has a good heart. Until now, sympathy and compassion have been his compass; he has listened to his more liberal advisors." Even *Der Freind,* the official organ of the Workman's Circle, endorsed Roosevelt; only a strong leader can rally America against the Fascists; the workers ought to vote for Roosevelt because he has put them to work.

Even more surprising endorsements came from the editors of small Hebrew journals, which had never before spoken out on politics. *Hadoar,* a secular weekly devoted to literary and cultural matters, endorsed Roosevelt, calling him "a leader and prophet, who had arisen to take the people from the desert to the promised land." They praised the President for his efforts in combating the economic Depression, and for his leadership for the "light and good" of democracy against the "darkness and evil" of Fascism. The most unexpected support appeared in *Hapardes,* a Hebrew monthly for rabbis. Its editor, Rabbi S. A. Pardes, endorsed Roosevelt not only as a champion of democracy and the savior of the country from the Depression, but as a protector of threatened Jews in Europe.

Roosevelt received a copy of this editorial in English translation. He responded with a letter thanking the author for "his pledge of loyalty and confidence and for his generous appraisal of his administration." But there was no response at all to Rabbi Pardes's concern about the Jews in Europe, not even a ritual expression of sympathy for their plight. The editor printed Roosevelt's letter, and added the hope that "we trust that President Roosevelt will stand by us [the Jews] not only in America but also beyond its borders." Rabbi Pardes had a hard time finding proof of this assertion from the very general letter that Roosevelt had written—but it was wonderful, so Pardes implied, that a president had responded to an Orthodox rabbi.

The near worship of Roosevelt was possible in the first five or six years of his presidency even among those, like Rabbi Pardes, who were most concerned about the Jews in Europe. In the mid-1930s, the temperature of anti-Semitism in Europe had not yet become uniquely searing. It was still possible for American Jews to think that the situation of their brothers and sisters in Europe was grave but not catastrophic, that there was still some time to find means of relief, and that Roosevelt, the "benevolent monarch," would take pity on his Jewish children. This was, in fact, a role he loved to play, and not only for Jews. He liked to hear his visitors call him "Papa," or Chief, and come to him as suppliants, asking for protection. It was unimaginable to Jews that such a leader would fail to protect the victims of the Nazis if their dangers increased. Therefore, Jews felt that they could in good conscience worry most about their own problems in America.

As the Depression hung on, anti-Semitism was on the rise in the United States. Public opinion polls showed that roughly one-third of the respondents thought that "Jews had too much power." There was substantial sentiment, on the order of one in five, to restrict the role of Jews in politics and even in business. Father Charles Coughlin, the radio priest from Royal Oak, Michigan, had an average of a quarter million subscribers to his largely anti-Jewish weekly, *Social Justice*. The Ku Klux Klan claimed more than one hundred thousand members. Though the Klan had begun in the South, which was still its major base, it was acquiring many members in the big cities where Jews lived. The German-American Bund, the Nazi party in America, though much smaller, was visible and virulent. There were many fistfights in those years between American Nazis in uniform and young Jews who were outraged by the presence of Hitler's followers on American soil.

In October 1935, the editors of *Fortune* magazine published a large study of anti-Semitism in America. This account argued that anti-Semitism was widespread, especially among the poor, and that the poor might turn violent if they remained hungry. A few months later, *Fortune*'s editors followed up their survey of anti-Semitism with an analysis of Jewish power. *Fortune*'s researchers had found that though Jews were concentrated in white-collar pursuits, they dominated nothing of any consequence in American life. This article was an attempt to answer the anti-Semites, and to calm the fears of Jews, who were described by the editors of *Fortune* as overreacting and thus inviting more trouble for themselves. But the Jews were not overreacting. *Fortune* itself soon proved that the Jews had real worries. In February 1936, the editors defined the Jew in America as still a "universal stranger." *Fortune*'s pundits added that the "Russian Jews" had not yet been absorbed in America, and that many insisted on retaining their Jewish identity. They were in need of "toleration and respect."

It was dangerous, then, for an embattled minority to push for the unpopular and losing cause, to try to open the door wider to refugees. Roosevelt's own political calculations produced essentially the same results. He could not annoy the labor movement, which was opposed to more immigration, and he did not want to lose votes to the anti-Semites, who had taken to calling him Rosenfeld. He had sinned in their eyes by appointing a number of Jews to visible roles in his administration.

The Zionists offered an alternative policy, to ask for the quick establishment of a Jewish state in part of Palestine which would accept those who were in danger in Europe. In 1936, there was reason for such optimism. The British commission under Lord Peel to consider the future of the land recommended in the spring of 1937 that Palestine be partitioned, and that a Jewish and an Arab state be established. It was not ignoble in the mid-1930s for some American Jews to take their energies away from a losing battle for large-scale immigration into America and to turn toward the fight for Zionist immigration into Palestine. There was a special dignity to pleading not for refugees but for a people who were reestablishing their ancient home. Roosevelt helped the Zionists by issuing declarations of support, especially at election time. In 1936, in their election platform, the Democrats did not advocate easing immigration restrictions, but neither did the Republicans. The Democrats demanded that Britain, the power that held the mandate to Palestine, refrain from restricting the immigration of Jews. Here, too, the Republicans agreed, but that could not gain them any votes away from Roosevelt. He spoke for this plank in public, and even in private representations to the British government. Roosevelt easily played the "benevolent monarch" for the Zionists, too.

II

American Jews have been accused in numerous recent studies of having done too little for the Jews of Europe. This charge is essentially not true. The one or two attempts that were made in the 1930s to loosen the restrictions on immigration backfired. The Congress of the United States was simply not susceptible to Jewish pressure. The only path that was open to Jews was to attempt to persuade Roosevelt.

The Jewish figure who was personally closest to Roosevelt was Felix Frankfurter. He was born in Vienna and came to the United States in his early teens. Hitler's attacks on the Jews of Germany were for him a very personal and painful issue. Frankfurter raised the matter with the President as early as April 7, 1933, barely a month after Roosevelt had assumed office and less than a week after the boycott of Jewish businesses that Hitler's government had organized for April 1. After hearing nothing for two weeks, Frankfurter sent the President a telegram, asking for "some word of progress." He finally received an answer, not from the President but from the secretary of state, Cordell Hull, who assured Frankfurter that there were plenty of unused quota numbers for people who were born in Germany who wanted to come to the United States. When Frankfurter wanted to save a relative of his from Vienna, he went to an English contact, Lady Astor, for help, and not to Roosevelt. After this effort succeeded, he sent a copy of the document to FDR. Frankfurter felt let down throughout the Roosevelt years by the lack of large action, but he believed, or wanted to believe, that Roosevelt was blameless and that the good intentions of the President were being blocked by State Department bureaucrats. Frankfurter, too, was behaving as a Jew who had been fashioned by the myth of the "benevolent king."

The leaders of the American Jewish Committee kept intervening in private. In the 1930s, that organization still spoke for the "German Jews," who believed that Jews should talk in universalist accents about the rights of individuals, and that anti-Semitism, as such, was best not mentioned. The leaders of the American Jewish Committee were afraid that given a choice between the cause of the European Jews and Nazism, the Jews would not necessarily win in American public opinion. In contrast, the major spokesman of the "Russian Jews," Rabbi Stephen S. Wise, insisted on public action. A coalition of organizations under his leadership organized a massive protest meeting at Madison Square Garden in New York on March 28, 1933. The tens of thousands who gathered there knew that they had little influence on Hitler; their main purpose was to move the newly in-augurated President to denounce the Nazi regime. They failed, be-cause the United States was still trying to have "correct relations" with Germany. But the American Jews were not indifferent. They raised impressive amounts of money in the years of the Depression to help the Jews of Germany emigrate. Between 1933 and 1939, the American Jewish Joint Distribution Committee spent nearly twenty million dollars, an impressive sum, particularly during the economic Depression.

After the election of 1936, despite the massive support he had received from Jews, Roosevelt did not move to do more for the "non-Aryans" who were being persecuted by the Nazis. He was limited by anti-Semitism, which was actually getting worse in the United States. In 1937, the American Institute for Public Opinion found that nearly two out of five Americans thought that anti-Jewish sentiment was increasing. In a poll in March 1938, forty-one percent thought that Jews had "too much power in the United States"; almost half thought the Jews were at least in part to blame for their perse-cution in Europe. In those days, everybody read the novelist Sinclair Lewis. It was Lewis's judgment that the triumph of anti-Semitism in America was a real possibility. That was the message of his topical novel, *It Can't Happen Here,* which appeared in 1935. American Jews read the book and they were both fearful and angry.

Soon after the election, Roosevelt himself was in a weakened political condition. In the first year of his second term, in 1937, he proposed adding to the number of justices in the Supreme Court, in order to overcome the existing conservative majority, and he lost the fight. The years 1937–38 were a time of economic depression—the "Roosevelt depression"—and parts of his own party, especially the Southerners, were in rebellion against the New Deal. The limit of Roosevelt's power was evident on the one occasion when he actually proposed a major act to help the Jews. In March 1938, Germany invaded Austria and its Jews were immediately in danger: some were mistreated or beaten up; others were sent to concentration camps. Within a few days Roosevelt floated the idea at a cabinet meeting of special aid for refugees from Austria. The cabinet advised him that he could not get a bill passed in Congress to increase the immigration quota. The public opinion polls proved most Americans were then opposed to such action. In April 1938, Roosevelt called for a conference of all concerned governments to find ways of helping the refugees. This meeting was convened in Evian-les-Bains, France, in July.

It came to very little. Few of the assembled nations, some thirty-two of them, wanted any new immigrants. Australia promised to admit 15,000 in the next three years, and it actually did admit some 5,000 before war broke out in the Pacific on December 7, 1941. The Dominican Republic made a dramatic offer to accept 100,000 refugees, but the structure to receive them did not exist in the primitive economy of the island. Some 500 families did arrive. The Netherlands, which had already accepted 25,000 refugees from Germany, offered temporary housing to those on their way to other countries. Denmark, with its already dense population, announced that it would continue to be as hospitable as it could to refugees. No other country responded with anything more than words. The United States, the principal convener of the meeting, did not offer even to consider changing its restrictive immigration policies.

Even Rabbi Stephen Wise was upset when a Jewish congressman from Brooklyn, Emanuel Celler, introduced a bill to waive all limitations on refugees who wanted to come to the United States. Wise was certain that such a bill would arouse the many enemies of immigration, and the ensuing outcry would block all possibility for quiet acts of favor by presidential instruction for all the refugees, including not only Jews but also other opponents of Nazism. The only real hope, against an increasing majority of the people, and the insensitivity and hostility of many of Roosevelt's advisers, was the personal benevolence of the President.

On the night of November 9–10, 1938, when the Nazis made a massive, nationwide pogrom in Germany, called Crystal Night, the problem became more acute. Almost all of the synagogues in Germany were burned or vandalized, and many Jews were beaten. After this outrage, it was clear to all the world that the Jews had to be gotten out, and quickly. Roosevelt recalled Ambassador Hugh Wilson, and issued a strong statement condemning Nazi barbarism, but he did not move to change the immigration laws. Under pressure from the secretary of labor, Frances Perkins, who, along with Henry Morgenthau, Jr., was most concerned about the victims of the Nazis, Roosevelt did extend visitors' visas for German refugees, for many had come to the United States on such visas. This action amounted to letting nearly fifteen thousand people stay on in the United States, almost all permanently.

By late 1938 Roosevelt was already mentally prepared for war in Europe. He did not want to add to the venom of the isolationists by being too involved in the question of Jews; he did not want to annoy the large majority of Americans who professed some sympathy with the victims of the Nazis but did not want them in the United States. In a radio speech in late November 1938, Myron Taylor, Roosevelt's principal representative to the Conference on Refugees in Evian, assured the American people that nothing would be done for the Jews who wanted to get out. The language was very thinly veiled:

> Our plans do not involve "flooding" of this or any other country with aliens of any race or creed. On the contrary, our entire program is based on the existing immigration laws of all the countries concerned, and I am confident that within that framework our problem can be solved.

Nonetheless, more was done for Jewish refugees that year than ever before. Roosevelt was behaving with far more concern in private than in public. The bureaucratic delays in issuing visas were made much less severe. For the first time, the whole of the quota that had been assigned to Germany and Austria by the immigration law of 1924, nearly twenty-eight thousand, was used in 1939. A bill to add twenty thousand additional places in the next two years for children under fourteen failed to get anywhere in Congress. In this very bitter time for Jews, Roosevelt nominated Felix Frankfurter to a seat on the Supreme Court, in actual, though not direct, succession to Louis D. Brandeis. Though Frankfurter was then perceived to be a radical, as Brandeis before him, Roosevelt insisted on appointing him. This action was widely interpreted both in America and abroad as an assertion by Roosevelt that he would not countenance the downgrading of Jews in America. The "Chief" had refused to be intimidated by anti-Semites. The difference between nominating Frankfurter and avoiding the issue of the immigration law was political calculation: the arguments about Frankfurter would soon go away, for they involved very few people directly; a more liberal immigration policy could have cost Roosevelt votes.

The most pointed and most poignant proof of Roosevelt's unwillingness to fight with the enemies of immigration on behalf of Jewish refugees was the St. Louis affair, in May 1939. At that time the Nazi government was pushing out every Jew who held a document which might entitle him to land somewhere. The St. Louis, which was owned by the Hamburg-America Line, sailed for Havana, Cuba, carrying more than nine hundred people, most of them Jews. Well over seven hundred were eligible for admission to the United States; they had already filed affidavits of support with American immigration officers, and were awaiting a "quota number." These refugees proposed to land in Havana, with the prior agreement of the Cuban government, until there would be a place for them in the United States. While the ship was at sea, however, the Cubans changed their minds. The "tourist letters" of admission to Cuba that the passengers had bought from the steamship line were no longer acceptable. When the St. Louis arrived in Havana harbor, almost no one on board was permitted to land. Privately, the American embassy in Havana tried to persuade the Cubans to let the passengers disembark. The American Jewish Joint Distribution Committee offered to pay bond so that the passengers would not be a public charge in Cuba, but the amount that the Cubans demanded kept rising, and the request for large bribes became increasingly more outrageous. All the negotiations failed, and the St. Louis was ordered out of Havana. The captain of the ship then headed for the coast of Florida, but the United States Coast Guard made sure that he would not make port in America and that no passenger would swim ashore.

This drama became headline news in America. The White House and the State Department were barraged with telegrams. At one stage of the negotiations with the Cubans, while the *St. Louis* was still in Havana harbor, American Jews tried to guarantee the bond. Leaders of the Joint Distribution Committee asked the embassy in Havana to arrange for them to see Cuba's president, Federico Laredo Bru. The head of the visa division of the State Department, Asa Warner, telephoned the counsel general in Vienna, Coert du Bois, to instruct him that "under no circumstances" should he "intervene in the landing of the *St. Louis.*" Warner made it clear that this instruction came directly from the secretary of state and the White House. Roosevelt and Cordell Hull had thus been willing to say a private word to the Cubans, but not to act in public. The desperate passengers on the *St. Louis* telegraphed the President, but he ignored them. The ship had no choice but to go back to Hamburg; most of its passengers ultimately perished in Nazi-held Europe.

It was not noticed at the time that the voyage of the *St. Louis* was an eerie, but tragic, reenactment of the very first journey of a boatload of Jews to America. In 1654, the *Ste. Catherine,* carrying twenty-three refugees from Recife, Brazil, had stopped in Cuba and been turned away, like the *St. Louis* almost three centuries later. But, when the *Ste. Catherine* arrived in New York, Peter Stuyvesant did not send out the "Coast Guard" to force the ship away. He eventually agreed to let them stay, on the assurances by the Jews of Amsterdam that they would not become a public charge. In 1939, a more "enlightened" government in America was infinitely less decent.

III

By 1939, when the Second World War began, and the situation of the Jews in Europe became catastrophic, Roosevelt had already defined and redefined this attitude to Jewish refugees. He was personally sympathetic, provided he could express that sympathy through quiet administrative action. In fact, Roosevelt had become more sympathetic personally, as the situation of the Jews in Europe was becoming radically worse. The proof is in the immigration statistics. In the years 1933 through 1937, fewer than 40,000 Jews had been allowed into the United States. These numbers represented less than twenty percent of the room for immigrants that existed even under the Immigration Law of 1924. From 1938 through 1941, when America entered the war, 110,000 Jews entered the United States as immigrants. The numbers increased because the visa section of the State Department knew that the President wanted to stop putting obstacles in the way of refugees. Roosevelt could change administrative procedure, as an act of conscience and to satisfy his Jewish constituents, without courting political trouble.

The onset of the Second World War essentially relieved Roosevelt of this problem along with many others. He was soon claiming the United States was "the arsenal of democracy," and he insisted that the defeat of the Nazis was now the democratic world's only concern. The Jews, who were the targets of Hitler's fiercest invective, certainly could take no exception to Roosevelt's seemingly single-minded passion for victory, especially because he promised that after the war all the wrongs that the Nazis had inflicted would be righted. At the beginning of the war, almost all the Jewish leaders in America agreed that the Jews of Europe should not be a "special case." The first bitter fight within American Jewry began in October 1939, over this very issue: Should Jews obey the blockade of Nazi Europe that Great Britain had announced, or should they, as neutrals, send food packages and other help to the Jews in Poland? The Jewish Labor Committee, which had direct links with occupied Poland, insisted that it was the duty of American Jews to send all possible help into Poland. But Dr. Joseph Tenenbaum, who was both the president of the Federation of Polish Jews in America and the chairman of the Joint Boycott Council, insisted in agreeing with the British that "the responsibility for feeding occupied Europe rightfully rests with Germany." Tenenbaum, therefore, urged Jews to cease contributing to the relief of their brethren in Poland. Rabbi Stephen Wise was even more vehement. He thundered that Jews could not afford "to run the risk of alienating the already dubious good will of the British government to our people," and therefore, as "president" of the American Jewish Congress, he issued "the order of immediate discontinuance."

The Socialists of the Jewish Labor Committee defied Tenenbaum and Wise, but they eventually directed their help to Jews who were taking refuge in neutral countries or in Vichy France. Uncompromising defiance came from ultra-Orthodox of the Agudath Israel. By the summer of 1941, only the Agudath Israel was still sending food packages directly to Poland. The Joint Boycott Council, which represented most of the organizations in America, picketed the offices of Agudath Israel in New York for three weeks—but this Orthodox body refused to knuckle under. At the beginning of the war, while America was still neutral, choices were made: almost all of the leaders of the Jewish establishment were loath to proclaim the Jews to be a special case. The Socialists and the Orthodox (in both groups most still spoke Yiddish) were emotionally closest to the Jews of Eastern Europe; they cared least about offending London or Washington.

This quarrel during the two years of American neutrality was conducted in the awareness of some random murders of Jews in Eastern Europe, but before the decision by the Nazis in January 1942 to establish the death factories. It was therefore still possible to believe that the Jews of Europe would come out of the war battered but not destroyed. The news of systematic murder began to leak to the West by July 1942. The Jewish Labor Committee received a report from Poland that seven hundred thousand Jews had already been killed. (We know, now, that this number was an underestimate.) But this report was not believed. By the fall of 1942, such accounts could no longer be disregarded. The government of the United States knew, as did the leaders of the American Jews, that the Nazis had embarked on systematic mass murder and that the killings had begun in January 1942 in makeshift gas chambers near Auschwitz. By midsummer the operation was at full speed. The news was brought to Switzerland by a German industrialist, Eduard Schulte. Through intermediaries the story soon reached Gerhart Riegner, who represented the World Jewish Congress in Geneva. Riegner brought this seemingly unbelievable information to the American consulate in Geneva and asked that it be sent on to Rabbi Stephen Wise in New York.

Riegner's story was not believed by anyone in the State Department's chain of command; it was characterized in an internal document in Washington as a "wild rumor" inspired by Jewish fears. Several levels of bureaucrats, reaching up to the under secretary of state, Sumner Welles (who was personally very sympathetic to the plight of Jews in Nazi Europe), decided that Riegner's story was inflammatory, and that such questionable information should not be passed on to Rabbi Wise. But Wise soon heard the story. Riegner had also informed another official of the World Jewish Congress, Samuel Sydney Silverman, who was a member of the British Parliament, and Silverman sent the telegram on to Wise. Almost immediately Wise called a meeting of leaders of the major American Jewish organizations to tell them of the Riegner cable, and to relay news from other sources, that there was mass carnage in Warsaw. In early December, a delegation of American Jewish leaders was received by President Roosevelt at the White House. He assured the delegation that he would do all in his power "to be of service to your people in this tragic moment." Two weeks later, on December 17, he and Churchill issued the one statement that the Allies ever made in the course of the war in which they expressed their concern for Jews by name. Rabbi Wise and the others had left the meeting with Roosevelt encouraged, but all that the President had really promised was punishment for the Nazi criminals after the war. In actual practice, Roosevelt reassured Congress, at the very moment of these expressions of sympathy and concern, that he had no plans for proposing the lifting of immigration restrictions.

Roosevelt may not yet have been aware of the full extent of the tragedy in December 1942, though there is abundant evidence in wartime intelligence documents that the American government was well-informed, both directly and through the Vatican. But there cannot be the slightest doubt that by midsummer 1943, Roosevelt knew everything. He heard directly in July 1943 from an eyewitness to the horrors. Jan Karski, a lieutenant in the Polish underground, gave the President a personal account of what he had witnessed some months before in Belzec. Karski actually had seen railroad cars full of corpses; he attested, as beyond doubt, to the existence of gas chambers. Karski told the President that the horror tales reaching the West were not exaggerated: more than half of Polish Jewry was already dead; the Nazis intended to exterminate every Jew in Europe. Roosevelt didn't comment on what he'd heard; he simply assured Karski that the Allies would win the war.

It is equally beyond doubt that the Jewish leadership in America knew the extent of the tragedy, as it was happening. Riegner and Karski were not the only sources. The Polish government-in-exile in London included two Jewish members, Szmul Zygielbojm and Ignacy Schwarzbart. They tried desperately to make the West pay attention to the news of the slaughter of the Jews, but they were ignored. On May 12, 1943, Zygielbojm committed suicide, leaving behind letters condemning the Allies for their failure to do anything to stop the murders. Zygielbojm already knew that his family in Poland had been completely wiped out, and that the Allies were refusing to do anything directly to save the Jews who were still alive. The day before he committed suicide, Zygielbojm was told by a young officer of American intelligence, Arthur Goldberg (who would later become a member of Kennedy's cabinet and a justice of the Supreme Court), that the American Air Force would not be instructed to bomb the railroad line to Auschwitz. Goldberg did not know who had made this decision, and so he could not have named names, but he suspected privately that the question had been decided by Roosevelt himself. Zygielbojm went home from his meeting with Goldberg—it was dinner at Claridge's—knowing that the Allies would not use force to symbolize any specific concern for Jews. The Western press took note of Zygielbojm's suicide, but it largely ignored the cause.

Among the Jews in America, all the leaders knew. The Orthodox Jewish community was particularly well-informed. Jacob Rosenheim, the international president of the Agudath Israel, the most Orthodox Jewish organization, was in close touch with developments in Europe through his representatives in Switzerland. The Labor Zionists in America knew, because they were told over and over again by the intellectual leader of the movement, Hayim Greenberg, through their publications, *Jewish Frontier* and *Yiddisher Kemfer*. Greenberg wrote in *Jewish Frontier* in 1943 that he was in shock that "Jews have not produced a substantial number of mentally deranged persons." The "full even temper" that prevailed was much more abnormal than "hysteria."

Knowing as much as they did, why did Roosevelt—and the Jews—do so little? When the United States entered the war at the end of 1941, it was far from certain that the Allies would win. During the first eighteen months of American participation, the Japanese dominated eastern Asia; the Germans were deep into Russia, and their Afrika Korps had driven across North Africa very nearly to Cairo. The Allies were the losing side until November 1942, when Montgomery stopped Rommel at El Alamein, and February 1943, when the Germans surrendered at Stalingrad. Roosevelt and Churchill began to feel like winners in Europe in the course of that year, as the Russians kept rolling back the Germans, and the Allies made their first landings in Italy. Millions were dying on all the battle fronts; it was difficult to cast the Jews as a special case. Indeed, until the death camps were opened after the German surrender, American public opinion did not believe the accounts of the atrocities. The one poll that was taken before the end of the war showed that most Americans guessed that perhaps one hundred thousand Jews in all had been killed by the Nazis. Jews in Europe were imagined to have been victims of the massive pogrom, but that was not unprecedented; some sixty thousand Jews had been killed between 1919 and 1921 in the wars on the Russian-Polish border. Such suffering, if that was all, was minor, by the standards of the mass slaughter of the war.

Roosevelt's convenient and comforting answer to others—and undoubtedly to himself—was that he was concentrating on winning the war, and he was hoping that victory would come quickly enough to save many of the Jews of Europe. In fact, if the war had been one year shorter, this hope would have been realized, for in mid-1944, two million of Europe's Jews were still alive. Roosevelt refused to permit the use of money or supplies to bribe Nazis to let some Jews live. He did repeatedly alert the Nazis that they would be held accountable for their murder of the Jews, but only once did he mention the Jews as such. Though Roosevelt has been severely criticized in retrospect by many historians, it is hard to see what a specific statement could have accomplished. The Nazi "war against the Jews" was so central to Hitler and to his followers that they pursued it to the very last days of their power. This was the "war" that they could win, and, as Martin Bormann is reputed to have said, they would "jump into their graves laughing." The Nazis knew that Roosevelt would treat them as war criminals for all of their crimes, and not only those against the Jews. Some lower-ranking officers occasionally behaved better than they might have, because they feared Allied retribution, but those who ran the Nazi government took no notice of these threats until the very last months of the war, when total defeat was imminent.

The pained and elaborate discussions in recent years about whether the Jews of the United States did enough to save their brethren in Europe are therefore essentially unhistorical. Jews had no power to do more. Jews protested in public many times during the war years. Individuals and delegations went to see the President and many high

officials of the government. Coordinating committees were organized several times by the major national Jewish organizations to
work to rescue the Jews in Europe. These bodies fell apart over
differences in policy and tactics. The Orthodox went their own way,
insisting on contravening the law against sending bribe money into
Nazi-held territory. The Zionists agitated for making a Jewish state
in Palestine the "war aim" of the Jewish people. Though they succeeded in winning overwhelming endorsement for their platform in
the meeting in January 1943 at the American Jewish Conference, a
body in which all the organizations participated, the endorsement
was not unanimous. The representatives of the American Jewish
Committee walked out rather than agree to this nationalist aim. The
dissenters preferred to hope, then, for the restoration of democracy
all over the world and the repatriation of the people whom Hitler
had displaced.

But even if the groups had been united and single-minded, it is
hard to imagine a different outcome. Had the American Jews dared
to stage a sit-in at the White House or to engage in civil disobedience
in the major cities of the country, the catastrophe in Europe would
have received much more attention. Indeed, one such effort was made
by the Orthodox, in alliance with the Palestinian representatives in
America of the right-wing Revisionist party. Four hundred rabbis
marched from the Capitol to the White House on October 6, 1943,
the day before Yom Kippur, "to protest the silence of the world
when an entire people is being murdered," and to assert that this "is
a crime and that all who tolerate it are equally guilty." Roosevelt
did not receive the rabbis, in large part because his closest Jewish
advisers did not like the organizers of the protest march. This action
did move some members of Congress to consider a special, separate
effort for the rescue of Jews, but nothing happened until Roosevelt
was persuaded to act—and he did not change his mind until victory
seemed secure.

In January 1944, Roosevelt was persuaded by Henry Morgenthau,
Jr., to create the War Refugee Board. This body was allowed to
"trade with the enemy." Its major success was to save the lives, by
bribery, of tens of thousands of Jews out of Hungary and Romania.
In Hungary, in the spring of 1945, Raoul Wallenberg, a young Swedish diplomat, protected thousands of Jews in Budapest from depor-
tation, only to disappear at the end of the war behind Russian lines;

Wallenberg operated with American Jewish money. The work of the War Refugee Board was the one major achievement of the Roosevelt administration in rescuing Jews from the Nazis. It was possible because the fears of domestic disunity had lessened, as worry about the outcome of the war was essentially gone.

Roosevelt ran again, for his fourth term, in the fall of 1944. He again lost votes among most of the minorities; five percent of the Irish and ten percent of the Italians moved to the Republicans. But the Jews gave him the largest proportion of their vote ever: ninety-three percent. They wanted to believe that he was extending himself to save the Jews in Europe. Most Jewish leaders knew even in 1944 that Roosevelt had done much too little, but the Jewish masses were more adoring than ever of the "benevolent king."

The experience of American Jews with Roosevelt was paradoxical. After his death, when the Jews began to reflect on the Roosevelt years, they discovered that he had taught them a deep truth about America: it is power that really counts, and they had not had enough. Roosevelt had paid his political and emotional debts to Jews by opening doors in government and in the economy—and they were deeply grateful. But, during the Holocaust, Jews had not been powerful enough among all the factions and fractions of America to make the President and Congress feel their Jewish pain. In the 1940s, this knowledge was not yet spelled out in public. Jews continued to speak the language of goodwill, and of "Americans all," but Jews would spend the next two decades making sure that power in America was not the monopoly of the uncaring.

17.

After the War

During the Second World War, the Irish had no love for Great Britain, many of the Italians admired Mussolini, most of the Slavs hated Stalin, and the blacks were still victims of almost total segregation. The Jews were different—they hated Hitler—but they shared with the other minorities the feeling of being outsiders in America. Yet everyone rallied to the flag with enthusiasm. The rhetoric of the war effort promised everyone equality in America after the war, if only the children of minorities would behave like "Americans." Most accepted this bargain and, at the war's end, they demanded payment. But they soon felt betrayed when the deal was not honored.

The bargain between the majority and the minorities was made by the new wartime American nationalism. Roosevelt took the lead in proclaiming America's mission as the "Bearer of Democracy" for all the world. This nearly messianic self-image reached back to one of the deepest themes in American history—the certainty of the Puritans that they had come to the New World to create a society which would redeem the Old. In a time of total war, this vision could no longer be defended by American aristocrats alone. The United States could save Europe from the Nazis—and itself from the Japanese—only if everyone, without exception, fought in the common cause. The "Bearer of Democracy" could succeed only with the participation of "Americans All." During the war, blacks continued to protest against the indignity of segregation in the military; Americans of Japanese origin were put in concentration camps as security risks. But even blacks and Japanese, who had the greatest immediate scores to settle with the American majority, eagerly enlisted. They were sure that in victory they would not be excluded again from all the benefits of America. Very consciously, they were earning due bills on the American future.

The war movies made during this era expressed this new American nationalism. The three major outsiders in American society were Catholics, Negroes, and Jews. Every embattled platoon contained at least one of each: a second-generation Irish Catholic who still spoke with a light brogue, or a Polish Catholic from the coal mines of Pennsylvania; a street-smart Italian-American, an inner-city or southern black, and a white-collar Jew who turned out to be as heroic as the rest. These heroes, regarded as aliens by their white, southern sergeant, usually started out distrusting each other. But under fire, in the movies' final scene, the protagonists coalesced. After one of them died heroically saving the sergeant's life, they were transformed into equally worthy examples of "Americans All."

There was thus room in America for people of diverse backgrounds and origins—but this ideal could be interpreted in contradictory ways. Did it mean that there was now a new, triumphant "religion of democracy" to which all Americans were supposed to belong? Or would each group now be free to be itself, at its most angular? The wartime vision of American nationalism was basically assimilationist. The standard movie plot contained more than a hint of the suggestion that the fast-talking kid from Brooklyn was learning to behave like the archetypal American from Kansas, or perhaps even a Yankee aristocrat from New England. All past separate accounts with the American majority would end, if only society agreed to accept suitably assimilated individuals of whatever origin.

But the separate accounts of the minorities of Jews with America could not be ended so easily. For Jews in 1945 it required a conscious act of looking away, of instant group amnesia. Perforce, American Jews looked at the death camps which had been discovered by the Allies in 1945, but they preferred to bury the issues raised by the newsreels of bodies stacked like cordwood in Bergen-Belsen, or of the ashes in the ovens of Auschwitz. American Jews did not want to stand aside from the rest of America. In their deepest souls, the sight of the death camps had suddenly made them very lonely in the world. As "cobelligerents," the Jewish people had lost their war. But American Jews needed to feel that they were part of America, that they were among the victors. Possible American complicity, by inaction, in the murder of the Jews of Europe could not be discussed. If such an accusation were true, America's Jews would have had to continue to think of themselves as deeply alien. In the midst of the euphoria of the spring of 1945, American Jews would have been left to imagine themselves as stepchildren, more of a nuisance than a source of pride, to America as a whole, and even to the "gracious king" Franklin Delano Roosevelt.

Nor did Jews want, then, to examine their own conduct. They could have offered the excuse immediately that as outsiders, beset by anti-Semitism and concerned about their own status, they had been powerless to act boldly, but they preferred to suppress the subject. The Jewish agenda was dominated by one desire, to expand the place of Jews in America. They wanted to be accepted by the Gentiles, not to confront them—at least not then.

This was the message in those years of the most talked about novel about anti-Semitism, Laura Z. Hobson's *Gentleman's Agreement*. (It was published in 1947.) The hero of the story is a Gentile who disguises himself as a Jew. This thoroughly likable and decent Gentile is mistrusted only because he is thought to be Jewish. The point of Hobson's story is that the hero, who was played in the movie version by Gregory Peck, one of Hollywood's cleanest-cut "American" actors, was really no different from everyone else, that his Jewishness was label-deep. This treatment of anti-Semitism in America encouraged Jews to behave like Gentiles, and it avoided the question of whether Jews really were different from Gentiles, or whether America should be hospitable to those who did not play the game of assimilation. According to *Gentleman's Agreement,* for Jews to succeed in America, the remains of their immigrant and ghetto past had to be driven deep underground.

No one had any illusions that *Gentleman's Agreement* was an important work of literature, but it did express the dominant mood, even among serious writers. During and immediately after the war many younger Jewish intellectuals, who had been born and raised in the immigrants' ghettos, were eager to accept what the new American nationalism seemed to offer: minorities would be allowed into society if they adopted the manners and culture of Protestant Christians, or if they became "universal men." This "bargain" was accepted then, with variations, by two brilliant young Jewish writers of the war years, Arthur Miller and Saul Bellow.

Bellow's first book, *Dangling Man,* appeared in 1944. Joseph, the protagonist and narrator of the novel, is caught in a state of ambivalence and self-questioning, torn between the desire to find a "group whose covenants forbade spite, bloodiness, and cruelty" and his own anger at what he perceives to be violations of the rules of humanity. The author reveals nothing about Joseph's origins. What we know about Joseph is that he is an ex-Communist, that he wants a life which is not hemmed in by choices which are made for him, and that he wants to find his way to the moral leadership of a regenerated humanity. This description is unmistakably that of a Jewish intellectual in 1944, who had become disillusioned with Communism.

Arthur Miller, who began his career in the war years, was equally uncomfortable with his Jewishness. Miller's early novel, *Focus,* which appeared in 1945, is the story of Lawrence Newman, a bigoted organizational man of the 1940s. Newman is especially repulsed by Jews, until he needs to wear glasses and begins "seeing a Jew" every time he looks in the mirror. His self-loathing creates paranoia; he hears and sees everything as anti-Semitic reaction to him. Newman tries to return to mainstream society by joining a group to drive away a Jewish neighbor, but ultimately, he cannot bring himself to persecute someone who has done him no wrong. The anti-Jewish group assaults him. At one point, Newman addresses the Jews and wishes that they would "for God's sake go away, let everybody be the same! The same, let us all be the same!" Nor does Finkelstein, the sole Jewish character in the novel, defend his right to be a Jew. He pleads only that people not be lumped together under one stereotype. He wants to be seen as an individual without any reference to his Jewishness: "You can look at me and you don't see me. You see something else." In an early issue of *Commentary* magazine, *Focus* was praised for attempting to enlighten the non-Jewish community about the evils of anti-Semitism. There was no ringing defense in the review of the right of Jews to be themselves, but rather an acceptance that Jewishness is best forgotten. Jews would arrive in America in the name of "brotherhood," that is, by finding acceptance in the existing bourgeois society.

Miller has confirmed the assimilationist thrust of his early work. In his autobiography he recounts that as a college student he struggled to identify himself "with mankind rather than one small tribal fraction of it." He asserted that for him Judaism had become "dead history." For Miller, Orthodox Jews "had always seemed like atavisms, fossils of a long-dead past . . . they were either collecting alms or were too sharp as businessmen." Such a memory had gone beyond assimilation; it had internalized more than a bit of the anti-Semitism of the WASPs. Bellow and Miller thus announced a new direction for their generation: some of the intellectual children of the immigrants no longer railed against America or wanted to make the Communist revolution. They had abandoned the community of the political Left, but they had not moved to the Jewish community. They simply wanted to make their way, then, into the existing post-war America.

This agenda of seeking acceptance was never central to Bellow, but it is at the core of Arthur Miller's most famous work, *Death of a Salesman* (1949). Though Willy Loman and his son, Biff, are presented as Americans, we are given no clues as to their provenance. Here again, Miller suggests a smoothed-out society in which people have jettisoned their pasts and belong to no subgroup. And while Willy Loman was portrayed as a "general American" type, he is most intelligible as a Jewish immigrant. Of the many productions of this play, perhaps the most memorable was in Yiddish in the mid-1960s. Willy Loman was played by Joseph Buloff, one of the last great classical actors of the Yiddish stage. Watching Buloff's performance, one knew that the family's deepest, most repressed pain came from the Jewishness Willy had surrendered. Biff knew, perhaps better even than the author who created him, that the sacrifice had been wasted, that the approval of the Gentiles did not offer the content of a life and, above all, such approval would not be offered.

In their rush to arrive in America, the Jews of all varieties were embarrassed by the Communists. They needed to say to America as a whole that Jews abhorred Communism even more than other Americans. The more sophisticated knew that most of the Jews who had survived Hitler owed their lives to the Soviet armies, and that the vote of the Soviet Union at the United Nations in November 1947 was crucial to the creation of the State of Israel. These were historic debts, and they would be acknowledged some decades later, in different times, but in the immediate years after the war, the domestic needs of American Jews took precedence. The Jews wanted to get rid of their image as outsiders in America.

The lure of revolutionary ideologies that had seemed attractive to much of the Jewish intelligentsia in the 1930s was fading in the 1940s. Most of the Communists of the 1930s and 1940s simply drifted out of any strong ideological commitment as they found a place in America's booming, postwar capitalist system. Others were frightened out of left-wing ideology by the Cold War. When Senator Joseph R. McCarthy was roaming the country, conducting hearings to hunt Communists, many youthful believers in Communism tried to bury their past; others made public recantation. The most interesting group of all was a handful of Jewish intellectuals who had been Trotskyites before the war. As believers in Trotsky's vision of world revolution, they had been bitterly opposed to Stalin's imperialism. When the war was over, world revolution of the proletariat was clearly not going to happen, for capitalist America was the world's dominant power. Though Communism was spreading through Eastern Europe, it was Stalin's Communism. To oppose Stalin's imperialism, this group thought that they had only one option—to join the American side in the Cold War. Under the leadership of Elliot Cohen, the editor of the newly established monthly *Commentary,* they organized the Committee for Cultural Freedom. In 1951 the flagship publication of this body, *Encounter,* was launched in London. The budget of the Committee for Cultural Freedom came from American intelligence sources. From the perspective of the American cold warrior, this money was well spent. The committee was the most sophisticated intellectual front against the Russians. Through this association with the American Establishment in the battle against Stalin, some ex-Trotskyites, such as Irving Kristol, began the journey that would take them to neoconservatism.

The transformation of the Jews into respectable American bourgeois society was symbolized in 1951 by the conviction of the Rosenbergs. Julius and Ethel Rosenberg, a Jewish couple in their early thirties, were tried and convicted as spies who had given the Soviet Union sensitive atomic secrets. They were sentenced to death, and, after repeated appeals, were executed in 1953. The nature and the extent of their guilt have remained in controversy. It is clear, in hindsight, that the making of atom bombs could not have remained an American monopoly for very long. Any help the Soviets got from spying on the Americans had little effect on their entry into the atomic age. In the atmosphere of those years, however, the Rosenbergs were judged guilty of fundamentally altering the balance of power. They became the only Americans ever put to death for spying in peacetime.

Whatever the actual extent of their contributions to Soviet knowledge, the Rosenbergs' trial gave the Jewish community the opportunity to prove its patriotism. Near the surface of the trial there was a Jewish motif. The case was heard in New York, before Irving R. Kaufman, a district judge, who in his personal life was very much part of the Jewish establishment. The prosecuting lawyers (and, for that matter, the attorneys for the defense) were all Jews. An unmistakable message was being conveyed: the Jewish community was not to be identified with the Rosenbergs. Judge Kaufman announced that he prayed for divine guidance before passing the death sentence. He certainly was aware of the fears in the Jewish establishment that Jews as a whole might be held responsible for this act of treason. The Rosenberg case was the purgation in which Jews "proved" to the country that the political radicals who had once dwelt among them had either converted or that they had been cast out.

It is unfair and untrue to suggest that the young writers and intellectuals of those days, children of immigrants, were motivated simply by the desire to surrender their Jewishness to America on any terms. On the contrary, during the years immediately after the war, the passion to enter the mainstream swept along even some writers whose language was Yiddish. America itself had become an ideal rooted in the same premises that Jews had once heard from the God of their ancestors. H. Leyvik, the leading Yiddish poet, had been seared by the Holocaust, and inspired by the creation of the State of Israel. In September 1954, near the end of his creative life, Leyvik wrote a poem, *To America,* in which he made his final peace with his adopted country:

For forty-one years I have lived under your skies,
For over thirty years I have been your citizen,
And until now I have not found in me the word, the mode
For painting my arrival and my rise on your earth
With strokes as broad and revealing as you are yourself,
America
As soon as speech would shift toward you, I would curb
My words, rein them in with austere restraint,
Bind them in knots of understatement.
My whole world and my whole life
I held under secret locks, far from your wide open breath

Leyvik continued to imagine that "the moment of farewell" could happen within America's boundaries, that he might again be an alien in America; or he might choose to leave and be part of the new Jewish life being born in Israel, but these options now seemed more imaginary than real. The new reality was America. At the end of the poem a faint trace of ambivalence remained, but his last lines were an affirmation of this land in which neither he nor his ancestors had been born:

In days of old age, when I stand in the bright vision
Of one or another shining farewell, I recall again
The moment, forty-one years ago, when I reached
Your shore, America, and I wanted to and should have
Fallen prostrate to your earth and touched it with my lips,
And in confused embarrassment I did not do it,—
Let me do it now—as I stand here truthfully,
Embracing the glare of intimacy and farewell, America.

II

After the war, however, the promises of equality were not kept. Racial segregation continued, and there remained prejudice against Catholics. Jews were no better off, at least not in the public regard. In February 1946 nearly sixty percent of all Americans surveyed agreed that anti-Semitism was increasing in America. During the war, anti-Semites had claimed that Jews were either avoiding service or were finding their way into rear-echelon jobs. In 1946 the Jewish Welfare Board, the body which had served the Jewish soldier in all the theaters of operation, felt the need to publish two volumes of lists of Jews who had distinguished themselves in combat. Nearly 11,000 had been killed, 24,000 had been wounded, 36,000 had been decorated. All told, more than 500,000 Jews served in uniform during the war. Such lists (like those which Haym Salomon had made in 1784 and Simon Wolf in 1891) were necessary not simply as a memorial to the dead and as a celebration of living heroes; they were evidence that the Jews had earned an equal share in America's future.

When the vast wartime bureaucracies were disbanded, Jews feared and even half-expected that they would be beaten back into the ghetto. This did not happen. On the contrary, Jewish academics, professionals, artists, and technocrats maintained their newly earned intellectual status. After the war, there was a sudden expansion in higher education, publishing, and other semiacademic endeavors. Through the GI Bill of Rights of 1946, the government offered returning veterans the cost of their higher education in America's colleges and universities. Hundreds of thousands of young men were coming home to finish college. Hundreds of thousands more, who had previously not thought of higher education, entered the colleges on government scholarships. Jewish veterans comprised a strikingly large proportion of these students, and especially those among them who were studying for advanced degrees. The existing faculties were far too small to cope with this influx, and thus Jews who had waited in vain to be hired by academe in the 1930s were now in demand. The new availability of academic jobs attracted thousands of Jews to the graduate schools; by the mid-1950s, many had acquired doctorates. In 1940, Jews had comprised less than two percent of the faculties in all the institutions of higher education in America; by the 1960s the number had risen to at least 20 percent of all the faculty appointments in the schools which were not church-related. Young Jews were an even higher proportion of those newly hired by the most prestigious faculties.

Jews in retail business had made a significant jump during the war. Consumer goods were scarce and rationed, even in America. It was a seller's market. Stores which had made no money in the 1930s turned their owners into rich men by the mid-1940s. The newly well-off could expand their businesses and move into new endeavors. They had the money to begin the flight from apartment buildings in the cities into houses in the suburbs.

One bastion of established America where circumstances of the war did not forge opportunity for Jews was the corporate and industrial world—the banks, the insurance companies, the steel mills, the motorcar manufacturers. American big business was doubling and redoubling in those years. Between 1945 and 1959 the gross national product of the United States quadrupled, but the bureaucracies of the major companies continued to exclude Jews from upper-level jobs. Unlike colleges and universities, the giants of "free enterprise" could not easily be brought to book. But there was hope that big business would accept "White Jews," that is, those who behaved like "general Americans."

But what did it mean in the 1940s and 1950s to become a "general American"? Who were the other Americans? Some parts of the organized Jewish community, especially the elements that were led by the American Jewish Committee, continued to believe that doors would be opened wider for Jews through persuasion and appeal to democratic conscience. It published together, in 1950, five volumes on anti-Semitism which had been prepared under its auspices by several Jewish scholars who were refugees from Nazi Germany. The essential thrust of these volumes, at least in the public mind, was a definition of anti-Semitism as a disease, an expression of an "authoritarian personality." This analysis suggested that healthy people—like, presumably, the Americans—could not possibly be guilty of such prejudice. If there were any pockets of hatred, these were a residue from less enlightened, past ages. Anti-Semitism would be dissolved by education, goodwill, and appeal to democratic principles. These learned volumes were, of course, a restatement of an old assimilationist theme: the Jews would be accepted by society if they and the majority together gave up most of their past memories and behaved like "enlightened" bourgeois.

The counterview was held by the old enemies of the American Jewish Committee, the "Russian Jews," for whom Stephen S. Wise still spoke. These forces believed that the Gentile majority would yield only if it had no other choice. The reigning Establishment might give away positions which it had not preempted, but it would yield a share in what it already had only if it was forced. The American

Jewish Congress, under Wise's leadership, accepted a suggestion of several brilliant young lawyers who were on its staff in the mid-1940s: use the courts; demand the equality that was promised in the Constitution of the United States. The first public expression of this new tactic was the threat by Wise to sue to deny Columbia University its tax-exempt status. Wise's legal staff argued that undeniable evidence existed of quotas both in admissions and in hiring policies; the university was, therefore, not a public body but a private club. Wise's argument did not reach the courts, for Columbia preferred to drop the quotas. The shock waves went out to the rest of academe: discrimination against Jews, either as students or as faculty, became a risky proposition. For a number of years thereafter, many of the colleges and universities continued to discriminate against Jews, but the practice was fading. The universities became the first established American institutional arena in which Jews entered and even joined the elite.

Wise had shown the way to force doors open, but the activist and confrontationist appeals to law had as their purpose the very same agenda as the assimilationist preaching of goodwill and democracy: to ease the entry of Jewish individuals into careers equal to their talents. Their Jewishness was their own private business, which America as a whole was not supposed to notice, at least not in the job market. Jews thus cast themselves as the greatest partisans in America not only of equality but also of the total separation of church and state. Jews thus assumed the role again (as Isaac Mayer Wise had in the 1850s, when he went to court in Ohio against prayers in the public schools) of constitutional purists.

But America was not simply a Jew-Gentile country. There were Catholics and blacks, major "outsiders" like the Jews, who represented one-third of the American population. They had their own postwar agendas, and their desires clashed not only with the wishes of the Protestant majority but also with the aims of the Jews. The Catholics were the clearest, and the boldest. They interpreted their American situation as offering them the right to be themselves. No matter that they were annoying other groups who comprised, together, a large majority of all Americans. In 1947, the Supreme Court decided *Everson* v. *the Board of Education,* the first major case involving public education. Though it set forth a strict definition of the "wall of separation" between church and state, it sanctioned the use of public funds to bus parochial schoolchildren. The immediate response from Protestants and secular liberals was outrage; it was feared that Catholics would ultimately find a way of gaining tax support for the parochial schools, at least for their teaching of reading, writing, and arithmetic. Even James B. Conant, then president of Harvard, attacked the Catholics; he called the parochial schools a threat to national unity, and he praised the role of the public schools in assimilating immigrants (even as he looked away from his own college, where the dominant minority of its students came from boarding schools). The attacks upon the Catholics were all the more pointed, because the liberal community had long been angry with the Church: Catholics had been perceived as major supporters of General Franco against the Spanish Republicans. They had not silenced Father Coughlin, who had opposed the New Deal after 1935 and had become a public anti-Semite by 1938. The Catholics had crusaded in the 1930s against birth control and they were even more intransigent in the 1940s and 1950s about very strict standards of public propriety.

These Catholic positions had evoked vehement opposition, but the Church had chosen to fight rather than to draw in its horns. In the words of its most eloquent and most liberal spokesman, Father John Courtney Murray:

> The American Proposition makes a particular claim upon the reflective attention of the Catholic insofar as it contains a doctrine and a project in the matter of the "pluralistic society," as we seem to have agreed to call it. The term might have many meanings. By pluralism here I mean the coexistence within one political community of groups who hold divergent and incompatible views with regard to religious questions—those ultimate questions that concern the nature and destiny of man within a universe that stands under the reign of God. Pluralism therefore implies disagreement and dissension within the community.

Murray was very much aware that there had to be a set of principles on which religious groups participated in one community, but he felt that these common grounds did not have to conflict with any group's individual expression. To be sure, there were younger Catholics who disagreed with the Church. As early as 1953, the liberal Catholic journalist, William P. Clancy, accused both Catholic authoritarianism and doctrinaire secularism as "the fruit of that totalitarian spirit which, hating diversity, demands that all existence be made over to conform to its own vision." The Catholic position was itself, thus, judged to be too intransigent. Catholics were asked to pull in horns and to put less pressure on the rest of America, but Clancy spoke for a minority then. The thrust of the Catholic mainstream, or, at very least, of the clergy, was toward using the new freedom and equality as the chance to buttress and secure Catholic separateness.

In those very years, blacks inevitably made the contrary choice. They had started so far outside American society, as the National Association for the Advancement of Colored People asserted in its program statement in the early 1940s, that the troubling immediate questions—discrimination in "jobs, housing, the vote, education"— had to be their primary concerns. This agenda remained constant until the mid-1960s, when serious advocates of black separatism appeared. Before then, most of the efforts of the black community were variations on a theme that had been stated in 1944 in the anonymous preface to a collection of essays entitled *What the Negro Wants*: "Race relations in the United States are more strained than they have been in many years. Blacks are disturbed by the continued denial of what they consider to be their legitimate aspirations and by slow, grudging grant of a few concessions."

The earliest "official" strategy of blacks had been that of Booker T. Washington. At the turn of the century, Washington had counseled his brethren to make themselves "worthy" of acceptance by the white majority. By the 1930s, the black organizations, and especially the intelligentsia, knew very well, and with great bitterness, that white racists were not waiting for the appearance of black men and women with polished manners, so that they could cease practicing racism. In the 1930s, a few blacks, like some of the Jewish intellectuals, had flirted with the revolutionary Left. Even a Swedish Social Democrat, Gunnar Myrdal, insisted that the mass of the blacks everywhere could be helped, as he proved in his study of *An American Dilemma* (it was published in 1944), only by radical change of the whole social structure.

Myrdal's book was one of the turning points in moving the black community away from Washington's philosophy. Even during the war there were race riots in several black neighborhoods. The expression of black impatience had, thus, become overt and even shocking. The declared purpose of the Negro community had become at once grandiose and simple: to make race irrelevant to the life and career of every individual in America. One of the leading black intellectuals, the historian John Hope Franklin, defined this purpose in an immediately famous essay that he published in 1964, entitled "The Transformation of the Negro Intellect":

> Surely, one of the great tragedies of American life has been the manner in which one's intellectual resources, whether they be of the order of a moron or a genius, have been used up in the effort to survive as a decent, self-respecting human being. Negro intellectuals in increasing numbers have come to appreciate this as one of the stark, grimly tragic facts of life. In increasing numbers they have come to regard this fact as a challenge which they would not escape, even if they could. Until they can live as other human beings—pushing back the frontiers of knowledge, writing a great novel, composing a beautiful symphony—Negro intellectuals have come to realize that they must carry on the fight, in concert with others, to make America true to her own ideals of equality and democracy. The realization of this fact and the continued preoccupation with a program to achieve success constitute the transformation of the Negro intellectual.

In the postwar years, black leadership thus moved away from any hope of acceptance by the America that had existed in 1939. The battle was to make society live up to its rhetoric about equality. The battle was not for black culture; it was for jobs, education, and an end to segregation.

The major Jewish organizations vied with one another to be helpful, even filing supportive amicus curiae briefs in the cases the Urban League and NAACP brought to strike down poll taxes in the South and to end segregation in education. The rationale was that ending any form of discrimination was also a victory for Jews in their own fight for total equality. And yet, Jews were different from blacks. In the 1940s most blacks were little concerned about "black culture." Most Jews, even when they were rapidly on the rise after the war, never abandoned some pride, even if it was ill-defined, in their Jewishness.

Inevitably, also, Jews chose up sides against the Catholics in the battle over state aid to parochial education. This was not a new battle. Jews had made the decision in the nineteenth century to enter the public schools; Catholics had chosen to put their efforts into keeping their children out of these Protestant-dominated institutions. These choices were rooted in each group's reasons for coming to America. The Irish, who were the dominant element among the Catholics, had fled the Protestant British. On arrival, they labored hard to stay away from the pressure of Protestant institutions which dominated America—and never mind that the price included an extra generation or two of remaining in the blue-collar classes. During their mass migration, Jews had come to America to escape the czar of Russia and the king of Romania, both of whom belonged to the Orthodox Christian faith. The ancestors of the American Protestant majority had not recently oppressed Jews. One had no reason for erecting barriers against this culture, and especially not if the main purpose of coming to America was to succeed in the "Golden Land." Therefore, after 1945, when the choices had to be made, the Catholics reenacted their earlier decision, and so did the Jews—but with a difference.

Catholics could not easily make the distinction between public devotion to the religion of "freedom and democracy" and private allegiance to the teachings of the Church—but that is what they were soon constrained to do. The hierarchy and much of the laity wanted to secure a separate Catholic culture, but Roman Catholics in America were haunted by the memory of Alfred E. Smith. Smith had run for president in 1928 as the nominee of the Democratic party. He had lost in a very ugly campaign in which the Protestant majority had made it clear that it did not regard a Catholic as a true American. By the 1940s and the 1950s the Protestants had not relented; their passionate battle against state aid for parochial education proved that their anti-Catholic emotions had not weakened.

In the years immediately after the Second World War, the blacks campaigned to enter the majority. Their ideal, then, was the day when the black organizations and the black community as a whole would dissolve into America. The Catholics wanted to make America accept, and make room for, their separate identity as a community. Most Jews tried to have it both ways: to become part of the majority society while keeping some kind of Jewish communal life alive.

18.

The Conquest of the Suburbs

I

The children of the East European immigrants were now, in the 1940s and 1950s, in midcareer. They were numerous and increasingly wealthy, and ever more "Jewish." Every sociological study made in the 1950s (and they were made by the dozens) attested to the fact that they were most comfortable with other Jews, and that they regarded the Jewish community as their primary home. Yet, they were deeply ambivalent, often without admitting it even to themselves, about their most Jewish emotions. They eagerly seized the pragmatic, "American" responsibilities of philanthropic and political leadership of world Jewry, but they regarded it as unthinkable, and even anti-American, to use any part of their new wealth to create boarding or parochial day schools in which separatist Jewish culture and values might be cultivated. What they did as Jews—and, more revealing, what they chose not to do—had to fit their dominant purpose: to "arrive."

The transforming moment for this generation can be dated precisely: the three years between 1945 and 1948, the time of the creation of the State of Israel. The children of the immigrants took the lead in this fight, and in the process, they settled their scores with other Jews. In the 1940s the "German Jews," well into their third generation, were still the richest members of the Jewish community. Though the "Russians" had comprised the vast majority of the Jewish population in the 1930s, dominating the community's public agenda since Brandeis's days, they had remained poor relatives. They were patronized too by Europe's Jews. Before the war, the European Zionists, without exception, regarded the Americans as intellectually and even politically irrelevant. They were the source of a few dollars, but the real action was in Europe and Palestine. The United States was largely on the margins in the fierce battle waged in the 1930s by the moderate Chaim Weizmann and the militarist Vladimir Jabotinsky over the future of the Zionist movement. The Halutzim, the pioneers who settled Israel, came from Europe and not the United States.

The first battle within American Jewry erupted over the future of the refugees in Europe. Little more than a million Jews remained of a European community that before the war had numbered over seven and a half million. The attempt was begun everywhere to reconstitute the broken pieces of Europe's Jewish communities. The "German Jews," represented primarily by the American Jewish Committee, felt that the refugees should return to their former homes. Those who could not return, they thought, could go to Australia, or the United States, or perhaps, as individuals, to Palestine, but not to a Jewish state there. A more extreme ideological group, the American Council for Judaism, split off from the American Jewish Committee. This group, led by Rabbi Morris Lazaron of Baltimore and Lessing Rosenwald of Philadelphia (an heir to the Sears, Roebuck fortune), was loyal to the pronouncements of "classic Reform Judaism" as enunciated in the Pittsburgh Platform of 1885: Judaism was a religion, and not a nationality; to constitute a Jewish national community in Palestine would make every Jew in the Diaspora suspect of dual loyalty. The "Russian Jews" were furious. They took to reprinting Brandeis's pronouncements that Zionism is the best form of Americanism. They knew that establishing a Jewish state was a popular cause. Americans admired fighters. More negatively, it was an open secret that the United States, which was engaged in demobilizing and finding place in the economy for some fifteen million soldiers, was in no mood to open its own door to hundreds of thousands of immigrants. The Zionists had little trouble persuading America that the Jewish state was a moral necessity—and that those who were supporting this endeavor were good Americans.

The "Russian Jews" in America especially identified with the Jews in Palestine. Most of the heroes who fought the battles of Israel's first war were from Eastern Europe. To be sure, young Jews from Germany, and from the rest of Central Europe, were doing their share, and perhaps even more, in the dramatic battles for the creation of the Jewish state. In the mid-1940s, Teddy Kollek, of Viennese origin, was the emissary of the Haganah, the mainstream Zionist army, to the gunrunners in America. The fabled Brecha, the underground which guided thousands of Jews across European frontiers and past the British blockade into Palestine, had many young Jews of Central European birth among its emissaries. But the dominant majority of the Jews in Palestine in those days, and almost all of their leaders, from David Ben-Gurion to Golda Meir, were from Eastern Europe. So were most American Jews. There was, of course, no equality of sacrifice between Americans and Israelis. The Jews in the United States were providing money and political support, but the Jews in Palestine were fighting the war. The Americans played a supporting role, and they knew it—but this role was sufficiently dramatic to make their leaders the most important Jews in America.

The successful battle for a Jewish state was not only a victory over the "German Jews"; it was, on many levels, a very American endeavor. These were the years of the Marshall Plan and the rebuilding of Japan by American occupation forces under General Douglas MacArthur. The creation of Israel was the equivalent task for American Jews. Those who engaged in it felt themselves cutting no less a figure in the Jewish realm than the American leaders were cutting on the wider stage. What a metamorphosis this was for the children of the immigrants who had been poor in the Bronx in the 1930s.

The effort for reconstituting a Jewish nation was even more "American" because of the Holocaust. The murder of six million Jews in Europe had been the ultimate demonstration of Jewish powerlessness. American Jews were doubly uncomfortable: they were suppressing their own immediate memories of not being able to help, and they suspected that American anti-Semites were more contemptuous than sympathetic to Jews who had not fought back in Europe.

It would take a generation before American Jews would even want to understand the impossibility of armed valor by the victims of the Nazis. In the years immediately after the war, only the few examples of armed resistance, such as the revolt in the Warsaw Ghetto, in April 1943, were remembered and celebrated. In American terms, the Warsaw Ghetto was the Jewish Alamo.

The fighting Jews of Palestine, at war with both the British and the Arabs, were even stronger proof that Jews were a heroic people. They were having their own Valley Forge and crossing of the Delaware—and the Jews of America were sharing in the glory. Settlers fighting Indians and establishing civilization in unfriendly territories were another American myth, and the battle for the State of Israel could be told in those terms. The Jews of Palestine could be cast as pioneers on an unfriendly frontier. The story of the creation of Israel soon was made into the Wild West in the Middle East by a Hollywood writer, Leon Uris, in his novel *Exodus*. As soon as the book was published in 1956, it became very nearly the "Bible" of American Jews. In the film version, the hero, Ari Ben-Canaan, was played by Paul Newman, a young American Jew. During those heroic, early years of Israel, American Jews were hoping to imitate the Israelis. They wanted to be believable to themselves as "cowboys" in America, as active wielders of power on American soil.

The Zionist effort in the mid-1940s was helped by a deep anti-British strain in American history. Had not the United States been created in rebellion against Britain? Never mind that America had just fought a war as Great Britain's ally. At war's end, the British still held a worldwide empire, and the United States was no defender of British power. It wanted that empire to dissolve—in large part so that America might inherit the role of primacy in the world. Various American ethnic groups, and especially the Irish, had more immediate reasons to dislike the British. Indeed, American sympathizers with the Irish Republican Army announced their admiration in the 1940s for the Zionists. For American Jews to help push the British out of Palestine was, therefore, on several levels a very "American" act.

The creation of Israel solved another basic problem for American Jews, the question of a homeland. In the immediate postwar years, it was no longer "anti-American" to remember one's origin. Individuals now looked with fondness to their ethnic pasts. All of these

Americanized ethnics, precisely as they were becoming more American and more remote from immigrant life and culture, needed the legitimacy of a homeland. They could not be less than the descendants of the earliest settlers who looked back to England. The Irish marched on Saint Patrick's Day; the Italians gloried in their kinship with the country which had been the home of culture and art since Roman times. Even the Germans claimed descent from the tradition of Goethe and Beethoven, as they insisted that Hitler had been a temporary aberration.

America's Jews, however, had no homeland in which they could take some pride. The vast majority of recent immigrants had never had positive feelings about their countries of origin. They could not look back to anti-Semitic Czarist Russia, or to interwar Poland. And many of the places from which they had come had either been destroyed by the Nazis or taken over by the Soviet Union. As Marc Chagall hinted at in his paintings of Jews floating in the air, Jewish life in prewar Europe no longer existed in the towns and villages to which Jews had clung for a thousand years.

The creation of Israel thus offered the Jews of America a place, a homeland, in which they could take pride, and thus nurture both their Jewish inner selves and their need for "normal" status in America. It was inevitable that American Jews would conceive of their old-new homeland as uniquely heroic. This nation had arisen again after a hiatus of two thousand years. This "miracle" had more than a hint of "chosenness" about it. Those who identified with the new State of Israel could feel very special as Jews, even as they were becoming Americans with roots in a homeland of their own, just like all other Americans.

All of these themes were symbolized in the fall of 1947. Abba Hillel Silver, the elected leader of the American Zionists, took a seat at a table in the United Nations. He was one of the speakers, along with Moshe Shertok, the political secretary of the World Zionist Organization, to present the case for creating an independent Jewish state. Silver was a distinguished and striking figure, of matchless eloquence. Though a Reform rabbi, he was an East European who had been brought to the United States as a child. Silver was an American, but he spoke not on behalf of the United States but rather as a principal representative of the Jewish people. As Silver spoke for Zionism in an American accent before the United Nations, he carried with him the ultimate dream of his generation: he had shifted the leadership of American Jewry away from the "German Jews." This son of immigrants to America was speaking for all the Jews of the world, as an equal to princes and prime ministers.

II

In less dramatic ways the children of the immigrants remade themselves on the domestic scene to suggest that, in their very Jewishness, they were behaving like all other Americans. Even as they were constructing institutions to serve their inner needs, the newly rich of the 1940s and the 1950s used these institutions as their "calling card" into America.

They began by repeating a maneuver used by the "German Jews" nearly a century earlier. The "Germans" had become rich during the Civil War, and they soon fought their way into the "best neighborhoods." They announced their success by building ornate synagogues on prominent thoroughfares in all the major cities of America. In the era after the Second World War, the East Europeans followed suit. Between 1945 and 1965, about a third of all American Jews left the big cities and established themselves in suburbs. The small-town synagogues which already existed in these areas were transformed into large, bustling congregations, and hundreds of new communities were created. The new synagogues were located in very visible places. The formula was an old one: American society might be prejudiced against Jews, but it respected religion. In the 1950s and 1960s, at least a billion dollars were raised and spent building a thousand new synagogue buildings. It was the largest building boom in the history of American Jews.

In the transplantation of Jews to suburbia in those decades, the Orthodox synagogues were essentially left behind. The bearers of Orthodoxy were the immigrant parents who continued to live in the Jewish enclaves that they had established in the big cities. As the Lower East Side in New York City was being taken over by Spanish and Chinese speakers, the electric sign in Yiddish atop the building of the *Jewish Daily Forward* on East Broadway became increasingly forlorn. Few among the aging immigrants moved to the suburbs. The older generation was attached to the established institutions of

Jewish life, to the older synagogues, the kosher butchers, and the meeting places in the corner candy stores. Even in areas of second settlement, such as the Bronx in New York or Park Heights in Baltimore, the sermons were still, at least some of the time, in Yiddish. Of all of the institutions of the Jewish ghetto, the Orthodox synagogue was the most vehement that Jews stay out of the American mainstream. Such separatist rituals as the Sabbath and kosher law expressed and enforced an attitude: to be a true Jew meant to live apart in a Gentile world, even in America.

Such sensibilities rarely came along to suburbia in the 1950s. The move from the old neighborhood into upper-bourgeois areas, where Jews had never been before, was a move into America. The Conservative and the Reform synagogues were suited to the task of helping this move. Their rabbis, trained in America, were more versed in the arts of congregational leadership than in the difficulties of Talmudic law. The inner convictions of these rabbis were, more often than not, as separatist as those of the older, Yiddish-speaking Orthodox rabbinate. This younger generation (and of course those of their peers who had remained Orthodox) still thought that America, like all of the rest of the world, was divided into only two camps: "we," the Jews, and "they," the Gentiles. This emotion was shared by the bulk of the laity, but it was a feeling held in reserve. The public policy of the new communities in suburbia was to "arrive." The synagogue of the 1950s (like the temples of the 1870s and 1880s) acted out a lead role in a very heady drama: Judaism was now being legitimized as a major American faith, on a par with the Protestant and Catholic versions of Christianity.

Though the Jews who were moving into suburbia were often invading restricted enclaves, the cult of "Americans All" dictated to the churches that they had to exercise neighborliness. Whatever the theological differences, they were now expected to behave, in practice, as if they accepted each other as equals. President Dwight David Eisenhower drove home this point. Just before coming into office, Eisenhower had joined a church. He never defined the specifics of his own religious view, and he did not seem to want to be troubled by any angular doctrines of other people's faiths. The President, acting as leader of opinion, and even as "High Priest" of Americanism, had pronounced all religion to be good, provided that the sects did not squabble with each other, and that they joined in teaching their believers to take pride in the United States. Eisenhower himself provided the best definition of this ideology: "Our government makes no sense, unless it is founded in a deeply felt religious faith— and I don't care what it is."

This "civil religion" that had been fashioned during the Second World War was now the "official" religion of American society. It was best expressed and symbolized by the story of the four chaplains. In 1942 an American troop carrier, the *Dorchester*, was sunk in the North Atlantic by a German submarine. There were not enough life jackets to go around. The four chaplains on board gave up theirs to four enlisted men. The chaplains—two Protestant ministers, a rabbi, and a Catholic priest—were last seen standing together in prayer on the deck of the ship. This heroic tale was told and retold in the 1940s and 1950s. In the postwar years the ministers and the priests were not called upon to die together with rabbis, but, at very least, they had to welcome the newly arrived Jewish clergy as colleagues.

The time was right in the 1950s for a social theorist, Will Herberg, to sanctify these events by pronouncing America a tri-faith society. Herberg had come to Judaism as religion in those very years, after spending all of his adult life as a secularist in the service of the labor movement. In 1955, Herberg published a book entitled *Catholic, Protestant, Jew*. The recent declaration of the State of Israel, and its heroic early years, made little impact on Herberg, for his prime concern was the state of American society. Herberg argued that religious differences were not only tolerated in America, but even expected. The synagogue could be cast as the most "American" of all Jewish institutions. Jews were less than three percent of America, but as a religious group, they could be defined as one of the three major faiths which the society had recognized and respected. Joining the synagogue was the way to be a respectable "American" in those Eisenhower years.

In the 1950s and 1960s, the rate of synagogue affiliation climbed from twenty percent in the 1930s to nearly sixty percent of all American Jews. Membership was highest in smaller and middle-sized cities and lowest in New York and Los Angeles. For example, in 1963, in Providence, Rhode Island, including the suburbs, eighty percent of the men and seventy-five percent of the women reported themselves as members of synagogues. In New York itself the enrollment never reached fifty percent, but in the suburbs, everywhere, it averaged two out of three Jewish households. These figures were even larger than they seemed, because of the "revolving door" nature of synagogue enrollment. Many joined synagogues when it came time to prepare their oldest child for bar mitzvah or bat mitzvah, and they left soon after the celebration of that ritual for their youngest child. All of the communal studies of the 1950s showed that more than eighty percent of American Jewish children were receiving some kind of exposure to Jewish religious education and that, therefore, at one point or another, their parents had belonged to a synagogue. The supplementary schools which taught Yiddish, under the auspices of what remained of the Jewish labor movement, were waning in numbers, and the few Jewish day schools were just beginning to increase in the 1950s by those founded by the newest arrivals to America, the survivors of the death camps who had arrived after 1945. The dominant form of education was the synagogue school which offered supplementary classes on weekday afternoons, after public school, or on Saturday and Sunday mornings.

But was this boom in affiliation a religious revival? There was no return to such traditional values as observance of the rituals and the study of sacred texts. Even as synagogue enrollments were increasing, fewer of their members obeyed the restrictions on forbidden foods or observed the Sabbath. The adult groups in the suburban synagogues were much more likely to discuss current events, or busy themselves with bowling, than to study the Bible. What was reviving, or, to be more exact, what was being expressed in a new way, was Jewish group feeling. The children of the immigrants were reexpressing, in wealth, the Jewish emotions of their parents.

In their youth, they had dreamed of both entering American society and retaining a closeness with other Jews. The suburban synagogue was their "city on the hill," the symbol of the achievement of this dream. In the new suburbs, as Nathan Glazer observed at the time, the synagogue was necessary even to Jews who had never attended its door when they were young in the ghetto. In Flatbush in Brooklyn, or in Rogers Park in Chicago, the candy stores and the delicatessens had been places of assembly for Jews. In suburbia people lived in one-family houses, surrounded by grassy lawns. There was little street life. This new environment was not like the Bronx; one could not walk out the front door of one's apartment house and encounter only Jews. Therefore, Jews built synagogues to swim together, to play mah-jongg, or to attend an almost endless variety of meetings.

Even those Jews who affirmed neither religious nor ethnic identity admitted that they were most comfortable with other Jews. Even the most "anti-Jewish" Jews reported that at least four out of five of their friends were Jews. This was true even of people of Jewish origin who had converted to one of the branches of Christianity. Jewish businessmen and professionals did establish themselves by the tens of thousands in the middle class, and they did business much of the time with Americans of all origins and persuasions. They lunched often with their customers or clients, but they went home to have dinner and play cards, or to play golf on weekends, or to go to the theater and the symphony, with other Jews.

In the spring of 1953 the United Synagogue of America, the central lay organization of Conservative Judaism, did a self-study of the leaders of the synagogues. Though 9,100 questionnaires were mailed out, only 1,800 questionnaires were returned. The professionals at Columbia University's Bureau of Applied Social Research were persuaded that the sample, though skewed because the leaders of the smaller congregations were not adequately represented, presented a picture that was essentially correct. About one in three of these synagogue leaders attended "the main Sabbath services" of their congregations with any frequency. About one in five came often, and nearly half showed up infrequently or not at all. Essentially, this profile of the synagogue leadership is not different from the results of a questionnaire about synagogue attendance among the laity as a whole.

The private religious habits of the leaders of the congregations were equally revealing. The Sabbath candles were lit in three-quarters of their homes, but three out of five did not make a sufficiently festive affair of the family dinner to chant the kiddush, the prayer over wine which is ordained by ritual custom. Only one-third of these board members kept a kosher home; there was a middle of one-fourth that was "partially kosher" and another third which made no effort whatsoever toward the ritual restrictions on diet. This profile of typical children of the immigrants is to be compared with the 1880s and the 1890s, when at least four out of five immigrant homes kept kosher. The figures from 1953 mean that the next generation (for Conservative Judaism was, then, the majority option) had largely moved away from obedience of this ritual—and that the stage had been set for further erosion in the next generation. There is a hint of this in the 1953 survey in the answer to the question about the attendance of children at the synagogue service. Only twenty-eight percent of the board members usually took their children on the occasions when they went to Sabbath services; as many as fifty-eight percent went by themselves, leaving their children the option to go shopping, to play in Little League baseball, or to attend ballet classes.

The force of the religious commandments of the Jewish tradition was weakening even among the leaders of the Conservative syn-agogues. In the survey they were asked whether they would support a requirement that board members regularly attend synagogue. Less than a third, probably those who themselves did come regularly, were for such a proposal; almost all of the rest were opposed. Indeed, there were wars in the boards of synagogues of all the denominations over the issue of what the requirements were for admitting a child to the rituals of bar mitzvah or bat mitzvah. Rabbis and religious school principals, and some of the lay leaders, wanted to make it mandatory that the child, and preferably the entire family, attend Sabbath services for a year or two prior to the ceremony. Wherever this rule was proposed, there was controversy. The parents were overwhelmingly in opposition. Most wanted to "buy" a service from the synagogue. Had not many of these parents themselves been "bar mitzvahed" (to use the phrase that was coined in those days) in a synagogue to which their parents did not belong, after instruction by a tutor who was hired for the occasion? Now, as adults in the 1950s, they wanted essentially to rent such facilities for their children, to let an institution "prepare" their children for bar mitzvah or bat mitzvah without any pretense of accepting any religious authority. Most synagogues did not dare impose such a rule.

The impression that most of the board members of the Conser-vative synagogues had become board members in order to be board members is illustrated by the behavior of these men and women outside the synagogue. Only a quarter of them claimed to read books or magazines of Jewish content, except for the information bulletin of the congregation which they helped lead, but most were active in some other Jewish organization, and often in more than one. The author of the survey summarized the figures with a certain sadness:

True, the bulk of community involvement shows a heavy concentration on fund-raising efforts, such as the U.J.A. or the local community chest! Yet, the active "side interests" in Zionist endeavors, fraternal associations, service organizations and other national agencies are formidable. The figures of participation add up to "astronomical" percentages (totaling 290) and indicate a pathetically harassed leadership group, relentlessly driven by the forces of social pressure and relentlessly driving itself to the point of exhaustion. They further demonstrate a fragmentization of attention which accounts for the present character of our communal organizations.

The writer of the report could not refrain from adding that no one complained that organizational meetings interfered with the time that these men and women wanted to set aside "to acquire information about Jewish affairs and to study them."

These synagogue leaders were asked what motivated them to work for the synagogue. Three-quarters asserted that they regarded the synagogue as the most important of all Jewish institutions. Many asserted that the synagogue is the primary agency for "perpetuating a Jewish way of life," but just as many said that the synagogue "raises the level of Jews in the American community" and that its existence "makes for a better America in which the Jews shall be well integrated." The suburban synagogue was thus defined as both a temple of Jewish togetherness and a bid for acceptance by the Gentiles.

This study was published in mimeograph form in 1953 by the sponsoring organization, but it was almost immediately buried. The results were too plain; they pointed to many problems which the author of the report, Emil Lehman (he was then assistant director of the United Synagogue), did not cover over with the rhetoric of self-congratulation. The people whom Lehman surveyed were of the second generation, the children of the immigrants. The members of this generation were then at the zenith of their lives. Nine out of ten of these board members of synagogues were between thirty and fifty-nine years of age; their children were still young. Educationally, almost half of the respondents had been to college and three out of ten had graduated (be it remembered that these men and women had struggled their way to an education before World War II, in the Depression years). Family income was reported as being over ten thousand dollars a year for a quarter of the respondents, and over fifteen thousand dollars a year for three out of ten. These were high figures in those years, when middle-class incomes were still under ten thousand dollars. No doubt, the synagogue board members were chosen for being, on average, wealthier than the bulk of the members of the congregation, but these respondents were most likely to have been even wealthier than they admitted. There certainly was enough money around those days to build hundreds of new synagogues. By the spring of 1953, among the Conservatives alone, the membership of the United Synagogue, their association of congregations, had risen from less than 200 in 1945 to 443 congregations.

This passion for belonging was a reflection of the problem of rootlessness, of anomie, which pervaded much of American society in the postwar years. In 1956, at the bicentenary of Columbia University, J. Robert Oppenheimer, the physicist who had been chief scientist among the makers of the atom bomb, described the present as a time when "diversity, complexity, richness overwhelm the man of today." His prescription was: "Each . . . will have to cling to what is close to him, to what he knows, to what he can do, to his friends and his tradition and his love, lest he be dissolved in a universal confusion and know nothing and love nothing." Oppenheimer spoke from very high philosophical ground about the need for educated men and women, intellectuals like himself, to define their values and to live by their ideals in the company of fellow believers.

Lesser souls had more tangible problems. America as a whole was moving to new neighborhoods, and thus new associations had to be formed by tens of millions of people. Membership in Christian denominations was rising in those years as dramatically as among the Jews. The Protestants claimed that for the first time in American history over half of those who had been born into Protestant families were formally associated with organized congregations. This would seem to indicate a religious revival, especially in the light of the results of a *Time* magazine poll in 1952 that almost all Americans of Christian birth believed in God.

The difficulty with this explanation is that the 1950s were not a period which was marked by religious fervor. On the contrary, middle-class America, which furnished the laity for the "main-line" Protestant churches, was increasingly self-satisfied and materialist.

In the South, in the Bible Belt, the young Billy Graham, the first of the modern revivalists to achieve a national audience, had barely made his mark before the mid-1950s. Whatever tremors were being felt within American Protestantism involved the issue of race. The central establishments of the main-line churches, especially as represented by the National Council of the Churches of Christ in the U.S.A., were strongly on the side of equal rights for all, but the bulk of the individual congregations, even in the North, did not make fighting for the rights of blacks into a central concern. Those who were joining the congregations, then, in unprecedented numbers were not repentant sinners who had suddenly become twice-born. By joining churches they were asserting not their Christianity but their Gentileness, just as the new, large synagogues of the Jews were an assertion not of their faith in Judaism but of their Jewishness.

Only seventy percent of the Jews answered the *Time* pollsters that they believed in God—and so, clearly, some, perhaps even many, unbelievers were joining synagogues. The difference between Jews and Christians in their answers to the *Time* poll was essentially rhetorical. When Jews were asked about their identity, it was possible for many of them to assert that their loyalty was to the Jewish people, and never mind faith in God. The sense of being one people, one family, as the seed of Abraham, had always been central in Jewish consciousness. This self-definition had become more pervasive in the 1950s, as American Jews increasingly identified with the new State of Israel. In Israel, all Jews belonged to the nation, even though many were indifferent to the Jewish religion.

Christians had no such readily available self-definition; they had always thought of themselves as belonging to a church, to a community of believers, and not to a people. When American Christians wanted to say, in a changing America, that they were Gentiles and not Jews, the rhetoric of Christianity dictated that this be expressed through asserting a belief in God. In the 1950s the Protestant Church in America, which had traditionally represented the dominant American Establishment, housed a laity which was being severely threatened in its role as the unquestioned American elite. Catholics, blacks, and Jews were all on the attack. The churches, even though they joined in an occasional interfaith service, became, like the country clubs, defensive bastions against the attackers. Looking back in 1968, in an essay entitled "Social and Intellectual Sources of Contemporary Protestant Theology in America" (published in a work by many hands entitled *Religion in America*), the Christian scholar and theologian Langdon Gilkey wondered why an increasingly secular America had been experiencing a revival of the churches:

> In recent decades this has created in this least of all ecclesiastical cultures a new species of ecclesiasticism, one stripped of all the dogmatic, priestly, and sacramental elements that have characterized other kinds of ecclesiastical systems. As of now, the variety of American church life has little theological, liturgical, pietistic, or even Biblical content, but it is nonetheless burgeoning with air-conditioned sanctuaries, ladies' and men's societies, large Sunday-school plants, "holy name" baseball teams, and innumerable suppers and dances. It is a "religious" institution of immense power, wealth, and prestige, but one characterized largely by secular values such as recreation, sociability, and sporadic good works in the community. The social value of such an institution is undoubted in our mobile, rootless, suburban culture. Whether it has any real religious character—whether it manifests a presence of the holy in its midst or offers a higher ethical standard for man's daily life—is something else again.

These words could, of course, have been applied without change to the contemporary synagogue. The main-line Protestant Church in decline, and the suburban synagogue on the rise, thus were mirror images of each other—temples of competing ethnics, bastions not of Judaism and Christianity but of Jewishness and Gentileness. Jews would feel more equal and even contentious in the next decade as their power grew and as they became less likely to think of the Protestant Church as everybody's host in America.

III

But there were limits, as much self-imposed as imposed by anti-Semitism, as to how far these Jews could go in becoming "just like everybody else." Jews were marked as Jews, at very least, by their drive to escape their early poverty. Jews were uniquely visible in this stampede toward wealth because they were moving more rapidly upward from the poverty of their youth than any other group in America. This intense passion for success was noted by others, and not always with approval.

The great majority of Jews willingly proclaimed that they were "proud to be Jews." But this American Jewishness was radically different from any Jewish experience of the past: it was situational; it had little to do with a tradition of Jewish learning which had been at the center of the life of all previous communities in the Diaspora. Eli Ginzberg, one of the most astute observers of the American Jewish scene, defined it in those very years. He published a short book in 1949 entitled *Agenda for American Jews*. Ginzberg was more concerned than almost anyone else in those days with strengthening the historical consciousness of the next generation of Jews. He was pointedly critical of the almost total preoccupation with anti-Semitism by the organized Jewish community.

> Today at least among large numbers of American Jews, the "defense activities" have usurped a position of priority. This was more or less inevitable since many of these Jews have lost all interest in positive Jewish values; their entire adjustment is externally oriented. Finally, we are confronted with the amazing belief among American Jews—and it is quite prevalent though it contradicts the inner wisdom of Judaism—that the basic attitudes of the Gentiles toward the Jews can be significantly altered, if only the right "techniques" are discovered and employed.

Nonetheless, Ginzberg concluded his book by insisting that "as Americans, we have not only the right, but the responsibility to be concerned with the future of our democracy." Ginzberg knew that Judaism and democracy were not the same. He used the most immediately available rhetoric of cultural pluralism: "The true strength of a democracy is its highly variegated and diversified culture which permits each sub-group to develop its maximum potentialities and thereby contribute to the whole." Ginzberg had thus paid some lip service to the clichés of cultural pluralism, but what really concerned him was the shallowness of a Jewish community which was largely organized on the domestic front as a society of anti-anti-Semites.

If the Jews to whom Ginzberg was speaking had paid any heed to his agenda, they should have thought about the question of schools. Ginzberg was writing at the beginning of an era when Jewish education was in the ascendant; the 1950s and the 1960s were the heyday of the supplementary Jewish school in America. Ginzberg expressed the hope that these schools would have intensive curricula and that they would succeed in imparting some classic Jewish learning. It was a vain hope. The after-hours schools in the synagogues were being used by the Jewish parents for their own ends. What the mass of parents wanted, apart from a decent performance at bar mitzvah, was that the school impart to their children enough of the sense of Jewish loyalty so that they would be inoculated against intermarriage, that is, that they should remain part of Jewish togetherness. Once that inoculation had supposedly taken hold, the Jewish child could then be launched on his next task, to succeed in being admitted into a prestigious college.

It is revealing that Eli Ginzberg, in his *Agenda for American Jews,* had not recommended, or even mentioned, the educational institution to which his analysis pointed, the Jewish parochial school. If the deepest problem of Jews was, in Ginzberg's words, "to strengthen the historical consciousness of the next generation," the institution within which such sensibility is best formed is a Jewish parochial school. There were a few such schools in existence in 1949, under Orthodox auspices, but Ginzberg's imagination did not have to be tied to this model. The American elite, the seemingly unattainable WASP Brahmins, had been educating their young for almost three centuries in elegant boarding schools which were avowedly Christian, or in their counterparts in private schools in the cities, such as the one conducted by Trinity Church in New York City, for students who lived at home. The creation of Jewish equivalents of these educational institutions was not a question of money, for the generation to which Ginzberg was speaking was finding hundreds of millions with which to build new synagogues and Jewish community centers. The fundamental decision about education, not to engage in private Jewish education, was not even discussed. It was self-evident to the newly affluent East Europeans that their children had to go to the public schools, or to the private schools which would admit them, for there they would encounter their Gentile peers.

In 1949 Ginzberg was pleading for Jewish intellectual seriousness. The tone of his writing suggested that he expected not to be heeded, but that he was sure that he was at least keeping some bad conscience alive. He was wrong. The truth was being foreshadowed by the board members of the synagogues: American Jews were going to make their "spiritual life" out of solving their problems or other people's problems. They would become the audience for numerous novels, sociological surveys about themselves, and for a growing literature about Israel. The American Jewish community had decided, with little deliberation and very much as a matter of course, that its inmost Jewish content was activism.

19.

With JFK, to Power

I

By the late 1950s American Jews imagined that all would soon be for the best in the best of all possible worlds. Anti-Semitism in America had not yet vanished, but it was consistently decreasing, and Jews could imagine that the problems were vestigial. American Jews had adopted Israel as their homeland and blacks as their principal allies. These were the Eisenhower years, when America was at the height of its power and its horizons seemed unbounded. Jews shared in the optimism. But, even as Jewish power and influence were cresting, snakes were growing in their Garden of Eden. The problems came from blacks and Israelis, the very people who were the closest allies of this generation of American Jews.

The established leaders of the black and Jewish communities still agreed, in the 1950s, that they shared the same agenda, but the official words barely masked the differences in real life. The agency which spoke for the Jewish community was the National Jewish Community Relations Advisory Council. This coordinating group included all of the Jewish organizations, both national and local, which dealt with American domestic affairs. Each year, these bodies met to redefine their objectives and priorities for action. In 1953, the NJCRAC asserted: "A fundamental objective of Jewish community relations is equality of opportunity for all, regardless of race, religion, color or national origin. In a still imperfect democratic society, Jews, together with many other groups, suffer from inequalities of opportunity and other forms of discrimination. They are among the victims of the intergroup tensions and antagonisms that exist in our society." In the text, the NJCRAC went on to argue that it was to the advantage of Jews to fight side by side with blacks against discrimination in housing and in jobs. This was true in law, for antidiscrimination legislation applied equally to every social and economic level, but it was not true in fact. Jews were then doing battle in suburbia, or in posh neighborhoods for apartments in the cities, against "restrictive covenants," which obligated the owners not to sell to Jews or other "undesirables," but the Jewish upper middle class was not out on the street, without possibility of buying adequate housing. Blacks were trapped in crowded slums. The drive to move out was motivated mostly by the sheer need for space. Jobs, too, were a different kind of issue for Jews and blacks. Jews were troubled by still existing discrimination at the very top of the American economy, in "executive suites." Blacks were fighting to leave the most menial jobs in America.

In those years, at the very height of the alliance, there was one marked note of dissonance among Jews. The southern Jewish communities were under fire from southern racists, who were angry with the Jews for leading in the battle against segregation. This ire was directed at the national Jewish organizations, which were all without exception based in the North and run by leaderships and bureaucracies which were overwhelmingly northern. A few southern Jews were prominent in the battle for racial integration. In Nashville, Tennessee, Dan May, a leading industrialist, was chairman of the school board in 1954, and he took the lead in fostering a plan for integrating the public schools, one grade at a time. This modest suggestion did not endear him to the local racists, and he had to be guarded by police for a while. In Atlanta, Jacob M. Rothschild, the rabbi of the Reform congregation, was an ardent supporter of the cause of blacks. He was himself in some danger, and the temple building was dynamited in 1958. Nonetheless, despite such exceptions, the overwhelming majority of southern Jews tried to avoid the racial controversy. Almost none shared in the most rampant prejudice. Many had close personal relations with blacks, because the typical southern Jew in the 1950s was a storekeeper whose clientele was often in part or even entirely black. The mainstream position among southern Jews was "gradualism," that is, that the progress toward racial equality should proceed in such fashion as not to evoke rage in the white majority—the very "gradualism" that Martin Luther King would mock and denounce at the end of the period, in 1963, in his letter from a Birmingham jail, which was addressed, in the first instance, to a coalition of clerics of all three faiths.

Southern Jews often suggested to the national Jewish organizations to which they belonged that they dampen their rhetoric in support of blacks, but, even as these pleas were not heeded, there were few defections. In their conscience, the Jews in the South knew that the misery of the blacks cried for better treatment, and so, even as they did very little, the southern Jewish communities did not dissociate themselves from the official Jewish position of alliance with the blacks. In 1955, the NJCRAC reaffirmed the alliance with some pride. The framers of the NJCRAC plan for the year took note of the discomfort of Jews in the South, but proposed an additional reason for remaining firm. The price was worth paying because "As the Asian and African colonial peoples pursue their inevitable course toward emancipation and political independence, they will grow increasingly aware of the role of distinctions based on race and color in most parts of the world; and their attitudes toward various nations and peoples—including their attitudes toward Jews—will be deeply influenced by their observations." Thus, strengthening international support for Israel became, probably for the first time, a reason for Jews to support America's blacks.

Still, the "black-Jewish alliance" was not, in the 1950s, and it had never been from its very beginnings as self-evident as the NJCRAC would have liked to think. On the contrary, the formal alliance had arisen only after the Second World War and, even as this cooperative relationship was being defined and celebrated, the memory of past difficulties was very much alive. Blacks, the weaker partner, remembered even better than Jews all of their hurts and disappointments. In the 1930s, as Walter White, the executive head of the National Association for the Advancement of Colored People, had attested, "Negroes were concerned only when Negroes were attacked; Jews became alarmed only when Jewish toes were trod upon." In those years, Jewish leaders, so he told, refused to join the NAACP against antiblack housing restrictions, even though White pointed out that such restriction "would in time be used against Jews and other minorities." Later, in 1943, White still did not think that the time was right to suggest joint action: "I do not advocate here a Jewish-Negro coalition." But he pleaded that Jews should at least learn from their own experiences not to "indulge in any form of prejudice or superiority to others who are victims of the same evil forces of oppression."

The race riots in Detroit in late June 1943 and the even more devastating outbreak in New York's Harlem in August of that year had marked components of black anti-Semitism, but this knowledge was largely unreported. Most of the businesses on the main shopping streets of black Detroit and of New York were then owned by Jews. In its lengthy account of the Harlem riot, the closest that *The New York Times* came even to hinting at these facts was to mention the destruction of a pawnshop on 125th Street owned by someone called Sobel. During the riot in Harlem a number of stores had put out signs NEGRO-OWNED AND OPERATED. Such establishments were not looted. Though the Jewish-owned stores soon called in the glaziers to install new windows and reopened for business, most of the owners had decided to get out. Jewish businesses in Harlem were now up for sale; they ceased being enterprises that fathers might hand on to their children. This was all the more true because by the 1940s there was almost no remnant of the earlier Jewish population in Harlem. Those who had founded the stores when they lived in the neighborhood had already moved out in the 1920s and 1930s, as the population of Harlem was becoming entirely black. They had left behind many ornate synagogue buildings, which were now black churches. Jews still owned much housing, which they were renting out to black tenants, who were often too poor to pay the rent and who, even more often, complained that they were not being provided with adequate services.

All of these tensions persisted in the years after the Second World War, even as the black-Jewish alliance was being made formal. In 1946, Kenneth B. Clark, a young sociologist, published a blunt description of the difficulties between blacks and Jews. He asserted that "in practically every area of contact between the Negroes and Jewish people, some real or imagined ground for mutual antagonism exists." Blacks, of course, were aware that the black entertainer who was antagonistic to his agent also knows that "if the Jews didn't give us bookings or parts we wouldn't work—but they make a gold mine out of us." Clark documented the proposition that blacks were more bitter toward Jews because they were more in contact with them— as merchants and as landlords—than with any other element in the white community. When Jews called conferences about "the Negro in the United States," blacks felt patronized.

Black leaders knew that they needed the Jews, for this was the only white community in which there was almost total support for their cause. But the "patronizing" Kenneth Clark spoke of was becoming ever more irritating. Jews seem to have been largely unaware, then, of these angers. They were persuaded in their own minds that their passion for the cause of blacks was entirely idealistic: Jews were remembering their own past suffering, and thus they were predisposed to be more identified with the blacks than any other group in America. But there was more than a little truth in Kenneth Clark's complaint. Jews were far better educated than blacks, and they presumed without question that they could provide a significant proportion of the highest caliber of leadership for the black cause.

Jews had cast themselves in the 1950s in the role of doing for blacks what blacks supposedly could not do for themselves. This notion seems to have appeared simultaneously both among the intelligentsia, especially among scholars in the social sciences who were Jewish, and among the bureaucrats of several of the national Jewish organizations. The scholars were troubled by the assertion that blacks are, in the aggregate, of lesser intelligence than whites. Writing in 1952, the sociologist Charles I. Glicksberg surveyed the literature on blacks in America. He found that "The Jewish scholar, be he a psychologist, an anthropologist, historian, or a student of public opinion, is drawn to the problem of racism because it furnishes another flagrant example of the violation of the American Dream." Glicksberg quoted Franz Boas, the leading American anthropologist of the previous generation, who had described the Negro past in America as fruitful and creative. Glicksberg listed a number of Jewish scholars of his own time, from the anthropologist Melville Herskovits to the Marxist historian, Herbert Aptheker, as disproving "the myth concerning the Negro past" and establishing "that the charge of inherent racial inferiority is utterly without warrant." Otto Klineberg, who tested blacks who had come to the North from the South, proved that intelligence rose when blacks lived in a freer environment. Glicksberg gloried in the fact that not a single Jewish scholar was to be found among the apologists for prejudice against the Negro. On the contrary: "The Jewish intellectual, steeped in the prophetic tradition of his people, is necessarily a defender of democracy, a champion of justice for all people."

In the mid-1950s, the rhetoric of the Jewish organizations began to shift. They were facing serious trouble within the Jewish community itself. The NJCRAC was forced to fight on behalf of blacks with some of its own Jewish constituents. It had to acknowledge that "when Negroes moved into formerly all-White communities" even some Jews were opposed. These attitudes were condemned because they ran counter "to the Jewish stake in the integration of housing and schools." The opposition among Jews to blacks came up again two years later, as did the same argument: that Jewish interests required them to oppose all forms of housing discrimination. But the Jewish organizational leaders, who were advancing this argument, were not convincing those of their brethren who were fighting against the penetration of blacks into lower-middle-class neighborhoods in New York and Chicago. The Jews opposed to blacks were aging workingmen, or small businessmen, who still lived in the cities. Unrestricted housing was not in their immediate interest. The Jewish leaders urging them to side with the black community were, overwhelmingly, rich suburbanites. Their own immediate, personal interests were not threatened, for blacks were not then competing for their jobs, or bidding for homes on the streets to which the well-to-do had moved.

To be sure, the involvement of Jews in the cause of blacks did not come cheap. Jews paid an outsize share of the financial bill for the black organizations. Few statistics are available, but it is a fair guess that at least a third of the money that financed the NAACP and the Urban League in the 1950s came from Jewish contributors. Thousands of Jews helped organize and participated in the protest marches in the South and in the North. These men and women were most often passionately convinced idealists—but their efforts for the black revolution served Jews in a very deep way. The era after the Second

World War was the time when Jews were on the march, with the intention of arriving at the very top of American society. By the mid-1950s, they had made base camp, through their rapid economic rise, for the final assault on the Mount Everest of elite status in America. Now, through their role in the black revolution, Jews were making their first overt bid for a major place in the American elite. They were announcing themselves as a major force for solving America's worst problem, racial tension. The Jews were the only white community in America that was very nearly united—in support of blacks. The great and passionate participation of Jews in the battle for blacks was the very first time, in all of American history, when Jews were not pleading for themselves. They were leaders at the very cutting edge of social change—and thus they had "arrived" at the center of American life.

But blacks would not allow Jews to enjoy this "triumph." The young among them, in particular, could not abide the thought that any whites, and especially the Jews, were an elite to whom they should defer. In 1960, young blacks organized the Student Non-Violent Coordinating Committee. They believed in direct social action, and insisted that the black struggle be led by blacks alone. SNCC led in lunch counter sit-ins and boycotts of businesses which discriminated against blacks. Whites were soon excluded from the organization—but nonetheless, for the next several years, Jews continued to furnish a quarter to a third of its financial support. Some admired the activism of SNCC. Jews were even officially indulgent of more radical black elements, such as the Black Muslims, with more than a hint that adults should understand the growing pains of less-advanced people.

The Jewish establishment and the liberal Jewish intelligentsia were reluctant to stop thinking of themselves as the patrons of the blacks. This attitude colored the NJCRAC program for 1960. But the framers of the "program plan" knew that radical changes were taking place, not only in the relation between whites and blacks in general, but especially between blacks and Jews. They predicted that there would be violence even in the North, and that this was all the more likely because of the new black nationalism: "Taking various forms, these movements are essentially alike in their Negro chauvinism, in their 'anti-Whiteism.' The Negro Muslim movement is also anti-Christian and anti-Jewish. All share the conviction that Negro rights can be achieved only through Negro efforts, that White cooperation or help is a poor reed on which to lean or even a fraudulent and deliberately deceitful mask for White domination and exploitation." The Jewish leaders knew that "the rank and file of the Negro community" had become alienated from Jews, and felt little gratitude for the contribution of Jews to the black struggle. Blacks were boycotting Harlem liquor stores and emphasizing that most of the proprietors were Jewish; there were charges in Harlem that black numbers racketeers were being arrested while Jews and Italians were not being bothered. The Jewish community had to take a new attitude toward blacks and not only by establishing relationships with the newest, most activist, and least "respectable forces" among the blacks.

The Jewish establishment thus admitted as early as 1960 that the relationship with blacks could no longer be defined as comradeship of excluded peoples, as in the first years of the alliance in the 1940s and early 1950s, or as the paternalistic concern of Jews for the less fortunate blacks, as in the late 1950s. The young activist black leaders had revolted, and the black masses were on their side. Blacks were well on the way to becoming a power group in America, if only because of their capacity to make trouble. Other groups in America would have to learn how to deal with blacks who could not be patronized, even by their friends. The Jews, who were closest of all, would have to learn the lesson first. Jews had bid for the role of an elite in America by taking care of the blacks—but the essential meaning of the black revolution had become clear by 1960. Blacks were insisting that America was the place that James Madison had once defined as an untidy collection of conflicting interests. There was no elite to which blacks would defer. Jews could rise in America only to the degree that they, like all other groups, acquired and held onto some power in the continuing jostle of American society.

II

The relationship of American Jews with Israel was just as booby-trapped—with difficulties and conflict—but the American Jewish community had a much larger emotional investment in pretending that this was not so. When conflicts arose, they were swept under the rug as quickly as possible. The essence of the matter was that, even as American Jews were adopting Israel as their "homeland," they were refusing to be Zionists.

In the 1890s, at the beginning of modern Zionism, Theodor Herzl had predicted the absorption of most Jews into a Jewish state and the disappearance of the rest; Ahad Ha-Am, the founder of "spiritual Zionism," had insisted that most Jews would live as Jews in the Diaspora. He suggested that the relationship between the Jewish society in the homeland and the rest of the Jews of the world would be primarily secular and cultural.

It was clear as early as 1949 that the Jews of America were not going to emigrate en masse to the State of Israel, and it was equally clear that this community resented any reminder of Herzl's thesis that those who chose to stay in the Diaspora should help "normalize" the Jewish people by assimilating. Those who made this suggestion, such as the writer Arthur Koestler, were bitterly attacked in the Jewish press as traitors. American Jewry was going to survive, so the critics insisted, by deepening its relationship to Israel. In defense, the name of the founder of "spiritual Zionism" was invoked and reinvoked: the Diaspora would be warmed by the blazing sun of the new Jewish center in the State of Israel. But there was no cultural content to this assertion. The Zionists in America were inventing a peculiar kind of Ahad Ha-Amism. Support for Israel, and not learning Hebrew, was the "spiritual content" of the relationship.

This American version of Zionism—to admire and work for Israel but not to move there or participate in its culture—surfaced in several stormy encounters. On May 14, 1948, when the State of Israel was declared, the World Zionist Organization ceased to be a "government in exile," but it did not cease wanting to exercise political functions. The leader of the American Zionists, Abba Hillel Silver, wanted to continue to have a roll in Israel's political life. Silver argued that the Jews of the world had a very special relationship to the State of Israel; they should have a voice in the decisions that Israel would make about itself. Soon after the War of Liberation was won, David Ben-Gurion, the prime minister of Israel, made an end of this anomaly. He thundered that no one "could sit in Cleveland and give directions to Tel Aviv." Let Silver come to Israel to live, let him join its political process, and then he would be entitled to whatever influence he could gain at the polls. Otherwise, so Ben-Gurion insisted, Silver's claim to a voice in Israel's life was impertinent; it was an assault on the basic character of the independent Jewish state.

Ben-Gurion won this argument because he insisted that the state was now sovereign over all partisan interests in the Jewish world. And yet, the question of the relation between the Diaspora and Israel remained. Ben-Gurion soon "solved" the problem by applying to it the rhetoric and ideology of basic Zionism, in its most uncompromising form. The "founding father" of Israel ruled that Zionism means the demand that all Jews, and not only those in immediate danger, must remove themselves to Israel. Since the Jews of the West were not coming in any appreciable numbers, the hundreds of thousands who continued to call themselves Zionists were simply misusing the term. Jews who remained in the Diaspora would, without exception, be treated as "friends of Israel."

In 1950, a year after Ben-Gurion ended Silver's Zionist career, he began to treat Jacob Blaustein, the president of the then non-Zionist American Jewish Committee, as the effective leader of American Jewry. The two of them soon made clear the meaning of their entente: Ben-Gurion wanted financial and political support from American Jews, but he was intractable in insisting that only the State of Israel could determine the use to which such support should be put. Those who disagreed with what Israel was doing had the right to walk away, but they had no right to object. The Zionists in America chafed under this formula. Even those who had made no claim, as Silver had, on major influence on the life of Israel, resented being downgraded to minor-level fund-raisers, but this unhappiness made little difference. Israel was nearly overwhelmed in the 1950s with the task of absorbing well over a million newcomers. It needed money badly, and most of its major donors were not associated with the Zionist organizations.

Ben-Gurion's solution to the question of Israel-Diaspora relations worked well for thirty years. It was widely accepted, at least in the Diaspora, that the leadership role of Israel's Labor party was permanent. American Jews belonged mostly to the moderate center of the Democratic party. They were sure that Israel, under Labor's management, would pursue policies which they themselves could accept and defend. Even as the Labor party began to splinter in the 1950s, American Jews preferred to know as little as possible about that quarrel. They were essentially happy with Ben-Gurion's formula of support without interference; thus, they could, in good conscience, avoid knowing any uncomfortable facts. The relationship between the official American Jewish community and official Israel was thus defined as an involvement which could be maintained only as long as distance was observed. American Jews were entitled to be proud of Israel, but not to meddle in it. Members of "missions" of the United Jewish Appeal often visited Israel in those years and expressed their identification with its brave new life by donning the tembel, the crushed cloth hat of the kibbutzim, and shouting "we are one" from their tour buses. On occasion, the Israelis asked these Americans whether they were truly one: the Israelis were fighting wars; Americans would fly home to safety in a couple of days.

The first hit movie to be made in Israel in the 1950s, *Salah Shabati*, mocked the American Jews, who arrived one after the other in tourist cars to inspect the name plaques on the trees they had given to the afforestation of Israel. It was the job of the hero to change the plaques in advance of each arrival; of course, he got confused, and thus he upset the self-important donors, who could not find their names on any honorific inscription. But such uncomfortable incidents were soon forgotten to permit each of the parties, American Jews and Israelis, to get on with their separate agendas. Israelis needed help, and American Jews needed to love Israel.

American Jews were sure that the involvement in Israel guaranteed the survival of their Jewishness. The surface rhetoric was the proposition that if things ever got bad in America, Jews could find haven in their own state, but this notion was brushed aside by most American Jews. For many, the labors for Israel provided the major content and the emotional highs of their immediate existence as Jews. It was ever more widely held in the 1950s and 1960s that the effort for Israel would somehow guarantee the Jewishness of the next generation of American Jews. Newly appointed heads of the fund-raising drives for Israel spoke, in the words of one such chairman in northern New Jersey, about "handing on the task of raising money for Israel to my children and grandchildren, so that they will remember that they are Jews."

The labors for Israel had one other important meaning for American Jews. These activities began to be recognized as a vehicle for Jews to rise to prominence in America. It was considered to be an act of anti-Semitism, in the 1950s and the 1960s, for anyone to talk about a "Jewish vote," and any Gentile who did was reprimanded by Jewish organizations, which insisted that Jews voted as individual Americans. This was, of course, not true. American Jewish politicians were very much engaged in cementing the power of the Jewish vote and of Jewish political activity. Increasingly, and ever more overtly, Jews were making the support of Israel into an American political issue, and they were rising to the heights of American politics precisely because of their involvement in Israel.

This did not happen all at once. In the first two decades of Israel's existence, there was almost no direct aid from the United States. Israel's deficits could still be met by privately raised funds, and it was not regarded as politic to push the American government during the Eisenhower years, when the war in Korea remained an ever less popular and more costly foreign entanglement. It was too soon after the poverty of the 1930s and the fears of the Hitler era for Jews, even as they were on the rise in America, to take on a very popular president over a few million dollars of possible aid to Israel.

These fears were evident in the American Jewish response to the events of November 1956. England and France tried to reverse by force the decree of Abdel Nasser, the president of Egypt, nationalizing the Suez Canal, and Israel acted in concert with these two powers by moving southward through the Sinai to the banks of the canal. Eisenhower was angered by this adventure, and he ordered the British and the French out of the region. They quickly complied, for both countries were then very dependent on American aid, but Israel did not. It had entered the war to make an end of terrorist raids from Gaza, and it insisted on holding all the territory that it had occupied until it was sure that it had won an end to hostilities.

The administration in Washington became ever testier with Israel. John Foster Dulles, the secretary of state, called in leading figures in the American Jewish community to put pressure on Israel. At this testing time, Eisenhower and Dulles achieved their immediate objective: the Jewish leaders insisted that Israel had a right to its objectives, but they were willing to tell the government of Israel that it ought to moderate its position. The voices grew louder when the rumor got around in February that the Soviet Union was supposedly preparing armed intervention in favor of the Egyptians. Israel withdrew to its original borders in the spring of 1957, under American pressure and with guarantees from the United Nations that an international peacekeeping force would henceforth safeguard quiet on the border of the Egyptian-controlled Gaza Strip. Israel felt itself too weak to defy the major powers. Its supporters in America were not inclined, then, to oppose the government of the United States, but they were sullen.

John Foster Dulles had played the old-line aristocrat, the representative of long-standing American legitimacy, when he leaned on American Jews. He had suggested, on behalf of an angry President Eisenhower, that the American Jewish community had to choose between defending Israel or following the policy of the government in Washington by joining him in forcing Israel to withdraw. The Jewish leaders waffled, but they resented the trap. It reminded them of their feelings of powerlessness in earlier decades, when they did not dare confront Roosevelt on behalf of the endangered Jews of Europe. It was clear that American Jews had not yet acquired enough power to talk back to Washington. Abba Hillel Silver (a longtime Republican) returned to politics to intervene at the White House, but Sherman Adams, the President's principal assistant, brushed him off with some testiness. He came home to Cleveland repeating an old conviction that Jews could not depend on goodwill.

III

Despite their difficulties with blacks, Israelis, and with the American government in the 1950s, American Jews entered the next decade with confidence and pride. They had ceased being an endangered species, and they had become wealthy and secure enough to have some real power in America. The seal was set on this achievement by the presidential election of 1960. This was the moment when the "outsiders," with Jews very prominent among them, conquered America. John F. Kennedy, the Catholic, won the presidential election by a handful of votes. The breakdown of the vote between him and Richard M. Nixon was striking: Nixon, who had infinitely less charisma than Dwight D. Eisenhower, got as much of the white, Protestant vote as Eisenhower had received in the previous election; Kennedy put together his bare majority by getting just about nine-tenths of the vote of Catholics, blacks, and Jews, and of the blue-collar workers, many of whom belonged to ethnic minorities. Thus, the older America was outvoted for the first time by a majority constructed out of the very elements which had been told, for at least two centuries, that they were on approval in America.

It was particularly significant to Jews that the election was so close that Kennedy could not have been elected without them. Jews, even though they were then already less than three percent of the population, cast at least five percent of the votes, for Jews were almost twice as likely to go to the polls as all other Americans. Jewish votes were the margin of victory in several of the swing states. Jews had been of some electoral importance in Roosevelt's coalition, but they had not been indispensable to any of his four presidential victories. The Kennedy election was different. Jews were proud that they had been so crucial to helping the first Catholic into the presidency and that they had thus helped reshape America. In 1960 Jews had a share in the new national administration, as they never had before.

In office, John F. Kennedy surrounded himself with members of the intelligentsia from the major universities. These included not only such figures as Arthur Schlesinger, Jr., who had Jewish immigrants in his immediate family tree, but also McGeorge Bundy, who was descended from the oldest Puritan families. Kennedy's "Camelot" was, thus, not an unvarnished overturn of the older America by an ethnic "pol" who transferred to Washington the machine politics of his grandfather, the first Irish mayor of Boston, John F. Fitzgerald. The minorities were not now simply being given their turn to stuff themselves at the political trough. Kennedy's "Camelot" thought of itself as a meritocracy, as a national leadership of the ablest mandarins, who were recruited regardless of their origins. This theory of merit was satisfying to Jews, for they had been pushing for two centuries for careers based on talent.

Moreover, the White House as "Camelot," with Kennedy as young "royalty," was a reenactment of Roosevelt's White House in which he had played the "gracious king," especially for Jews. There was a critical difference, though, between the new generation of Jewish advisers in "Camelot" and their predecessors who had followed "good king Roosevelt." The Jews in the Kennedy administration represented independent power. The Kennedy years were the moment when the East European Jews finally reached the top of the mountain and saw the promised land. John F. Kennedy brought with him to his cabinet two Jews, Arthur Goldberg and Abraham Ribicoff, both of whom were American-born children of East European immigrants; they were exact representatives of the generation that was then cresting as the dominant element in American Jewry.

The Kennedy era came to a tragic end when the President was assassinated in Dallas on November 22, 1963. These were the years when Jews became a normal, and even unremarkable, part of the American political scene. But Jews had been moving with equal passion toward the upper reaches of American society. In the early 1960s, the black revolution was denying Jews the special role of patron, but Jews could and did associate themselves with those white leaders, and especially the clergy, who fought for the cause of blacks. The great symbolic pageant had taken place just three months before Kennedy's assassination. On August 28, one of the great moments of American history, the march for civil rights took place in Washington. This was a climactic event not only for blacks but also for Jews. It was strikingly evident that Jews were playing a far larger role in pushing for equality than any other white group. There were many Jews among the leaders and members even of the older black civil rights organizations, and the organized community was represented by many delegations. A rabbi walked at the head of the parade, hand in hand with the leader of the march, Martin Luther King. But Jews and blacks were not even pretending to be in the same situation.

On the platform that day Martin Luther King asked blacks not to "distrust all White people" and he pleaded that "in the process of gaining our rightful place we must not be guilty of wrongful deeds." But the thrust of his historic speech was in a confrontationist early paragraph which was really no different from the angry, Black Power outcries of Malcolm X: "There will be neither rest nor tranquility in America until the Negro is granted his citizenship rights. The whirlwinds of revolt will continue to shake the foundations of our nation until the bright day of justice emerges."

The Jewish speaker that day was Rabbi Joachim Prinz, who had come to America in 1937 as a refugee from the Nazis. As a Jew, he invoked "our own painful historic experience, most recently under the Nazis." What the world should have learned from "those tragic circumstances is that bigotry and hatred are not the most urgent problems; the most urgent, the most disgraceful, the most shameful and the most tragic problem is silence." He pleaded that "America must not become a nation of onlookers." This was required "for the sake of the image, the idea and the aspiration of America itself." Martin Luther King was that day the prophet who chastised America for what it had done to his people. Joachim Prinz, even as he remembered the Holocaust, was not speaking in the accents of a minority. He sounded much like his colleagues from the Catholic and Protestant communions. They too—in the persons of the Roman Catholic archbishop of Washington, Patrick O'Boyle, and of the immediate past president of the Protestant National Council of Churches, Eugene Carson Blake—were speaking from that platform of the duty of white America to bring justice to the blacks.

The March on Washington was a high moment for blacks—but also for Jews. They believed that August day that the future was unbounded—but the worst turmoils of racial tensions were soon to come, and so were the divisions over the war in Vietnam.

20.

Turmoil at Home, Glory in Israel

In the mid-1960s, most of American Jews wanted to stop the clock. The dreams of their immigrant ancestors had been realized: Anti-Semitism no longer troubled their business careers, and their children were going to the best colleges. It was also a quiet time for Israel. The raids from Gaza had been ended by Israel's war with Egypt in 1956. American Jews raised money and visited Israel with quiet satisfaction that all was well with the Jewish homeland. Martin Luther King was beginning to have his troubles with younger militant and sometimes even anti-Semitic blacks, but, in the mind of the Jewish community, he was the leader whom they knew and liked. He was, like them, a liberal and not a revolutionary—and he was a great admirer of the State of Israel. Christianity seemed better disposed to Jews than ever. Interfaith activities had become so routine and institutionalized that the major Jewish organizations were vying with each other to "control" the field. In New York, the Interreligious Affairs Office of the American Jewish Committee and the Synagogue Council of America were at war, inconclusively, over who could properly claim to be the Jewish representative in interfaith activities, but these were squabbles over "turf" and publicity. No one, not even among the English-speaking Orthodox Jews, disagreed with the proposition that Jews ought to find some common ground for meeting and working together with Christians. The atmosphere was all the more positive because the Jews revered Pope John XXIII. The pope was reliably rumored to feel contrite about the role of the Church in the Nazi years and to deplore all the elements in Christian theology which were hurtful to Jews. Vatican Council II that John called together in 1962 issued a near-unanimous declaration against anti-Semitism. The Jewish experts and lobbyists, most of them American, who were present in Rome exulted in the coming of a new age.

Inside the Jewish community, the situation was equally comforting. Intermarriage did not yet seem threatening: it was 1 percent of the grandparents and 5 or 6 percent of the parents. But, some worry was beginning to creep into the organized community. Among the Jewish faculty in the colleges and the universities, the rate was much higher, one in three; these were the people who were often the most admired by the hundreds of thousands of the Jewish young in the colleges. The young, the grandchildren of the immigrants, were already marrying out at the rate of one in three, but few of them were old enough by the early 1960s to be marrying. Thus intermarriage had become a topic for discussion, but it was not yet frightening.

In the congregations, there was increasing bustle, but an essential placidity. The dominant problem was how to take care of ever-expanding budgets and how to pay off the mortgages of the newly built synagogues and Jewish community centers. Rabbis were being called to pulpits, in the rhetoric of those days, not to lead or to teach but to "serve." They were expected to be neither prophets nor teachers of Talmud, instructing their students in how to live. The suburban rabbi was cast as a pastor, but he was not a mentor for troubled souls. That task had been entrusted to psychiatrists who were then in ever greater vogue among the educated urban middle class, in which Jews were so prominent. The English-speaking rabbi of the 1960s often tried to become a "pastoral psychiatrist," but he really existed as synagogue functionary.

In the public life of the Jewish community, confrontations had ceased. In the 1930s and the 1940s, American Jews had been led by colorful rabbis such as Stephen S. Wise and Abba Hillel Silver; feisty labor leaders like David Dubinsky and Adolph Held, and capitalists like Felix Warburg and Jacob Blaustein, who fought with Brandeis or Ben-Gurion about Zionism. By the 1960s, some of these figures were dead, and the rest were inactive and irrelevant. The fights had ended, or seemed to have. "Class struggle" between Jewish workers and Jewish bosses was over, because the children of the immigrants who had worked in the needle trades had become businessmen, or lawyers or doctors. All the polls showed at least nine out of ten American Jews were pro-Israel. The vestiges of anti-Zionism among some of the old-line reform Jews, small circles of Socialists and Communists, and some of the intellectuals had become so marginal that no one even bothered to fight with these elements.

The national Jewish organizations were therefore becoming totally bland. Leaders were being chosen almost everywhere because they were likable and moderate. Almost inevitably, the organizations were soon dominated by professional bureaucracies. The executive directors and executive vice presidents were on the scene every day. They were the natural guardians of public policy, and, to ensure that they had the largest possible outreach, they were geared to mass sentiment. A generation earlier, Jewish organizations had "specialized" in competing causes. By the 1960s, they were all doing the same thing. Everyone of the major bodies was for civil rights, for the cause of Israel, and, of course, against anti-Semites. The competition for money and volunteers was among organizations, each of which claimed that it could do all of these things better than any of its rivals. Both in the local communities and on the national scene, this "end of ideology" (in the contemporary term coined by Daniel Bell, the political thinker and social critic) bred not charismatic leaders but institutional managers.

Amidst this self-satisfaction, some social discomfort continued to exist. Jews expressed their annoyance by founding their own country clubs—and by remaining Democrats in politics. The Republicans whom Jews encountered in the suburbs usually had controlled local politics for generations, but these were often the same people who had tried, just a few years before, to uphold "restrictive convenants," to make it impossible for Jews to buy real estate in the neighborhood. The Republican party continued to hold many of its fund-raisers and social affairs in clubs which did not admit Jews. In some places it was tactically wise to be a Republican on the local scene, but the social distance between Jews and Gentiles, between newcomers and older settlers, was sufficient ground for voting present and past resentments, at least in national elections. Irving Kristol, the leading theoretician of neoconservatism, observed ruefully that "Jews are as rich as Episcopalians but that they vote like Puerto Ricans." In the 1960s, when the Jews became as "rich as the Episcopalians," they were the only group in America which had social prestige that was far lower than its income level. And so the Jews—out of memory of the New Deal, pride in their role in the Kennedy administration, resentment at the remains of social exclusion, and sympathy for the poor (for they had recently been poor themselves), and a continuing re-echo in the Jewish soul of prophetic injunctions to love justice and do mercy—became the richest Democrats in the 1960s.

But even so, Jews had become a special kind of Democrat. They wanted the party to be stable and orderly. They wanted negotiated settlements among all the factions in the party and in the country. The majority of American Jews, as Democrats, had become the party of order: they were the true conservatives. Subject only to some minor changes, they liked their world as it was.

But what was the content of inner Jewish life in these years of quiet? The question of self-definition was being posed in the mid-1960s, but most Jews paid no attention. They were interested in their families, in business, and in their social engagements with each other. They did not hear the radically opposed suggestion that the intellectuals and the ultra-Orthodox were making. Most intellectuals wanted the Jewish community to dissolve. The ultra-Orthodox proposed a return to the ghetto; the Jews should live apart from the rest of America. The mainstream refused to listen to either suggestion. Most American Jews preferred to affirm their togetherness without quite being sure what they meant.

The intellectuals were prime disturbers of the peace. Some were wrestling with their Jewishness, and others were indifferent, but almost all of them disliked or were even contemptuous of the existing American Jewish community. In 1961 Norman Podhoretz, who the year before had become editor of the monthly *Commentary,* organized a symposium on "Jewishness and the Younger Intellectuals." Half a generation earlier, in 1944, the *Contemporary Jewish Record,* the predecessor of *Commentary,* had published a comparable symposium and had found almost total alienation from the Jewish community, and from the Jewish religion, among such figures as literary critic Lionel Trilling, art critic Clement Greenberg, and the essayist/novelist Isaac Rosenfeld. Podhoretz reopened the subject for a younger group, under forty, to find a somewhat less angry version of the same result. These grandchildren and even great-grandchildren of immigrants felt "that they properly belonged to a much larger world than is encompassed by the Jewish community—or, indeed, by America itself." The youngest of the contributors almost totally rejected the idea of the need for attachment to any community of tradition. Summarizing the answers, Podhoretz was encouraged by "the atmosphere of idealism." He found that these young intellectuals were asserting with almost one voice "that the essential tradition of Judaism became to be embodied in modern times not in the committed Jewish community, but in the great post-emancipation figures who rushed out of the ghetto to devour and then to recreate the culture of the West: Marx, Freud, Einstein."

These names kept recurring in the symposium. Raziel Abelson, then an assistant professor of philosophy at New York University, mentioned these names, along with Spinoza, as the figures "to which I feel most directly linked"; the modern Jew, he noted, should be "spokesman for a nationally organized, democratic world society, unfettered by parochial traditions and superstitions." Werner Cohn, then assistant professor of sociology at the University of British Columbia, invoked Marx, Freud, and Einstein, and added Jesus and Trotsky, as role models for the Jews as the "outsider," the one who stands alone. Jason Epstein, then editor in chief of the Modern Library, was detached from the Jewish community: "I have the impression that the traditional human groupings are on the way out . . . Perhaps it would be good to feel oneself engaged in a highly auspicious tradition. But I happen not to and do not feel as one with those who do." Nat Hentoff, a regular columnist in *The Village Voice*, echoed this view: "I feel no more involvement with the Jewish community as a whole than I do with any community." Only two symposiasts were clearly on the other side, Enoch Gordis, a physician whose father was a rabbi, and Malcolm Diamond, who was teaching religion at Princeton and writing on Martin Buber. Neither was Orthodox, but both found their Jewish identity in the Jewish tradition, in its texts and practices.

The fundamental issues about contemporary Jewishness had been raised seriously and precisely in these essays. These questions would appear again two years later in a comparable discussion in the Zionist journal, *Midstream,* which published a symposium on the question of whether American Jews were "in exile." Henry Roth, who had fallen totally silent since the publication of his novel *Call It Sleep* (1934), asserted that he had abandoned the "fairly intensive conditioning of [his] own childhood with regard to Judaism," and now felt himself attached to humanity. He knew that his life and the life of his children were inescapably affected by prejudice, but, because his children had not freely chosen to be Jews, they owed Judaism no allegiance: "I can only say, again, that I feel that to the great boons Jews have already conferred upon humanity, Jews in America might add this last and greatest one: of orienting themselves toward ceasing to be Jews." Though some of the other participants in the discussion in *Midstream* agreed with Marie Syrkin, the Zionist intellectual, that American Jewish life was being strengthened by the growing centrality of Israel in the concerns of the community, the younger Jewish intelligentsia agreed with what the novelist Philip Roth said in the exchange in *Commentary,* that "I cannot find a true and honest place in the history of believers that begins with Abraham, Isaac and Jacob on the basis of the heroism of these believers, of their humiliations and anguish. I can only connect with them, and with their descendants, as I apprehend their God." Since Roth was not a believer, "nostalgia or sentimentality" or even "a blind and valiant effort of the will" cannot connect him to Jews as he is not connected to other men.

Roth was correct: only the religious believers had a clear and unshakable answer to the question of why be a Jew, and such believers had recently appeared in the United States, for the first time in all of American Jewish history, in their most ultra-Orthodox version. They were mounting a serious attack from the religious right on conventional American Jewish life. They asserted the most uncompromising, separatist version of the Jewish religion. This doctrine was brought to America during and after the Second World War by leaders who had previously refused to come to the United States—heads of yeshivoth (the schools for advanced Talmudic studies) and Hasidic rebbes. A few, such as the rebbe of Lubavitch, Rabbi Joseph Schneerson, and Rabbi Aaron Kotler, the head of the yeshiva in Kletzk, Poland, had been saved in 1940–41 from Nazi-occupied Poland and brought to the United States. Most other leaders arrived after the war, when the remnants of European Jewry decided that they could not reconstitute the communities which the Nazis and their collaborators had destroyed.

The Talmudic scholars and the Hasidic rebbes who had survived, and their followers, could choose only between Israel and the United States. Many chose the United States, because they were uncomfortable with or strongly against the new secular Jewish state. In their minds, states were a non-Jewish affair. Rabbi Joel Teitelbaum, the rebbe of Satmar, went first to Jerusalem, but he soon left for New York. A number of other Hasidic figures came directly to America. These rebbes reestablished their "courts" in several neighborhoods in Brooklyn. Satmar and several less renowned groups settled in the Williamsburg section where by the mid-1960s the Hasidic community was estimated at five thousand families. Lubavitch established its headquarters in the Crown Heights section; many other branches of the ultra-Orthodox moved into Brownsville. In less than twenty years, all three neighborhoods were dominated by the ultra-Orthodox. Williamsburg, in particular, had become the urban equivalent of an East European shtetl.

The new arrivals were not necessarily at peace with each other. On the contrary, they brought along to the United States many existing sectarian quarrels. The legalists of the yeshivoth and the more mystical Hasidim continued to feel the distance which had arisen between these two versions of Judaism in the late 1700s in Europe. The adherents of Satmar and Lubavitch quarreled violently over a very contemporary issue; the rebbe of Lubavitch was not totally opposed to the State of Israel; the rebbe of Satmar regarded Zionism as the ultimate sign of rebellion against God, who had commanded the Jews to wait for the Messiah. Nonetheless, despite their quarrels, the ultra-Orthodox held one fundamental value in common: they had come to America not to "arrive" or even to succeed (though some were becoming rich by the 1960s), but to be uncompromisingly religious by their own standards.

In the twenty years after the end of the war, less than one hundred thousand Orthodox came to the United States, but this was the first group of Jews in all of American history to come not primarily in search of bread but to find refuge for its version of Jewishness. The new ultra-Orthodox were reenacting, in mid-twentieth century urban America, and mostly in New York, what the Puritans had done three centuries before in the New England wilderness; they were escaping a hostile Europe and coming to the New World in order to create their own separatist theocracy. Their neighborhoods in Brooklyn were being fashioned as their own "city on the hill."

All the sects of the new Orthodoxy insisted on entirely separatist education. Upon arrival, the ultra-Orthodox had found that the existing, "modern Orthodox" community was educating its children largely in the public schools. Like the Conservative and Reform groups, the "modern Orthodox" depended on supplementary classes in the afternoons and on Sunday to impart the teachings and practices of Judaism. Before the Second World War, there were fewer than 20 Jewish day schools in the country, almost all of which were in New York. By 1944, the number had grown to 55, for the existing Orthodox community had begun to move toward educating the young under Jewish auspices. Nineteen years later, in 1963, according to a survey by the Jewish Education Committee of New York, there were 257 Orthodox day schools in the United States, 132 in greater New York and 125 in other cities. In about half of these schools the language of instruction was Yiddish; these were the institutions that the newly arrived ultra-Orthodox had created. From their poorest beginnings, they had insisted that their children be raised in an all-Jewish and uncompromisingly Orthodox environment. The "modern Orthodox" had little choice but to follow the example of the newest arrivals. Within a decade, by the mid-1970s, almost all children of Orthodox families, including the older, Americanized ones, were attending Jewish parochial schools.

The ultra-Orthodox community was the one group in American Jewry which was opposed on principle to having the young go to college. They were especially opposed to the college under Jewish auspices which had been founded a generation earlier by the oldest yeshiva in the United States, and had become Yeshiva University. Its school for the study of Talmud no longer dominated Orthodox learning in America. By the mid-1960s four out of five of the advanced students of Talmud were attending the ultra-Orthodox yeshivoth. These numbered more than three thousand in all. Television sets were forbidden in the dormitories of these schools, and newspapers were frowned upon. The necessities of making a living forced those who ended their studies into contact with the non-Jewish world, but the alumni of the ultra-Orthodox yeshivoth remained convinced that one meaning of American freedom was the right not to participate in American culture. Other Jews who did not share this view were excluded from their fellowship. This, too, was reminiscent of the Puritan attitude, three centuries earlier, toward all other Protestants.

The ultra-Orthodox picked their leaders just as the Puritans had, by consensus. An individual or several individuals were recognized as possessors of profound Talmudic scholarship and charisma. Such leaders were to be obeyed because they represented the true meaning of "Torah," the cumulative teaching of the whole of the sacred tradition. Among the teachers and students of the American yeshivoth, and the thousands of laymen who belonged to this subcommunity, Rabbi Aaron Kotler was the undoubted religious authority. His decisions were widely accepted in most of the other camps of the Orthodox community in the United States, and they were respected in Israel. After his death in 1962, the mantle passed to Rabbi Moshe Feinstein, the head of a yeshiva on the East Side of New York. The modern Orthodox group increasingly revered Rabbi Joseph Soloveitchik, who was the premier figure among the teachers in the yeshiva of Yeshiva University, but Soloveitchik's authority was not recognized by the ultra-Orthodox. He was exactly the kind of figure they opposed, a rabbi with a doctorate in philosophy. No one doubted Soloveitchik's Talmudic learning, or his Orthodox piety, but he was a man who lived intellectually in both the Jewish and the secular world—and the new ultra-Orthodoxy in America refused to compromise with secular culture or even acknowledge its existence.

Rabbi Menachem Mendel Schneerson, the rebbe of Lubavitch, was an extreme separatist, but he was a unique figure, because he was more involved than any other ultra-Orthodox leader with the non-Orthodox majority of American Jews. He had succeeded as the rebbe of Lubavitch on the death in 1950 of his father-in-law, Rabbi Joseph Schneerson. Though the new rebbe had himself attended university in Berlin and Paris, he had long left that phase of his life behind. As rebbe, he insisted, as vehemently as all other ultra-Orthodox leaders, that his followers should be educated entirely in institutions of his movement, and that secular education should be given only to the degree necessary to satisfy the laws of the state. But the new rebbe turned his movement into a "mission" to the rest of the Jewish world. His disciples were sent out into the "wilderness," to all five continents, to do good works and to propagate the faith. By the 1960s, young emissaries of Lubavitch were to be found on street corners handing out prayer shawls and other ritual objects, and asking Jews to join in saying the prescribed benedictions. Any Jew who was moved to perform even one of the commanded rituals, so the rebbe taught, was opening a gate which would lead him to Lubavitch Orthodoxy. The rebbe had thus announced a new policy: his Orthodoxy was a missionary faith which was now setting out to convert all other Jews.

The prestige of this endeavor was rising in the 1960s. The rebbe was widely revered because he was rumored to control the only effective underground Jewish network in the Soviet Union. But there were deeper, less tangible reasons for the success of Lubavitch, and for the increasing influence of all the ultra-Orthodox. Within the non-Orthodox mass of American Jews, many had always felt that Orthodoxy was the true Jewish religion, and that the more modern forms of Judaism, those that admitted the existence of the secular world, were essentially compromises. Had not the "reformed" Jacob Schiff, a generation earlier, said kaddish for his parents in an Orthodox synagogue? The self-confidence of the rebbe of Lubavitch attracted many. Some joined him, at least in part. The renowned sculptor Jacques Lipchitz made no secret that under the influence of the rebbe of Lubavitch he had returned to saying morning prayers every day in the Orthodox manner. Many others basked in the glow of the rebbe's virtue by giving money to his endeavors.

The new ultra-Orthodoxy in America broke with the modern Orthodox by refusing to cooperate with the more liberal religious groups. The fight began over the Synagogue Council of America, a national organization founded in the 1920s as a joint endeavor of the central bodies of the Orthodox, Conservative, and Reform groups, to be the peer group of the Protestant National Council of Churches, and of the National Conference of Catholic Bishops. Belonging to this body suggested that the three Jewish "denominations" were willing to accept each other as equals, if only for limited representational purposes. In 1962, however, the leading ultra-Orthodox religious authorities ruled that belonging to any body which admitted Conservative and Reform rabbis was forbidden. Though that did not stop the modern Orthodox from continuing to adhere to these institutions, the ruling made clear that the ultra-Orthodox felt secure in the future of their own separate community. One could join the "elect" by conforming to its rules, but this "elect" would never adjust to other Jews—or to secular American culture. The mainstream of the American Jewish community thus had been urged by its intellectuals to dissolve, and by the ultra-Orthodox to live apart from American society. The mass of Jews refused to think such radical thoughts. What came naturally and easily was the customary, well-established option, to affirm "togetherness."

But if Jews were "other" from Gentiles, what made them so? Why did they need to remain together? Was it simply the label Jew, pinned on them by anti-Semites? Was it a residual sense of being unwelcome in Gentile America? It was already clear in the 1960s that the older American elite had lost interest in anti-Semitism. Black angers against Jews had become more overt, and sometimes poisonous and violent, but no one in the Jewish community, not even the poor who were fighting housing battles in changing neighborhoods, could imagine being antiblack as a continuing principle of cohesion.

Jewish "otherness" needed positive justification. American Jews had to find a way of persuading their children to be "proud to be Jews," and not merely to be angry with the enemies of the Jews. A "usable past" had to be constructed.

In the seeming quiet of the early 1960s (when racial confrontations were still confined to the South), this Jewish "past" could not be presented as angry, defiant, and revolutionary, nor could it be based on Prophets and Talmudists who had demanded obedience to the law that God had pronounced at Sinai. This past, edited for American Jews, needed to be sanitized so that it would be uplifting and inoffensive.

This editing of memory had begun almost as soon as Jews began to "arrive," after the end of the Second World War. The Rosenberg affair (a Jewish couple, Julius and Ethel Rosenberg, were convicted of spying for the Soviet Union and passing on atomic secrets) had "corrected" the notion that any substantial number of Jews had ever been Communists. Indeed, Jews insisted that they had always been the most respectable of Americans. The Broadway hit, *Fiddler on the*

Roof, was evidence of this trend. The tens of thousand of American Jews who came to see the play were both remembering and inventing an ancestor. They were remembering correctly that their European grandfathers had been poor and semiliterate like the hero of the play, Tevye, the milkman in the mythic village of Anatefka. There was psychological truth, also, in the village's fatuous rabbi: the poor of Europe had old scores to settle with the traditional leaders of the community who had failed to save them. But, as Irving Howe, the essayist and socialist intellectual, said at the time, *Fiddler on the Roof,* unlike the Sholem Aleichem stories on which it was based, had very little of the blazing anger of the poor toward the rich. Class struggle was not a "nice" subject. Moreover, it was not a piece of Jewish history that the newly well-to-do wanted to remember as they were joining the middle class. Tevye's piety, in the Broadway version, was equally sanitized. It bore little relation to the original figure in the Yiddish tales, for Sholem Aleichem's hero, even as he misquoted the Bible, knew that it enjoined commandments, and not some vague and sentimental "tradition."

The earthy Tevye was a Jewish version of an American theme. Tevye belonged together with De Lawd, the dignified black man who was God in *The Green Pastures,* Marc Connelly's play of the 1930s about simple black folk; an Irish leprechaun in Lerner and Loewe's *Finian's Rainbow* (1947); and with Zorba the Greek. Like them, Tevye was quaint and undemanding; he was, at once, Jewish and American. Jews in New York and Chicago did not have to ask themselves to behave like Tevye, any more than the Irish in Boston could be expected to take leprechauns seriously. The Jews who flocked to *Fiddler on the Roof,* and brought their children to see the show, were proud of Tevye. He was Jewish in a very American way.

This new American Jewishness of the masses who flocked to Tevye was all too respectable—and boring. By the beginning of the 1960s, the problem was unmistakable. In 1963, sociologist and historian Nathan Glazer summed up his essay on the Jews in *Beyond the Melting Pot,* the book that he wrote together with now Senator Daniel Patrick Moynihan, by asserting:

Neither the synagogues and temples, nor the charitable and phil-anthropic work, nor the fund-raising for Israel and defense seems sufficiently vital and relevant for the most gifted young people

who are emerging from the community. Nor does that other community that was scarcely less Jewish, that of the radical movements
and the unions, engage them much.

Speaking of the mainstream of the younger generation, those who
were not intellectuals, Glazer added that "a satisfying pattern of
Jewish middle-class life has not yet emerged." The Jewish community as a whole had not yet found the balance between its Jewish
and American identities. Nat Hentoff echoed this view. He asserted
that the vast majority of American Jews possessed an identity with
little substance; they have "no permanent psychological barrier to
joining the other hollow men."

The middle-class Jews of the mid-1960s might have seemed "hollow," or uncertain of their values, but within themselves they remembered why they were Jews. They had been taught by their
immigrant parents that being a Jew meant having *tsuris* (troubles)
and complaining about them to other Jews. They had been reminded
of this Jewishness by Tevye, whom they had just seen on Broadway.
He had been saddened by a daughter who went off with a Gentile
revolutionary; he had problems with the Russian peasants who sometimes got drunk and made pogroms. A reenactment of such problems
in their own time, here in the United States, was thus an almost
comforting reminder to the suburbanites that they, too, were Jews.
There were such worries to be complained about in the mid-1960s.
Some Jews, and some blacks, were disturbing the peace.

Some "clever" Jews were becoming a problem to the Jewish mainstream. Intellectuals and writers were giving Jews a "bad name."
Norman Mailer was a famous novelist, the author of an acclaimed
war novel, *The Naked and the Dead* (1948), but the Jewish community
deplored him. He was looking for the "apocalyptic orgasm," and
he was insisting that affirming the body, and even lust, was a daring
proclamation of marginality to American culture. Mailer imagined
an individual who left society to set out on an "uncharted journey
into the rebellious imperatives of the self," even if that meant "to
encourage the psychopath in oneself." He did exactly that in those
very years. In a frightening passage in *Advertisements for Myself* (1959),
Mailer had found value in the murder of "a candystore keeper," no
doubt a Jew, by "two strong eighteen-year-old hoodlums." The
murderers have displayed "courage of a sort," because they were

murdering "not only a weak fifty-year-old man but an institution as well, one violates private property, one enters into a new relation with the police, and introduces a dangerous element into one's life."

Norman Podhoretz was even more troubling to the Jewish community, because he had *Commentary* as his platform. Early in 1963, Podhoretz published an essay titled "My Negro Problem—and Ours." He argued that the "Negro Problem can be solved in the country" only through "the wholesale merging of the two races." He did not flinch from the conclusion that, despite his own upbringing as a white and a Jew, he would give his daughters parental blessing if they decided to marry blacks. This assertion was denounced from almost every synagogue pulpit in America. How dare a Jewish editor advocate intermarrying and the dissolution of the Jewish people? Those who denounced Podhoretz did not stop to hear the torment in his essay. He had not been at ease with blacks since his childhood, and he refused to make himself comfortable in 1963 as a "white liberal" who wished blacks well from a distance. The mainstream Jewish community heard none of this: it heard only that the most prominent Jewish editor of the day was an anti-Jew.

Even the most serious Jewish novelists made the mainstream community unhappy. To be sure, the literary world, which had long seen Jews as aliens, was now very nearly dominated by them. They were establishing that Jewish immigrant habitations, whether in Saul Bellow's Chicago or Bernard Malamud's New York, were as valid a "region" of American experience as William Faulkner's Yoknapatawpha County in Mississippi, or J. P. Marquand's Yankee Connecticut. But Faulkner could write about drunks and perverts and Marquand could tell stories of disintegrating Yankee aristocrats freely, because they were Gentiles. Was it really necessary to tell the non-Jews about quack psychiatrists, like Dr. Tamkin in Bellow's *Seize the Day* (1956)? For that matter, were Isaac Bashevis Singer's earthy stories "good for Jews"?

Many of the writers and intellectuals were disturbing, but they did not threaten the immediate peace of the Jewish community. Blacks were different. They were no longer willing to accept what the white liberal community, where the Jews were so prominent, was eager to offer them: personal equality, a place at the same starting gate as everyone else in the race for success and honor in American society. In the mid-1960s blacks were articulating a radical new program: not equality at the beginning but equality of result. Blacks insisted that the ladder of "merit" was a set of tests invented by whites to measure not intelligence but assimilation to white culture. The poor results of black children in the schools was the direct fault of an educational system which was, by its very nature, racist: it taught black children to be underclass.

These propositions were articulated in their most challenging form by Malcolm X, the leader of the most uncompromising black nationalists, the Organization of Afro-American Unity:

> What do we want? We want Afro-American principals to head these all-black schools. We want Afro-American teachers in these schools. Meaning we want black principals and black teachers with some textbooks about black people. We want textbooks written by Afro-Americans that are acceptable to our people before they can be used in these schools.

The most nationalist element in the black community had thus been told by its leader, at the founding rally of the OAAU on June 28, 1964, that the New York schools, in which Jewish principals and teachers predominated, were an arena in which blacks could wrest control of programs and jobs for themselves. This demand was made by blacks not as individuals but as a community: they were proclaiming themselves to be a national group in America with ethnic roots in Africa.

Six months later, Nathan Glazer told the Jews that there was "a new challenge to pluralism" in their encounter with blacks. The demand by blacks for special consideration, for equal share in all of society, was a direct challenge to the Jews. Glazer was aware that Jews were particularly the gainers of the move "into a diploma society, where individual merit rather than family and connections and group must be the basis for advancement, recognition, achievement. The reasons have nothing directly to do with the Jews, but no matter—the Jews certainly gain from such a grand historical shift. Thus Jewish interests coincide with the new rational approaches to the distribution of rewards." The new demands by blacks, so Glazer asserted, did not simply threaten the "merit system"; they undermined the existence of the Jewish subcommunity and of all other American subcommunities. The demand by blacks for equality of results meant that the neighborhoods, professions, and businesses that the various subcommunities had created for themselves would be breached. "The force of present-day Negro demands is that the sub-community, because it either protects privileges or creates inequality, has no right to exist." Glazer insisted that Jews, despite their concern for the advancement of blacks, were now opposed to blacks: "Thus Jews find their interest and those of formally less liberal neighbors becoming similar: they both have an interest in maintaining an area restricted to their own kind; an interest in managing the friendship and educational experiences of their children; an interest in passing on advantages in money and skills to them."

Glazer was not yet confronting the blacks' nationalism for which Malcolm X spoke, even though it was then transforming most of the black intelligentsia. Glazer focused on the majority view among blacks at that particular moment, the demand for a percentage of place in white schools, neighborhoods, and jobs. But the blacks who had gone to war against "merit"—even the majority, then, who wanted integration with whites—were not at war with the idea of subcommunities in America: they simply wanted the rules to be changed so that their subcommunity could arrive.

Glazer's defense of the Jews was, as he knew himself, unhistorical. Three decades earlier, Jewish intellectuals had been arguing that English literature was not the particular province of Christians, who supposedly best understood its spirit. Blacks were arguing, forty years later, that the system of preferment in America had to change, again, to take account of their particular situation. The supposed culture-free and color-blind exactness of "merit" examination had produced, so Glazer was asserting, a community of Jewish bureaucrats and teachers with an ethos of its own, a subculture which had the right to defend itself—against blacks who wanted to seize the schools for their own subculture! The relationship of American Jews to blacks had now changed; the consistency of the arguments was unimportant. What mattered was that the theories were rationalizations by some Jews, who were fighting to retain posts which blacks were demanding.

To be sure, the Jews on the immediate firing line were middle-class bureaucrats and teachers whose jobs were products of civil service exams in the era of the New Deal. They were threatened, as their richer Jewish relatives in business and the professions were not.

But the genie was out of the bottle: some Jews and some blacks were on their way to open war. Jews could no longer assume that, having fought their way to the top of American society, they would not be attacked from below by blacks on the march into the middle class.

In 1966, the situation became more pointed, when Stokely Carmichael became president of the Student Non-Violent Coordinating Committee (SNCC). Carmichael insisted in the early months there was no anti-Semitism in his "Black Power" outlook. Some Jews, such as the journalist I. F. Stone and the entertainer Theodore Bikel, remained in public support. There were even rabbis, such as Harold Saperstein, who was then in the Reform congregation in Lynbrook, New York, who, while unhappy with the insistence on "Black Power," continued to support SNCC. The real break with black nationalists would not come until the next year, in June 1967, when the Israel-Arab war broke out, and the black radicals and their supporters in the white community sided with the Arabs. Until then, specific groups of Jews—the not very rich who still lived in the cities and the white-collar bureaucrats—were in direct battle with blacks. The richer and better established elements could continue to talk the older language of social conscience. Rabbis had gone by the planeload to join the march on Selma, Alabama, in 1964. Albert Shanker, the head of the American Federation of Teachers in New York, which was beginning to be embroiled with blacks over control of the schools, had joined the march. The National Jewish Community Relations Advisory Council persisted in believing that the riots in the cities, in which Jewish stores in the black ghettos were main victims, were of little importance. In "program plan" after "program plan" the doctrine was reiterated that Jews should remain committed to every form of help for blacks. In late May 1967, the Anti-Defamation League published a study in five volumes of black anti-Semitism, to assert that there was less such prejudice among blacks than among whites. The Anti-Defamation League would soon change its estimate of black anti-Semitism, but in May 1967, this was the dominant "orthodoxy" of the American Jewish establishment. It took until 1969 for Bertram Gold, the executive vice president of the American Jewish Committee, the organization which published *Commentary,* in which Glazer had written in 1964, to say that the Jewish community could no longer remain silent and forgiving of angry blacks. Until 1967, the leaders of the organized Jewish community, those who spoke for the mainstream, wanted to believe the Jews were, somehow, still where they had briefly been in 1963, an elite which no longer had to battle other groups in an often rancorous America.

Important elements of the Christian intelligentsia were siding with the most radical blacks. In the spring of 1968, one of the riots in the cities was in Washington, on Easter weekend. Rosemarie Reuther, a young Catholic theologian who was a partisan of the blacks, wrote a column in the *National Catholic Reporter,* in which she pronounced the burning of the Jewish stores in the black ghetto to be a contemporary celebration by the poor of Christ's Resurrection. This was Reuther's version of a theme from Malcolm X: blacks in the American ghettos were the victims of white colonialism. The exploiters, so he insisted, were none other than Jews, who were "colonizing" the blacks, while the Jews themselves had moved away to better neighborhoods. The implication was clear that burning down stores, some of which Jews might own, was a liberating act.

What was least troubling then, in the mid-1960s, were the young Jews of the New Left. As the political thinker and sociologist Seymour Martin Lipset estimated at the time, these were not very many: less than ten thousand of the nearly four hundred thousand Jews who wer students in the colleges and universities. Thus, very few Jewish families were directly affected by the young radicals. But these Jewish activists did make up a very large proportion of the total leadership of all of the various movements of the New Left. The Jewish community, which was always measuring the temperature of anti-Semitism, feared that the prominence in the New Left of Jews such as Saul Landau and Paul Jacobs in Berkeley and of Abbie Hoffman and Jerry Rubin, who were the founders and the leaders of the Yippies, would arouse anti-Jewish feelings among Gentiles. This did not happen. In the mind of America, the New Left was an American and not a Jewish problem.

A study done in 1968 showed that 82 percent of all Americans regarded Jews as the least troubling and troublesome of American minorities. These opinions were being expressed at a time when Abbie Hoffman was screaming at a Jewish judge in Chicago that judging him for his role in the riots at the Democratic National Convention was a "*shande* [disgrace] before the Gentiles." Hoffman was dragging in his Jewishness; it did not matter even in those most superheated days. Jews had "arrived"; they would not be blamed for outbreaks which some of their children were making together with contemporaries from good or even the best old-line Protestant families.

Until June 1967, when large parts of the New Left became anti-Israel, the mainstream of the American Jewish community had substantial sympathy with its purposes. The first manifesto of the New Left, which was written at Port Huron, Michigan, in early summer of 1962, was, in its language and ideals, a very "Jewish" document: "We are the people of this generation, bred in at least modest comfort, housed now in universities, looking uncomfortably to the world we inherit." What the drafters of the statement affirmed was "human independence . . . a quality of mind not compulsively driven by a sense of powerlessness." They pleaded for community which could be achieved "by improved gadgets but only when the love of man by man overcomes the idolatrous worship of things by man." Their social ideal was proclaimed to be "participatory democracy" in which the individual would "share in those social decisions determining the quality and direction of his life." The group that met at Port Huron was opposed to the "military-industrial complex," to the "cold war," and to "colonialism." It was vehemently opposed to discrimination against blacks. Salvation was to be found in remaking society.

The major drafter of the Port Huron Statement was Tom Hayden, who was a Catholic, but the text echoed the committed language of previous generations of Jewish radicals, in the labor unions and in several varieties of the Socialist movement. A substantial proportion of those who came to Port Huron were, indeed, Jews. The Students for a Democratic Society (SDS) had been founded two years before at a convention in New York, and Robert Alan Haber had been elected its first president. Haber came from the University of Michigan, where his father, William, had been teaching since 1936. The elder Haber was an economist and labor arbitrator, who had helped create the Social Security system in the era of the New Deal. In 1948, the family had spent a year in Frankfurt, Germany, while William Haber was adviser on Jewish affairs to the general who commanded the American forces. These were the very days when the survivors of the concentration camps were finding ways, with some quiet American help, to break the British blockade of Palestine and to help in the battle to create Israel. Haber was thus raised in the home of an American Jew who was a social democrat and a Zionist. When he became "Ann Arbor's resident radical," as James E. Miller called him in *Democracy is in the Streets* (1987), Robert Alan Haber had no opposition at home. On the contrary, the SDS, at its founding, was supported by the League for Industrial Democracy, of which his father was a leader.

Dozens of memoirs, histories, and sociological analyses of the New Left, in all its complicated and often warring parts, have appeared. The explanations vary from psychoanalytic interpretations of Oedipal rebellion by the young, to the "red diaper" theory that many protesters were children of radicals of the 1930s, to the thesis that the young copped out of serious politics by protesting without a serious political program. But the New Left as a whole is not the subject here; it is rather the question of the Jewishness of these young radicals and of their affect on the Jewish community as a whole. The adult Jewish supporters—or indulgers—of the New Left were not only some older radicals. The American Jewish establishment never really distanced itself from these young Jews.

Racial equality was a cause which all Jews shared—or said they did. The war in Vietnam did divide American Jewish opinion down the middle, exactly as it divided all of the rest of America, but by 1968, when the college draft was instituted, American Jewish parents were transformed into opponents of the war, along with the parents of much of the rest of the students of the colleges. The occupation of university buildings and the violence were disturbing, but the mainstream of the Jewish community, as represented by these parents, was more indulgent of the young protesters, who were their children, than were most of the Jewish faculty members. The professors had almost all come to their jobs very recently, in the 1950s when academic appointments were opened wide to Jews; they did not want disruption of the institutions through which they had just entered one of the American elites. Thus, some Jewish professors, such as Edward I. Levy in Chicago, were prominent in opposing the students who took over university buildings: others, like Henry Rosovsky in Harvard, led in the effort to conciliate and to bring peace.

Very "established" Jews figured among the early ideological opponents of the war. The women's division of the American Jewish Congress passed an antiwar resolution in the fall of 1965, associating

itself with the demonstrations against the war which had been organized by students and especially by the SDS. Clergy and Laity
Concerned About Vietnam (CALCAV) was formed in the next year;
rabbis led by Abraham Joshua Heschel, the theologian, were prominent among its leaders. That fall the Reform lay body, the Union
of American Hebrew Congregations, passed a resolution at its bien-
nial convention which asked the President "to declare to the world
that as of a given date, our armed forces would cease firing, our
planes would cease bombing and our representatives would proceed
forthwith . . . to meet with the representatives of the opposing
forces in Vietnam, with the view toward finding a peaceful solution
to this conflict." In January 1966, the Synagogue Council of America,
despite the Orthodox, who tended to be more prowar than all the
rest, issued a statement calling for an immediate cease-fire. There
were countervoices to this opposition to the Vietnam War, especially
among the Orthodox. Michael Wyschogrod, who taught philosophy
in the City University of New York, wrote in the Orthodox quarterly *Tradition* (Winter 1966), that America's presence in Vietnam
was part of the war against the Soviet Union, and that Jews had to
support this war as part of their defense of Israel, which was safe
only if the United States included it under its protective, anti-Soviet
umbrella.

American opinion as a whole, and especially the White House,
was aware that Jews, both established figures and young protesters,
were central to the opposition to the war. This issue came to a head
on September 6, 1966, when Malcolm Tarlov, the national commander of the Jewish War Veterans, reported that President Lyndon
Johnson was "disturbed by the lack of support for the Vietnam War
in the American Jewish community at a time when he was taking
new steps to aid Israel." Inevitably, there was an outcry about this
statement, and the White House soon let it be known that Johnson's
remarks had been "misunderstood" or "poorly interpreted" by the
news media. Tarlov soon took back his words. The essential result
of this incident was to harden the views within the Jewish community
on both sides. The supporters of the war in Vietnam insisted that
the protest movement was "bad for Jews" and "bad for Israel." The
opponents of the war became all the more vehement in their insistence
that Jews should not be singled out by a president who wanted to
quell dissent. So long as the young in the New Left remained con-

cerned with race and Vietnam, the older Jewish community was essentially friendly or at least understanding. The atmosphere changed in May–June 1967. Theodore Bikel and Rabbi Arthur J. Lelyveld, the president of the American Jewish Congress, resigned from SNCC, which was most vociferously anti-Israel. The American Jewish community still cared about social justice in America, and about ending the war in Vietnam, but Jews cared most, and with unique passion, about Israel. This emotion had been largely hidden, even from itself, by the Jewish establishment in the mid-1960s. But suddenly, these newly minted American bourgeois, these "hollow men," as Hentoff described them, were full of Jewish anxiety. The children of the immigrants looked like their parents again. They were no longer solving America's problems; they were worrying about Jews.

Many Jews would never have believed that grave danger to Israel, which was being threatened by Egypt and by all of its other Arab neighbors, could dominate their thoughts and emotions to the exclusion of all else. Many were surprised by the depth of their anger at those of their friends who carried on as usual, untouched by fear for Israel's survival and the instinctive involvement they themselves felt. Almost every observer said, then and later, that American Jews had never behaved this way before. The magnitude of the response was without precedent, because Jews were more numerous, richer, and more powerful than they had ever been—but the response was not new.

Jews had been fighting their government on behalf of Jews in danger since they first quarreled with James Buchanan in 1858 over Edgar Mortara, the child whom the papal authorities refused to return to his parents after a maid had secretly baptized him. In 1903, when a bloody pogrom took place in Kishinev, Russia, the Jews in America protested in mass meetings all over the country, and they raised much money for relief. Since the 1890s, Jews had fought with nativists and some aristocrats, and with most of Congress, to keep the doors to America from closing on other Jews. Thus, the passion for Israel was not born in 1967, and it had not even been born as a passion for Israel. It was the immediate, contemporary version, then, of all the earlier campaigns for overseas relief and for political pressure for Jews in trouble. The Nazi years had been the only exception: Jews had been too weak, too concerned about themselves, and too trusting of Roosevelt to go to war with major elements of American power and public opinion.

In May–June 1967, some atonement was made for those years. The response to the Middle East crisis was a way of saying that, come what might, Jews would not repeat such conduct—but that conduct, in the 1930s, had not been the norm; it had been the sole exception in all of American Jewish history.

The immediate reaction to the Middle East crisis was to give money. Much more money was given by many more people than ever before in history. There were numerous stories from every Jewish community throughout the United States not only of giving on a fantastic scale by people of large means but also of the literal sacrifice of their life's savings by people of modest means. During the little more than two-week period which marked the height of the crisis—between the day when President Gamal Nasser of Egypt closed the Gulf of Aqaba on May 23 and the end of the war on June 10—well over *one hundred million dollars,* the bulk of it in cash, was realized for the Israel Emergency Fund of the United Jewish Appeal. This was a fund-raising effort unprecedented not only in Jewish experience but also in the history of private philanthropy in the United States. Ultimately the UJA drive that year realized the unheard of amount of six hundred million dollars, more than any such appeal in all of American history.

The drive did not begin from the top. On Monday May 29, the national board of the United Jewish Appeal met in special session in New York to launch its nationwide emergency campaign, but by that time—six days after the inauguration of the blockade by Egypt of Israel's southern sea-lane—local campaigns were already under way in dozens of communities which had not waited for anyone to ask them to move. Moreover, it was not only the old-line, late-middle-aged leadership of these communities who were acting in this way. Many people in their thirties and forties who had never participated in organizational Jewish life suddenly emerged to take the lead in giving and in working. The financial contributions of these newer elements were astonishingly large—perhaps because of a desire to make up for past neglect and a wish, or even a need, to be counted in during a moment of manifest danger. If in Israel more reserves showed up in some places than had been ordered to mobilize, American Jewish fund-raising was, in its own way, a comparable phenomenon.

In the last days of May, Israeli consulates and the Hillel directors in the colleges were overwhelmed by hundreds of young people who wanted to go to Israel to take over the civilian jobs of their peers who had been mobilized for the army. By June 5, the day war broke out, some ten thousand such applications had been recorded throughout the country, more than half of them in New York at the offices of the Jewish Agency, the Zionist central body, despite the American ban on travel to the area. A high official of the Jewish Agency told that as he arrived at his office early that morning, a cab drew up and a man jumped out, followed by two younger men. He stopped the agency official and said to him: "I have no money to give but here are my sons. Please send them over immediately." That day this was no isolated incident.

Dr. Arnulf Pins, executive director of the Council on Social Work Education, offered his services to help process the volunteers at the New York office of the Jewish Agency. He had some questions included on the forms they filled out concerning their Jewish educational and organizational background and their involvement in such causes as Zionism, race, and peace. Those who came in May, and who therefore constituted the large majority of the young people who actually did get to Israel before June 5, were Orthodox from yeshivoth, and from the relatively small circle of American Jewish youth whose main interests were Jewish. At least a third of all the ten thousand who ultimately came to volunteer had had a substantial Jewish education and a continuing Jewish concern. In their answers to the political questions, another third showed that they had spent their young adult years worrying about race and Vietnam, and that they now lacked any organizational Jewish ties. Yet even this group had had some Jewish education in childhood or even into the teens. What seemed to be happening to them was that a dormant loyalty had suddenly been stirred, and that it had become at that moment an overriding passion.

The Six-Day War thus united the Jews of America but it also made them somewhat lonelier and even angrier. Most American opinion was enthralled by Israel's victory, but the opponents of the war in Vietnam were divided, and so were the churches and the blacks.

Among Jews, the question of Vietnam was instantly swept aside. But there were immediate jibes at the Vietnam doves now transformed into Middle East hawks. No one had the time or the inclination to produce a theoretical case which would harmonize the two positions. American Jews and some of their friends acted instinctively in the face of a threat to the survival of Israel. Their concern for the life of the beseiged Jewish state was not to be compromised by any embarrassment that might come to them out of any other views on other matters, even one so serious as the war in Vietnam.

Within a very few days, however, a rationale began to be developed. The pro-Israel Vietnam doves argued that American support of the government of South Vietnam represented an involvement in a regime which had no popular roots. The last thing that could be said of the State of Israel, by contrast, was that it lacked popular roots. A similar contrast was drawn between American diplomatic commitments in the two cases: they had always been less than perfectly clear in Vietnam, whereas no one could possibly deny that to support the integrity of Israel had been a solemn American obligation for nineteen years. Why then was it inconsistent to demand that America honor its commitment to a rooted democracy fighting for its life and to withdraw from a dubious venture to prop up an unpopular military clique? This "case" helped persuade even many Jewish radicals, but not all of them. A significant and vocal minority clung to sympathy with the Palestinians as Third World victims of Western colonialism.

The churches were especially troubling to the very Jews who had been most involved in Jewish-Christian dialogue. Despite some vocal opposition among the Orthodox to the broadening of the Jewish-Christian dialogue, the majority view within both religious and secular Jewish organizations had cherished the increasing contact between Jewish and Christian groups. When the crisis broke, Jews found that leading individual figures within the various Christian denominations, such as Reinhold Niebuhr, Alexander Schmemann, and George Higgins, were quick and firm in their public commitment to the cause of Israel, and so were Martin Luther King and John Bennett, the president of Union Theological Seminary. But the formal establishments of both the Protestant and Catholic churches remained largely silent. In the last days of May, as the crisis was building toward war, almost no statements in support of Israel could be elicited from any of these communions. As soon as the war was over, several emergency meetings were arranged between Jewish figures with a large stake in the dialogue and their Christian peers. As individuals (though not as spokesmen for their churches) some of the Christians present had supported Israel's right to exist, but the prevailing Christian sentiments in those tension-filled rooms were directed toward the question of Arab refugees and the status of Jerusalem. Israel was denounced as the aggressor in the conflict, and there was much discomfort in being pressed hard by Jews to think differently.

The Jewish participants in these discussions had not prepared any statements in advance, and yet they were as one in their answers: the existence of Israel was not a negotiable matter for any Jew, and Jews would regard Jewish-Christian relations in America as greatly damaged if the organized Christian community failed to support Israel's right to live. It was made very clear that Christian emphasis on the Arab refugees, no matter how correct the argument might be both morally and politically, would be taken by Jews as an evasion, or worse, if it was not linked to Israel's right of existence. The day had now come when Jews could afford to dispense with goodwill from the churches, if that was the price they might have to pay for their passion for Israel. The Jewish ecumenists did concede that they had been at fault in having failed to make clear to their Christian colleagues in the past that Israel was more important to Jews than the concerns for racial justice and peace that they shared with other Americans. The identification with Israel was their "religion." This connection was the ultimate meaning of contemporary Jewish "togetherness"; this was what set them apart from all other men. And oddly enough, at the same time, the new shining pride in Israel brought American Jews, in one sense, closer to the majority. American Jews were identified with the most successful army in the world. At a time when the United States was bogged down in Vietnam, Israel had again "proved" to the world that Jews were a race of fighting heroes.

The events of 1967 answered some questions that the mainstream of the community had been asking themselves for the several years before: how to define Jewishness in America's open society. In June 1967, the Jews of America were "saved" from having to think about issues of meaning and value that the intellectuals and the ultra-Orthodox had posed. They did not have to face the question that Philip Roth had asked: what is Jewishness to the unbelieving Jew? There was a ready answer: it is glory in Israel.

The spirit of the high drama of June 1967 lasted for months and even years. American Jews thought that they had solved their problems as Americans and Jews. But they had not. They were, in fact, ever more comfortable with their place in the jostle of American society, and ever less secure within themselves.

Conclusion:

The End of Immigrant Memory— What Can Replace It?

After 1967 the Jews in America were freer, bolder, and more powerful than any community of Jews had ever been in the Diaspora. And yet, amid the bustle of success, the Jewish community was eroding. Those who had been young in the 1930s still remembered Hitler, and Coughlin, but their children had much less sense of embattlement as Jews. Some took up causes, such as fighting for the rights of Soviet Jews or rallying to support Israel. Those who took part in the "student struggle for Soviet Jewry," or in the agencies which supported Israel, felt both virtuous and important, but they and their parents knew, if only deep in their hearts, that American Jews would eventually run out of causes. They would have to face the question of meaning. American Jews had solved their problem with the Gentiles, but they did not quite know what to do with themselves.

Jews could be bolder than they ever had before because America was different. There was no longer a stable, self-confident American majority. The oldest American population, which had lost the election of 1960, could not regain its majority status. Many of the minorities were busy emphasizing their angularities: some blacks were taking to wearing dashikis; Orthodox Jews in the colleges were insisting on wearing skullcaps at all times. The young Woody Allen began making film comedy out of the persona of an undersized Jew from Brooklyn who did not know how to behave at dinner in the home of his WASP girlfriend. Though this clash of cultures had been a cliché of the American stage since the beginning of the century, the tone was now different. The wearers of dashikis and of skullcaps were saying that there were no arbiters left in America of what was proper and improper.

America, moreover, was becoming less Western and Judeo-Christian. Large numbers of Asians and Muslims were arriving. The time was coming near when a Buddhist priest and a Muslim imam might be included with ministers, rabbis, and Catholic priests at the most sacral event in America's political life, the inauguration of a president. For the first time in American history, Jews were no longer the only non-Christian minority.

In this untidy America, Jews were a striking and accepted part of the political landscape. In their support of Israel, they were asserting Jewish interests with almost total unconcern as to what the Gentiles, or the government in Washington, might be thinking. In the America of the 1970s, the pro-Israel lobby behaved like the lobbies of big business, or labor, or the farm interest, or the China lobby; each was defending a "special interest."

In 1981, 50 percent of those polled believed that at a moment of confrontation between Israel and the United States, American Jews would side with Israel. Six years later, in answer to the same question, a large majority thought that American Jews would support American policy. These opinions were expressed in the years when all Americans, very nearly nine out of ten (including some of those who thought Jews were more involved in Israel than in America), were willing to vote for a Jew for president of the United States. Obviously, underneath the rhetoric of these seemingly contradictory attitudes, there were two awarenesses: America had become a place in which individuals and communities were affected by conflicting loyalties; Jews were therefore "entitled" to be a one-issue lobby.

In domestic policy, too, Jews behaved like everybody else; they made bargains in their own interest. The most lasting arrangement was with the blacks. Jews were well aware that there was more anti-Semitism among blacks than among whites in America, including greater support for the enemies of Israel, but the organized Jewish community chose to ignore these feelings. In Congress, the Jewish members were consistent and nearly unanimous in voting for social programs; the black caucus was equally consistent and almost equally unanimous in voting for all of the aid packages for Israel. In the election campaigns of 1984, and again in 1988, when Jesse Jackson was a candidate for the Democratic nomination for president, he expressed some public distemper with Jews, and he actively supported the political aspirations of the Palestinians, but he pulled back, very visibly, from questioning the compact that Jews and blacks had made in Congress.

Such enlightened self-interest was basic to the commitment of Jews to the Democratic party. The mainstream remained liberals, at very least, because they feared social disorder. In the 1970s, the circle of writers around *Commentary* preached at American Jews that their interests had changed. They were now one of the richest communities in America; they should be voting their pocketbooks, for lower taxes and for decreased social spending. But the bulk of American Jews did not agree. In every presidential election Jews were securely and sometimes overwhelmingly on the side of the Democrats. In 1968, almost 90 percent of the Jewish vote went to Hubert Humphrey; in the next several elections, Jews voted on the order of two to one against the Republicans. In 1984, when Ronald Reagan defeated Walter Mondale in a landslide, the Jews were the only white community to vote Democratic; in 1988 George Bush received less than 30 percent of the Jewish vote.

But there was also, in this commitment to the welfare state, a reecho of the prophetic commandment to "do justice and love mercy," and to protect the weak, "for you were once slaves in the land of Egypt." Even some Jewish Republicans believed in social welfare. In 1968, in the very midst of the battle between Jewish teachers and blacks over teaching jobs and control of the schools in the Ocean Hill–Brownsville district in Brooklyn, Max Fisher, who was then both president of the United Jewish Appeal and the leading Jewish Republican, insisted that Jews had to continue to support the programs of aid for blacks. "If Jews truly believe that advancing social justice is a Jewish obligation," he said in 1968, "there can be no lingering doubts that helping people in the inner city . . . does represent a genuine Jewish commitment." The pragmatic and materialistic Jewish community of the 1970s could not quite become just another collection of well-to-do Americans with ethnic memories of their own. The social conscience that the Jewish religion taught still lived among them.

But in white America, anti-Semitism was disappearing as an effective force. College students in the 1930s had all known that anti-Semitism barred them from many careers; by the 1970s, this was no longer true. A 1988 survey of the Jewish students at Dartmouth College found not a single respondent who thought that being Jewish made any difference to his or her future. Other studies showed that very few people, less than one in ten, continued to believe that Jews had too much power in America. Other Americans still thought of Jews as Jews, but they were equally likely to think of them as businessmen, physicians, or college roommates.

Even when they admitted to themselves that anti-Semitism was negligible, many Jews kept worrying, deep within themselves, whether the America of the 1970s and 1980s was forever. One could interpret the rise of Jews in America in economic terms: throughout all of their history in America, Jews had leaped forward when the economy was expanding. The "German Jews" had become well-to-do on the frontier. The "Russian Jews" had broken out of poverty after the Second World War, when the United States was booming. In some future economic depression would Jews again be under the kind of attack that they last experienced in the 1930s? No one knew the answer to this question, but few really believed that the 1930s were likely to recur.

The economic boom in America in the 1970s and 1980s was less important for Jews than the fundamental change in the nature of the society. A majority in the Supreme Court had excluded prayer from the public schools and crèches during Christmas from the lawns of public buildings. These decisions reaffirmed that America was not a "Christian country," a point Jews had been arguing since the 1840s when they protested the invocation of the Trinity in a Thanksgiving proclamation by the governor of South Carolina. In the 1970s and 1980s, the "born-again" led a counterattack to permit prayers in the public schools and, in general, to increase the Christian flavor of public life, but Jews remained in the forefront of the forces which resisted this latest attempt to re-Christianize America. They were unwilling to compromise with the fundamentalists even when the prime minister of Israel, Menachem Begin, made them his allies in the cause of Israel.

Jews in America felt they were nearer than ever to helping to make the kind of society that they had last experienced in the third century, in the Roman Empire. Rome had ceased insisting that its culture and state religion must dominate everywhere, and it had not yet itself been dominated by Christianity. Rome's "golden age," however, did not last much more than a century. Will it last longer in America? There is some reason for hope that it will last, for such structures are at this moment the wave of the future. Western Europe is moving toward this third-century Roman model; it is organizing itself as one economic market, and looking toward the possibility of becoming a "United States of Europe." The difference from the past is already apparent among the Jews of Western Europe. Because an increasing number of Muslims from North Africa and Turkey, Buddhists from Indochina, and political refugees from Communism now live permanently in Western Europe, Jews are no longer the only persisting religious and ethnic minority.

America and the West as a whole are still essentially Christian. Some Jews would regret to see the end of the dominant role of Christianity in the West. Christians are supposed to have a special reason for protecting Jews: orthodox Christian theology commands that Jews be present to witness and to be converted at the Second Coming. In the 1970s and 1980s, however, this special relationship was becoming an ever less important concern for Jews. In "foreign policy," Communists and Arabs were more prominent as opponents and as interlocutors than Christians. At home in America, most Jews opposed the entire domestic agenda of activist Christians, including their effort to forbid abortion. American Jews were fighting in the 1970s and 1980s for an objective beyond their old purpose, a neutral public life. Jews wanted a post-Christian American society. It seemed to them to be the logical conclusion to the end of the dominance in American life of those who claimed descent from the overwhelmingly Christian colonial America.

American Jews had thus very nearly achieved their dreams of equality and influence, and they believed, despite some residue of fear, that their future was secure. Moreover, they tried to construct an equally lasting bargain with their own Jewishness. They used the "material" that they knew: they invoked anti-Semitism at a time when it was essentially irrelevant, and they preached and practiced togetherness at a time when Jews were associating more and more with anyone they pleased. By the mid-1980s, it was beginning to be clear that these techniques that were being used to preserve Jewish identity would fail.

In the 1970s, after a generation of avoidance, the Holocaust was reevoked. There were many reasons, but one was the need for the memory of anti-Semitism. The young in the colleges were the most prone to believe that their generation was free of danger, and that they had the opportunity to blend into the American scene. In the many new centers of Jewish studies that were being founded in the 1970s, the Holocaust was the subject that was most taught. In the deepest recesses of their hearts, young Jews were being exhorted to live a contradiction: they should accept, joyously, the liberal America which Jews had helped make, but they should remain afraid. The teaching was that Jews stood, ultimately, alone. This inner, more than half-hidden isolation was their "Jewishness." By 1975, when the interest in the Holocaust was reaching its height, Lucy Dawidowicz published *The War Against the Jews, 1933–1945*. Based on a clear, "Jewish" thesis—"Hitler's idea about the Jews was at the center of his mental world. They shaped his world view and his political ambitions, the matrix of his ideology and the irradicable core of his Nationalist Socialist doctrine"—Dawidowicz depicted a Holocaust that gave grandeur to the rule of the Jew as the persecuted combatant who had to continue the fight.

The Holocaust was a shattering memory. It evoked guilt, compassion, and fear. It said to American Jews, in an essentially optimistic time, that being Jewish is to know that life itself is often about tragedy, suffering, and murderous hatred. Even the new State of Israel, the center of Jewish hope and power, was not merely about glory and triumph; it was endangered by Arab enemies. Jews were called to rally to Israel in the name of the slogan "Never Again." This "army" was united not only in the camaraderie of combat but also in some rituals, such as the Passover seder or the lighting of Hanukkah candles which expressed good feelings about other Jews, past and present. Jewishness in America was thus fashioned, de facto, not as religion but as ethnic community. America's Jews would define themselves by fighting their enemies and clinging to each other.

In the 1980s some Jewish sociologists, led by Calvin Goldscheider, were busy hailing this development. Their basic contention was that American Jewry had "transformed" itself into a form of Jewishness appropriate to America. They insisted this very American Judaism had stabilized: it was being continued, unweakened, by the third and fourth generations. American Jews were not assimilating. On the contrary, some of these sociologists maintained that the rate of intermarriage had leveled off at about thirty percent, and American Jews were observing a few of the festivals—Passover, Hanukkah, and Yom Kippur—as fervently as ever. This generation had even added to its observances a new, unparalleled passion for Israel.

This optimism about continuity was not true. Intermarriage, the single most sensitive indicator of the stability of the Jewish community, was continuing to rise in the 1980s. Even Goldscheider was becoming less positive. In 1987, he conducted (together with a collaborator, Sidney Goldstein), a demographic survey of the Jewish community of Rhode Island. The figures for intermarriage in Rhode Island were 14 percent in the 1960s, rising to 27 percent in the 1970s—and rising again in the 1980s.

> Among the couples married between 1980 and 1987, 38% intermarried. These data do not suggest, as some other studies have, that the rate of intermarriage has plateaued. Indeed, there have been increases in every decade since 1960.

The figures from Rhode Island were part of a pattern. In Boston the overall percentage, for all the marriages including those that were contracted half a century ago, rose steadily from 7 percent in 1965 to 13 percent in 1975 and 18 percent in 1985; in San Francisco in the mid-1980s intermarriage was, overall, 40 percent.

The "transformationists" made much of the fact that younger Jews said that they observed the High Holidays as much as their parents and even their grandparents. But did they, really? As the sociologist Charles Liebman asked: Was there equivalence between the college students who absent themselves entirely on Yom Kippur, and those who drop in on the service on campus between classes? Is a seder on Passover the same when it is observed with all the prescribed rituals as when it is simply an elaborate family dinner? Does the most widely observed of all the holidays, the very minor festival (in the Jewish tradition) of Hanukkah, represent a rebirth of piety, or is it a creation of a Jewish equivalent for Christmas?

In the 1980s, the observance even of the new Jewish *mitzvah*, the commitment to Israel, was becoming more tepid. In 1973, when Israel was attacked on Yom Kippur Day by Egypt, American Jews were less involved than they had been in June 1967. Contributions were just as massive, but there were fewer volunteers among the young. Some American Jews had already begun to question Israel's policies. In 1973, a few hundred American Jews had banded together in an organization that was named Breira ("alternative") to insist that Israel should make peace on the basis of a Palestinian state in the West Bank and Gaza. Breira was effectively "excommunicated"; it was blackballed as an organization by every coordinating Jewish body which it tried to join. Nonetheless, for the first time since the euphoria of June 1967, the government of Israel was under attack on the most sensitive of all issues, its policy toward the Palestinians.

In June 1977, when Menachem Begin took office as prime minister, he insisted that he had been elected to enact the ideology of his Likud party that the land of Israel, west of the Jordan River, was indivisible. But the mainstream of the American Jewish community wanted to believe that Begin was really a hard bargainer, a pragmatic politician in the American mold, who was announcing these ideological propositions in order to negotiate from strength. When Israel went to war in Lebanon in 1982, the American Jewish majority insisted that Israel's move was really an incursion to clean out terrorists from southern Lebanon; any criticism of Israel's actions or motives was misrepresentation by the media. But the war in Lebanon was the first in all of Israel's history that did not evoke massive donations from American Jews. They seemed to have been unhappy, at least subconsciously, in this attempt to end by war any need to negotiate with the Palestinians.

This increasing disaffection was evidence of a deeper process that had been at work for a long time. Near the very beginning of the State of Israel, as early as 1949, several observers had predicted that Israeli and American Jews would inevitably move apart. The cause would not be some definable quarrel, such as Israel's demand upon the Diaspora for manpower to come to settle, or some disaffection in America from specific policies, domestic or foreign, in Israel. Rather, Israelis and American Jews were fashioning two different cultures. The life of a minority in a democracy would be radically different in another generation from the life of the majority in its own, Hebrew-speaking, Jewish state.

Forty years later, Steven M. Cohen, a sociologist who is himself part of this next generation of American Jews, concluded that this had indeed already happened:

> Policymakers in American Jewish life and Israel need to confront the challenge to Israel-Diaspora relations posed by long-standing processes: the fact that Israeli and American Jewry have been parting company politically, culturally and religiously, . . . I would suggest that educators place more emphasis on how Israelis differ from their American Jewish counterparts, and how the possibilities for Jewish living in Israel are really very different from those in the Diaspora. . . .

And yet there are statistics which say that the majority of American Jews, at least nine out of ten, are still as devoted to Israel as they used to be. Indeed, they are—but ever less intensely than in earlier years. The situation is essentially parallel to the commitment of the third and fourth generations to a Passover seder or to fasting on Yom Kippur. Some attention is paid to these observances, but the commitments are impressionistic. The love of Judaism, and of Israel, cannot rest for the future on such unsafe ground. But, the Jewish experience in America could not, so far, have produced a more secure kind of Jewishness. Like almost all the other migrants who came to the United States throughout the centuries, Jews arrived in America as individuals and not as communities. There was no Jewish equivalent of a "Mayflower Compact" until after the Second World War, when organized groups of Orthodox Jews replanted themselves in the United States. American Jewish history is thus the story of Jewish individuals who banded together to form communities, to express their memories, or serve their immediate needs. The ancestors of American Jews did not come to the United States to create a base for a rebirth of their religion or to become the other front for Israel. They came to succeed in America. Their Jewish commitments, including their involvements with other Jews, were ultimately bounded by this vision of themselves. The problem was that Jews kept trying to convince themselves that they had come to America for some good higher than their own success and they kept wanting to believe that they were united by something stronger than fear and memory.

Disillusionment was growing in the 1980s, and anger at the shallowness of the seemingly busy life of the Jewish community. Ethnic tasks and memories, some warm and some angry, could not stop the erosion of Jewishness even at a time when Jews had become powerful and accepted. Ethnic identity is, by its very nature, a free association. It has recurrently become a mix of sentiment and surface decoration. When Armenians move out of their neighborhood in Fresno, California, or Jews leave Borough Park in Brooklyn, or when the young of all the ethnic groups go to college with each other, most associate with people who are not of their own kind. In America, after a few generations, ethnic identities have been either forgotten by individuals or remembered in Saint Patrick's Day parades or Steuben Day observances. Even those who march do not necessarily feel commanded to support the political line of their original homeland. Jewish ethnicity has had a stronger hold than almost any other because Jews had been more alien for centuries, as non-Christians, than any other minority. In fact, the mass of American Jews are only fifty years out of the ghetto, and the form of assimilation has changed. American society no longer forces assimilation into a dominant culture. It is possible in this new age of America to evaporate out of being Jewish without making a decision to be anything else. In fact, the drift of life in contemporary America is toward free association. The older generation of Jews still finds most of its friends among other Jews; the young, so they have told in all the polls of the 1980s, do not. They remain "proud to be Jews" but they are less and less likely to live their lives within the ethnic community.

After nearly four centuries, the momentum of Jewish experience in America is essentially spent. Ethnicity will no doubt last for several more generations, but it is well on the way to becoming memory. But a community cannot survive on what it remembers; it will persist only because of what it affirms and believes.

In the 1970s some American Jews were becoming uncomfortable and even despairing. A few of the young who had participated in the movements of the 1960s were demanding that the organized Jewish community be less pragmatic and more spiritual. Arthur Waskow, who had made his reputation as a leader of the 1960s counterculture, became a kind of rebbe who taught hundreds of followers that such forms as the Passover seder could be made both more immediately political and more mystical. Still, the overwhelming bulk of American Jews were unaffected. Ninety percent of the young continued to receive their Jewish education in some hours of supplementary schooling, essentially as training for bar or bat mitzvah. The Reform movement created almost no day schools. The Conservative group, which did, could not get beyond the number of sixty countrywide; in these schools they were educating less than ten percent of the children of affiliated families. Nonetheless, even in the midst of "business as usual" the question of religion was troubling the mainstream of American Jews. The leaders of the Jewish establishment, those who ran the national organizations and the local fund-raising drives, were busy congratulating themselves that their institutions were the true "synagogue" of American Jews—but they did not quite convince themselves. In 1983 Jonathan Woocher, a sociologist who had praised Jewish activism as the "civil religion" of American Jews, studied the "Jewishness" of these leaders of the establishment. He found one astonishing result: two out of three insisted that the Jews were God's "chosen people." Such an assertion did not belong together with their usual rhetoric about ethnic pluralism. An ethnic group cannot assert "chosenness" without falling into chauvinism or worse. In a democratic society, only a religion dare use this term and only to describe believers who are committed to live spiritual lives. Perhaps a desire to be commanded by God, rather than to keep devising various forms of Jewish togetherness, troubled the people whom Jonathan Woocher interviewed.

Jews who cared about being Jewish knew, if only in their bones, that they had to turn to religion—and most did not know how to begin. They were not heirs to a religious past. Their ancestors who had come to America had brought little learning in Bible and Talmud, and they had imparted less still to their descendants. Mainstream Judaism in America, at its most religious, had emphasized the tangible rituals, the practices, and not the learning that had been accumulated for three millennia. Thus, a community which was uniquely "American"—that is, pragmatic and not intellectual or spiritual, even in religion—knew only that it ought to become "more observant."

The most observant sector, the ultra-Orthodox, who had arrived in recent decades, were an available home for some—but only for a few. Ultra-Orthodoxy was attractive because it posited authority and certainty, but the rationale of that authority could not be accepted by most Jews. The intellectual base of this orthodoxy was unabashed religious fundamentalism. The rebbe of Lubavitch, the most striking leader of the Orthodox revival, had defended the faith by asserting that the world is indeed in its fifty-eighth century since creation, the date given in the Jewish sources. The rebbe insisted that, all of the scientific evidence to the contrary, from dinosaurs to atomic clocks, was planted by God in the universe, in His act of creation, to test men's faith. Most Jews could not accept such fundamentalism. They finally had to ask the inescapable question: can Judaism as religion be renewed? What does Judaism say to modern men and women who come to its texts and to its practices from the outside?

American Jews may be the descendants of not very learned, poor immigrants, but they are Jews, and thus they know that being Jewish is indissolubly connected to moral responsibility and to the inner life of the spirit. Tevye in all his quaintness had not read much Bible, and he misquoted wildly, but it reechoed within him, and the memory of that memory is present among his descendants. They still worry about the poor, and they still think that they are "chosen," perhaps to suffer. The embers of the classic Jewish faith still smolder, but they may be dying among the mainstream of American Jews. The rational evidence is that these Jews will continue, with growing unhappiness, to bet their future as Jews on what they know, their ethnic togetherness. But Jewish experience through the centuries has often been surprising and unpredictable. The need for and the possibility of a spiritual revival are clear. If it does not happen, American Jewish history will soon end, and become a part of American memory as a whole.

When Asser Levy and all the other refugees from Recife arrived in New Amsterdam in 1654, they did not know that the fundamental questions of meaning were then being asked in Amsterdam by Baruch de Spinoza (who contributed that year to the fund for the relief of Levy and all the other stranded Jews). Spinoza insisted that by the light of reason, Jews had only two options, either to assimilate to the majority or to reestablish their national state in the land of their ancestors. But Levy had chosen to come to America, and to remain a Jew. He had fought to join the militia as an equal, but that fight, in all its permutations, is over. Three-and-a-half centuries after the oblique encounter between Levy and Spinoza, the question of faith remains open. It will be answered, if at all, not by politicians and bureaucrats, but by men and women who hear voices—even in America.

Notes on Sources

In both American and American Jewish history, there is no lack of comprehensive bibliographies. The works mentioned here are those that were used directly and that made a specific difference to the arguments that are advanced in the text.

Chapter One: The authoritative work on the early history of Jews in North America, from the beginning of the settlement to the Revolution, was done by Jacob R. Marcus. My account of this period is heavily in his debt, though my interpretations vary some from his. Marcus's most important synthetic work, in three volumes, is *The Colonial American Jew, 1492–1776* (Detroit, 1970). This work supersedes his first attempt at synthesis, *Early American Jewry*, 2 vols. (Philadelphia, 1951, 1953). The early pages of Morris U. Schappes, *A Documentary History of the Jews in the United States, 1654–1875* (New York, 1950), were a useful source. The many volumes of *The Publication of the American Jewish Historical Society* (*PAJHS*), a quarterly which was founded in 1893, are full of detailed information. The following articles were of particular help here: Leon Huehner, "Asser Levy," vol. 8, pp. 9–23; Max J. Kohler, "Jewish Activity in American Colonial Commerce," vol. 10, pp. 47–64; Samuel Oppenheim, "Early History of the Jews in New York," vol. 18, pp. 1–91; Arnold Wiznitzer, "The Exodus from Brazil and Arrival: New Amsterdam of the Jewish Pilgrim Fathers, 1654," vol. 44, pp. 80–97. Another instructive series is the semiannual, *American Jewish Archives*, published by the institution of the same name. J. S. Emmanuel, "New Light on Early American Jewry," vol. 7, pp. 3–64, was particularly useful. The existing overview of the earlier history of the Jews in New Amsterdam, and, later, New York, is in Hyman B. Grinstein, *The Rise of the Jewish Community of New York, 1654–1860* (Philadelphia, 1945). This book was helpful also to Chapters 6–8.

Chapter Two: This study of Puritans and Jews is based on direct reading of many seventeenth-century tracts, some of them to be found only in the British National Library. A technical version of this chapter appeared in *Israel and the Nations: Essays Presented in Honor of Shmuel Ettinger* (Jerusalem, 1987), pp. xxxii–lxvi, under the title, "The New England Puritans and the Jews," with citation of all the sources, both primary and secondary. My views on Puritans and Jews parallel the opinions of Sacvan Bercovitch, *The Puritan Origins of the American Self*, New Haven, Conn., 1975.

Chapter Three: The older Jewish communities which existed in colonial times have all been the subject of numerous books. In addition to Grinstein on New York, see Charles Resnikoff and U. Z. Engelman, *The Jews of Charleston* (Philadelphia, 1950), and Edwin Wolf II and Maxwell Whiteman, *The History of the Jews of Philadelphia: From Colonial Times to the Age of Jackson* (Philadelphia, 1975), and Morris A. Gutstein, *The Story of the Jews of Newport (1658–1908)* (New York, 1936). See also *Letters of the Franks Family 1733–1748*, edited by Leo Hershkowitz and Isidore S. Meyer (Waltham, Mass., 1968). On Ezra Stiles, the early book by George A. Kohut, *Ezra Stiles and the Jews* (New York, 1902), contains all of the relevant diary entries; on Carigal, see Lee M. Friedman, *Rabbi Haim Isaac Carigal* (Boston, 1940). The most recent work on Ezra Stiles was done by Arthur Chiel. See especially "Ezra Stiles and Rabbi Karigal," *Yale Alumni Magazine* (March 1974), pp. 16–19; "Stiles and the Jews: A Study in Ambivalence," in *Jews in New Haven*, vol. 3, edited by Barry E. Herman and Werner S. Hirsch (New Haven, Conn., 1981), pp. 118–34. The standard biography of Stiles is by Edmund S. Morgan, *The Gentle Puritan: A Life of Ezra Stiles, 1727–1795* (Chapel Hill, N.C., 1962). There is no adequate biography of Haym Salomon.

Chapter Four: The single most interesting article, because it contests the myth that all Jews were partisans of the American Revolution, is Cecil Roth, "Some Jewish Loyalists in the War of American Independence," in *PAJHS*, vol. 38, pp. 81–107. Aaron Lopez's biographer is Stanley F. Chyet, *Lopez of Newport: Colonial American Merchant and Prince* (Detroit, 1970). There is much information on Judah Touro in Gutstein's monograph on Newport, mentioned above. There are numerous articles on this period in the *PAJHS*; in other publications, see especially Albert M. Friedenberg: "The Jews of America, 1654–1787, With Special Reference to the Revolution," in *American Jewish Yearbook*, vol. 17, pp. 193–218. David Nassy, before coming to Philadelphia, lived in Surinam and even published a book: see Sigmund Seeligman, "David Nassy of Surinam and His 'Lettre Politico-Theologico-Morale Sur Les Juifs,' " *PAJHS*, vol. 22 pp. 25–38. On the echoes in France of the American Revolution, see Arthur Hertzberg, *The French Enlightenment and the Jews* (New York, 1969). See also the documents in "Miscellaneous Items Relating to Jews in Wars of United States and Correspondence with Washington," in *PAJHS*, vol. 27 pp. 494–96. As always, the work of Jacob R. Marcus is instructive. See *Memoirs of American Jews: 1775–1865*, vol. 1 (Philadelphia, 1955).

Chapter Five: The prime source for American Jewish history in the period immediately after the Revolution is Joseph L. Blau and Salo W. Baron, editors, *The Jews of the United States, 1790–1840: A Documentary History*, 3 vols. (New York, 1963). See also the following articles: Abraham Lewis, "Correspondence between Washington and Jewish Citizens," in *PAJHS*, vol 3, pp. 87–96; Anita Libman Lebeson, "Hannah Adams and the Jews," *Historia Judaica*, vol. 8, pp. 113–34. The discussion by Raphael Mahler of messianic dreams in early America is in Hebrew, *Zion*, vol. 15, pp. 107–31: "The Jews of America and the Idea of the Return to Zion in the Era of the American Revolution." For some thinking of the Founding Fathers about Jews, see Thomas Paine, *The Age of Reason*, edited by M. D. Conway

(New York, 1924). The other quotations in the text are from *The Complete Writings of Thomas Paine,* edited by Philip S. Foner (New York, 1945). Of Irving Brant's multivolume biography of James Madison, the third volume, *James Madison, Father of the Constitution, 1787–1800* (New York, 1950), was relevant here.

Chapter Six: The "hero" of this chapter is Mordecai Manual Noah, on whom an excellent modern biography has been written: Jonathan D. Sarna, *Jacksonian Jews: The Two Worlds of Mordecai Noah* (New York, 1981). See also Sidney M. Fish, "The Problem of Intermarriage in Early America," in Gratz College *Annual of Jewish Studies,* vol. 4 (1975), pp. 85–95. See the early biography by Leon Huehner, *The Life of Judah Touro (1775–1854)* (Philadelphia, 1946), and the material in Bertram W. Korn, *The Early Jews of New Orleans* (Waltham, Mass., 1969). For Isaac Harby, see Resnikoff on Charleston cited above. Two illuminating articles were by Abraham Peck, "That Other 'Peculiar Institution': Jews and Judaism in the 19th Century South," *Modern Judaism,* vol. 7, pp. 91–114, and Edward Pessen, "The Egalitarian Myth and the American Social Reality: Wealth, Mobility, and Equality in the 'Era of the Common Man,' " *American Historical Review* (1972), pp. 989–1034. Despite some inevitable errors, the genealogies by Malcolm H. Stern are important: *Americans of Jewish Descent: A Compendium of Genealogy* (Cincinnati, 1960); and *First American Jewish Families: 600 Genealogies, 1659–1977* (Cincinnati, 1978).

Chapter Seven: The most recent study of the "German Jews" is by Naomi W. Cohen, *Encounter with Emancipation: The German Jews in the United States, 1830–1914* (Philadelphia, 1984). On Belmont, see C. Irving Katz, *August Belmont: A Political Biography* (New York and London, 1968). On politics, see the early pages of Lawrence H. Fuchs, *The Political Behavior of American Jews* (Westport, Conn., 1956). Of the many articles in various places by Rudolph Glanz, the most important for this chapter is "German Jews in New York City in the 19th Century," *YIVO Annual of Jewish Social Science,* vol. 11 (1956–57), pp. 9–39. See also Barry E. Supple, "A Business Elite: German-Jewish Financiers in Nineteenth Century New York," *Business History Review* (Harvard), vol. 21 (1959), pp. 143–78, and Bertram W. Korn, "Jewish 48'ers in America," *American Jewish Archives,* vol. 2, pp. 3–20.

Chapter Eight: Isaac Mayer Wise has been the subject of several biographies. The most extensive is by James G. Heller, *Isaac M. Wise: His Life, Work and Thought* (New York, 1965); it contains much material but it is a chronicle and not a history. There are also biographies by Israel Knox, *Rabbi in America: The Story of Isaac M. Wise* (Boston, 1957); and an early one by Max B. May, *Isaac Mayer Wise: The Founder of American Judaism, A Biography* (New York, 1916). Wise's orthodox opponent-to-be, Isaac Leeser, published some of his early sermons under the title *Discourses, Argumentative and Devotional, on the Subject of the Jewish Religion* (Philadelphia, 1841). See also *Selected Writings of Isaac Mayer Wise*, edited by David Philipson and Louis Grossman (New York, 1901); Guido Kisch, "A History of the Isaac M. Wise Temple of Cincinnati," *Historia Judaica*, vol. 7, pp. 205–7; and Bertram W. Korn, *Jews and Negro Slavery in the Old South, 1789–1865* (Elkins Park, Pa., 1961). The monographs most useful to this chapter, and the next, were Leon Jick *The Americanization of the Synagogue, 1820–1870* (Hanover, N.H., 1976); Betram W. Korn, *American Jewry and the Civil War* (Philadelphia, 1951); and Jeanette Baron and Salo W. Baron, "Palestinian Messengers in America, 1849–79, a Record of Four Journeys," *Jewish Social Studies*, vol. 5, pp. 115–62, 225–92.

Chapter Nine: On Reform Judaism in general, the two standard works in English are David Philipson, *The Reform Movement in Judaism* (New York, 1967), and W. Gunther Plaut, *The Growth of Reform Judaism* (New York, 1965). Three biographies were helpful: R. L. Duffus, *Lillian Wald, Neighbor and Crusader* (New York, 1938); Benny Kraut, *From Reform Judaism to Ethical Culture: The Religious Evolution of Felix Adler* (Cincinnati, 1979); and Eli N. Evans, *Judah P. Benjamin: The Jewish Confederate* (London, 1988). The most recent overview is in Marc Lee Raphael, *Profiles in America Judaism: The Reform, Conservative, Orthodox and Reconstructionist Traditions in Historical Perspective* (San Francisco, 1984).

Chapter Ten: The central argument of this chapter, that the mass emigration from Eastern Europe represented the poor, exists in far greater detail from literary and rabbinic sources, with substantial reference to statistics for the period, in a paper that I presented at The Eighth World Congress of Jewish Studies, Jerusalem, 1981. It was published in the *Proceedings of the History Section* (Jerusalem, 1984), under the title "*Treifene Medine*, Learned Opposition to Emigration to the United States." In addition to the sources cited in that article, see also H. E. Jacob, *The World of Emma Lazarus* (New York, 1949), and Mary Antin, *The Promised Land* (Princeton, 1969). On immigration as a whole, see especially John Higham, *Send These to Me: Jews and Other Immigrants in Urban America*, Revised Edition (Baltimore, 1975), and Oscar Handlin's first book on the subject, *Boston's Immigrants* (Cambridge, Mass., 1959). On nativism, see Higham, *Strangers in the Land* (New York, 1973). On the debate about the nature of immigration, see John R. Commons, *Races and Immigrants in America* (New York, 1907) and Roy Garis, *Immigration Restriction* (New York, 1927).

Chapter Eleven: The battle against limiting immigration waged by American Jews is best described in an unpublished doctoral dissertation done at the University of Wisconsin, 1969: Sheldon Morris Neuringer, "American Jewry and United States Immigration Policy, 1881–1953." The history of the American Jewish Committee was written by Naomi Cohen, *Not Free to Desist* (Philadelphia, 1972). See also John Garraty, *Henry Cabot Lodge* (New York, 1953), and a prime source, Henry Adams, *The Education of Henry Adams* (Boston, 1918). See also Louis Harap, *The Image of the Jew in American Literature: From Early Republic to Mass Immigration* (Philadelphia, 1974). Another prime source is *The Voice of America on Kishineff*, edited by Cyrus Adler (Philadelphia, 1904).

Chapter Twelve: The literature on the Jewish "Lower East Side" is vast. The most famous contemporary account is by Irving Howe, *World of Our Fathers* (New York, 1976). A somewhat earlier book, less well-known, covers the same ground in an interesting way: Ronald Sanders, *The Downtown Jews: Portrait of an Immigrant Generation* (New York, 1970). See also *The Early Jewish Labor Movement in the United States,* edited by Elias Tcherikower (New York, 1961); Jeffrey S. Gurock, *When Harlem Was Jewish, 1870–1930* (New York, 1979); Stephan F. Brumberg, *Going to America, Going to School: The Jewish Immigrant Public School Encounter in Turn-of-the Century New York City* (New York, 1986); Neal Gabler, *An Empire of Their Own: How the Jews Invented Hollywood* (New York, 1988); and Sherry Gorelick, *City College and the Jewish Poor* (New Brunswick, N.J., 1981). On crime, see Edward J. Bristow, *Prostitution and Prejudice: The Jewish Fight Against White Slavery, 1880–1939* (Oxford, 1982); and Jenna W. Joselit, *Our Gang: Jewish Crime and the New York Jewish Community, 1900–1940* (Bloomington, Ind., 1983). On the family, see Reena Sigman Friedman, "Send Me My Husband Who Is In New York City: Husband Desertion in the American Jewish Immigrant Community, 1900–1926," *Jewish Social Studies*, vol. 44, pp. 1–18.

Chapter Thirteen: All of the major actors in the dramas described in this chapter have been the subject of biographies. See: Cyrus Adler, *Jacob H. Schiff: His Life and Letters* (New York, 1922); Alpheus Thomas Mason, *Brandeis: A Free Man's Life* (New York, 1946); Allon Gal, *Brandeis of Boston* (Cambridge, Mass., 1980); Philippa Strum, *Louis D. Brandeis: Justice for the People* (Cambridge, Mass., 1984); and Norman Bentwich, *For Zion's Sake: A Biography of Judah L. Magnes* (Philadelphia, 1954). Magnes is the "hero" of the account by Arthur A. Goren, *New York Jews and the Quest for Community: The Kehillah Experiment, 1908–1922* (Philadelphia, 1970). See also the two volumes on *Cyrus Adler: Selected Letters*, edited by Ira Robinson (Philadelphia, 1985); and Morton Rosenstock, *Louis Marshall: Defender of Jewish Rights* (Detroit, 1965).

Chapter Fourteen: The discussion on the limitation of immigration in 1924 owes much to Neuringer's unpublished dissertation, mentioned above, and to the statement by Dr. Harry H. Laughlin, *Hearings before the Committee on Immigration and Naturalization, House of Representatives, March 8, 1924* (Washington, 1924). For the texture of Jewish life, see especially Deborah Dash Moore, *At Home in America: Second Generation New York Jews* (New York, 1981), and Gurock's book, mentioned above. On conflicts among the ethnic groups see Ronald H. Bayor, *Neighbors in Conflict: The Irish, Germans, Jews, and Italians of New York City, 1929–1941* (Baltimore, 1978). On the Jewish left, see especially Nathan Glazer, *The Social Basis of American Communism* (New York, 1962). On academic anti-Semitism, see the two most recent discussions, Tamar Buchsbaum, "A Note on Antisemitism in Admissions at Dartmouth," *Jewish Social Studies*, vol. 49, pp. 79–84, and Dan A. Oren, *Joining the Club: A History of Jews and Yale* (New Haven, Conn., 1985).

Chapter Fifteen: In addition to the direct citations in the text, see also *The East European Jewish Experience in America*, edited by Uri D. Herschler (Cincinnati, 1983), and *Images and Ideas in American Culture: The Functions of Criticism—Essays in Memory of Philip Rahv*, edited by Arthur Edelstein (Hanover, N.H., 1979), especially the contribution by Alan Lelchuk. Irving Howe, Sidney Hook, and Arthur Miller have written autobiographies: Irving Howe, *A Margin of Hope: An Intellectual Autobiography* (New York, 1982); Sidney Hook, *Out of Step: An Unquiet Life in the Twentieth Century* (New York, 1987); Arthur Miller, *Timebends: A Life* (New York, 1987). There is a biography of Clifford Odets, Margaret Brenman-Gibson, *Clifford Odets, American Playwright: The Years from 1906 to 1940* (New York, 1981). On religion, see the book by Marc Lee Raphael mentioned above; Moshe Davis, *The Emergence of Conservative Judaism* (Philadelphia, 1963), and Nathan Glazer, *American Judaism* (Chicago, 1957).

Chapter Sixteen: On Roosevelt and the Jews, the literature keeps growing: Henry L. Feingold, *The Politics of Rescue: The Roosevelt Administration and the Holocaust, 1938–1945* (New York, 1970); David Wyman, *The Abandonment of the Jews* (New York, 1984); Deborah E. Lipstadt, *Beyond Belief: The American Press and the Coming of the Holocaust, 1933–1945* (New York, 1986); Richard Breitman and Alan M. Kraut, *American Refugee Policy and European Jewry, 1933–1945* (Bloomington, Ind., 1987). There was even in 1984 a privately organized American Jewish Commission on the Holocaust which published a collection of studies by various hands: Seymour Maxwell Finger, editor, *American Jewry During the Holocaust* (New York, 1984). For the New Deal and Yiddish writers, see the publication by the Works Progress Administration in the City of New York in Yiddish of the Jewish Immigrants Association of New York (1938) and Jewish Families and Family Circles of New York (1939). On anti-Semitism, see the study *Jews in America*, published by *Fortune* in 1936, and Charles Herbert Stember, "The Recent History of Public Attitudes" in his *Jews in the Mind of America* (New York, 1966).

Chapter Seventeen: On Jewish-Christian relations see: Leo Pfeffer, *Creeds in Competition: A Creative Force in American Culture* (New York, 1959), and Arthur Gilbert, *A Jew in Christian America* (New York, 1966). See also Mary T. Hanna, *Catholics and American Politics*

(Cambridge, Mass., 1979). From this chapter forward, the factual account (but not the interpretations) leans heavily on the summaries year by year of public events of significance to Jews that were published in the *American Jewish Yearbook (AJYB)*. On blacks in this period, the most important single essay was written by John Hope Franklin, "The Transformation of the Negro Intellectual." It is to be found in *Assuring Freedom to the Free: A Century of Emancipation in the U.S.A.*, edited by Arnold M. Rose (Detroit, 1964). See also, William L. Katz, *Eyewitness: The Negro in American History* (New York, 1967). On American culture, see David Riesman, *The Lonely Crowd: A Study of the Changing American Character* (New Haven, Conn., 1950). On the understanding of the changing nature of American society and American nationalism during and after the Second World War, see the article by Philip Gleason, "Pluralism and Assimilation: A Conceptual History," which is chapter 8 of John Edwards, editor, *Linguistic Minorities, Policies and Pluralism* (London, 1984), and his article "Americans All: World War II and the Shaping of American Identity," in *Review of Politics*, vol. 43, pp. 483–518.

Chapter Eighteen: On the question of "arriving," I read in a vast literature, and the books and articles mentioned here are even more selective than in earlier chapters. On interreligious and intergroup sociology, see the following: Gerhard Lenski, *The Religious Factor: A Sociological Study of Religion's Impact on Politics, Economics, and Family Life* (New York, 1963); E. Digby Baltzell, *The Protestant Establishment, Aristocracy and Caste in America* (New York, 1964); Will Herberg, *Protestant Catholic, Jew: An Essay in American Religious Sociology* (New York, 1955), and Nathan Glazer and Daniel Patrick Moynihan, *Beyond the Melting Pot: The Negroes, Puerto Ricans, Jews, Italians, and Irish of New York City* (Cambridge, Mass., 1963). On the Jews, see: Emil Lehman, "National Survey on Synagogue Leadership" (mimeographed) (New York, 1953); Alexander M. Dushkin, and Uriah Z. Engelman, "Jewish Education in the United States" (mimeographed) (New York, 1959); Marshall Sklare and Joseph Greenblum, *Jewish Identity on the Suburban Frontier: A Study of Group Survival in the Open Society* (New York, 1967), and Marshall Sklare, editor, *The Jews: Social Patterns of an American Group* (Glencoe, Ill., 1959). On economic changes, see Simon Kuznets, *Economic Structure of U.S. Jewry: Recent Trends* (Jerusalem, 1972), and Nathan Goldberg,

"Occupational Patterns of American Jews," *Jewish Review* (1945–46), pp. 3–24, 161–85, 262–90. One cannot think about the American Jewish culture of this generation without reference to two books which were "scandalous" when published, Norman Podhoretz's autobiographical *Making It* (New York, 1967), and Philip Roth's novel, *Portnoy's Complaint* (New York, 1969). On majority-minority tensions see Benjamin B. Ringer, *The Edge of Friendliness: A Study of Jewish-Gentile Relations* (New York, 1967). The "mainstream" view that Israel and American Jewry are forever united without any fundamental differences was best expressed by Melvin I. Urofsky, *We Are One! American Jewry and Israel* (New York, 1978); for a more even-handed account, see Peter Grose, *Israel in the Mind of America* (New York, 1983).

Chapter Nineteen: Most of the books mentioned in chapter 20 are relevant to this one. See also, Oscar Handlin, *Fire-Bell in the Night: The Crisis in Civil Rights* (Boston, 1964). My own views, as a participant in the "actions and passions" of the time, were collected in *Being Jewish in America* (New York, 1979).

Chapter Twenty: For the situation of the Jews in the 1960s, in addition to the survey articles in the *American Jewish Yearbook*, see Jack Nusan Porter, editor, *The Sociology of American Jews* (Washington, D.C., 1978). On the ultra-Orthodox, my account is greatly indebted to an article by Charles S. Liebman, "Orthodoxy in American Jewish Life," *AJYB*, vol. 66, pp. 21–97. See also the first book-length accounts by Solomon Poll, *The Hasidic Community of Williamsburg* (Glencoe, Ill., 1962), and George Kranzler, *Williamsburg: A Jewish Community in Transition* (New York, 1981). On black-Jewish relations, see Shlomo Katz, editor, *Negro and Jew: An Encounter in America* (New York 1967); Nat Hentoff, editor, *Black Anti-Semitism and Jewish Racism* (New York, 1969); Max Geltman, *The Confrontation: Black Power, Anti-Semitism and the Myth of Integration* (Englewood Cliffs, N.J., 1970). For the black perspective, see George Breitman, editor, *By Any Means Necessary: Speeches, Interviews, and a Letter by Malcolm X* (New York, 1970), and James Forman, *The Making of Black Revolutionaries* (New York, 1972). On the younger generation of Jewish radicals, see: Percy S. Cohen, *Jewish Radicals and Radical Jews* (London, 1980); James L. Wood, *The Sources of American Student Activism*

(Lexington, Mass., 1974); and Richard G. Braungart, *Family Status, Socialization and Student Politics* (San Diego, 1979). On the reactions to the war in Vietnam see in general Nancy Zaroulis and Gerald Sullivan, *Who Spoke Up? American Protest Against the War in Vietnam 1963–1975* (New York, 1984). Diana Winston, "Viet Nam and the Jews," pp. 189–209, in Jack Nusan Porter's book mentioned above was especially valuable. On the counter-culture within the Jewish community, see Chava Alkon Katz, "Jewish Radical Zionists in the United States, 1968–72," in the *Year Book of the Encyclopedia of Judaica,* 1975–6, pp. 115–33.

Conclusion: On the changes in American society, see, most recently, Robert C. Christopher, *Crashing the Gates: The De-Wasping of America's Power Elite* (New York, 1989). The annual declarations of the National Jewish Community Advisory Relations Council are an instructive barometer of what the Jewish "establishment" is thinking. This is a printed series of pamphlets called *Joint Program Plan.* On the neo-Conservatives, see Peter Steinfels, *The Neo-Conservatives: The Men Who Are Changing America's Politics* (New York, 1979). On the question of the nature of the "third generation," the rate of intermarriage, and the supposed stabilization of American Jewry, see Calvin Goldscheider and Alan S. Zuckerman, *The Transformation of the Jews* (Chicago, 1984); Calvin Goldscheider and Sidney Goldstein, *The Jewish Community of Rhode Island: A Social and Demographic Study, 1987* (Providence, 1988), and Egon Mayer, *Love and Tradition: Marriage Between Jews and Christians* (New York, 1985). The views of these authors were popularized by Charles E. Silberman, *A Certain People: American Jews and Their Lives Today* (New York, 1985); they were reassessed in an unpublished honors thesis in the Department of Religion, Dartmouth College: Jevin Seth Eagle, "Jewish Students at Dartmouth College: A Study of Third and Fourth Generation American Jews" (Hanover, 1988). The frequent mimeographed reports on Jewish opinion about Jews and Israel issued by the research office of the American Jewish Committee are a prime and trustworthy source. On religious stirrings among mainstream American Jews, see Jonathan Woocher, "The Civil Judaism of Communal Leaders," in *AJYB,* vol. 81, pp. 149–69, and the moving autobiography by the late Paul Cowan, *An Orphan in History: Retrieving a Jewish Legacy* (New York, 1983).

Index

INDEX

INDEX

INDEX

INDEX

WPA (Works Progress Administration), 283
Wright, James, 63
Wyschogrod, Michael, 370

Yeshiva College, 279
Yeshiva University, 357
Yiddish
  culture, 165, 215, 216, 241, 280
  as language, 118, 189
  newspapers, 165, 175, 213, 222, 240, 265, 285
  theater, 165, 198, 212–13
  Western Europe, 170
  writers, 166, 201–2, 283, 307
Yiddisher Kemfer, 297
Yippies, 367
Yishuv, the (Palestine), 226, 227, 231, 232, 280
Yom Kippur, 211–12, 299, 383, 384, 385
  See also Day of Atonement
Yulee, David, 108, 135

Zangwill, Israel, 244, 257
Zanz (Poland), 158
Zion, 37, 73, 76, 96, 97, 257

  See also Israel
Zionism, 158, 215, 219, 225, 257, 278, 280–81, 317–18, 320–21, 342–43, 356
  beginnings of, 84
  creation of, 165
  and East European Jews, 228, 230, 233
  nationalist theories of, 224
  respectability of, 217–18
Zionist Organization of America, 262–63, 278
Zionists, 166, 222, 223, 226–27, 228–31, 238, 287–88, 299, 319, 327, 373
  and American Jewish Congress, 233–35
  organizations, 262–63
  and Reform Judaism, 276–77
Zion Mule Corps, 231–32
Zorba the Greek (film), 361
Zukor, Adolph, 209
Zukunft, 221, 285
Zunz, Leopold, 86
Zvi, Shabtai, 37, 38
Zygielbojm, Szmul, 296–97

428

Steel at the Sault:
Francis H. Clergue, Sir James Dunn,
and the Algoma Steel Corporation 1901–1956

Canada's achievement of nationhood in 1867 brought in its wake the desire for a diversified and self-sufficient national economy. At a time when industrial might was commonly equated with national virility, Canadians looked longingly to the prospect of a flourishing iron and steel industry within their borders. A century later Canada possesses a steel industry that stands as one of the unqualified successes of the economic development policies initiated in the era of the National Policy. Canadian 'Big Steel' is not only able to meet a major proportion of our national steel demand but also internationally competitive, technologically advanced, and in large measure indigenously controlled.

Steel at the Sault focuses on the emergence of steelmaking at Sault Ste Marie, Ontario. As Canada's third-largest primary producer, Algoma Steel originated in the adventures of its two founders – the flamboyant American promoter F.H. Clergue and 'the last of the multimillionaires,' Sir James Dunn. Algoma's troubled but ultimately fruitful evolution cannot be explained in terms of daring, if at times devious, entrepreneurship alone. The dictates of geology, corporate management, and industrial economics also play a crucial role, as do the intricacies of Canadian federalism. By the time of Sir James' death in 1956, these varied influences had combined to make Algoma a well-rounded, profitable, and modern steel company. It has not relinquished that status in the intervening years. The principal thread in the pattern of development, McDowall argues, has been the symbiotic relationship of businessmen and politicians – a relationship typified by the friendship of Sir James Dunn and C.D. Howe, who joined forces at the Sault to pursue the common goal of increased steel production, albeit for different reasons and rewards.

DUNCAN MCDOWALL is a Senior Research Associate with the Conference Board of Canada.

DUNCAN McDOWALL

Steel at the Sault:
Francis H. Clergue,
Sir James Dunn, and the
Algoma Steel Corporation
1901–1956

UNIVERSITY OF TORONTO PRESS
Toronto Buffalo London

© University of Toronto Press 1984
Toronto Buffalo London
Printed in Canada
Reprinted in paperback 1988

ISBN 0-8020-5652-0 (cloth)

ISBN 0-8020-6736-0 (paper)

Canadian Cataloguing in Publication Data

McDowall, Duncan, 1949–
    Steel at the Sault

    Includes bibliographical references and index.
    ISBN 0-8020-5652-0

    1. Algoma Steel Corporation – History. 2. Steel industry and trade –
Ontario – Sault Ste. Marie – History. 3. Clergue, Francis H. (Francis Hector),
b. 1856. 4. Dunn, James, Sir, 1875–1956. I. Title.

    HD9524.C24A43 1984   338.4'7672'0971312   c84-098599-1

For Jocelyn, in loving memory
For Sandy, in enduring love

Contents

Acknowledgments

Sir James Dunn died on New Year's Day, 1956. The death duties on his $66 million estate, together with those garnered from the estate of Montreal financier Izaak Walton Killam, gave the federal treasury an unexpected windfall. Rather than pay these monies into the general revenues, Ottawa used them as seed money for the Canada Council. It is no small irony that my first debt of gratitude should be to the Canada Council, which, twenty years after Sir James' passing, generously provided a doctoral fellowship which enabled me to study Dunn's stewardship of Algoma Steel.

I owe much to Blair Neatby of Carleton University under whose thoughtful and incisive guidance this book originally took shape as a doctoral thesis. Special thanks are due to Michael Bliss for his unstinting encouragement and the fine example set by his own adventures in business history. This book has benefited formatively from criticism which was tendered in a spirit of encouragement. In this respect, the contribution of Tom Traves, Viv Nelles, John Taylor, Ken Hart, Derek Chisholm, and Jim Frank deserve special recognition. What criticism the book may attract is my responsibility alone.

Lady Beaverbrook graciously allowed me permission to read certain restricted sections of the Dunn Papers. Thoughout my research and writing, the Algoma Steel Corporation exhibited an open and cooperative attitude. Access to their archives and conversations with their executives, most notably the late David Holbrook, enhanced my appreciation of the company's evolution.

This book has been published with the help of a grant from the Social Science Federation of Canada, using funds provided by the Social Sciences and Humanities Research Council of Canada, and a grant from the Andrew W. Mellon Foundation to the University of Toronto Press. Wendy Cotie typed the manuscript with precision and cheerfulness. My thanks also go to Liz Stewart, Jocelyne Lapensée, and Ruth Kirkpatrick for their assistance in preparing the manuscript. Gerry Hallowell and Judy Williams of the University of Toronto Press handled the editorial arrangements for this book with a skill that was professional in every respect.

Under most circumstances, the simultaneous preparation of two doctoral theses under one roof is a recipe for anything but bliss. My love, respect, and thanks therefore go to my wife, Sandy Campbell, for her support and companionship through seven happy years.

DUNCAN MCDOWALL

'New Ontario' on display: Ontario legislators tour the Sault industries, June 1899.
(PA52772 Public Archives of Canada)

Francis Hector Clergue, 1856–1939 (Algoma Steel)

Sir James Hamet Dunn, 1874–1956 (Algoma Steel)

The Helen mine, 1906 (PA 17695 Public Archives of Canada)

The 'All-Curves and High Bridges Railway': a trestle on the Algoma Central and Hudson Bay Railway, early 1900s (Ontario Provincial Archives ACC4113)

The interior of the Algoma rail mill, 1911 (Ontario Provincial Archives L2037, p. 5)

Unloading coal and ore at the Sault, 1911 (Ontario Provincial Archives, L2037, p. 3)

Open-hearth plant no. 1: Algoma makes steel for war, 1918. (PA29355 Public Archives of Canada)

Loading iron ore from the Helen mine at Michipicoten harbour, 1918 (PA29349 Public Archives of Canada)

Steel at the Sault: a 1928 aerial view of Algoma Steel, the St Mary's River, and
Sault Ste Marie (PA15588 Public Archives of Canada)

Two men in the driver's seat: Premier Mitch Hepburn of Ontario and Sir James
Dunn in the late 1930s (Neil McKenty)

Salvador Dali's 1949 portrait of Sir James Dunn
Salvador Felipe Jacinto Dali
La Turbie: Sir James Dunn, 1949
oil on canvas
52¼ by 35⅝ inches
The Beaverbrook Canadian Foundation
Beaverbrook Art Gallery
Fredericton, New Brunswick, Canada

Sir James Dunn and C.D. Howe on a November 1953 visit to Wawa, Ontario
(The Sault *Star*)

STEEL AT THE SAULT

Introduction

The history of steelmaking in Canada is the story of an infant industry that grew. Since the 1950s, the iron and steel industry has enjoyed a status which few other sectors of the Canadian economy have ever attained. It is a diversified, modern, profitable, and Canadian-owned industry. Canadian steel mills produce a broad range of steelwares, which are generally competitive in price and quality with those of European, American, and even Far Eastern steelmakers. While the tariff remains a necessary safeguard of the industy's prosperity, it has ceased to be its *raison d'être*.

'Big steel' in Canada offers the unusual example of a well-rounded, mature sector of the economy capable of serving most areas of domestic demand, while at the same time venturing into world markets. It stands in stark contrast to the pattern of technological dependence, foreign ownership, and low productivity that pervades much of Canadian manufacturing. Even in times of economic recession, such as the early 1980s, when the world steel industry is plagued with overcapacity, dumping, and escalating costs, Canadian steel producers have maintained a relatively even keel, while other less mature and diversified sectors of the ecomomy have foundered or stagnated.

'The Canadian steel industry is a vital link in the Canadian economy,' a 1978 task force report has concluded, 'and provides the fundamental base for the continuing expansion of a competitive, Canadian secondary manufacturing sector.'[1] Other commentators in the ongoing debate over the direction of Canada's industrial policy have argued that the steel industry offers a 'model for emulation.'[2] In short, steelmaking is seen as a Canadian industrial success story.

If the steel industry has prospered in Canada, it is because of a complex set of circumstances. The successful evolution of the country's four leading primary steel producers is not a testament to the unfettered operation of Canadian corporate capitalism. The propensity of many early steel promoters to rely on foreign capital and their urge for quick profits more often than not led to stunted growth, if not collapse, rather than industrial success. Neither is the steel industry's progress to maturity primarily the product of government intervention or stimulation. Despite the fact that the government has had to rescue the weakest of Canada's primary steelmakers, the state has not played a primordial role in the development of the industry.

The state has instead played a facilitating role – as a provider of incentives, a protector from external influences, and, at times, a principal customer. The emergence of a well-rounded, profitable, and technically advanced steel industry in Canada has in essence been the product of an amalgam of influences. Benevolent and at times competing governments, aggressive and at times reckless entrepreneurs, and the pattern of natural resource endowment have all contributed to, and occasionally impeded, the industry's progress. The principal thread in this pattern of development has undoubtedly been the symbiotic relationship of businessmen and politicians, who joined forces to pursue the same goal of increased steel production, albeit for differing reasons and rewards. Human coalitions of this sort none the less depended for their success on immutable patterns of geology and on fickle patterns of consumption and international competition. Like the precise blend of ingredients needed for each crucible of new steel, the success of the industry in Canada has resulted from a formula of complex dimensions.

This book is the story of the Algoma Steel Corporation, Canada's third largest producer of crude steel, surpassed only by the Steel Company of Canada and Dominion Foundries and Steel (now Dofasco) in Hamilton. Algoma produces more than seven hundred different specifications of steel in a wide range of products ranging from automotive sheet steel to seamless tube. It is therefore able to compete for over 70 per cent of the steel required by the Canadian market. Algoma Steel is, at first sight, an unlikely candidate for industrial prosperity. Perched on the shores of Lake Superior at Sault Ste Marie, the company seems to defy the popular wisdom about the ideal location of a steel industry. This is to say, it lacks access to coal and is well removed from its primary markets. While the American shore of Superior abounds with high-grade hematite ore, Algoma on the Canadian shore has had to subsist on lower-grade ores, which have been difficult to locate and expensive to process. Algoma has also had to contend with absentee ownership, a burden which it was able to shed only in 1935. The Philadelphia promoters who conjured up the dream of steel at the Sault at the turn of the century were never able to translate their dreams into a sustained and profitable reality. Addicted to short-term profits and incapable of progressive management, Algoma's American owners condemned the enterprise to submarginal performance for the first thirty-five years of its existence. In addition to the operation's inherent weaknesses, the obstinate opposition of the consumers of crude steel to any measure aimed at establishing the primary industry within Canada's borders also blocked Algoma's road to maturity. Protected by its own wall of tariffs, the secondary steel industry was loath to give up its assured supply of imported iron and steel. As long as the flow of low-duty foreign steel served the Canadian market, aspiring Canadian primary producers were condemned to a paltry existence. These were the odds with which the Algoma Steel Corporation has contended for much of its existence. The repeated incidence of plant shut-downs, layoffs, and a fateful slide into receivership in the Depression brought the company close to extinction.

But Algoma survived. The price of survival was high by any measure. No amount of subsequent diversification or solid profits can erase the record of grim working conditions, prolonged unemployment, and fruitless investment from the minds of those who staked their lives and money on a company that failed to turn a steady profit in human or financial terms for the first four decades of its corporate existence. None the less, Algoma ultimately succeeded, much to Canada's economic betterment. Any attempt to understand the company's initial failure and eventual success must encompass many factors.

In this regard, it would be tempting to explain Algoma's fortunes solely in terms of the two entrepreneurs who played so formative a role in the company's emergence. There is indeed a fascination in the careers of Francis Hector Clergue, the American entrepreneur who established the Sault industries at the turn of the century, and Sir James Hamet Dunn, the Canadian financier who seized control of the bankrupt steel company in 1935 and guided it to subsequent prosperity. Any attempt to understand the fortunes of Algoma Steel must of necessity focus in some detail on the life and methods of Clergue and Dunn. Neither was an especially competent business manager, but each possessed particular talents by which he capitalized on the industrial possibilities of steel-making on the shores of Lake Superior. In Clergue's case, both the dream and its pursuit were flawed. Despite the recklessness which underlay the initial establishment of the Sault industries, Clergue's motives and methods bear close examination. Much of the history of Algoma from the collapse of the Clergue empire in 1903 to the 1935 reorganization can be explained in terms of Clergue's early misadventures.

This is not a study of the life and times of Sir James Dunn. No account of the rebuilding of Algoma Steel after 1935 can, however, stray far from the personality of Sir James, who as principal owner and president quite literally ruled the company until his death in 1956. Dunn's performance on the job at the Sault was predicated on attitudes and patterns of behaviour which he had acquired long before 1935, during his ascendancy to millionaire status in the City of London; his early career as a merchant banker has therefore been given a prominent place in this study. It is ironic that Algoma's emergence as a profitable and diversified steel company – a positive achievement in terms of nation-building – was at root based on Dunn's self-serving methods and dubious ethics.

This said, it must be observed that the tragedy and glamour of Clergue's and Dunn's respective careers reveal only one aspect of the story of steel at the Sault. Despite their autocratic ways, Clergue and Dunn needed professional managers to run their empires. Algoma's evolution must therefore be seen in terms of the emergence of a cadre of professional managers, men who were trained to operate a modern, integrated steelworks. Their presence was a *sine qua non*. For all his millions, Sir James did not in 1935 know the crucial difference between hematite and siderite. The contribution of paid managers was complemented by that of other professionals. The geologists who pioneered the Helen mine – Canada's first successful large-scale iron mine – contributed to Algoma's livelihood as much as did Dunn's mastery of the financial world. The corporate lawyers in Toronto also played a crucial role, not just as writers of contracts but also as political go-betweens. Ironically, the steelworkers who sweated out their days inside the plant had the most to lose from Algoma's possible demise. Labour was, however, very much a quiescent factor in the business history of Algoma Steel. There were few strikes and, as long as the company tottered on the edge of collapse, the workers seemed to share management's perspective on the company's best, and only, course of action. This is not a history of Algoma Steel from the labour perspective. Labour's role enters into the narrative only when it impinged on the calculations of management and threatened to deflect the company from the course they had determined for it.

Algoma's development must also be explained in terms of the perennial conflict between Canada's federal and provincial politicians. Clergue's grandiose dream of an integrated industrial complex on the edge of the Canadian Shield capitalized on the Ontario government's dream for a 'New Ontario.' The steelworks were also the direct result of the federal government's wish to foster a primary steel industry. Both Clergue and Dunn quickly learned the art of playing one level of government against the other. Algoma's faltering existence touched the political careers of Ontario premiers from Ross to Drew and figured in the policies of prime ministers from Laurier to St Laurent. Some premiers, like Mitch Hepburn, were better friends to Algoma than others. Laurier visited Clergue's 'miracle' at the Sault, but Mackenzie King instinctively distrusted Dunn and avoided contact with him. Yet what Laurier did for Clergue, C.D. Howe, King's senior economic minister, did for Dunn.

The human actors in this study played out their roles against an inanimate backdrop – coal, ore, the shifting pattern of Canadian steel consumption all play a part in this analysis. Some amount of geological detail is therefore unavoidable because, in a sense, the scouring of the Ice Ages was the first significant event in the story of steel at the Sault. From geology, the story proceeds to technology, economics, and politics. Together they combine in the history of one Canadian company. It is a tale worth telling, because, when all is said and done, Canadians have succeeded in building their own steel industry.

1

The Iron and Steel Industry in Ontario: Troubled Beginnings to the 1890s

The coming of the frontier of settlement to Upper Canada in the late eighteenth century brought inevitably in its wake the age of iron. Many of the essential implements which supported the rough and ready existence of the early backwoodsmen reflected the ever-growing iron technology of the European and American cultures which they had brought to their new land. The axes, plough points, and chains with which the settlers tamed the forest and built their new life were all products of the iron furnace and forge.[1] These tools made possible the colony's early exports of potash, wheat, and timber, the staple commodities which provided the colony with the purchasing power to finance further imports of the necessities of frontier life. Just as they depended upon England and the American Loyalists for their political culture, these earliest Ontarians relied heavily upon the mother country and the young American republic for their supplies of iron goods. As the colonial society developed a sense of identity and a desire for a greater measure of political independence, a parallel drive for a greater degree of economic independence emerged in areas of the colonial economy. Eager to reduce the cost of weighty imported pig iron, Upper Canada embarked on its first efforts to mine, smelt, and fashion its own iron.

From the outset it was apparent that the production of crude pig iron in Upper Canada could only be profitably undertaken in those few locations which offered readily accessible raw materials and at the same time afforded inexpensive access to the province's scattered markets. Small pockets of bog ore lying in swampy ground or exposed veins of higher-grade ore attracted the promoters of the first crude furnaces, provided nearby sources of running water, for power and cooling, and hardwood for fuel could be found. Proximity to navigable water was also indispensable in a colony lacking all but the most primitive roads. These dictates of geography and geology imparted a distinctly local character to the production and distribution of iron goods in early Upper Canada. Although iron had been successfully refined at the St Maurice forges of Lower Canada as early as 1729,[2] the first sustained smelting enterprise in Upper Canada was initiated at Lansdown, near Brockville, in 1799, followed closely by one at Furnace Falls on the Gananoque River in 1800. Of the numerous small furnaces that sprang up in the wake of these early ventures, the Normandale smelter in Norfolk County was perhaps the most illustrious. Founded about 1815, the Normandale forge was taken over in the early 1820s by Joseph Van Norman, an American who gained considerable repute over the next three decades as Upper Canada's preeminent iron master. Elsewhere in the colony, the Marmora Iron Works, established north of Belleville about 1820, survived precariously, even after the Montreal entrepreneur Peter McGill acquired ownership in the early 1830s.[3]

From its inception, the Ontario iron industry laboured under most trying circumstances. Successful ironmaking depended on a propitious combination of suitable and readily accessible ore, flux, and coal, together with sufficient capital, entrepreneurship, and demand. In early Ontario, most of these factors were conspicuously absent. Non-renewable timber resources adjacent to most furnace sites were also quickly exhausted and the complete absence of coal in Ontario deprived furnaces of any alternative fuel supply. Distance from other sources of fuel and ore precluded the economic importation of supplementary raw materials. An early attempt mounted by an American syndicate in 1865 to exploit reported iron deposits in the Michipicoten area on the shores of Lake Superior foundered because of its distance from southern markets.[4] Montreal capitalists also speculated on the unknown mineral wealth of the rocky Superior country, chartering companies that bore little fruit except for the isolated silver bonanza on Silver Islet[5] in the late 1860s.

Lack of entrepreneurial and technical expertise further debilitated the fledgling industry. The whole thrust of the colony's economic development lay in the commercial possibilities of staples such as wheat and timber that paid quick returns on capital invested. Few in the agrarian colony had the technical knowledge to operate even the most rudimentary furnaces. John Mason, the original proprietor of the Normandale furnace, complained in 1817 to Robert Gourlay that there was 'not a man in the country that I know capable of working in the furnace.' Mason also bitterly noted the 'many experiments' and 'enormous expense' needed to perfect his smelting technique, a task made all the more difficult by the unwillingness of the government to subsidize the passage of English workmen to operate the furnace.[6] The provincial government was also subject to incessant petitioning from the owners of the Marmora Iron Works, who in the 1830s saw the provision of cheap prison labour from Kingston and improved water transport on the Trent River, both at government expense, as the solution to their woes. From an early date, would-be Ontario iron producers developed the habit of looking longingly to the provincial government for succour.

Besides these inherent obstacles, the Ontario iron industry in the second half of the nineteenth century experienced a decline in its ability to compete with foreign producers as a result of the rapid and radical changes in the technology of ironmaking. The decades between 1850 and 1890 witnessed a dramatic acceleration in the rate and scope of technological innovation in the manufacture of iron. In the first place, the iron industry now became the iron and steel industry. The work of Henry Bessemer, Charles Siemens, and Thomas Gilchrist revolutionized the industry by introducing relatively inexpensive and efficient methods of smelting a metal of great strength, plasticity, and hardness – steel. The Bessemer converter and the open-hearth furnace dramatically increased the applications of ferrous metals and at the same time progressively lessened the cost of the industry's products. As David Landes has commented, 'the primary feature of the technology of the last third of the nineteenth century' was 'the substitution of steel for iron and the concomitant increase in the consumption of metal per head.'[7] One of the greatest stimulants to these technical advances was the almost insatiable appetite of the growing railway networks of both Europe and North America for iron and steel. The advent of steel sealed the fate of the brittle iron rail and hastened the adoption of the heavier, more durable steel rail. Moreover, unlike iron, steel could be rolled and shaped, making it an ideal substance for rails, fishplates, and the endless variety of shapes and angles demanded by railway builders.[8]

Tremendous as they were, the advances of 'the age of steel' remained almost exclusively within the purveyance of the British, German, and American economies. Production of iron in the United States increased from 919,770 tons in 1860 to 4.3 million tons in 1880, the year which saw 681 blast furnaces operating in twenty-five states. By 1874, there were sixty-nine rail mills churning out the staple ingredient of the sensational expansion of American railway network. Throughout the period of 1867–80, the average price of rails dropped from $135.60 to $65.42 per ton.[9] Under the pressure of this expansion, the American industry shed its localized character and gravitated to geographically more advantageous locations, where better economies of scale and cheaper transportation could be exploited. These years witnessed the growing preeminence of Pittsburgh and the industrial northeast as the steel heartland of the United States. Blessed with abundant local supplies of bituminous coal, Pittsburgh relied on the railway and waterways to supply its flux and ore requirements. Responding to this demand, the American canal at Sault Ste Marie was opened in 1855, thereby allowing eastern steel centres to draw upon the newly discovered rich hematite ores of the Superior ranges to such an extent that by 1880 Superior ore constituted 33 per cent of American iron ore consumption.

The American iron and steel industry experienced not just a quantitative transformation in the second half of the nineteenth century but also a qualitative one. The birth and rapid growth of the steel industry reflected crucial changes in the nature of American capitalism. Together with the railways, the steel industry acted as a precursor of modern 'big business' with its reliance on mass production, scientific management, and industrial integration. At the centre of this process was the application of the Bessemer furnace, which appeared in the United States in the 1850s, to the production of steel for rails. Henry Bessemer's leading apostle in America was a New England engineer named Alexander Holley. Holley strove to reduce the high cost of making steel rails by centralizing production, coordinating the supply of natural resources, maximizing heat use and emphasizing what he called 'throughput,' or the velocity of production. Notwithstanding his success in these endeavours, Holley's integrated steel mills required huge injections of capital and consequently attracted the attention of financiers, whose opinions carried increasing weight in the affairs of the growing American steel industry. Similarly, the day-to-day management of the industry required new managerial skills to oversee every aspect of steelmaking from procurement of resources to the marketing of the end product. 'The history of the American steel industry,' Alfred Chandler has noted, 'illustrates effectively how technological innovation, intensified use of energy, plant design, and overall management procedures permitted a great increase in the volume and speed of throughput and with it a comparable expansion in the productivity of operation.'[10] By the turn of the twentieth century, the American steel industry was embarking on its second technological wave – the open hearth furnace. With such innovation and maturity, tariff protection ceased to be a bone of contention for steelmakers. As steel magnate Joseph Wharton put it in the early 1890s: 'We are not pleading the baby act.'[11] In Canada, the situation was totally different. Steelmaking had yet to become even an infant industry north of the border.

Emasculated by its own internal weaknesses, the infant Ontario iron industry simply buckled under the pressure exerted by the bounding expansion of the American and British industries. The production of steel remained a dream. Britain's industrial expansion from the 1840s had left the colonies virtually defenceless in the face of the onslaught of cheap foreign rails. In the years after 1847, the embryonic Canadian tariff policy provided only negligible protection and encouragement for the Canadian iron industry. Although duties inched gradually upwards in 1847, 1849, 1856, and 1858, the protection given the Canadian industry afforded little shelter from the influx of cheap foreign iron goods, especially during the 1854–66 period of American reciprocity. The Cayley tariff of 1859, the first acknowledgment of the primacy of tariffs for protection over tariffs for revenue, imposed duties as high as 20 per cent on iron goods, although an extensive free list was maintained.[12]

Early tariffs tended to provide more generously for the protection of secondary iron and steel goods, such as nails, wire, and agricultural implements, while leaving the primary stage of production 'to be conducted on its own merits at practically all times.'[13] This gaping hole in the Canadian tariff wall was principally due to the inability of the local smelters to supply Canadian consumers with sufficient quantities of pig iron. Unable to match American supplies of ore and coal or to equal the cheapness of English pig iron, the Canadian industry specialized increasingly in the secondary levels of production in which it could compete on nearly equal terms.[14] Indicative of the primary industry's flimsy existence was the failure of Van Norman's attempt to forge railway wheels at the Houghton Iron Works in the 1850s.[15] About 1860, railway promoters Casimir Gzowski and David Macpherson established a plant to produce bar iron and to reroll rails, but this too failed by 1873. The Toronto Steel, Iron and Railway Works Company, founded in 1866, lasted only until 1872, despite the fact that it used prison labour. Canadian ironmakers never managed to duplicate the success of their American counterparts in supplying the needs of their nation's growing railway system. In the early 1850s, for instance, the promoters of the Bytown and Prescott Railway ordered their rails and fishplates from the Ebbw Vale Iron Company in Wales. Not surprisingly, B.J. Harrington of the Geological Survey of Canada concluded in 1874 that 'the history of iron smelting in this country is neither a long one nor a brilliant one.'[16] In the age of steel and railways, Canada was failing to supply the sinews of its own industrial growth.

Undoubtedly the most debilitating weakness of the Ontario iron industry in the mid-nineteenth century was its failure to locate alternative domestic ore resources to replace the now depleted or economically unviable pockets of ore in southern and southeastern parts of the province. With the American industry employing its efficient water and rail networks to tap both eastern coal and Lake Superior ore, the Canadian industry took the course of least resistance by relying upon ever-larger importations of British and American pig iron. Scattered evidence suggests that American firms surveyed and attempted some exploitation of Canadian ores at Madoc and Marmora, but in almost every other sense the Canadian primary iron and steel industry came to occupy a peripheral and submarginal position in the continental economy. As long as the level of tariff protection remained low, there seemed little alternative for the Ontario industry but to remain enslaved to this continental resource pattern. Reviewing the development of the industry to 1885, one publicist gloomily concluded that the position of the few iron manufacturers remaining in the province had not only deteriorated but that 'in fact they can hardly be said to exist.' From being *the most important manufacture in the late Province of Canada*, fifty to seventy-five years ago, when iron and stoves were articles of export,' the iron trade had fallen off to such a point that 'a sort of hopeless feeling has been engendered, and a great number of people believe that we have not the facilities to enable us to manufacture iron in Canada.'[17]

The move to confederation by four of the Canadian colonies in 1867 signified the first consolidated attempt to provide the proper conditions for sustained industrial growth in a nation almost totally overshadowed by the feverish industrial activity of England and the United States. 'Federation,' as Harold Innis once perceptively noted, 'was a device to secure ample supplies of capital for the construction of railways from the Atlantic to the Pacific in a region handicapped by concentration on staples such as fur, timber, and agricultural products and without an iron and steel industry.'[18] Equally clear was the belief at Confederation that the new federal government's role in stimulating industrial growth extended no further than that of fostering an enlarged national market and of subsidizing a national transportation network. Most Canadians, however, came to regard protection as 'an ambitious gamble for success,' as one historian of economic thought has noted, 'and free trade as stoical acceptance of combined dependence on Great Britain and the whims of world markets.'[19] Despite the prodding of such isolated protectionists as Issac Buchanan, the pre-Confederation tariff structure remained essentially intact. Tariff revision in 1868 shifted many iron goods, such as bars, sheets, and rods, off the free list, but gave them only nominal 5 per cent protection. Even when the Mackenzie government, with its distinct free-trading bias, was forced to hike tariff levels in the mid 1870s for revenue purposes, iron and partially manufactured iron goods were given only a 5 per cent revenue duty. The effectiveness of such low levels of tariff protection was predictably unimpressive, especially in light of the tremendous competitive advantage enjoyed by the American iron and steel industry.

Other forces conspired to stifle the progress of Canadian iron smelting. Continued technological sophistication in the English, American, and awakening German steel industries gave these countries an almost insurmountable lead in terms of diversified, large-scale production of steel goods. Coupled with the deflationary economic depression that pervaded the late decades of the century, the efficient size of foreign industry accounted for the continuing steady drop in the price of industrial goods. Under such conditions, only those areas of Canada that were naturally endowed with ready supplies of iron ore and coal and adjacent to substantial markets or cheap transportation could survive. Few did. The venerable St Maurice forges persevered until 1883 in Quebec, while in Nova Scotia, with its abundant supply of Cape Breton coal, the Londonderry Iron Works and the Hope Iron Works produced small quantities of pig iron throughout the 1870s.[20] In Ontario, the primary industry lay dormant. There was little incentive either to search for iron ore or to smelt it. Surveying the provincial industry in 1874, the geologist B.J. Harrington lamented the lack of surveying for ore bodies in the northern area of the province and complained that the known ore in Ontario was too 'titaniferous' and would require mixing with imported ores if it was ever to be brought into production. 'So long,' Harrington concluded, 'as other ores can be obtained in abundance the demand for the highly titaniferous ores cannot be great.'[21] By 1879, there were no blast furnaces in Ontario.

As faith in the precepts of free-trade economics crumbled, the demand for tariffs to encourage industry became more insistent. Tilley's National Policy budget of 1879 heralded the first concerted attempt to foster an indigenous iron and steel industry in Canada through protection. A panoply of tariffs was imposed on iron and steel goods, including a $2 a ton duty on pig iron and scrap, duties on coal and coke, and duties of between 12½ and 20 per cent *ad valorem* on puddled iron, beams, forgings, and other iron and steel goods. Notable exceptions from dutiable status were iron ore and rails. The government argued that supply for railway steel was too imperative to be tampered with. Advocates of protection none the less prophesied that the National Policy would supply the elixir to rouse the Canadian iron and steel industry from its slumber. In many minds, steel offered a road not only to prosperity but also to nationhood. When Sir Leonard Tilley brought down the 1879 National Policy budget, he spoke in terms of the necessity of clothing his young nation in some industrial armour: 'We find in every country that has risen to any position of wealth and commercial greatness ... [that] the iron interest is one of the most important interests of that country. I would also instance the United States. It may safely be said that it is the basis of every other industry. It is true we have not developed it to a great extent yet.'[22] In the minds of many late-nineteenth-century Canadian nationalists, iron and steel thus occupied an important symbolic position, looming large as a *sine qua non* in their schemes of national survival. 'In the great age of steel, this was the fondest of hopes,' two historians have recently noted. 'Iron and steel was at once the prestige symbol of industrialization and the base of any respectable industrial power.'[23] In the Commons, the Hon. John Beverley Robinson confidently but naively predicted that since in the United States there were seven hundred blast furnaces sustained by a population of forty million, Canada could soon rightfully expect to support seventy furnaces with its population.[24]

Steady increases in the iron and steel tariff in the early 1880s were capped in 1887 by a wholesale upward revision, including provisions for establishing minimum applicability levels for *ad valorem* tariffs to guard Canadian producers against falling international prices. The thrust of these tariff adjustments tended to improve the competitive position of the secondary or 'finishing' level of iron and steel production. Agricultural machinery, for instance, was now dutiable at rates as high as 35 per cent. On the other hand, many of the basic products of the primary industry were exempted from tariff coverage. A federal act of 1881 empowered the government to transfer by order-in-council items from the dutiable to the free list, a provision that was liberally employed to afford the CPR duty-free fishplates, steel plate, and railway bars. This tendency to differentiate between the primary and secondary sectors of the industry revealed at an early date a basic flaw in the practice, if not the conception, of the National Policy. Pressured by the demands of the railroad builders and the owners of a growing number of factories processing iron and steel into a myriad of finished goods,[25] the government reneged on its original intention and allowed the primary iron and steel products to flood freely into the country. Defending this lenience in the tariff, the government took refuge in the argument that, should the primary industry begin to show signs of life, adequate protection would be provided or, as Finance Minister Tilley put it, 'there was a proposition to establish a steel manufactory in this country and it was left in that manner ... as a declaration of the policy of the Government if the manufacture was undertaken in the meantime.'[26]

To combat the increasing discrepancy between the stillborn primary industry and the maturing secondary sectors of the trade, the Macdonald government in 1883 devised a system of bounties on the production of iron and steel. Adopted only as a temporary expedient, a bounty of $1.50 per ton of pig iron smelted from domestic ore was to be paid for three years. Extended for another three years in 1886, decreased to $1 per ton in 1889 and subsequently increased in 1892 to $2, the bounty shed its impermanent character and became a fixture in both Conservative and Liberal government policy until it was finally jettisoned in 1912. Bounties provided an excellent political expedient, for they extended a stimulus to primary producers while not placing an undue burden on consumers of crude iron and steel. Introducing the measure, Leonard Tilley spoke of the 'richest quality of ore' available in Canada and said that he hoped the bounty would reduce the nation's dependence upon imported pig iron, which amounted to 63,431 tons in 1882.[27] Although Edward Blake, in his free trading zeal, prophesied that no government or tariff could protect the unaccomplished entrepreneur from disaster, the bounty scheme was well received, especially by one government member who cockily predicted profitable iron mines within five miles of Parliament.

Despite its enthusiastic promoters, the policy of tariff protection and bounties was by no means an unqualified success in stimulating the growth of a well-rounded primary iron and steel industry in Ontario. By any measure, the primary industry failed to gain ground on the more established secondary levels of steel processing. Ensured of a fairly solid shield of tariff protection, the Canadian rolling mill and finishing industry had begun to take root throughout the 1880s. Nail, screw, and bar rolling mills were established with considerable success in urban areas of Ontario, Quebec, New Brunswick, and Nova Scotia.[28] Exemplary of this trend were the Montreal Rolling Mills and the Pillow-Hersey plant in Montreal, firms that had their beginnings before the National Policy but quickly expanded and diversified under the protective tariff.[29] Similar establishments sprang up in Ontario at Hamilton, Toronto, and Belleville. The nascent iron and steel finishing industry remained for the most part reliant upon imported pig iron and scrap, using domestically smelted pig iron only where competitively available. Staunchest support for the *status quo* in the National Policy tariff structure thus came from this secondary sector of the iron and steel industry. When, in 1888, demands were made for greater protection for the primary industry, representatives of bar and plate rolling mills from Halifax to Hamilton informed Sir Charles Tupper of their belief that the tariff was 'on the whole satisfactory.' Since, the petition continued, 'the present capacity of those interested in developing the resources of the country in the making of Pig Iron, Puddle Bars etc., is yet limited ... you will see at once that the time has not yet come for making any advance in the rate of duty on wrought Iron Scrap or Steel Scrap.'[30]

The affection of secondary manufacturers for the established iron and steel tariff was not shared by would-be primary producers. A.T. Peterson of the Londonderry Iron Works vented the frustration of the primary producers when he wrote to Justice Minister J.S. Thompson in 1887 to complain that the existing tariff structure 'was a piece of patchwork inconsistent in itself, and therefore incapable of developing the Home Industry of Iron making from Canadian ore, although possibly well calculated to put money into the pockets of manufacturers who employ a small amount of Canadian labour in manipulating foreign Iron.'[31]

Between 1879 and the early 1890s, the record of Canadian iron and steel producers was studded with many failures and few successes. Nova Scotia sustained the most successful activity on this front, principally because of its indigenous sources of ore and coal. A resurrected Londonderry Iron Company operated intermittently from 1887 to 1896, by which time it was 'hopelessly embarrassed' financially and hampered by low-grade ores.[32] The Nova Scotia Steel Company, founded in 1882, utilized an open hearth furnace, and, when amalgamated with the Nova Scotia Forge Company at Trenton, became the first integrated steelworks in Canada capable of producing pig iron through to finished steel goods. In 1888, the New Glasgow Coal, Iron and Railway Company secured a sufficient supply of local hematite ore to operate a large capacity furnace totally reliant upon local ore. With the opening of the rich Wabana ore bodies in Newfoundland and the more intensive exploitation of Cape Breton coal fields near Sydney, the Nova Scotian industry found itself on a firmer footing. Progress in the Maritime industry up to 1900 was characterized by vertical and horizontal integration which capitalized on the natural community of interest between primary iron and coal producers and the finishing stages of the industry, a movement best typified by the emergence of Nova Scotia Steel.

The progress of the Nova Scotia industry contrasted starkly with the faltering progress of iron smelting in Ontario. In the *Canadian Magazine* of May 1893, W.H. Merritt, a prominent mining engineer and son of the founder of the Welland Canal, reminded Ontarians of the 'shame' that there was not a single blast furnace in their province. 'I boldly make the assertion,' Merritt persisted, 'that Canada's greatest deficiency lies in not producing her own iron and steel.'[33] The members of the 1890 Royal Commission on Mineral Resources noted with regret that in their travels only the Wilbur iron mine, north of Kingston, was in operation, while 'the other deposits visited were either undeveloped or lying idle and full of water.'[34] In the years since the closing of Van Norman's pioneer furnace in the 1850s, however, the challenge of smelting had not gone untried in Ontario. Throughout the 1880s, numerous attempts had been made to establish furnaces in Ontario towns such as London, Toronto, and Kingston. All met quick and dismal ends. The 1890 Mineral Resources Royal Commission attributed 'this hapless record of failure' to the persistence of American tariffs which blocked export of Canadian ore to American furnaces, thereby denying the would-be Ontario industry sufficient demand to sustain production on a profitable scale. The exploration for ore that did take place was largely dependent upon initiative and expertise supplied by American capitalists eager to locate high-grade ore which could be profitably shipped south despite the American tariffs on imported raw materials. Between 1886 and 1894, 150,800 tons of Canadian ore were in fact exported, primarily to the Pennsylvania heartland of the American steel industry.[35]

Attempts to initiate smelting in the populated areas of southern and southeastern Ontario foundered because they perpetuated the old pioneer reliance upon isolated pockets of bog or vein ore of varying quantity. Readily exhaustible, these reserves of ore provided a flimsy base for the primary industry. Exacerbating the situation was the ever-quickening development of the American iron ore industry. As early as 1856, the first shipments of Marquette Range ore made their way by lake and rail to the eastern furnaces. In the remaining decades of the century the iron frontier of Superior moved progressively westward into the Menominee, Gogebic, Mesabi, and Vermilion Ranges, so that by 1895 the region had shipped 10.4 million tons of high grade ore to eastern consumers.[36] It was a classic example of high-grade ore coupled with low-cost bulk transportation serving expanding demand. The prosperity of iron ore mining on the American shore of Superior did not, however, sponsor the growth of an integrated iron and steel industry in the same locale. Mindful of the lack of markets in the northwest, American steelmakers opted to bring the ore and flux to the coal in Pennsylvania, thereby relegating the Superior area to the status of a resource hinterland.[37] It was Ontario's inability to develop a comparable resource hinterland that blocked early efforts to foster a smelting industry in the province.

Writing in 1891, W.H. Merritt complained of the reluctance of Ontarians to scour the northern reaches of their province for iron ore. This reluctance, he suggested, was attributable to 'the great bug-bear held before our prospectors or investors that there is no certainty as to the persistency of the magnetite deposits of north-eastern Ontario.' If the province could develop 'a permanent demand and a systematic mining development,' Merritt predicted, there could be 'no question whatever, geologically speaking, about the ultimate permanent supply to be derived from the magnetite deposits of north-eastern Ontario.'[38]

Merritt's prophecy was for the time being an act of faith, for there was little point in engaging in costly exploration in the wilds of northern Ontario while iron ore remained ensconced on the free list of the Canadian tariff schedule. Penetrated by only one railway and far distant from Ontario's infant industrial community in the south, the geologically unexploited reaches of the province's northland were destined to remain untapped for some years to come. Dr A.R.C. Selwyn of the Geological Survey of Canada boldly declared at Ontario's Mineral Resources Royal Commission hearings in 1890 that not 'one-tenth part of the country has been explored.' The Royal Commission *Report* likewise complained that 'knowledge of the extent of our natural resources is necessarily imperfect' and that much of the mining industry's 'slow progress' was due to the lack of systematic surveying. Too much reliance was placed on 'aimless' prospecting by surveyors who travelled 'through the region at random, trusting to chance to make a discovery.' While reiterating the belief that the mineral potential of the north was 'simply incalculable,' the commissioners lamented that so far there were only 'indications' of this wealth and little specific knowledge.[39]

Another major factor militating against smelting in Ontario was the province's total lack of coal. In both Ontario and Quebec the obsolescence of charcoal-fired furnaces and distance from American or Nova Scotian bituminous coal supplies placed severe constraints on attempts to utilize domestic ores.[40] In the 1890s Ontarians must have at times questioned God's beneficence in apparently bestowing such bounteous supplies of ore and coal upon their American neighbours while leaving them without coal or iron ore at the foot of the barren and inhospitable Canadian Shield. Surveying the period from his vantage point in 1915, political economist W.J.A. Donald crystallized the Canadian dilemma. 'In short,' he said, 'there was little hope for good returns on an investment in the Canadian pig iron business, and no matter what the ambitions of Canadian producers, Canada could not have got along well without importing some American or British pig iron.'[41]

When Merritt declared in the early 1890s that he could not 'point out any great nation which does not manufacture its own iron and steel,' he was underscoring the failure of the National Policy to stimulate the growth of an autonomous primary iron and steel industry in Canada.[42] Ontario by 1894 could boast of no blast furnaces and only paltry amounts of iron ore mined within its boundaries. Quebec's few scattered furnaces subsisted on ever-diminishing ore supplies, while sharing with Ontario central Canada's acute lack of fossil fuel. Only in Nova Scotia had relatively abundant sources of coal and ore combined to sustain a nascent primary industry. The Maritime sector of the industry thus constituted the productive backbone of Canadian steel. Between 1886 and 1894, of the 793,137 tons of iron ore mined in Canada, 562,732 tons or 70.9 per cent was mined in Nova Scotia. Ontario contributed 6.8 per cent while Quebec's ore represented 17.5 per cent. British Columbia's 4.7 per cent contribution was mainly comprised of ore from Texada Island, a mine which closed in 1891. In terms of pig iron output, Nova Scotia enjoyed a susbstantial lead over Quebec, producing 82 per cent of the country's 238,005 tons in the years 1886–94.

Resource deprivation was not the only impediment to central Canada's aspirations for a solid foundation at the primary level of the ferrous metals industry. Under constant pressure from the producers of secondary iron and steel goods not to allow any upward adjustment in existing tariff structures, the federal government maintained a tariff wall behind which potential primary producers could take only insufficient refuge. Cowering in the face of insuperable British and American competition, the incipient Canadian steel industry had also to contend with several debilitating gaps in the façade of the tariff wall, most notably exemptions of duty on such key items of Canadian growth as steel rails. During the 1881–7 period, years in which the Canadian Pacific was constructed, Canada imported $5,397,204 worth of steel rails, 67 per cent of which came from Great Britain and the rest from the United States. In the same span of time, Canada imported a total of $95,255,585 of primary and secondary iron and steel goods, both dutiable and free under the tariff schedule. Further evidence of Canada's lack of self-sufficiency in primary iron and steel output was the $12,615,483 of imported bar and ingot iron, equivalent to 13.2 per cent of total iron and steel imports throughout 1881-7. Although Tupper proposed a duty of $13 a ton on steel rails to Macdonald as early as 1889,[43] the Conservative government stood resolutely by its contention that protection would only be bestowed once the industry began to show signs of life. In the meantime Canada's 'national dream' would run on foreign-made rails. Like secondary producers, the railways vigorously sought to preserve this generously lenient tariff structure. When, for instance, American promoter S.J. Ritchie applied to Ottawa in 1891 for a federal subsidy to build a Central Ontario Railway with provision for an iron smelter along its route, the request was rejected after vehement protests from Van Horne of the CPR.[44] By the time the Conservatives fell from power in 1896, the iron and steel tariff had already become a contentious political issue, a discomfort for whatever party found itself in office. Newly installed Trade and Commerce Minister Richard Cartwright was given little repose before being confronted by the pent-up frustrations of would-be primary producers. 'I say,' one irate industrialist told him, 'the Government ought to recognize that fact and to give us a fair chance to establish this industry here ... It is an awful thing to think that all the rails used in our street railways as well as our steam railways are brought in from other countries. The money they cost has got to go out of this country.'[45]

While federal policies offered a convenient target for the barbs of thwarted Ontario steelmakers, there was considerable wisdom in W.J.A. Donald's 1915 judgment that it was not only the protective policies of the federal government but, more important, 'other conditions, such as high cost of production and sometimes the low price of iron' that were the 'real factors' checking the growth of the iron industry in Canada.[46] These technological and economic forces, governed by continental and at times global conditions and coupled with the inadequacies of the protective policies of Ottawa, stunted the growth of Ontario's primary iron and steel industry. This failure must be balanced against the imperatives of nation-building. In the 1880s and 1890s the primal necessity of a nation drawn together by railways outweighed, in the mind of the Macdonald government, the necessity of autonomous production of iron and steel. In later years, the tension between the established and relatively prosperous secondary iron and steel industry and the precariously balanced existence of the primary industry would plague the tariff calculations of future politicians. Sympathizing with the plight of early primary producers in the 1890s, W.H. Merritt reiterated his concern that Canadians were 'practically standing still, if not actually receding, in our manufacture of pig iron,' whereas the Americans were 'advancing with marvellous strides.' It was, Merritt concluded, a question of 'immense, nay, of vital importance' for the citizens of Ontario to convert the annual volume of imported pig iron equivalent to the output of twenty-seven or twenty-eight blast furnaces into domestically mined and smelted pig iron.[47] By the mid-1890s the iron and steel industry found itself in the largely anomalous position, for the Canadian economy, of relying upon foreign staple exports to feed the demands of the indigenous secondary and tertiary levels of production. As the Ontario Bureau of Mines *Annual Report* gloomily reported in 1892: 'Iron ore has been discovered in numerous localities, east and west, but mostly in association with the Huronian rocks, and some of the deposits are known to be very large, and the quality of the ore is claimed to be good. During recent years however there has been no inducement to explore the country for iron, and little progress has been made in our knowledge of its occurrence, saving in two or three localities beyond Lake Superior.'[48]

2

Iron and Steel in 'New Ontario'

Up to the 1890s, the policies designed to stimulate a Canadian iron and steel industry had fallen almost exclusively within the domain of the federal government. The lacklustre response of would-be industrialists to Ottawa's proddings, however, soon prompted the provincial and munici-pal governments of Ontario into providing their own inducements. While federal policies were predicated on Ottawa's constitutional hegemony over trade, commerce, and certain aspects of industry, the provincial and municipal levels of Canadian federalism saw their opportunity in the active promotion of natural resouce exploitation and remission of certain direct taxes. In the last decade of the century, Ontario began drawing up its own blueprint for industrial development. 'Encouragement of the industry, not its discouragement, is the office and duty of governments,' concluded the commissioners of the 1890 Ontario Royal Commission on Mineral Resources. 'To instruct, to inform, to ascertain and publish facts, to lighten the industry, to enlighten the men employed in it and deal with them in a generous spirit,' they insisted, 'is the true national policy for governments to pursue in promoting the development of our mineral resources.'[1] The councils of innumerable Ontario municipalities echoed these sentiments in near-perfect harmony. The promotion of an iron and steel industry in Ontario from the 1890s was therefore to be a *pas de trois*, with the three levels of government sometimes performing in unison and more often vying for the leading role.

Federal tariff and bounty policies dating from 1879 enjoyed a remarkable durability, outliving their Tory creators after the defeat of 1896 and remaining more or less intact throughout the regime of the Laurier Liberals. Despite the hammering previously administered by Grit critics to Tory tariff policies and bounty largesse, the Liberals, once elected in 1896, reluctantly accepted the role of protector and rewarder of industry.[2] Scepticism about the efficacy of protectionism, however, did persist in Liberal ranks. 'But the fact remains,' Sir Richard Cartwright told Toronto manufacturers in late 1896, 'that though an immense amount of duty has been levied and an immense sum paid in bonuses, the result, up to the present time, is nothing like what was promised.'[3] Citing the overwhelming competitive advantages of American iron smelters, one irate industrialist protested at the same time that 'the government ought to recognize that fact and to give us at least a fair chance to establish this industry here. We want at least five years without being interfered with at all.'[4] Caught on the horns of this dilemma, Finance Minister W.S. Fielding adroitly juggled the tariff and bounty clauses of his 1897 budget in order to appease free trade interests, a traditional bulwark of Grit support, and at the same time satisfy the masters of Canada's 'infant industries.' Sizeable cuts in duty were applied to imports of pig iron, scrap, and steel ingots, while an extensive duty-free list of steelwares was preserved.[5] The brunt of these reductions was borne by the primary level of the industry, while the secondary level of production, already firmly entrenched in the Canadian economy, was less affected. To offset the impact on would-be primary producers, the bounty system was generously expanded. Pig iron smelted from domestic ore was to receive a $3 per ton bounty and iron produced from imported ore, previously excluded from the schedule, now qualified for a $2 per ton bonus. Bounties on puddled bars, ingots, and steel billets were hiked from $2 to $3 a ton. The effect of these changes was to heighten the incentive for the primary iron and steel industry while lessening the stimulus for the local iron ore industry. By admitting imported ore to the bounty schedule, the federal government invited Canadian furnaces to import duty-free American Lake Superior ore to be smelted in Canada where it qualified for a $2 bounty, just a dollar less than the bounty on iron smelted from Canadian ore. A one-dollar differential hardly made the ore from a virtually non-existent Ontario iron ore industry competitive with that of the booming American industry.

The Ontario government first adopted the role of sponsor of a provincial iron and steel industry in an effort to promote the hitherto neglected extractive industry. Responding to the awakening consciousness of the vast northern reaches of the province, the Liberal government of Oliver Mowat had appointed a royal commission to investigate the mineral resources of the province in 1888. The commissioners, including eminent Canadian geologists W.H. Merritt and Robert Bell, advised the government to adopt an active role in the exploitation of the province's mineral resources. 'Explorers, prospectors and miners,' they recommended, 'deserve just consideration and liberal treatment. Mineral lands should be held for development, not for speculation.'[6] In the wake of these proposals, Ontario initiated measures intended to prod the prospector and mining entrepreneur into action. A Bureau of Mines was created in 1891, followed in 1893 by a provincially subsidized School of Mines in Kingston. A year later a Provincial Iron Mining Fund of $125,000 was established to provide a $1 bonus on each ton of domestic ore smelted in Ontario, although this measure was limited to an annual ceiling of $25,000. Queen's Park complemented its encouragement of the iron industry in the early years of the new century with the less direct but equally important subsidization of the Temiskaming and Northern Ontario Railway, which was designed to link the resource-rich wilds of 'New Ontario' with the capital-rich commercial and manufacturing centres of southern Ontario. The provincial government thus created for itself an active role in promoting the exploration and exploitation of the Ontario northland, acting, as H.V. Nelles has perceptively put it, 'as intellectual entrepreneurs, carrying information, ideas and opportunities to labour and capital.'[7]

If Queen's Park was chiefly responsible for fostering a climate in which the primary iron and steel industry might germinate, municipal governments provided the specific conditions in which the industry could actually take root. With the coming of the railway and industrial age in the mid-century, many Ontario towns had indulged in an almost fanatical bout of 'boosterism' in hopes of breathing economic life into their slumbering environs. Civic inducements in the form of tax exemptions, free land, guaranteed loans, and straight cash grants had done much to dictate the location of Ontario industry and to introduce foreign capital to Canadian industrial opportunities.[8] This localized drive for industrialization served to reintroduce the primary smelting of iron and steel in Ontario in the 1890s. In 1893, Hamilton City Council dangled tax exemptions, free land, and a cash bonus before would-be industrialists who were invited to erect a blast furnace and open-hearth steel plant in the city. Once the offer had been eagerly accepted by a New York syndicate, Hamilton extended additional inducements to manufacturers, notably Westinghouse Electric, in a bid to create secondary production dependent on the output of the Hamilton Blast Furnace Company.[9] On the shores of Georgian Bay, the civic fathers of Midland pledged themselves to support of the Midland Iron Company to the extent of a

$50,000 cash bonus and a ten-year exemption from all but nominal municipal taxes.[10] Similar municipal munificence towards aspiring industrialists first brought the hum of industry to Sault Ste Marie in the Algoma District.

From the earliest days of the European penetration of the Canadian interior, the rapids between Lakes Superior and Huron had left an indelible impression on the mind of the explorer. The St Mary's River falls between twenty-one and twenty-three feet, depending on year and season, along its sixty-four-mile length. At the Sault rapids, the river tumbles twenty feet and, when measured in 1890 by a young Canadian engineer, Alan Sullivan, was found to disgorge 125,000 cubic feet of water per second into Lake Huron.[11] Cradled in a trough cut into the Laurentian Shield, the rugged and spectacular terrain surrounding the St Mary's figured prominently in the accounts of the early Jesuit missionaries, not because of its geophysical potential, but because it acted as an impediment to navigation and therefore served as a natural gathering place for the unconverted native peoples. From the beginning, however, there was also a sense of the commercial potential of the area. In 1670–1, for instance, the French explorer Louis Joliet wintered at the Sault after a fruitless search along Lake Superior for copper.[12] Although the reach of the fur trade soon supplanted that of the Bible, the Sault rapids remained an unavoidable part of the voyage to the interior. An awkward but not insurmountable obstacle to the missionary or the *canot du maître*, the St Mary's rapids proved a more formidable obstacle to the larger vessels so necessary for opening up the commercial possibilities of the western interior. In 1798, the Northwest Company constructed a crude canal and lock system to circumvent the cascading waters, but not until 1855 was the first large lock and canal opened on the American side. The American lock, enlarged to a commodious 515 feet in 1870, was a technological response to the demand for cheap bulk transport of iron ore from the pitheads of the Superior ranges to the Lake Erie railheads and on to eastern smelters. By 1872, over a million tons of ore annually moved through the canal.[13] Americans were quick to exploit other aspects of the rapids' potential. In the early 1880s American entrepreneurs sought to harness the St Mary's for hydro power generation. By 1890 the Edison Sault Light and Power Company was feeding the Michigan Sault's appetite for 'white coal' as well as supplying the power needs of a giant Union Carbide plant which produced calcium carbide. American progress in converting the rapids from obstacle to industrial base produced a state of mind in which 'a combined Chicago and New York was believed by every citizen to be the immediate future of the two Soos.'[14]

Progress on the Canadian side of the rapids since the mid-nineteenth century had, however, proceeded at a drowsy pace. With the fur trade in eclipse and the absence of any concerted pressure to open up arterial routes to the west, Sault Ste Marie slumbered in the shadow of its American neighbour. As the adminstrative centre of the Algoma District, the Sault benefited from being made the district judicial seat in 1866, but this did little to enliven the local economy.[15] An attempt was made in the 1870s to open the Canadian side of the rapids by canalization. With the arrival of the Canadian Pacific at the Sault in 1887 the rapids ceased to be a practical impediment to westward expansion. The coming of the railway also served to arrest the gradual decline in the Sault's population, which had shrunk from 879 in 1871 to 780 in 1881.[16] Under the stimulus of the railway, the Sault was incorporated as a town in 1887 and grew to 2414 by 1891, but at this level the town seemed to have reached its limits to growth. If the town was unable to seize economic advantages from canals or railways, the barren, uninviting Algoma hinterland dissuaded all but the hardiest settlers from leaving the train at the Sault. While the settlement literature of the Department of Crown Lands advertised 'lands for thousands of settlers,' the pamphlets could not avoid mentioning that the 'only serious drawback' of the area was the 'broken character' of the land.[17] Such euphemistic descriptions of the Canadian Shield deluded few, with the result that by 1891 there were only 41,856 people spread over the 143,517 square miles of the largest district in the province.[18]

Inhospitable to the farmer, the Algoma District was more attractive to prospectors and miners. Scattered reports of the presence of precious minerals had lured occasional prospectors to the area throughout the 1870s. In 1880, for instance, the English-financed Michipicoten Native Copper Company began operations, only to fall into liquidation by 1887. In evidence given before the 1890 Ontario Royal Commission on Mineral Resources, numerous prospectors and mining engineers, inspired by the Silver Islet bonanza, spoke optimistically of a treasure house of valuable minerals within easy distance of the Sault. Engineer Thomas Keefer described the richness of gold, zinc, galena, and copper ores in the Huronian rock of the north Superior shore. Although one prospector decried the 'general apathy' displayed towards the resources of the area, he prophesied that 'as soon as capitalists fully realize the mineral wealth of the Algoma and Nipissing districts there will be a great improvement.' W.H. Plummer, a prominent Sault businessman and booster, protested that, although several American and English mining firms had come to the Sault area, he did not 'think that so far any company has given the district a fair trial.' The companies, he concluded, had failed because of 'their injudicious expenditure' and lack of 'proper men.'[19] In 1897 the Bureau of Mines *Report* stated that although there were ample indications of valuable ore in the Sault area, 'almost nothing is yet known definitely as to the occurrence of any of these.'[20]

Amid these somnolent circumstances, the civic leaders of the Sault adventurously, if somewhat desperately, took the initiative into their own hands. In 1888, a group of local promoters, spearheaded by W.H. Plummer and the extraordinary politician-cum-promoter James Conmee, purchased a rudimentary power plant erected on the river by an unsuccessful American syndicate. After securing a provincial charter for the Sault Ste Marie Water, Gas and Light Company the municipal promoters attempted to harness the rapids and use the resultant power to attract industry to their stillborn city.[21] Renamed the Ontario Water, Light and Power Company in 1889, the company began construction of a power canal and power house. After the unfortunate cave-in of the head race channel, the company itself collapsed, saddling the municipality with an unfinished power plant and a debt of $263,000.[22] Lacking capital and expertise, the Sault's vision of entering the age of electricity flickered out.

The 'experience, money and imagination'[23] necessary for sustained industrial growth, civic attributes that the Sault seemed unable to muster by itself, soon forcibly presented themselves to the local citizenry in the form of Francis Hector Clergue, an ebullient, hard-selling American entrepreneur. F.H. Clergue was born in Brewer, Maine in 1856, the son of Huguenot parents who had come to the United States in the 1840s.[24] After studying law at Maine State College, Clergue was called to the bar in 1876 and joined a local legal firm. Despite his legal training, Clergue's energies were soon diverted into engineering and promotional activities. Legal work, especially after he became city solicitor, brought him into close contact with the local business community. These men, including future Secretary of State James G. Blaine, provided Clergue with his first circle of backers. In 1880, the Bangor Street Railway was incorporated. A power station on the Penobscot River was built to furnish electricity for the city's new streetcars. The company was an engineering success but was forced into receivership by the heavy cost of building the system. The city inherited the street railway and Clergue turned his attention to new ventures.

Clergue's career from 1885 to the early 1890s was an entrepreneurial pot-pourri. Sensing the tourist potential of his native state, he promoted a resort hotel complex near Bar Harbor. The scheme, which included a ferry to Nova Scotia and a railway up the side of Cadillac Mountain, was never profitable and eventually petered out. The Eastern Trust and Banking Company and a company to export Penobscot ice to New York and Philadelphia met similar fates. Undeterred, Clergue began to look farther afield for opportunities to exercise his promotional skills. In Mobile, Alabama he encoutered an opportunity for industrial integration on a scale much grander than Maine had to offer. Backed by English capital, Clergue founded a bank and then launched plans for a shipyard and drydock complex. Failure again stalked the Maine promoter.

Unable to find an outlet for his promotional skills in his native land, Clergue began to look abroad. In 1888, he formed the Persian Railway and Construction Company with the intention of exploiting the Persian government's desire to acquire railways and public utilities. Buffeted by the imperial aspirations of England and Russia, Persia was an unstable investment bet. None the less, Clergue pushed ahead, using financial backing from, among others, James G. Blaine, now secretary of state in the Harrison administration. The Persian Electric Company and the City of Tehran Waterworks Company were soon added to Clergue's Persian portfolio. In 1889, the whole venture collapsed when Clergue failed to secure a long-term railway concession from the Persian government. Despite the active support of his friends in high office in Washington, Clergue lost out to Russian promoters. He returned to the United States and, in the 1890s, promoted mining ventures in the American West and a power development in Maine. 'This was a period of time,' Clergue later remarked, 'when my good fortune brought me to Sault Ste. Marie, where my good sense has kept me ever since.'[25]

Clergue's greatest promotional weapon was the overpowering salesmanship with which he disarmed potential investors of their doubts and instilled in them the profoundest confidence in both his own abilities and the merits of his schemes. To one contemporary, he was one of the 'greatest word painters in the line of modern promoters.' 'His well-disciplined mind, scientific knowledge, calm, tireless enthusiasm,' commented Principal G.M. Grant of Queen's University, 'along with remarkable powers of exposition, made me say "There is no such word as impossible in the dictionary of that man."'[26] Clergue was thus an archetypal 'captain of industry' of the Veblen mould, 'a man of workmanlike force and creative insight into the community's needs, who stood out on a footing of self-help, took large chances for large ideals ...'[27] He would undoubtedly have won lasting repute as a capitalist of the classic American variety, bringing capital and opportunity together for profit, if it had not been for the tendency of his ventures to fail with 'such monstrous regularity.'[28] Caught in the spell of his own visions, Clergue seldom measured up to the practical challenge of his bold plans and all too often embroiled his backers in reckless overexpenditure on grandly conceived but poorly implemented projects. 'As his meteoric career subsequently revealed,' Ontario Deputy Minister of Mines, T.W. Gibson later noted, 'Clergue's vision occasionally outran his judgment, and at times he took things for granted which had not been proven.'[29] 'Mr. Clergue just willed that a wilderness should become an industrial community,' Sir James Dunn somewhat more kindly noted years later, 'and laid it out on a broad and generous scale and the chinks are gradually being filled in.'[30]

Clergue's initial attraction to the Sault was not for its potential as a base for iron and steel production but as a source of plentiful and cheap hydroelectric power. Touring central Canada at the behest of American capitalists in search of investment opportunities, Clergue was invited to assess the incomplete Sault power project. Loosing his eloquent and persuasive selling talents, he sought the backing of the Sault civic fathers and Philadelphia capital to harness the unused energy of the rapids, which to this time had remained little more than 'a health resort for the whitefish,' as he picturesquely described them. Clergue bought the town's stake in the defunct power company in late 1894 and promised to pump $200,000 into the local economy within a year. In return for this, the city council extended a twenty-year exclusive franchise for its water and electricity supply and a ten-year tax exemption on Clergue's endeavours.[31] Returning to the United States, Clergue secured the financial backing of eastern coal and railroad financiers E.V. Douglas, E.J. Berwin, and John Terry, using their resources to incorporate the Lake Superior Power Company under Ontario charter with a capitalization of $2 million.

From this kernel Clergue built his sprawling network of Sault industries, all dependent on and integrated by the power generated by the rapids. After the power company was supplemented by the Tagona Water and Light Company and the Sault Ste Marie Pulp and Paper Company, the Consolidated Lake Superior Company (CLS) was incorporated under Connecticut law to act as an umbrella or parent company for future additions at the Sault. With a capitalization of $117 million, the CLS was used by Clergue in the years up to 1902 as a corporate brood-hen to hatch a wide range of subsidiaries encompassing pulp and paper, transit, railway, and, most significantly, steel activities.[32]

Clergue's ability to attract Philadelphia capital to back his Canadian ambitions was in many ways not surprising. In the years since the Civil

War, Philadelphia had emerged as a centre of American mercantile wealth and entrepreneurship. The city's business and social elite became a driving force in American railroading, coal-mining, and steelmaking. Philadelphia gentlemen, one historian has observed, became an American business aristocracy in the gilded age and, as such, exercised a powerful sway over the nation's business.[33] Philadelphian businessmen like Joseph Wharton helped, for instance, to shape the transition of ironmaking into steelmaking as the late nineteenth century unfolded. While the city itself did not experience the brunt of the steelmaking revolution, its business leaders were active in promoting the growth of steel mills in Bethlehem, Harrisburg, and Johnstown. From this base, some Phildelphians went on to become absentee owners of more distant steelworks.[34]

The Philadelphian names which appeared in Clergue's promotional literature were prominent representatives of the city's business caste. Although born in Philadelphia, Edward Julius Berwind lived in New York where he presided over an extensive empire of coal and realty companies. Samuel Frederic Houston was president of the Real Estate Trust Company of Philadelphia and chairman of the board of Pennsylvania Sugar Company. John Taylor Terry was a New York lawyer with ties throughout the banking and trust company community. Samuel Rae was a vice-president, later president, of the Pennsylvania Railway. Simon Gratz was a member of one of Philadelphia's wealthiest Jewish mercantile families.[35] It was Clergue's persuasive promotional talents that induced 'capitalists' of this stature to back a hitherto unknown company in a northern Canadian town far beyond the social and business pale of Philadelphia. Through these patrons of industry Clergue was able to establish the credentials of his fledgling enterprise in the minds of the myriad small investors who would eventually stake their savings on the venture. In later years, Clergue made frequent reference to the capital generated by Philadelphia, 'that enlightened community' which was 'really responsible for the present happy auguries of Sault Ste. Marie.'[36]

If Philadelphian capital augured well for the civic fortunes of Sault Ste Marie, it soon also brought hope to the stillborn provincial iron ore industry. Clergue's interest in exploiting the iron ore potential of the Algoma district was first aroused in the late 1890s at a time when many of the governmental incentives designed to foster a Canadian iron industry were beginning to show signs of fruition in Ontario. With the prospect of both federal and provincial bounties and the municipal sponsoring of blast furnace companies, the search for iron ore in Northern Ontario had intensified.[37] Canadian prospectors were joined in their search by Americans eager to locate exploitable sources of ore to supplement or competitively undercut Superior ores. By 1894, the Cleveland Rolling Mill was backing exploration at the Stobie mine east of the Sault while the Belmont iron mine near Cobourg had been leased to American interests.[38] Canadian exploitation of iron ore also accelerated in the late 1890s with mining activity at scattered southeastern mines, such as Calabogie and Madoc, and in isolated northern locations near the Seine, Michipicoten, and Matawin rivers.[39] In 1896, for instance, iron ore of 47.26 per cent purity was reported in the basin of the Montreal River, north of the Sault.[40] While overshadowed by more valuable nickel and silver discoveries, iron was in its small way contributing to the unfolding of 'New Ontario.'

The growth of Ontario iron mining was paralleled and prodded by the progress of the primary smelting industry. In December 1895, the Hamilton blast furnace was 'blown in' and in the next three years produced 165,653 tons of pig iron.[41] Although the Bureau of Mines' *Annual Report* proudly noted that the technical advisor at the Hamilton furnace was trained at the Kingston School of Mines, the fledgling operation was in fact heavily reliant on Mesabi ore, Pennsylvanian coal, and American technical expertise. Ontario's other two blast furnaces, at Deseronto and Midland, also imported large quantities of Michigan ore, only 'experimenting' with native ores.[42] While dependence on foreign ore and coal remained high, the Ontario iron and steel industry had at last developed a primary capacity for smelting pig iron. As a result, provincial furnaces produced a total of 543,762 tons of pig iron between 1896 and 1902 and, in the three years after steel production began in 1900, 86,092 tons of steel. 288,381 tons of native Ontario ore were fed into provincial furnaces in these years, as compared with 496,472 tons of imported ore. Such progress aroused hopes for national self-sufficiency in this vital industry. 'It may be hoped,' the Bureau of Mines *Report* stated in 1903, 'that when the time comes for mining iron ore on a large scale in Ontario, the demand for pig iron and steel for use in our Province and country will have correspondingly increased, and that we may see the ore smelted into pig, the pig converted into steel, and the steel worked up into manufactured articles – all within the bounds of Ontario or at any rate of the Dominion of Canada.'[43] A tremendous stride in this direction was made by F.H. Clergue's development of the Helen mine in the Michipicoten area, north of the Sault. For the next six decades the fluctuating fortunes of the Helen were to serve as a barometer of the whole Ontario iron ore industry, a history of long droughts and brief periods of frantic activity.

In the summer of 1897 two itinerant prospectors stumbled on a vein of hematite ore beside a lake several miles inland from Michipicoten harbour.[44] Reported to be 58.7 per cent pure, the ore was an immediately attractive commercial proposition. 'In general,' the Bureau of Mines *Report* boasted, 'one may say that the Michipicoten iron bearing rocks resemble, often quite closely, those of the famous iron ranges of Minnesota and Michigan, the greatest producers of high grade iron ore in the world.'[45] Aroused by the prospect of an exploitable body of rich, brown hematite, Clergue purchased the Boyer Lake claim, named it the Helen mine after his sister and proceeded with his usual bravado and confidence. 'Scientists,' he told the Toronto Board of Trade, 'have said that there was no real hematite on the Canadian side of Lake Superior; that God had put it all on the American side of Lake Superior. I always thought that a mistake and now I am ready to prove it. We will show you an iron mine up there equal to anything on the other side.'[46]

To tap the Helen's wealth, Clergue reasoned, a railway was absolutely necessary. Once again the dominion and provincial governments proved eager and generous benefactors of private enterprise. In 1899, a federal charter was obtained for the Algoma Central Railway and surveys were hastily initiated. Renamed the Algoma Central and Hudson Bay Railway in 1901, the line was endowed with a $6400 per mile federal subsidy and a provincial land grant of two million acres.[47] Clergue reciprocated the government's largesse with an extravagant promise to implant ten thousand settlers in 'New Ontario' and to exploit the Helen's iron ore potential. By 1903, fifty-six miles of tortuously twisted and steeply climbing track had been laid north from the Sault, including a fifteen-mile spur line from Magpie Junction past the mine to Michipicoten harbour. The start of mining operations at the Helen in 1900 dramatically increased the amount of iron ore mined in the province. The meagre total of 16,911 tons of native ore mined in 1899 grew steadily through the early years of the new century to 357,288 tons in 1902, of which the Helen provided 334,231 tons. Four iron mines in eastern Ontario contributed a paltry 23,057 tons.[48] An exploration department of the corporation, established by Clergue to ferret out additional sources of iron ore, spent over $100,000 in 1901; 'an amount,' the Bureau of Mines reproachfully pointed out, 'quite in excess of that which the Government devotes yearly to similar surveys for the whole province.'[49]

To complement the Helen, Clergue chartered the Algoma Steel Company in April 1901 and began erection of American-made Bessemer steel converters and blast furnaces.[50] Inexplicably, Clergue opted to construct the steel furnaces before the iron smelters, thus forcing the infant plant to rely on costly pig iron purchased from other primary producers, notably the Canada Iron Furnace Company in Midland.[51] Clergue's vision of steelmaking at the Sault thus defied the traditional wisdom that the ore, the least weighty ingredient in the process, should be brought to the fuel supply. On the American side of Lake Superior this wisdom had prevailed and, despite a brief attempt to smelt Mesabi ore in Michigan in the 1870s, the smelting of American ore took place in close proximity to eastern coal.[52] The production of steel at the Sault, Clergue reasoned to the contrary, could be profitably undertaken because of the abundance of hydro power and ore, coupled with the ease and cheapness of water transportation. He also, rather naively, planned to minimize the Sault's coal requirements by operating his blast furnaces on large quantities of local charcoal. Besides the fact that the Sault steel plant had Lake Superior as its 'mill pond,' the process of making iron and steel was now, as one like-minded observer commented, under 'scientific control' and therefore 'the suitability of any given place for producing pig iron or steel resolves itself into a question of proximity to raw material and to the market for the finished product.'[53] Clergue needed fewer words to convey the same message: 'From the days of the first baboon there has never been an industrial failure where the raw material existed to the best advantage, combined with the force necessary for its transformation into practical use.'[54]

On 18 February 1902, Algoma's Bessemer converter was 'blown-in' and fed with Midland pig iron made from Helen ore. With the rolling of the first steel rails in Ontario in May 1902, Clergue's vision of an integrated steelworks at the Sault was virtually complete, although the blast furnaces were still under construction. When Premier Ross visited the Sault in April 1902, Clergue boasted that seven thousand people were engaged in the operations of his industries and that a monthly payroll of $170,000 was being pumped directly into the community.[55] At the same time he confidently assured the Sault citizenry that there was 'no industrial undertaking on the globe where there is a more complete absence of recklessness, and a more complete presence of the soundest and most conservative and logical business reasoning.'[56] The subsequent history of Algoma Steel was to belie the rosy predictions of Francis H. Clergue.

Algoma had found its origins in the inducements of the Sault municipality, but it was in the largesse of the federal and provincial governments that it found its means of survival. Once in production, Algoma became eligible for federal and provincial bounty payments on both its pig iron and steel output. Through the period of July 1902 to June 1906, Algoma collected $988,433 in federal payments.[57] The bounty was seen as the birthright of the infant iron and steel industry, one which had grown increasingly more permanent as Liberal Finance Minister Fielding became more reluctant to remove the industry from the crib of government assistance. While Clergue could be sure of the cooperation of the other Canadian primary producers, especially the Hamilton Blast Furnace and Nova Scotia Steel and Coal companies, in pleading with Ottawa for continued bounties, there was less unanimity on the question of increased tariff protection for the nascent industry. Clergue perceptively argued that Algoma Steel could best carve out a prosperous industrial future for itself by capitalizing on the enormous Canadian demand for steel rails, a demand previously conceded to foreign producers.[58] With plans afoot for two new transcontinentals and a steady demand for track renewal and branch lines, a vast potential existed for the Canadian production of rails, provided adequate tariff protection could be secured. This quest for federal tariff and subsidy assistance for steel rail manufacture first brought Algoma Steel to the corridors of power in Ottawa.

Ministers of finance in the National Policy era had habitually taken refuge, whenever pressured for a tariff on steel rails, in the proposition that tariffs would be applied whenever a railmaking industry displayed signs of life. Pointing to the Consolidated Lake Superior Corporation's large investment in the Sault works by 1901, Clergue persistently reminded Prime Minister Laurier that the time had come for the government to honour its promise. 'We are just starting in operation on a steel rail mill, costing with its blast furnace and other accompanying plants over five million dollars,' Clergue wrote to Ottawa. 'We have solicited business of all the railroads in Canada, but are confronted with the statement that American manufacturers do not propose to allow us to take any orders ... There being no duty on rails into Canada what is the prospect of successful operations of our plant under such conditions?'[59] Clergue alleged that American producers were 'dumping' rails at $25 a ton, three dollars below the prevailing price. He thus introduced a theme that would long typify debates between Canadian steel producers and their legislators, that of the American steel industry as predator, ever circling and ever ready to devour the struggling Canadian industry. Domestic producers, Clergue insisted, could not hope to compete with the integrated giants of the United States industry, primarily because the Canadian firms would 'get to the end of our purse long before the American rail makers will.'[60]

This line of argument had an ironic double twist, for while it held out the gloomy prospect of the abrupt extinction of the Canadian industry, it also implicitly reminded Laurier that extensive American investments in Canada could not be left unguarded. 'I am satisfied that if disaster should overtake this company,' A.E. Dyment, Algoma East Liberal MP and Soo booster, told his federal leader, 'it would be impossible to secure any further capital for the development of what is known as "New Ontario" for many years to come.'[61] To impress these propositions on the federal government, Clergue lavishly entertained Laurier and various other Canadian political luminaries at the Sault, where the Algoma works were displayed as living proof of the wisdom of federal policies and where the politicians could be introduced to Philadelphian financiers, each to form confidence-inspiring impressions of the others' integrity and ability. On one such occasion, Clergue invited the Lauriers to the Sault, where they would enjoy a private guest house, guard dogs, and a 'French family' to wait on their table and make them feel at home.[62] Especially close to Clergue in federal Liberal ranks were Public Works Minister J. Israel Tarte and Senators J.K. Kerr and Raoul Dandurand, all of whom accompanied the industrialist to public functions and made representations for him abroad.[63] Kerr and Dandurand, in particular, proved tireless stalwarts for the Sault industries, incessantly urging Laurier to nurture Clergue's steelworks with sturdy tariffs. 'C'est un question de vie ou de mort pour sa compagnie,' Dandurand bluntly told Laurier in early 1903.[64]

Clergue's persistent lobbying in Ottawa won him two early concessions from the Laurier government. In late 1901 the government amended the Railway Act to stipulate that all federally subsidized railways be required to use Canadian-made steel rails, when competitively available. This rather 'lenient regulation' was followed by a more substantial piece of government assistance, a federally sponsored rail contract for the Intercolonial Railway.[65] Under PC 2303 of 9 October 1900, the Lake Superior Power Company was contracted to supply 150,000 tons of rails over five years at a guaranteed price of $32.50 a ton. The contract was remarkable in several respects. Unlike earlier federal measures to foster the industry, the contract applied not to the industry as a whole but to one specific company. Furthermore, the contract was granted to a company that had yet to roll a single rail, although Clergue promised full production by 1902. Finally, the contract was let without tender or parliamentary debate just a month before the federal election of November 1900. Like the bounty system, the rail contract was an adroit attempt to pacify the demands of primary steel consumers with those of primary steel producers intent on a larger share of the home market. As a compromise, it proved a dismal failure.

In the session of 1901, Laurier and his minister of railways, A.G. Blair, were exposed to withering criticism from the Tory benches. Led by their new leader R.L. Borden, the Conservatives castigated the 'secret' rail pact as a piece of pre-election chicanery. Borden pointed out that since the contract had been made the price of rails had dropped and the government was now obliged to pay Algoma as much as $7 a ton above the current American price for rails.[66] Discomfited by the attacks, Laurier spoke of the 'misfortune' of Canada's reliance on foreign railmakers, while obliquely admitting that Blair had erred in letting the contract in so surreptitious a fashion. For his part, Blair defended the contract because it would serve to establish a 'permanent' rail industry in Canada and to generate employment, goals he felt 'would appeal very strongly to the sympathetic consideration of the Canadian people.'[67]

By the early years of the new century, Laurier had little option but to support Clergue's ventures. Fearful that failure at the Sault would scuttle an important new national industry and deeply tarnish Canada's attractiveness to American investors, Laurier reluctantly gave in to the implications of the situation which Clergue had placed him in. Hounded by the Kerr-Dandurand lobby and advised by Premier Ross in Toronto of the 'great benefit to the Province and to the Dominion' of the Sault enterprise, the prime minister accommodated Clergue's *fait accompli*, although not without serious misgivings about the Soo King's integrity. 'J'ai dit dix fois à Clergue,' he grumbled in early 1903, 'que j'étais prêt, pour ma part, à imposer des droits sur les rails d'acier du moment que nous pourrions en fabriquer au Canada, et Clergue n'est pas encore en état de le faire.'[68]

Laurier's inclination to succour the vision of F.H. Clergue was further demonstated in October 1903 when legislation was passed to allow Ottawa to impose by order-in-council a $7 a ton duty on imported rails. In August 1904, with rail mills at the Sault and Sydney finally in operation, the $7 a ton duty was enacted.[69] A major concession to Clergue and the Sault industries, the tariff instantly raised the hackles of many Canadian steel consumers. Even before the official announcement, railway interests rallied in defence of their long-standing right to low-duty steel imports. An irate Sir Thomas Shaughnessy of the CPR cabled Fielding in April 1903 that Clergue 'cannot make rails to meet the requirements of ourselves nor could anybody else in Canada. Time enough to talk of duty when efficient rail mill established ... Mr. Clergue has been unable to turn out rails that we could use although given an opportunity of doing so.'[70] C.M. Hays of the Grand Trunk sternly warned Fielding that a $7 a ton duty would 'add to the burden the railway companies already are carrying.'[71] Retaliating against such allegations, Clergue assured Ottawa that the capacity of his Algoma works 'exceeds all the requirements of street and steam railway uses in Canada last year,' and that an upward tariff hike was imperative 'to prevent the United States Steel Trust from destroying the usefulness of the industry so established.'[72] Most compelling in Clergue's arsenal of arguments was the calculation that, while the Algoma works would annually generate $2.5 million for the Canadian economy, this could only be achieved behind a tariff wall. 'Steel plants *must* operate at full capacity,' he lectured the prime minister.[73] Laurier proved a dutiful student and, with the imposition of the $7 duty on heavy rails, Clergue won a major victory for Algoma and the young Canadian steel industry.

The first rails rolled at the Sault were the product as much of the policies of sympathetic Liberal governments in Ottawa and Toronto as of F.H. Clergue and Philadelphia capital. Clergue's plans for a rail mill had flattered the hopes of federal politicians for an autonomous Canadian primary steel industry and at the same time appealed to provincial aspirations for the well-rounded economic development of 'New Ontario.' The Sault industries were befriended by the Liberal government of George Ross, who saw in the endeavour a potential industrial base for Northern Ontario, a coordinating centre in the bid to colonize the alleged agricultural richness of the 'Clay Belt,' and a beachhead for an assault on the mineral wealth of the northern hinterland.[74] Appreciative of the support of the provincial Liberals, the Lake Superior Corporation had backed the Grit candidate, C.N. Smith of the Sault *Express*, in the 1902 provincial election. Unable to unseat the Tory incumbent that year, the corporation again promoted the candidacy of Smith in a 'more flagrant manner' during a 1903 Algoma East by-election.[75] Smith took the seat, but only after the *Minnie M*, a small steamer owned by the corporation, was employed to ferry Americans to the Helen polling station to cast fraudulent ballots. After losing the seat in an election trial and being exposed to considerable political embarrassment over the questionable navigations of the *Minnie M*, the Liberals amazingly regained the riding in the 1905 provincial election. Despite the decisive shift in provincial loyalty from the Ross Liberals to the Whitney Tories in that year, Sault voters backed the party that had given their town industrial life.

For an infant industry on which federal and provincial Liberal politicians had staked so much, Algoma Steel had a disappointing childhood. It failed both operationally and financially. Despite Clergue's assurances that Algoma would fulfil all the rail requirements of Canada's railways, the company did not achieve full operational capability until June 1904. By that time it had failed to meet its contract obligations to the Intercolonial. Similarly, when an early batch of Algoma rails was found to be of deficient quality, the Canadian Northern, Mackenzie and Mann's new transcontinental, reneged on its Algoma contracts and turned to German suppliers. In the wake of this cancellation Clergue was forced to shut down the steel plant in December 1902, after only 33,950 tons of rails had been rolled. Chastened in his zeal for Clergue's rosy promises, Laurier wrote to the Algoma president in April 1903 to call his attention 'to the fact that similar statements were presented to us last year, and even the year before, which proved to be over-sanguine. I do not say this merely for fault finding, but simply to remind you that circumstances can arise ... to put back these circumstances.'[76]

Unfortunately for Clergue, similar unforeseen circumstances continued to arise with such embarrassing frequency that on 18 September 1903 the entire Sault complex closed down when the parent company could not cover its payroll. Up to that date in 1903, only 1243 tons of rails had been rolled. At the root of Clergue's problems lay two basic flaws in the conception and implementation of his enterprise, flaws which undid the logic of his industrial strategy for steelmaking at the Sault. In the first place, Algoma was not a balanced industrial operation. Because its own blast furnaces were as yet incomplete, the company's Bessemer converters were forced to depend on costly pig iron smelted at Midland and elsewhere.[77] There was no smooth, cost-efficient flow of iron from pithead to finishing mill at the Sault. Not until 1905–6 did Algoma complete its own blast furnaces. While the absence of furnaces was overcome in relatively short order, the second flaw in Clergue's imposing industrial edifice was to have a more permanently debilitating effect on corporate fortunes. From the smelting of the first steel at the Sault, Clergue had conceived of Algoma as a rail producer. This dependence on the needs of the national railways proved to be both its greatest strength and its greatest weakness. Bound to rail manufacture by an inflexible and heavy capital outlay, Algoma was destined to live a precarious boom or bust existence, ever reliant on the fluctuating demand of the railways for rails. A wise business strategy in the heady years of railway expansion at the turn of the century, Clergue's commitment to rolling rails shackled Algoma to an industrial orientation unsuited to the steel demands of future periods of national growth.

Algoma's dependence on rail production was given added rigidity by the Liberal tariff revisions of 1906–7 which enshrined the $7 duty on heavy rails as the protected mainstay of the primary steel industry in Canada. Clergue's hope had been to use rail production to gain sufficient momentum to diversify the plant's product line. This ambition over-looked certain political realities. Faced with the increasingly vocal demands of the agrarian and secondary manufacturing lobbies for low-duty imports on raw steel, the Laurier government struggled to accommodate the divergent interests of primary steel producers and steel consumers. Clergue, joined by Henry M. Whitney, the American pro-moter of Cape Breton steel, persisted in his demand for continued tariff and bounty assistance on rails while holding out the promise that 'a year or two should see this industry permanently and successfully established, when it may be assumed that this bounty will be discontinued.'[78] Acutely aware of the dangers of overreliance on a protected rail market, Clergue launched a campaign for a more extensive panoply of protection. Carrying his case to the Fielding tariff inquiry in 1905, he assailed the low tariff demands of western farmers, whose fields 'require but a little tickling of the plow to yield almost a fortune in a single season.' After sketching the rigorous life of industry on the Shield, where nothing could survive 'except the Indian,' Clergue was forthright in declaring that 'our industries require special action by the Government.'[79]

Clergue's request for 'special action' to allow Algoma profitable manufacture of structural steel for bridges and rail cars elicited a visceral reaction from steel consumers. As early as 1902, the president of Canadian Bridge had flatly declared that it was 'perfectly safe to say that no steel producing company in Canada will be able to cut any important figure in furnishing our raw materials for many years to come ... Mr. Clergue will not be able to supply any portion of our wants until he has installed open hearth furnaces.'[80] Clergue had in fact established his steel plant with Bessemer technology just when the American industry was rapidly converting to open-hearth steelmaking. While Bessemer steel was ideal for railmaking, open-hearth steel was better suited to the increas-ingly varied uses to which the metal was being put in the new century. Further opposition to Clergue's demands came from the president of Massey-Harris, who concluded that 'time' and 'experience' were neces-sary to produce 'reliable output' in a steel industry in which 'too much capital had been hurriedly expended.'[81] Faced with Clergue's already fractured credibility, Fielding sided with the secondary manufacturers. 'There is,' he told Clergue in 1905, 'an important difference between what you propose and the condition that existed in reference to the duty on rails. In the case of steel rails you were asking for a duty for a particular article which was your finished product. No other manufacturer was standing at the door with a club to object but if you propose to affect the price of what would be the material of some other manufacturer he will be standing at the door ready to object.'[82]

While Clergue protested that the railways were intentionally victimizing the steelmakers,[83] Fielding's patience was exhausted. The tariff revision of 1906 put into solid, and what was to prove lasting, form the tariff tinkering of the previous decade. Products in which the Canadian steel industry had shown some proficiency, notably rails, were afforded considerable protection at all levels of the tariff and the anti-dumping schedules. Products in which the Canadian industry had yet to show any prowess but for which secondary producers had a healthy demand were left either duty-free or with low protection. Having left iron ore on the duty-free list, Fielding announced that the bounty system was to be phased out over a period that was eventually stretched to 1912. '[T]hese industries.' he declared, 'should become self-sustaining – at all events, they should no longer have any claim for bounties.'[84] Primary steel producers vigorously protested this retraction, contending that the industry lacked the stamina to withstand American competition.[85] When the stream of bounty payments eventually dried up in 1912, representatives of the primary steelmakers petitioned the newly elected Borden government for compensating tariff increases, 'declaring that the protection afforded the iron and steel industries ... was not quite inadequate to enable them to hold the business they had hitherto had under the assistance of the bounties.'[86] Confronted by western antipathy to any further assistance for the eastern steel industry, the Tories adhered to the decision of their Liberal predecessors.[87]

The solidification of the iron and steel tariff structure in the 1906 revisions had a crucial, lasting significance for the Canadian economy. On the one hand, a small core of steel products, notably rails, had been adequately protected, thereby placing Canadian producers on a competitive footing with foreign producers. The security of a relatively impregnable market in some products had to be balanced against the broad spectrum of steel items still permitted low-tariff entry to Canada. Relations within Canadian steel were hereafter characterized by the constant struggle between the primary producers, anxious to minimize their precarious reliance on a restricted line of products, and the consumers of steel in the manufacturing sector, zealously guarding their right to low-cost imports of raw steel. Progress at the primary level of the industry would in future be governed by its ability to establish sufficient productive capacity to displace various iron and steel imports.

These tensions within the steel industry repeatedly caught the federal government on the horns of a dilemma. In 1912, for instance, representatives of the primary producers reminded Borden that the 'manufacturing of the most important lines of agricultural implements, of springs, axles, tools, bedsteads, windmills, etc., have in effect, free iron and steel ... These exemptions are one of the main causes of the difficulties in which we find ourselves ...'[88] From the other flank, Ottawa was confronted with vehement opposition to tariff alteration from steel consumers in secondary industry. H.S. Howland, of the Graham Nail Company, warned Borden that, should primary producers be afforded adequate protection to enter into the production of wire for nails, the effect on established nail producers would be disastrous.[89]

Whereas the established secondary iron and steel producers were fairly cohesive in their defence of high protection on finished steel goods and low duties on raw steel, the primary producers often suffered from a lack of common purpose. The secondary manufacturers were ably represented on the federal scene by the Canadian Manufacturers Association.[90] The primary producers frequently could not find common ground on which to stand. There could be, for instance, little accord between Ontario and Nova Scotia primary producers on the question of duties on coking coal. Nova Scotia Steel and Coal was anxious to exclude American coal from Canada, thereby enlarging the market for Maritime coal. Ontario producers like Algoma, on the other hand, lobbied intensively for free entry of American coal.[91] Further differences could be seen among the Ontario producers themselves. Algoma, with its heavy emphasis on primary production, eagerly sought to broaden the base of its protection, whereas the Steel Company of Canada, the product of a 1910 merger, had less reason to seek added protection because of its limited primary production and its already well-diversified output in the protected areas of secondary production.[92] From the beginning Algoma therefore learned that it would be forced to stand alone in its struggle for industrial survival.

F.H. Clergue had in one sense acquitted himself admirably as an industrial pioneer. He had won a high degree of tariff protection for rails, on the production of which Algoma had so heavily staked its future. But this strategy augured well only as long as Canadian demand for rails remained high. Any downswing in railway demand would expose the corporation's lack of diversification. Thus, despite the boldness and verve of his original conception, Clergue had bequeathed the Sault a steel industry lacking in well-rounded productive capacity. This deficiency was to haunt Algoma's operations for the next three decades. 'Whatever credit is due to Mr. Clergue,and I give him first place for courage and a boundless imagination,' Sir James Dunn recalled in 1934, 'the fact remains that neither he nor his successors built a sound steel industry. Its earning power from the start was the rail mill. I am speaking at random but I suppose two thirds of the present rail mileage of Canada was rolled at the Soo.'[93]

Clergue's troubled legacy at the Sault lay not only in the unbalanced nature of the Algoma plant, but also in the snarled and overextended financial structure of the Consolidated Lake Superior Corporation. On 18 September 1903 the corporation went bankrupt and was forced to turn its workers away at the gates, thereby bringing its varied operations to a standstill. The Toronto *Daily News* reported on 22 September that the company's liabilities totalled $11,070,000. Clergue's dream had been dashed by a combination of factors, most of which had their roots in his overzealous and headlong approach to corporate management and organization. In a Herculean but futile bid to maintain personal control over all aspects of Sault operations, Clergue had simultaneously tried to play the role of promoter, financier, and executive, predictably failing in all tasks. In the course of his slide to defeat he managed to tangle the financial and managerial affairs of the corporation in such a way as to hobble its operations for the next thirty years. In the words of the Toronto *Daily News*, Clergue was 'an indomitable promoter, an ingratiating canvasser, a buoyant and slightly irresponsible manager ... in whose intellectual bias must be sought the reasons for the financial and commercial peculiarities of the Consolidated Company.'[94]

While the original vision of a family of industries mutually dependent on the water power of the St Mary's had a general economic validity, there was little economic benefit and great liability involved in Clergue's rapid diversification of the corporation into railways, steamships, traction companies, and even an express company. Many of these subsidiaries were launched in such a reckless and ill-considered fashion that their ultimate profitability was clearly never considered. The Algoma Central and Hudson Bay Railway was, for instance, routed over such rugged territory that it soon encountered exceptionally high construction costs, forcing Clergue to plead for special aid from both Toronto and Ottawa. The local citizenry were soon jokingly referring to it as the All Curves and High Bridges Railway. In 1905, Clergue begged Laurier to guarantee the principal and interest of the Michipicoten branch line at the rate of $30,000 per mile, claiming that this was 'not an ordinary line into a wilderness.'[95] Clergue's successors were to discover that the weaker links in the chain of Sault industries were a permanent liability to those which managed to sustain themselves profitably. Clergue's Consolidated Lake Superior Corporation was little more than an unstable symbiosis, brought together by the joint desire of Philadelphian investors to exact a profit from their investment and of Ontario politicians to see their vision of 'New Ontario' flower.

In retrospect, it was easy to criticize the financial venality of Clergue's Sault industries. What bears remembering is the euphoria that surrounded the birth of the corporation; the sense of confidence which Clergue engendered in politicians, citizens, and investors alike. Aroused by his powerful rhetoric and overawed by his flamboyant displays (which included fireworks and welcoming bands for those arriving to inspect the Sault industries), few retained their better judgment. To the people of Sault Ste Marie and Ontario in general, F.H. Clergue was an industrial messiah, sent to lead them to the same land of prosperity which their American neighbours occupied.[96] As one Toronto newspaper put it, Clergue 'thought in centuries.' One suspects, given lack of evidence that he was strongly motivated by personal financial gain, that Clergue was himself often caught up in his own rhetorical spell. Until the cracks began appearing, few doubted the integrity of the Clergue empire. One prominent exception was Byron Walker, the president of the Bank of Commerce in Toronto. From the outset, Walker refused to make advances to the corporation.[97] Few shared his scepticism.

Byron Walker's misgivings about the financial underpinnings of the Sault venture began to be widely shared only belatedly. By July 1903 the corporation had issued $102 million in capital stock of which $70 million was held by Philadelphia interests.[98] Although the corporation claimed in June 1902 to have assets of $99,987,654.50, there was considerable evidence to suggest that the Sault industries were 'overcapitalized' or 'watered.'[99] Opponents of the primary industry's tariff demands revelled in maligning the motivation of steel promoters. As one incensed steel consumer charged, the promoters of the Sault enterprise deserved little sympathy because they 'started their business and ran it, not on business principles, but for the sake of what they could make out of it in a stock-jobbing way.'[100] The discrepancy between the earning power of the corporation's subsidiaries and its financial obligations to its investors finally brought the giant at the Sault to its knees in September 1903. In April 1903, investors alarmed by the faltering fortunes of the Sault industries had forced the replacement of Clergue as general manager by

Cornelius Shields, formerly general manager at Dominion Steel.[101] Poor corporate structure and inadequate management were symptoms of the deeper problem of absentee ownership. As E.H. Bronson privately noted to Premier Ross at the height of the Sault 'smash-up,' it was 'the original shareholders, who seem to have made themselves more or less culpable in that they have so largely watered the stocks of the various companies as to make the consolidation unwieldy and in that way precipitate the present crisis.'[102]

The immediate cause of the stoppage was the failure of the corporation to honour a $5,050,000 loan from Speyer and Company of New York. Severely shaken by the fact that 350 militia men had to be called in from Toronto to contain the wrath of 3500 unpaid Sault workers,[103] Clergue embarked on a whirlwind campaign to restore financial confidence in the industries. As he later told Laurier, he had 'solicited the cooperation' of Senators Dandurand and Kerr to visit England and the United States 'for purpose of assuring capitalists in these money centres of the commercial importance of these industries.' Dandurand carried with him a letter signed by Laurier expressing the 'sincere hope' that the Algoma mill would reopen, while Kerr was 'especially commissioned' by the Ontario goverment to impress on foreign investors 'the strong desire of the people of Ontario and of Canada for the successful establishment of this rail mill.'[104] Interim assistance was forthcoming from the Ontario government on 1 October when Premier Ross guaranteed by order-in-council the corporation's now overdue wages. Trying desperately to ward off the sale of the Sault properties by Speyer and Company in New York, Clergue dashed between New York and Philadelphia proposing various schemes for the refinancing of the corporation. Although he was successful in gaining reelection to the corporation's board in late October, Clergue was unable to stave off the mounting corporate debt, with the result that the corporation was put into liquidation by court order on 14 December 1903. At a court sale in New York on the following day certain holdings of the Clergue empire were bought by Speyer and Company for $4.5 million.[105]

Not until late February 1904 was Clergue able to reconstruct the shattered corporation. Rechristened the Lake Superior Corporation (LSC) with head offices in New York, the new company had a dehydrated capitalization of $40 million stock, $3 million income bonds, and $10 million first mortgage bonds,[106] a considerable reduction from the bloated $117 million of the previous corporation. Control of the Sault complex remained firmly in Philadelphian hands, although it was now chartered under New Jersey law. The debts of the old company were funded with fixed charges 'of about $600,000,' an obligatory encumbrance for the new corporation. When the directors of the LSC found in early March of 1904 that there was a discrepancy of $8 million between the $35 million share capital subscribed and the $27 million actually paid in, the corporation was again in jeopardy. The reorganization committee was able to supply $6 million of this money on an *ad hoc* basis and turned to the Liberal government of Ontario for the remaining $2 million, 'not as a bonus,' Clergue stressed, 'but merely as a loan of credit.'[107] Premier Ross presented a bill to the legislature on 8 March stipulating that a two-year, $2-million guarantee was to be extended to the corporation on the surety of the Algoma Central Railway together with various promises on the part of the corporation.[108] Ross vigorously defended the government's action on the grounds that, first, the province's toehold in the iron and steel industry must be protected and, secondly, that the security the government had extracted from the corporation was eminently safe. 'This is the first large industry, or combination of industries I may say, of the kind, which ever attempted to establish itself in the Province of Ontario,' Ross told the legislature, 'and endeavoured to get under its wings such a series of cognate industries ... [which] would have contributed immensely to the advancement of the country.'[109]

Led by James Whitney, the Conservative benches fought every aspect of the bill, attacking the Sault industries as an 'inflated bubble' that deserved to be pricked. Clergue himself attracted considerable criticism from the Opposition. Among other allegations, he was described as a friend of 'stock jobbers and boomers.'[110] The Tories questioned the propriety of a loan they described as a 'book-keeping extravaganza' and an 'open and scandalous bribery' of Sault voters, pointing to the fact that two Liberal members, James Conmee and C.M. Bowman, held contracts from the Algoma Central. Whitney could see no reason why government should bolster the fortunes of private enterprise and warned the House that it would 'create a precedent whereby other struggling institutions will have just as much right to come to the Legislature for assistance.'[111] With Conmee and Bowman barred from voting, the bill was passed by a two-vote margin amid an uproar, one of the crucial deciding votes being cast by an invalid Grit member transported to perform his duty on a stretcher.[112] Once the bill passed, Ross secured a pledge from Laurier that the Algoma Central guarantee would receive 'sympathetic consideration' from Ottawa.[113] To represent the province's newly reaffirmed faith in the Sault complex, Ross stipulated that Queen's Park have the right to appoint three directors, including Toronto lawyer N.W. Rowell, to the new corporation's board.

The electoral landslide that brought Whitney and the Conservatives to power in 1905 wrought surprisingly little change in the provincial attitude to the Sault industries. During the campaign, Tory leader James Whitney fully aired the 'notorious and unsavoury memory,' as the *Canadian Annual Review* described it, of the *Minnie M*, a scandal Whitney likened to the record of a 'rotten South American Republic.'[114] Eager to escape such invidious comparisons, the Liberals upheld the Sault industries and the beneficence of Queen's Park towards them as cornerstones of provincial prosperity. N.W. Rowell told a Toronto audience at the height of the campaign that the province's $2 million loan guarantee to the corporation had sparked a 'revival' of the Sault's fortunes, transforming 'clamouring creditors' into 'enthusiastic investors' once again and fostering 'the renewed activity of great industrial institutions where before was the deathlike silence of stagnation and idleness.'[115] While the campaign abounded with charges that the Grits toadied too much to swashbuckling northern developers to the neglect of broad and balanced growth of the province, Whitney embraced the hope of 'New Ontario' as eagerly as any of his Liberal predecessors. Although the new ministry housecleaned many of the province's northern timber agreements and introduced new mining legislation, it respected the terms of the Ross guarantee to the Lake Superior Corporation.[116] Installing a politically sympathetic nominee, R. Wilson-Smith, as its representative on the Lake Superior Corporation board, the new Conservative government cooperated with Lake Superior president C.D. Warren, a Toronto promoter and financier less prone to recklessness than his predecessor. Buoyed by the knowledge that the corporation was receiving hefty rail orders, the province released half of its collateral holdings in the corporation in May 1906, allowing the Canadian Improvement Company to assume responsibility for $1 million of the loan without a guarantee. It then passed an act guaranteeing 5 per cent interest on the remaining portion of the 1904 loan held by the Morton Trust in New York.[117] In January 1909 the provincial treasurer, A.J. Matheson, travelled to New York where the remaining $1 million was finally paid off.[118]

F.H. Clergue, his entrepreneurial and financial credibility deeply tarnished, was gradually eased from the reins of control of the Sault Corporation. As soon as C.D. Warren had taken over as president of the corporation in April 1904, he assured the press that 'this company will have new managers and an entirely new method of doing business. Mr. Clergue's connection with it will be an advisory one only.'[119] Clergue remained in this capacity until he was dropped from the board of directors in 1908. Despite the debacle at the Sault, Clergue did not resign his entrepreneurial ambitions. Neither did he forsake his sense that Canada was a land of opportunity. Canadian politicians and investors were not quick to forget Clergue's deviousness and in future years treated him with extreme suspicion. 'It has been said of him,' Mackenzie King privately noted after a 1936 encounter with Clergue, 'that he has tried to pull the legs of most Governments in Canada but has never been able to reach either Mr. Bennett or myself.'[120] Such scepticism did little to deter Clergue. Maintaining his residence in Montreal, he reappeared in Ottawa in 1912 with a scheme to build a transcontinental railway across the north of Canada. The North Railway was to follow the Ottawa Valley before veering north via the Nottaway River to James Bay. Ferries would then transport the trains across the bay to a port at the mouth of the Nelson River, from whence the tracks would follow the sixtieth parallel across the frozen northland. In spite of obvious obstacles in the form of ice and muskeg, federal, Ontario, and Quebec politicians seriously entertained Clergue's requests for subsidies, land, and loan guarantees for this bizarre venture. As usual Clergue looked to others to shoulder the burden of risk. Amazingly, such politicians as Quebec's premier Lomer Gouin accepted the risk. The economic slump of 1913 and the outbreak of war combined to extinguish the North Railway before a single track could be laid.[121]

Clergue never gave up. In 1915, he travelled to tsarist Russia in hopes of selling rails and shells made at the Sault and by the Canadian Car and Foundry Company in Montreal. At the same time, he served as president of a tool company in Waterbury, Connecticut. In the late 1920s and early 1930s, he became a lobbyist in Ottawa and Washington for an improved St Lawrence Seaway. Clergue's sense for business adventure was untiring. In the mid-1930s he followed the invading Japanese into Manchuria in hopes of selling railway equipment to the Japanese-controlled puppet government. Few of these ventures bore fruit. One that quite literally did bear fruit for Clergue was his attempt to introduce the Red Delicious apple to Canadian orchards, using his own farm in the Eastern Townships as a personal experimental farm. When he died in 1939, Clergue was described by the Montreal *Gazette* as the 'Cecil Rhodes of Canada.'

Like Rhodes' imperial vision, Clergue's dreams were never realized. He left behind him a monument that on one hand honoured his precocious vision of creating an industrial complex on the edge of the Canadian Shield and on the other bore damning witness to his spendthrift excesses. For the next three decades, Clergue's successors would labour to undo many of the consequences of the 'Soo King's' original vision. Algoma Steel, the productive backbone of the corporation, battled to overcome its overreliance on rails and the accompanying federal tariff structure that Clergue had given it, while the parent corporation searched vainly to extricate itself from the financial maze into which Clergue had led it. Despite their growing doubts of Clergue's integrity and proficiency as a captain of industry, federal and provincial politicians had little choice but to support the Sault industries. To Clergue's credit, he had almost singlehandedly made the corporation with its diverse subsidiaries an economic reality with lasting national and provincial implications. His dream of industry at the Sault masterfully flattered the hopes of all three levels of Canadian government. Welcomed by municipal politicians as an elixir for local stagnation, the prospect of thriving industries by the rapids coincided perfectly with provincial aspirations for a northern hinterland in 'New Ontario.' At the federal level, the whole thrust of the National Policy predisposed federal politicians to favour the emergence of Algoma Steel as a railmaker. Once committed to Clergue's vision, there was little escape from the ongoing implications of the initial decision to succour Clergue's *fait accompli* for any of the three levels of government. The federal tariff and bounty structure and the emergency financial aid to the corporation from Queen's Park in 1904 bore witness to the way in which Clergue had conscripted federal and provincial developmental policies for duty in the service of a foreign corporation. As the Lake Superior Corporation *Annual Report* noted in 1905: 'The disposition of the Canadian government and people to foster and protect home industries, particularly those which are developing the mineral resources of the Dominion has been generously manifested towards the enterprise.'[122]

3

Rails and Shells: Algoma Steel and the Precarious Rewards of National Prosperity 1905–1919

The financial reorganization of the Lake Superior Corporation in 1904 brought to a close what its *Annual Report* described as 'a long period of idleness with its attendant demoralization and accumulating disadvantages.' It also set the stage for a period of sustained activity and relative prosperity for steelmaking at the Sault. This prosperity was not only the product of less profligate and more conservative policies on the company's part but was also clearly predicated on the overall prosperity of the Canadian economy in the years down to 1913. Mammoth export shipments of wheat, two new transcontinental railways, and the myriad demands brought forth by industrialization and urbanization created an unprecedented demand for iron and steel. Algoma Steel felt the full brunt of this demand as its rail mill struggled to meet the demands of Canadian railways.[1] The commercial collapse of 1913 and the ensuing brief depression abruptly ended this spurt of national growth; but prosperity quickly returned, induced by the different stimuli of the Great War. It was a period of paradox for the Sault industries. The activity induced by national prosperity and a war economy served to mask deep-seated industrial and financial deficiencies at the Sault and give the period a deceptive sense of unity and prosperity. Revealed briefly in the depression of 1913–15, Algoma's inner weaknesses of lack of product diversification and foreign ownership would not be fully exposed until the exhaustion of national prosperity in the early 1920s.

Clergue's decision to specialize in rail production brought sizeable short-term rewards to Algoma. Throughout the years 1905–15, the plant rolled 2,179,795 tons of rails, and in only one of those years, 1909, did Algoma produce less than half of the total national output of rails. This demand effected a speedy recovery of Algoma's fortunes. By April 1906, the Sault steel plant had rail orders totalling 146,000 tons from the Grand Trunk Pacific, Canadian Pacific, Canadian Northern, and Michigan Central and could boast that its mills had produced a record 1004 tons of rails in a single day.[2] Newspapers and magazines honoured this feat with photos of huge stockpiles of finished rails awaiting shipment to the railheads in western Canada. Although the 'panic' of 1907 did reduce production in 1908 and 1909, the high demand for rails remained steady through 1913, when national production peaked at an all-time record of 506,709 tons, 289,343 tons of which were rolled at the Sault. At times the demand nearly overwhelmed the company. Although Premier Whitney could boast to a potential investor in September 1908 that Algoma had a backlog of 85,000 tons of rail orders, Lake Superior president T.J. Drummond later confided to Prime Minister Borden that he was 'inclined to think that the disposition of some of the railways is to overcrowd some of the rail manufacturers' in hopes of obtaining some relaxation of tariffs on foreign rails.[3] Despite this persistent suspicion of the railways' motives, company management was undeniably pleased with the relative financial health that rail business brought to the corporation. By 1908–9, the parent corporation reported net earnings from its subsidiaries of $1,083,482, the bulk of which was generated by the steelworks.

Beneath the surface of railway-induced prosperity lurked many potentially crippling dangers for the Sault industries. In the first place, the steel complex was not self-sufficient. Once again the logic of industrial integration asserted itself. If Algoma was to emulate the success of American steelmakers, it would have to ensure an efficient 'throughput': that is, an assured and uninterrupted flow of materials through the blast furnaces, to the rolling mills and to Canadian markets. The 1907 annual report pointed out that 'the output of the two blast furnaces is not nearly sufficient to supply the rail mill with pig iron.' If costly and unreliable outside purchases of pig iron were to be avoided in the future, Algoma would have to expand its primary iron capacity and diversify away from Bessemer steel into open-hearth steel with its more varied uses. The subsequent installation of open-hearth furnaces cut seriously into the earnings of the corporation and in the years up to 1910 precluded the payment of dividends to investors. Another weak link in the Algoma chain of production was the necessity of mixing the hematite ore from the Helen mine with imported ores in order to make satisfactory Bessemer steel. Of the 1,584,571 tons of Helen ore mined in 1909, only about 175,000 tons was consumed at the Sault, the rest being sold to other companies. Moreover, when the company opened the Magpie mine in

1913 to exploit lower-quality siderite ore, it was faced with heavy expenses for crushing and concentrating the ore.

Other ventures proved more beneficial. Algoma attained greater self-sufficiency through vertical integration into the furnishing of coal and limestone for its furnaces. In 1910, the Cannelton Coal Company of West Virginia and the Fiborn Limestone Company were bought outright and made subsidiaries, as was the Lake Superior Coal Company in 1914. Such incursions across the American border ensured that by the outbreak of the First War the company had insulated itself to a significant degree from the uncertainties of external sources for its raw materials.

The two most debilitating factors affecting corporate vitality were the steel company's inability to widen its productive output and the shaky scaffold of subsidiaries surrounding the parent company. 'It is increasingly evident,' the directors of the corporation reluctantly told their investors in 1915, 'that in order to have a balanced and thoroughly commercial steel plant, another mill is necessary, otherwise the operation is confined practically to the manufacture of steel rails alone, and to the comparatively small tonnage that can be made on the existing merchant mills.'[4] Stelco and Dominion Iron and Steel, Algoma's chief rivals in primary steel production, enjoyed a far greater measure of diversification in finishing their primary steel output.[5] Stelco, for instance, not only made steel but rolled it into a wide variety of shapes and then finished it into products ranging from nails to fencing. In an effort to reduce its own lopsided reliance on rails, Algoma began construction in 1910 of a new merchant mill to enable it to roll various steel shapes. When the merchant mill began operation in 1912 it produced 39,466 tons of steel shapes. This output dwindled to a meagre 8903 tons by 1915 in the face of the commercial depression which set in in 1913. Although plans were unveiled in 1916 for a 32-inch billet mill, the directors warned that even greater amounts of capital would be needed in the future to put the plant 'on a proper footing in reference to the manufacture of a much more diversified product.'[6]

The corporation's inability to implement a more rapid diversification of steel output was partly attributable to the financial constraints placed on it by its motley collection of subsidiaries. Since the Lake Superior Corporation acted as the common purse for all the Sault industries, guaranteeing their securities and paying their interest in return for their earnings, it was frequently forced to juggle its finances to accommodate the less profitable enterprises. The original rambling group of companies was in fact added to in the years preceding the First War with the inclusion of the Lake Superior Iron and Steel Company, the Algoma Iron Company, both ancillary to Algoma Steel, and the Manitoulin and North Shore Railway. Some attempt was made to streamline the unwieldy corporate structure either by amalgamation or sale. In 1912, the Algoma Steel Corporation Limited was incorporated to amalgamate the old Algoma Steel, Lake Superior Power, and the Algoma Commercial Company. In 1914 the Tagona Water and Light Company was sold to the city. While the corporation sought to shed those subsidiaries it could not profitably integrate, it could not circumvent the financially dismal performance of the Algoma Central and Algoma Eastern railways. As guarantor of both railways' securities, the parent corporation had to sustain the high construction and operating costs of the lines in the face of skimpy earnings. By 1915, the LSC had advanced $317,489 to the Algoma Central to cover its costs and was forced to admit the 'inability of this railroad to earn its fixed charges.'[7] Unable to stave off the inevitable, the corporation allowed the two railways to fall into liquidation and consequently into the hands of a bondholders' committee. Since the railway bondholders had a lien on the corporation's holdings, little corporate rationalization could be attempted by the parent company until a settlement, which was to prove elusive, was made.

Financial woes plagued even the steel company, the profit-earning workhorse of the corporation. In constant need of capital to finance plant extensions, Algoma Steel stretched its finances to such a point that in 1915 a committee of bondholders was formed in London 'for the purpose of protecting their interests and advising with the Board of the Steel Corporation from time to time.' Forced to surrender its Algoma holdings to the committee, the parent corporation urged in its 1915 report a 'readjustment' of the steel company securities, resulting in a 'voting trust' arrangement that continued to 1917. The effect of these several predicaments was to force the corporation into a cautious and conservative stance in policy matters, which, although it might avoid the excesses of the Clergue period, impeded sensible attempts to rectify corporate shortcomings. Faced with such conditions, the corporation's foreign owners frequently succumbed to the temptation of reaping quick profits from the plant's existing assets and shunning any thought of costly expansion.

Largely because of the unsettled financial and operational condition of the enterprise, management of the corporation proved an exacting and unrewarding task. Confronted with the assumption of the LSC presidency in 1905 by C.D. Warren, F.H. Clergue had rallied his forces in opposition but was finally ousted from the board in 1908. Warren, with his broad experience in Canadian banking and promotional activities, was much more acceptable in the presidency to both Queen's Park and the majority of Philadelphia investors. To signify Warren's triumph over the old management, the corporate headquarters was moved, albeit temporarily, from Philadelphia to Toronto. While Warren, as president, and the Canadian directors appointed by the Ontario government gave the corportation a nominally Canadian executive, financial control remained rooted in Philadelphia.[8] As late as 1923, a trade journal sarcastically noted that the corporation's legal and financial situation was 'so tangled that it will take a Philadelphia lawyer to unravel it.'[9]

In 1908, however, a chink appeared in the armour of Philadelphia's monopoly. From this developed the first major shift in the control of the corporation away from American and into English hands. The key to the financial dealings of late 1908 was the Canadian Improvement Company, the Toronto investment firm which had acted as the intermediary between the Ontario government, the defunct Consolidated Lake Superior Corporation, and the new corporation in the $2 million loan of 1904. The Ross government had made the loan to the Canadian Improvement Company under a deed of trust with the United States Mortgage and Trust Company of New York acting as trustee. Queen's Park held a large amount of collateral in trust. Although $1 million of the loan had been shifted from the Improvement Company to the Sovereign Bank of Canada, the Ontario government renewed its loan on the remaining $1 million and extended the due date to October 1908.[10] As the date neared, it became apparent that the Improvement Company would be unable to make payment. The Ontario government countered by refusing to perpetuate its commitment 'on the ground that if the Philadelphia banks which are in control of the management of the Corporation did not consider the enterprise of sufficient merit to justify them in carrying its securities as collateral, the Government was not justified in assuming a risk which they declined.'[11] Caught in the middle ground between two intransigent parties, the Improvement Company, with collateral in the corporation and its subsidiaries totalling over $19 million, presented a delectable financial plum for any group intent on seizing a controlling interest.

The opportunity of capturing this collateral block was seized by the Scottish investment trust banker Robert Fleming and an American engineer and promoter, F.S. Pearson. Also prominent in the transaction were two young City financiers, James Dunn and Walter Whigham. The group represented a partnership of English capital and American promotional skill. Fleming possessed a canny mastery of the investment trust and had used it to channel millions of pounds of Scottish savings into North American investments. Fred Pearson's reputation as an innovative electrical engineer was built on public utility ventures in the United States, Canada, Mexico, and Brazil. Success in electrical engineering had drawn Pearson into the world of business promotion, where his name became synonymous with the rich promotional possibilities of the age of electricity. The need to attract capital to Pearson's widespread enterprises had brought him to London where he soon came to rely on underwriters such as Fleming and Dunn to float the shares of his electric enterprises.

The Fleming-Pearson group was encouraged to intervene in the Sault investment by H.S. Fleming, president of the Improvement Company, who intimated that, when the loan was defaulted upon, 'If friendly interests were at that moment ready to take the place of the Government, repaying the $1,000,000, they would become the owners of the property.'[12] Pearson was dispatched to inspect the works at the Sault, from where he pronounced that with alterations costing $2.5 million the Sault industries could become profitable on a continuous scale. 'Bear in mind,' Dunn emphasized to Pearson, 'that we are really getting control for a few million dollars and on a basis that it will not be difficult to find the money for a group of enterprises in which something like $35,00,000 has already been expended and to which in addition belong valuable Government rights and concessions.'[13] With this incentive, Fleming, joined by Dunn and Robert Nivison, another City investment banker, bought out the Canadian Improvement Company at a greatly deflated price and promptly lodged their newly found holding in the Sault corporation under the aegis of the Lake Superior Investment Company, a New Jersey holding company.[14] In a move signifying the switch to English control, Montreal businessman T.J. Drummond[15] was installed as president and Whigham was given a seat on the board to represent English interests. With Philadelphia interests in eclipse, Fleming utilized his prowess in English investment markets to underwrite, on generous terms for himself and his syndicate, a series of securities issues for the corporation and its subsidiaries, most notably $5 million of 5 per cent collateral trust gold bonds to finance plant extensions in 1909.[16]

Throughout this period of prosperity and reorganization, the Sault industries remained a favoured child of the Ontario and Ottawa governments. 'The practical evidence of our goodwill exists in the Statute Books,' Laurier informed George Drummond in 1904, 'which show that we have offered a substantial bonus in cash on steel manufactured in Canada, that we have provided for a $7 per ton duty on rails ... and ... required the subsidized roads to give the preference to Canadian made rails.'[17] While the Ross Liberals remained in power in Ontario, liaison between Ottawa and Toronto in matters pertaining to the Sault was expedited by intermediaries such as N.W. Rowell, the Toronto corporate lawyer already conversant with the industries' needs.[18] By the time the Whitney Tories took power provincially, the fortunes of the Sault industries had become synonymous with those of the whole of 'New Ontario' in the minds of politicians and investors. Descriptions of the northern complex were couched in bold adjectives whenever politicians, foreign investors, and journalists toured the 'immense industry.'[19] Members of the Whitney government, especially Frank Cochrane, minister of lands, forests, and mines, and W.H. Hearst, member for the Sault after 1908, waxed lyrical in describing the agricultural and mineral potential of the 'Clay Belt' and Shield country in the Sault's hinterland.[20] An eloquent advocate of northern development, Hearst, like Rowell, had done legal work for the Lake Superior Corporation before seeking political office.[21]

The province's commitment to the Sault industries extended beyond the painting of visions. As the Canadian Improvement Company neared financial collapse in 1908, Premier Whitney actively cultivated the interest of the English syndicate, cabling Hearst at the Sault to afford every convenience to F.S. Pearson on his inspection tour. Whitney also assured Dunn of the corporation's profitability and ordered the provincial treasurer to open the company accounts 'for the information of the British capitalists anxious to understand the situation.'[22] Quick to detect the importance the government placed on the success of the enterprise, the capitalists operated from a position of strength. '[B]y helping the Government in taking care of this loan,' Whigham pointed out to Fleming, 'we would put ourselves in a very good position with the Government party, and also strengthen their hands in giving us facilities in the future.'[23]

The federal government played a less prominent role in the encouragement of iron and steel production in the years from 1905 to the war. Satisfied with a steadily growing volume of rail orders down to 1913, primary steel producers prospered under the now firmly established federal development policies set in place by Finance Minister Fielding, although they were still quick to plead for a broader base of tariff protection and the retention of the bounty system. Ottawa was also frequently called on to arbitrate frictions arising between the railmakers and rail consumers, especially the financially plagued Canadian Northern. T.J. Drummond remained a frequent correspondent with the prime minister and Senator Dandurand was retained as a corporate solicitor in Ottawa. When Dandurand's name was forwarded as a potential director, however, James Dunn objected on the grounds that 'if he were a Director and outside of the political influence, I cannot conceive that he will be of any value to the Company.'[24]

If Ottawa was unresponsive to suggestions that it provide further direct assistance to the corporation, its sponsorship of experiments in the electrical smelting of iron ore at the Sault revealed a willingness to assist the Sault industries indirectly. Under the direction of the Department of the Interior, tests conclusively proved in 1907 that the electric smelting of iron ore was economically prohibitive, thereby belying much of Clergue's original contention that the power of the rapids alone could support the whole Sault complex. The Sault, like the rest of Ontario, would continue to rely on imported coal.[25] Apart from such peripheral assistance, the overriding contribution of the federal government to the iron and steel industry lay in facilitating the tremendous pre-war railway boom that satiated the rail mills of Sydney and the Sault with orders.

The corporation for its part developed a pragmatic response to most political situations. During the reciprocity election of 1911, a contest fraught with implications for much of the Canadian business community, the Lake Superior Corporation remained seemingly untroubled by the prospect of free trade, especially where it did not affect the staples of its steel production. Only in the natural products in which the corporation's subsidiaries dealt did President T.J. Drummond, a staunch protectionist and opponent of reciprocity, take a firm stand, insisting that in its export policy for pulp and paper 'Canada is right in the position she has so far taken and that any withdrawal would be hurtful.'[26] Algoma undoubtedly welcomed the advent of the Borden Tories to power, primarily in the hope that some reprieve could be won for the iron and steel bounties or, failing this, that some degree of added tariff protection over and above that afforded by the Liberal schedule could be obtained. In both aspirations, the corporation was summarily disappointed. The federal government, under both the Liberals and Conservatives, had been prepared to give the company a helping hand in terms of tariffs and bounties, but by the 1910s it was not prepared to put its hand any deeper into its pocket to aid the young steel industry.

If the burdens of acting as salesman, guarantor, and bounty payer for the Sault corporation were often onerous and at times politically embarrassing for Ottawa and Queen's Park, the results were by the same measure gratifying. By 1913, Algoma produced about 56 per cent of the provincial output of pig iron or about 32 per cent of national production. Although the Atikokan Iron Company had begun iron-mining and smelting near Port Arthur, Algoma clearly dominated the iron industry in 'New Ontario.'[27] By 1910, Algoma had three of Ontario's eight blast furnaces. On the ore front, Algoma was the province's sole success story. As its appetite for iron and steel grew, Ontario found itself less able to supply its own needs in iron ore. While it could satisfy 56 per cent of its ore needs in 1901 it could only muster 17.4 per cent in 1910.[28] Only the hematite and siderite production from the Lake Superior Corporation's Helen and Magpie mines kept the province from near-total dependence on imported iron ore.[29]

By the end of the first decade of the century the Sault industries provided tangible proof to both federal and provincial politicians that a nascent primary iron and steel industry was finally taking root in Canada. In October 1910 this achievement was honoured at a Sault banquet attended by Frank Cochrane and W.J. Hanna, representing the province, and the young W.L. Mackenzie King, representing the federal government. Before an audience which included A.M. Grenfell, the London financier, and company executives W.C. Franz and T.J. Drummond, Provincial Secretary Hanna praised the loans and bounties that had brought industrial life to the Sault and prophesied unbounded growth for its hinterland, 'a reservoir of untold wealth.'[30] The bountiful prospects of 'New Ontario' were underscored by the fact that the Sault's 1901 population of 7169 had grown to 10,984 by 1911 and, by the *Canadian Annual Review*'s calculation, the value of the Sault's annual industrial production had expanded 610 per cent in the first five years of the new century.[31] W.H. Hearst, minister of lands, forests, and mines, told the Canadian Club in 1912 that the Lake Superior Corporation was 'employing an army of ten thousand men, paying in wages more than $6,000,000 a year ... What does that mean not only to the Sault and the whole Province of Ontario? It surely means that the Province at large must be benefitted by these industries.'[32]

Such confidence in the corporation, built up as a result of a decade of relative prosperity, was suddenly dashed by the commercial depression of 1913. Always the creature of foreign capital, the corporation soon found itself starved for capital on the increasingly unresponsive European and American markets. As early as 1912, underwriters were unable to float £1,130,000 of Lake Superior First and Refunding Mortgage Gold Bonds on the London market. With 93 per cent of the bonds unsold, it was, said the *Financial Times*, 'simply a case of investors ... having been offered too many good things at once.'[33] On the heels of this tightening of credit in London and New York, the corporation announced in its 1914 report that capital expenditure had been 'curtailed as far as possible.' Far more serious was the impact of the slump on the railways, Algoma's primary customer. By 1915, the directors reported a 'sharp falling off in demand' as rail production tumbled 46 per cent from the previous year. The war made matters worse. In late 1914, Algoma president J. Frater Taylor ruefully described his worries to federal Finance Minister White: 'I had arranged to discuss finance in October with London, in connection with our contemplated extensions to the mills here, but all our schemes were of course upset by the European situation, and my great difficulty now is to keep our plant going at all, seeing that we manufacture only steel rails. We are operating at 40% of our capacity, and as matters stand I regret to say that we cannot even operate from now on without some assistance. ...'[34] The Canadian Northern Railway, which was chronically in arrears in payments for delivered rails, was largely responsible for the corporation's woes. Mackenzie and Mann's insolvency, coupled with the lack of CPR rail orders, made Algoma's future outlook, Frater Taylor emphasized, 'exceedingly depressing.' A request for federal guarantees for Canadian Northern rail purchases was flatly rejected by White, because the railway was 'in control of its own affairs until default in payment of principal or interest of the guaranteed securities.'[35] Suddenly the Sault corporation's prospects had become 'somewhat uncertain,' in the words of the 1914 *Annual Report*, as the effects of commercial and financial depression laid bare its innate weaknesses.

While the outbreak of the First War brought a sharp change in many spheres of Canadian economic activity, the effects of the pre-war depression lingered in the steel industry. Once the delayed-action effect of hostilities was felt, however, it dramatically changed the face of Canadian iron and steel production. The steel industry lay at the heart of the enormous Canadian contribution to the allied munitions industry, bringing forth from the industry new techniques, new anxieties, and a new relationship with government. In other significant ways, the war perpetuated and often enlarged the pre-war pattern of the industry. Algoma Steel felt the brunt of both these developments. If the war fostered short-lived prosperity, its long-term implications were often detrimental for the Sault steelmaker. The war thus fulfilled few of the politicians' and businessmen's dreams of a self-sufficient and diversified steel industry and in many ways exacerbated its traditional shortcomings.

In the initial stages of the war Algoma hoped that the diplomatic wall which had cut German steelmakers off from their export markets would create a 'German vacuum' into which the company could pour its rails. In this hope the company was sadly disappointed. Canada soon had no rails to export. The end of the pre-war railway boom coincided with wartime demands for steel for military applications that seldom included railways. Railway building in Canada was put in abeyance. In 1916, only 84,497 tons of rails were rolled[36] as the government shunted railway needs ever lower on its list of production priorities. As a result, the shortage of rails became acute. Despite wartime constraint, the railways still needed rails to replace worn sections of track. Consequently, the railways brought heavy pressure to bear on the government to alleviate the severe rail shortage by permitting the duty-free import of rails,[37] alleging that domestic producers were failing to meet orders. 'Steel rails can be obtained,' Algoma president Frater Taylor retaliated, 'by those who have placed their orders in good time.'[38] Irritated by the tardiness of the railways' response to his requests for rail orders, Frater Taylor pointed out that 'Algoma might have pursued a selfish policy and have booked nothing but high priced shell steel and high priced war orders but, generally, we have deliberately gone out of our way to reserve tonnage for all of our Canadian customers.'[39] None the less, the Canadian Northern was permitted duty-free rail imports during 1916, in the face of intense western pressure to see the line completed. In 1917, despite having dismantled parts of their rail mills, Algoma and Dominion Steel were permitted to roll 32,500 tons of rails.[40] So acute was the rail shortage that by that year track was actually torn up from secondary lines to provide mainline replacements.[41] The war thus intervened in the close relationship of Algoma and the railways, but did not fracture it completely.

Instead of rails, the steel industry was called on to produce massive amounts of shells for the munitions industry. Although rails and shells were both standardized products, the transition from one to the other placed severe strains on the industry, especially because shell manufacture entailed new equipment, skills, and materials that had not been generated by traditional steel production.[42] Munitions and war *matériel*, for example, greatly accelerated the adoption of open-hearth steel production, as opposed to the Bessemer method with its reliance on high phosphorus ore. Canada's 645,062-ton open-hearth output of 1912 grew to 1,245,488 tons by 1916, while Bessemer output withered from 207,509 tons to 10,968 tons by 1916.[43] Algoma had specialized in Bessemer steel almost exclusively before 1914, principally because of its suitability for rail production. Now it was forced into an expensive and rapid furnace conversion program, an exercise made doubly difficult by the company's tight finances and the high price of new steelmaking equipment caused by the war. Despite such problems, Algoma rose to the challenge given it by the Imperial Munitions Board. By March 1916, for instance, the chairman of the board, Sir Joseph Flavelle, noted to Prime Minister Borden that Algoma had 'recently placed at our disposal the entire output of steel for 1916 (110,000 tons).'[44] Out of over four hundred munitions contractors, Algoma was consistently the leading producer, producing 825,200 tons of finished steel between 1916 and 1918 and in 1918 alone just a fraction under a half million tons of steel ingots.[45] In 1917, Flavelle confided his esteem of Algoma's 'patriotic' contribution to Borden. 'The Algoma Steel Corporation has a rather remarkable record with this Board,' Flavelle emphasized. 'They have consistently taken the ground that it was wrong for the steel manufacturers in the United States to seek to extort the last price possible from the Allies for this basic requirement of war. They have supported their view by contracting for their complete output of steel at a price much below the value at which contracts were made by this Board in the United States and in Canada. ... The whole attitude of the company has been one to command our respect and confidence. They have cooperated to the full in all our mutual responsibilities, and have placed us under real obligation.'[46]

Flavelle's lavish praise did not offset the problems that shell production created for the company. The feverish pitch at which munitions production was conducted accentuated the lack of self-sufficiency in the Canadian steel industry. Forced to compete for ore, coal, and iron ore with other, better-integrated producers in the overstraining North American steel industry, Algoma often found its operations restricted by scarce raw materials. Although its American subsidiary, the Lake Superior Coal Company, had acquired additional American coal holdings in 1913, Algoma still required sizeable outside purchases of coal. Similarly, the exhaustion of the known deposits of hematite and siderite ore at the Helen and Magpie mines forced Algoma back onto a costly and precarious reliance on foreign ore. The war thus boldly underlined the lesson that success in the steel industry was predicated on the thoroughgoing vertical integration of the whole steelmaking process. Unlike the Steel Company of Canada in Hamilton and most of American 'Big Steel,' Algoma's chain of production still had missing links.

On a broader scale, the national industry was afflicted by the same lack of self-sufficiency. Faced with a prospective continental 'steel famine,' a confidential report to Flavelle estimated that of the 2,150,000 tons of steel ingots needed in Canada during 1918, only a million tons of the basic pig iron could be domestically produced. Flavelle commented that he feared even these estimates would 'break down through the difficulty of securing the necessary raw product from which to secure a full supply of steel from the present equipment in Canada.' 'To remedy this shortcoming,' he suggested', 'low phosphorus pig iron from the United States is an absolute necessity if the cast steel plants are to produce the tonnage necessary for their side of the programme.'[47]

Algoma's production shortcomings, coupled to the sense of 'real obligation' felt by officials of the munitions program, brought the federal government to the aid of the national steel industry. Besides the federally operated 'national' munitions plants,[48] Ottawa proffered assistance to private-sector producers to help alleviate their deficiencies and expedite munitions production. There was an acknowledgment on the part of both business and government that the war constituted a national emergency under which the *ad hoc* intervention of the state into business could be sanctioned. Such intervention was not founded on compulsion but instead on a spirit of voluntary compliance. In 1917, the Union government had established the War Trade Board, staffed it with prominent businessmen, and given it a mandate to alleviate production and trade problems besetting the national economy. A similar sense of mutual advantage and cooperation was evident in the steel industry. If Algoma cooperated willingly and energetically in Flavelle's munitions program, it did so because it had certain *quid pro quo*s in mind. 'We feel that owing to the abnormal conditions,' Algoma president Frater Taylor told Finance Minister White in 1916, 'we must all be prepared to give and take and to recognize the fact that all the time war orders (shell steel, etc.) must have precedence.'[49] Ottawa, for instance, provided incentives for Algoma to accelerate its transition from Bessemer to open-hearth steel, offering an interest-free $500,000 loan to enable a third open-hearth furnace to be brought into operation at the Sault. The loan was to be amortized out of the proceeds of a 162,000-ton shell order.[50]

Government intervention was also solicited by Algoma to alleviate its labour problems. With its skilled labour force severely denuded by military enlistment, Algoma complained in 1916 to federal officials 'that having undertaken serious contracts for the Imperial Munitions Board. there should be some measure of protection which would enable us to secure ourselves in respect of sufficient labour, skilled and unskilled, to enable us to rise to our obligations.'[51] Facing reduced labour productivity from inexperienced labour, Algoma became a staunch advocate of rationalizing the national labour situation. 'This is something,' Frater Taylor urged, which under conscription, we should not in all probability have to ask.' When, in January 1917, Algoma production was abruptly halted by an enginemen's strike, Flavelle and Borden vigorously intervened to restart production.[52] All such direct government involvement in the business of making steel was predicated on the belief that peace would see an immediate 'return of normalcy.' When, for instance, W.C. Franz of Algoma, frustrated by chronic labour shortages, suggested 'some form of Government control at their works,' he was met with astonished silence from Ottawa politicians.[53]

A return to normalcy did not, however, preclude an attempt on the part of the government, or at least one branch of it, to ensure a more diversified normalcy for Canadian steelmakers. 'Those of us who are in daily contact with this work,' Joseph Flavelle of the IMB wrote early in 1917, 'hold the opinion that the steel corporations in Canada will make a mistake if in addition to securing important profits which betters [sic] their financial position, they fail to establish during this period of high prices such further additional capacity to serve the country after the war as will lend added character to their enterprise when the immediate war business has passed.'[54] This perceptive judgment prompted Flavelle to undertake a one-man crusade within the federal government to broaden the base of Canadian steelmaking. Shells would not assure this. What the industry needed was the capability to roll plate and structural steel. These steel shapes, hitherto imported, would furnish the material necessary to sustain a national shipbuilding industry. It would also open the way for the production of locomotives and other equipment requiring heavy steel shapes. The addition of these new steel forms to the national steel inventory, Flavelle repeatedly stressed to members of the Borden government, was a matter of 'vital importance to Canada.'

Throughout 1917, Flavelle urged the two principal Nova Scotian steelmakers, Nova Scotia Steel and Coal and Dominion Iron and Steel, to consider constructing a plate mill. The companies reacted cautiously, citing the high cost of new rolling equipment and the uncertainties of post-war demand. Caution soon turned to demands for government assistance in the form of tariff remissions on imported machinery for the would-be plant and government-guaranteed orders for plate steel. Lack of progress in the Maritimes prompted Flavelle to turn his attention to Algoma, to which he was already favourably disposed. In October 1917, he initiated negotiations with Algoma president J. Frater Taylor. Algoma, Frater Taylor announced, would consider building a structural mill capable of rolling steel shapes up to 24 inches in width. Flavelle was elated.

Algoma was not prepared, or indeed able, to build the mill alone. The 'heavy cost of such a mill' coupled with the uncertainty of continued high steel prices made it imperative 'to see in what way we can pare down the capital costs.' 'I feel quite sure,' Frater Taylor told Flavelle, 'that with a little encouragement we could grapple with the problem outlined.'[55] So did Flavelle. 'We think,' he told the steel president, 'that an argument can be presented which would establish a reason for preferred treatment.'[56]

Unfortunately, Flavelle was not able to carry his case with the Union government. Late in November 1917, Algoma presented plans for a 24-inch rolling mill which would not only be able to produce 'the necessary shapes for shipbuilding' but also 'a great portion of the general steel requirements of the Country.'[57] It was clear, however, that the company wanted the government to shoulder much of the risk entailed in the plant. The plant, Algoma stipulated, was to be financed on a three-year government loan bearing 6 per cent interest. The government was also to guarantee the initial production of sixty thousand tons of structural steel and to waive all duties on the machinery imported for the mill. The tariff schedule was also to be corrected to exclude foreign structural steel and the Excess Profits Tax was to be waived from the mill's early earnings.[58] Such onerous demands Flavelle could not bring the federal government to accept, especially when plate and structural steel could readily be imported from Canada's allies. Post-war problems could wait for post-war solutions.

Algoma clung to the idea of a structural mill as the key to post-war stability and prosperity. Negotiations continued in a desultory fashion with little result. In the summer of 1919, the company actually commenced construction of the plant. 'The Algoma Corporation,' *Iron and Steel of Canada* editorialized, 'is to be congratulated on its vision in commencing the manufacture of structural steel and small commercial sections.'[59] In doing this, the company was probably hoping to force the government's hand into providing financial assistance. Ottawa would not budge. At least one cabinet minister, N.W. Rowell, believed that peace had made a 'difference' and doubted whether government help was now warranted. When Sir Henry Drayton, the minister of finance, visited the Sault in 1920 to discuss the tariff situation, Franz told him that the company had already spent $2 million on the unfinished plant. 'You have to get financial help in order to finish it?' Drayton asked. 'Yes, sir,' Franz replied.[60] Drayton was unmoved and shortly thereafter work on the mill was halted. Throughout the 1920s the concrete shell of the structural mill stood beside the main Algoma works as a reminder of what might have been.

The spurt of activity induced by the war thus did little to correct the lack of industrial balance from which the company had suffered since the days of Clergue. Shell production was an industrial cul-de-sac which would close as soon as hostilities ended. The 1918 *Annual Report* reported the directors' resolve 'to have the Algoma Steel Corporation emerge from the war times as a well balanced plant, able to hold its own with any competitors.' The new structural mill was seen as the centre-piece in this plan. While the war had seen a marked increase in pig-iron capacity, including the purchase of a fourth blast furnace, coking facilities, and open-hearth furnaces, the company had not developed new capacity to finish steel. There was little doubt that the ability to finish basic steel into a wide range of shapes, angles, beams, sheets, and channels would be the key to prosperity in the post-war world. Despite some additions to its pre-war merchant mills, Algoma was easily outdistanced in finishing capacity by Stelco, with its 290,000-ton capacity in billet, sheet, and bar milling. Algoma was left with its pre-war reliance on railmaking.

Further progress towards diversification at the Sault was barred by the continuously perilous state of the Lake Superior Corporation's finances. While most Canadian steel companies had suspended dividends in the depressed pre-war years, Stelco, Dominion Steel, and Nova Scotia Steel were all declaring handsome profits by 1916-17. The Lake Superior Corporation similarly recovered from pre- and early-war doldrums and reported healthy net earnings thoughout the war, peaking at $6,973,433 in 1918. Unfortunately, these earnings did not filter through to the corporation's shareholders. Once again the corporation's ability to cope effectively with its shortcomings was severely restricted by the tangled financial affairs of its subsidiaries, especially the two Algoma railways, which by 1918 were $2 million in arrears to their bondholders.[61] The railways' insolvency therefore intruded on all the parent corporation's financial plans. After they defaulted in 1916, a railway bondholders' committee was formed and given the right to place a representative on the parent corporation's directorate. Coupled with the voting trust on the steel company's securities, these financial arrangements shackled the parent company's management to the demands of the least profitable components of the corporation. In a bid to lighten corporate indebtedness, the International Transit, the Lake Superior Pulp and Paper, and the Lake Superior Power companies were all sold. The jettisoning of the power company, to a Chicago syndicate for $1.1 million, irreparably damaged the steel company's self-sufficiency by estranging it from an assured source of electric power.[62]

Underlying these recurrent financial woes was the ongoing contest for control of the corporation waged between Philadelphia and London. With the death of T.J. Drummond, the English syndicate had installed J. Frater Taylor, a British engineer later described as 'a tough individualistic Scotsman with a reputation as a company doctor,'[63] as president, backed up by W.K. Whigham as chairman of the board. London's grip on the corporation was considerably weakened by the collapse in June 1914 of Chaplin, Milne, Grenfell and Company and its Toronto wing, the Canadian Agency, both of which provided financial support for the Fleming group's block of Sault securities. With most of the corporation's bonds held in England and the stocks predominantly held in America, the wartime struggle revolved around which group could impose its strategy on the company's affairs. London's insistence on corporate rationalization and a more integrated steelworks was squarely opposed by Philadelphia's inflexible insistence upon maximizing profits from the existing works. By 1918, the American group had gained the upper hand, displacing Frater Taylor and installing W.H. Cunningham, a Philadelphia banker, as president. Although Cunningham clung to his office until 1928, he by no means assured enlightened and progressive executive control. Against this background of internecine strife, Algoma was unable to capitalize on all the opportunities presented by the First War and found it necessary to finance its expansion on the basis of a $3 million government loan.

As early as 1919, at least one Philadelphia director of the corporation had concluded that the kind of close financial control exercised over the company by absentee interests was one of the corporation's endemic problems. 'I think that all of these [Philadelphia] people,' J.S. Dale confided to Robert Fleming in London, 'have about concluded that running a steel plant at Sault Ste. Marie, Canada, financing it, keeping it up to the mark, and making some money out of it, is no easy job.'[64] Less charitable in his assessment of Philadelphia management was an American investment broker, who commented that the 'Lake Superior management was very happy to take their salaries, enjoy a trip to the Soo once a year, and etherize the stockholders with honeyed words and long promises ... Those interests had been barnacles. They put nothing in and took out as much as they could without upsetting the boat.'[65] With, on the one hand, the railway bondholders threatening to exercise their lien on corporate assets and, on the other, the service charges on its various other liabilities awaiting payment, the Lake Superior Corporation entered a period of post-war stalemate, during which the imperatives of corporate survival would at all times supersede any concerted effort at corporate reform. It was, as journalist B.K. Sandwell put it, 'a fine example of the evils of absentee ownership.'[66]

With the armistice of 1918, Algoma Steel, like the rest of the Canadian iron and steel industry, faced the future with great apprehension. Frater Taylor warned the board of directors in 1918 that 'whilst the financial situation is vastly improved, great care will have to be taken to conserve finances, especially against the unknown conditions that may have to be faced in these times.'[67] At a meeting of the federal Reconstruction and Development Committee in late 1918, Sir Joseph Flavelle candidly admitted 'that he viewed with frank apprehension the domestic situation in Canada incident to the stoppage of the munitions industry,' noting that a capacity of thirty thousand tons of steel a month would be freed when the munitions business ceased.[68] As if to underscore Flavelle's anxieties, the *Canadian Annual Review* for 1919 pointed to the fact that of all the war industries, iron and steel had 'the greatest adjustments' to make in the post-war economy.[69] Fearful that war production had saddled them with a monstrous overcapacity in lines for which there was little peacetime demand, Canadian steelmakers, sharing Flavelle's apprehension, instinctively pinned their post-war hopes on a resuscitation of the pre-war mainstays of production. For Algoma this meant an unavoidable reliance on rail production and a small amount of merchant mill business. In this expectation, Algoma's hopes were bolstered by the prediction of the federal deputy minister of railways and canals, G.A. Bell, that the national railways would generate two hundred thousand tons of rail orders in the wake of hostilities.[70] It was to prove a false hope.

Less willing to revert to traditional and at times precarious patterns of production, more optimistic Canadian steelmakers concluded that the safest future for the industry lay in diversifying their output to capitalize on the growing steel demands of the many 'new industries' spawned by the war and by the overall process of urbanization and industrialization. Consequently, many steelmen looked eagerly to Ottawa for tariff alterations and federal assistance to achieve this goal, believing that the 'present equipment and capacity' of the industry was 'a great deal more than sufficient to supply the total Canadian demand.'[71] David Carnegie, an English businessman prominent in Imperial Munitions Board administration, pointed the way to the future in a speech of early 1919.

If Canadian manufacturers will follow Britain's example by determining to supply its domestic trade more fully than in the past, Canada will go a considerable distance in using its surplus steel capacity. Canada should have at least one structural mill for rolling heavy structures. The home demands, alone, of the electrical industry for higher quality steel sheets is not by any means insignificant. The growing demands for alloy steels for motor cars, tractors, and all kinds of engines and high class machines ... should arouse the most earnest attention of the makers of electric and crucible steel ...[72]

By 1919, this vision of a prosperous future for steel already seemed to be vanishing. With no landslide of post-war orders, the Algoma rail mill was by mid-1919 working at 46 per cent capacity. Operating at less than 50 per cent of productive capacity throughout 1919 and 1920, the corporation reluctantly informed its shareholders in 1921 of a 'marked decline' in profits 'due wholly to conditions that could not be surmounted and were not foreseen.' Faced with this worsening situation, Algoma entered the 1920s frantically trying to retrieve the bygone prosperity of rail production and bitterly witnessing the fading of its hopes for diversification. While Algoma's prodigious output of munitions had won it broad acclaim in the industrial effort 'to smother the Hun,' the war and ensuing commercial depression had done little to alleviate its corporate ills.

More broadly viewed, the war had only marginally accelerated the drive for national self-sufficiency in iron and steel that had persisted since the framing of the National Policy. As early as 1916, the *Monetary Times* remarked that the lack of self-sufficiency should 'provide a moral to the country at large to build up what is one of the most fundamental national assets – a strong, well-rounded and self-dependent iron and steel industry.'[73] 'One fault of the larger steel companies in Canada,' *Iron and Steel of Canada* grudgingly admitted in 1919, 'has been their reliance on one main product, necessitating large tonnage production for profitable operation, and somewhat out of balance with the requirements of Canada itself.'[74] Algoma's fortunes in the succeeding decade would do little to challenge this judgment.

4

Frustrated Ambitions:
Algoma Steel in the 1920s

Canadian iron and steel producers faced the new decade of the 1920s with considerable trepidation. Plagued by internal deficiencies and assailed by external challenges, steelmen concluded that 'it would look as if a very quiet time were to be experienced in Canadian steel circles in the near future' and that the industry had entered 'a waiting period.'[1] Consequently, Algoma made little headway during the decade towards balanced and self-sufficient production and in fact slipped deeper into the financial morass that had threatened to engulf it since the days of Clergue. Only in 1930, when the country was settling into economic depression, did the federal government extend a helping hand. The promise of tariff changes, however, came ten years too late. In the interim, Algoma struggled under the burden of financial, organizational, and operational defects, all induced by the callous indifference of an absentee ownership and faltering national policies of industrial development.

Instead of major plant extensions and modifications, the first five years of the 1920s bought a steady increase in corporate indebtedness. Construction of new merchant and structural mills, which had been envisaged as a sure remedy to post-war depression, was reluctantly abandoned in 1920 as Algoma, like other Canadian steel concerns, found that reduced sales forced curtailment of large expenditures.[2] In these years, Algoma made only some small additions to existing machinery. Failure to supplement its physical plant in a major way was the direct result of the vicious economic circle in which the corporation found itself trapped. In times of national prosperity when the steelworks were fully and profitably employed in rail production, Algoma had short-sightedly exploited its reliance on rails to the hilt. In less halcyon times when the rail mill simply idled on piecemeal orders and when the need to diversify production became acutely obvious, the corporation found itself starved of the capital necessary to break its dependence on rails. The early 1920s were not years of national prosperity and consequently Algoma lived a kind of half-existence, unable to regain past prosperity and incapable of fostering a more secure future.

The crucial factor depressing Algoma's fortunes was the slow recovery of railway demand for iron and steel and an inability to apply its excess capacity to new areas of finished steel production. 'No one would suggest,' *Iron and Steel of Canada* had somewhat mistakenly predicted in 1920, 'that we have finished building railways in Canada, not to mention deferred replacements of track.'[3] Unfortunately, the decade brought no new transcontinentals. By 1922–3 the Sault rail mill was subsisting on small and infrequent orders from the CNR, CPR, and Temiskaming and Northern Ontario, none of which were sufficient to warrant steady operation of the mill.[4] The minutes of the board of directors through these years record how Algoma president W.C. Franz reported to his Philadelphia masters on his frantic efforts to secure rail orders.[5] The relatively meagre quantities that were booked imparted a highly uneconomic stop-start character to operations at the Sault. When CPR and CNR orders were booked in late 1922, a thousand men were hired to work the rail mill for two ten-hour shifts a day, only to be laid off when the order was completed.[6] Steel firms with broader product ranges, notably Stelco, were partially cushioned against the danger of such sporadic production and, because of their linkages with the secondary industry, tended to feel the effects of any recovery before the solely primary producers.[7] Moreover, reduced railway orders affected Algoma's other facilities. With the rail mill operating for only 194 days in 1922, Algoma made continuous use of only one of its blast furnaces, a situation that mirrored the national scene, where as few as two of Canada's twenty blast furnaces were, on average, in blast. In steelmaking, profits are made only through continuous operation. Blast furnaces cannot, for instance, be turned on and off like appliances, but must be maintained at constant temperatures whether they are being charged or not.

The steel situation was further depressed by the steady fall in iron and steel prices from wartime highs. New lows were reached in the early 1920s. During 1922, for instance, pig iron plunged from $45 a ton to $24; while the price of steel ingots sank from $58 to $40 a ton. Under this pressure, Algoma's 18-inch and 12-inch rolling mills remained idle thoughout 1922.[8] Other factors commonly cited by company executives to explain the dismal performance of the steel plant included high exchange rates on American currency which inflated the cost of coal and ore supplies, shortage of railway freight capacity, and the cancellation of orders as a result of the general economic *malaise*. By 1921, earnings of the parent corporation had tumbled to a meagre $5962.35 and by 1923 to a deficit of $1,307,949.48.[9] Desperate for capital, the Lake Superior Corporation sold over a half million acres of Algoma Central lands for $1.3 million to ease the financial pressure. Despite this injection of cash, no dividends were paid thoughout the 1920s by any of the Sault industries, except by the miniscule express company.

Exasperated by the unprofitable nature of their investment, the U.S. Mortgage and Trust Company, trustee of the Algoma Steel bonds, commissioned Coverdale and Colpitts, New York consulting engineers, to appraise Algoma. The conclusion of the 1923 Coverdale and Colpitts report was blunt and damning: 'The Algoma Steel Corporation plant is unbalanced, its working capital is inadequate for its needs, and its normal income is inadequate to meet its fixed and current interest charges.'[10] Estimating Algoma's operational losses over the decade 1913–23 at $1,021,503, the report made the obvious point that added structural steel and finishing capacity was urgently required. The $11 million necessary to construct a structural mill, Coverdale and Colpitts emphasized, 'cannot be furnished with the present financial structure. The corporation's working capital was insufficient for its needs in 1913 and it is insufficient for its needs today.' While the report painted a grim picture, it was not enough to force the issue of corporate reorganization. Even a subsequent report by the Chicago engineering firm of Freyn, Brassert and Company, tabled in May 1924, failed to jolt the corporation's executive with its conclusion 'that inability to operate at full capacity is undoubtedly directly responsible for the unsatisfactory earnings of the plant and is almost entirely due to a lack of diversity in output of rolled steel products.'[11] Discussing mooted plans for a Sault structural mill in 1923, *Iron and Steel of Canada* pointed out that the 'investment required will be large, but not prohibitive. The trouble is the company has not the money, its credit has been stretched to the limit, and the involved state of its finances, with numerous conflicting interests, is enough to frighten new capital.'[12] Inability to tackle the corporation's structural and financial maladies in the mid-1920s was once again attributable to the centrifugal pulls of London and Philadelphia for corporate control, forcing management to vacillate ineffectually between the jealousies of the vying interests. 'The unfortunate thing now,' complained Algoma president Franz in 1927, 'is that there is as much or more deadlock between London and Philadelphia as there has been at any time in the past.'[13]

Algoma's inability to advance in the 1920s was therefore not only the product of economic hard times. The corporation was also constrained by the cautious and conservative inclinations of its foreign owners. Saddled with an unprofitable rail mill, the board of directors saw little reason to increase its liabilities by venturing into new and expensive areas of steel production, no matter how much their hired managers urged them to do so. As a consequence, Algoma's managers, notably its president, W.C. 'Billy' Franz, worked with their hands tied behind their backs, and Algoma Steel executives somewhat unjustly acquired a reputation for lacklustre performance. R.B. Bennett, for instance, later stipulated that his government would provide no aid to the troubled company until the old managerial cadre, headed by Franz, was dismissed. In short, Algoma during the 1920s suffered from a kind of managerial paralysis.[14]

There was near-universal accord among Canadian steel producers in the depressed years of the early 1920s concerning the underlying maladies of their industry. Seeking a scapegoat for their poor fortune, primary iron and steel men pointed to the failure of the Canadian industry to become self-sufficient. The concern for self-sufficiency focused in the 1920s on two crucial deficiencies: the dwindling supply of native iron ore for the primary industry and the domination of much of the Canadian primary steel market by foreign producers. A sense of vulnerability pervaded the industry. Canadian plants had to compete with the American industry for coal and ore and at the same time face the influx of foreign steel through what they pictured as an imperfect tariff wall. Furthermore, the prospect of foreign 'branch plant' steelworks in Canada seemed very real in the wake of the war. In 1913, a subsidiary of United States Steel, the Canadian Steel Company, had begun construction of an integrated mill at Ojibway, Ontario. After $3 million had been spent, work on the plant was suspended, primarily because E.H. 'Judge' Gary of uss was unable to extract special tariff concessions from Prime Minister Borden to permit the duty-free importation of machinery for the plant.[15] Lying dormant, the Ojibway mill served as a potential Trojan horse for American penetration of the Canadian industry throughout the 1920s. Even if Americans stayed at home, Canadian steelmen feared their competition. As early as 1918, one observer had warned that, although there were sixteen rolling mills in Canada, domestic producers could not compete with American 'specialty mills' in turning out 16-inch, 18-inch, and 20-inch special shapes. The cost of producing a gross ton of structural shapes was, for instance, $20.45 in the United States and $29.40 in Canada, a difference which was hardly obviated by the $3 a ton Canadian tariff on such shapes.[16] One of the prime considerations behind the attempts of 1919–20 to merge various Nova Scotian steel concerns into the British Empire Steel Corporation (BESCO) was the desire 'to have something big enough in Canada to compete with the gigantic iron and steel interests of the United States.'[17] By the end of the First War, the American steel industry had acquired, in the opinion of Alfred Chandler, 'its modern look.' As a result of mergers, both vertical and horizontal, American steelmakers enjoyed unparalleled economies of scale. Against these, the 'infant' Canadian industry was unable to compete.[18]

Broad agreement that self-sufficiency and a fortified tariff were the key issues retarding the industry did not necessarily lead to a working consensus within Canadian 'big steel.' Steelmen discovered that while it was easy to treat national problems with rhetoric, regional differences and the conflicting interests of the primary and secondary level of the industry often impeded any cohesive attempt to remedy the industry's problems. 'There is no unanimity, and no common policy,' complained *Iron and Steel of Canada.* 'A provincial outlook has obscured the national aspects of the case, and we all drift along, we know not whither.'[19]

Hope of satisfactorily solving the steel industry's problems was further dimmed by the delicate balance on which federal political power hung throughout the 1920s. Any positive federal action on contentious issues such as the tariff or natural resources development might have seriously aggravated the smouldering antagonism between Ottawa and the provinces or offended the susceptibilities of the largely western and agrarian-based Progressive Party. Throughout the 1920s the iron and steel industry was schooled on the realization that it could no longer automatically expect favoured treatment from Canadian governments. Other more successful economic interests in the country, many of them also the fruit of the National Policy, organized and brought to bear their demands, jealousies, and counter-proposals on the government. Caught in the middle of these pressures, Prime Minister Mackenzie King trod his cautious way, ever mindful that any act of assistance to central Canadian manufacturers might have severe political repercussions in the aggrieved West or the depressed Maritimes. Unable to muster a solid phalanx of their own, Canadian steel producers, especially Algoma, therefore made little progress towards making a more diversified and self-sufficient industry.

Ontario's bid to emulate the prosperous American iron ore industry on Lake Superior died a quick death with the close of the Great War.[20] In April 1918, with its high grade hematite ore exhausted, the Helen mine was abandoned, so that by 1919 only 4.3 per cent of ore charged into

Canadian furnaces was of Canadian origin. Canada had returned to 'the beaten path of imported ore.'[21] With the closing of the Magpie and Moose Mountain mines, both low-grade ore sources, the province surrendered its last vestige of iron mining.[22] From 1921 to the eve of the Second War, Canada mined no iron ore, relying instead on imported Wabana ore from Newfoundland or high-grade American ore. Between 1919 and 1925, for instance, the United Stated exported 6,176,199 tons of ore to Canada at an average price of $4 per ton. Such dependency had potentially dire effects, for although Ontario was actually importing less iron ore in the 1920s than it had before the war, it was paying a considerably higher average price per ton for it.[23] The economic squeeze lay in the fact that Canadian steel prices generally fell throughout the early 1920s, meaning that while more was paid for the foreign-controlled raw materials, less was received for the domestically consumed finished product. Since an ever-increasing amount of American ore production was integrated into the big United States steel firms, Canadian firms enjoyed a low priority when ordering, especially at times of shortage induced by strikes in the United States. 'The iron and coal trades in Canada,' warned *Iron and Steel of Canada*, 'therefore are in a position of much uncertainty. We are so entirely at the mercy of events in the United States, and so unable to control these events in the slightest degree as to suggest that those who have the management of Canadian steel enterprise must make careful study of tendencies below the line, if they are to anticipate events at home.'[24]

For the more prescient observers of the Ontario steel industry, there was another inherent danger in dependency on foreign resources. As the provincial deputy minister of mines, T.W. Gibson, bluntly put it: 'The mines south of Lake Superior will not last forever.'[25] Canadian furnaces could not depend on American altruism when ore supplies ran short. Already by 1921, smaller furnaces at Atikokan, Midland, and Deseronto had been closed, leaving the two Stelco and four Algoma furnaces as the last bastions of provincial smelting.[26]

The absence of an indigenous iron ore industry had significant implications for the national economy. In the first place, it aggravated the national balance of payments by making a primary national industry dependent on foreign raw materials. As *Iron and Steel of Canada* graphically put it, 'what we get for wheat we pay for coal and iron.'[27] The iron and steel industry in the 1920s turned the classic Canadian economic conundrum on its head. Instead of hewing and drawing Canadian staples for foreign manufacture, Algoma and Stelco imported American coal and ore to work them in Canada. In the second place, the lack of an indigenous extractive industry gave one of Canada's crucial industries an essentially unbalanced structure. The relatively flourishing secondary level of the steel industry had as its foundation a primary level that, in the words of Algoma general manager J.D. Jones, was no more than 'an overflow of the industry in the American side of the lakes.'[28] Too much finishing of imported raw steel and too little smelting of domestic ores had resulted in what *Iron and Steel* described as 'the inverted nature of our industrial pyramid.'[29] From the political perspective of Mackenzie King in Ottawa, the conundrum was how to broaden the base of the primary industry without incurring the disfavour of the many well-developed branches of the secondary steel industry.

The complete quiescence of the Ontario iron ore industry in the inter-war years was the product of several unfavourable factors. There were, in the first place, sound geological reasons favouring the American side of Lake Superior. When R.J. Manion plaintively asked the Commons in 1927 'surely the good God did not let all the good ore stop at the 49th parallel,' he had unwittingly struck a vein of basic geological truth.[30] The rich and relatively pure hematite ore extracted from the Superior mountain ranges like the Vermilion and Mesabi explained the vitality of the American steel industry. The richness and concentration of these ores was the product of a unique set of geological circumstances that were not generally duplicated on the Canadian shore. What pockets of high-grade ore did exist on the Canadian shore of Superior, such as the Helen hematite body and, later, the Steep Rock discovery, were scattered and presented awkward problems of extraction.[31] The Huronian and Kee-watin rock in which the laying down of rich iron deposits had taken place in the American ranges was largely superseded in Canada by the old pre-Cambrian, Laurentian rock which constituted the Shield.[32] Since the sparse Canadian deposits had not benefited from the same intensive leaching and concentration as most American ores, they tended to be 'lean,' or low in iron content, and full of impurities.[33]

Ontarian iron ores therefore tended to be hard and dense magnetites or siderite, neither of which had the commercial attractiveness of the soft brown and red American hematites. Since the 1890s, Ontario miners had faced the frustrating fact that as long as easily accessible, high-grade American ore was plentiful and as long as the Canadian government allowed duty-free entry of iron ore into Canada, there would be little hope of a profitable local iron ore industry. Ontario's few hematite deposits allowed mines like the Helen to eke out an existence on the periphery, but when the hematite veins petered out and only siderite remained, these mines were abandoned and left, as one prospector complained, to become 'a mere moose-run.'[34] 'I believe that someday high grade iron will be found,' Algoma's Franz told Finance Minister Drayton in 1920. 'I cannot believe that the Helen mine is the only deposit of ore of this kind that we have along this north shore.'[35]

Modern mining technology in the period after the Great War brought some hope of breaking the supremacy of American high-grade iron ore. As premium-grade iron ore began to be exhausted and more low-grade ore was encountered on the American shore, attention focused on practical methods of 'beneficiating' or concentrating and purifying lean ores. Benefication entailed the treatment of lean ores such as siderite by heat to effect 'the removal of such impurities that will leave a product admitting of economical transportation, qualified for proper smelting, yielding good iron and yielding a profit to the ore producer.'[36] During the ore-hungry years of the Great War, experimental benefication had been attempted at special mills in Duluth and Babbitt with encouraging but uneconomical results.[37] In Canada, low-grade ores were 'sintered' into higher-yield briquettes at the Moose Mountain and Magpie mines. Feasibility tests conducted by Stelco in 1922 on Moose Mountain briquettes concluded that there was 'no reason why a large percentage of Moose Mountain briquettes could not be used in place of Lake Superior ores.'[38] A 1917 geological survey of the siderite ore body at the Helen mine enthusiastically concluded that, if beneficiated, it could satisfy 40 to 60 per cent of Algoma's ore needs and would 'make available to Canada the largest and highest grade iron product yet known within its boundaries.'[39] If the quality was acceptable, costs made beneficiation prohibitive. Despite Ontario's extensive low-grade ore deposits, there was little profit to be gained from them once the costs of beneficiation were added, as was the case when the Moose Mountain mine closed.[40] As one Ontario geologist reluctantly noted in 1925, 'the cheaply-mined, high grade American ores render impossible at present the exploitation of low grade deposits yielding ores requiring benefication'; instead of siderite Ontario should look 'with confidence to the eventual discovery of large bodies of high grade iron ores.'[41] Thoughout the 1920s many in Ontario disputed this judgment.

The staunch advocates of a Canadian iron ore industry as the base of a self-sufficient national steel industry argued that if all that held Canada's iron ore mines back from profitable production was the small margin between their operational costs and American costs, some level of

Canadian government should cover this small margin and thereby launch a Canadian industry. In true 'infant industry' fashion, it was alleged that a great industry was 'ready to spring up in Canada as soon as the conditions are made just a little more favourable for its development.'[42] A renewal of the bounty system was seen as the key to this future. 'The alternative to assistance and progress is idleness and decline,' warned the Honorary Advisory Council for Scientific and Industrial Research in 1924. 'The establishment of an iron mining industry in Canada is possible of realization at a small cost by utilization of known resources.'[43]

Agitation for new bounties had begun shortly after the cessation of the old bounties in 1912. In 1913, a non-party motion calling for federal assistance to the iron ore industry was passed in the Ontario assembly. Speaking to the motion, Premier Hearst said that it was Ottawa's place to aid the industry, not Toronto's. Liberal leader N.W. Rowell stressed that it would be 'trenching' on federal powers for the province to provide direct aid.[44] Interest in Canada's iron-ore industry was again rekindled in 1920 when Toronto lawyer G.E. Kidd petitioned Prime Minister Borden for a 75¢ a ton bounty 'on the immense deposits of low-grade ore' in Canada.[45] Kidd's request was echoed at a Northern Ontario Development Convention in January 1920, and later in the year before federal politicians at tariff hearings in Fort William and the Sault.[46] Also in 1920, the Ontario Mining Association formed a committee, including George Cowie of Algoma's mines department, to lobby for a 75¢ per ton bounty on ore mined and beneficiated in Ontario.[47]

Support for the bounty came from three sources: the steel industry, the mining industry, and a loose group of proponents of northern development. Among the arguments used to bolster the pro-bounty case was the ingenious claim that an industrially vibrant northern Ontario would 'wipe out the "East and West" in Canada' by erasing the hitherto barren gap that had divided the industrial east from the agricultural west.[48] 'Canada holds within her bosom what might be called without exaggeration, the key to the solution of her national economic problems,' contended the president of the Sault board of trade.[49] In 1921 the Sault city council, backed by local labour groups and the board of trade, requested the Ontario Bureau of Mines to survey the iron-bearing district to the north of the city. The request for bounty aid was soon being echoed by the Canadian Manufacturers Association, the Ontario Mine Operators Association, and the Canadian Institute of Mining and Metallurgy.[50] Algoma Steel's perspective on the ore problem coincided perfectly with that of the northern development lobby. Proper methods of concentrating lean Canadian ores would 'drive American ores out of the Canadian market.'[51] In short, there was a persistent and broadly based demand for government intervention at the extractive level of the iron and steel industry and Algoma took a leading role in promoting the case of what former Algoma president Frater Taylor dubbed 'the doctrine of aggressive government action.'[52]

Requests for a renewed bounty system were directed at both the federal and provincial governments. At first, they elicited little response. Ontario's minister of mines, Harry Mills, told the 1920 meeting of the Canadian Mining Institute that the United Farmers government 'did not feel disposed' to offer a bounty until it was deemed 'really necessary' to open up domestic ore supplies.[53] In the federal house, R.J. Manion and T.E. Simpson, Tories from northern Ontario ridings of Thunder Bay and Algoma East, performed an annual ritual of urging the federal government to provide bounty assistance for the iron ore industry. Charles Stewart, federal minister with responsibility for mines, perfunctorily replied each year that the matter was under consideration.[54] Foiled in its attempt to chivvy the federal government into action, the iron ore lobby encountered some success at Queen's Park in 1922 when Mines Minister Mills convened a conference of 'representative interests' to discuss the iron ore question, 'the most serious single problem' confronting his department.[55] J.D. Jones of Algoma vigorously argued at the conference that American experience showed that low-grade ore, like Helen siderite, could be sintered, although 'a very large outlay of capital' would be needed. While making no formal resolution on the bounty, the conference did resolve that 'the present methods of beneficiation are satisfactory' and that the 'known and probable ore reserves' of Ontario could sustain profitable iron mining.[56] In November 1922, Mills followed up the conference by appointing a committee 'to investigate the commercial possibilities of mining ore in Ontario,' appointing G.S. Cowie of Algoma as one of its members.

After meeting through the first half of 1923, the Iron Ore Committee's report recommended that a bounty of one cent per ton of iron ore, natural or beneficiated, produced and actually marketed from Ontario ore be jointly paid by the federal and provincial governments.[57] Together with other recommendations calling for a 'properly qualified geologist' to study provincial ore deposits and a mining engineer to study sintering methods, the report prodded the new Conservative government of Howard Ferguson into action. Spurred by the knowledge that British Columbia had offered a bounty on provincially mined and smelted pig iron, Ferguson announced in October 1923 that Ontario would follow suit.[58] Significantly, Ferguson made the announcement at Sault Ste Marie, making it clear that the Ferguson Conservatives would take up the same vision of 'New Ontario' that his Tory predecessors had pursued so vigorously. In February 1924, Charles McCrae, minister of mines, introduced the Iron Ore Bounty Act, a measure that provided a one cent per unit bounty on iron ore beneficiated in Ontario, with the proviso that the federal government contribute half the payments.[59]

The bounty scheme was conceived by the Ferguson government with Algoma Steel as the chief prospective beneficiary. In late 1923, the company duly promised that, once a bounty was enacted, it would build a plant to beneficiate Helen siderite. Two years later, Ferguson described his own ambitions for the Sault to a consultant he had dispatched to study Algoma. 'I am still extremely anxious to give some impetus to the development of our iron ores,' he wrote. 'I am convinced that therein lies the foundation of the greatest and most widespread industrial activity in the Province.' For Ferguson, the Algoma Steel Company at the Sault was 'the logical nucleus for the formation of a proper kind of organization. It has the strategic location and already possesses a plant that would play a large part in the creation of a more symmetrically developed metal industry.'[60] The bond of shared interest between Queen's Park and the developers of New Ontario had reemerged.

Ferguson's desire to see the Sault industries thrive was further displayed in his willingness to consider guaranteeing the steel company's capital requirements for steel plant extensions. In October 1924, E.R. Wood, of the National Trust Company, and J. Frater Taylor visited the premier to sound him out on the possibility of some form of financial backing for the company's urgently needed diversification program. 'We quite realize,' Frater Taylor cabled Wood, 'we have perhaps asked for something exceptional but the situation is such that it demands exceptional treatment.'[61] Although he considered the request one of 'tremendous magnitude,' Ferguson was sceptical of Wood's suggestion that Queen's Park back a corporate bond issue, calling the idea a 'somewhat radical departure.'[62] Ferguson none the less commissioned a special private study of Algoma and appeared willing to act, except that 'in the expenditure contemplated by the company no provision has been made for iron ore development.'[63] Ferguson's hesitancy to commit the government was increased by the corporation's chronic inability to reorganize itself.[64] In the end, neither the bond issue nor the government guarantee materialized. Crippled by its corporate affairs and unable to live up to its promise to reopen the Helen mine, Algoma lost the help of an all-too-willing provincial premier. In early 1927 Sault lawyer J.A. McPhail wrote Lake Superior Corporation president Cunningham that:

He [Ferguson] certainly has been holding out the right hand to us and we have not been in a position to make any response. He is more than anxious to do all that he can to assist the steel Company in getting on its feet and reviving Sault Ste. Marie and it is difficult for him to understand why our people are so dilatory. It is clear that he is determined upon the establishment of a real steel plant somewhere in Ontario ... I believe that unless we do something in the comparatively near future his kindly feeling will be diverted elsewhere and we may find ourselves in a much less favoured position.[65]

Algoma's failure to prosper under the financial aegis of the province coincided with its failure to reap any benefit from what became the stillborn bounty system of 1924. The federal government never rose to the challenge of contributing its half of the bounty. Federal obstinacy stemmed from the grating friction that developed between the federal Grits and the Ontario Tories over the whole question of natural resource development in the 1920s. The failure of provincial and federal politicians to find common ground on the question of economic development was by no means a new feature of Confederation. The creation of a national economy had given rise to internal jealousies and conflicts over the direction of economic policy, a rivalry which soon became tainted with personality clashes.[66] These persistent frictions were reinforced by the fact that the two most prominent pro-bounty spokesmen in Ottawa were Tory MPs Manion and Simpson and by the fact that Ferguson was a trusted confidant of federal Conservative leader Meighen.

Whenever Manion pounded the government front bench about 'its twilight sleep so far as the development of iron is concerned,' Interior Minister Charles Stewart curtly replied that beneficiation was not yet 'commercially workable.'[67] Finance Minister J.A. Robb pointed out that a bounty on Ontario ore would discriminate against mining in other regions of the nation and, taking a verbal jab at Sault MP Simpson's ties with Algoma Steel, 'the government has to do with all the iron and steel industries throughout the Dominion. We cannot legislate for one industry alone.'[68] With the free-trading Progressives holding the balance of power in the Commons, it would have been politically inadvisable for Ottawa to bonus Ontario iron ore. Within federal Liberal ranks, there was also some residual *laissez-faire* antipathy to bounties. W.S. Fielding, active in the finance portfolio until 1923, would have vigorously opposed the reintroduction of the system he had dismantled under Laurier. Further-more, Ottawa was still committed to a free-entry policy for raw materials. As Minister of Trade and Commerce James Malcolm told the Toronto Board of Trade in 1927: 'The expediency of ever increasing imports of raw materials for use in Canadian factories can hardly seriously be called in question.'[69] Angered by Malcolm's views, Tories like J.A. Fraser described the speech as a 'positive intimation that they have absolutely no consideration for the iron and steel industry. We must get our supplies from outside because we are not capable of producing them here.'[70]

The provincial response to the federal policy of 'no man liveth to himself'[71] was to increase its share of the proposed iron ore ante in 1930 from the 1924 half-cent bonus to a full cent 'per unit of metallic iron contained in each long ton' for a period of ten years.[72] The offer had little effect. Federal intransigence on the bounty issue, Algoma's chronic shortage of capital, and an unusually light market for iron ore in the mid-1920s ensured that the Helen remained dormant.[73] Throughout these years the fear persisted that dwindling supplies of foreign ore would eventually strangle Ontario's iron producers. 'Iron ore, coal and steel are the three main roots that give life to and support the trunk of the iron trades tree,' a Tory MP from the Lakehead warned in 1929. 'No matter how widespreading and fruitful its branches, if this tree has its roots outside of Canada it is not a Canadian possession.'[74]

Algoma's other overriding preoccupation throughout the 1920s was its desire to broaden the roots of the Canadian iron and steel tariff. Like the campaign to secure some measure of assistance for iron mining, Algoma's bid for diversification through tariff reform was thwarted by its own far from glittering corporate record, the failure of steel producers to close ranks in a common front, and the general instability of national politics. Only in 1930, after almost a decade of criticism directed against the strait-jacket of the 1907 tariff schedule, did Ottawa concede a belated measure of tariff relief. Ironically, from Algoma's perspective, Ottawa acted out of political concern for the Nova Scotian steel industry, *not* for the plight of Ontario's steelmakers. Regardless of its auspices, the gesture of tariff reform was soon nullified by the onslaught of the depression.

The 1907 primary iron and steel tariff had been tailor-made to allow big steel in Canada to purvey the needs of the rapidly expanding railways. This specialization, typified by Algoma's reliance on rails, had become the source of dissatisfaction in the subsequent decades of the new century as the place of the railways as principal steel consumer was usurped by an ever-increasing diversity of steel demands generated by new technologies and industries, most notably the automotive and canning industries. The huge skyscrapers which began to crowd the skylines of Montreal and Toronto rested, for instance, on steel girders, practically all of which were imported. Canadian steel producers were thus faced with the prospect of satisfying the huge appetite of these new industries for sheet, plate, and structural steel. Not only were new sizes of steel required, such as heavy structural steel for construction, but new types of steel, like alloy steel, were needed to supply the elaborate needs of the burgeoning motor trade. While wartime shell production had provided a prosperous, if temporary, aberration from this gradual shift from old to new staples of production, the 1920s brought ever-louder demands from Canadian primary iron and steel firms that the structure of the tariff must be altered to accommodate the changing nature of steel demand. If the primary industry was to break out of the rut of its infant industry reliance on narrow, specialized production, the transition to diversified production needed to be helped by alterations to the tariff structure. 'The iron and steel tariff as it now exists,' stated Thomas Cantley, a Nova Scotia Tory MP with considerable steel affiliations, 'is the most irrational and confusedly mixed mass of out-of-date schedules imaginable.'[75] Or, as the vice-president of Stelco described it in 1924, the iron and steel tariff was 'a thing of shreds and patches,' so tatty that the industry was intent upon a new suit of protective clothing.[76]

Steel producers employed a series of stock arguments in their dealings with Ottawa during the Liberal administration of 1921–5. Canadian steelmen were, in the first place, angered by the extensive list of drawbacks that enabled Canadian manufacturers to invoke substantial tariff reductions when importing steel for specific purposes, whenever such steel was unavailable from domestic producers. Under drawbacks number 1007 and 1008, for instance, spiral and flat-spring steel together with axle bars, all vital ingredients in autos, were permitted a 99 per cent rebate if imported by Canadian automotive or rail car producers. In 1926, C.H. Cahan condemned the Liberals for the 'covert way of removing a fair protection from one of the great basic industries of the country,' estimating that between 1920 and 1924 $144,000,000 had been lost by Canadian steel producers 'due to the insidious and deceptive' policy of drawbacks.[77]

Steel producers were further annoyed by the failure of the government to extend tariff protection to areas in which the industry felt that it had acquired some degree of productive competence. The 1907 tariff acknowledged that lightweight rolled iron and steel beams, channels, and angles 'weighing not less than 35 lbs. per lineal yard' could be manufactured in Canada and dutied them accordingly at $4.25–$7.00 per ton, but left heavier sections of the same shapes at only $2.00–$3.00 per ton. By the 1920s, Canadian producers were clamouring to produce these heavier shapes, so necessary to modern construction and railcar manufacture. Algoma's planned structural mill, aborted in 1920, was based on the hope of capturing part of the estimated three hundred thousand tons of structural steel imported into Canada each year.[78] Even in the depressed markets of 1925, when only 73,488 tons of structural steel was imported, Algoma pressed for a boost in protection on structurals.[79]

Another cause for loud complaint was that the incidence of many of the 1906 specific tariff rates had not kept pace with increases in the value of the products dutied. *Iron and Steel of Canada* calculated in 1924 that the level of protection afforded light structural forms represented 24 to 26 per cent of the prevailing market price in 1911–15, but by 1924 this had sagged to 15 to 18 per cent.[80]

Discontent over drawbacks and the lack of tariff reform was indicative of the much deeper belief that the needs of the iron and steel industry were being discriminated against by Ottawa Liberals in favour of other economic interests in the country. Once the 1921 federal general election had delivered the balance of political power into the hands of the Progressive Party, Mackenzie King was obliged to take that party's low-tariff predilections into account. Steel executives consequently complained bitterly that Liberal tariff and economic policy was indecisive and pandered too much to the whims of western farmers. In a memo prepared in 1924 for Opposition leader Arthur Meighen, R.H. McMaster of Stelco argued that tariff policy was 'based upon no settled policy –experimental taxation subject to constant change, and ill-administered, half-baked legislation with unconstitutional and uneconomic bills. Necessity and expediency have formulated our policies instead of sound judgment of what was best for the country's interest.'[81] That McMaster's conception of what was good for the country differed from Mackenzie King's was verified by the horrified reaction of steelmen to J.A. Robb's tariff-reducing 1924 budget, or what McMaster described to Meighen as the industry's 'annual dose of fears.' Tariff reductions on agricultural machinery and machinery for primary production dealt a direct blow to steel production for machinery, second only to the railways in steel consumption.[82] The 1924 budget put the capstone in place on what the industry viewed as a betrayal by the Liberals of the principles underlying the 1907 schedule. *Iron and Steel* decried 'the fact that successive governments reacting to various sectional demands have tinkered with the tariff; they have not revised it wholesale nor as a part of a well-thought-out plan, they have tinkered with it, in patches, first here, then there, according to the loudness of the demand for action on some particular article, but always – downward.'[83]

Liberal perfidiousness in the industry's eyes was reinforced by a host of other complaints. The steadily expanding volume of steel imports to Canada, which reached $245,625,703 in 1921 before slipping to $181,196,800 by 1926, was cited as a serious contribution to the national balance of trade deficit.[84] The severe deficit situation in Canada's trade in steel was depicted as a direct result of Ottawa's failure to insulate the industry with tariffs. In 1925, for instance, former Algoma president Frater Taylor complained to Premier Ferguson that it was no wonder American bankers were 'not keen on aiding development of the Canadian iron and steel industry. *Canada is too good a market for them.*'[85]

By 1924–5, the steel lobby in Canada was incessantly warning that the 'ruin' of the industry could only be avoided by 'a wise and just protective tariff,' 'one that really protects, one that is not a compromise between the demands of different section of the country.'[86] Such a 'wise' or, as it was often called, 'scientific' tariff would also have to compensate producers for the exigencies of the Canadian market, notably its sparse and scattered nature. In 1929, for instance, Opposition leader R.B. Bennett visited the Algoma plant and reported that alloys being made there 'could not possibly be produced in open competition with the plants engaging in mass production in the United States.' Castigating the government for letting Canadians become 'economic slaves' of United States Steel, Bennett called for a surtax on alloy steel imports.[87]

Steelmen and Conservative tariff critics did not have far to search to understand why the steel tariff had become 'a thing of shreds and patches.' Caught in a precarious minority situation, the Liberals could not afford in the years 1921–5 to court the displeasure of the Progressives, who viewed any upward revision of the tariff as a direct addition to the cost of making a living on the farm. John Morrison, a Saskatchewan Progressive, after welcoming the reductions of the 1924 budget, lectured the Commons on his philosophy of tariffs. 'My observation,' he observed, 'leads me to the conclusion that it is about as logical for us to enrich Canada by the bonus and the tariff route as it is for a man to go on a prolonged drunk to overcome his financial difficulties.'[88] Further anti-tariff sentiments were voiced by J.S. Woodsworth and A.A. Heaps, independent Labour members. Heaps in 1927 pointed out that Algoma

Steel workers were required to work eleven- to thirteen-hour shifts for wages between 35¢ and 51½¢ an hour. 'All tariff protection in this country,' Heaps alleged, 'is for the benefit of capital, and nothing else.'[89] From Algoma's perspective, the intransigence of the Progressives and the cautiousness of Liberal tariff tinkerers left the Conservatives as the only political choice. The steel industry as a whole eagerly looked to the Meighen Conservatives in the 1925 and 1926 elections to free them from their economic plight.[90]

With the election victory of 1926 and the removal of the Progressive threat from immediate concern, the Liberal government was somewhat freer to entertain the demands of the steel industry for a 'scientific tariff.' The easing of western and agrarian political pressure was quickly superseded, however, by the emergence of the Maritime Rights movement in the east. Aggrieved by the decline of their economic fortunes in Confederation, Maritimers began to agitate for some redress of their most pressing problems. Besides demanding lower railway freight rates and improved harbour facilities, the Maritime Rights movement took up the cry of economic rejuvenation for the Atlantic region. The ailing Nova Scotia coal and steel industry was a prime candidate in this respect. From Mackenzie King's perspective in Ottawa, the movement was cause for political alarm. The establishment of a federal royal commission on the Maritimers' claims was not sufficient to avert the electoral defeat of the long incumbent Liberal government of Nova Scotia at the hands of provincial Tories, inspired by Maritime Rights, in 1925. King was now prompted to ponder other means of righting Maritime wrongs. As the federal Liberals embarked on the delicate task of appeasing the east while trying to hold their support elsewhere, the steel industry took solace in the fact that in this political manoeuvring its interests could not be completely overlooked.[91]

The years after the 1925 election at least brought an upturn in national economic activity which by 1928 had pushed steel production out of its depression to the highest level of production since 1918.[92] Much of the revived demand for iron and steel was stimulated by growth in the automotive, construction, agricultural, and power generation industries, together with a reawakened demand for rails.[93] The prospect of a resuscitated national economy hardened the desire of steelmen for a broadened tariff to ensure an even greater share of the domestic market. The Liberal response to these demands was to point out that the return of national prosperity provided ample business for the existing industry. Since 'the prevailing prosperity' was well distributed over the various provinces, King argued that tariff changes would only upset the balance.[94] Like a sphinx, he evasively answered the prodding query of a Nova Scotia steel representative: 'I made no intimation of any assistance to the steel industry, neither did I say there would be none.'[95] As early as 1924, the Liberals had realized that the only solution to the whole thorny question of the tariff was to remove it from politics to a non-partisan arena in which it could be 'scientifically' settled. Finally in 1926, with the Maritime Rights movement at its peak, King convened the Advisory Board on Tariffs and Taxation as his vehicle for removing the tariff from day-to-day politics. Accepting the chairmanship of the board, W.H. Moore, an Ontario lawyer, publicist, and Liberal, told King that he saw it as an opportunity to 'weld the diversified interests of the country into an economic whole.'[96]

If the intent of the board had been to mould national economic unity, its hearings unfortunately soon resembled a cockpit in which various economic interest groups wrangled over their proprietary rights in the Canadian economy. Although the board's hearings focused on tariff items ranging from frozen rabbits to bituminous coal, the sessions on iron and steel, especially the presentations of Algoma and BESCO, were among the longest and most vituperative of the board's four-year history. For the Liberal government the board did at least remove the tariff from politics, protecting it from the kind of direct, intensive lobbying that F.H. Clergue had skilfully applied to the Laurier cabinet. Flanked by paid publicists and commissioned academics, the steel industry's captains now did battle with the opponents of higher tariffs in a largely non-partisan arena, while the politicians looked on as spectators.

Algoma Steel presented its application to the board in April 1926 and, without exception, solicited a wholesale upward revision of the iron and steel tariff. Submitted by Algoma president W.C. Franz, the application began with a long recitation of the economic adversities besetting the company. The brief explained that Sault steel had a competitive advantage over its competitors in terms of freight rates only in western Canada, while in serving the industrial heartland of Ontario it was at a considerable disadvantage *vis-à-vis* Stelco and BESCO. Algoma was further penalized in the lucrative central Canadian market by insufficient tariff protection, which allowed Buffalo and Pittsburgh steel to sell in Ontario's industrial corridor at a lower price than Sault steel.[97] American steel producers had the further advantage of the economies of scale afforded them by their home market. While Canadians demanded the same diversity of iron and steel products, Algoma pointed out, 'the demand for particular sections and sizes is not large, hence the necessity for frequent mill roll changes and such changes add very materially to the production cost per ton of finished product.'[98] The need for upward tariff revisions to stem the flood of imported steel was reinforced by other alleged injustices to the industry, such as out-of-date 'specific' duties and the overabundance of drawbacks. In every respect, the 1907 tariff was portrayed by Algoma as an antiquated policy that had reached an unproductive old age through the neglect of Canadian politicians. To add a human dimension to the Algoma application, a delegation of Sault steelworkers (who appeared, quite literally, with caps in hand) submitted a handwritten statement describing the plight of Algoma workers whose payroll and numbers had dropped dramatically in the 1920s.[99] The stage was thus set for Algoma's tariff demands.

Drawn up by company management and presented by Norman Guthrie, an Ottawa lawyer, Algoma's application represented a bold prescription for industrial health. In its general outlook, though not in all its specifics, Algoma's brief closely paralleled that of BESCO, the other primary steel producer in Canada located outside the central industrial heartland. At the primary level of the industry, Algoma demanded hefty increases in the pig iron duty to $5 a ton and on billets, slabs, and blooms to $7 a ton. A 35 per cent *ad valorem* duty on all alloy steel was requested, together with a boost of 35¢ per 100 pounds on the general tariff for structural steel angles, beams, and channels. Abolition of drawbacks and exemption was demanded on many items, notably special steel forms for the automotive and agricultural implements industries. Tariff hikes, the application concluded, must be accompanied by stiffened anti-dumping regulations. Taken as a whole, Algoma's application represented a strong bid by the primary level of the steel industry to ensure itself stability and diversified production through tariff increases that would markedly broaden the captive market for Canadian steel in the automotive, agricultural implement, construction, and other secondary industries.

The Tariff Board subjected all tariff applications to two forms of assessment, one by 'expert' analysis and the other by public hearing. Relying on academics and professional consultants, W.H. Moore commissioned studies to investigate the claims of each applicant and to provide overall assessments of specific industries. Professor H. Michell of McMaster University studied the steel tariff schedule and produced the damning conclusion that it was full of 'glaring inequalities and inconsistencies.' 'The truth appears, as far as I can see,' Michell observed, 'that the tariff has never been thoroughly revised since 1907, and has been subject ever since to a series of patching and cobbling operations which have left it in a pretty bad state.'[100] W.G. Wilson, chief of the Mineral Resources Division of the Mines Department, surveyed the general state of the Canadian steel industry, pointed out how much idle basic steel capacity existed in the country and how many diversification projects, designed to soak up excess steel, hovered on the verge of realization.[101] Personal inspection of Canadian steelworks by the board members was supplemented by a report on the European steel situation. The Franco-Belgian industry was described as benefiting from inexpensive labour, modern equipment, and steady production runs. Of the huge German Vereinigten Stahlwerken, one Canadian engineer enviously noted: 'they roll almost everything under the sun.'[102]

If some reports tended to substantiate the general complaints of Algoma and besco, others cast considerable doubt on their claims for better treatment. One study of Algoma's plans to accommodate a larger slice of the structural market concluded, for instance, that though ample raw materials were available, the impossibility of cost-reducing, long production runs precluded economic production of large structurals in Canada. The prospective position of Canadian consumers of structural steel relying on Algoma Steel 'will not be as desirable as at present, when they are able to draw their supply of steel from several rolling mills in the United States.'[103] An economist, W.A. Mackintosh of Queen's, inspected the Cape Breton primary steel industry and noted that it was poorly located to serve the central Canadian market and its plant was 'badly proportioned' and subject to 'bottlenecks.' The troubles, Mackintosh concluded, 'seemed very much more numerous than the hopes' for the Cape Breton industry.[104]

Further damage was done to the aspirations of the primary producers by their own lack of solidarity before the board. No two steel producers in Canada shared the same perspective on the industry's problems and frequently their differences outweighed their similarities. The weakest plate in the primary industry's armour was the aloofness of Stelco from the requests of its two chief rivals, Algoma and besco. Stelco, well diversified into secondary steel finishing and less reliant on primary processing, did not wholly share Algoma's enthusiasm for more protection. Although it did table specific demands for upward revisions on sheet steel and skelp duties, Stelco vice-president H.T. Diplock smugly informed board chairman Moore that Stelco was generally satisfied with the existing tariff.[105] Stelco's passivity was attributable to the fact that its corporate fortunes had, in comparison with besco and Algoma, remained buoyant throughout the 1920s. In 1928, for instance, Stelco unveiled a

$6–$7 million program of plant additions and instituted a 4:1 stock split.[106] Embittered by critics' unflattering comparisons of Algoma with Stelco, newly elected Lake Superior Corporation president Robert Dodd told the board in 1928 that if 'we had the same [established] tariff protection that the Steel Company of Canada had, we could exist without trouble.' Dodd added candidly that it was possibly 'a foolish thing for the people who started this [Algoma] not to go into those things that were highly protected.'[107]

Other differences gnawed at the solidarity of the primary producers. besco's demands for federal subsidization of its coal production grated against central Canadian steel producers' long-standing reliance on an unrestricted flow of cheap American coal. The request of Dominion Foundries and Steel Limited of Hamilton, a steel-plate producer with no blast-furnace capacity, for abolition of duties on pig iron for steelmaking welded Stelco, besco, and Algoma in tight opposition to any relaxation.[108] At no time did a solid phalanx of steel interests emerge and confront the board. 'Big Steel' in Canada was characterized by bickering and internal jealousies, rather than a cohesive spirit. Although *Iron and Steel of Canada* admitted to feeling 'puzzled' and 'a little ashamed' about the divided front, the cause of disunity was not difficult to isolate. The problems of the industry were too deep-rooted and too varied in character to be banished by any one easy solution. A fossilized tariff structure and the exigencies of regional economics militated too completely against easy solutions and common fronts.[109]

When Algoma attempted to pilot its tariff proposals through the board's public hearings, it encountered an impregnable wall of opposition. In seeking protection for products that had previously enjoyed low-tariff or drawback status, it had antagonized large sections of secondary industry that had traditionally relied on low-cost imports of such steel. Algoma's assurances that its mills could produce the same goods at comparable prices were greeted with extreme scepticism by Canadian steel consumers. Not unexpectedly, farmers' groups with their traditional antipathy to protection opposed Algoma's brief as a matter of course. J.J. Morrison of the United Farmers of Ontario told the board that farmers were 'unalterably opposed' to all tariffs and were tired of the steel industry's tales of 'impending disaster' that never came.[110] The Canadian Council of Agriculture, the National Dairy Council, and the United Farmers of Canada, Saskatchewan Section, all reiterated this sentiment. Labour, although poorly represented before the board, complained that increased tariffs would only propel the workingman's cost of living upwards.[111] The Consumers' League of Canada, represented by R.J. Deachman, doggedly criticized the steel companies' requests, alleging that the already lush steel profits in the 1920s would grow even larger behind a heightened tariff wall. Deachman mustered a wealth of statistics to assail Algoma's case and was able to back top Algoma executives into embarrassing corners by charging that the company's present predicament was the product of 'bad judgment' in the past.[112]

Farmers, workers, and consumers were the steel industry's ultimate clients, but, as Deachman pointed out, 'you reach him by way of the secondary manufacturers'[113] and it was from these consumers that Algoma encountered the stiffest opposition. In the words of one irate sheet-metal consumer, BESCO and Algoma were to be blamed for 'their rather cold blooded way of looking over the field of steel industry in Canada and selecting what they judge to be luscious plums grown by someone else.' This therefore 'rather justifies the use of plain unadorned language from the intended victim.'[114] Afraid that less efficient Canadian producers would push up prices, the Steel Fabricators of Canada informed the board that they would be pleased to 'obtain all our requirements in rolled shapes, sections and slabs in Canada on a basis of competitive production within the country, with satisfactory deliveries.' Unfortunately, 'the country would have to have a very much larger population before that object can be attained.'[115] The Canadian Locomotive Company of Kingston estimated that increased tariffs on plate and structurals would add $2500 to $3000 to the cost of each locomotive, while Dominion Forge and Stamping, a maker of auto parts, warned that any tariff hike would lead to the 'crucifixion of their drop forge customers.'[116]

Another tactic adopted by secondary industry was to disparage Algoma's ability to supply the Canadian market.[117] 'It is our absolute, firm conviction,' stated the John Morrow Screw and Nut Company, that 'the Algoma Steel Corporation are not in a position of being the sole provider of certain steel goods in Canada ... it would be unsound, uneconomical and unfair to tie us down to one source of supply in Canada.'[118] The unkindest blow of all for Algoma to bear was dealt by the railways, its oldest customer. Apprehensive about requested hikes in duty for plate and boiler steel, the CNR insisted that 'it would not be in the railway's interest to add anything to the duty which already requires to be paid on articles which we have to import.'[119]

The general attitude of Algoma's critics was that the company was seeking government aid to extricate itself from a predicament of its own making. Algoma was depicted as an industrial 'lame duck' whose tariff demands would jeopardize the prosperity of companies that 'had the courage to pioneer this new field in Canada without special promises of government aid.'[120] If Algoma's demands were acceded to, 'inexperience, inefficiency and geography will combine to produce industrial chaos.'[121] In the face of such criticism the company was in an awkward position. In late 1926, W.C. Franz publicly admitted that the corporation would never 'show enough profit to pay $1,000,000 annual interest on its bonds.'[122] Just as its overreliance on rails was the legacy of its founders' headlong exploitation of railway prosperity, so too Algoma's reputation as the puppet of foreign ownership in the 1920s was the logical outcome of its reckless financial inception. Vainly trying to offset the company's low credibility, Algoma officials struggled to provide an *apologia*, citing poor location, dependency on rails, and plain bad luck to explain corporate failures. 'We are victim, perhaps, of the prevailing optimism of the day,' Lake Superior president Dodd reluctantly admitted, 'if you cast your mind back you will recall that Northern Ontario was looked at through very rosy glasses.'[123] 'Your calculations as to your tonnage of ore were hopelessly wrong,' board chairman Moore angrily replied. 'Your ore petered out. Then you found yourself located at Sault Ste. Marie without ore and away from your market. Your competitor, the Steel Company of Canada, located in Hamilton, is not here today ... We have to take these things into account ... Are the people of Canada to pay for your lack of balance of industries?'[124]

When W.H. Moore initiated the board's hearings, he had declared that it was his object to present 'a clear picture to parliament' of the real tariff needs of industry. Although the board never tabled a comprehensive report, much of the controversy surrounding the Algoma application filtered through to the federal cabinet. Faced with anything but a 'clear picture,' the government excused itself from tariff reform, citing the fact that the board was still deliberating and hoping that reviving national prosperity would dissolve the discontents bred in the depressed early 1920s. In Ontario, this political gamble would probably have worked. Algoma's demands could conveniently have been ignored as the province's industrial heartland returned to fuller production. In Nova Scotia, it was otherwise. The provincial steel and coal industries continued to suffer. Labour strife abounded. Afraid that social and economic discontent in the Maritimes would translate into political disaffection, Mackenzie King finally acted in response to eastern demands. In 1927, freight rates for Maritime rail traffic were reduced and in 1930, with a federal election fast approaching, Ottawa moved to aid the steel industry. Unable to discriminate between the Ontario and Nova Scotia primary steel industries, the Liberals used the 1930 federal budget to raise the protective tariff wall around the Canadian steel industry.

There is little to suggest that the increases in the steel tariff introduced in Charles Dunning's 1930 budget were the direct outcome of the primary industry's persistent attempts to entrench itself behind stiffened tariff protection. The primacy of regional political pacification, not the dictates of sound national economic planning, had carried the day. Just as Progressive discontent in the early 1920s had militated against the steel industry's interests, the Maritime Rights movement now, somewhat fortuitously, worked in the industry's favour.

If anything, the budget of 1930 reflected trade policy more than industrial policy. While Finance Minister Dunning acknowledged 'the national necessity of maintaining an efficient and self-reliant iron and steel industry supplying Canadian consumer demand at reasonable prices,' he confessed elsewhere that the budget was 'frankly framed to enable us to buy more freely from these countries which buy from us most freely those commodities which are of vital importance to us.'[125] This generally entailed aligning more of Canada's import trade with the chief source of her export trade; that is, increasing British trade at the expense of American trade. For Liberal trade policy-makers, Canada's massive deficit in steel trade with the United States loomed large in this respect. The 1930 budget therefore left the British preference intact, but improved the relative competitiveness of English steel by boosting the level of the general and intermediate protection on many steel items, including new sizes of structural steel, rolled steel, steel plate, and skelp for pipe. A bounty was placed on Nova Scotia coal used in steel production. To pacify farmers, agricultural machinery was allowed duty-free status under the British preference.

The 1930 budget was in theory a masterpiece of compromise. It had realigned trade priorities and moved to placate Maritime grievances. In doing so, the budget had extended tangible inducements to Canadian steel producers to enter some of the new lines of production they had so vigorously pleaded for before the Tariff Board.

Writing from Toronto, Liberal senator James Spence wrote Mackenzie King that Dunning's budget was a 'knockout' from the steel industry's point of view, especially since it had stolen the Tories' thunder.[126] Spence's enthusiasm was indicative of the budget's reception by most steel interests. W.C. Franz of Algoma, writing in *Iron and Steel*, spoke enthusiastically of the fact that the government had finally 'recognized the needs of a properly coordinated iron and steel industry' and had thereby given assurance for large expenditures on equipment for structural, sheet, and skelp steel. *Iron and Steel* editorialized that the tariff changes coupled with coal bounties would provide 'just sufficient protection from foreign competition,' although the British preferential rates might tend 'to take back with one hand what has been given with the other.'[127] In the Commons, although R.B. Bennett complained that the budget did little for 'the development of the great resources of Canada,' the Conservatives were left with little to criticize. T.E. Simpson, Tory MP for the Sault, frankly admitted that he would vote for the Dunning budget, regretting only that the changes had not come earlier. Only A.A. Heaps, J.S. Woodsworth, and a handful of Progressives took violent exception to the budget's steel tariff changes, arguing that they constituted a 'class policy' by which capital benefited at the expense of labour and the farmer.[128]

In calling a federal election for July of 1930, Mackenzie King hoped to capitalize on the popularity of the Dunning budget at the polls. As a political gambit, the budget failed. It won the support of neither the steel industry nor the disaffected Maritimes. Of the twenty-five seats in Nova Scotia and New Brunswick the Tories took all but five. At the Sault, T.E. Simpson retained his seat for the Conservatives. As for Algoma Steel, with its close ties with Ontario's Conservative government and the federal Tory caucus, the Liberals' last-minute conversion to protection had not dampened its ardent belief that steel's interests would be best served by R.B. Bennett. 'I think we are in a good position,' W.C. Franz wrote a week after Bennett's election victory, 'to get a fair protective tariff on a number of articles that we had to keep away from the old government so as not to bring opposition from the west.' Franz reported that Bennett had asked to see him in Ottawa 'within the next two weeks,' confidently adding that the new prime minister was 'fully familiar with our requirements in the way of tariff protection.'[129]

Algoma had much to expect from Bennett. The previous decade of Liberal rule had seen little progress towards overcoming the two chief operational obstacles to its prosperity – self-sufficiency in iron ore and diversification of production. This period of stasis had its origins not only in the limitations imposed by the exigencies of national politics but also in the corporate paralysis created by the tangled and overextended financial affairs of the foreign-owned corporation. While the brief return of prosperity in the last years of the decade served to push corporate finances out of the red, allowing some expansion of Algoma's rail and merchant mills,[130] the onslaught of the depression soon obliterated these temporary advances. By 1931 the corporation's directors ruefully reported that a 'severe depression has been experienced in all lines of business, but in none more so than the steel business.'[131] The tariff changes of 1930 had not necessarily been a case of 'too little, too late,' they were simply too late.

The 1920s witnessed no appreciable change in the position of Algoma Steel as a primary steel producer. Shackled to an outmoded industrial strategy predicated on the railway-building imperatives of the National Policy, Algoma Steel now found itself encircled by the hostile forces of secondary industry and unable to initiate a diversified industrial strategy better suited to the demands of the post National Policy Canadian economy. As *Iron and Steel* sardonically noted in 1927: 'It may be set forth as an axiom, therefore, that steel companies in Canada have prospered in inverse ratio to the extent that they have entered into the production of the primary forms of iron and steel and its products, and in inverse ratio to the extent they have utilized in such production the raw materials of Canadian mines and quarries.'[132]

5

A New Brunswicker in the 'Financial Aristocracy' of Europe: Sir James Hamet Dunn 1900–1930

The history of steel at the Sault is a reflection of many factors, some deterministic, others fortuitous. The fortunes of Algoma Steel in the 1920s were, for instance, largely dictated by forces beyond its control, principally the faltering national economy and regional imbalances in federal politics. At other times, the company had forged its own destiny. Francis Hector Clergue's bold promotion of the Sault industries illustrated the ability of a determined entrepreneur to turn broad national tendencies, such as the mania for railway building and the latent political desire for a national steel industry, to the advantage of one locality and the capitalists who invested therein. Without Clergue and his entrepreneurial daring, one of Ontario's largest steelworks arguably might have found itself in Midland, Port Arthur, or some other location nearer the province's industrial heartland. Algoma had therefore occasionally prospered and more habitually struggled under the auspices of forceful personalities and the fluctuating influence of broader economic and political conditions.

In the 1920s, Algoma Steel's misfortunes were to a degree attributable to the absence of a strong personality in its corporate affairs, an individual able to promote its interests with vigour and resourcefulness. With the possible exception of Ontario premier Howard Ferguson, who saw Algoma as the keystone of an economically invigorated northern Ontario, the company's affairs throughout the decade were presided over by a group of lacklustre hired managers and a boardroom of cautious absentee owners. Under such leadership, Algoma was swept along by the force of national economic and political circumstances. After the brief recovery of the late 1920s and the Liberals' unexpected eleventh-hour conversion on the tariff question, the company was plunged into the

Depression late in 1929. Still lacking dynamic leadership and constrained by the legacy of Clergue's original overfinancing, Algoma and its parent corporation entered the 1930s as poor candidates for corporate survival. The Depression did in fact push Algoma into receivership – a result of economic determinism on a global scale.

The company's demise would have been permanent had it not been for the reemergence of forceful personality as a factor in Algoma's affairs. Just as Clergue had dominated the first decade of the company's existence, Sir James Dunn would command the next three decades, a period in which Algoma not only survived but built itself into a profitable, well-balanced, and Canadian-owned steel company.

Until his death in 1956, Dunn acted as the galvanic force behind every decision affecting the company's affairs. After seizing control of the bankrupt company, reorganizing it and bringing it under his near-complete financial control, Dunn served as Algoma's unchallenged president through depression, world war, and post-war recovery. To understand 'Jimmy' Dunn's indelible impact on the company and the Canadian steel industry as a whole, one must examine his life in its entirety. Dunn's authoritarian presence in the Algoma boardroom was the product of years of experience in the world of merchant banking, a training which began long before the Canadian millionaire ever entertained thoughts of a career as a captain of industry.

To a slight degree, the careers of Dunn and Clergue at Algoma overlapped. Throughout his presidency, Dunn was always very conscious of Clergue's legacy at the Sault, in both its positive and negative lights. In his own mind, Dunn conceived of his 'greatness' as Algoma's president in terms of his ability to rectify Clergue's original sins and to realize the potential of the American promoter's original vision of Sault Ste Marie as an industrial centre. In 1946, seven years after Clergue's death, Dunn commissioned Alan Sullivan, the author of an earlier, fictionalized account of Clergue's adventures at the Sault, to write a biography of Algoma's founder. Dunn imposed few conditions on the ageing writer, except the stipulation that the book be entitled 'Before the Tide.' Dunn, as the book's last chapter was to make clear, was the 'tide' which brought prosperity to the city by the St Mary's rapids.[1] Sullivan died before a publishable manuscript was completed. If he lacked a book to illustrate his achievement, Dunn was seldom at a loss for words when asked to compare himself to his predecessor. 'Clergue was a man of great faith,' Dunn wrote in 1945, 'and his conception, based on rather scanty evidence of the iron ore resources of the Sault Ste. Marie hinterland, is proving to be true even to a greater extent than Clergue ever thought and he was a big thinker.'[2] The Sault, in Dunn's mind, lived and died by the acts of 'big thinkers.'

James Hamet Dunn was a member of a small but illustrious band of Canadians who emerged from the forests of New Brunswick in the late nineteenth century and went on to build stellar careers in business, law, and politics thoughout the Empire. They were all driven men. Andrew Bonar Law and R.B. Bennett captured prime ministerships on either side of the Atlantic. Although born in Ontario, Max Aitken, later Lord Beaverbrook, was raised in Newcastle and was always a New Brunswicker at heart. From Nova Scotia, the Maritime exodus was joined by Izaak Walton Killam and Cyrus Eaton. Of the group, Dunn had the humblest origins. Born in St Peter's village outside Bathurst on 29 October 1874, Dunn was immediately confronted with the unpleasant realities of life in late-nineteenth-century Maritime Canada. His grandfather and father, first- and second-generation Irish-Canadians, had seen the New Brunswick timber trade, the source of their livelihood, steadily decline since mid-century. When Robert H. Dunn, the father, died from pneumonia caught from a winter spill into Bathurst harbour, young Dunn's upbringing fell to his hard-working and self-reliant mother, Eliza. Mrs Dunn's wages as a telegraph operator provided the boy with adequate but by no means sumptuous surroundings.[3] For both mother and son, life in Bathurst was, without exaggeration, a struggle to keep daily bread on the table and to maintain some semblance of social standing.

Dunn's early years, he always claimed, were moulded by two predominant influences: the Presbyterian values inculcated by his church and the stimulation provided by his exposure to the world of learning. Beaverbrook later claimed that, like himself, Dunn was indelibly impressed by the message of the Presbyterian Shorter Catechism which made a 'bold virtue of getting on in the world.'[4] 'Getting on' for Dunn first took shape in the classroom, where he apparently proved an 'apt and conscientious' student, a status that grew from a lusty appetite for work and a self-assured cockiness. A voracious reader with a taste for historical writing, young Dunn soon displayed a prodigious, if not photographic, memory. When honoured with an honorary doctorate from Sacré-Coeur University in 1954, Dunn informed the graduands that they, as he had decades before, should seek inspiration from the Book of Ecclesiastes: 'What thy hand findeth to do, do it with thy might.'

If history gave Dunn an awareness of broader horizons, the bleak parochialism and economic grimness of North Shore New Brunswick must have shown him that Bathurst offered little opportunity for 'getting on' in the world. In later years, he claimed that he made his first dime by retrieving stray logs from the beaches of Chaleur Bay. This was obviously not enough: Dunn's adolescence in the 1890s was marked by brief sallies into the wider world in search of employment and experience, first to the American shore of Lake Michigan to work as a deckhand and then to Lynn, Massachusetts to wrap armatures for the Thomson Houston Company. Finally he made his first trip to England as assistant to a travelling 'professor of memory.' 'From that time on fortune buffeted me about,' he later recalled, 'and I've always thought the buffets were the best possible things that fortune ever did to anybody because they make you more determined to do something different.'[5] From an early age, Dunn displayed a knack for striking up friendships with fellow adolescents imbued with similar ambitions and energy. In Michigan, for instance, he befriended Bob Lafollette, Junior, the future reform politican. In his native New Brunswick, Dunn's closest boyhood friend was the precocious Max Aitken.

Returning to Bathurst, Dunn determined that a legal career offered the best chance of advancement to one without wealth or social standing. He articled under a local solicitor in Bathurst, where, while on a legal errand to Chatham, he first met Dick Bennett. On Bennett's advice, Dunn enrolled in Dalhousie Law School in 1895. Jimmy had wanted to read law at Harvard, but Bennett advised him that his meagre savings would go farther in Nova Scotia. Once in Halifax, he never looked back, except nostalgically.

Throughout his life, Dunn harboured a deep nostalgic yearning for New Brunswick. 'One thing every decent ordinary person never wants to throw off,' he reflected shortly before his death, 'is the land of his birth.'[6] The memory of a North Shore childhood served to remind him, as it did Beaverbrook, of his humble origins, thereby embellishing the 'success' stories he relished telling in the cosmopolitan circles in which he later found himself. 'Are there any New Brunswickers in Jerusalem?' Dunn once cabled Beaverbrook.[7] More important, the maritime orientation of the New Brunswick economy provided Dunn and Beaverbrook with a world view that had a decidedly oceanic perspective, an attitude that gave parochial New Brunswick much greater meaning in the world of the Empire than in continental Canada. This transatlantic frame of mind was reinforced by the belief, clearly held by Dunn, that New Brunswick's Loyalist heritage gave it a distinct political role to fulfil in the empire. From London, Dunn saluted R.B. Bennett's 1930 election victory as 'a great day for New Brunswick and the Empire.'[8] Similarly, Dunn welcomed Beaverbrook's Empire Free Trade crusade as the portent of 'a new Elizabethan age'[9] and told the Montreal *Star* in 1928 that 'England regards Canada as the first hope of the British Empire in the future and the eventual centre of Anglo-Saxon power and culture.'[10] New Brunswick thus bred in Dunn the habit of thinking in expansive imperial terms, much the same outlook that was required in the world of international high finance which he was to frequent for the next four decades.

Hard pressed to finance his legal education, Dunn resorted to casual jobs as a librarian and harbour worker. An opinionated and argumentative student,[11] he caught the attention of both his professors and Haligonian lawyers, with the result that he was taken on at graduation by the firm of Pearson and Covert. It was Benjamin F. Pearson, promoter of the Halifax Tramway and ally of American industrial promoter Henry M. Whitney, who first showed Dunn that the legal profession could serve as an entrée to many other realms of activity. The interlude at Pearson and Covert supplied the young lawyer with adequate contacts to draw him away from Halifax and into the vortex of central Canadian economic life.[12] Through the Pearson offices, Dunn glimpsed the brightest stars of industrial promotion in Canada, ranging from railway mogul William Mackenzie to utilities wizard Fred S. Pearson. Advised by B.F. Pearson to establish a legal career in Alberta, Dunn did a brief stint in Edmonton as a legal counsel for railway promoters, notably those of the Edmonton, Yukon and Pacific Railway.[13] Although his two young friends Max Aitken and R.B. Bennett lingered in the burgeoning West, Dunn chose to return east to lobby for various railway schemes before the Department of the Interior. 'The west must pay tribute to the east,' he is said to have quipped to Aitken, 'and I'm off to the east where I can collect tribute.'[14] Again on Pearson's recommendation, the ambitious young lawyer found work with the preeminent Montreal legal firm of Greenshields, Greenshields and Heneker, where under the tutelage of J.N. Greenshields he handled the firm's railway lobby in Ottawa and Quebec City.[15] By 1901, Dunn's peripatetic career had come to a halt in Montreal, only, however, after he had been called to the bar in Nova Scotia, the Northwest Territories, and Quebec.

Montreal provided an environment in which Dunn's professional and social ambitions blossomed rapidly. In August 1901, he married Gertrude Price, daughter of a wealthy Quebec City lumber merchant.[16] The marriage soon proved propitious in both social and financial terms. Dunn borrowed $20,000 from his father-in-law, H.M. Price, and purchased a seat on the Montreal Stock Exchange in 1902. He then established a brokerage firm under the name of J.H. Dunn and Company. Association with Greenshields had given him a new set of contracts and brought him one step nearer the complex financial network that serviced the immense capital needs of Canada's growing economy. It was a business world predicated on a heavy reliance on English capital, supported by the transatlantic financial fellowship of promoters, financiers, and lawyers. As a railway lobbyist, Dunn had seen the potential for profit and power offered by this fellowship, and he now determined to join it rather than serve it as a lawyer. A novice in this world, Dunn initially specialized in two brokerage activities: arbitrage and flotations. Arbitrage was an age-old traffic: the art of capitalizing on minute differences in price for the same commodity or stock on different markets. To exploit the full potential of this trade, Dunn established a London office in 1905 in partnership with a Swiss-born investment broker, C.L. Fischer, under the name of Dunn, Fischer and Company.[17]

While immense profits could be made by capitalizing on fractional differences in price between two markets, arbitrage operators stood to diminish their risk and increase their profit if they could in some measure manipulate market movements. Trust and secrecy were indispensable. Groups of brokers or 'syndicates' were formed with the purpose of cornering a stock, seizing control of it, and then juggling the price up in a 'bull' market or down in a 'bear' market. 'Do not try [to] clean up [the] Canadian market,' Dunn typically instructed London in code, 'until I advise you to, as I may need to force some selling here.'[18] If a syndicate did not have control, such attacks on the market could backfire miserably, as once happened when Dunn tried to force up the price of Dominion Iron and Steel stocks only to see the price collapse, entailing considerable losses. Dunn's arbitrage dealings covered many of the popular Canadian securities of the day, including the Electrical Development Corporation, various Latin American utilities ventures, Canadian street railways, and national railways. In each case, the syndicates sought to inhibit the free play of the market and to induce artificial prices. This cynical exploitation of the market secretly undermined any pretence of equal opportunity for the small investor. As Robert Horne-Payne, the English financial lieutenant of railway promoters Mackenzie and Mann, told Dunn in 1907: 'As soon as we find that there are no more [Rio] bonds offered in Canada, we must set to work to draw all the attention to them in Canada that we can, because when once the Canadian public finds that there is no supply with their speculative inclinations, there is nobody like them to run a price up. I think one fine day we shall find there is not a Bond to be had either in Toronto or Montreal and then you must fix fireworks in the local press.'[19]

From arbitrage, it was logical that Dunn would progress to the field of flotations and underwriting. Here again the key to profits lay in gaining control of a new security by forming a tight syndicate to underwrite its issue. The underwriter stood to enhance his investment either by manipulating prices or by taking stock bonuses on bond issues, gambling that a rising market for bonds would pull the stocks' value up in its wake. One of Dunn's first underwriting participations was in Sir William Van Horne's Havana Electric Company, a Canadian-incorporated venture capitalized on the London market.[20] Participation in such syndicates provided Dunn with invaluable contracts among Canada's legal and financial élite, an illustrious group including Sir Henry Pellatt, Mackenzie and Mann, Z.A. Lash, Sir George Drummond, E.J. Clouston, and lesser but expanding lights such as Aemilius Jarvis and Izaak Killam. Despite occasional setbacks, Dunn quickly exhibited the perspicacity and driving ambition to survive in this Darwinian world of finance. In later years, he would wistfully refer to this halcyon period as 'the old developing days' when he imbibed the wisdom of established financiers, most notably William Mackenzie and F.S. Pearson, men who 'carried out great enterprises and gave some of us younger men a chance.'[21]

Tempted by the success of Mackenzie and Mann's Canadian Northern, Dunn approached Prime Minister Laurier in June 1904 as a supplicant for the position of secretary to the commission appointed to build the government section of the Grand Trunk Pacific. Citing his 'good legal and business training,' Dunn assured Laurier that he was 'comfortably independent of financial returns.'[22] Rebuffed in this bid for a career as a railway promoter, Dunn made the momentous decision to leave Montreal and to seek the greener financial fields of London. He departed Montreal in 1905, crossed the Atlantic, and consolidated himself in the Dunn, Fischer firm in the City of London, leaving his junior partners in Montreal to oversee the Canadian terminus of what he hoped would grow into a thriving transatlantic arbitrage and investment business. For Dunn it was a natural step closer to the centre of world finance, a step soon to be taken by other young Canadian financiers, notably Max Aitken, Izaak Killam, and E.R. Peacock.

While London offered a much broader and more appetizing field for investment, Dunn's oceanic shift was chiefly prompted by his growing friendship with Fred Stark Pearson, the dynamic American engineer, promoter, and financier who did more to mould Dunn's formative years than any other person. Born in Massachusetts in 1861 and schooled as an engineer at Tufts and MIT, Pearson possessed an uncanny ability to visualize the application of electric power to the urban transport needs of late-nineteenth-century America.[23] This proclivity for invention and adaptation of a new technology was first displayed in his harnessing of 'white coal' to the needs of municipal power and streetcar companies in Boston and New York, where he built generators of a size and efficiency that defied the imagination of more timid engineers. Pearson's abilities drew him on assignment to tasks outside the United States, including a stint at Cape Breton's Dominion Coal Company in the 1890s and the construction of the Lac du Bonnet power station outside Winnipeg. By 1905, Pearson had become a familiar face on Toronto's Bay Street and his name regularly surfaced as a consulting engineer to many Canadian companies.

The emerging public utilities barons of the United States, men like the English-born Insull brothers, built their empires on the rudimentary but convincing dictum that, to be exploited efficiently, electric power must be produced monopolistically, as a 'natural monopoly.' The bigger the producer, the greater the saving to the public. Whereas in Canada this logic led to the people's power movement, culminating in Adam Beck's Ontario Hydro,[24] in the United States it fostered the growth of giant utility conglomerates like the Insull's Middle West Utilities Corporation. Such corporate monsters glittered in the imaginations of financiers. Because his projects required massive amounts of capital, Pearson was inexorably drawn into league with financiers who stood ready to promote and exploit the engineer's genius. Following in Pearson's path was the more flamboyant but less gifted Percival Farquhar, a Pennsylvannian Quaker trained in law, whose ambitious railway promotions brought him to the London and New York money markets to capitalize his grandiose schemes.[25] It was to ambitious and well-connected financiers like James Dunn that Pearson and Farquhar turned in the City.

Pearson and Farquhar were quick to realize that if handsome profits were to be made from public utilities in North America, even greater profits were to be earned in the technologically starved and capital-poor areas of Latin America. The surge of interest in foreign investment began with the 'new Cuba' of 1898. American syndicates calculated that with the promise of supplying relatively cheap electricity, water, and public transportation to sprawling Latin American metropolises they could extract from grateful, if unsuspecting, municipal governments monopolistic rights to these services, in some cases in perpetuity. Besides this 'inestimable advantage,' as Farquhar put it, Latin American enterprises were free of all the entanglements of government regulation that had come, in businessmen's eyes, to plague American railways.[26] The best means to achieve these ends was often found in a charter obtained under lax Canadian laws, Canada being a country with which European investors were familiar and disposed to invest in generously. In the early years of the new century, a steady stream of Latin American, Caribbean, and Central American enterprises were chartered under Canadian law.[27] Incorporation in Canada afforded a company a nominal domicile and a good reputation, and subjected it to minimal legal obligations, provided the company guaranteed 'that their operations will be carried on entirely without the Dominion of Canada.'[28] These foreign utility companies, carefully incorporated and administered by such leading Toronto lawyers as Zebulon A. Lash, often exploited legal loopholes permitting the publication of imprecise prospectuses, skimpy audits, and irregular annual reports.[29] Control being the crucial factor in promoters' eyes, Canadian laws endowed the small investor with paltry rights. 'The minority shareholder is rarely the subject of compassion,' complained one critic of the law. 'He is usually regarded as a "kicker" or a noisy fellow who has lost in the game and deserves no consideration.'[30] As Dunn's partner Fischer once arrogantly boasted about a proposed bank: 'We will control the board, and, if we find it necessary we can at anytime issue another 100,000 or 200,000 f[rancs] of shares and subscribe them ourselves.'[31]

Since the Canadian investing public could provide little of the capital needed for these foreign ventures, Canadian brokerage firms, like Dunn's in Montreal, participated in syndicates that steered their bonds and stocks on to the London and New York markets. 'I do not see that Canada has done anything for this enterprise,' Dunn noted of the Mexican North Western in 1910, 'and the directors he [Pearson] has there outside the firm of Blake, Lash and Cassels who are paid for their work are mere figureheads.' 'London,' Dunn concluded, 'is entitled to any profits that are to be made on the financing of the company as London will eventually get the bonds any way whether they are sold here or in Canada.'[32] Immense profits were generated for the brokers of these issues through under- writer's commissions, stock bonuses, and what could be skimmed off by arbitrage.[33] Dunn was instrumental in flotations of numerous Pearson and Farquhar enterprises, ranging from the Rio de Janeiro Tramway, Light and Power to the Denver and Northwestern Railway. In doing so he dramatically expanded his financial horizons and ambitions from the rather narrow possibilities of Canadian finance to the unbounded potential of investment banking on many continents. After 1904, Dunn had only a minimal interest in the possibilities of financing Canadian endeavours. In fact, Dunn's Canadian connection was greatly damaged in the years 1907–9 by the collapse of the Sovereign Bank and J.H. Dunn and Company, in Montreal. The episode vividly exposed the ruthlessness with which the financial world punished those who abused the implicit trust on which syndicates and transatlantic partnerships were built.

Dunn, who by 1907 was a director of the Sovereign Bank, relied very heavily on the bank to supply 'call loans' with which he financed further investments, using securities already held on margin as hypothecated collateral. Such precarious arrangements worked well in times of financial vitality, but any downswing, such as the 'panic' of 1907, caught the borrower overextended. Faced with $282,876 in call loans from the Sovereign by mid-1907 and a stern demand for repayment, Dunn found his ability to make good his liabilities severely restricted by the financial crisis. Sovereign president D.M. Stewart had little option but to cover Dunn's position, arranging special terms with the bank's foreign allies, J.P. Morgan and Company and the Dresdner Bank. Surrounded by 'whispers of pessimism and criticism of his methods,'[34] Stewart's position became untenable and he fled the country to Alaska, later telling Dunn it was '*solely* for my health.'[35] Fortunately for Dunn, Stewart was replaced as president by Aemilius Jarvis, a Toronto stockbroker friend, and by the time the Sovereign collapsed for good in 1908, Dunn had extricated himself from his debts.[36]

Less propitious was the collapse of J.H. Dunn and Company. Caught in the 1907 'panic,' Grey and Hughes, Dunn's Montreal surrogates, had financially overextended themselves without consulting their senior partner. Fearful of Dunn's reaction to this state of affairs, Victor Grey committed suicide. Alleging that Grey personally owed him 'more than $60,000,' Dunn insisted that the remaining partner, Hughes, take out life insurance to the extent of his liabilities.[37]

Dunn's ruthless proficiency, tireless energy, and insatiable appetite for profit pushed him to meteoric success in the financial world. The years 1906–14 were for Dunn a period of rapidly escalating success leading to millionaire status, a dazzlingly lavish style of life, and a much-heralded international reputation. To his social acquaintances, he was a 'galvanic force,' a 'human dynamo.'[38] To the artistic world which he opulently patronized, Dunn was 'the friendly financier,'[39] 'a man of blustering tempers, kind impulses and excellent business acumen.'[40] The brash young Canadian's reckless behaviour in his many Rolls-Royces and the revelry of his country house parties frequently figure in the memoirs and diaries of the rich and influential of Edwardian society.[41] Whether in social or in financial circles, Dunn sought to control and manipulate. For those who were willing to play or to do business on Dunn's terms, the rewards were large. To those who were not, Dunn showed the litigious and unforgiving side of his character.

Most important, Dunn was, in the words of the preeminent Otto Kahn, 'a greater financier than all of us.'[42] From his Threadneedle Street office he coordinated and participated in financial syndicates with investments from South America to Norway and from Spain to Mexico. The financial substructure of these enterprises encompassed millions of small investors in Europe and America, all bound together by the salesmanship of brokers in New York, London, Brussels, and Berlin. In the dizzy years before the Great War, Dunn had solidly established himself in what a friend dubbed the 'financial aristocracy' of Europe. Writing to Dunn in 1912 from what must have seemed relative exile in Davidson, Saskatchewan, one of his old Dalhousie schoolmates noted that he was 'glad to note that you and my old friend Max Aitken, now Sir Max, are top notches in the financial world of the old country, and my best wish is to see you ... a member of what our old friend the Dean called "the most exclusive club in the world."'[43]

Dunn, Fisher and Company thrived in the charmed circle of merchant banking. Since the Napoleonic wars, the merchant banker's activities had been sheathed in an aura of mystery and respect. The great houses of Speyer and Baring became synonymous with the spread of industrialism and British economic hegemony, serving to give the term 'London banker' a 'charmed value,' in the words of Stanley Baldwin, and so Lombard Street, 'which received money from one part of the world and lent it to the other, became ... a world conception.'[44] With the twentieth century, the role of the merchant banker began to diversity so rapidly that although Speyers, Barings, Seligmans, and Rothschilds continued to thrive, they did so in the presence of a new type of merchant bankers whose activities defied generalization. The classic definition of merchant banking became debased to the point that conversationally 'the word "merchant banker" has come to cover any type of financier, financial adventurer, or promoter of mergers, of whatever standing or achievement.'[45] James Dunn's London career exemplified this development.

The Pearson-Dunn partnership was on the edge of this new frontier of merchant banking, for while Pearson was not a member of a financial house himself, their activities broke down the old barrier that barred the banker from participation in the actual entrepreneurial process. Not content to be a mere purveyor of capital, Dunn actively cultivated projects which would generate capital demands and, whenever possible, dextrously manipulated both the promotional and the financial aspects of the same project through a common syndicate. Hence, while 41 Threadneedle Street acted as head office of the English Construction Company, a Costa Rican firm established by a Dunn syndicate in 1912, it was also the brokerage firm handling the company's flotations.[46] Adopting Pearson's style, Dunn himself commissioned agents to ferret concessions out of Latin American governments.[47] He was also constantly in receipt of proposals forwarded by technological missionaries, like Pearson, Farquhar, and Sir Robert Perks, outlining lucrative opportunities stretching from Havana to St Petersburg, all in need of capital.[48] While Dunn was involved at times in as many as several dozen such syndicates, the real fulcrum of his activities was the Pearson enterprises: the Spanish, Mexican, and Brazilian utilities ventures so well regarded by the investing public. Increasingly assisted by Alfred Loewenstein, a shrewd and ambitious Belgian broker, Dunn used this investment pipeline to pump profits out of commissions, stock bonuses, and arbitrage.[49] For years afterwards it was said that Brazilians described their tramcars as 'bondes,' honouring the bonds of the Canadian companies that established their urban utilities.[50]

The profitability of any syndicate promoting such utility companies hinged on two crucial factors: an airtight and monopolistic concession and absolute control of its financial promotion. The extraction of concessions from foreign state and municipal governments was the forte of F.S. Pearson. Hungry for the civilizing touch of technology and untutored in the intricacies of modern science, foreign governments readily succumbed to the blandishments of the promoter, often yielding concessions of incredible latitude. The Mexican Tramways syndicate, for instance, secured a franchise for the sole right to operate trams in downtown Mexico City until 1982, together with a perpetual lease of the city's suburban routes.[51] In 1912, Pearson negotiated a hydro concession with exclusive rights for the Spanish city of Barcelona. After securing Canadian incorporation and establishing 'excellent relations' with the Spanish government and King Alfonso XIII, Pearson launched the Barcelona Traction, Light and Power Company. Through concessions and purchases of existent companies, it soon enjoyed a near complete hold on the power potential of the Ebro River, from which Pearson envisaged net annual earnings of £1,184,000 by 1917.[52]

With an ample concession assured, the syndicate's next objective was to ensure itself the inside track on the road to profits. A syndicate could exploit a flotation for much more than the usual underwriter's commission. When contracting the flotation of a 1911 loan for the state of Santa Catarina in Brazil, Dunn was, for instance, able to buy bonds *en bloc* from the state at 85½ and to sell them in Europe at between 89⅛ and 94⅝, leaving him with an automatic 6 per cent profit. Most industrial flotations were accompanied by the promise of further earnings from stock bonuses. These stocks, valueless at the time of issue, represented a windfall profit when and if the enterprise in question became popular in investors' eyes. 'Our final position in the business,' Fischer reported to Dunn on their commitment to the Havana Docks Company, 'will therefore be that we get as [stock] bonus with the bonds 37½% and in addition, ½ of the surplus stock which is 18¾% together with 10% of the construction profit in cash.'[53] This whole strategy of syndicate flotation depended on majority control, a condition which enabled the participants to induce a 'bullish' market onto which they could dump their bonds and stocks. 'One must find the psychological moment when the market can be turned and driven in the way that will make the short cover and induce independent buying,' Dunn once advised Farquhar.[54] When a 'bear' attack intent on depressing prices materialized, Dunn adroitly marshalled his syndicate's 'friends' to dike his position. ' The different friends of the company,' he once reported to Toronto stockbroker F.H. Deacon, 'seem to be working much more in harmony and the bear party have used up their ammunition in the way of scarce rumours.'[55] Dunn was not always so lucky. Having invested heavily in a 1910 bid to refinance the Rock Island Line, a Pearson-Farquhar bid to build a US transcontinental, Dunn lost substantially when two unreliable partners sold on a rising market. 'Next time,' Dunn bitterly concluded, 'we will be more sure of our associates and stick to the things that we absolutely control.'[56]

The object of all Dunn's intricate and secretive orchestration of the market was to induce independent buying by the small investor, 'the most permanent class of investor.'[57] Since this mass of unorganized buyers formed the ultimate core of any company's ownership, it was imperative to cultivate and retain their confidence in the projects into which they so trustingly poured their money. In this respect, the 'paid puffing' or 'fireworks fixing'[58] of the press was invaluable. In 1909 Dunn dispatched a *Financial Times* reporter from London to the Sault industries 'for the purpose of acquainting the English public with the Lake Superior property.'[59] If good news could be manufactured, bad news could be suppressed. When the Nexaca dam, the linchpin of the Mexican Light and Power grid, partially collapsed in 1909, Dunn valiantly tried to downplay the news, fearful that a 'strong bear party' would take advantage of 'the vulnerable bull position.'[60]

James Dunn's astonishing ascendancy in the City was at root founded on this manipulative, greedy, and ruthless approach to finance, an approach fuelled by unflagging energy, an unerring memory, and a keen intelligence. Some indication of Dunn's vindictiveness to those who impeded his progress was revealed in 1913 when Charles Fischer, always very much the junior partner to Dunn, fled London after overextending himself in the complex web of the firm's affairs. Charging that Fischer had left him bowed under 'extraordinary burdens,' Dunn dispatched detectives to scour Europe for the culprit, took possession of his home and art collection, and called his family 'liars.'[61] When the ruined Fischer returned to London in 1922, Dunn reinstated him in his junior position, reminding him constantly of his past transgressions.

If the demands of business on Dunn were onerous and at times unpleasant, the sybaritic style of life they supported made the effort worthwhile. Country homes, French villas, a fleet of Rolls Royces, and a well-indulged appetite for art catapulted the New Brunswicker to the centre of English social life. Through fellow expatriates Max Aitken and Hamar Greenwood, Dunn was soon socializing in the distinguished company of Bonar Law, Asquith, Lloyd George, and the young Churchill, all of whom seem to have held the bumptious Canadian in considerable esteem. On Dunn's advice, Violet Asquith, daughter of the prime minister, invested £1,000 in Pearson's Mexican North Western Railway.[62] After meeting Dunn on a transatlantic passage in 1918, Prime Minister Borden pegged him as 'an exceedingly capable businessman and his interests and connections are much wider and much more important than I realized.'[63] As Margot Asquith, the notorious social snob, told Dunn some years later: 'I *am* glad to hear you have become rich.'[64] (It has been alleged that Rex Mottram, the abrasive Canadian millionaire in Evelyn Waugh's novel *Brideshead Revisted*, was modelled after Dunn. In all probability Mottram was a composite of Dunn and Beaverbrook. Waugh was acquainted with both and treated both with snobbish disdain.)

Wealth served to develop and accentuate in Dunn certain eccentricities, which when observed in any but the rich would have occasioned alarm if not hilarity. From an early age, the Canadian millionaire displayed an obsessive interest in his health, especially with respect to his prospects of long life. Huge sums were spent on vitamins, health bread, yoga lessons, pillows stuffed with spruce boughs, and mysterious elixirs.

At one point, Dunn sought the opinion of a New York 'doctor' as to whether his circulatory system fared better from vigorous rubbing with a towel after a bath or from simply patting himself dry. Dunn did not hesitate to pass such wisdom on to his friends. Churchill, for instance, was advised to steam cook all his food and to avoid frying at all costs. Such dietary advice was by no means wrong-headed. Dunn, it must be admitted, lived to the age of eighty-one. In many ways, he was a pioneer health food addict. It was not his prescience in these matters but his determination to beat life's odds that commanded attention.

James Dunn's interest in Canadian affairs never flagged during these years of London success. Although Beaverbrook later insisted that Dunn was a 'lifelong Liberal,'[65] he welcomed the 1911 election victory of the Tories as the 'best evidence of the intelligence and patriotism of the Canadian people triumphing over the superficiality of active commercialism.'[66] Almost simultaneously, he dispatched condolences to Liberal W.S. Fielding, later coaching the deposed finance minister on land purchases in New Mexico.[67] Essentially apolitical in his approach to politics, Dunn cabled 'heartiest congratulations' to Borden, Mackenzie King, Meighen, and Bennett through the years without distinction. Politicians, in his mind, were simply a means to an end.

After his scrap with the Sovereign Bank in 1907–8, Dunn exhibited little enthusiasm for underwriting Canadian securities, except the nominally Canadian Pearson utilities. In 1909, he accepted the position of Agent-General for Alberta in London, not so much because of the salary it offered but for the prestige and 'the fact that these high class [provincial] securities bring with them a following of similarly high class investors.'[68] Otherwise, Dunn studiously avoided Canadian industrial securities, claiming they were 'so difficult' to handle in England.[69] Only with the tottering Lake Superior Corporation was Dunn prepared to break his resolve. In many ways, what F.H. Clergue had done at the Sault was essentially what Pearson had so masterfully done in Latin America. Like the Pearson 'group,' the Sault industries were planned around a hydro-power base, financed and controlled by foreign capital and incorporated under the auspices of company laws of convenience. Dunn reasoned that the application of Pearson's engineering skills and the backing of syndicated London finance could radically transform the fortunes of the Sault corporation and realize Clergue's vision. 'I was just young enough to feel that he was right,' Dunn later told Beaverbrook.[70]

As early as 1906, Dunn had observed Clergue's frantic efforts to secure European loans to buoy up the Sault complex. Noting that he did not have 'a good opinion of this business under its present control,' Dunn fell back on the hopeful strategy that 'a condition might arise when these friends of mine could get possession of the property on a different basis, at which time it would be a profitable enterprise for us to embark in.'[71] When conditions at the Sault became financially unstable in 1908, Dunn turned to Pearson and London financier Robert Fleming.[72] Seizing the initiative, he canvassed Pearson and Fleming, pointing to the 'great opportunity here' and the 'excellent option for control' and stressing that the Clergue works were 'the most important undertaking in Canada after the great railway systems.'[73] To a degree, Dunn himself seemed to have succumbed to Clergue's persuasive rhetoric. He brought Clergue to London to assist in lobbying Fleming and Pearson. Control, Dunn assured his two seniors, could be secured through purchase of the Canadian Improvement Company's liabilities and offered the chance 'to make of this group of enterprises what Clergue and his Philadelphia friends originally set out to do. We would then have right at home on the American continent a business to employ our energies for the next ten years to come.' Like others before him, Dunn soon learned to distrust Clergue's extravagant claims. Late in 1908, he scolded the American for 'putting me in a position to make statements that are so different from the facts.'[74]

Aided and abetted by Premier Whitney of Ontario, the Pearson-Fleming syndicate bought into the Sault industries with much the same set of expectations that had accompanied Pearson's Latin American and Iberian ventures. Yet even with a bloc of approximately $19 million (nominal value) in Lake Superior Corporation securities, the London syndicate never managed to wrest permanent control of the corporation away from Philadelphia. While London control did pare off some of the unprofitable subsidiaries and facilitated corporate borrowing on the London market, it never addressed itself to the obvious task of radical surgery on the Sault corporation. With Pearson's attention soon diverted again to his other ventures, Philadelphia gradually reasserted its hegemony, finally reinstating its own management in 1917. Dunn, always a junior partner in the syndicate, was powerless to revive London's interest in the Sault. In 1908, he had insisted that Fleming regard him 'as a continuing factor in the business' and when he first visited the Sault complex he admitted his surprise at 'their extent' and 'their structure.' Dunn's commitment to the Sault was, however, one of speculative finance, not industrial management. He frankly confessed to being 'personally ignorant of what it should cost to make rails.' He told Fleming that his principal contribution to the Sault venture lay in his 'acquaintance with

Canada and with the local and federal governments.'[75] By 1910, Dunn's ardour for his Sault investment had cooled. He complained that Fleming had no 'definite plan' for the Sault and confided in a New York financial friend that the Lake Superior Corporation had 'an excellent future but I think as far as the common stock is concerned the future is a long way off yet. I am not speaking from the market point of view but from the point of view of intrinsic value.'[76]

The inability of Pearson and Dunn to capitalize on their Sault investment was largely the result of their troubles elsewhere. The last years before the First War saw Pearson's overseas investments bedevilled by revolution in Mexico, financial and construction problems in Spain, and the debilitating effects of the 1913 economic slump. The three crowning gems in Pearson's Mexican tiara were the Mexican Tramway Company, the Mexican Light and Power Company, both serving Mexico City, and the Mexican North Western Railway, a hinterland line tapping northern Chihuahua state. Based on concessions won under the indolent regime of Mexican president Porfirio Diaz, the success and profitability of these ventures hinged on political stability, regardless of ideological hue or brutality of method. When the Mexican republic began to crumble into anarchy in 1910–11 so too did the profits of Pearson's Mexican operations.[77] A nightmarish succession of unstable regional regimes held sway over Mexican affairs from 1910 through the early 1920s. In the midst of this turmoil, Pearson found that his once successful formula for foreign investment had gone sadly awry as waves of 'ruffianly generals' swept over his power and railway installations. This banditry reached a climax when one particularly sadistic insurgent, Castillo, backed a train-load of American nationals into a burning tunnel. Amid such upheaval, the 530-mile Mexico North Western Railway simply ground to a halt, severing Pearson's rich stand of soft pine from American markets. 'The man who can operate the Mexico North Western Company successfully,' Dunn dolefully told an English banker in 1913, 'must be something of a politician, railwayman, lumberman, and generally a good businessman.'[78]

Desperate to restore stability, Pearson instructed his Mexican managers to lobby the Mexican government for protection of foreign investments. Despite lavish contributions to 'friends at court,'[79] these endeavours proved as futile as trying to run the trains on schedule. 'At the present time,' one Pearson confidant reported, 'it is absolutely impossible to have anything done in any of the Government departments ... The President [Huerta] is drunk and incapable of conducting business for two or three days in a week as is also the Minister of Communications, who aside from being a drunkard, is a drug fiend ... The only people today making money in Mexico are the officials and army officers who pocket the pay that should go to the soldiers, steal and sell government supplies etc.'[80] 'I think the time has come,' Pearson told Dunn in 1912, 'when we must get the English government to intervene.' Without intervention, Pearson stressed, English investors stood to lose investments totalling £5 to £6 million.[81] Working through his friend Hamar Greenwood, an influential Liberal MP, Dunn applied pressure on the British government, seeking additional support from Canadian Prime Minister Borden.[82] Caught in the rather anomalous position of being a Canadian company seeking protection from foreign governments for its far-flung operations, Dunn's pleas fell on deaf ears. 'The prospect is a terrible one indeed,' one Foreign Office official placidly noted, 'but I fear there is no action we can take, and the U.S. government evidently prefer that Mexico City should be sacked rather than attempt to avert such a calamity.'[83] Learning that the American occupation of Vera Cruz would not be extended further inland, Dunn and Pearson railed against President Wilson's 'mollycoddlers' and 'Washington's pusillanimous policy.'[84]

By 1914 events in Mexico were rapidly moving beyond the pale of solubility. The tramway system had been expropriated by the Carranza government and the railway and power companies had passed into receivership. Dunn did not allow his Mexican aspirations to evaporate without a struggle. In 1919, he urged Borden to seek justice for Mexican investors at the Versailles talks.[85] He briefly toyed with the idea of forming a private air force to patrol the concessions with which he was associated in northern Mexico. As late as 1926, Dunn could still confidently predict that the Mexican North Western would 'come back in a very big way.'[86] By the 1930s his predictions had turned completely sour. 'I have however so lost confidence in that country,' he conceded, 'that I do not feel that any effort on my part by employing Mexican lawyers or fighting the Mexican processes would get me anything but further expense and troubles so I must take the consequences of what happens in that God-forsaken land.'[87]

The abiding lesson of the Mexican fiasco was that of loss of stability brought not only the end of profits but loss of control, the essential element in all the Pearson undertakings. This message was reinforced by the decline of Pearson's Iberian ventures. Incorporated in 1912 under Canadian law, the Barcelona Traction, Light and Power Company quickly outdistanced the ability of its investors to finance it. Faced with this escalation of construction costs, Pearson's solution was simply to increase the capital of the already overcapitalized enterprise. Astonished by this folly, Toronto financier E.R.Wood protested that his Canadian syndicate was 'groaning under the load' and would not 'sail under false colours.'[88] Similarly, European backer Alfred Loewenstein expressed his 'profound feeling of dissatisfaction' with Pearson's practices and the escalating cost of construction in Barcelona.[89] Although the Seros power plant was completed in 1913, Pearson's position was so attenuated that he defaulted on bonus share commitments to his backers. Consequently, he was squeezed from the direction of Barcelona's affairs in early 1915 and control was lodged in a London committee headed by E.R. Peacock.[90] The crucial element of control had once again slipped from Pearson's hands. Of all Pearson's scattered endeavours, only Brazilian Traction ultimately escaped the ravages of revolution, nationalization, and financial collapse.

In the unstable years of 1913–15, Dunn learned that membership in the 'financial aristocracy' could at times be a precarious and impoverishing experience. Financial losses inflicted by Pearson's reverses in Mexico and Spain were exacerbated by the commercial slump fo 1913. 'I need not point out to you,' he wrote to United Fruit Company mogul Minor C. Keith in April 1914, 'how seriously the credit of all Latin American countries has been shaken by conditions in Mexico and Brazil and how necessary it is at this time to do nothing that can shake public confidence any further in Latin American countries.'[91] The prospect of war cast an even darker pall over the Pearson empire. As early as spring 1914, Dunn was bemoaning 'the utter inactivity of markets in Europe and the utter inability to sell or interest one's usual friends in anything.'[92] The paralysis of international finance induced by the German onslaught at least gave Dunn and Pearson a reprieve from clamouring investors,[93] whose claims on the Pearson enterprises went into suspended animation until the war's end. In desperate straits up to that point, Dunn had sought a £150,000 loan from American steel magnate Henry C. Frick in July 1914, using his Lake Superior holdings and 110,000 pounds' worth of his art collection as collateral.[94] Any hope of resurrecting the Dunn-Pearson syndicates after the war came to a watery end off Ireland in May 1915, when Pearson went down on the *Lusitania*. Even though he was left to unravel his mentor's tangled and debt-ridden affairs, Dunn later reflected that 'it may be some years before we have similar world conditions again but I doubt whether the like of ... Dr. Pearson will [again] rise in our circle of friendship.'[95]

With his carefully cultivated network of financial connections shattered and the arteries of international capital completely blocked, Dunn adroitly adapted his methods to the demands of the war economy. If capital could not be traded, then commodities could. In 1915, he told Sir Frederick Williams-Taylor of the Bank of Montreal that it was his 'great regret' that 'the absolute necessity and duty of devoting myself to my business interests had prevented me from going to France.'[96] Aside from a hurried trip to inspect battlefront hospitals with Violet Asquith and the loan of his Daimler to Prime Minister Asquith, Dunn's patriotism was limited to commercial battlefields. Commodity trading for Dunn began quite literally in 'horse trading.' After promising 'satisfactory fees' to his political friends for their assistance, Dunn secured a substantial contract to supply horses to the French army.[97] By mid-1915, he was delivering between three and four thousand horses a month, purchased in the American mid-west, to French docks.[98] As the war progressed, Dunn continued to offer the British, French, and Russian governments large quantities of blankets, ammunition, Algoma steel rails, Argentine beef, and military clothing.[99] Dunn's friendship with British politicians such as Asquith, Bonar Law, Beaverbrook, and Churchill opened many doors in these negotiations. Other schemes hatched by the expatriate Canadian attempted to convert 'frozen' German investments into securities of neutral countries, to reorganize the Aetna Explosives Company and Algoma Central Railway in Canada, and to forge financial and trading links between England and Scandanavia.[100] War, for Dunn, was chiefly a case of 'business as usual.'

The war afforded Dunn one significant opportunity to marry his talents as an investment broker with the demands of industrial management. The British American Nickel Company (BANCo), established by Ontario charter in 1913, was the product of an Anglo-American syndicate, composed of F.S. Pearson, E.R. Wood, Sir William Mackenzie, James Dunn, and others who were intent on breaking the tight monopoly held on nickel production by International Nickel (INCO) and Le Mond.[101] BANCo was predicated on the hope that a new electrolytic method of nickel smelting invented by a Norwegian, Victor Noach Hybinette,[102] could be used to produce large amounts of nickel at prices lower than the patented Orford process and thus loosen INCO's grasp on the nickel trade. Cheapness was not BANCo's only appeal for, unlike INCO, it promised to erect its smelter within Canada, thus flattering the strong nationalistic impulse for self-sufficiency that had surfaced around the turn of the century. From the outset, however, the BANCo syndicate argued that they could only overcome the initial advantage of its entrenched competitors through some measure of government largesse. The short and calamitous existence of BANCo was characterized on the one hand by its ongoing efforts to extract assistance from the Canadian and imperial governments and, on the other, its struggle to ward off bankruptcy and the predatory advances of its jealous rivals.

Dunn initially confined his activities to managing the European end of the syndicate's finances. Wood and Pearson secured the North American rights to the Hybinette process, assembled various nickel-laden properties near Sudbury,[103] and gave the company a capital of $25 million in stock and $5 million in bonds, with the usual generous stock bonuses for the promoters. The syndicate tried hard to extract bounty assistance from the Borden government to match the existing provincial bounty on nickel. This hope was abruptly quashed in 1913 when Finance Minister White rejected E.R. Wood's blandishments on the subject.[104] Without federal aid, BANCo soon worked its way into a precarious financial position with over $5.7 million expended, large debts with the Bank of Commerce, and not an ounce of nickel yet refined. Under this strain the syndicate began to lose cohesion. By early 1914, E.R. Wood told Dunn that he could juggle BANCo's finances no longer and that it was 'absolutely impossible to proceed further on present lines with this nickel business.'[105]

The outbreak of war dramatically changed the complexion of the nickel question by bringing a sensational acceleration of demand for the metal and at the same time intensifying demands for Canadianization of nickel refining. Exploiting these tendencies, Dunn lobbied the Restriction of Enemy Supplies Committee in London, urging its chairman, Sir Francis Hopwood, to declare the BANCo scheme of 'great Imperial importance.'[106] Dunn and Pearson resolved to use this declaration as leverage to persuade the dominion government to guarantee a bond issue backing construction of the BANCo refinery, thereby allowing the syndicate to extend the promise of 'reasonable prices' for nickel to the British government.[107]

In Ottawa, Pearson exposed Borden to the most persuasive of his promotional charms, stressing that BANCo would be 'the first to undertake the refining of these metals in Canada' and that the Canadian government would have 'first call on a large part of its production at less than market price' and 'a very large interest in the equity' in return for a bond guarantee.[108] Assured by George Perley, high commissioner in London, that imperial authorities now viewed the nickel question as 'really a domestic question for Canada to decide for herself,' Borden bluntly told London that Ottawa saw 'no necessity for regarding [the BANCo] proposals as a war measure.'[109] 'It is an industrial corporation whose success will depend in large degree upon its management,' not on a philanthropic government, Finance Minister White emphasized.[110] Ottawa, the syndicate learned, was not Mexico City or Havana. In the midst of this transatlantic lobbying, the syndicate's kingpin, F.S. Pearson, was lost on the *Lusitania*.

With Pearson gone and Ottawa uncooperative, Dunn proceeded to write his own prescription for BANCo's future. Relying upon British hopes of severing Germany from foreign supplies of nickel, Dunn boldly proposed to travel to neutral Norway and attempt to redirect its nickel from Germany to the allies. In Norway, he sought to buy control of the Kristiansands Nikkelraffineringsverk (KNR) from a syndicate centred around Victor Hybinette, hoping to redirect KNR-refined nickel to England and ultimately forge some corporate link with BANCo. 'I act,' Dunn told the British government, 'without remuneration in the acquisition of these [KNR] shares and solely with the object of carrying out the purpose of the Government but that if the Government desire to part with this property after the War they will sell it to me at cost to be arrived at equitably.'[111] Profit and patriotism blended perfectly. It was a brilliant strategem, especially because it afforded BANCo a monopolistic hold on both an ore supply and a smelting process, just what 'the Nickel Combine has endeavoured in everyway to prevent being developed and brought into competition with them.'[112] In return for Dunn's services, the British government provided a $6 million guarantee of BANCo's securities. As with so many of Dunn's business promotions, somebody else accepted the immediate risk and he stood to reap the ultimate reward. From this apogee, the fortunes of BANCo slipped steadily downward, turning Dunn's dream of a profit-making monopoly into a nightmare from which there was no waking.

Dunn's inability to capitalize on his BANCo strategy stemmed primarily from his failure to impose unified control. He had, in the first place, to contend with the basically irreconcilable interests of the Norwegians, the British government, and his Canadian backers. Anxious only to keep nickel out of German hands, the British pursued a cautious, almost disinterested role once that end was achieved, while the Norwegian and Canadian financiers were perpetually at loggerheads over company profits. Victor Hybinette proved especially irascible and petulant and, because he was the controlling factor in the situation, prevented Dunn from exercising vigorous control. BANCo's fate was sealed by the continued reluctance of the Ontario and federal governments to extend any assistance to the fledgling company. In a desperate bid to induce federal assistance, Dunn attracted Edgar Rhodes, a prominent federal Tory, to the syndicate as a director. This did nothing to shake federal intransigence.

Against the impregnable monopoly of INCO, British American Nickel made but small inroads. A Hybinette smelter was finally opened at Deschenes, Quebec in 1920. This spark of life was extinguished by the post-war economic slump, forcing a halt to operations until 1923.[113] By 1925, BANCo was defunct and its assets were triumphantly brought up by INCO lawyers for $5 million. Dunn himself had bailed out of BANCo in early 1921, surrendering the presidency, most of his holdings, and the whole tangled skein of the corporation's affairs to Rhodes and the Norwegians. Dunn attributed his failure to rising costs and the perfidiousness of his partners and Canadian politicians, but in reality it was also the result of a lack of unified control. In an environment in which he controlled neither his own syndicate nor the INCO-dominated nickel trade, Dunn had never stood to profit from BANCo. J. Frater Taylor of Algoma observed the whole fiasco. The would-be nickel company lacked 'well balanced commercial direction.' 'Believe me,' he lectured Dunn, 'it is just the same in a commercial undertaking as it is in the European war, organization and aggressiveness are the things that must count.'[114] 'It was always a will-of-the-wisp anyway,' Dunn explained to E.R. Wood, 'but perhaps it made me exert my best efforts on occasions on which I was running the show.'[115] Wood, who like Dunn had lost heavily on the venture, scornfully replied: 'For the love of mike be careful after this where you write your name.'[116] Dunn learned his lesson well. Ten years later, the sorry memory of BANCo was never far from his thoughts as he angled for control of Algoma Steel.

Dunn greeted the return of peace with apprehension. He heartily endorsed Joseph Flavelle's view that 'the problems of peace seem more difficult and more ominous than those of war,' especially when they gave rise to 'a reawakened class spirit and class consciousness.'[117] Despite this unease, Dunn resolved to return to the proven and lucrative paths of syndicate financing. 'I have gone back to my old business of public issues,' he told Otto Kahn in early 1920. 'There will need to be a lot of business among energetic people to rehabilitate this broken-down world.'[118] Within a year this optimism had turned to despondency. 'You say that your markets are weak,' he confided to a Montreal friend. 'Ours are practically non-existent and I do not see the turn because real prosperity depends on the resumption of international trade which the present depressed and fluctuating exchanges make extremely difficult.'[119] Despite a close reading of J.M. Keynes' *The Economic Consequences of the Peace*, Dunn dejectedly admitted that 'no-one seems to have solved the riddle of how to build a new international bridge over which the exchange of commodities can take place at all freely.'[120] This gloom was broken temporarily by the bestowal of a baronetcy in 1921, awarded in honour of Dunn's wartime services.

In trying to solve the post-war 'riddle,' Sir James indulged in a staggering variety of business schemes designed to rekindle the fires of prosperity. A favourite ploy was to offer the services of Dunn, Fisher and Company as a financial agent for the new states of Europe, notably Eire, Finland, and the Soviet Union. (Responding to wartime xenophobia, Dunn had dropped the 'c' from Fischer's name.) 'I have a full and complete abhorrence of Bolshevism and the whole idea of Bolshevism,' admitted Dunn later, 'but I still think we have got to try to do business with them.'[121] In one improbable scheme, he sought to inveigle Soviet trade commissar Leonid Krassin into a film deal with Hollywood czar Sam Goldwyn.[122] In 1924, Dunn hired Loring Christie, a quick-witted young Canadian lawyer and confidant of Robert Borden, in a bid to facilitate the repatriation of German assets seized during the war by the Canadian government.[123] Christie had accompanied the Canadian delegation to Versailles and knew the new diplomatic road map of Europe intimately. Despite much lobbying in Berlin and Ottawa, the proposed repatriation deal collapsed in 1925 under the weight of innumerable complications.

Dunn's inability to recreate the extensive and profitable network of financial ties that had characterized his early years in the City was not only the product of a slumbering international economy in the early 1920s. It was also the result of the altered position of London in the financial world. While Dunn, Fisher and Company did continue to reap rewards from arbitrage and flotations in the City, London's pre-war prowess as the financial capital of the world was under challenge from New York. In 1920 Dunn confided to Montreal financier I.W. Killam that, while he remained 'hopeful' that the London market for Canadian securities would soon revive, he could not 'yet see any practical opening' in London which could compare with the promotional opportunities on the North American side of the Atlantic.[124] Despite this 'long period of difficulties,'[125] new avenues to profit did open up for Dunn in the 1920s, offering the chance to recreate the halcyon days of the Pearson ventures.

If foreign investment lacked resilience, the post-war period produced new areas of domestic investment. Industrial flotations, capitalizing on the new technology-based progress of the automotive, chemicals, electrical, and artificial fabrics industries, gave a new opportunity to English investment bankers. As investments, 'industrials' spurted immediately after the war, with such English companies as Dunlop, Lever Brothers, and Armstrong-Whitworth issuing £400 million in new securities in the first eighteen months of peace.[126] This initial burst of investment dropped off sharply in 1921–2 and only recovered gradually until the boom years of 1927–9. Dunn was quick to capitalize on this trend. Besides participating in the underwriting of new industries, he readily spotted the promotional potential of 'artificial silk,' or rayon. Although initially discovered in the late nineteenth century, the acetate method of making cellulose fibre was perfected on the eve of the First War by the Swiss chemists Camille and Henry Dreyfus.[127] With an insatiable consumer demand to be captured at the expense of England's ailing cotton industry, artificial silk offered a sterling opportunity for industrial growth. In sensing this potential, Dunn showed great perspicacity, but his subsequent experience in the rayon industry degenerated into a mire of mismanagement and distrust.

Dunn underwrote and issued the initial capital of the British Cellulose and Chemical Manufacturing Company Limited 'in a couple of hours' and was widely hailed 'on the brilliant success of [his] first issue after so many years.'[128] Heartened by this success, he predicted 'the quickest and most profitable returns,' only to see his aspirations crushed by the onset of economic recession in early 1921. Despite this setback, Dunn, together with his Belgian friend Loewenstein, moved to assert his control over the enterprise by setting up the Cellulose Holdings and Investment Company Limited, a holding company. Even with this close control, Dunn was unable to bring British Celanese, as it was now known, under tight rein. Managing director Henry Dreyfus refused to bend to Dunn's insistence that the largest profits would come from supplying raw rayon to the producers of finished goods and instead launched Celanese in the knitting of rayon clothing itself. 'In my opinion the way to develop the yarn trade is to concentrate all our efforts on increased production, lower costs and better deliveries, on pleasing our customers rather than becoming their competitors,'[129] Dunn told the company's chairman, Sir Harry McGowan. Dunn was beginning to show the instincts of an industrialist but, since Dreyfus held the crucial patents on the acetate process, could not work his will on the company.

By 1924 the situation at British Celanese had become bitterly polarized. In the intensely competitive textile industry, Dunn believed that Dreyfus' policy of producing fabric instead of yarn was suicidal. 'This company,' he alleged, 'instead of having established itself as an integral part of the British textile industry has never got its feet,but has remained outside alone, rightly or wrongly regarded as the rival and enemy alike of the spinners, weavers, knitters, wholesalers, and retailers and now I am told it is competing with the dressmakers.'[130] After an extremely acrimonious struggle for control, the Dreyfus brothers emerged victorious in mid-1927. Dunn and Loewenstein relinquished their Celanese holdings but recouped some of their investment through the sale of their royalties contract for what the *Times* estimated as 'upwards of £1,000,000.'[131] Dunn emerged from the British Celanese fracas much chastened. As with BANCo, he had once again lacked sufficient control to integrate financial and managerial direction of a fledgling industry.

The revival of the Pearson-style syndicates under the aegis of Alfred Loewenstein, the Belgian 'mystery man' whose meteoric post-war rise to financial prowess dominated the financial press on both sides of the Atlantic, offered Dunn a second new line of business in the 1920s. These syndicates largely represented a reshuffling of the old Pearson and Farquhar railways and utilities under new and more encompassing financial umbrellas. Outlining the theory behind his enormous Société International d'Energie Hydro-Electrique (SIDRO), Loewenstein instructed Dunn in 1926 to get all his 'hydro-electric enterprises under one incorporation. Spanish, if possible, if not Spanish, Canadian but in either case control the administration directly by your own immediate friends whose interests in the business are the same as your own.'[132] Like Pearson in his later years, Loewenstein succumbed to the folly of financial recklessness and overextension, vices that Dunn tried valiantly to curb. As early as 1922 Dunn complained of 'the danger of Alfred going too rapidly and committing his friends who wish to help him beyond the distance they wish to go.'[133] By late 1926 Loewenstein had launched the International Holdings and Investments Limited, his most ambitious scheme, under which he hoped to subsume all his varied interests. To achieve this, the Belgian had bought colossal holdings on margin, especially in Brazilian Traction, with which he hoped to assert his control. At the crucial moment the shareholders of SIDRO balked and at a meeting in Belgium vetoed his share exchange plan, forcing him to abandon his 'big project' and to liquidate much of his SIDRO holdings.[134] Dunn greeted his ally's defeat by admitting that 'doing business with him is not always perfectly smooth sailing.' Despite the setback, Loewenstein was 'a big constructive man' and had 'not been stopped in his career.'[135]

There was indeed no stopping Loewenstein. Rallying his forces,

Loewenstein launched another assault for control of Brazilian Traction. Loring Christie described for Dunn 'the Napoleonic trail blazed by our friend Alfred' through Toronto in 1927 in pursuit of this object, while Mackenzie King described the wealthy Belgian as 'a very generous and noble soul' after a visit for tea at Laurier House.[136] Loewenstein's financial trail came to an abrupt and tragic end when the 'Belgian Croesus' fell to a mysterious death from his private aircraft while crossing the English Channel in July 1928. Amid much sensational speculation, the *New York Times* linked Loewenstein's 'growing habit of absent mindedness' to 'the fatal step into empty space which sent his body spinning down through the sunset 4,000 feet to be lost in the blue waters of the Channel.'[137] Loewenstein's demise removed the vital centre from the syndicates. SIDRO stock plummeted overnight from 51½ to 25 and International Holdings dropped from $215 a share to $100. Although Loewenstein's estate was valued at $55 million, Dunn was left with a tangled mass of debts and litigation and a syndicate that had lost its pulse.

Despite heavy personal losses, Sir James remained an immensely wealthy member of the 'financial aristocracy' in the 1920s. He continued to exercise his lifelong passion for the fine arts, influential friends, and wine to the point of overindulgence. His walls at various times displayed masterpieces ranging from Holbein to Dali, while his cellar stocked the finest vintages that Berry Brothers and Rudd, London's exclusive vintners, could purvey. While his eldest daughter, Mona, carried on a torrid affair with English politician Lord Birkenhead, Dunn's own marriage succumbed to the pressures of his social life. A new marriage, to the former wife of the Marquis of Queensberry, followed.

Dunn's sybaritic lifestyle was thrown into bold relief some years later during the depths of the Depression. In 1932, while Britons reeled from savage unemployment, Sir James maintained a livery at Norwich House, his London home, of twelve servants, several occasional workers, two Rolls-Royces, and one Chrysler. As well as several transatlantic journeys to his Canadian retreat in the woods of New Brunswick, Dunn took a Christmas vacation that year in St Moritz.[138] Yet in February 1932, office salaries at Dunn, Fisher and Company were cut in response to the worsening economic situation. In May of the same year, Sir James severely reprimanded his chauffeur for his 'extravagant' electric bills and forbade him to use the Norwich House phone for private calls.[139] Few beyond the servants' quarters glimpsed the niggardly side of Dunn's character. Most shared the observation of Noel Coward, who remarked after a meeting with Dunn in Deauville in the 1920s that 'Jimmy Dunn's personality was strong, and I expect the atmosphere of the whole place had nurtured in me a reverence for riches which, even in my most poverty-stricken moments, I had not been aware of before.'[140]

The rewards of social and economic preeminence could not mask Dunn's growing uneasiness about his tenure in England. On the heels of Loewenstein's loss, the sudden death of his favourite daughter, Mona, in late 1928 emotionally devastated Dunn, sapping his usually boundless vitality for life and work. On a less personal scale, the decade also witnessed Dunn's growing pessimism about the future of England. Viewing the 1926 General Strike from his French villa, he ruefully concluded 'that there won't be much use going back to England unless the forces of law and order win.'[141]

Gloomy prognostications of a 'classless' English society, coupled with his own personal and financial troubles, gave rise in Dunn to a yearning to return to New Brunswick. In 1926, he had actively campaigned in the province for Arthur Meighen, a man whose high protectionism and 'charming' personality he greatly admired.[142] The prospect of a 'socialist' government in England forced Dunn's thoughts further homeward. 'I am beginning to think it is time I returned to my own country.'[143] Advising his son Philip on a prospective business career in 1927, Dunn admitted that he 'personally didn't see any great future for any young man over here as compared with the opportunities in New York and Montreal.'[144] Algoma Steel and the Depression would give Dunn himself the opportunity for a new start.

In 1929 Dalhousie University offered Dunn an honorary degree in recognition of his 'conspicuous success in the business world of the Motherland' and his 'rising eminence in the domain of international finance.'[145] While many knew of Dunn's success beyond the seas, few had the slightest idea of how his millions had been won. Dunn always revelled in painting his career as the struggle of a humble, underprivileged country boy from the colonial outback, who through innate ability and hard work had triumphed over great odds. It was, as Beaverbrook described it, 'a tribute to a man's courage.'[146] While this was all undoubtedly true, the corollary was not. Dunn never assumed that the interests of the economically and socially unprivileged could be reconciled with those of the privileged. Throughout his financial career, he always strove to operate from a position of power built on the weakness of the small and, in a sense, unprivileged investor. Through arbitrage, syndicate deals, and holding companies Dunn made millions subverting the free play of market forces, manipulating the pooled savings of small investors for ends that would seldom have met with their approval. Ironically, the speculative abuses of the 1920s, best symbolized by the Hatry and Insull 'crashes,' would eventually bring in their wake measures of reform intended to curb the excesses on which Dunn's fortune was founded.

What then was the achievement of financiers like Dunn and Loewenstein? In the words of Fritz Redlich, their contribution was of a 'daimonic' nature, the result of an ongoing process of 'creative destruction' by which no economic advance or creation is possible without concomitant destruction or abuses.[147] The Pearson, Farquhar, and Loewenstein syndicates, from which Dunn so handsomely profited, contributed railways, utilities, and the other trappings of industrialization and urbanization to what is today called the 'underdeveloped' world. The syndicates also facilitated the building of the economic infrastructure of modern European and North American life. That these advances were necessary or useful there can be no doubt. The question lies instead in the methods used to achieve these ends. Redlich suggests: 'If, as these men believed, the natural law ruling social life demanded the fight for survival of the fittest, there was no room for what today would be called high business ethics. Thus these men were both magnificent builders and ruthless destroyers and their creative concentrations on the organization and financial side of transportation and industry, while overlooking the human and strictly industrial aspects, gives their destructiveness "daimonic" character.'[148]

By making control the objective of their manipulations, the syndicates sought to minimize the free play of the market and render it no more than a screen for the machinations of high finance. For the mass of public investors on whom Dunn built his financial empire he felt only a thinly disguised contempt. If control was lost, 'the widows, orphans and bankrupts from the shareholders list,' as one of his Canadian confrères described them, would be allowed to reassert their timorous policies.[149] Dunn did not invent the art of control and manipulation, he merely learned its tenets and adroitly applied them to the financial needs of the early twentieth century. Dunn and Loewenstein unscrupulously preyed upon the small investor's trust and gullibility to build their fame and fortune. As one small English investor told Sir James in 1924: 'You fellows, who are dealing constantly in large figures, and who lose today ten or twenty thousand quid, do not worry so much about it, because you know that, tomorrow, you may make thirty or forty thousand. My little monies, however, come in over the desk, and represent more or less constant wear on my nose, due to its being constantly on the grindstone.'[150]

6

Cutting the Gordian Knot:
Sir James Dunn and the Takeover of
Algoma Steel 1930–1935

Until he assumed the presidency of Algoma Steel in May 1935, Sir James Dunn had never considered himself a captain of industry. His interest in Algoma up to the 1930s had been speculative, one not entailing a commitment to long-term industrial management. 'I am not an investor,' he categorically stated as early as 1910, 'but buy issues for the purpose of reselling them.'[1] After his initial bid for control of the Lake Superior Corporation in 1908, Dunn's ardour for the speculative prospects of the Sault industries had cooled. Unable to loosen Philadelphia's grip on the corporation, Dunn and Robert Fleming had consolidated their Sault holdings in the Lake Superior Investment Company, allowing their attention to shift to more profitable and more controllable financial opportunities. Without control, the Sault investment had become a risky proposition and one worthy of only casual stewardship. The futility of acting from a position of partial control was amply underscored for Dunn in his British American Nickel and British Celanese ventures. Dutifully dispatching his proxies for Lake Superior annual meetings, Dunn otherwise displayed distinct apathy towards the corporation's affairs throughout the 1910s. Twice, in 1914 and 1919, he offered his Lake Superior holdings for sale or use as collateral in frantic bids to shore up his position in other, more promising ventures.[2]

As the 1920s unfolded, events on both sides of the Atlantic conspired to rekindle Dunn's enthusiasm for the steelworks at the Sault. A creeping despondency overtook his English financial ambitions. In 1927, for instance, he declared his growing conviction that England 'must play a secondary part in international commerce for a long time to come. The North American continent has a big start and is creating wealth at a rate unheard of in the past.'[3] Against this backdrop, Dunn's attention gravitated towards North America where his eye soon alighted on new opportunities that invited his financial skills. Long-standing ties with firms like Dillon, Read and Company and Empire Trust in New York and the National Trust and Dominion Securities in Toronto gave him a ready-made entrée into the charmed circle of North American finance. Early in the 1920s, for instance, Dunn had joined Leroy Baldwin, president of Empire Trust, in taking control of the Equitable Office Building, lucratively situated in the heart of New York's financial district. By 1929, Equitable's annual earnings were nearly $2 million.[4] Backed by Empire Trust and Dillon, Read and Company, Dunn plunged into trading on the American and Canadian markets, speculating in railway, automotive, distillery, and other investments, all largely bought 'on margin.' By February 1930, his loan account at Empire Trust alone totalled $627,147.[5]

At first sight, it was strange that Dunn could have been lured away from the rewards of Wall Street to the dismal and unpromising prospect of Algoma Steel. Labouring under a depressed national economy, the Lake Superior Corporation, Algoma's parent, had reported a net annual loss of $1,325,136.08 in 1925. A year earlier, former Algoma president J. Frater Taylor had confided to Dunn that the outlook for Canadian steel was 'not good,' primarily because proper bounties and tariffs were not forthcoming from Ottawa.[6] Lake Superior Corporation annual reports left the indelible impression that Algoma was starved for capital and that this deficiency directly impeded the corporation's efforts to diversify. Algoma's plight none the less whetted Dunn's appetite. In 1925, Sir James confided in his Toronto financial friend E.R. Wood that he believed that many Algoma bondholders were becoming discouraged and would sell out 'pretty cheaply.' If he could acquire control through these bonds and win tariff protection from Arthur Meighen, Algoma could be reorganized and set on the path to recovery. Dunn's principal goal however remained a speculative one – 'to make some money out of reorganizing the position.'[7]

Dunn's appreciation of the virtue of integrating the financial and managerial control of an industrial enterprise had matured considerably since the days of his ill-fated nickel and rayon ventures. The dazzling industrial achievements of two of his European friends, Sir Harry McGowan and Hugo Stinnes, provided him with examples of forceful industrial management. Stinnes was Germany's most gifted practitioner of the vertical trust or combine. Rebounding from reverses inflicted by the First War, he organized the Rhine-Elbe Union in 1920, culminating in the gigantic Vereingte Stahlwerke, which Dunn had visited and admired in 1924.[8] With similar dexterity, Sir Harry McGowan and Sir Alfred Mond had created Imperial Chemical Industries in 1926 out of scattered British chemical firms.[9] These European examples, together with the memory of his friend Beaverbrook's wizardry in the Stelco merger of 1910, instilled in Dunn a belief that similar magic could be worked on Algoma.

It can also be suggested that as Sir James' ardour for the game of investment banking waned he developed a strong psychological desire to leave his mark on the world in a very tangible form. Arbitrage and stock promotions had allowed Dunn to amass a fortune which he ostentatiously disbursed on homes, cars, travel, and the good life. But none of these constituted a lasting monument to what Dunn considered his vision and hard work as a businessman. By 1925, he was entering his fifties and, unlike Beaverbrook with his newspapers or Stinnes with his German factories, he could not point to any single company which was indisputably 'his.' Dunn was always acutely aware of his own mortality – hence his abiding concern for his health and diet – and the thought of remaking Algoma according to his own dictates undoubtedly appealed strongly as a means of perpetuating his reputation. In later years, he took tremendous pride in Algoma's iron ore operation at Wawa. The extraction of ore was a brute physical action which Dunn could comprehend and which, he believed, would exhibit his personal achievement as an industrialist. To celebrate this, he built a guest house overlooking the mine and named it 'The Eagle's Nest.' Later, he allowed Salvador Dali to paint his portrait as a Roman emperor, clad in a toga, seated on a stone throne overlooking Lake Superior.

Besides a personal vision, vigorous management, and access to capital, Dunn felt he could contribute one other revitalizing element to the Sault industries. In 1925–6, he had vowed his support for Arthur Meighen's Conservatives and their pledge for higher tariffs for Canada's primary industries. 'I am all out to help [elect Meighen],' Dunn assured Loring Christie, 'being a thorough believer in the policy of high protection.' Mackenzie King's triumph over Meighen at the polls not only foiled Algoma's hopes for a dose of high protection but gave Dunn an early indication that his aspirations for a smooth assumption of power at Algoma could be easily frustrated. None the less, Dunn's familiarity with the mores of English and Canadian political life stood him in good stead to capitalize on political opportunities when they presented themselves. As he later told a Sault lawyer, 'I know of nothing more interesting than political intrigue when there is a purpose in it.'[10]

Towering above all other obstacles to Dunn's ambitions at the Sault was the paralysis of the corporation's financial and managerial structure. Overcapitalized since the days of F.H. Clergue, the corporation was afflicted with too many tiers of investors, each with a lien on some section of the Sault properties or assets and each reluctant to see another gain an upper hand in any corporate reorganization or collapse.

The capital structure of the corporation was still indisputably governed by the parent Lake Superior Corporation, which through stock ownership controlled its three principal subsidiaries: Algoma Steel, the Algoma Eastern Railway, and the Algoma Central Railway. Many of the other subsidiaries chartered by Clergue had been sold off or amalgamated in the two decades since the founder's departure. The relationship of the parent holding company and the steel company was legally complex and financially involved. In essence, the Lake Superior Corporation used its assets of approximately $47.5 million, book value, to control Algoma and its subsidiaries. The Lake Superior Corporation's capital structure consisted of $40 million in stock and a funded debt of First and Collateral Trust Bonds. Algoma Steel had $15 million in common stock, $10 million in 7 per cent preference shares, about $5.8 million in 5 per cent Purchase Money Bonds, and $15.3 million in 5 per cent Refunding Bonds, for a total book value in 1928 of approximately $45 million. Algoma in turn controlled four subsidiaries: Cannelton Coal, Fiborn Limestone, Lake Superior Coal, and Algoma Steel Products. The pivotal and controlling elements in this financial arrangement were the three sets of bonds, with the Algoma Steel Purchase Money and First and Refunding bonds having first lien on 'all the undertaking, property and assets' of the steel company.[11]

By the mid-1920s control of the parent corporation had solidified around several main blocks of securities, which more often than not were implacably opposed to each other. The majority of the parent Lake Superior Corporation's stock was in American hands, under the sway of Philadelphian financiers centred around W.H. Cunningham, president of the corporation since 1917. As the owners of the corporation, the shareholders would dictate the fortunes of Algoma as long as the parent corporation honoured its obligations to its bondholders. English investors held much of the corporation's funded debt, particularly the 5 per cent First and Refunding Bonds and the Algoma Steel Purchase Money Bonds. The largest cohesive block of London control lay in the hands of the Fleming syndicate, represented by the Lake Superior Investment Company, the New-Jersey-based holding company created by Fleming and Dunn in 1908. In controlling this block, Fleming and Dunn were joined in a minor way by Kuhn, Loeb in New York, Lord Glendyne in London, and E.R. Wood in Toronto. The interests of the English bondholders of the Algoma Central and Algoma Eastern railways also could not be overlooked. Long in arrears of interest, the railway bondholders had entrenched rights that put them in a position to veto any proposed corporate reorganization of the Lake Superior Corporation.[12] The contending financial interests behind the Sault corporation thus jealously vied for power to direct the corporate policies of their ailing investment. 'The financial structure of the Lake Superior Corporation,' the *Financial Post* observed in 1928, 'has not been simplified by the various reorganizations for the reason that the claims of various classes of bondholders have been conflicting to a great or less extent and this has necessitated the adoption of expedients and compromises until such time as properties began to earn sufficient money to pay bond interest, or until a comprehensive reorganization would be acceptable to all parties.'[13] Anxious not to jeopardize their already precarious position, investors in the Sault complex were predisposed to reject any reorganization scheme that might admit new capital to the financial structure with rights that ranked ahead of their own. Such reorganization schemes did not, however, fail for lack of trying.

In December 1923, J. Frater Taylor, acting on behalf of the London interests, forwarded a scheme whereby old bonds would be supplanted by preferred stocks in a new corporation and followed by a flotation of new prior lien bonds. This plan foundered when Philadelphian interests objected to the underwriting arrangements for the new issue and argued that too little had been done in 'affording the [present] Lake Superior stockholders an opportunity and an incentive to subscribe to the new bonds.'[14] Frater Taylor then proposed a combined new issue of prior lien bonds, second mortgage bonds, preferred and common stock with a value in excess of $25 million. This proposal was flatly rejected by Cunningham, who saw it as prejudicial to the interests of the American stockholders in the existing structure. Countering with their own proposal in April 1925, the Philadelphians suggested a $20 million issue of first mortgage bonds and nearly $30 million in preferred stock. This plan proceeded to the stage of a reorganization committee, only to be sabotaged by the Lake Superior Investment Company's insistence that the corporation default on its present bond payments.[15]

Dunn had not been an active participant in any of these frustrated negotiations, although he received reports on their progress from E.R. Wood, N.W. Rowell, and J. Frater Taylor. Frater Taylor informed Dunn in January 1925 that all attempts to secure new money had failed. One conclusion, he noted, was 'very certain': 'it is that every day's delay means an increasingly difficult situation and of course more money ... As I have repeatedly said, it is idle to think of any practical help from Philadalphia.'[16]

If help was not forthcoming from the two traditional bastions of control, other interests were eager to promote a reorganization. In Toronto, E.R. Wood of National Trust lobbied Premier Ferguson for a provincial guarantee for half of a mooted Lake Superior bond issue.[17] Further north in the province, John A. McPhail, a Sault lawyer, was trying to entice the American public utility magnates Martin and Samuel Insull to introduce outside capital to the Algoma situation. The Insulls had a vested interest in the survival of Algoma. The Great Lakes Power Company, in which they had considerable holdings, was the chief supplier of power to the steelworks. Backed by the Chicago financial house of Halsey Stuart and Company and assured by McPhail that the 'present Philadelphia crowd are pretty well at the end of their rope,'[18] the Insulls represented a potential flank attack on the Algoma situation throughout the late 1920s until the ignominious collapse of their Middle West Utilities empire removed them from the scene.

By the mid-1920s the affairs of the Lake Superior Corporation were in such a financial quagmire that it was unable to satisfy its need for capital and incapable of reorganization. The groups constituting its control remained locked in jealous equipoise. This state of affairs not only tarnished the corporation in the eyes of potential investors but also cooled the enthusiasm of both levels of Canadian government. The mauling administered to Algoma's tariff demands before the Advisory Board on Tariffs and Taxation added to the impression of the corporation as a 'lame duck,' riddled with inefficiency and profligacy.[19] Against this forlorn backdrop, Sir James waited for his opportunity.

In late 1926, Dunn determined to intervene actively in the control of Algoma, opting to increase his 20 per cent share of the Lake Superior Investment Company to a majority position by buying out his partners, Robert Fleming, E.R. Wood, and Kuhn, Loeb. While there was no profit to be made directly in this transaction, an immense strategic advantage was to be gained over the affairs of the Sault corporation through control of the holding company. In late June, 1927, Dunn purchased Kuhn, Loeb's shares, and followed this rapidly by acquiring most of E.R. Wood's block for $200,000.[20] The decisive *coup* came a few days later when he bought Fleming's interest in the syndicate. 'It is very hard to put a value on the Investment Company's shares,' he told Wood. 'They are really worth what one makes the Algoma Steel Company worth when the time comes to reorganize it.'[21]

These purchases gave Dunn, by his own estimation, control of 72 per cent of the investment company's shares and in turn power over $7.8 million in Algoma bonds. To reinforce his new-found strength, Dunn began to forge closer links with the managers, lawyers, and bankers who were intimately versed in Algoma's affairs. Algoma president W.C. Franz, for instance, acquainted Dunn with the day-to-day routine and deficiencies of the plant. Equally important were the lawyers retained in New York, London, Philadelphia, and Toronto to represent his holdings in the corporation. Typifying these 'hammer and tongs lawyers,' as one of Dunn's friends jestingly described them,[22] was Newton Wesley Rowell, who had kept a watching brief on the investment company's affairs for twenty years from his Toronto legal office. Rowell's facility with federal-provincial intricacies of law and his familiarity with the nuances and personalities of federal and provincial politics gave Dunn a perspective on the parameters of possible action in reorganizing Algoma. Dunn also cultivated financial allies. In particular, Leroy Baldwin of Empire Trust in New York extended generous loans on lenient terms, enabling Dunn to solidify and enlarge his Lake Superior holdings.[23] These were all shrewd acquaintanceships. To compensate for his lack of experience as a steel industrialist, Dunn had assembled his own *de facto* board of directors.

While he had assured himself complete control over the affairs of the investment company, Dunn was still not in a position to work his will on the corporation at large. Philadelphia shareholders, railway bondholders, and numerous unaffiliated investors could still thwart any reorganization. Furthermore, Dunn was still uncertain of his own plan of action. His overriding instinct was to persuade President Cunningham to let the corporation slip into default,[24] thereby delivering control of the corporation into the bondholders' hands. Not surprisingly, Philadelphia refused. 'Our Philadelphia friends,' Dunn noted, 'seem to be able to keep themselves cheered up by a good month now and then but the position has not really improved and sooner or later Algoma will go to pieces ...'[25] When the corporation punctually met its bond payment in 1927, Dunn fell back on a contingency plan designed to achieve the same end by different means. 'Failing this,' he told an English confidant, 'my plan is the formation of a new Canadian company and an offer of an interest in that new company to the bondholders of the Lake Superior Corporation, the Algoma Steel First and Refunding bonds, the Lake Superior shareholders with the object of getting control of the Lake Superior Corporation and making the default myself.'[26]

Dunn's plan for reorganization through default set him squarely at odds with the corporation's other investors who persisted in their attempts to patch up the corporation's rickety structure in hopes of attracting new capital. Dunn's goal was to secure a redoubtable position of control, knock several links from the corporation's financial chain, and then shorten it in his favour. 'It is not my idea to sell these bonds at all,' he told Algoma president Franz, 'but to sit with them until the reorganization occurs and control that reorganization.'[27]

Reorganization on Dunn's terms proved an elusive goal. In late 1927, he peevishly complained that he had 'thought out at least a dozen plans' for reorganization 'but they all show some defect or difficulty.'[28] Finally he opted for a plan by which the corporation would be refinanced under the auspices of the Lake Superior Investment Company. Bondholders in the existing corporation would be invited to exchange their bonds for Investment Company preferred stock with certain guarantees of dividends. The offer was vigorously opposed by the Philadelphia shareholders, who argued that corporate management had modernization plans well in hand and that an infusion of new capital was unneeded.[29] By early May, 1928, Dunn confided to E.R. Wood that the proposal of exchange had 'not been a great success' but, if reorganization had again been thwarted, the gambit had at least helped to fatten his holdings. 'I think I can safely say that the results of my efforts in the past few weeks have given us an unassailable position in Algoma Bonds.'[30]

Events on the Lake Superior front now began to turn against Sir James. The reviving Canadian economy in the late 1920s resuscitated iron and steel demand, thereby easing much of the financial pressure on the Sault corporation. Under this stimulus, Algoma recorded respectable profits in the last years of the decade. Improved profitability helped to keep the financial wolves at bay. In 1928 the Lake Superior Corporation was able to begin serious negotiations with the Algoma Central bondholders, resulting in some loosening of the financial guarantees that had bound the corporation to the unprofitable railway since the Great War.[31] The Algoma Eastern Railway was sold to the Canadian Pacific, netting $2.2 million. While Algoma could not match the steady performance of Stelco in the late 1920s, it at least avoided the ignominy of BESCO as it slipped beyond financial redemption, to be taken over and reborn in 1928 as the Dominion Steel and Coal Company (Dosco) under the auspices of Herbert Holt and J.H. Gundy.[32] Striking a note of optimism, the *Financial Post* described the Sault corporation in 1928 as 'full of promise for those who have faith and will yet be patient.'[33]

The misadventure of his first reorganization attempt coupled with the partial revival of corporate prosperity obliged Dunn to retire to a shadowy yet still influential position for the next few years. During this period, Dunn quietly persisted in buying whatever Algoma First and Refunding bonds, Lake Superior Income bonds, and Investment Company shares drifted onto the market. Strong as his bond position was, Dunn's position was still open to the unlikely challenge of any agglomeration of previously unattached shareholders. When, in early 1928, he first heard rumours of concerted buying of Lake Superior stock on the Montreal and Philadelphia markets, Dunn dismissed it as 'of no special significance' and simply 'a gamble in Algoma.'[34] This buying, which drove the depressed price of Lake Superior Corporation stock upward, proved far from chimerical when Montreal interests, headed by Robert F. Dodd,[35] seized control of the company via the stockholders' route late in the year. Toppling long-incumbent President Cunningham, Dodd brought the corporation under the sway of seven Canadian and three American directors. Dodd's purpose and backing remained shrouded in 'a deep veil of mystery,'[36] from which emerged grandiose promises of $50 million in additional capital for the steelworks. Dodd's tenure as president was a brief one. Dunn contemptuously viewed Dodd as 'an amateur president' whose commitment to Algoma was a speculative one, built on intricate 'stock jobbing' calculated to create a 'bull' market for stock bought at bargain prices.[37] Dodd was forced to resign in April 1929 because of some 'serious irregularity' on his part.[38]

Dodd's place as president was filled by Frank B. Common, a Montreal lawyer and investor, who completed the displacement of Philadelphia interests on the board, leaving a lone American to face ten Canadians. Built on a base of solid financial and engineering experience, it was a board that in no way invited the charges of lethargy and negligence that three decades of absentee Philadelphia management had often brought. Dunn initially welcomed it as 'an experienced Canadian board of high standing who will thoroughly examine [the] position and face the facts ... freeing [the] company of the stock jobbing reputation it has had lately.'[39] The folly of his initial blasé dismissal of Dodd's chances instilled in Dunn an abiding respect for the potential power of the company's common and preferred stockholders, a power he never again discounted. Despite this, his Algoma strategy remained unchanged. 'Everyone must see, who gives the subject close study,' he told one of the new Montreal directors in April 1929, 'that no real progress can be made at the Soo until $10,000,000 or $15,000,000 of new money is found for the Algoma Steel Company.' Dunn was quick to offer 'to get the new money' but only after a corporate reorganization.[40]

The Crash of October 1929 altered both Dunn's and Algoma's plans. As late as August 1929, Dunn was still predicting 'a great bull market this fall.' By December of the same year he was gloomily reporting 'dull skies, dull markets and tales of ruin and dismay.'[41] The Crash by no means marked the financial ruin of Sir James Dunn, but the lingering depression in its wake did drastically affect his activities as an investment banker and stock promoter. The atrophy of international finance severely cramped his style as a transatlantic financier. His position was further undermined when England suspended the gold standard in 1931 and moved to restrict various stock trading practices. In June 1933, the Chancellor of the Exchequer requested brokers to discourage English investment abroad because 'this country is not at present in a position to invest large sums on long-term abroad.'[42]

In the United States, Dunn's other financial arena, the Glass-Steagall Act of 1933 segregated investment and commercial banking into two separate entities.[43] In the wake of the spectacular Hatry crash of 1929, Ivan Kreuger's suicide, and the Insull débâcle, the once-gleaming reputation of the investment banker became deeply tarnished. 'Rarely,' one historian has commented, 'had a group lost so much status and respect so quickly. The folk hero of the boom years had become the scapegoat of the depression.'[44] The American Securities Exchange Act of 1933 and the British Prevention of Fraud (Investment) Act of 1939 clipped the wings of many of the more high-flying members of Dunn's financial fraternity. Later in the 1930s, Dunn himself became embroiled in an acrimonious tax evasion case with the British government. None the less, in the midst of depression and the growing thicket of regulation, James Dunn still found some scope for his investment skills. In 1933, he dazzled the English financial community by repatriating Boots the Chemists from the American control of Rexall Drugs.[45] Similarly, he aided and abetted his friends Lord Beaverbrook and Lord Rothermere in their efforts to seize control of Price Brothers Paper Company. None of these financial adventures seemed fully to reawaken Dunn's passion for investment banking. Dismayed by the collapse of the English economy and the failure of Beaverbrook's Empire Free Trade crusade, Sir James looked with increasing hope to Canada as a sphere for his future activities. Like his friend Edward Beatty of the CPR, he did not know 'of any country which can experience such a quick and permanent restoration of prosperity.'[46]

Dunn's interest in the Canadian economy was reinforced by the presence of R.B. Bennett's Conservative government in Ottawa. Sir James had long-standing legal, social, and business ties with many of the leading lights of Bennett's cabinet and found himself *persona grata* in Ottawa's corridors of power.[47] By 1933, Dunn was advising E.N. Rhodes, federal minister of finance, on his personal investments, engineering on one occasion a £2550 profit in distillery securities.[48] By 1934, G.H.Ferguson, the former Tory premier of Ontario and London high commissioner, was also entrusting some of his private investments to Dunn.[49] Dunn frequently interrupted his North American trips for confidential chats with his good friend Dick Bennett. Dunn's prestige in Tory eyes was indicated in 1934 when Prime Minister Bennett deputized him to refinance $6 million in City of Montreal Treasury Bills on the London market.[50] Aware that Canadian borrowing on English markets was strictly forbidden, Dunn and Bennett surreptitiously worked through Ferguson in London and Victor Drury, Beaverbrook's brother-in-law, in Montreal.[51] Hopes of clinching the deal were dashed by the vigorous intervention of the governor of the Bank of England, Montagu Norman, who, Ferguson reported, was 'very much annoyed' by Dunn's covert attempts to circumvent British financial regulations.[52] Bennett, claiming a 'misunderstanding of the situation,' hurriedly retracted his offer to Dunn and dispatched Ferguson to appease Norman.[53] His talents unrequired, Dunn moved on to pursue other schemes of profit. In the depression-ridden years of the early 1930s Dunn had suffered, but in the contest for survival he remained in the ranks of the fittest. For Algoma it was otherwise.

'The large bonded indebtedness of the Algoma Corporation,' the 1932 Lake Superior annual report announced, 'and heavy sinking fund requirements, together with lack of normal orders for that Company's principal products, have combined to render the profitable operation of the Company impossible during the past year, and have imposed a heavy drain of the Company's resources.'[54] By 1932, Algoma was rolling only 15.2 per cent of the rails it had in 1929, a catastrophic decline from 215,011 tons to 32,751 tons. The nadir came in 1933 when only 5052 tons of rails were produced at the Sault. Pig iron output dropped from 95,930 tons in 1929 to a meagre 8343 tons in 1932. Coke output slipped to 31,013 tons by 1932 or 16.3 per cent of its 1929 level. Total shipments of all iron and steel products plummeted from 630,804 tons in 1929 to 147,169 tons in 1932, a 76.7 per cent decline.[55] Once again Algoma was trapped by the continuing implications of Clergue's original industrial strategy, especially its overreliance on rail production. 'I agree,' Dunn frankly told Algoma president Franz in mid-1931, 'that tariffs do not matter much to you at present and that you are better without any merchant mill business until you can get a lot. Rails and more rails is what you must strive for to carry you through the bad period.'[56] Algoma's struggle for survival in the early 1930s can best be seen as a frantic search for rail orders. Dosco in Nova Scotia found itself in much the same position, while Stelco, with its broad range of finished steel goods, had the relative luxury of selectively channelling its primary output to a host of steel consumers.[57]

Faced with their steadily worsening industrial fortunes, Canada's primary steel producers engaged in feverish activity to convince Ottawa's politicians of the need for special tariff and subsidy assistance. The Bennett budgets of September 1930 and June 1931 quashed any hope of a wholesale restructuring of the iron and steel tariff. The Emergency Session budget of 1930 boosted duties on agricultural machinery and scattered iron and steel items, at the same time cancelling the countervailing duties of the Dunning budget. Subsequent budgets juggled some steel duties upwards and some downwards. Bennett's much-heralded economic miracle never materialized: the steel industry was left much like other primary industries, with traditional tariff walls heightened but not expanded. In their brief to Ottawa on the eve of the 1932 Imperial Economic Conference, primary steel producers emphasized the necessity of securing 'the existing primary steel industry of Canada a sufficient volume of business to reduce its operating costs and thus to enable it to earn a moderate return.' From Algoma's perspective, this 'strong urge and necessity for new lines of output' centred on a protection for structural steel and sheet piling. Despite such lobbying, the Imperial Conference broke no new ground for the steel industry, leaving Canada with a 'disproportionate import trade,' 'too many drawbacks,' and a 'decidedly low' tariff.[58]

As the Depression deepened and Algoma's fortunes sank lower, Dunn's attention was increasingly focused on the option of cutting the Gordian knot of the corporation's tangled finances. Placing himself at the centre of a network of informants who kept him well acquainted with Algoma's legal, operational, and financial position, Dunn embarked on a campaign to outwit and outmanoeuvre his rivals for control. In May 1930, he again offered Lake Superior president Common his services to underwrite a $5 million loan to facilitate plant extensions.[59] More candidly, he told his remaining partner in the Lake Superior Investment Company, Lord Glendyne, that he was 'very unhappy about the outlook as it would seem that Algoma is fated to fall into the control of one board of directors after another, none of which has grasped and dealt with its vital necessities.'[60] Dunn's opinion was confirmed by his friend the prime minister, who told him that Algoma's managers were 'dead on their feet.'[61] In a moment of exasperation, Dunn himself described the Sault rail mill as a 'fit piece of machinery for the British Museum' and bemoaned the failure of the board to construct a new combined rolling mill.[62]

Dunn's new impatience with the Algoma situation was also moulded by what he saw as the 'extreme danger' of the giants of American steel crossing the border and overpowering the vulnerable Canadian industry. 'Bennett believed the u.s. Steel Company are going into Canada,' he told Algoma president Franz in 1931, 'but just when and to what extent and in what lines of steel I did not learn. ... Bennett said that nobody could stop them from coming in or shape their policy for them.'[63] Dunn's growing boldness was further prompted by the example of decisive steel management set by close friends and acquaintances in the British steel industry, notably Hamar Greenwood, Sir William Firth, and Sir Andrew Duncan.[64] Additional encouragement was supplied by High Commissioner Ferguson, whom Dunn reported as 'a particularly good friend of the north country' and 'right behind Algoma.'[65]

Driven by these forces, Dunn redoubled his efforts to fortify himself in a position of control. Whenever possible, he added to his trove of Algoma and Lake Superior bonds. The strain of this continued buying forced Dunn to tax his financial resources to the limit. Throughout 1929–34 he drew sizeable loans on the Empire Trust Company and Central Hanover Bank and Trust Company, loans secured against collateral with very little market value. He frankly admitted that the loans were made 'as much on myself as on the stocks' he used as collateral.[66]

In 1930, Dunn's plans were once again upset by the appearance of yet another holding company, the Algoma Consolidated Corporation. It had been created under a Prince Edward Island charter as part of a deal with the Algoma Central bondholders. This new addition to the overextended corporate structure was to act as a repository for 94 per cent of the old Lake Superior Corporation stock as well as a controlling interest in the Algoma Central common stock.[67] Dunn was not fooled. He told a Bank of Montreal official that the Algoma Consolidated Corporation had been created by Montreal interests with no purpose but 'to entangle and befog the situation as much as possible.'[68] Unperturbed, Dunn continued to build his position, operating behind a screen of brokers and lawyers. He also continued to shroud his activities in anonymity, explaining to E.R. Wood that he saw no purpose in exposing his position 'to the Lake Superior directorate with whom we may before very long be sitting down on different sides of the table.'[69] His goal remained a default on the corporation's bonds.

The crisis that brought Dunn and the directorate to the conference table finally came in mid-1932. With only a 'few small orders' on hand and enormous 'idle expenses,' W.C.Franz reluctantly reported that he might have to 'bank in' the remaining operational furnaces.[70] Franz' anxieties were compounded by the refusal of the Bank of Montreal to advance the corporation, which already owed its banker $894,000, any further funds. Facing a payment of $145,000 in interest on its bonds, the parent corporation accepted the unavoidable and in June 1932 surrendered Algoma Steel into receivership. When a net operating loss of $817,139 for the fiscal year 1931–2 was announced on 30 June, it was apparent to all parties concerned that Algoma's fortunes had reached their lowest point.

Receivership elevated the holders of Algoma Steel Purchase Money bonds and First and Refunding bonds to an unassailable position of control over the shareholders. With his majority control of both these securities, Dunn seemed poised on the verge of financial victory. 'I very strongly urge you in the interests of Algoma and consequently in your own interests,' J. Frater Taylor urged him, 'to make as quick a job of it as possible, and without too many cooks … your aim, I suggest, should be a strong, impregnable steel corporation … with an uncomplicated capital.'[71] For Dunn in 1932, there were, however, still 'too many cooks' to give him any assurance of ultimate victory. In the first place, the cumulative preference shareholders still had to be borne in mind in any reorganization scheme. With the preference shares sixteen and a quarter years in arrears on dividends, Dunn was wary of any scheme of corporate refinancing that might draw opposition from these aggrieved shareholders. His Toronto lawyers also warned him that the Bank of Montreal's status as a 'substantial creditor' would give it some sway over any Algoma reorganization.[72]

Besides the possibility of investor friction, Dunn saw little gain in seizing a company incapable of paying its own way in the midst of a severe depression. 'My view is and I believe the Bank of Montreal holds the same opinion,' he admitted, 'that the Company is better in the hands of a Receiver until there is sufficient lifting of the depression to justify restarting operations.'[73] In the interim, he would content himself by using his influence to secure a cooperative board of receivers for Algoma. The appointment as receivers of Sir William Stavert, W.C. Franz, and Alex Taylor, all onetime business acquaintances, met with Dunn's unreserved acceptance. He next used his financial influence to ensure the sympathy of the bondholders' committees being formed in London and Philadelphia. The Philadelphia committee was chaired by William Lilley, a broker who had already told Dunn that he had the 'highest impression' of his 'ability and integrity.'[74] In London, the bondholders were represented by G.C. Cassels, R. Ashton Hamlyn, and Guy Ridpath, all intimate financial acquaintances of Dunn's.[75] The hub of Dunn's wheel of control was provided by Toronto lawyer N.W. Rowell and his nephew, Ward Wright, who counselled their client on his legal position amid a situation so tangled that even Dunn could not always grasp its intricacies.

By working behind the scenes in late 1932, Dunn had used his position as majority bondholder to install a group of competent and cooperative overseers at Algoma. His stealth at times verged on the paranoiac. Few had the least inkling of his intentions or even his interest in the Algoma situation. 'The popular idea,' a Sault lawyer confided to him, 'is that some reorganization should take place providing for a benevolent Santa Claus dropping millions of fresh money into prematurely considered schemes of enlargement at a time when the business of the country is not crystallized into a definite trend. We are all in the dark as to the immediate future.'[76] There was nothing precipitous or benevolent about Dunn's plans for the Sault. His objective was to nurse the corporation back to reasonable financial health under the receivership and then attempt a reorganization that would simplify and streamline the existing corporate structure to his advantage. The key would be to find some means of disinheriting a large number of the shareholders, thereby condensing financial control in his hands.

The financial recuperation of Algoma Steel was to a high degree at the mercy of the vicissitudes of the depressed Canadian economy. The steel industry reached its lowest ebb in the first half of 1933, when from March to May Canada produced no pig iron whatsoever. Only 34,970 tons of steel was made between February and April of the same year.[77] Per capita consumption of steel in Canada declined from 569 pounds in 1929 to 121 pounds by 1932. The winter of 1932–3 proved Algoma's darkest hour. With only one blast furnace and one battery of coke ovens in operation, Franz dolefully reported to Sault MP T.E. Simpson that the company's labour force had dwindled to 332 men by October 1932. By late 1932, 1052 Sault families were on direct relief.[78] In May 1933, the company arbitrarily reduced its employees' wages by 10 per cent, thereby giving it the lowest base labour rate, 27¢ an hour, in the steel industry.[79]

In 1933 steel began emerging from the doldrums, registering what the Monetary Times called an 'upward trend,' not dramatic but at least steady.[80] Pig iron production, only 67,899 tons in the first half of 1933, grew to 159,418 tons in the second half and then advanced throughout 1934 to a total of 404,995 tons.[81] The economic tide continued to turn in Algoma's favour during the second half of 1933 as orders for rails, merchant bars, and coke mounted. As a result, total shipments from the plant increased from 195,497 tons in 1933 to 342,956 tons in 1934. In the fiscal year 1933–4, the company once again crossed the great divide into the profit column, reporting profits of $862,036.[82] These gains gave the corporation sufficient financial headway to embark on a partial diversification program, commencing in late 1934 with the ordering of rolls for structural beams and channels up to 15 inches, followed by a decision to produce sheet piling for construction. 'We are very pleased to have demonstrated,' noted one of the receivers, 'that business can be carried on with some profit without rails. This never occurred before in the history of Algoma.'[83]

The partial return of solvency and activity to Algoma was not only the product of saner management and improved economic trends. It was also attributable to the intervention of Canadian politicians. Algoma's financial and operational crises had always tested the mettle of federal and provincial politicians' commitment to the Sault industries. The Depression proved no exception. Throughout the 1920s Algoma's provincial and federal political sympathies had been firmly planted in the Conservative camp. With Premier Henry in Toronto and Prime Minister Bennett in Ottawa, the corporation could therefore at least face the Depression with partial equanimity. Unable to secure better tariff protection, Algoma clamoured for some more practical measure of relief to tide the company over its bad times. In late 1932, T.E. Simpson, Tory Whip and Sault MP, approached Bennett and railways minister R.J. Manion with a request for a government rail order 'to relieve the serious unemployment situation at Sault Ste. Marie.'[84] Despite Sir George Perley's warning to Bennett that Algoma was 'not in good shape financially,'[85] Simpson's persistence eventually resulted in a government guarantee to pay Algoma's wages and cover certain interest charges on a thirty-thousand-ton rail order for the CNR. The guarantee was made by order-in-council under the terms of the 1933 Relief Act. When S.J. Hungerford of the CNR protested that the railway did not need the rails, the government agreed to pay its carrying charges until such time as the rails were required.[86]

The government's guarantee of a private corporation's contract was attacked by Liberal leader Mackenzie King, who alleged that 'the government has been using this legislation [1933 Relief Act] to further the interests of certain financial corporations rather than in the interests of the unemployed.'[87] Enacted without debate, 'this blank cheque authority,' King asserted, left the government with all the risk and gave a private corporation all the profit in a deal that no Canadian bank would have touched. Simpson, Bennett, and Manion responded to this criticism by asserting that it was a measure of unemployment relief and that the rails had been procured at the going rate. 'I know of nothing that any businessman would not have done,' Bennett asserted.[88] One businessman at least agreed wholeheartedly with this contention. Sir James Dunn privately boasted that the government's sanction made the deal 'ordinary banking business.'[89] Less than a month later, Bennett was informed by G.P. Fullerton, head of the Board of Railway commissioners, that the eighty thousand tons of Dosco and Algoma rails guaranteed by the government were costing 'approximately $200,000 more than they would have had they ordered them when they were required.'[90]

Unquestionably, the rail deal created jobs at the Sault – about 1600 of them through the winter of 1933–4. The biggest winners were, however, the bondholders of the corporation, who saw their investment continue to regain financial stability under auspices that would never have been sanctioned by private bankers. 'An investment of $45,000,000 is not lightly abandoned,' J.A. McPhail gratefully told T.E. Simpson. 'I must say in all fairness that the momentum was supplied by this deal to carry the Corporation over a difficult bump and into a more or less steady production.'[91] Significantly, Bennett's office staff filed the rail deal correspondence under 'patronage,' not 'relief.'

The import of these proceedings was not lost on James Dunn. It was clear that he, acting in the name of the majority bondholders, could increasingly count on one or even both levels of Canadian government to provide the decisive ingredient in any eventual resolution of the Algoma situation. 'The friendly cooperation of the Canadian or Ontario governments,' Dunn admitted to a Philadelphia broker in mid-1934, 'will be necessary to us and I am trying to accomplish something along these lines.'[92] In the early 1930s Queen's Park was not, however, the avid supporter of the Sault industries it had once been. The Tory government of George Henry had not inherited the unbounded faith of Howard Ferguson in 'New Ontario.' 'I feel,' J.W. Curran, owner of the Sault *Star*, told Henry in 1931, 'that it would be unfortunate if the north got the idea that its efforts to help the solution of its difficulties were to be treated lightly.'[93] Algoma's lacklustre performance in the previous decade had left a residual coolness at Queen's Park towards the Lake Superior Corporation. In the spring of 1934, W.C. Franz unsuccessfully approached Henry in search of a government-sponsored rail order for the Temiskaming and Northern Ontario Railway. Franz was quick to point out to James

Lyons, Tory incumbent in the Sault riding, that 'if the rail mill is down at election time it will be very difficult to elect a Conservative member in this riding.' J.A. McPhail, now an Algoma receiver, prevailed on T.E. Simpson in Ottawa for another federal rail order. In a bid to curry the favour of both federal and provincial Tories, company management decided 'to encourage the key men at the plant to support Lyons, having in mind particularly the keeping up of the proper relations at Ottawa.'[94] Not surprisingly, Lyons of the Sault openly attacked Premier Henry for his neglect of the north during the 1934 election.[95]

If politicians were to accede to Algoma's wishes, Dunn realized, a sympathetic mood of public opinion would have to be cultivated. Discussing the prospect of federal aid to the dormant iron ore industry, Dunn noted that 'it is not fair to ask Bennett to give aid till we ourselves convince the public. He will give what the public demands.'[96] The same undoubtedly applied to the recalcitrant provincial Tories. In this respect, Dunn made the lucky acquaintance of J.W. Curran, the ebullient editor of the Sault *Daily Star*, who greeted Dunn with the same unbounded enthusiasm as the previous generation of Sault residents had given F.H. Clergue. 'I feel in my bones that with your leadership we can put the steel plant over big,' Curran assured Dunn; 'we will have to build up a "rep" for the new regime as hustlers and men who know what they are doing ... I just love pushing the public around – for its own good. I know you'll succeed.'[97] More and more Dunn emerged from the shadows. Frequent trips to the Sault and speeches in which he proclaimed himself a 'Soo Booster' won him broad publicity. He was increasingly cast in the role of heir apparent at the Sault. 'I feel that we can put the plant over,' Curran told Dunn, 'if we can only use the right tools.'[98]

While public sympathy was important, Dunn's plan for his ultimate assumption of power at Algoma depended on the use of 'right tools' well hidden from the public's purview. A sense of urgency was imparted to this process during 1933 and early 1934 by the mounting pressure on Sir James' personal finances. Dunn's steady acquisition of Lake Superior securities had been made possible by loans, usually extended on generous and easy terms by Leroy Baldwin of Empire Trust in New York. These loans, at times exceeding $1 million, placed Dunn in a precarious financial position, a position that could not be prolonged indefinitely. Adding to Baldwin's pressure on Dunn, there was the growing reluctance of the Bank of Montreal to extend its already large advances to Algoma. These advances had hovered around the $1 million mark throughout 1933 and with the moderate upswing in corporate fortunes the bank became anxious to see Algoma removed from receivership and placed in a position to make good its indebtedness.

Any doubts Dunn may have entertained as to the eventual profitability of Algoma were eased by the tabling in the fall of 1934 of a consultant's study of the steel corporation. Charles G. Atha, an English engineer recommended by Frater Taylor and Winston Churchill, was commissioned by Dunn to divine the steel corporation's future. 'I am convinced there is an excellent prospect of satisfactory financial results being obtained from the operation of the Algoma works,' Atha reported, 'if proper steps are taken to reduce costs and improve the efficiency of the existing plant and to add to the present range of products new products for which there is an adequate market in Canada.'[99] Atha held out the tantalizing prospect that if $4,995,000 were expended on plant improvements, Algoma could confidently expect annual profits of $3,475,000 by 1938. Atha crowned his optimistic survey by noting his 'high opinion' of the 'capable body of men' who directed the steelworks' operations.[100]

Reassured about Algoma's industrial potential, Dunn turned in late 1934 to his legal and financial consultants. He needed an infallible means of converting his bondholding position into a position of absolute control. Uppermost in Dunn's mind was the fear of the disruptive effect that minority bondholders or maverick shareholders might have on any proposed settlement. His financier's instinct told him that he must secure the commanding heights at any cost. Throughout the early 1930s, he had, for instance, observed the unsuccessful efforts of his friends, Lords Beaverbrook and Rothermere, to wrest control of the Price Paper Company out of the hands of obstreperous shareholders. The tangled financial affairs of Abitibi Paper, another Sault industry in receivership, reinforced Dunn's impression of the folly of proceeding without absolute control. His Toronto lawyer, Ward Wright, was well aware of the dangers in the Algoma situation. Wright believed that Dunn as majority bondholder had the legal right to dictate to the receivers. None the less, Wright worried about the danger of 'not consulting the other interests who hold approximately one-third of the First and Refunding Bonds.'[101] Informed by N.W. Rowell that the bondholders' trustees were 'receiving a great many inquiries' from investors about their rights, Dunn deliberately downplayed the extent of his controlling interest, 'fearful opponents now sleeping might be roused.'[102] Only a dramatic change in Ontario politics and the keen legal mind of Ward Wright would eventually solve Dunn's conundrum.

The election of 'Mitch' Hepburn as Ontario premier in June 1934 at first sight threatened to upset all the schemes of Dunn and the Algoma receivers. Hepburn's populist rhetoric gave the business community in Ontario little to hope for and much to worry about. Having backed the renegade Tory Lyons at the Sault in the election, Algoma had bet on the losing horse. 'I presume you were somewhat surprised at the Ontario election results,' Franz wrote to Dunn. As a result of the Liberal victory, Algoma would not be 'looking for anything from the Provincial Government.'[103]

In the wake of Franz' gloomy prediction, it was a matter of considerable surprise for Algoma's executives to discover that a government dedicated to the 'little guy' could in fact be just as sympathetic to the interests of the Sault corporation as G.H. Ferguson had ever been. Within five months, Franz reported that Dr A.D. Roberts, the Liberal victor over Lyons at the Sault, had 'a good standing with the Government, particularly with the Premier, and is quite anxious to do anything he can for Algoma.'[104] The premier for his part was by November 1934 quick to assure Ward Wright that his government was 'prepared to support and facilitate'[105] any legislation that would expedite Algoma's reorganization. Hepburn's eagerness to assume the mantle of Ferguson as the patron of Northern Ontario industry was rooted to a large extent in a genuine desire to foster employment in the province's primary industrial base.[106] The north imposed certain political realities on all Ontario governments regardless of partisan hue. The greatest of these was the need to preserve employment in towns whose economies hinged on single or predominant industries. More compelling, however, were the pressures exerted on the new premier by Dunn's Toronto lawyers, N.W. Rowell and Ward Wright, both staunch Ontario Liberals with none of the taint of Toryism that might have stigmatized other Algoma representatives in the new government's eyes.[107]

In the unexpectedly warm climate of a Liberal government, plans for Dunn's final push for complete control of Algoma began to take shape. In October 1934, Wright visited Dunn in London and suggested a scheme whereby the dangers of a negotiated reorganization could be circumvented by means of a foreclosure sale. Such a sale would permit the transfer of the corporation's assets to a totally new steel company, especially established to absorb the old company's assets and to refinance them with none of the financial obligations of the old corporation. The plan immediately appealed to Sir James. It would place the whole reorganization 'beyond peradventure,' especially if the legal position of the bondholders could be confirmed by provincial law.[108] Convinced that private legislation confirming such a sale was 'the one shortcut to get on with the job,'[109] Dunn gave Wright the utmost freedom to implement the new strategy.

Wright's initial approaches to the government depended on the good will of Dr Roberts and on making the proposed legislation sanctioning the sale of Algoma's assets seem as equitable as possible and yet financially and legally airtight. This meant that the actual extent of Dunn's controlling position must be kept veiled in secrecy. ' The whole matter of negotiations with the Government has, I think, been kept secret,' Wright advised his anxious client. 'I was afraid that there might be some mention in the Press at some time and I want nothing said until I have the Government definitely committed.'[110] Besides Roberts, Wright's only other confidant was Stanley Norsworthy, assistant general manager of the Bank of Montreal, who was eager to see Algoma put in a position to clear its sizeable indebtedness with the bank. Not surprisingly, Norsworthy assured Wright of the 'full cooperation' of the bank in any reorganization.[111]

The government's only proviso was that it be given some tangible evidence that new capital for the corporation was in the offing.[112] Within twenty-four hours, Dunn cabled Wright from London to inform him that as long as 'Rowell and you are satisfied that perfectly sound legal situation results from proposed legislation,' he would provide, through bond subscription, $5 million for Algoma extensions. When Wright replied that this would clinch the deal, Dunn elatedly cabled back that the sale proposal would not only save time but would also close the doors to any 'nuisance by minority bondholders.'[113]

On 15 November, Wright wrote to Hepburn outlining the sale scheme in full detail. He assured the premier that 'the holders of the outstanding First and Refunding Bonds of the Algoma Steel Corporation Ltd. and the holders of the outstanding Collateral Trust Bonds of the Lake Superior Corporation' were the 'real owners' of the steelworks. Wright then stressed that it had been 'conceded,' although he did not specify on what grounds, 'that the bonded indebtedness of the Corporation (over $20,000,000) is so great that it wipes out any value in the common stock.' Exerting pressure for quick action, Wright mentioned that 'responsible parties' in England were prepared to advance $5 million for plant extensions. No mention of Dunn's name was made anywhere in the letter.[114] Hepburn's initial response to the Toronto lawyer's request was to seek the advice of his cabinet colleagues and the senior bureaucracy. After considering Wright's request, F.V. Johns of the provincial secretary's office voiced some reservation about the proposed legislation. 'To grant such undertaking, the Government without more information, must rely on the *bona fides* of Mr. Wright and those he represents,' Johns warned. As a measure of protection, he suggested that the proposed legislation describe the sale as not only 'necessary' but also 'equitable.'[115] Johns' opinion was reinforced by the deputy attorney-general, J.A. Humphries, who also urged the inclusion of the word 'equitable.' Humphries expressed some hesitation in that 'usually it is not advisable for the Government to give any assurance that any particular piece of legislation will be passed' in the House to the parties concerned, but in view of the 'extreme urgency' of securing capital from England, this consideration could be waived.[116] Less certain was Attorney-General Arthur Roebuck who bared his conscience to the premier in an undated, scribbled note: 'I do not like this because it is loose and indefinite and we are depending too much on one lawyer [Ward Wright], but the guard of the word "equitable" and the importance of the reorganization makes me recommend it.'[117]

At no point did Hepburn press Wright for the identity of the 'responsible parties' in England. Queen's Park was also seemingly blind to the fact that all talk of an 'equitable' settlement was in fact nonsense in the light of Dunn's overwhelming control of the bonds which would allow him to dictate any corporate restructuring. Hepburn himself seemed woefully ignorant of Dunn's controlling position, even though it had been bandied about in the provincial press. On 2 October 1933, for instance, the Sault *Daily Star* had proclaimed that Dunn 'now controls the destiny' of the steelworks. While the concurrence of two-thirds of the bondholders seemed 'equitable' in theory, Hepburn was in reality opening the way for a financial rout of the stockholders and minority bondholders of the Sault corporation. Implicitly trusting in the word of Wright, whom he had even allowed to draft the proposed legislation, Hepburn had given public assurance of the government's intentions before submitting the plan to the provincial legislature. It was little wonder that Dunn cabled Wright in early December to express that he was 'highly appreciative [of] your plan and remarkable progress.'[118]

Armed with the government's assurances, Wright applied in late November 1934 for a provincial charter for the new Algoma Steel Corporation Limited.[119] The new corporation was tailor-fitted to Dunn's ambitions with a bonded indebtedness of $5 million, exactly what Dunn had promised to provide, $2.7 million in preference shares and the rest of the company's $20.7 million capitalization in no par value common shares. The bondholders of the old corporation were to be compensated through the medium of a foreclosure sale with shares of the new. The fate of the old corporation was settled on 14 December at a Montreal meeting at which Dunn, Wright, and Lilley, of the Philadelphia bondholders' committee, agreed that legal sanction would be sought from the Supreme Court of Ontario for sale or exchange of the old bonds for the new shares, after approval had been won from three-quarters of the bondholders.[120] No provision was made to accommodate the interests of the old corporation's common and preferred shareholders. After consulting with Mr Justice Davis of Ontario, Wright arranged for the special bondholders' meeting to be advertised in Canadian, American, and English newspapers in early January 1935. The bondholders were to be asked 'to take action by extraordinary resolution sanctioning, authorizing and approving a scheme for the selling of the undertakings of the said Algoma Steel Corporation Ltd. (1907) to Algoma Steel Corporation (1934).'[121] For each $200 in bond principal one common share of no par value in the new corporation was to be issued, up to a limit of 74,718 shares. The whole transaction was then to be endorsed by provincial legislation. Responding to Dunn's fears of a last-minute miscarriage, Wright noted that 'the Government's majority is so overwhelming that the question of any effective opposition can be dismissed from our minds.'[122] It was, however, Wright stressed, 'most important that the public should understand that the Government are behind this reorganization.'[123]

The bondholders' meeting on 6 February set its predictable stamp of approval on the transaction. Fearing potential opposition from junior or minority bondholders that could have resulted in 'another futile re-hashing of the whole problem,' Wright hastily brought the Algoma sale before Chief Justice Davis of the Ontario Supreme Court on 12 February. Presented with no opposition, the court issued an order sanctioning and directing the sale of the old corporation's assets to the new steel company. With legal sanction secured and the bond exchange scheme ratified,[124] the last act of Wright's *tour de force* was to secure the provincial seal of approval on the whole reorganization. When the Ontario legislature convened on 20 February the Algoma reorganization bill was ready for tabling. Now in the home stretch, Dunn and his legal advisers encountered an unexpected piece of good fortune. Hepburn's arbitrary cancellation of Ontario Hydro's Quebec contracts completely overshadowed all other events of the legislative session, relegating the Algoma reorganization to the back pages of the provincial press.[125] Wright none the less told Dunn that he would 'bring Dr. Roberts down from the Sault, and keep him here for a while, so that he can be interviewing Members, but this will depend entirely upon the calibre of the opposition which may develop.'[126] When on 4 March, Premier Hepburn publicly avowed his backing for the bill, the chance of substantial opposition in a House packed with Liberals almost completely evaporated. 'Hepburn is a man,' McPhail confided to Dunn, 'who is not very tolerant of those who oppose him.'[127] The only visible ripple of dissent came in early April when Arthur Slaght, a Toronto lawyer and Liberal backer, spoke out against the bill on behalf of various American minority bondholders. Slaght demanded that the new corporation make a $1 million deposit with the Ontario treasurer to indicate that their purchase of the old corporation's assets was not 'just a shoestring trick.'[128] Slaght's opposition faded when his backers 'pulled him off as no further opposition developed.'[129] Despite this isolated protest, 'an act respecting the Algoma Steel Corporation Ltd.' was legislated with dispatch and proclaimed on 18 April 1935.[130] 'Algoma reorganization effected,' Dunn tersely cabled his son, 'am chairman and president. Company's outlook good.'[131] The Lake Superior Corporation ceased to exist.

Dunn's sudden arrival on the Canadian industrial scene was perhaps best exemplified by a quiet dinner at the Toronto Club arranged for the new Algoma president by Ward Wright, now an Algoma director. Around that table on 10 May 1935 gathered the wealthy and influential of Ontario industry, finance, and government. James Y. Murdoch of Noranda Mines, minister of mines Paul Leduc, provincial secretary Harry Nixon and Mr Justice Jeffrey of the Ontario Supreme Court joined in honouring Dunn with Thomas Bradshaw of Toronto General Trusts, John R. Lamb of the Bank of Toronto, and Harold Franks, president of the Toronto Stock Exchange.[132] Many of these men had played a part in Dunn's ascendancy and many would be needed in the near future to support Dunn and legitimize the new Algoma corporation in the public eye. This convivial assemblage, intent upon celebrating Dunn's Sault triumph, was strikingly reminiscent of the old bond of common interest that had united Bay Street and Queen's Park with the flamboyant promoters of 'New Ontario' at the turn of the century. Dunn, like Clergue, had not only used Toronto's financial and political power to achieve his ends but at the same time had epitomized a development strategy for Northern Ontario that subsumed the public interest to the needs of private enterprise in the hopes that they would eventually be synonymous.

Less appreciative of Dunn's rise to power were many of the investors in the old Lake Superior Corporation, whose investments had either been reduced to the proverbial 'worthless scraps of paper' or drastically devalued from bonds to common, no par value stocks. Stunned by the speed with which the final sale had taken place, investors were now faced with a *fait accompli* sanctioned by the Ontario Supreme Court and ratified by the province's legislators. For the holders of millions of dollars in the common and preferred shares of the old corporation there was virtually no hope for accommodation. These were the myriad small investors who had pinned their hopes on an overfinanced and ill-managed corporation and who had lost out completely in a game where they had no control of the rules. It was a classic case of *caveat emptor*, in which the rights of small investors evaporated in the face of the concerted efforts of clever lawyers and a wily and determined financier. Dunn summed up his attitude to these dispossessed investors when he asked Ward Wright to answer a letter protesting the reorganization in May 1935. 'I wish you would answer the enclosed letter for me,' he said. 'Apparently this poor misguided man invested his money in Lake Superior shares and afterwards changed them into Algoma Consolidated and on these subjects of course he had no advice from me.'[133]

Others sought redress in higher quarters. While the reorganization was still in motion, A.G. Costello of Philadelphia, a 'big stockholder of Algoma Consolidated,' wrote Prime Minister Bennett to protest the 'arbitrary foreclosure proceeding of Algoma Steel Corp. Ltd. led by Sir James Dunn depriving American investors of holdings in said Company.'[134] Bennett, a lifelong friend of Dunn, forwarded the letter to Secretary of State C.H. Cahan, another of Dunn's old acquaintances, for reply. Pointing out that the corporation had a provincial charter, Cahan suggested that Costello address his grievance to Queen's Park.[135] There can be little doubt as to the tenor of the reply Costello would have received from Mitch Hepburn's government. The professed champion of the 'little guy' had little inclination to ponder the lot of the small investor. 'You will doubtless be aware,' an irate investor told the Toronto General Trusts in 1936, 'that many English investors have brought away the most painful memories of the occasions when they entrusted savings to Canadian industry.'[136]

Dunn's arbitrary reorganization of Algoma Steel cast the legal and ethical position of the small investor in a harsh and revealing light. The completeness and speed of the reorganization was in large measure due to the inadequacy of the laws protecting junior or minority investors. The shareholders of the Lake Superior Corporation in particular had never been in a strong financial position. They had been so beguiled by

Clergue's powerful rhetoric that they had invested in a corporation whose securities had been flagrantly 'watered.' From this initial folly there was little hope of extraction. Even when detected, there were few penalties for devious financiers. As late as 1931, a widely read text on investment warned that despite efforts 'made in late years, by the Provincial Governments, the Investment Bankers' Association of Canada, and the Better Business Bureau, to eliminate such practices from the investment business ... they have not yet gone far enough to warrant complete confidence on the part of the investor, except after inquiry into the record of a firm and its members.'[137]

Dunn's campaign to gain control of the bankrupt corporation rested on two legal principles about which there was little dispute – majority rule and the right of bondholders to control the destiny of a bankrupt business. These were incontestable. Less definite was the question of minority rights in such situations. There were, by the 1930s, abundant legal precedents to support the contention that members of a specific class of security holders must be accorded equality of treatment. 'The key to the problem,' a contemporary legal text noted, 'is the principle that if ... a majority shareholder pushes his own interest so far as to vote a part of the company's assets into his own pocket, to the exclusion of the minority, he is not acting for the benefit of the company *as a whole*.'[138] This principle Dunn flaunted by not according equality of treatment to all bondholders and by trammelling whatever meagre claims the shareholders had on the insolvent enterprise. The province's ineffectual attempt to ensure equal treatment through the use of the word 'equitable' did little to protect minority rights. The speed with which the organization was executed precluded any concerted opposition.

The creation of the new Algoma Steel was not the only illustration of the inadequacies of company law provided by the Depression. In 1932, the Abitibi Power and Paper Company, another enterprise in which the Sault had a large stake, defaulted on its bond interest and went into receivership. For the next eight years a bondholders' protection committee tried vainly to affect a reorganization. Each attempt at reforming the company's capital structure succumbed to the jealousies of competing cliques of investors. In 1940, the Ontario government, anxious to restore a major provincial employer to financial health, named a Royal Commission to inquire into Abitibi's affairs. Premier Hepburn's desire to see Abitibi returned to prosperity prompted him to appoint Sir James Dunn as a commissioner. The commission's 1941 report drew attention to 'the inadequacy of existing legislation to meet situations that arise when companies find themselves in financial difficulties.' In particular, the bondholders should not be the 'sole judge' of any reorganization. 'As the law is now,' the *Report* pointed out, 'if bondholders for themselves concede there is no equity, they simply proceed to foreclosure through the unwholesome fiction of a sale.' Bondholders could thereby 'buy the property for much less than its real value not only to the detriment of the junior security holders but also to the financial disadvantage of bondholders who have not elected, perhaps for very excellent reasons, to place their bonds under the control of the Committee.' Such sales should have 'no place in corporation reorganizations today.'[139]

To these conclusions James Dunn signed his name. The man who had championed bondholders' rights in 1935 now felt free to criticize the very loopholes through which he had passed to capture Algoma. The reorganization of the steel company by means of a foreclosure sale had indeed been a 'wholesome fiction' in which Sir James had acted, in effect, as both auctioneer and sole bidder. Control of the new steel corporation rested entirely in its shareholders' hands. No bonds were created. As principal Algoma shareholder in 1940, Dunn saw every reason to cloak himself in the garb of the common shareholder and to speak out for his rights.

As Canada's newest steel president in 1935, Sir James Dunn received the generous accolades of the press. 'Algoma Steel has at last got clear of the mill-stone hung around its neck by the group who founded it a generation ago,' noted *Iron and Steel of Canada*. 'Sir James Dunn ... has done the steel industry of this country a notable service. His insistence on a revised capitalization strictly in accord with the earning power of the plant puts the company for the first time, on a sound financial footing.'[140] While the future lay uncharted, Dunn had staged a considerable financial and industrial *coup*. The Depression had pushed many Canadian corporations to the limits of their financial endurance, creating an unprecedented spate of receiverships and liquidations. Out of these circumstances, most companies slowly reemerged on a new basis, refinanced and restructured along lines acceptable and equitable to all parties concerned. Few, however, were refinanced by means of legislative fiat on a basis far from 'equitable,' as its political patrons had hoped. The Algoma refinancing was, as Arthur Slaght alleged, more a 'confiscation' than an equitable readjustment of corporate finances.[141]

Dunn's ability to 'freeze out' large sections of the old corporation's investors and to create for himself a tight grip on the reduced capital of the new corporation was in large measure attributable to the support given him by two prime allies. Ward Wright and the various other lawyers retained by Dunn performed brilliantly in plotting a legal strategy ideally suited to the financier's fundamental goals. Realizing that only legislation by the provincial government offered an infallible solution, the Toronto lawyers adeptly manipulated the new incumbents of Queen's Park, Dunn's other, albeit unwitting, allies, into acceding to the financier's wishes. Premier Hepburn's actions in one sense merely perpetuated a long tradition of provincial assistance to the Sault industries. What distinguished the assistance rendered in 1935 was the willingness of the government to provide support on a distinctly inequitable basis which, with a minimum of analysis and perception, could clearly have been seen to benefit the financial fortunes of one financier directly and only indirectly bring about the revival of a major provincial industry. In later years the provincial government would not have the luxury of a choice, for in the future Sir James Dunn *was* the Algoma Steel Corporation. Not surprisingly, Dunn would later assure Hepburn that 'Algoma Steel is always ready to belch a smoky welcome from many chimneys' whenever he passed the Sault's way.[142]

7

The Road to Recovery: Sir James Dunn and Algoma Steel 1935–1939

The transformation of Algoma from broad ownership to the control of a single shareholder can best be described as a throwback to an earlier phase of North American business. By the 1930s, the industrial economy of the continent was increasingly passing from the control of the great captains of industry and their families to a more dispersed investing public. While America's great industrial families were still much in evidence in boardrooms, their role in directing the affairs of the companies they had once created and solely owned was being challenged. The modern industrial corporation was becoming the creature of those who managed it, not those who owned it. In 1932, two American economists, Adolf Berle and Gardiner Means, identified and elaborated on this divorce of ownership from control. It heralded, they noted in *The Modern Corporation and Private Property*, 'a new form of economic organization of society.'[1]

At the heart of this change was the growth of the 'managerial' corporation. The entrepreneurs who had given birth to the modern integrated industrial corporation found themselves overwhelmed by the subsequent demands of their own invention. 'Neither the entrepreneurs, their close associates, nor their families,' Alfred Chandler, the leading exponent of the managerial revolution, has written, 'could carry on the multitudinous activities involved in producing, marketing, and purchasing a massive volume of goods for national and global markets.'[2] The founding entrepreneur often remained influential in the managerial corporation in terms of ownership, but in matters of setting corporate policy, the advice of paid managers became paramount. The power of the entrepreneur became 'essentially negative.' 'They could say no, but unless they themselves were trained managers with long experience in the same industry and even the same company, they had neither the information nor the experience to propose positive alternative courses of action.'[3]

Algoma Steel under Sir James Dunn was very much the exception that proved this rule. In the years up to 1935, Dunn's insistence on absolute control as the *sine qua non* in any reorganization was the one inescapable, if Draconian, solution to the corporation's ills. As president and principal owner after 1935, this same measure of control allowed Sir James to impose his own blueprint on the corporation. His authority was seldom 'essentially negative.' Those he hired to manage the steel company served at his whim and did his bidding. In this sense, Algoma was denied the fruits of the 'managerial revolution.' The corporation was governed along authoritarian and idiosyncratic lines. In the short run, this may ironically have been to the company's advantage. Even with its lean financial structure, the new Algoma was still locked in a battle for industrial survival. A single, unchallenged owner had the ability to dictate corporate policy with a minimum of interference. In the long run, however, the company was denied the benefits of management by trained executives who served with the confidence and compliance of those who employed them.[4] In later years, Sir James took inordinate pride in the knowledge that he was the 'last one-man steel company' in North America. What Dunn failed to realize was that he was not really upholding a proud tradition of business individualism but was in fact blocking the inevitable emergence of managerialism at the Sault.

Dunn's one-man rule at Algoma began on 4 May 1935, when E.G. McMillan, one of Ward Wright's Toronto legal partners and Algoma's interim president, stepped aside to allow Sir James' elevation to the company's presidency and chairmanship. Presiding over the first board meeting of the new company in the King Street offices of his lawyers, Dunn once again extended his all-important offer to facilitate the flotation of $5 million in bond capital.[5] This personal promise had clinched the reorganization deal at Queen's Park, thereby placing Dunn at the undisputed centre of the new corporation's affairs. This was exactly where Toronto's political and business élite wanted Dunn. Under Dunn, the rechristened steel corporation was to lead the economic resuscitation of the Sault. On 12 May, this hope was made manifest at a banquet in Dunn's honour at the Windsor Hotel in Sault Ste Marie.

Those present at the Sault dinner included local, provincial, and federal politicians, together with eminent lights of the Toronto business community such as J.H. Gundy. Dunn was introduced by John A. McPhail, the Sault lawyer who had loyally supported him throughout the takeover, as the 'man who made our dreams come true.' 'A period of expansion lies ahead of you,' Dunn assured his audience. Algoma would 'manufacture things never made in Canada before and for which there is a very growing market.' The company would also 'take more advantage of the mining industry to the north of us.'[6] In this atmosphere of praise and promise, Dunn made it clear that his 'silent partnership' of the last twenty-seven years had been superseded by an 'active partnership.' On the morrow Dunn departed the Sault, bound for London to minister to his many remaining obligations in the City. His visits to the Sault were to be few and far between, seldom averaging more than two a year. In one sense, his infrequent presence at the Sault was a scant departure from the practices of the displaced Philadelphian owners. It was none the less apparent that Dunn had a strategy for the Sault steelworks. His determination to implement this strategy was soon evidenced by the barrage of daily inquiries that he incessantly directed at his managers. Thus a regime of management by telegraph and telephone was initiated, a regime that was to last until the new president's death in 1956.

The rhetoric surrounding the transfer of power at Algoma did little to assuage the anxieties of those intimately associated with the problems of the steel corporation. While Dunn had arbitrarily removed the burden of the old corporation's financial obligations, serious and deeply ingrained problems still confronted Algoma. The introduction of new, heavier forms of structural steel, namely channels and I-beams, in early 1935 had only partially satisfied the need to market lines of finished and semi-finished steel and thereby diminish the company's vulnerability to fluctuations in the demand for rails.[7] Product diversification was accompanied by a need for vertical integration. Uppermost in this respect was the necessity of securing an assured supply of raw materials, especially iron ore, thereby reducing dependence on what was commonly believed to be the ever-shrinking reserve of American Superior ore. The dormant Helen mine loomed large in the minds of Algoma officials in the early 1930s as the potential centre-piece of the new corporation's resources policy. Solution of Algoma's diversification and vertical integration problems depended above all else on the availability of 'new money' to finance plant and mine expansion and on the infusion of new managerial talent. These decisions now rested on Dunn's shoulders alone.

The pace at which the national steel industry emerged from the Depression would also have a very direct bearing on Algoma's ability to put its house in order. Compared to the disastrous winter of 1933, the situation in 1935 for the steel industry flickered with hope. The national aggregate of iron and steel sales had expanded to $38,700,961 by 1935, an increase of 33 per cent from 1934.[8] None the less, only five of Canada's ten blast furnaces were 'in blast' in 1935. This represented only 42 per cent of available capacity and gave some indication that the road to recovery was still long. Of Algoma's four blast furnaces with a total capacity of 1600 tons daily production, only one 450-ton furnace remained in operation in the 1933–5 period. Its annual operation had, however, been pushed from a meagre 84 days in 1933 to a more encouraging 325 days in 1935. Dunn had timed his takeover at the Sault to coincide with what he perceived as the turning point in the Depression; to have seized control in the dark days of 1933 would have deprived him of even the slight leverage that the moderate demand of 1935 afforded. In 1935, the federal Public Works department had, for instance, placed substantial orders for Algoma's new steel piling for wharf construction – a sure sign of the wisdom of product diversification. Hopeful that this slow and as yet uncertain revival of the national economy would gradually work its regenerative effect on Algoma, Dunn was also aware that the company must promote its own rebirth through internal reorganization and by seeking the assistance of its two long-standing foster parents, the provincial government at Queen's Park and the federal power in Ottawa. While the Hepburn government had filled the role of *deus ex machina* during the crucial 1935 reorganization, much remained to be gained by the new Algoma in the arena of federal politics, especially in the realm of tariffs.

Dunn's ultimate success at the Sault would hang directly on his ability to capitalize on the inclination of both levels of government to foster the establishment of a prosperous steel industry in northern Ontario. Like Clergue, Dunn would have to exploit the areas of consensus as to Algoma's future that existed between Ottawa and Toronto, and, when no consensus existed, use the mutual suspicions and anxieties of the two political centres to the corporation's best advantage. Dunn soon developed an uncanny knack for convincing both Ottawa and Toronto politicians that the ends of Algoma Steel and those of their governments were largely synonymous. He had already used this equation during the 1935 reorganization by convincing Hepburn that Algoma's resuscitation offered the government a ready means of stimulating employment in the north. The government would only provide assistance in the future if Dunn managed to preserve this association of corporate and provincial interests.

The long-range solution of Algoma Steel's problems in May 1935 was overshadowed by the pressing problem of simple survival and here there was room for a political helping hand as well. Only after sufficient production had been stimulated, the crippling drain of 'idle expenses' reduced, and a modicum of capital flow restored, could Algoma hope to gain enough momentum, financially and operationally, to forge its new policies. 'The trouble in Canada is the slowness of orders,' Dunn explained to Charles Atha, his English confidant in technical steel matters. 'There is no use in kicking against the pricks or undertaking new financing before we have some important business in sight – in other words some important rail orders.'9

Ironically, therefore, Dunn's initial strategy at Algoma was to perpetuate the company's long-standing reliance on rail production. Like the receivers of the bankrupt company before him, he instinctively turned to Ottawa for assistance. 'The next thing for us to do,' Dunn instructed his new general manager, T.F. Rahilly, 'is to get the best part we can of the orders resulting from the Government relief finance and in this matter I hope to be of some use.'10

Dunn's usefulness in Ottawa lay in his close social and sometimes business ties with the prime minister, Finance Minister Rhodes, and Sir Edward Beatty of the CPR. Dispatching Algoma's new general manager, T.F. Rahilly, and Sault MP T.E. Simpson to Ottawa, Dunn insisted that they should impress on Ontario cabinet ministers like R.J. Manion that their province 'get at least as much from relief orders as Nova Scotia.'11 Rahilly conducted 'very satisfactory' interviews with Manion and Rhodes and was able to report to his president that an order-in-council had provided government guarantees on the interest charges of a forty-thousand-ton rail order for the Canadian National. A similar order was placed with Dosco.12 Bennett insisted on one concession from Dunn for his government's generosity. He stipulated that former Algoma president W.C. Franz, whom he held culpable for the old corporation's misfortunes, be removed from any effective influence over the company's affairs. Dunn, who harboured a genuine affection for Franz and had a realistic appreciation of the problems he had confronted, reluctantly acquiesced to Bennett's demand.

The rail order helped Algoma continue to gain momentum. In the first year of Dunn's presidency, the company rolled $3,835,530 worth of steel rails, constituting 42.5 per cent of the corporation's total net sales of $9,013,213.13 Like Hepburn, Bennett had shown his willingness to give Algoma a new lease on life. By August 1935, however, it was apparent to Dunn that, while Bennett claimed to be 'heartily in accord with what we were attempting to do here, and ... would give every assistance possible,'14

Tory political fortunes were on the wane. 'However I suppose,' Dunn noted of Bennett's various promises, 'a lot of things are said at election time.'[15]

The struggle for survival also extended to the financial sphere, where a two-front campaign was being waged. On the one hand, a rearguard action was carried on to wind up the involved finances of the old corporation. On the other hand, a vital drive to consolidate and extend the finances of the new corporation was conducted to facilitate expansion and diversification. Capably orchestrated by Ward Wright, the winding-up of the old Lake Superior and Algoma Consolidated Corporations lingered on until April 1939. With outstanding bonds still to be redeemed for common stock in the new corporation and the claims of a legion of junior security holders to be adjudicated, Dunn felt compelled to tie up all loose ends in order to protect fully his hold on the new corporation. In March 1936, Wright bought up $5.8 million of outstanding Lake Superior Purchase Money bonds at a trustee's auction for $1,055,000. He quickly converted these into Algoma common, in the case of deposited bonds, and into cash for non-depositing bondholders. Holders of Algoma Consolidated securities were less fortunate. After the appointment of the Montreal Trust as liquidator in October 1938, the assets of the Algoma Consolidated were deemed 'insufficient' to cover any claims by the common shareholders, while those of the more senior preference and bondholders were paid in a paltry fashion out of the proceeds of the sale of such assets as the Ontario Northern Lands Limited. 'I might say,' Algoma Central Railway president E.B. Barber noted years later, 'that so far as my knowledge goes, this equity is all the original Lake Superior shareholders received out to the Clergue enterprises.'[16]

These financial mopping-up operations were one facet of Dunn's unbending desire to place complete control of the new Algoma Steel Corporation in the hands of its common shareholders, namely himself. The pivotal feature of the 1935 reorganization had been the deliberate downgrading of the senior bondholders of the old corporation into common shareholders of the new, thereby protecting Dunn from the folly of his predecessors who had become hopelessly burdened by the obligation of servicing an overlarge, bonded indebtedness. Dunn's preoccupation with retaining his control of Algoma and with fending off any real or imagined challenge to his paramountcy rapidly assumed a paranoiac dimension. Despite the fact that he had utilized his position as a bondholder to seize control in the first place, he now donned the cloak of an outspoken advocate of the rights of the lowly common shareholder.

The inviolability of Algoma common was amply revealed by the zealousness with which Dunn marshalled and protected his own holdings. In July 1936, Algoma common was split 4:1, creating a total share capital of 480,000 of which 407,540 was issued. By 1 July 1937, Dunn had therefore been able to manipulate his original block of 50,456 common shares into 202,532 shares, which he tightly held together with sizeable holdings in Algoma preference shares.[17] Using the Lake Superior Investment Company, over which he had 69.3 per cent control, to maximize his grip on Algoma, he had in turn effective control over 66.6 per cent of Algoma common.[18] Dunn's only rival for control of the holding company was Lord Glendyne in London, whose 18.8 per cent interest overshadowed the small holdings of E.R. Wood and the general public.[19] Assured by Glendyne that he had no intention of actively intervening in Algoma's management or of disposing of his block, the president of the new steel company found himself in a position of unassailable, if not absolute, control.[20]

Dunn was now able to turn his attention to the implementation of new corporate policies. In this respect, his absolute financial control facilitated the adoption of practices that would never have met with the approval of a more diverse body of shareholders. Of cardinal importance was the decision, as inquiring minority shareholders were bluntly told by form letter, that there was 'no likelihood of this company paying a dividend in the near future.'[21] Even the preference shares of the new corporation had a five-year, no-dividend clause attached to them, ostensibly so as not to prejudice the interests of the common shareholders, who were the previous bondholders. In reality the cessation of dividends was intended to enable Dunn to plough back all profits and to reduce the need of resorting to long-term financing. While this policy brought allegations that Dunn and Algoma were bucking general corporate practice and shirking their ethical duty to the preferred shareholders, it did allow the corporation to build up its earned surplus from $541,814.63 in 1935–6 to $1,580,423.65 by April 1939, a luxury that the previous corporation had never enjoyed.[22]

Dunn also adopted the rather uncharacteristic habit, for a City financier, of disregarding the market value of Algoma common. Uninterested in selling his holdings or in inducing others to buy, he could afford to let the market find its own level. Dunn flatly announced to an old City friend in 1937 that he had 'no shares for sale and no interest in their being purchased in the market.' And by 1938 he was telling prospective sellers of Algoma common that he had 'such a large interest in the stock that a few shares more or less do not matter.'[23] Up to 1939, Algoma common was therefore never a particularly marketable stock. Dunn himself privately described it as a 'very second grade security' to J.A. McPhail in 1935 and it was not until late 1938 that application was made to the Toronto and Montreal stock exchanges for listing.[24] Even then, Dunn's old Montreal financial friend, W.P. O'Brien, reported that the market in Toronto for Algoma common was 'practically nil.'[25] After years of pumping securities up to inflated values on the London exchange, Dunn now settled on a policy of letting his securities find their intrinsic value. 'I am a complete believer,' he wrote in 1935, 'but it is going to take time. I have no doubt the price of the shares will be forced up way before its present value because other steel shares are going up and the speculating crowd always looks round for something cheaper than the average run of steel stocks.'[26] In the meanwhile, Sir James kept complete control of the company, an achievement that pleased him far more than a bull market in his stock.

Blunt refusals to issue dividends and an unresponsive market did little to soothe the anxieties of Algoma shareholders outside the pale of Dunn's controlling block, many of whom were investors in the former corporation still awaiting the first whiff of a return on their long-suffering investment. In 1936 one disgruntled shareholder inquired when an end would be put to the 'present grotesque position' by which 'a Bondholder, having lost 4/5ths of the money entrusted to this company on security and been given an equity interest only in exchange' was deprived of any return on his investment.[27] Dunn compounded such suspicions by veiling the company's activities in impenetrable mystery, issuing tersely worded annual reports, sometimes lacking even a president's statement. Ever distrustful of the press, he tried to dampen the press's curiosity, limiting press coverage of company affairs to newspapers whose biases were well known and undoubtedly sympathetic, like Curran's Sault Daily Star. Dunn's only exposure to the public came at sparsely attended annual meetings or in carefully edited, almost hagiographical, journalistic sketches in which he was depicted as the 'man of steel.'[28]

Dunn justified all these policies on the grounds that they increased the company's chances of survival. On a more psychological level they found their origin in the president's deeply felt fear of betrayal, and at times unbounded suspicion of all those about him. Every proposal placed before him was viewed in the light of both constructive policy advice and a potential bid to oust him from his hard-won position of power. This constant paranoia had been bred by years of wheeling and dealing in the City, a financial world notorious for its deviousness and perfidy. Dunn's sense of persecution and insecurity was at times so counterproductive as to obstruct constructive proposals made by his managers. It therefore enabled him to rationalize almost any procedure if it could be seen to increase Algoma's chances of survival and hold at bay those forces that threatened to put it back into the financial quagmire from which he had dragged it.[29] One aspect of this behaviour was the president's extreme reluctance to resort to any form of bonded indebtedness which could interpose the rights of more senior investors over his own. This reasoning prevailed even in the face of strong arguments from Algoma's managers that the capital attracted by a bond issue would expedite the company's modernization. Fear of a financial complication also tainted Dunn's receptivity to outside advice on the business of running a steel plant. When urged by George Humphrey, a seasoned American steelman, to conclude a cost-sharing agreement for the construction of a continuous strip mill with National Steel and the Mesta Machine Company, Dunn balked, fearful of some hidden motive on Humphrey's part.[30] Considering that National Steel was one of the few us steel corporations to stay consistently in the black during the Depression, Dunn would have been well advised to take this suggestion as an astute step towards diversifying Algoma's product mix. In fact, it was Stelco which moved in the late 1930s to construct Canada's first continuous strip mill.[31]

The first two years of the new presidency at Algoma can therefore be seen as a period that enabled Dunn to consolidate his financial paramountcy and further allow the gradual rejuvenation of the Canadian steel economy to coax Algoma's slow recuperation. The first fiscal year with Dunn at the helm saw a net operating profit of $1,264,142. The result of the second year's operations, $756,871, reflected a national downswing that was to spill over into 1938.[32] By relying heavily on sales of rails and industrial coke, Algoma was able to lessen costly 'start-up' and 'idle expenses.' The resultant profits and growing earned surplus afforded Dunn an opportunity to assess Algoma's problems from a broader perspective. This was a relative luxury quite unthinkable before 1935, when the crippling losses of 1932 and 1933, coupled with the conservative management of the steelworks under the recievers, had precluded any chance of even gradual change.

Dunn not only changed the atmosphere in which constructive policy could be contemplated but also altered the means of change by effecting a decisive reshuffling of Algoma's senior management. Reluctantly agreeing with Prime Minister Bennett that W.C. Franz, Algoma's president since the 1920s, had reached 'a certain age,' Dunn shifted him to the board of directors. Accompanying Franz to the board was veteran Soo booster John A. McPhail, who had earned his laurels during the takeover and came with the recommendation of Sir Edward Beatty of the CPR. Replacing Franz as the corporation's chief operating officer was Thomas F. Rahilly,[33] a talented American-born engineer, who had impressed Dunn as a 'rare young man' in his capacity as assistant to the receivers. Ambitious and perceptive about the company's shortcomings, Rahilly had subtly aided and abetted Dunn throughout his pre-reorganization man-oeuvres. This triumvirate of Rahilly, Franz, and McPhail, together with the president himself, comprised the board's executive committee. Ward Wright continued to direct Algoma's legal affairs. Assessing these key appointments in May 1935, Dunn concluded that 'our team is a good one,' a judgment that was borne out in 1938 by the first independent post-reorganization review of Algoma's affairs. The report by McClelland and Ker, London accountants, remarked on the 'most efficient group of officials, full of interest in and enthusiasm for the company's welfare' and credited Rahilly with creating 'an entirely new atmosphere.'[34] Despite such praise, Dunn was the undisputed boss and Rahilly soon learned the frustration of a trained manager whose advice frequently fell on deaf ears.

The process of divining what policies could best promote the 'com-pany's welfare' initially centred on the long-standing need to revive Clergue's vision of exploiting iron ore in the Sault's hinterland. Once this was achieved, Algoma could concentrate on diversifying its steel produc-tion. Control over iron ore supply would partially liberate Algoma from its uncertain reliance on foreign raw materials, while diversified steel production would insulate the company from the financial and opera-tional vicissitudes brought on by a dangerous overreliance on railway steel.

Long before his ascendancy to the presidency Dunn was intimately familiar with the problems of providing Algoma with an assured supply of ore. As early as 1916, he had travelled down the Algoma Central in Sir William Mackenzie's private car to inspect the Helen mine. He was therefore well aware that the initial success of the Helen mine was the product of combined private initiative and government incentive, a formula Algoma had vainly tried to reconstitute in the 1920s. 'I have had a lot of talk lately with Howard Ferguson on the subject of these ores,' Dunn reported to McPhail in 1934, and I am sure that if Howard Ferguson were back in Canada we would get strong Government assistance apart from the bounty now in the Statute Book.'[35] Reopening the Ontario iron ore industry for the mutual advantage of province and company alike could not be accomplished in the realm of *laissez-faire* economics, for in order to compensate for the massive advantage of American Lake Superior ores, some 'small help,' as Dunn put it, from Ottawa and Toronto was necessary. Sir James was convinced that a robust Ontario iron ore industry would induce employment, industrial expansion, and railway traffic in Northern Ontario, but realized that 'a favourable public attitude to the proposal' was first necessary.[36]

The cultivation of public support for a reborn Canadian iron ore industry was assisted by several compelling arguments. The danger of Canada's total reliance on foreign ores, amounting to 2,124,972 tons by 1937,[37] became increasingly evident as the resuscitating American steel industry placed ever greater demands on what was believed to be its own dwindling domestic supply of high-grade hematite ore. Increasingly concerned about their existing resources of ore, American producers on the one hand turned to beneficiation of low-grade taconites and siderites and, on the other hand, looked beyond their borders for new sources of exploitable high grade ore.[38] This development was to unfold over the next twenty years as the giants of American steel scoured Latin America and the northern half of their own continent in search of new ores to supplement the once unchallenged Mesabi ranges. This predatory interest in foreign ores, albeit still embryonic, aroused a sense of vulnerability in Canadian iron and steel circles. 'If there is iron in Ontario, even in those places where it is now supposed to be extinct,' J.R. MacNicol, a Toronto Tory MP, urged Mines Minister T.A. Crerar in 1936, 'and if iron can be produced in this province, the government should do whatever it can to assist in the development of the industry.'[39] On other occasions, MacNicol alluded to the 'tremendous possibilities for that fine city of Sault Ste. Marie' if only a local iron ore industry could be developed.[40]

The prospect of reviving Canada's iron ore industry found a broad response in the depths of the Depression. Many looked to a mining boom as an elixir for the dreary national economy. As Crerar himself told a nation-wide radio audience in early 1936, Canada was becoming 'mine-minded,' conscious of the potential of a thriving mining industry for the national balance of payments and northern development.[41] The federal government responded to this mood with caution. Despite his goal of a balanced budget, Finance Minister C.A. Dunning conceded certain tax breaks to operators of new mines in his 1936 budget. Otherwise the federal government extended no major incentives to Canadian mining.[42]

The government of Ontario, on the other hand, sensed in the potential of a prosperous mining industry an opportunity of adopting a regional approach to economic recovery, won at the expense of centralized, federal direction of the national economy. In this sense Mitch Hepburn was merely perpetuating the struggle of the Ferguson Tories in the 1920s to wrest the province's economic destiny out from under the influence of what now seemed the largely defunct policies of national economic expansion.

Despite the long-standing commitment of previous Tory provincial administrations, Premier Henry of Ontario had done little to encourage Northern Ontario mining up to 1934. Unlike Henry, new Liberal premier Hepburn showed an eager inclination to involve his government in the regeneration of the province's northern hinterland.[43] Egged on by political friends like Curran and Roberts and mining magnates like J.P. Bickell and Bill Wright, Hepburn took a growing interest in the province's northland. Dunn sensed this propensity on the part of the provincial government in the early years of his presidency and resolved to exploit it.

Hepburn was not alone in his interest in Ontario's northland. Geological surveys taken just after the First War had indicated the presence of large amounts of low-sulphur, high-manganese siderite ore at the old Helen mine site.[44] American ore companies began to look longingly northward to the Michipicoten region. As early as October 1930, Clarence Randall, vice-president of Inland Steel, visited the dormant Helen site and took samples, which he reported indicated a 'very large tonnage of ore' which could be sintered to 53 per cent iron content.[45] By 1935, Dunn could boast with smugness that the 'people who have been trying to buy into our Algoma ores' included the M.A. Hanna Company, representing the National, Weirton, and Great Lakes steel corporations, the Pickland Mather Company, representing Bethlehem Steel, and the Cleveland Cliffs Iron Company, representing the Otis and Republic steel corporations.[46] Herein lay the solution to Algoma's long-term ore procurement problems. If the Helen could produce five hundred thousand tons of siderite a year, one Algoma geologist reported in 1934, part of the output could be 'traded or sold' to an American steel company, possibly in exchange for 'high phosphorous ore.' With the Ontario bounty payment as an inducement, Algoma could profitably engage in this transborder trade.[47] Here, in embryo, was an early recognition of what later developed into Dunn's wholehearted advocacy of a continental or 'North American' economy based on the exchange of raw materials and regional industrial specialization. Sir James reasoned that Canada could never be wholly autonomous in iron ore, given that the wide variety of ores needed to feed any one 'blast' could not all be found in Ontario. With an increasingly sophisticated steel industry demanding ever more complex 'mixing' of ores of varying iron and mineral content, Algoma prepared 'to take the plunge,' as Dunn often said, into the continental ore market.

The years 1935–6 were devoted to ongoing feasibility tests of Helen siderite and to continued dickering with American interests. In February 1936 an Ontario charter was obtained for Algoma Ore Properties Limited, a wholly owned subsidiary of the steel company intended to coordinate Algoma's bid to resuscitate the Helen. Most consultants' estimates of the Helen's potential pointed to the fact that even with the one-cent bounty offered by the 1930 Ontario bounty act, additional assistance would be needed to boost production to a self-sustaining level. It was the classic Canadian argument for the protection of an infant industry. As T.F. Rahilly explained to Sault MP H.S. Hamilton, the added fuel and labour costs created by the sintering process made 'it necessary to seek aid in order to produce ore in competition with the iron ores found in the Lake Superior district of the United States where, in their natural state the iron content averages in excess of 50%.'[48] Furthermore, the bounty would have to be applicable not only to sintered ore destined for domestic smelting but also to exported ore.

The initial moves in sounding out the Hepburn government's reaction to the idea of a more generous bounty were made easier by Dunn. By early 1937, Sir James had drawn the premier into his high-living social circle, a circle frequented by men like J.P. Bickell and Ben Smith, the hard-driving élite of the booming Ontario mining industry. In their raucous way, these men were the reembodiment of the 'New Ontario' fever which Clergue had typified at the turn of the century. Now, thirty years later, at a time when Ontario's industry was stagnating, the lure of mining – especially for gold – in Northern Ontario was once again hard to resist. Dunn did his best to make it less resistible. In his appreciation of the 1935 reorganization legislation, Dunn had wined and dined Hepburn, praised his role in the Liberal federal election victory of 1935, and brought him as his guest to the Sault.[49] It was, however, in the salubrious winter climate of Arizona, where Hepburn had joined Dunn and Beaverbrook to have 'a grand time riding horses, flying dangerous planes ... and shooting craps with Sam Goldwyn and other magnates of Hollywood,' that the steel president made the first concrete suggestion that the corporation and the province renew their partnership in Northern Ontario.[50] Hepburn responded eagerly. Back in Toronto in early February, the premier wrote to J.W. Curran of the Sault *Daily Star* declaring that he was 'quite ignorant about the iron industry' and would have 'to be guided by the views of those who have given this matter a great deal of thought and study.'[51] Curran acted with alacrity and replied within three days that he had talked the matter over with Algoma general manager Rahilly, with whom he had agreed that the government should offer 'a bounty of 2¢ per metallic unit, or about $1.00 per ton.' Reminding Hepburn of the work of previous Ontario governments, Curran emphasized that 'the mining of iron ore has been a dream held ever since the old Helen Mine was started in 1899.'[52] Without waiting for an unbiased expert opinion and acting on the basis of this rather incestuously obtained advice, Hepburn assured Dunn that a bounty would be extended, on the condition that the company provide $1.5 million to finance sintering operations.

Elated by the premier's decision, Dunn made the news public at a civic dinner honouring F.H. Clergue in the Sault on 15 February 1937. As in the 1935 reorganization, Hepburn had singlehandedly committed his government to legislative action, basing his decision on rather dubious advice and ignoring the right of the legislature to debate the measure before any assurance was extended to concerned parties. Hepburn even failed to consult the local member of the legislature, A.D. Roberts. He had unquestioningly accepted Dunn's promise to provide $1.5 million, although not one cent of the $5 million in 'new money' pledged by Dunn in the 1935 reorganization had yet materialized. These shortcomings were not lost on A.D. Roberts, who bluntly informed his leader that he 'was astounded to hear a private financier announce government policy of the future while the people's elected representative who for two years loyally supported a supposedly democratic government sat idly but not supinely by.'[53] Roberts' outburst was not totally unexpected. He had already made himself a thorn in Dunn's flesh by complaining that due credit had not been accorded him in Curran's *Star* for his backroom efforts in the 1935 reorganization. While placating Roberts with praise for his actions, Dunn evidently agreed with Ward Wright's judgment that Roberts had gone 'a bit haywire.' In future Dunn decided to cast his lot with Curran, 'such a consistent optimist and boomer of everything concerning the Sault.'[54] Although Dunn did apologize to the premier in the wake of Roberts' latest outburst for the 'annoyance' he had caused, it was Roberts who suffered in the long run, losing the backing of his riding association for 'seeking his own ends to the exclusion of the interests of his constituency.'[55]

Not until 3 March, the same day the new bounty act won approval in the Ontario house, did D.H. McDougall, a Toronto consulting geologist, report to the government on the geological prospects of Algoma sinter. McDougall noted that there were 'ample ore reserves to permit mining operations at the rate of 450,000 tons per year for a much larger period than for which government assistance is asked.' He therefore concluded that, despite the heavy capital outlays required, sintering would ultimately prove 'economical.' The Helen was thus an infant industry worthy of protection. As to the 'national aspects of the proposal,' McDougall judged that an Ontario iron ore industry supported by a 'fair bonus' would provide insurance against any cessation of imported ore.[56] Heartened by these conclusions, Hepburn plunged ahead on his predetermined course. The Act to Encourage the Mining of Iron Ore granted a 2¢ bounty on each unit of metallic iron in each ton of beneficiated or natural ore mined in Ontario, effective January 1939.[57] Although the act was general in its application, the company for which it had so obviously been created made application for its benefits on the day before its official promulgation.[58]

Work on the New Helen was initiated without delay in the summer of 1937. In a feat of considerable engineering daring, a shaft was driven diagonally up through the hill containing the siderite ore body to a point which subsequently served as a funnel at the base of what was, over the years, to become a cavernous open-pit operation. Phoenix-like, the town of Wawa sprang up three miles from the mine site. Removing the calcinated ore to Michipicoten harbour from the Wawa sinter plant presented serious problems. Ore from Clergue's old hematite mine had been brought to Michipicoten along a spur of the Algoma Central, then a subsidiary of the parent Lake Superior Corporation. By 1937, the Algoma Central, no longer under the steel company's control, was much less willing to cooperate in carrying Algoma ore. The railway's president, E.B. Barber, complained that the prospective contract for carrying coke to Wawa and sinter to Michipicoten offered only 'a very small margin of profit' and he therefore felt entitled to a guaranteed annual payment.[59] Infuriated by this inability to have his own way, Dunn retaliated by having Hepburn apply pressure on the financially troubled railway. Queen's Park pressed the railway for payment of over $1.3 million in back taxes, ultimately forcing it to surrender some of its granted land in payment. For its part, Algoma was able to circumvent Barber's intransigence by chartering an aerial tramway to carry ore from the mine to the sinter plant. After these opening affronts, the Dunn-Barber relationship became a simmering feud that would last almost a decade.[60] Dunn would have liked to reincorporate the Algoma Central into the Sault complex. Vertical integration into ancillary railway and steamship services would, Dunn envisaged, diminish the steelworks' dependency upon external services. Unfortunately, Barber of the Algoma Central proved a sturdy impediment to Dunn's dream of a well-planned and well-executed reconstruction of the Clergue complex.

The commencement of operations at the Helen in July 1939 coincided with the conclusion of an ore exchange contract with the M.A. Hanna Company of Cleveland. The ten-year agreement, negotiated by Dunn and George MacLeod of Algoma's mines section with George Humphrey of Hanna, called for Hanna to supply Algoma with at least 150,000 tons of non-Bessemer ore in exchange for an equal amount of Helen sinter which it would in turn market to American steel firms.[61] Dunn confidently calculated that the contract, once signed, would bring an $801,000 annual profit to Algoma on the basis of an annual output of three hundred thousand tons of sinter.

In later years Dunn looked on the revival of the Helen mine as the crowning achievement of his Algoma presidency. Departing from his usually terse and unadorned public vocabulary, he frequently talked of having reopened Clergue's ' Treasure House' in Michipicoten and in late 1938 abandoned his habitual avoidance of press coverage by contributing an article, 'The Romance of the Helen Mine,' to the *Financial Counsel*.[62] The Helen appealed to Dunn because he could so readily grasp its significance. Unlike the intricate complexities of steelmaking, the extraction of iron ore from the Shield was a relatively simple operation with direct tangible results, well within Dunn's limited technical ken. Dunn later fell into the habit of flagrantly overestimating the Helen's potential, often pushing its supposed reserves beyond a billion tons. It became a well-known fact among Algoma executives that the president's violent temper was most easily soothed and that policy was most fruitfully discussed at Wawa, or 'Jamestown' as its benefactor called it, while Dunn perched at the 'Eagle's Nest' overlooking the Helen mine.

Algoma's contribution to Northern Ontario development at the Helen went much deeper than its president's vanity. The first shipments of Algoma sinter marked a small but decisive break in the old pattern of dependency on external ore sources that had characterized almost two decades of Canadian steelmaking. The 414,603 tons of ore mined in Ontario during 1940 was meagre in comparison with the still-enormous output of the Mesabi ranges, but it did represent the vital first step in the direction of restoring a healthy and competitive iron ore industry in Canada, a 'new industrial epoch in Canada' as Dunn put it in the *Financial Counsel*.[63] Followed by Steep Rock in the 1940s and Labrador in the 1950s, the New Helen helped to elevate the Canadian iron ore industry from the status of dependency to that of interdependency. The New Helen was eloquent testimony to the long-standing partnership between business and government in the development of Northern Ontario's resources. Although there is every indication that Hepburn had been unwittingly seduced by the blandishments of Algoma's president into perpetuating this alliance, his bonus legislation had alleviated in one stroke the problems of company and province alike. No matter how dependent the company later became on federal economic prerogatives, Dunn never stinted in his praise of the 'vision and courage' displayed by Ontario's premier in revitalizing iron-mining. 'I will never cease to be grateful for your action,' he wrote to Hepburn in 1945, 'in enabling Algoma to take an active part in making the Soo hinterland one of the great iron countries of the world.'[64]

For the solution of its diversification problems, it was to Ottawa, not Queen's Park, that Dunn and Algoma first looked. The study prepared by Charles Atha on the eve of the reorganization had vigorously advocated a broadening of Algoma's product mix as the *sine qua non* of corporate recuperation. After warning that Canadian steelmakers could not expect the railways to generate demand for more than two hundred thousand tons of rails a year, Atha urged that Algoma ought to move with haste to install a plate mill capable of rolling flat steel for the construction and engineering trades and strip steel for the automobile, engineering, furniture, and canning industries.[65]

Algoma had historically believed that the surest route to a better product mix lay through the tariff clauses of the federal budget. Indigenous growth took place through a process of import displacement by which tariffs were judiciously used to remove steel goods from the importers' list and bring them within the realm of domestic production.[66] This process had worked smoothly in the early years of the enterprise, but as Canadian industry matured into a complex structure with built-in prejudices against tariff alteration, the process became increasingly inoperative. None the less, one of Dunn's first sorties as Algoma president was to the Ottawa office of C.D. Howe, the minister of railways, canals, and marine in the newly elected government of Mackenzie King. He explained to Howe that Algoma proposed 'to take the plunge, and only ask from the Canadian Government such reasonable protection on sheets and tinplate as Liberal Governments have given to the steel trade generally since W.S. Fielding's time.'[67] Howe responded that the matter 'very much interested' him, especially with its implications for Northern Ontario, and that the King government was disposed to give 'every possible encouragement in bringing the flat steel industry to Canada.'[68]

Howe's inclination to assist Algoma was evidently not shared by the rest of the King cabinet. The thrust of the new Liberal government's fiscal policy was toward reciprocal tariff reductions, culminating in the 1935 American trade pact and the renegotiation of the 1932 UK trade agreement in 1937. Learning that Finance Minister Dunning was amenable to low duties on imports of British flat steel, Dunn complained that it was impossible for him 'to conceive that Canada will hang such a millstone round the neck of its struggling steel industry.' No country aspiring to be a nation, he concluded, 'can afford to sacrifice its steel industry.'[69] Despite Algoma's representations made to the Tariff Board,[70] it became painfully apparent that Charles Dunning was not inclined to alter the Canadian tariff to accommodate the company's diversification plans. Dunning was quick to point out that the steel industry was recovering sufficiently well along traditional lines. In his 1936 budget Dunning stressed that tariff reform would only be based on the principle of 'orderly progress.' 'Extremes,' he declared, 'defeat their own purpose, violent fluctuations one way or the other are mere leaps in the dark.' Tariff changes would be secured through 'deliberate, considered and related stages,' but Dunning left little doubt that these would be in the direction of a 'thorough-going downward revision.'[71] While reassuring the industry that countervailing tariff reductions would not be allowed to erode established patterns of steel production, Dunning made it clear that many shapes and sizes of Canadian steel could simply not compete with those produced by the huge American and British industries.[72] After Algoma finally took its plunge into tinplate production in 1938, Dunn noted bitterly that 'Mr. Dunning is not to help the people who had the courage to do something last year.'[73] Such bitterness revealed a deeper truth. The company's chances of recuperation and prosperity would be significantly improved when and if it succeeded in aligning its interests with those of the national or, at least, the Ontario regional economy. In the late 1930s, Ottawa's interests did not encompass the steel industry's desire to expand into new product areas. The revival of existing industrial capacity and the freeing of trade outweighed all other considerations. 'King and Dunning apparently have decided they must pay this country for the trade she gives us,' Dunn complained about the tariff changes made in Britain's favour, 'and it happens to be at our expense.'[74]

Elsewhere in Ottawa the news was not good. In October 1936, Rahilly and H.S. Hamilton, the Sault's Liberal MP, lobbied C.D. Howe for further government guaranteed rail orders, only to be told by the chairman of the Board of Railway Commissioners that there would be no rail orders until late 1937. Rahilly and Wright reacted to this rebuff by suggesting to Dunn that 'it might be a good thing to have Billy Franz down in Ottawa and just sitting around the Rideau Club, so that we would get the atmosphere, and if anything important turns up I will get you on the telephone at once.'[75] In 1937, Sir Edward Beatty assured his old friend Dunn that 'pretty big rail business is not far off' from the CPR.[76] By 1938 Hamilton was, however, still pressuring Howe for assistance, with little apparent result. These setbacks in Ottawa exasperated Dunn to the point that by 1939 he was castigating the federal government as 'a damn rotten lot,' a government capable only of temporizing and devoid of the decisiveness of a Hepburn or a Bennett.[77]

The realization that diversification was not to be won with special federal assistance bred more than a passing animus in Dunn, who alleged that Ottawa was actively discriminating against Algoma. As early as 1936, he was marshalling statistics to reveal how Dosco basked in the warmth of federal coal and freight subventions which allowed it to compete both in external markets and in central Canadian markets, while unsubsidized and landlocked Algoma struggled to survive. A ton of rails, Dunn pointed out, could be delivered in Montreal from Sydney for $4.50 while Sault rails reached Montreal, a journey three hundred miles shorter, for $5.40.[78] Dunn used such evidence not only to browbeat federal politicians, especially Ontario cabinet ministers, but also to exploit and fuel Hepburn's incipient rivalry with Ottawa. 'I see that Ontario and Quebec money,' Dunn reminded Hepburn in 1938, 'is being used by Ottawa to pay a bigger subsidy to our rivals the Dominion Steel and Coal Co.'[79] This 'favouritism' meant that Algoma had to meet competition 'both fair and unfair' and was being denied at least an 'even break.' It was because Algoma was 'not feeding from the public trough' that Dunn trumpeted Algoma's success in marketing rails to South Africa in 1939 with no federal aid. He told Hepburn, 'It must be more important for Canada that Ontario industry reaches world markets than Nova Scotia industry reaches Ontario markets.'[80] Hepburn frequently echoed Dunn's resentful opinions, speaking out publicly and using Algoma's maltreatment as solid evidence of Ontario's too onerous burden in Confederation.[81] By 1939, Dunn was openly intimating that he favoured Bob Manion, always a stalwart Northern Ontarian, in the next federal election. He was also fanning the flames of discontent in the premiers' offices of Toronto and

Quebec City. After one of his frequent breakfasts with the Quebec premier, 'Jimmy' confided to Maurice Duplessis that Quebec's position and that of Hepburn 'harmonized and ... together you could do as fine a service to Canada as Macdonald and Cartier did seventy odd years ago' by bringing about a National Government in Canada.[82]

Ottawa was not oblivious to Dunn's part in the worsening of federal-provincial relations in Central Canada. Mackenzie King was certainly aware of Dunn's animus towards him and the latter's role as an avid promoter of the Duplessis-Hepburn 'conspiracy.' In November 1938, Senator Raoul Dandurand met Dunn en route to England and later described for the prime minister how Dunn had met with Duplessis before the voyage in a meeting 'arranged a day in advance so that he might carry a message from Hepburn to Duplessis concerning the two combining together for the next general elections.' 'Sir James said I was slow in dealing with matters and difficult to get to make decisions,' King wrote in his diary, 'and that Hepburn was right, etc., etc.' King also noted that 'Dandurand reminded me that Hepburn had given Dunn two million dollars subsidy on his Algoma steelworks. We had declined to do anything for him.'[83] King's coolness towards Dunn was not shared by C.D. Howe. Although unable to extend any tangible assistance to Algoma in the late 1930s, Howe was already exhibiting admiration for Dunn's work at the Sault. Howe represented a Northern Ontario riding and understood the region's peculiar problems. In July 1936, he visited the Sault and the Michipicoten area to its north to inspect Algoma's operations. The visit marked the beginning of a long and fruitful association between the steel president and the federal minister.

Ottawa's lack of ardour for a remodelling of the tariff brought with it the growing conviction that Algoma would have to 'take the plunge' into diversification by itself if it was to capitalize on the appetite of the reviving automotive, mining, construction, and canning industries for steel. In 1935, Algoma initiated production of certain sizes of structural steel and steel piling. Pursuing this trend away from rails, Algoma decided to diversify into tinplate production. A consultants' report in early 1936 revealed that in 1934–5 Canada consumed eighty-two thousand tons of imported sheet and tinplate.[84] Despite warnings that without 'sympathetic treatment' from Ottawa in establishing a tinplate mill Algoma was risking 'serious losses,'[85] Dunn negotiated a five-year contract in 1937 with the Continental Can Corporation's Canadian subsidiary. Under the contract Algoma was to receive the benefit of Continental Can's tinplate technology in return for a guarantee to sell 80 per cent of its output to that company. While at first sight a decisive breakthrough, the contract was in many ways ill considered. By stipulating that Algoma pay a royalty of 25¢ per box of tinplate produced, an amount not to fall below $50,000 annually, Continental Can had ensured itself a guaranteed supply of tinplate at 25¢ below market price.[86] While Dunn was not oblivious to these shortcomings, his eagerness to boost Algoma's finished steel output led him to accept the contract and to approve the subsequent expenditure of $1.7 million for a tinplate mill.[87]

Like the Hanna ore contract, the tinplate agreement represented another move to expand and diversify Algoma's production through bilateral arrangements with other producers and consumers in the ladder of iron and steel production. Despite his fruitless clamouring for tariff protection from the King government, Dunn increasingly displayed a continentalist perspective on the problems of the Canadian steel industry, arguing that by entering technology- and production-sharing agreements the American and Canadian industries could mutually solve their difficulties without compromising their autonomy.

The tinplate mill proved to be an unmitigated disaster. The second-hand mill erected at the Sault was of such elderly vintage that a further $700,000 was needed in 1939 to overcome innumerable breaking-in problems. At a time when tinplate production was rapidly being automated, Algoma had 'plunged' into the market with an antiquated, labour-intensive mill, the profitability of which was completely undermined when wartime tin shortages placed a premium on efficient tinplate production. By December 1942, Dunn reluctantly admitted that the tinplate mill was draining corporate profits and ordered it closed. The failure of the tinplate venture revealed Dunn's flimsy understanding of the technical side of steelmaking. He had sensed an opportunity but had failed to capitalize on it. Much of this was due to his unwillingness to seek and heed the advice of his own managers. The episode instilled in Dunn a deep and often counterproductive fear of bold policy departures at Algoma, especially if he in any way construed them as jeopardizing his control. In future, Dunn's policy advisers at Algoma would be confronted by a near-paranoiac cautiousness in response to any suggested departure from the established pattern of production. A grinding ball mill, to serve the mining industry, a wider selection of structurals, to serve the construction industry, and new coke ovens, to cater to INCO's smelting needs, all marked less dramatic but productive operational initiatives in the late 1930s. Progress towards diversification had therefore not been great by 1939, but on the other hand there had been no backsliding to an overdependence on rails. Gross sales for 1939 revealed that 24.5 per cent of Algoma output went to railways, 20 per cent to mining and smelting, 16 per cent to construction, 10 per cent to automobiles, and 7.6 per cent to sheet metal consumers.[88]

Where production could not be diversified, Algoma sought to diversify its customers, hoping to break down the company's traditional reliance on Ontario markets. Here Algoma fell back on rails, its tried mainstay of production, to win its new markets. As early as 1934, Dunn had used the good offices of Howard Ferguson, Canada's high commissioner in London, to ferret out possible rail orders in South Africa. After several rebuffs in the highly cartelized world rail market, Algoma eventually secured a sizeable South African rail contract in 1938 and in 1939 won membership in the international rail cartel. 'This is international recognition,' Dunn exulted to a friend, 'of Algoma's place in world markets.'[89] Although the export sales were not particularly lucrative, Dunn revelled in their 'psychological effect in the province of Ontario.' He boasted to Premier Hepburn that 'it is pretty good for our organization at Algoma right in the heart of the continent that they can pay their way to the seaboard and fight for and get as good a place in world markets as Dominion Steel.'[90] Export sales, totalling 8.5 per cent of total sales in 1939, only slightly loosened the grip of the central Canadian market on Algoma. With 73.5 per cent of sales in Ontario and 14 per cent in Quebec, Algoma was still unshakably tied to the central Canadian economy.

Algoma's slow recovery from the grim days of the early Depression was governed not only by product and market diversification but also by Dunn's stewardship of corporate finances. The steel corporation found itself with a president whose personal finances were virtually synonymous with corporate finances. Soon after the 1935 reorganization, Dunn was under great pressure to honour his pledge to underwrite $5 million in bonds for the company's expansion. Although quick to pocket the guaranteed commission on twenty-five thousand common shares, Sir James began to procrastinate, adopting the stance that his bond promise was not so much a pledge as an 'option.' When and if the circumstances warranted it he would act. Consequently, Dunn combed through his financial acquaintances in search of the necessary backing for a bond issue. Requests to Lord Greenwood, Lord Glendyne, and Seligman Brothers brought cool responses, all tempered by the tight London money market. In Toronto, J.H. Gundy apparently shunned Dunn's request for a three- to five-year loan of $2 million.[91]

The 'wait and see' attitude of the financial community was rooted in the belief that Algoma under Dunn was still a risky proposition. Dunn was personally heavily indebted to Empire Trust in New York and the corporation itself was beholden to the Bank of Montreal for $2,399,000 in the fiscal year 1935–6.[92] Algoma was not viewed as a gilt-edged investment opportunity, a fact Dunn discovered in June 1936. After signing an initial agreement for a $6 million bond issue, Boenning and Company of Philadelphia reneged on their agreement with Dunn, citing passive money markets as the cause.[93] This news prompted the Bank of Montreal to demand repayment of Algoma's swollen debt. With astounding good fortune, Dunn was able to convince Morris Wilson of the Royal Bank to take on the steel company's account in July 1937, a reprieve that brought with it an advance of $5 million, backed by Dunn's personal surety and the renewed promise of a bond issue.[94]

Riding on the cushion of credit afforded by the Royal Bank, Dunn was able in the fall of 1938 to conclude an underwriting agreement for a $3 million first mortgage bond issue with a Toronto syndicate headed by his old friend J.H. Gundy.[95] These were the only bonds Dunn ever created for Algoma. The issue was speedily oversubscribed, an indication that the investing public were beginning to take note of Algoma's gradual recovery. No other aspect of the first years of Dunn's presidency was so striking as the steady turnabout of Algoma's finances. Unlike his absentee Philadelphia predecessors, Dunn was committed to the hilt in Algoma, meticulously poring over every detail of the steel plant's operation, even though often thousands of miles away in London. Algoma was never for Dunn an adventure in watered stock and absentee ownership; it was a make-or-break commitment to the resuscitation of a once irresponsibly managed enterprise. Indirectly, a profitable Algoma would also contribute to the industrial maturation of the Canadian steel industry by repatriating one of its largest companies from foreign control and by broadening its product base.

Saluted in 1939 by his longtime friend Lord Greenwood as 'the King of Algoma Steel,' Dunn's grasp on Algoma after four years was none the less still tenuous. He was heavily reliant on the Royal Bank's line of credit and the continued recuperation of the national steel economy. Dunn's immense wealth was tied up almost exclusively in the common stock of Algoma, a stock yet to show much buoyancy on the stock market. So tight were Dunn's personal finances that in 1938 he sought and won a $50,000 annual salary as president from his board.[96] Inured by a lifetime's experience in speculative high finance, he was ideally suited for the financial side of his Algoma gamble. On the other hand, Dunn found himself less advantaged, indeed temperamentally ill suited, in dealing with the delicate problems of labour-management relations at the Sault.

If Dunn had staked everything on the company, so too had the men who spent their working lives within its walls. Reasonable pay, the guarantee of steady employment, and decent working conditions had been policies that the management of the financially crippled old corporation had never been able to pursue. 'I think it has now ended,' A.A. Heaps of the CCF charged in the Commons in 1936, 'but I know that at this Algoma factory the conditions are not too good. It is impossible for the men to organize. They are paid low wages, and ... I venture to say without fear of successful contradiction that the wages paid at this particular mill are lower than those paid for the same class of labour in the United States.'[97] Algoma management could not have contested Heaps' claim. The 2238 men working at the Sault mills in October 1935 received the lowest base labour rate in the Canadian industry, 30¢ per hour, besides having to work shifts as long as thirteen hours. Algoma's labour was entirely unorganized. The last concerted effort to organize the Sault steelworkers as a lodge of the Amalgamated Association of Iron, Steel and Tin Workers of North America had ignominiously collapsed in the depressed 1920s. Within weeks of his assumption of the presidency, Dunn was told by Rahilly that petitions demanding higher wages were circulating through the steelworks. Rahilly's response to these demands was to acknowledge that Algoma's wages were 'low' but to say that the company could not afford to increase them. Once the product line had been broadened, Algoma would be in a position to 'assure continuity of employment at higher wages.' Rahilly reported that the majority of Algoma's workers were prepared to accept this reasoning.[98]

Rahilly's attitude was symptomatic of a consensus that existed between Algoma labour and management, a consensus built on the belief that wages would not improve until new business materialized and that labour strife could irreparably damage such a recovery. 'I appreciate the difficulties of the wage question,' Dunn told Rahilly in 1938, 'but one thing is evident – operating at 25% of capacity in iron and 40% in steel we cannot afford either Dominion or Steel of Canada wages, companies generally working at double our operating percentage.'[99] Labour participated in this understanding by negotiating wage increases contingent upon continued rail contracts and actively backing management's search for orders. 'Don't fight against this Company but with it,' a 1937 company handbill urged Algoma workers, 'come to Ottawa with us and get a 100,000 ton rail order.'[100]

Under the terms of this tacit understanding the lot of the Algoma worker improved steadily in the years up to 1939. Management did not actively oppose the growth of the independent Algoma Steelworkers Union as an affiliate of the All-Canadian Workers Union. As the steel labour force grew to 2989 in 1938, base labour rates inched upwards from 33¢ an hour in July 1935 to 45¢ in 1939.[101] By late 1936, all Algoma departments had instituted an eight-hour day. Although a federal conciliation board hearing at the Sault in August 1936 denied labour a wage hike on grounds of the company's slim profits, it did remark that 'they very rarely found such good feeling existing between a Company and its employees.'[102]

Credit for Algoma's relatively smooth labour relations lay with T.F. Rahilly and the union officials with whom he dealt. Constantly reiterating that the men were 'extremely loyal' to the company in its adversity, Rahilly tempered Dunn's trenchant views on the subservient role of labour in a capitalist economy. In 1936, for instance, Dunn bluntly rejected Rahilly's proposal that a ten-dollar Christmas bonus be distributed to the workers. 'Unless steel mills are run exclusively for the workmen,' Dunn declared emphatically, 'there seems very little purpose in running this steel mill at all if we must raise the wages of the men while the Company is losing money.'[103] Organized labour had wrecked English industry, Sir James firmly believed, and it was not going to be given an opportunity to ruin his steel company. Dunn's determination not to 'lie down before labour' and sacrifice 'the rights of capital in this enterprise' was intensified by the incursion of the American CIO into Canadian labour in the late 1930s. Describing the John L. Lewis style of labour organization as an invitation to 'class warfare,' Algoma's president was heartened by Hepburn's 'courageous battle' at Oshawa in 1937 and even more invigorated by the news from Rahilly in late 1938 that there was little sympathy in the Algoma Steelworkers Union for the CIO.[104]

Sault labour, much like the capitalists who had come to the Sault, had developed along unique lines, often quite autonomous from 'Old Ontario' in the south. Cut off from other concentrations of industrial labour and working in an enterprise whose perpetual precariousness threatened their very jobs, Algoma labour shied away from hard-line militancy and organized along lines that emphasized the seemingly common plight of both labour and management. Only with the full order books induced by war production did the consensus between employer and employee begin to show strain. As Dunn remarked to Rahilly in 1938, 'The relationships prevailing between employees and direction which permit of these amicable conversations must be a matter of deep satisfaction to all the varied interests of our company.'[105]

Dunn's use of the phrase 'all the varied interests of our company' was significant. By the late 1930s he was increasingly inclined to picture his work at Algoma as his 'life's work,' an attempt to tie together the loose ends left by his predecessors into a magnificent industrial tapestry. As president of Algoma, Dunn conceived of himself as a dynamic captain of industry, who, like F.H. Clergue, marshalled the forces of capital, labour, community, and management in pursuit of a single goal, the resuscitation of steel at the Sault. By 1939, he had moved towards this goal, although the ultimate victory was yet to be clinched.

Dunn's greatest triumph in these early years of his presidency was his ability to convince 'all the varied interests of our company' that they *did* in fact share a common goal. 'The North Country,' he told C.D. Howe in 1936, 'had got into my blood a bit.'[106] The long-cherished and now much tarnished dream of industry in Ontario's northland allowed Dunn to imbue forces as disparate as the Liberal government of Mitchell Hepburn, the leaders of Sault labour, and the financial powers of Toronto with a sense of common purpose. This commonality was, of course, in many ways illusory, for each party involved was subject to different risks and prospective rewards. For Queen's Park, the risk was borne by the public purse and the reward was to be garnered in terms of job creation, regional development, and, ultimately, votes. For the steelworkers, the risk and the reward were their daily bread. For Dunn, with his overwhelming stake in Algoma's equity, the risk was of course large – a millionaire's fortune wagered on a single industrial bet – but the degree of risk was in many ways diminished by the willingness of government and labour to share in the wager. The prospective financial gain, on the other hand, would accrue to Dunn alone, who, as majority shareholder, could dominate corporate policies to his own, as well as the company's, best ends. After 1939, the ultimate success of Dunn's bold gamble at the Sault would depend on whether he could induce the federal government, in the frenzied atmosphere of the wartime and post-war economies, to share in this ostensible parallelism of goals and thereby accept the same set of inequitable risks and rewards.

8

Algoma Steel and The Second World War: Steel in a Regulated Economy

The second global conflict of the century decisively changed the nature of the iron and steel industry in Canada. Before the war, the fortunes of the Canadian steel industry had been governed not only by the general economic climate of the nation but also by a limited consensus between government and the industry, a consensus built on commonly agreed areas of interaction. Tariff tinkering, bonuses, freight subventions, tax exemptions, government-guaranteed purchases, and relief work had provided the grist for the milling of policies between industrialists and politicians in both the provincial and federal spheres. Beyond these well-defined areas, the steel industry's operations were sacrosanct. Except where subject to anti-combines regulations and aspects of labour legislation, Canada's primary steel producers functioned in a *laissez-faire* environment, setting prices and establishing product lines as they saw fit, appealing to government for assistance only in those fields where joint endeavour between business and government was mutually acceptable.

Algoma's chequered industrial career reflected this hybrid consensus. Brought to life under the auspices of tariffs, bonuses, and incentives of mixed federal and provincial parentage, the corporation had then been left to fend for itself in terms of diversification and vertical integration. It had fallen back on government succour only in periods of extreme hardship, such as during the early Depression, or when, as Dunn had adeptly done in 1935, the state power could be coopted to sanction an essentially private reorganization. In many ways it had been a 'school of hard knocks' for Algoma's management, but they, like the politicians with whom they dealt, shared the view that the consensus that had pragmatically evolved since the days of the National Policy stopped well short of any direct or pervasive intervention in the internal affairs of the steel industry.

Straining under the pressure of unprecedented wartime demands, the old consensus between steel producers and politicians crumbled, to be replaced by a new government-imposed basis of understanding and cooperation. On all sides the steel industry was challenged by the intrusions of the federal government into matters of labour, production, distribution, prices, and even profits. This forceful imposition of a new and more pervasive consensus governing the affairs of the steel industry was met with considerable apprehension and at times hostility on the part of those who owned and managed the industry.

Sir James Dunn, who had long depicted himself as a *laissez-faire* disciple of Cobden and Gladstone, although ever ready to enlist government's authority to serve his own ends, initially shared this sense of mixed anxiety and resentment. It soon dawned on him that there was to be no post-war 'return to normalcy' and that the Canadian steel industry had instead entered, albeit reluctantly, a new era. Dunn learned to cooperate with government within the terms of this emerging consensus and in time, as was his penchant, to exploit its terms to his fullest advantage. Especially after the pressures of war on the industrial front began to ease in 1943–4, industrialist and politician alike began to seek ways to convert this consensus of expediency into a new and lasting basis of understanding for the post-war steel industry. While this process had begun in the early war years as one of government dictation, it evolved into one of mutual consultation and accommodation. The government's motivation in this process was rooted in a desire for an orderly return to a prosperous peacetime economy. The steel industry participated because it wanted at all costs to avoid a return to the days of unused capacity and frustrated ambitions which had characterized the two pre-war decades. The relationship of Sir James Dunn and C.D. Howe, Canada's economic overlord through both hostilities and reconstruction, was not only symbolic of this new relationship, but was in many ways also instrumental in shaping it. In Howe, the steel industry found a forceful arbitrator of business-government relations as well as the creator of a revitalized federal response to the problems of the national economy. For Algoma in particular, Howe signified the reemergence of the decisive national economic leadership that it had vainly sought from Ottawa throughout the 1920s and 1930s.

The outbreak of war in 1939 came as no shock to Sir James Dunn. Even as president of Algoma after 1935, he had maintained his permanent residence in London from where he could oversee his still myriad financial affairs in the City and indulge in the glittering social life of England's political and financial élite. As a close confidant of Beaverbrook and friend of Brendan Bracken, Lord Greenwood, and Churchill, Sir James kept abreast of English political and industrial affairs. Annual visits to his villa at Cap Ferrat on the Coté d'Azur also gave him a personal window on developments on the Continent. Throughout the late 1930s, Dunn's correspondence echoed the Churchillian refrain of 'no appeasement.' 'My contacts in the political world,' he told Algoma president W.C. Franz early in 1935, 'lead me to believe that Europe is now in the period 1911–14, in other words preparing for war again. This would gradually mean increased employment in industry and a rise in raw materials. Don't get caught short of the raw materials you bring in from the u.s.'[1] While Dunn rightly imagined in 1935 that war was 'three or four years away,' he was already fully cognizant of its implications. 'I don't like the outlook,' he confided to a Philadelphia friend, 'but if it must come to war it will sell a lot of steel.'[2] Algoma's new president subtly employed the spectre of impending war when bargaining with Ontario's Liberal government in the late 1930s. A bounty on Helen sinter, he assured Premier Hepburn in 1937, would protect Ontario steelmakers from any sudden wartime disruption in the flow of Mesabi ore. As the prospects of appeasement dimmed in 1938, Sir James suggested to the premier that 'our defence preparations should include a Canadian "Woolwich" where the nucleus of our armament can be created and maintained, situate[d] well away from the seaboard and close to the American border ... My mind naturally turns to the Soo with deep water frontage both above and below the canals and within reasonable distance of the nickel mines at Sudbury.'[3] This pandering to provincial sensibilities reached its height on the eve of the war as Dunn urged Hepburn to employ his rhetorical skills to rouse the patriotic fervour of Ontarians. At the same time he egged Maurice Duplessis of Quebec on to take a common stand with Hepburn against the federal Liberals.[4]

Dunn's coaching of the Ontario premier stemmed from a hope that a provincial industrial strategy might stimulate continued recovery in the steel industry, as it had done for the iron ore industry in the late 1930s. Dunn's sense of pique also found its origin in his belief that the federal government had failed since 1935 to come to the assistance of his reorganized steel company. 'Are we going to take part in helping the Empire get ready in time and give our people employment instead of relief and idleness,' he lectured Hepburn, 'or are we going to lag and do nothing as has been the policy at Ottawa for so long on so many things?'[5] Despite his hopes for provincial assistance, Dunn was under no illusions that when Canada was eventually sucked into the European vortex the fortunes of his steel company would be drawn magnetically into the orbit of the federal power. This was pointedly brought home shortly after war broke out when Dunn tried unsuccessfully to fend off the imposition of the federal Industrial Disputes Investigation Act on all labour disputes in the munitions industry. Sir James told federal Labour Minister McLarty that Algoma preferred to keep its existing provincial machinery as a proven basis of 'friendly arbitration of differences.' In doing this, he undoubtedly believed that Hepburn's government would be inclined to take a more resolute stand against the incursion of the American CIO into the ranks of Algoma labour.[6] Despite Dunn's vigorous lobbying, Hepburn reluctantly informed Algoma that it would be *ultra vires* under the War Measures Act for Queen's Park to attempt to undermine federal authority in labour matters. Much as Dunn may have railed against the Ottawa Liberals, it was clear by late 1939 that the war he had so long anticipated would force Algoma to come to terms with the federal government, which by virtue of its wartime emergency powers could decisively outmanoeuvre or overrule any provincially initiated program of industrial advancement. While Hepburn continued to be the butt of Dunn's patriotic prodding through the early years of the war, it was to the less hospitable powers in Ottawa that Dunn and Algoma were now forced to take their case.[7]

Dunn's initial response to the prospect of wartime steel production was coloured by the legacy of Algoma's role in the munitions industry of the Great War. In that conflict the corporation's headlong commitment to shell steel had produced handsome short-term rewards but had done little to diversify its product mix away from railway-oriented production or prepare it for the post-war economy. The folly of adopting a similar strategy in the new conflict pervaded Dunn's thinking. His own memories as an investor in the defunct Lake Superior Corporation and the advice of past presidents Franz and Frater Taylor underlined the wisdom of specializing in steel types that fostered diversification and had a definite post-war utility. Ideally, Algoma's wartime effort should be directed towards building capacity in a wide range of semi-furnished steels which would find broad and stable appeal among post-war consumers.

Ironically, Algoma's first inclination on the eve of the new war was to exploit its old reputation as shellmaker to the Imperial Munitions Board in a bid to utilize some of its underused capacity. In late 1937, a committee of the Canadian Defence Department had visited the Sault to investigate Algoma's war steel capacity. By October 1938, Dunn was lobbying Sir Thomas Inskip, Britain's minister of defence coordination, in search of munitions orders. To underline the company's repute as a munitions maker Dunn forwarded copies of old letters of commendation from Sir Robert Borden and Sir Joseph Flavelle.[8] General manager Rahilly hastened to assure Dunn that shell steel production could be undertaken 'within 24 hours' but that the government should be expected to bear the cost of machinery that could finish shells 'to the point where they only require loading with explosives.'[9] Dunn confided in Hepburn that he was making a 'big fight' for English munitions orders and even inveigled his old friend in the English steel industry, Lord Greenwood, to impress on British officialdom the wisdom of patronizing the Canadian arms industry.[10] Dunn's efforts to foster a Canadian 'Woolwich' bore little fruit, primarily because they flew in the face of the Ottawa Liberals' initial desire to avoid binding defence production pacts with London. Algoma's one wartime plum in this respect was a small British munitions contract in 1940 for howitzer shells, the cost of which was jointly borne by the Canadian and British governments.[11]

Blocked by his inability to secure a slice of the imperial munitions trade and stymied by Ottawa in his hopes of continued provincial sponsorship, Dunn ultimately had little choice but to submit to whatever course the federal government set for the national economy. He none the less remained determined not to commit Algoma to product lines with little potential for post-war diversification. In Ottawa, the Algoma president encountered a government initially willing to cooperate in matters of steelmaking but ever ready to dictate if circumstances required. It was because Dunn would only cooperate on his own terms and had never brooked dictation that the wartime relationship of Algoma Steel and the Department of Munitions and Supply was one of incessant friction and at times explosiveness, but one that eventually proved productive to both parties.

In April 1940, as the phoney war in Europe began to be overtaken by the reality of total warfare, Howe had been chosen by Mackenzie King to head a new federal department which was to spearhead and coordinate Canada's wartime economy. As minister of munitions and supply, one of Howe's first concerns was to ensure that the nation's war industries had a sufficient supply of steel. Already by the spring of 1940 there were clear signs that, after two decades of underutilization, Canada's ability to make steel was about to be tested to the limit. To assess the situation, the new minister convened a meeting in his Ottawa office on 4 July 1940. The presidents of Canada's four principal steel companies – Stelco, Algoma, Dosco, and Dofasco – were all invited. There was no question of declining the minister's summons. Howe used the gathering to introduce Canada's leading steelmen to H.D. Scully, the recently appointed steel controller, one of nineteen control offices he had hurriedly established to regulate the wartime economy.[12] Faced with a rapidly deteriorating steel supply situation in Canada as the war intensified, Ottawa had empowered Scully 'to conserve, coordinate and regulate the steel resources and industry of Canada.'[13] Scully was equipped with a formidable array of bureaucratic powers, ranging from the right to investigate a steel producer's facilities or financial statements to the Draconian right of seizure of any steelworks or equipment.[14] From the industry's perspective, Steel Control presented a frightening spectre. The pervasiveness of its powers over the production, pricing, and distribution of steel would be felt at all levels of the industry and where Steel Control lacked jurisdiction, other regulatory agencies under Howe's purview, notably Coal Control, infringed upon the industry's once inviolate right of self-regulation. The steel industry could at least take solace in the fact that Scully had once been a businessman himself and could be expected to sympathize with the industry's concerns in the new regime of government intervention. Although he had served as the federal commissioner of customs since 1933, Scully came from a business background, having worked in Toronto investment houses and various Ontario manufacturing firms and as assistant secretary of the Canadian Manufacturers Association.

Specific controls on steel given to Scully were reinforced by the economic leverage given the government under the Excess Profits Tax (limiting corporate profits to $116^2/_3$ per cent of 1936–9 averaged profits), the War Exchange Conservation Act, and the price and wage stabilization powers of the Wartime Prices and Trade Board.[15] Industrial labour was also placed under tight control. On all sides, the steel industry was the apparent captive of the federal government. Coordinating all aspects of this federal economic suzerainty, the Wartime Industries Control Board brought together all Howe's controllers with the overseers of price and wage control to form an economic control mechanism unprecedented in Canada's history. In comparison, the crude economic control mechanisms of the First War paled in their imperfection. Caught in this web of control, Algoma Steel was but 'one of the small cogs in your wheel,' as Dunn once coyly flattered Howe.[16]

To assuage the industry's apprehensions, Howe and Scully were quick to point out that a spirit of cooperation lay behind their foreboding wall of regulation. Cooperation was necessary because Howe was determined from the outset to adapt and expand existing steel capacity to wartime needs rather than create new capacity extraneous to the existing industry.

'With the object of producing "the greatest quantity of steel in the shortest possible time at the lowest possible cost,"' an official history of the wartime economy later noted, 'the government took advantage of existing facilities, trained staffs, and technical knowledge.' Expediency ruled the day. 'With the mills producing at capacity,' Steel Control reflected in 1943, 'time and steel were synonymous, and there was uncertainty as to the exact time when construction projects would actually commence, or when those for the manufacture of equipment requiring steel would be in production.[17] In this world of uncertainties, Howe assured the primary steel producers that if their cooperation was forthcoming in expanding capacity and channelling output on a priority basis to critical areas of the economy, they would never experience the full brunt of formal, rigid regulation. '... [M]y policy,' Howe later told coordinator of controls J.G. Godsoe, 'is that controls are associated with scarcity and should be removed when the reason for the control disappears.'[18] Scarcity was best alleviated, Howe reasoned, by informal cooperation with the various controllers, the 'connecting link between government and industry.'[19] Informal liaison between industry and government in the case of steel was institutionalized in the Steel Advisory Committee, a body created in July 1940 to ensure regular contact between the senior officials of Steel Control and the large primary producers. Supplemented by the Scrap Iron and Steel Advisory and Technical Advisory committees, this caucus of business and bureaucratic officials met infrequently to tackle the primary task set for it by its minister, namely 'a radical readjustment of our steel supply situation from Canadian sources.'[20]

Throughout its history, Steel Control's activities were characterized more by compromise and cooperation than by the arbitrary thrust of legislated authority. During the entire course of its operations, the Steel Controller resorted to only forty formal orders, many of which dealt with relatively trivial matters. This atmosphere of cooperative consultation, while never wholly free of friction and apprehension, not only lay at the foundation of the phenomenal expansion and diversification of Canadian steel during the war but also contributed to the building of a new and lasting consensus between 'big steel' and government. Initially Dunn and Algoma stood somewhat aloof from this development, distrustful of Ottawa's intentions and jealous of their own financial and operational autonomy. Unlike the other primary producers who delegated their senior vice-presidents or presidents to attend the Steel Advisory Committee, Dunn deputized T.F. Rahilly, his managing director, to represent Algoma's interests. Sir James had other hopes. He immediately began plotting to circumvent rule by committee and to build a private and direct line of communication to the minister's office. Dunn rationalized his quest for special status in the department's eyes by employing the now well worn argument that Algoma's northern location, unbalanced product line, and recuperating finances marked it apart from Canada's more profitable, or, in the case of Dosco, more subsidized, primary steel producers. The chaffing of these sensibilities against the policies of Steel Control dominated and irritated the early years of the Dunn-Howe relationship.

Fearful that tight restrictions on steel consumption would engender 'a strong tendency to bogging down in a bewildering maze' of bureaucracy, Steel Control opted for control at the place of production rather than consumption.This ensured 'the utmost flexibility' in regulation and allowed 'a fine adjustment of civilian supply according to the position of the mills in respect to war orders, which necessarily received preference, with a minimum of arbitrary prohibitions.'[21] To effect firm control at source, Steel Control employed various mechanisms to govern production and distribution of wartime steel. At the July 1940 meeting in Ottawa, the primary producers voluntarily submitted to the freezing of all iron and steel prices, including those of raw materials. Coupled with the Excess Profits Tax, the price freeze placed a ceiling on corporate profits and also allayed widespread anxiety about a recurrence of industrial profiteering on the scale of the First War.

Steel distribution was regulated by a system of priorities and licences issued to consumers, reflecting the relative importance of their needs. No steel purchase could be accepted by a primary producer without authorization. Items in perilously short supply, such as structural steel, were placed under separate and especially rigorous control, while consumption of steel for luxury purposes was often wholly proscribed. To minimize gluts and hoarding, stiff regulations governing steel inventories and warehousing were instituted.[22]

To streamline Canadian steel production and to minimize costly delays and redundancies, Steel Control rationalized some aspects of national iron and steel production, insisting, for instance, that Steel of Canada not sell pig iron to outside consumers and that Algoma and Canadian Furnace, at Port Colborne, fill the void created by the Hamilton mill's withdrawal from the market. To facilitate inter-company transfers of raw steel, the Department of Finance and Steel Control subsidized shipping costs between regions, thereby allowing Dosco and Algoma, both deficient in rolling capacity, to 'compete' in the central Canadian market and supply large volumes of steel billets to Stelco for its rolling mills.[23]

The administration of these and a myriad of other guidelines for steel production was handled by Steel Control's small staff of sixty-six persons (as of December 1943). That such a small group could cope with a task of such complexity bore witness to the degree of cooperation and consultation that developed between the war bureaucracy and the steel industry. Steel Control orders seldom represented arbitrary fiats by the government, but were more accurately simply the formal acknowledgment of arrangements already decided informally at the Steel Advisory Committee. Symbolic of this willingness to cooperate was the presence of nineteen 'dollar-a-year' men, many of them drawn directly from the ranks of the peacetime steel industry, in Steel Control's Ottawa offices. W.E. Morley of Algoma was, for instance, seconded to oversee the government's pig iron control program. Far from being the steel industry's Trojan Horse in Ottawa, ready to manipulate the levers of wartime government for the advantage of the private sector, the 'dollar-a-year' men were more a group of economic engineers, pragmatically building up a new and more broadly applicable set of ground rules for the mutually advantageous interaction of business and government. In the crisis-filled days of 1940–1, few could have viewed Steel Control's work as anything more than a temporary expedient, but, as the urgency of the steel crisis began to ease by late 1943, the irrevocable nature of their actions began to emerge.

The changes wrought by Steel Control would have been unconscionable in the pre-war Canadian economy. Before the war, planning of the national steel industry had taken place on a pell-mell company-by-company basis. Now the industry's shape and direction was centrally decided, requiring statistical and economic expertise. Admitting that it had been 'working somewhat in the dark as to the overall total steel requirements,' Steel Control instituted a 'steel budget' in the fall of 1941 to project Canadian production and consumption of steel for 1942 and thereby calculate prospective import and domestic production requirements.[24] With its steel budget Ottawa was able to give priority to areas of extreme scarcity, to allocate existing steel output as equitably as possible, and to create enhanced capacity in the shortfall areas of domestic production through capital assistance and special tax concessions. The federal government's efforts to rationalize and stimulate the national steel economy constituted a clear infringement of pre-war economic freedoms. As such, they simultaneously aroused the industry's suspicions as to the future sanctity of its operations and drew its applause as the solution of long-standing impediments to its progress. While Sir James Dunn eventually came to share both these attitudes, his initial response to the initiatives of Howe's department was one of hostility alone.

Dunn's obstinacy in the face of the directives of Steel Control was first occasioned by Ottawa's refusal in 1940 to permit Algoma to export rails to the foreign markets that the company had so painstakingly built up in the late 1930s.[25] Furthermore, Steel Control's domestic rail purchases posed a dire threat, in Dunn's eyes, to Algoma's traditional mainstay of production. Fortunately, the productive capacity freed by this restriction was soon completely taken up by war production.[26] The ultimate encroachment on Algoma's freedom to determine the allocation of its own productive capacity came with the imposed diversion of Algoma ingots and pig iron to Stelco for rolling and final finishing. Dunn argued that Ottawa was taking unfair advantage of Algoma's sizeable primary capacity and, by shipping its raw steel elsewhere for processing, was denying it an opportunity to realize its own finished steel potential. The situation was exacerbated in May 1941 by Steel Control's adamant refusal to allow Algoma a price increase on the steel it supplied to Stelco. Unappeased by Scully's appreciation of Algoma's 'spirit of cooperation' in the matter, Dunn went directly to Munitions and Supply Minister Howe and protested that Algoma resented 'the role of "hewers of wood and drawers of water" for any other steel company while a full market exists for our output.' At Howe's request, the steel president tempered the final wording of his written presentation to read that the company was 'sensitive to taking a subsidiary role in the war economy of the country.'[27]

Dunn's exasperation with Steel Control's supposed insensitivity to Algoma's needs led him, from an early date in the war, to seek to bypass its offices and to communicate directly with the minister. Sir James contacted Howe in person, by incessant telephone calls, and by what he called 'entirely unofficial note[s],'[28] sent directly to the minister's Rockcliffe home in Ottawa. He complained to Howe in one of these notes,

I do not find that I get anywhere by exchanging letters with the Steel Controller who quite naturally is not intimate enough with industrial affairs to realize the millions of dollars that Algoma has invested in coke ovens, blast furnaces and open hearths in order to be able to supply Mr. McMaster [Stelco] with pig iron at about $12 a ton and ingots at about $6 a ton cheaper than he could get them but for Algoma's investment. These pig and ingot deliveries to Mr. McMaster provide him with raw materials to carry on his ordinary business and to make the products that enter into competition with ourselves and the other steel producers and not to make any special war product. ... This is off the record but I feel better at having said it.[29]

As the tempo and volume of war orders picked up, other issues began to inflame relations between Algoma and the government. Since the profit ceiling imposed by the Excess Profits Tax was calculated on 116 per cent of normal pre-war profits averaged over 1936–9, Dunn argued that in view of the company's lacklustre financial performance in the late Depression some special allowance should be made to compensate it for its abnormally low averaged profits. After much pressure from Dunn and adjudication by a board of referees, Algoma's 'standard profits' were set at $1,311,098.63 in June 1942.[30] This concession was due, as Howe's financial adviser F.H. Brown told Deputy Finance Minister W.C. Clark, to the minister's personal guarantee to Dunn that 'the company's earnings would be lifted to a reasonable standard provided he continued to be satisfied with the output and cooperation received.'[31] Dunn's hectoring of the minister and his controllers clearly ensured that Algoma's rights in the Canadian steel industry were never overlooked. By the same token, Howe never buckled under Sir James' pressure – Algoma got what its performance warranted.

Another burden under which Algoma laboured, Dunn complained, was the inequitable incidence of controls on the economy. As early as 1941, Algoma and Dosco protested that while their profits were rigidly held down, the ever-increasing cost of raw materials, labour, and transport was eroding corporate profits to the point of insolvency. Algoma and Dosco claimed that the cost of ingot production had risen by 30 per cent since 1939 and in late 1941 sought a $6 a ton price hike for ingots.[32] Such representations eventually brought a 25¢ per 100 pounds price rise on most steel forms in January 1943, an increase that was not adopted by Stelco. Rail prices were permitted to rise by $5 a ton in May 1943. While these concessions temporarily alleviated the situation, the creeping and uneven advance of costs in the steel industry was to remain a problem, frequently introducing friction into business-government relations.

Not surprisingly, the Howe-Dunn relationship throughout these early war years had a chameleon-like quality about it. Neither could do without the other. Howe desperately needed steel and Dunn could not operate without the sanction of Howe's officials. Given the implacably iron-willed character of both men and the unique pressures of war, such skirmishes were unavoidable. 'The Department of Munitions still has at least one crisis every day,' Howe flippantly remarked to one of his officials at the height of the production crisis in 1941.[33] The basic bone of contention between Howe and Dunn was that the minister viewed the steel economy in essentially *national* terms while Dunn examined every proposal solely from Algoma's perspective. Tension developed whenever common ground between the two positions did not materialize. In the final reckoning, Howe held most of the winning cards. Dunn's freedom of action was not only restricted by the blanket of wartime government control but also by Algoma's continued corporate indebtedness and the collapse of his health in 1941–2.

Algoma entered the war with a large indebtedness to the Royal Bank, an indebtedness totalling $2.3 million by April 1940. Furthermore, Dunn's position of personal control in Algoma's stock was still balanced on a financial knife-edge. Fortunately, most of Sir James' personal creditors were within his circle of business friends and did not press for prompt repayment, but, as he told his son in late 1940, 'For myself I have no income and require to cash in capital from time to time as I cannot afford to pay dividends which the various taxes exhaust.'[34] Adding to his troubles, Dunn faced an extremely embarrassing tax evasion charge in the British courts. Her Majesty's Government alleged that Dunn owed back taxes of forty-one thousand pounds.[35] Sir James countered this charge by alleging that his principal residence since 1935 had been in Canada and that he should pay only Canadian taxation. Under such intense pressure, Dunn's health gave out to a bout of cystitis in the late spring of 1940 and a near-fatal thrombosis in the summer of 1942.[36] So as not to attract undue attention in government and financial circles, Dunn's illness was kept secret, with a furtive Algoma directors' meeting even being held in a Montreal hospital room.[37]

The pressures of wartime production provided an illuminating contrast in the managerial styles of Dunn and Howe. As minister of munitions and supply, C.D. Howe administered his department like a multi-divisional business corporation. The minister was a superb delegator of authority. He recruited men with proven records of achievement from the business and bureaucratic communities. Each was then invested with sufficient authority to pursue the goal set for him and left alone. Above all else, Howe wanted results. Day-to-day operational decisions did not bother him; he confined his energies to planning Canada's overall strategy for wartime production. If a manager in a crown corporation or a munitions and supply program failed, Howe acted quickly to supplant him.

Sir James Dunn, by contrast, was by nature incapable of delegating authority. Since Algoma was *his* company, every decision of any significance had to pass across his desk. Delegated authority and managerial autonomy constituted a potential challenge to his rule. Consequently, Sir James came to be more feared than respected by his employees. In many ways, he treated all those on the company premises as his chattels. As the years passed, Sir James' eccentric and dictatorial managerial style became memorialized in anecdotes which enjoyed broad currency at the Sault and in the Canadian business community. Dunn's infrequent visits to the Sault occasioned panic in the head office. On seeing a secretary who in any way might be accused of daydreaming, the steel president would rap the offender's desk and inform her that she was wasting *his* time and *his* money. Other clerks chose to avoid such unpleasant reprimands by hiding in the closets and the elevator machinery room.

The war brought changes in Dunn's personal life. Following his thrombosis in 1941, Sir James divorced his second wife, Irene, and married, in 1942, his long-time personal secretary, Marcia Christoforides. The new Lady Dunn provided Sir James with a quick-witted and intensely loyal companion, who shared his perspective on life and defended his interests with tenacity. Throughout the war, Dunn divided his time between his New Brunswick forest retreat, the Ritz Carlton Hotel in Montreal, and, most important, the Seigniory Club in Montebello, Quebec. From the club on the Ottawa River, Dunn was but an hour's drive from the offices of the steel controller and his minister. Annoyed by the steel president's frequent, unannounced appearances in his office, Howe trained his secretary to intercept Dunn and to put him off with prearranged excuses. The servants who attended Dunn back in Montebello found life little easier. Sir James made incessant demands and was quick to level criticism. In particular, he insisted that his two pet dogs be accorded excessive attention. One club employee later admitted that he kicked the little beasts once he had them out of the steel magnate's sight.[38] At times Howe must have thought of Dunn as a terrier, always nipping at his heels.

In the midst of these personal and financial developments, Dunn obdurately opposed many of Steel Control's directives. His pugnacity was at times so fierce that it was widely rumoured that he was a defeatist, unwilling to back the Allied cause. Such rumours filtered through to the highest levels of Allied leadership. When informed in late 1940 by his Washington representative that Canadian officials were 'inclined to take action to intern Sir James Dunn, as a result of his continual defeatism,'

Lord Beaverbrook felt compelled to inform Prime Minister Churchill that Algoma's president was his 'oldest friend' and that to his best knowledge had displayed 'no spirit of defeatism.'[39] Beaverbrook came to his old compatriot's assistance on other occasions. In the spring of 1943, in the midst of negotiations over the terms of Algoma's government-financed expansion program, Howe and Beaverbrook met in New York to discuss their mutual friend Dunn. Later Howe confidentially replied to Beaverbrook that Dunn had 'expressed complete satisfaction with the arrangements that have now been completed. Your work on his behalf helped him considerably.'[40] Significantly, many of the senior British representatives in Washington during the war were mutual acquaintances of Dunn, Beaverbrook, and Howe. Most notable in this respect were Arthur Purvis, the head of the British Supply Mission; Morris Wilson, a Royal Bank executive representing the British Ministry of Aircraft Production; and E.P. Taylor, Howe's man in Washington. Gossip flowed freely between these men. This was especially true of Morris Wilson, who, with his ties to the Canadian banking community, kept Howe and Beaverbrook intimately informed of the precarious state of Dunn's finances. Another of Dunn's cronies, Ontario mining magnate J.P. Bickell, performed valuably in ATFERO, the Atlantic aircraft ferry set up by Howe and Beaverbrook.

Howe's reaction to Dunn's unrelenting campaign to let Algoma fight the steel war on its own terms was to stand resolute and not succumb to the Algoma president's mixture of bullying and seduction. Cases of Krug 1926 champagne delivered to Howe's London hotel suite brought the minister's thanks but did little to loosen his resolve.[41] F.H. Brown, Howe's financial adviser from April 1941, recalled that the Howe-Dunn relationship was 'cool' and then 'warm,' despite the fact that Dunn was 'a great old charmer.'[42] In later years, Howe himself was guardedly ambivalent about the nature of the association, telling Beaverbrook on one occasion that he 'hardly knew' Dunn by 1942 and on another that he had 'worked closely with Sir James from 1940.'[43] The most serious conflict between the two occurred in late 1942 when Dunn decided to exploit the wartime situation to settle his simmering feud with E.B. Barber of the Algoma Central Railway. Determined to break the railway's monopoly over Algoma's transportation needs, Dunn had his Toronto lawyers obtain a charter for the Algoma Southern Railway, a corporate subsidiary designed to link Algoma's yards with the CPR's Sudbury mainline and thereby circumvent Barber's railway. If he were successful in this ploy, Dunn hoped, the financially plagued Algoma Central would fall into his lap. Sir James delighted in portraying the Algoma Central as 'an uneconomic railway system' dating from Clergue's days of reckless financing, 'a general tax against Algoma Steel' resulting in severe 'bottlenecks' in its wartime production.[44]

Rather than approach Howe directly about the railway problem, Dunn despatched Tom Rahilly, Algoma's general manager, to deal with Ottawa. It was an unfortunate choice. Not only was Rahilly a personal friend of E.B. Barber, but he was opposed to Dunn's scheme of broadening Algoma's activities beyond steelmaking into railroading. Tension between Algoma's president and its general manager had existed for years, engendered by Dunn's innumerable and often intemperate intrusions into Algoma's daily operations. Rahilly's initial approach to Howe and the Board of Transport Commissioners in November 1942 was sharply rebuffed. 'It is difficult to see,' Howe wrote to Rahilly, 'that any considerable savings in freight charges will result to the Algoma Steel Corporation from the proposed new connection.'[45] At this point Dunn entered the fray and dispatched a blistering letter to 'Mr. Howe' reiterating what he claimed was Algoma's incontestable right to a rail link with the CPR.[46] At this point, Rahilly had an irreparable falling-out with Dunn, culminating in a nervous breakdown that forced the general manager to take an extended leave of absence on the West Coast.[47] Deprived of his chief witness, Dunn let the Algoma Southern case fall into abeyance. Despite the president's assurances to Rahilly that he could 'take hold again with me,' by August 1943 Rahilly was said to have rejected a new position in the corporation and was let go.[48]

Rahilly's dismissal alarmed Howe.[49] Fearful that the capable general manager could not be replaced and that operational control might fall completely under the sway of Algoma's sixty-eight-year-old president, Howe contacted Morris Wilson, now returned from Washington to the presidency of the Royal Bank, and asked him to investigate the situation discreetly. It was understandable that Howe should have taken such an initiative, especially since labour troubles at Algoma in January 1943 had already unexpectedly curtailed steel output. In later years Dunn concocted a story that Howe had in fact delegated Wilson to lay the foundations for a government takeover of Algoma.[50] The whole notion was antithetical to Howe's understanding of the relationship of business and government: private business could be influenced but never directly controlled by government. Crown corporations were established only where private enterprise feared to tread. When Beaverbrook later gave credence to the notion of an anti-Dunn *putsch* in his biography of Dunn, Howe protested vigorously: 'At no time did I threaten that the Government would take over the operation, nor did I have any thought it would do so. Algoma was a vital part of Canada's war machine, and I simply wished to make sure that there would be continuity of operational management of the enterprise. What Morris Wilson told Sir James I do not know, but if he stated the Government intended to take over the enterprise, he had no suggestion from me that could be so interpreted.'[51]

Howe's apprehensions were eased in February 1944 when Dunn, on the advice of Algoma's American consulting engineers, Coverdale and Colpitts, hired David S. Holbrook, a promising young American steelman trained at United States Steel, to replace Rahilly. Howe was so anxious to see Holbrook at Algoma that he personally tried to expedite his release by the US Selective Service Board.[52] Talented and able to stand up to Dunn's harassment, Holbrook soon restored Howe's confidence in Algoma. It was a mark of Howe's intuition as an engineer that he sensed that Algoma's prosperity depended not only on Dunn's financial acumen but also on the solid technical advice provided by Rahilly and later Holbrook. As Dunn himself admitted, Holbrook was 'the most promising young man I have come in contact with in many years.'[53]

After the Rahilly crisis, there was growing evidence of warmer relations between Howe and Dunn. By August 1943, as the intense pressure of the 'steel crisis' eased, the Minister confided in Beaverbrook that Dunn was 'doing a first-class job and deserves to be well treated.'[54] As the friction with Ottawa diminished, a tacit understanding between minister and Algoma president began to evolve on the much broader question of the overall role and function of the Canadian steel industry in the national economy. Howe's task at Munitions and Supply had entailed not only marshalling existing industrial resources but also promoting a rapid increase in their capacity. Industrial expansion proved a crucial task, for not only did it directly affect Canada's war effort but there was, especially after 1942, a distinct realization that it would formatively influence the post-war Canadian economy.

Howe and Dunn were in perfect harmony in their belief that the problems of Canadian steel must be viewed in a continental context. It was illusory, both agreed, to talk of Canadian industrial self-sufficiency. As his early experience in marketing Algoma iron sinter to American buyers had illustrated, Dunn firmly believed that Canada must capitalize on its industrial strengths and seek equitable trade-offs in those areas where it was deficient. Howe harboured the same view. 'The Minister has been here since Friday,' E.P. Taylor reported to Dunn from Washington in late 1942, 'and we have had some good talks. I find that his ideas, regarding the way in which the post-war economy should be arranged, entirely line up with mine, and yours. He agrees that the key to the whole situation rests with Canada and the U.S.A. and that the time to make the deal is now because it will be next to impossible after the peace, or when peace is in the air. He has undertaken to have a chat with the Prime Minister.'[55] Mirroring the diversification policy Algoma had set as its goal in the late 1930s, Howe believed that Canadian steel should build up a well-rounded basic capacity and specialize only in those areas for which there was sufficient Canadian demand to warrant efficient and profitable production. What Canada could not undertake should be left to foreign producers, whose imports could be balanced by exports of Canadian surplus production or raw materials. For both men this entailed the thoroughgoing orientation of the Canadian steel economy towards mutual dependency on American iron and steel. As a late-war Victory Bond poster, sponsored by Algoma and depicting an early French map of the continent, proclaimed: 'The men who made this map many years ago conceived the North American continent as one economic whole.' In 1941 Howe told the Commons that it was 'a matter of judgement whether at a time like this we should go all-out to make ourselves self-contained in steel for war requirements.' He concluded that this was not a justifiable goal 'particularly as we have obtained every assurance that the usual source of supply will be available to us at least up to the amount we nominally [sic] take.'[56]

Underlying this acknowledgment of the virtue of continental dependency was the extreme reluctance of Canadian steelmakers to overexpand to the point where they would once again be saddled with unusable post-war capacity. Largely through the Steel Advisory Committee, a consensus was slowly built between government and the industry. Expansion of Canadian capacity would continue to reasonable limits, usually to the level that was construed by the industry as normal peacetime consumption, leaving marginal and specialized steel production to foreign producers. There was a general recognition that any further expansion would invite serious imbalances not only in the internal operation of the steel industry but also in the national economy, notably in the supply of labour. This cautious attitude towards expansion of national steel capacity was the product of the industry's residual insecurity from the Depression. Indelibly marked by their experience in the 1920s and 1930s with underused capacity and low profits, the steel industry insisted on distinct limits to its wartime growth. The steel companies were ready to respond to any of the incentives a regulated economy might offer, but they staunchly defended what they conceived of as their inalienable right to set the limit of those changes.

The implications of too large and too hurried an expansion of the steel industry also aroused the anxieties of Howe's fellow cabinet ministers. As early as 1942, Finance Minister J.L. Ilsley sternly warned the minister of munitions and supply that 'these large additions to plant capacity' were creating a 'competitive scramble for men' which might soon affect the military manpower situation. 'My departmental interest in the matter is as a Minister trying to prevent inflation,' Ilsley added. 'If we undertake too much, it will become impossible to keep wages and prices down and the whole situation will get away from us.'[57]

Amid these varied pressures, C.D. Howe and his officials were able to engineer a remarkable expansion and diversification of Canadian iron and steel capacity. From total production of 755,731 tons in 1939, Canadian pig iron output more than doubled to just under two million tons by 1942. Steel ingot and casting production over the same period burgeoned from 1,384,870 tons to 3,110,264 tons. The value of rolled steel production virtually trebled to $157,973,074 over 1939–42, while capital employed in the iron and steel industry increased from $697,893,720 to $1,446,215,017 in 1942.[58] From the outset of the war, Howe's officials also learned to augment the Canadian steel supply by means of increased American imports. Success in this direction was, however, somewhat curtailed after Pearl Harbor. Despite growing domestic capacity and American imports, the steel crisis that lay at the heart of Canada's wartime economy intensified until the winter of 1942–3. Wartime demand for steel was created in two principal ways. There was, in the first place, the huge demand for munitions and war materiel, all of which required steel. At the same time, steel was an indispensable ingredient in building the factories and machinery which produced other raw materials for the munitions industry.

In meeting this double-barrelled demand for steel, Ottawa moved first to ensure a large and stable level of American steel imports and then to structure domestic expansion to meet the shortfall between imports and existing domestic production. The 'steel budget' projections for 1941 estimated a prospective consumption of 3,390,000 tons, of which 1,140,000 tons could be furnished through imports. By 1943, projected consumption had grown to just over five million tons, with Canadian output at 3.4 million tons.[59] Such statistics served to mould the continentalist strategy for solving Canada's wartime steel problems that both Dunn and Howe embraced. Faced with the enormity of the domestic shortfall,

Howe admitted to the Commons that since it 'has been our custom to import from the United States about a third of our steel requirements,' his department had 'determined to plan our programme on continued importations in the same proportions.'[60] This strategy received great impetus from the Ogdensburg and Hyde Park production-sharing agreements, whose integrationist tendencies were soon felt in defence planning and also in the overall streamlining and coordinating of the neighbouring economies.[61] The establishment in November 1941 of the Joint War Production Committee, co-chaired by two General Motors executives, H.J. Carmichael of Canada and C.E. Wilson of the US, paved the way for the maximization of labour, raw materials, and technical resources in all areas of industrial production. This harnessing of Canadian and American industry under the same yoke hastened the integration of the American Production Requirements Plan priorities system with that of the Canadian Steel Control administration. By July 1942, the PRP priorities, soon to be superseded by the Controlled Materials Plan, was made obligatory for Canadian industry, except railways and public utilities.

As the Canadian-American grid of controls and product exchanges was refined, Canadian steel consumers were guaranteed a sizeable and steady supply of American steel on a regular allotment basis, averaging approximately 375,000 tons per quarter through the first three years of the war. Although constant vigilance was needed by Canadian officials in Washington to prevent any curtailment of this essential flow of American steel, Howe was confident that guaranteed imports provided a large and ongoing measure of relief for Canada's critical steel situation. 'We do not anticipate,' he assured Defence Minister Ralston as early as December 1941, 'that the time will ever come when, due to shortage of steel or other raw materials, we will find it necessary to slow down any part of our war production.'[62] By 1943, the 'steel crisis' had passed. 'It has been an almost impossible task to make ends meet,' Associate Steel Controller Hoey reported to Howe, 'but most of the new construction is finished. From now on, more of our steel supply can be used to make implements of war in those plants where the tonnage was previously used to build the plants themselves.'[63]

Hoey's optimism was also anchored in the mammoth program of government-assisted expansion of Canadian steel capacity. The incentives for expansion extended to industry by Ottawa emphasized flexibility and adaptability to the needs of each recipient. When criticized in 1942 before the Commons for the seeming lack of an overall industrial blueprint in his department's policies, Howe defended the necessity of a pragmatic approach to problems of wartime industry: 'But I think all we can do is try reasonably to anticipate the requirements of the war and plan our course from week to week and month to month accordingly ... We have found that certain lines of production are particularly adapted to this country, and we have gone full out on these lines.'[64] To implement this flexible response, the federal government fashioned a wide range of fiscal and contractual tools to remedy the shortcomings of the national steel economy. These instruments ranged from relatively straightforward munitions contracts to complex 'target cost' and 'ceiling price' contracts. Each respected the fundamental integrity of free enterprise but at the same time gave the government sufficient leverage to influence primary steel production.[65] Common to all these contracts were the profit ceiling and foreign exchange regulations imposed at the outset of war. Because of these constraints, it soon became apparent that if the private sector was to be induced to expand under such abnormal conditions, especially in capital-intensive areas of primary production with questionable post-war utility, special incentives would have to be extended. One such instrument was the capital-assistance contract, under which Ottawa assumed the cost of plant additions, vested title in the contractor, and bound him to a low-cost production contract for the duration of the war.

Much more pervasive and subtle in application were the numerous fiscal arrangements extended by the government to stimulate wartime investment. Fearful that any relaxation in price and profit ceilings would create serious inflationary pressure, the finance department devised special depreciation allowances under which companies could amortize new capital expenditures at accelerated rates, thereby advantageously redistributing their taxable income. Such depreciation allowances were administered by the Wartime Contracts Depreciation Board, which took into account the added cost of plant expansion in a wartime economy, the potential post-war utility of any project, and its export dollar-earning capability.[66] Once the accelerated depreciation allowance had been exhausted, the amortized plant became liable to taxation at the full rate. The government also extended tax breaks to natural resource companies, notably tax moratoriums on new mining and oil projects. In allowing private initiative some freedom of response to investment opportunities despite the Excess Profits Tax, the government provided ample room for the growth of cooperation between Algoma and Ottawa.[67]

Algoma and the federal government first came to terms on the thorny matter of steel expansion in the frenzied atmosphere created by the steel shortages of late 1940 and early 1941. Any assessment of the benefit ultimately derived by both government and Algoma from the ensuing agreements must take cognizance of the extreme sense of urgency that prompted the government's willingness to sponsor industrial expansion. Hounded in the Commons over steel shortages plaguing his department's shipbuilding and munitions programs,[68] Howe searched for some expedient to alleviate the chronic shortage of rolled steel. At this crucial juncture in February 1941, Sir James Dunn appeared in Ottawa with a proposition that Howe impetuously seized. Pointing out that Algoma's greatest pre-war weakness lay in the lack of balance between its 700,000-ton capacity for producing unfinished steel and its 450,000-ton rolling capacity, Dunn proposed the erection of a government-financed rolling mill that would at one stroke ease the national steel shortage and facilitate Algoma's diversification. Howe accepted the steel president's claim that the company's sizeable indebtedness to the Royal Bank made it 'incapable of furnishing on its own credit more than a portion of the amounts required for such purpose' and moved with alacrity to draw up an agreement that by any measure was highly beneficial to the corporation.[69] Algoma was authorized by the agreement of 18 February 1941 to begin construction of a 44-inch blooming mill, a 25-inch continuous billet mill, and all the necessary ancillary equipment needed to roll these new sizes of finished flat steel. The estimated cost of the project was $5,250,000. The government provided a guarantee of capital assistance for the project up to $4,000,000 and a special depreciation rate of 33 $1/3$ per cent, beginning in April 1942, on 50 per cent of the cost of the plant. Title was to be vested in Algoma, but the government retained this right to dictate the wartime use of the mill. By company calculation, the government would pay 76.2 per cent of the plant extension program with Algoma reimbursing Ottawa for the 'residual value' of the plant at the cessation of hostilities. Not surprisingly, a hastily assembled quorum of Algoma directors met in the Chateau Laurier and set the corporate seal of approval on the pact.[70]

Throughout 1941 the Munitions and Supply Department concluded a series of similar assistance agreements with other primary steel firms. The government thus took an active role in making good such deficiencies in the chain of Canadian production as the lack of plate capacity, while at the same time sponsoring a wholesale expansion in overall national steel capacity.[71] This latter desire brought Algoma its second substantial government contract in the dying days of 1941. When Steel Control informed Howe's officials that it was 'imperative' to increase national pig iron capacity, they suggested that this could be 'most economically and expeditiously' achieved by erecting a thousand-ton-a-day blast furnace at the Sault. Under the contract of 19 December 1941, Ottawa agreed to bear the entire cost of the blast furnace, $17,299,000, on the condition that the pig iron output of the new furnace be distributed at the discretion of the government until five years after the cessation of hostilities.[72] Title to the whole complex was vested in the steel company, although the government had certain rights of intervention. Algoma was to receive 60¢ per ton of pig iron produced under the operating contract.

The two government contracts of 1941 made possible remarkable advances at Algoma with a minimum of risk for the company. Without resort to internal or external financing, the company had acquired title to over $20 million in new assets. Erection of the enormous Number 5 furnace, the largest in the Empire, solidly established Algoma as Canada's leading pig iron producer, with a daily capacity of 2912 tons by 1943. The new rolling mills handsomely increased Algoma's potential for product diversification. By the end of 1943 Algoma was the leading beneficiary of government-financed industrial expansion in Canada with a total commitment of $20,999,000. By the end of 1944, this had increased to $23,105,840. Although Alcan's Shipshaw expansion project ultimately proved the largest recipient of government capital assistance, Algoma received considerably more wartime capital assistance than all other Canadian steel producers combined. Of the $28,002,190 earmarked for expansion of privately owned and operated steel plants by the close of 1944, 82.5 per cent went to Algoma.[73] The corporation received further 'invisible' benefits from the special depreciation allowances permitted by Ottawa on its expansion. Eventually totalling $2,728,331 through 1942–4, this special depreciation was deducted after normal depreciation totalling $3,450,126.[74] While relations between Algoma and Ottawa continued to bristle with tension over many operational aspects of wartime regulation, a new, still tentative consensus, hurriedly brought into being by the 'steel crisis' and adroitly capitalized on by businessmen like Dunn, had emerged and pointed the way to a new post-war relationship between government and primary industrial producers.

Howe's headlong drive to bolster Canada's industrial capacity did not, however, escape criticism. Alarmed by the magnitude of the Munitions and Supply Department's commitment to industrial expansion and its potential for destabilizing the finely tuned war economy, Finance Minister Ilsley urged Howe in September 1942 to apply the brakes. 'My own view is that the time has gone past when we should expand our capacity,' Ilsley exhorted Howe. 'It seems to me that the only way to stop expanding is to stop instead of going on as we are at present.'[75] Howe acknowledged the 'undesirability of further expansion,' but vigorously defended past expenditures on the grounds that the shortage of steel in Canada had had 'a far reaching effect on our munitions programme.'[76] By Howe's own rudimentary standard of expediency, the steel expansion policies had produced results.

More explosive and less easily defused were the criticisms aimed at the industrial expansion program from outside the cabinet. Reiterating CCF scepticism of the ends of big business, M.J. Coldwell called for a Truman-style investigation of capital-assistance projects by assuring the Commons that 'someday we may find that a few trusts and corporations have so increased their power over the economic life of Canada that the individual, unorganized consumer is entirely at their mercy.'[77] Coldwell repeatedly charged that accelerated rates of depreciation made some expansion projects virtual 'gifts' to the private sector. Other critics homed in on steel shortages in critical areas of the economy, demanding to know why Canada remained so reliant on US steel imports. Angus MacInnis of the CCF assailed domestic steel producers for their reluctance to expand capacity beyond 'discernible future needs.'[78]

Howe staunchly defended his department's record on industrial expansion. In response to the CCF's gibes about profiteering and favouritism to certain companies, the minister emphasized the openness of the contract system. 'We have not singled out a few industries and said "We will expand you", but your competitor will have to stay as he is,' Howe told the Commons. 'Any industry that has had the desire and the ambition and courage to expand to meet war needs has been encouraged to do so by my department and perhaps financially assisted to do so.'[79] That Howe rewarded the aggressive and efficient was vividly illustrated by the comparative wartime fortunes of Algoma and Dosco. Whereas Dunn and Algoma seized every opportunity thrown up by the 'steel crisis,' Dosco's lethargic response to wartime incentives irritated Howe to such a point that he unofficially directed Steel Control to 'use that company to the minimum extent possible even if we have to buy the steel in the United States.'[80] A subsequent departmental inquiry concluded that Dosco plant 'as a whole reflects a degree of disorganization,' suffered from 'bad' costs, and was in danger of collapse without government aid.[81] In April 1945, Howe publicly reproached Dosco in the Commons for its 'unsatisfactory' financial performance.[82]

Allegations of overgenerous treatment of big business through the use of accelerated depreciation were examined by a special Commons committee on war expenditure. Initiated by the prime minister in March 1941, the committee's investigations were hampered by somewhat restricted terms of reference and the sheer magnitude of its task. None the lesss, after a thorough examination of government contracts and the mechanism established to monitor them, the committee felt compelled to do little more than point out that 'the checks and controls exercised over the cost of contracts do not operate as well in practice as they appear to in theory.'[83] Careful examination of Coldwell's charge that Alcan had reaped 'exorbitant profits' through depreciation write-offs brought a judgment that the company had enjoyed 'no special privilege of any nature.' Not only was Coldwell's grasp of accounting principles shown to be flimsy, but the work of the Wartime Contracts Depreciation Board was upheld and praised.[84]

The litmus test of Howe's steel program came when its results were examined. In 1942, the most critical production year of the war, actual pig iron production of 1,773,337 tons surpassed the estimated target of 1,767,900 tons while steel ingot output bettered its estimated target of 2,943,082 tons by 15,824 tons.[85] The number of blast furnaces in operation doubled from six to twelve between 1939 and 1942, while thirty-three pre-war open-hearth steel furnaces increased to forty-eight by 1942. By June 1943 Howe could comfortably boast to the Commons that 'Canada's steel production had been doubled since the war began, and this country is now the fourth greatest steel producer among the united nations exceeded only by the United States, Russia and Great Britain ... we have succeeded in meeting our heavy obligations. At no time has there been a single serious interruption in the operation of a munitions plant or a vital industry owing to lack of steel.'[86] Canada's new-found prowess in steelmaking bred a kind of crude economic national pride, at least in the government's official propaganda. 'Every time,' a 1944 publication from Howe's department boasted, 'a Canadian-made gun blasts at an enemy position in Italy, or a Canadian destroyer fires at a U-boat, the chances are five to one that "Made in Canada" steel is being let loose at the enemy.'[87] On the home front, Canadians became familiar with pictures of a grinning C.D. Howe standing beside the ten thousandth tank or fifty thousandth truck produced by a Canadian factory. All were built of Canadian steel.

By the time the new Algoma Number 5 blast furnace began its first campaign in November 1943, the 'steel crisis' was generally believed to have passed. Production in 1943 fell from the record high levels of 1942 to 1,758,260 tons of pig iron and 2,846,736 tons of steel ingots, levels that were to prevail generally through the closing stages of the war.[88] Regulating steel production from Ottawa now became a process of periodically relaxing and tightening controls so as to direct existing steel capacity to areas of wartime scarcity as well as to the gradual alleviation of the immense backlog of civilian demand.[89] Although the steel controller continued to emphasize the 'gravity of the steel situation,' by October 1943 Howe felt sure enough of the steel supply to suggest to WICB chairman Henry Borden that 'as we are closing down steel productive capacity, controls might be lifted in certain directions.'[90] Steel Control subsequently began to ease some of its regulations on steel consumption and production. In February 1944, for instance, the compulsory order system for structural steel was abolished. Howe and Steel Control resolutely resisted pressure exerted by the industry to dismantle some of the major regulatory controls on steel. When Algoma moved to discontinue structural steel production in the spring of 1944, the Steel Advisory Committee blocked the company, ordering it to devote at least four thousand tons per month to structurals.[91] Steel Control's panoply of authority thus remained essentially intact until November 1945.

Algoma's wartime performance can only be judged against this general pattern of wartime steel production. In the years of peak production between 1941 and 1945, munitions-oriented production overshadowed all other work at Algoma, ranging from a peak of 80 per cent of total output in 1942 to a low of 63 per cent in 1944. There is no evidence to indicate that the steel from the Sault was ever of substandard quality or that contracts were ever seriously breached. By 1943 Howe and his officials generally acknowledged that Sir James and Algoma were 'doing a first-class war job and deserved to be well treated.' By 1943, however, the two enormous capital assistance contracts awarded to Algoma at the height of the 'steel crisis' could be scrutinized under a somewhat more critical light. While satisfied with the results of the contracts, Howe began to feel some uneasiness about the generous terms exacted by Dunn in the hectic days of 1941. Frank Brown, the minister's financial adviser since April 1941, later explained that 'C.D. gave me the job of trying to undo some deals that had been made in Jimmy's favour.' Dunn was 'a great old charmer' who, Brown alleged, had enlarged his steel company 'for free.' 'And Mr. Howe suddenly realized that if this were looked into, this would look pretty damn bad.'[92]

While the claim that Algoma's expansion had been won 'for free' was an exaggeration, Brown did succeed in forcing the corporation to start amortizing its government debt before the war's end. When Algoma complained that it could not meet the inflated costs of the rolling mill project 'without serious prejudice' to its financial position, the government agreed to a new contract under which the company was to pay off its debt at the rate of $100,000 per year, subject to certain minimums and maximums of annual profit. In December 1943 the blast-furnace contract was modified so that Algoma would become the lessor of the new complex, paying 6 per cent of depreciated 'fair value' annually.[93] The revamped contracts put the government in only a marginally better position, but as Brown later pointed out, 'it was a mixed business – we also gave them some subsidies. We gave them with one hand and took away with the other.'[94] Algoma's financial situation, for instance, was lightened in July 1943 when an order-in-council authorized reimbursement for cost increases in its raw materials and for increases in the average cost of freight.[95] In February 1945 Ottawa undertook to finance a $3.7 million rehabilitation of a Bessemer converter deemed 'superfluous to the present and normal business of Algoma' but necessary for national production.[96] Once again, title was vested in the corporation.

Howe's beneficence to Algoma and its hard-bargaining president was rooted in several factors. In the first place, Algoma's industrial performance had consistently fulfilled the minister's expectations. This impression was solidly reinforced by the late-1943 report of Coverdale and Colpitts, an American engineering consultancy. Commissioned by the corporation but clearly intended for the minister's eyes, the report left an impressive picture of Algoma's new-found vitality. Noting that the management at the Sault 'on the whole is composed of experienced and capable men,' Coverdale and Colpitts concluded that the company had 'gained substantially' in comparison to the rest of the Canadian steel industry, especially in pig iron production.[97] The report pointed to 'an unanimous feeling of optimism regarding the future' at Algoma and estimated a steady post-war production of 232,000 tons annually based on 'an unusually high rate of business activity.' Refraining from any comment on Dunn's stingy husbandry of corporate profits, the report did draw attention to the 'steady improvement since 1935' in Algoma's balance sheet and earned surplus.

Howe's positive opinion of Algoma was further reinforced by the knowledge that the corporation was not profiteering from the war. Throughout the war the company never exceeded the ceiling imposed by the Excess Profits Tax and was on occasion well below the mandatory limit. These profit levels were confirmed when Algoma's wartime contracts were submitted to 'renegotiation' by federal accountants after the war. After auditing all direct war sales and special depreciation allowances, E. Winslow-Spragge, associate financial adviser, certified that 'on an overall basis, your [Algoma's] prices on War Business have been fair and reasonable and we are, accordingly, recommending that no overall refund is required in the case of your company.'[98] Howe was also aware that throughout the war the corporation had borne the brunt of steadily escalating costs for materials, freight, and labour.[99] By 1942 Algoma's financial position was so acute that, as Dunn told Howe, without some increase in prices, frozen since 1940, the company would suffer a net loss in 1942–3.[100] Such evidence impressed Howe with the degree of Algoma's wartime contribution.[101]

Algoma's progress during the Second War cannot be adequately measured in terms of financial gain. Although the corporate earned surplus grew from $2,380,663 in 1939 to $6,118,371 by April 1945, the crucial advance of the war years lay instead in the tremendous growth in company assets accomplished without any recourse to outside financing. While C.D. Howe was aware that Dunn had in some ways bettered Ottawa's bureaucrats at the bargaining table, he was prepared to tolerate the 1941 contracts as long as Algoma fulfilled its part of the bargain. He was also able to tolerate Dunn's often tempestuous behaviour because Algoma's expansion loomed large in his blueprint for Canada's post-war economy. Convinced that Canada's ultimate prosperity lay in jointly exploiting the benefits of a continental economy with the United States, Howe believed that it was imperative for Canada to possess a solid and competitive base in those primary industries in which she could efficiently participate. Steel fell squarely into this category. While Stelco already assured Canada a broad and well-established capacity in finished steel, and firms like Atlas Steels offered specialized output in alloy steel, Dosco, Dominion Foundries, and Algoma offered the potential for a solid base at the primary level. Dosco, with its long history of government subsidization, never impressed Howe as a worthy candidate. On the other hand, Algoma and to a lesser degree Dominion Foundries in Hamilton had advanced unremittingly throughout the war. By 1945, despite all the friction *en route*, Howe readily acknowledged that one of the healthiest candidates to shoulder the burden of post-war economic expansion was Algoma Steel.

The crucial ingredient in the changing fortunes of Algoma was the persistence with which Dunn pursued, protected, and extended Algoma's interests in Ottawa. Through most of the war, Dunn mounted his frequent sorties from the Seigniory Club at Montebello into Ottawa to badger government officials or press for an interview with the minister. Junior officials were inundated with correspondence from the audacious Dunn, while more senior bureaucrats and politicians were hounded by telephone. The steel president was, as F.H. Brown rather politely put it, 'a great adventurer and a ... and so on.'[102] While doing business with the irascible Dunn always proved a volatile affair, there is little to suggest that Howe ever succumbed to Dunn's intemperate blandishments. He measured his concessions to Dunn by national necessity not personal favouritism. As the war progressed, a strong working relationship nevertheless grew between the two men, tempered on Howe's part by a degree of circumspection. By the end of the war, minister and steel president were exchanging confidential correspondence concerning Algoma's stalwart wartime performance and its post-war role. Howe later admitted to Beaverbrook that he had destroyed his files of this correspondence, because it might 'be regarded by many as improper for me to have written such a letter.' At the same time, he vehemently objected to the suggestion that 'while a minister, I extended any special favour to Sir James Dunn, or anyone else, because of personal friendship.'[103] This is not to say that Dunn did not make the effort. As Norman Lambert, the Liberal party's chief organizer, recorded in his diary just after the crucial conscription plebiscite of 1942: 'Howe told me that [National Revenue Minister] Gibson had arranged exemption from income tax for every person who contributed to plebiscite. He also said Sir James Dunn had approached him with $5000 but he wouldn't touch it ...'[104]

Towards the end of the war, Howe began insisting that his ties with Dunn were 'a private matter' involving the exchange of views between two like-minded men with much the same end in sight. A glimpse into this bond of common-mindedness was caught and set down in the diary of Adolf A. Berle, the eminent economist and wartime adviser to the American secretary of state. Berle was brought by plane from Washington in July 1944 for 'a rather fantastic weekend' with Howe, Dunn, Beaverbrook, and British Secretary of the Treasury Assheton at 'Dunn's Camp' in the New Brunswick forest. Amply fortified by Dunn's private stock of whisky and champagne and sumptuously dined on an 'Alice-in-Wonderland' schedule, these men of state and business 'proceeded to take up the broad subject of economic reconstruction and how much the Government would have to support the situation.'[105] Others were more sceptical of Dunn's offers of friendship. Another diarist, Prime Minister Mackenzie King, who while happy to exchange official greetings with 'my dear Sir James,' privately noted in 1945 that 'I believed we were now in an era where great world enterprises were taking shape, where a few wealthy interests were combining together to seek to control those organizations. That I thought Beaverbrook was one who would not hesitate to put money into Canada to get control for his friend. I might have added: Sir James Dunn.'[106]

Despite Sir James' rather ambiguous position in the eyes of Ottawa's politicians, there was no question whatsoever that the war had brought Algoma Steel and its fortunes almost completely under the federal sway. Howe with his extensive array of wartime emergency economic powers made Ottawa the *sine qua non* of Algoma's future, while Toronto, constitutionally outgunned in the war crisis, assumed a second-rate importance in Dunn's eyes. The irresponsible departure, as Dunn saw it, of Premier Hepburn from office in 1942 had deprived the steel president of a close personal friend at Queen's Park and at the same time left the provincial government a 'rudderless hulk of former greatness.'[107] There was pathos in Hepburn's departure from public life, a departure to which Dunn had in no small way contributed. While C.D. Howe had resolutely rejected a place in Dunn's hard-living social circle, Mitch Hepburn had readily succumbed to the good life which Sir James' hotel suite invariably offered. Dunn noted with unconscious irony in 1944:

If Mitch will keep emotionally stable and not allow himself to be rushed into decisions, I think he can come back in the estimation of his friends and of the country ... he cannot maintain the dignity of a great political position by harbouring drunks who drop in at all hours of the day and night to hinder his repose and interfere with his serious engagements. A man with two kidneys and two hearts could not again go through what Mitch went through for many years before his collapse – so Mitch with only one kidney and one heart although very big and generous cannot successfully come back to a great leader in the dragging attachments of a few years ago. ...[108]

Dunn never established close ties with Hepburn's successors, Premiers Conant and Nixon, and instead began to cultivate the friendship of Ontario politicians and businessmen who displayed the kind of decisiveness he found so lacking in other Canadian politicians. George McCullagh 'with his *Globe and Mail* battleaxe' and Tory leader George Drew, 'a fine fellow and a good Britisher,' were men in Dunn's eyes of sufficient mettle not only to prosecute the war vigorously but also to hold at bay the 'socialist' CCF threat in Ontario.

In the face of the unfolding federal supremacy during the war, one act of the Hepburn government put Algoma in excellent stead. The Helen mine, brought to life by the 1937 iron bounty act, cushioned the corporation from the impact of scarcities and price increases transmitted by the American ore producers to Canadian iron ore consumers. In the years of peak demand between 1940 and 1942, the Helen mine supplied on average 21 per cent of the iron ore requirements of the Sault blast furnaces. Surplus Helen sinter was traded through the Hanna company to US steelmakers in return for Mesabi ores to mix with lower-grade Ontario ore. 'I am not immodest,' Dunn states in 1944, 'in claiming to have established iron ore mining in Ontario which I could not have undertaken without this iron ore bounty of Hepburn's.'[109]

The impression that the 1937 bounty act was a private deal between Hepburn and Dunn was evidently held by Premier Conant, who abruptly cancelled the bounty in 1943. Conant argued that the Helen operation had achieved self-sufficiency and no longer merited assistance. 'The government,' Dunn bitterly complained, 'contracted with me – I have fulfilled my contract – I expect the Government to do likewise and to continue to pay me my Bounty for the ten year period.'[110] When Queen's Park refused to budge, Dunn acquainted provincial Tory leader George Drew with the problem and obtained a vague promise that, if elected, the Tories would restore the bounty. John Bracken, the federal Tory leader, visited the Sault and was reportedly 'very interested in the iron ore situation.' The Tories had, however, aroused false hope in Dunn. Soon after the Tories reclaimed Queen's Park in 1943, Dunn disconsolately recorded that the new premier kept 'putting me off for one reason or another.'[111] The province's abrogation of an active role in the development of Algoma's iron ore supply left the corporation to fall back on its own resources and ultimately to look to Ottawa for relief and incentives, even though Dunn angrily pursued Algoma's moral and legal claim for continued bounties from the province well into the post-war period.

It was obvious by 1944 that readily accessible bodies of Helen siderite were near exhaustion and that American high-grade ores were believed to be approaching exhaustion. Algoma's first reaction to the American situation was to maximize its existing iron ore supply. Foiled by Steel Control in a bid to boost the price of Algoma sinter,[112] Dunn turned cunningly on the 1939 ore exchange agreement with the M.A. Hanna Company. He alleged that the Hanna Company was extracting maximum American value for ore obtained at a fixed Canadian price and abruptly terminated the contract, arguing that government price controls in Canada had invalidated the agreement. Despite the questionable legality of this ploy, it succeeded in forcing Hanna to submit to a new contract in July 1944. By pegging Algoma sinter prices to prevailing American, non-Bessemer ore prices, the new contract in effect gave Algoma a *de facto* price increase.[113] Such unscrupulousness was typical of Sir James' ability to seize on any expedient that served his purpose.

Anxiety over the security of future ore sources impelled Algoma as early as 1943 to intensify its search for new ore bodies in the Sault hinterland. A study of the feasibility of exploiting a previously untouched ore body adjacent to the Helen concluded that there was sufficient ore to 'take care of production needs for probably fifteen years in the future.'[114] Encouraged by this prediction, Dunn opted in May 1945 to exploit this low-grade siderite ore body beside his cherished Helen mine. The new Victoria mine thus ensured Algoma a continuing stake in the extractive stage of the industry and a degree of control over its primary raw material.

Dunn's late-war preoccupation with securing a protected source of iron ore for Algoma had much broader implications. Once again Dunn envisaged Algoma's resources policy as part of a national strategy designed to integrate Canadian and American mineral production on as equitable and advantageous a basis as possible. Aware of Canada's industrial shortcomings, notably the complete absence of exploitable coal in central Canada,[115] Dunn believed that national deficiencies should be counteracted by exploiting areas of strength. Sir James thus kept a keen eye on the progress of the Steep Rock iron ore project, another of Howe's forced-growth, wartime projects. At the same time, he endorsed the view of Mines Minister T.A. Crerar that the 'mineral possibilities of Canada, not only with regard to iron but with regard to other metals' had been 'little more than scratched ... He would be a bold man who would attempt to place any limit upon the possibilities of mineral development in this country.'[116]

What Dunn, Howe, and Crerar all agreed on was the general premise that the federal government must stimulate and direct mineral production. On the eve of the war Tory leader R.J. Manion had praised the 'gambling spirit necessary to build up the mining industry of Canada,'[117] holding up Algoma's Helen mine and the Steep Rock project as shining examples. By war's end, there was a growing recognition that solid progress in mining could only be won if the federal government reduced the gambling element in the industry. While rejecting Opposition demands for a federal bounty on iron ore, Ottawa did extend certain tax concessions to new mines in the first three years of their operation.[118] Algoma was quick to apply for such concessions in 1945 for the Victoria project. This new-found consensus between the mining industry and the federal government was to set the framework for much of the vigorous growth in the resources sector of Canada's post-war economy. Just as Steel Control had fostered an irrevocable change in the relation of business and government in the steel industry, so too was there a developing consensus at the extractive end of the industry. This commitment by prominent businessmen and politicians to national growth in the continental context lay at the very root of Canada's post-war industrial expansion. Symbolic, in its small way, of this alliance for national progress was the appointment of T.A. Crerar to the Algoma board of directors in August 1945. Now retired from politics, Crerar moved with ease into the boardrooms of the nation. Similarly, the induction of Frank Brown, Howe's wartime financial adviser, and Gordon Fogo, former associate coordinator of controls, to the board in early 1946 reinforced the link between the federal government and Sault steelmaking.[119] In this ebb and flow of businessmen, 'dollar-a-year' men, and politicians between Ottawa and the corporate boardrooms, the ground rules for Canada's post-war economy were to be discussed, agreed on, and pursued.

The evolution of this new commonality between 'big steel' and the federal government during the war coincided with the progressive tightening of Dunn's control over Algoma and consequently his ability to set the corporation on any course he deemed fit for it. 'I am going to stay through,' he told Lord Glendyne some years later, 'as Algoma has become my life work and I could not "touch" [my shares] to any considerable extent without risking loss of control of the shares which condition would spoil my hopes of building a great Empire.'[120] After his early-war illnesses, his still tightly stretched finances, the loss of Rahilly, and the simmering feud with Barber of the Algoma Central, Dunn's commitment to his 'great Empire' had become obsessive. Only men like C.D. Howe, who dared to challenge Dunn's judgment, had any chance of turning Algoma's president from his determined course. Many fell by the wayside. Allan Aitken, Beaverbrook's brother, stormed off the Algoma board after criticizing some of Dunn's 'unusual' methods of getting his own way at board meetings.[121] Thomas Hobbs, another director, admitted that he was 'not comfortable as a director' especially because of the infrequency of Algoma board meetings.[122]

Viewed from the outside, Algoma's affairs continued to be wrapped in an enigma. When Arthur Meighen requested a consolidated balance sheet for Algoma and its subsidiaries in 1943, he was curtly informed that it had 'never been our practice to publish balance sheets of these subsidiaries.'[123] In fact, Algoma made frequent and sizeable transfers of capital to its subsidiaries, notably Algoma Ore Properties, thereby clouding any clear understanding of corporate finances by an outsider. Improved wartime earnings did little to shake Dunn's resolve to spurn dividends and plough back all Algoma's profits. In late 1940, he won permission from the board to buy up the corporation's outstanding preference shares, on which dividends had to be paid.[124] The few common shareholders outside Dunn's controlling block were quick to voice their pique at the lack of a return on their investment in a corporation which was clearly in much improved financial health. Dunn was impervious to such criticism. His only concern for Algoma stock was control, not dividends. 'If you are buying or selling shares,' Dunn requested Glendyne in 1944, 'I would appreciate business being done through me so that I can keep some control of the market.'[125] Dunn could rationalize all these practices with the knowledge that the ultimate success of his 'great Empire' would be built out of accumulated earnings, applied where and when he alone deemed fit. A position of such unbridled control also left him free to commit Algoma almost unilaterally to whatever post-war economic strategy best suited the steel company's interests.

On 25 November 1945 Sir James joined the members of the Steel Advisory Committee at a dinner in Montreal's Mount Royal Club to honour the services of steel controllers Kilbourn and Hoey. Four days later all Steel Control powers and appointments were rescinded. Nobody that evening was celebrating the return of the steel industry to the norms under which it had existed in 1939. Instead the conversation and speeches revolved around the prosperity brought by the war, the prospect of continued high activity, and the acknowledgment of a new relationship between the industry and government. As Dunn had told Hoey even before the war had ended, 'I am strongly in favour of continuing Steel Control when the war is over as far into the future as I can see. I feel that the Steel Control has done a splendid piece of work for the country ... and I think that at least in the first few years following the end of the year its authority as a regulatory body within the trade itself in its relations with the Federal and Provincial Governments ... will be of very great service to the country and to the industry.'[126] Algoma Steel was never 'one of the small cogs' in C.D. Howe's wheel. It was instead at the centre of a tremendous transition in Canadian economic life, a change it both helped to make and used to its own advantage. Sir James Dunn, who had clambered and scratched his way to unassailable control of Algoma, represented at one and the same time the last gasp of hardy and irresponsible old-style capitalism and the first breath of post-war regulated capitalism.

9

An Empire Realized:
Dunn and Algoma Steel 1945–1956

As the ultimate fate of the Axis became apparent, Canadian politicians and businessmen determined to avoid a repetition of the haphazard economic transition which had followed the First War. 'Reconstruction' became the key to a prosperous post-war society which married the massive wartime gains in productive capacity to the needs of a peacetime economy. 'To a large extent,' a late-war government report on Canada's industrial prospects emphasized, 'success of the whole programme of reconstruction relates to, and revolves about, the attainment of a high and stable level of industrial employment and income.'[1] The first step in this process was 'a smooth, orderly transition' from industrial production for war to production for peaceful purposes.

The steel industry found itself at the centre of this post-war transition. Over the next decade, steel mirrored many of the central developments of the Canadian economy. The welfare of the nation's steel corporations would, in the first place, reflect continued state intervention in the economy. The attainment of full employment and low inflation was predicated on the application of many of the tools of fiscal and economic management developed by the federal government during the war. As in the war, business and government were in broad agreement about the necessity of such intervention. There was, none the less, persistent friction over the specifics of its application. Mindful of the lessons of the 1920s and 1930s, the steel industry adopted a conservative approach to the prospect of expanding national steelmaking capacity past limits which they construed as sufficient for peacetime demand. The state, particularly in the fearful days of the early Cold War and the Korean crisis, construed the necessity of steel expansion in a different light. Once again under the auspices of C.D. Howe, Ottawa responded to the consequent impasse by extending incentives which served to shift part of the risk from private shoulders onto those of the interventionist state. Algoma's response to these incentives opened the way in the early 1950s for a wholesale modernization, expansion, and diversification of the company. While the procurement of these benefits in Ottawa was largely Sir James Dunn's doing, their application at the Sault was the work of the corporation's professional managers led by David Holbrook. The Howe-Dunn friendship was the product of the fortuitous combination of two forceful personalities and, as such, would pass with time. The emergence of competent management at Algoma under Holbrook was a more long-lasting achievement.

Algoma was intimately involved in other post-war developments on the industrial front. The war marked a watershed in the corporation's relations with its labour force. The business-government relationship, which lay at the heart of the war economy, had operated largely to the exclusion of labour's interests. Labour's desire for recognition of its right to bargain on an industry-wide basis with full collective bargaining – a right held in check until late in the war – surfaced with a vengeance with the coming of peace. In many ways, Algoma was a bystander to the acrimony of the 1946 national steel strike – peace prevailed on the Sault picket lines – but the outcome of the conflict permanently altered the relationship of steelworker and management at the Sault.

The post-war decade also witnessed the flowering of a continentally integrated economy. Here there was little disagreement between Dunn and Howe. Algoma was part of a North American economy, a Canadian-owned company capable of trading its iron ore and steel across the border while at the same time helping Canada become self-sufficient in many areas of steel production. Where self-sufficiency was unattainable, American imports would fill the breach. The formula sometimes faltered – especially when the American steel industry was strike-bound in 1952 – but on the whole it served to accelerate Canadian steel's coming of age.

Amid these crucial developments, Sir James was both an anachronism and a moving force. His ability to dictate Algoma's corporate policy without recourse to the consent of shareholders and at times even the advice of his own managers was unparalleled in the North American steel industry. The company's whole existence depended on his whims. In most respects, his managers were more in touch with the realities of modern steelmaking. Dunn, however, possessed the trust and friendship of Canada's most influential maker of economic policy, C.D. Howe. This liaison played a crucial role in Algoma's post-war expansion and prosperity. None the less, the close relation of steel president and minister of the Crown was a transitory phenomenon. The subsequent emergence of articulate and resourceful special interest groups, the growth of conflicting regional economic aspirations, and the evolution of a keener sense of political conflict of interest would make the recreation of a similar friendship a future improbalility.[2] None the less, by the time of Dunn's death in 1956 and Howe's departure from Ottawa in 1957, the steel industry had come of age as a competitive, Canadian-owned, and technologically advanced sector of the national economy. For Algoma, the years after the war made possible the revivification of Clergue's original dream of steel at the Sault – a dream now confirmed by the reality of a well-rounded and integrated industrial complex on the shores of the St Mary's River.

The steel industry greeted the advent of peace with cautious optimism. 'We are closely controlled,' Dunn confided to a friend in early 1945, 'as seems to be the case in allied countries, but although at times so much control is irksome we all realize here that it is essential.'[3] Steelmen and bureaucrats both pinned their hopes on the assumption that pent-up civilian demand for steel coupled with that of primary sectors of the economy would buoy up post-war steel production, precluding any return to the depths of the Depression. 'Following cessation of hostilities,' F.B. Kilbourn of Steel Control had assured the post-war planners in 1944, 'I am of the opinion that the steel capacity of this country will be ample to take care of all domestic demands ... and also be in a position to supply a substantial tonnage of steel for the rehabilitation of the countries formerly occupied by the Germans.'[4] Algoma's own outlook on the post-war economy was moulded by the optimistic conclusions of the 1943 Coverdale and Colpitts investigation of the company, which had held out the prospect of steady peacetime production of 323,000 tons annually.

What in fact followed in the wake of these predictions was a decade of hot and cold relations between Ottawa and the industry: a period of initial cautiousness, followed by compromise and intense cooperation. The decade culminated in the tremendous expansion of steel capacity in the tension-filled days of the Korean War.

Divergence of opinion between the steel producers and Ottawa sprang initially from disagreement about the purpose and application of controls on steel distribution, not from differing estimations of post-war demand. The federal economic controls policy was aimed at 'creating conditions under which private enterprise might restore prosperity to the industry.'[5]

Operating on the belief that post-war capacity would match post-war demand, Steel Control had initially advocated scrapping all direct government control over steel after the war. 'In my opinion,' F.B. Kilbourn urged his superiors in 1944, 'post-war price control should be indirect rather than positive.' In keeping with this advice, controls on steel production and consumption were rescinded in November 1945. A month later the Excess Profits Tax was relaxed.

Continued but indirect government influence over Canadian steel production found ready acceptance among the captains of Canadian steel, who had envisaged the perpetuation of direct and pervasive supervisory control with some trepidation. 'Reduction in the cost of Government and lower taxes will confer more practical advantages than the expansion of Government interference with economic developments,' noted Stelco's McMaster.[6] Dunn too uged the government's retreat from the business of the boardroom. Believing that Algoma had at times been forced by Steel Control into unprofitable lines of production and transfers of unfinished steel, Dunn had warned Associate Steel Controller Hoey in 1944 that there was 'one freedom that I think we should all have in view – the freedom to refuse business that is not suitable to the economy of the company concerned. In this of course I refer to the post-war period.'[7] Government, in Dunn's mind, should act as an insurance policy, intervening directly only when there was some disjuncture between national steel supply and demand.

Ottawa's ability to pursue a policy of indirect influence through fiscal measures and subsidization was dependent on steel production and consumption staying in relatively close alignment, not only in the Canadian context but also in the continental context. As in the war, post-war steel calculations were predicated on the continued availability of large inflows of American raw materials and finished steel to supplement Canadian output. In the heady months of victory in mid-1945, few doubted that this formula could cope with post-war demand.[8] Many were inclined to believe that after the backlog of civilian demand had been satisfied, some measure of overexpansion would be discovered. Even the usually bullish Sir James characterized the period as an 'emergence from big volume war business to low volume peace business.'[9]

By mid-1946 the confident expectations of both government and industry had gone sadly awry as joint hopes for 'a smooth, orderly transition' to peacetime production were thrown into disarray. The rhythm of post-war readjustment in steel was initially upset by severe disruptions in the continental steel economy, closely followed by the effects of a national strike of Canadian steelworkers. A four-week American steel strike in January and February 1946 was the first factor to destabilize the Canadian steel economy. It curtailed American steel output by six million tons. A coal strike later in the spring cramped steel production by a further two million tons.[10] The ensuing scarcity of American coal and finished steel upset the delicate balance between imports and domestic production that underlay the Canadian steel economy.

The American coal strike exacerbated an already precarious energy situation for the company. Even during the war, Algoma's coal-producing subsidiary in the us, the Cannelton Coal Company, had been plagued by Washington's arbitrary requisitions from its coal stockpiles. By July 1945 the parent company in Canada was roughly 270,000 tons of coal short. The 1946 American coal strike seriously aggravated this situation. In July 1946 Howe's Coal Control officials reported an 850,000-ton coal shortage in Canada. This deficiency not only jeopardized Algoma's steel operations but also hurt its sizeable trade in domestic and industrial coke. Scarcity of coal and coke coincided with the increased demand on domestic steel-makers created by the abrupt curtailment of steel imports resulting from the us steel strike. After consulting with the industry's leaders, Martin Hoey reported to Howe in May 1946 that a deficit of 405,000 tons of steel existed in Canada and predicted that 'the future domestic distribution of steel will grow steadily worse and must result in the most serious consequences for a large part of Canadian industry.'[11]

The federal government responded to this threat to its post-war reconstruction plans by reverting to direct controls. 'I am completely frustrated by shortages,' the new minister of reconstruction and supply noted. 'Every industry in Canada is trying to expand and everyone wants a house, but no one can get materials; for this, I seem to be the goat.'[12] Eager to shed this image, Howe reinstituted both Steel and Coal Control in early 1946. Moving to protect the 'extremely grave' domestic coke situation, Coal Control ordered Algoma to 'make available to the government' fifty-four thousand tons of its coke per month for domestic heating and foundry purposes even if such shipments imperilled its own steel production.[13] Algoma was promised a 'satisfactory formula for compensation.' Steel Control then exercised its right to distribute national steel production by requesting Algoma to allocate twelve thousand tons of steel slabs monthly to Stelco and to augment national pig iron output. At the same time, Canadian steel exports were vigorously curtailed. Within months of the disappearance of the last vestiges of wartime control, a new panoply of direct control over the steel economy had thus materialized. Not unexectedly, friction soon developed between business and government.

The fissures that opened between Algoma and Ottawa during 1946 stemmed largely from the incompatibility of broad federal controls designed to surmount a national steel and coal shortage and the more narrowly defined interests of the corporation. While a bond of cordiality remained between Howe and Dunn, a measure of adept manoeuvring and hard bargaining entered their relationship. Reacting to Steel Control's directives for the diversion of his steel to other mills, Dunn railed against Ottawa's intrusions:

Putting Algoma on any of these extreme operations for what Martin Hoey might consider the general advantage of Canada would disrupt our routine business and throw much of our skilled labour out of employment and generally disorganize our future. The perilous raw material position of North America including coal, ore and scrap is in my opinion more important to keep in view in guiding the decisions of Steel Control than futile efforts to meet a variety of accumulated demands throughout the country beyond the capacity of Canada's steel mills to quickly overtake. We must each of us go on producing the things for which we have capacity and getting a good backlog of coal, iron ore and limestone.[14]

Foremost in Algoma's post-war priorities was the desire to bring its primary and finishing capacities into alignment and, using this productive base, to pursue its pre-war ambition of diversifying its market. Wartime sales of Algoma rails as far afield as Russia had whetted Algoma's appetite for export sales to war-devastated Europe. Using his personal contacts with English steel magnate Sir Andrew Duncan, Dunn was able to secure export orders for steel billets from the British Iron and Steel Corporation throughout 1947 and 1948. These hopes were rudely arrested when Steel Control reminded Dunn that 'Mr. Howe was adamant in stating that domestic requirements must be taken care of before consideration would be given to the export of steel in primary form.'[15] 'My chance to put Algoma on its feet financially will be lost,' Dunn irately replied, 'if we lose this British order ... Algoma Steel has no modern finishing mills out of which we can make a profit when times get normal ... I want Algoma to get rich enough to be able four or five years from now to build out of its accumulated profits the kind of mills necessary to put it in the front rank for competitive business.'[16]

In the face of Dunn's protests, Howe stood his ground, insisting that Algoma put its aspirations into abeyance and comply with Steel Control's directives. In return for his compliance, Dunn exacted a heavy toll from the minister. After repeated trips to Ottawa by Dunn and Holbrook, backed up by the lobbying of Algoma vice-president Fogo from a Wellington Street office, Howe settled on compensation to cover the cost of diverting Algoma products from their 'natural markets.' Payments ranged from $1.50 per ton on domestic coke redirected by government orders to $3.50 a ton paid on diverted pig iron.[17] Subsidies were granted to defray abnormal freight and production costs occasioned by the diversions. Howe prided himself on this enforced rationalization of the Canadian steel market and boasted in the Commons that the subsidies had 'increased the production of secondary steel by at least 20 to 25 per cent over what it would be without government intervention.'[18] Dunn accepted Howe's thanks for 'revising your operation along the lines requested by our Steel and Coal Controllers' and later confided to J.S. Duncan, president of Massey-Harris, that while he regretted the necessity of steel controls he was reconciled to them as 'healthy and reasonable.'[9] At Christmas 1946, Howe informed the Algoma chief that he was 'much in your debt' and that he wished 'our friendship will continue as long as we both may live.'[20]

If the post-war reintroduction of controls had temporarily strained relations between the industry and Ottawa, the national steel strike of 1946 tended to reunite them in common opposition to the concerted efforts of steel labour to exert a greater influence on its fortunes in the industry. The issue of what wages and prices should prevail in the post-war Canadian steel industry unleashed volcanic tensions in the relations of industry, labour, and government, tensions that were intensified by the determined efforts of the steelworkers' union to obtain recognition of its status as a national bargaining agent.

The labour issue had deep and tangled roots. War and the ensuing steel crisis of 1940–2 had catapulted steel labour out of the languid position it had occupied through much of the last two decades and given it a crucial role in the battle for war production. Steel labour's indispensability placed it at the fulcrum of the wartime economy, exposed to the full brunt of emergency wage and price controls and subjected to a gruelling burden of work dictated by labour shortages and the imperative necessity of squeezing optimum output out of Canada's overstrained steelmaking capacity. Steel labour therefore provided a barometer of the success of business and government stratagems for the Canadian war economy.

While crucially affected by the outcome of these strategems, labour was 'unrepresented and unheard' in their formulation.[21]

On 22 May 1940, C.D. Howe had directed all producers of war *matériel* to 'speed up' production schedules to an around-the-clock basis.[22] With the establishment of various agencies to oversee national labour requirements and the imposition of a wage freeze, steel labour found itself blanketed by regulation. Within the constraints of these new circumstances the relatively amicable relations between Algoma and its workers dating from pre-war days came under increasing strain. Much to the disgust of its president, Algoma did, however, recognize the Steelworkers' Organizing Committee (swoc), the cio affiliate that had just absorbed the independent Algoma Steelworkers Union, as the official bargaining agent at the Sault for steel labour.[23] In December 1940, the corporation concluded its first wage agreement with local 2251 of swoc. The cio's presence in the Sault confirmed the worst suspicions of Dunn and his Liberal friends at Queen's Park. Fortunately, the steel president maintained a shadowy role in Sault labour matters, leaving negotiations to his able and liberal-minded general manager, T.F. Rahilly.

With the 'steel crisis' of 1941–2 exerting pressure on the industry, amicable relations between Algoma, swoc, and the federal government disintegrated. Antagonism centred on several contentious issues. swoc criticized business and government strategies of wartime steel production. swoc director C.H. Millard charged in 1942 that 'The experience of our Union during the past two years and eight months of war has ... produced grave disappointment and a feeling of frustration.'[24] Frustration, Millard alleged, stemmed from low morale, the business-oriented industrial policies of government, the slipshod execution of these policies by 'big steel,' and management's overcautious attitude to the expansion of steel capacity. Steel's salvation, in swoc's judgment, lay in national organization, not only of production, but also labour. Through national planning and collective bargaining the industry could be rationalized and the prevailing 'chaotic' and 'indefensibly low' wages could be supplanted by a uniform national wage rate that would eradicate the 'harmful and unjust variations in wages and working conditions' that militated against steel labour's interests. To substantiate swoc's case, Millard alleged that by the fall of 1942, 40 per cent of Sault steelworkers received less than 55¢ per hour.[25]

Algoma reacted intransigently to labour's demands. Citing the frozen prices of its steel products, management maintained that increased labour costs would place an undue burden on the corporate balance sheet. Dunn himself grew increasingly belligerent, confiding to Lord McGowan in England that North American labour lacked 'patriotic and studious' leadership and was motivated by 'an undercurrent of bitterness.'[26] Ottawa's response to the growing discontent in steel labour was conditioned by the imperative need to ensure uninterrupted steel production and to avoid any major breach in the wage freeze that lay at the heart of the regulated wartime economy. When informed in August 1942 by Millard that steelworkers' dissatisfaction threatened 'an imminent stoppage in the steel industry,' Prime Minister Mackenzie King pointed out that by adopting such a course steelworkers 'would forfeit the sympathy of the people generally if they occasioned any avoidable interference with the production of the tools of war.'[27] Although King privately noted his desire to 'have the men get justice,' Ottawa's anxiety to avert any steel stoppage predisposed it to the management's point of view, particularly in its insistence that labour's grievances be settled by regional, as opposed to national, war labour boards.[28]

When the Ontario War Labour Board refused to sanction a base labour rate of 55¢ an hour at the Sault, Millard defiantly took an illegal strike vote at the Sault and Sydney in August 1942. He used the resulting pro-strike mandate to halt production at Algoma from 29 August to 3 September.[29] 'Banked' furnaces and immobilized rolling mills shook Ottawa to its senses. A full-scale strike was only averted by Labour Minister Mitchell's pledge of a three-man Royal Commission to investigate the plight of steel labour.[30] To this point, Millard's strategy had focused on Algoma and Dosco, where the lowest labour rates prevailed, in hopes that pay hikes won there would boost their labour to parity with Stelco, where the highest rates were paid and the union had made the least impact. This achieved, Millard would have won an implicit acknowledgment of steel as 'national employer.'

swoc's ambitions were dealt a harsh blow by the majority 'findings of the three-man Royal Commission headed by Mr Justice Barlow. Tabled in December 1942, the majority report of Barlow and J.T. Stewart quenched union demands for a 55¢-an-hour base rate at Algoma and Dosco, maintaining that Algoma's existing 50½¢ rate with a cost of living bonus was 'not substandard but in fact above the average rates generally prevailing for that class of labour.'[31] After concluding that Algoma's unskilled labour rates were the highest ever paid by the corporation and were in line with other rates at the Sault, Barlow and Stewart sternly warned that it would be 'manifestly unfair' to boost steel wages out of alignment with other industrial workers elsewhere in the country. The majority report contrasted starkly with the sympathy of the third commissioner, J. King Gordon, for the plight of the steelworkers. Gordon argued that his fellow commissioners had adopted too 'strictly legalistic' an approach to the problem. He reminded the government that steel was not only the product of inanimate raw material but 'of the lives of men and women.' For the 40 per cent of Algoma labour receiving less than 55¢ an hour, Gordon alleged, a stake in this vital industry meant little more than 'a story of hardship and privation, of overcrowding, of financial worry, of acute distress occasioned by illness against which there was no financial protection.' In light of 'inhumanly long hours' and the frequent absence of a 'bare subsistence income,' Gordon strongly advocated that a boost to 55¢ an hour was 'not only justified but actually required.' This would not only 'remove injustices' and eradicate anomalies 'throughout the industry,' but would stabilize the operations of a vital wartime industry.

Gordon's impassioned plea on behalf of labour did little to assuage the wrath of Millard and swoc at the majority recommendations that seemed to uphold the *status quo* in the steel industry. When Labour Minister Mitchell moved to implement the majority recommendations he triggered what swoc described as 'the swift, irresistible climax of 22 months of delay and evasion.'[32] Between 12 and 14 January 1943, swoc pulled 11,613 steelworkers off the job at Sydney and Trenton in Nova Scotia and at the Sault in an illegal strike that struck at the jugular of war production. While the crisis called for quick and decisive political action, the federal cabinet was deeply divided on the subject. Prime Minister King, impressed by Gordon's reformist views, 'felt a strong case had been made out for increasing the wages of the sub-standard employees, but not a case for those receiving higher rates.' C.D. Howe, although less motivated by humanitarian concern than by industrial efficiency, plumped strongly for recognition of steel as a national employer and 'a levelling up of the lowest wage groups in other industries as well as in the steel.' Arrayed against this viewpoint was a strong body of cabinet opinion, led by the labour and finance ministers, firmly convinced that 'any compromise would mean the destruction of the policy of wage stabilization and price ceiling.' Ilsley candidly confessed 'that even if there were injustice in the wage stabilization policy, we would have to continue injustice if the policy were to be maintained.'[33] Dosco president Arthur Cross and Dunn of Algoma reinforced this stance by informing the government that 'they would be financially embarrassed having to meet extra demands' and that they expected government assistance if any concession was made to labour.[34]

Intense negotiations in Ottawa led to a compromise that brought the steelworkers back to the mills on 27 January. Under the 'memorandum of agreement' Algoma and Dosco were tentatively designated national employers who were to recognize the 55¢ national base rate. Provision was made for future disputes to be settled by the National War Labour Board, whose new chairman, C.P. McTague, a Toronto justice, was to reconsider the workers' case. In the hearings before McTague during March, E.G. McMillan, Algoma's legal counsel, vigorously opposed the steelworkers' application for a rate of 55¢ plus a cost of living bonus by arguing that varying regional costs in other phases of steel production should hold true for labour. Millard later charged that the companies had mounted 'an intensive lobbying campaign.'[35]

McTague's 31 March decision reversed much of the January agreement by rejecting the notion of steel as a national employer, chopping the base rate to 50¢ plus bonuses, and excluding the Trenton workers from the agreement. 'What can be expected on the industrial front in Canada,' Millard protested, 'if promises solemnly made are so lightly broken?' By respecting wage differentials throughout the industry, this 'perverse and fantastic decision' had severely checked swoc's ambitions of encompassing all steel labour under one union umbrella. The attempt to hoist Dosco and Algoma workers to parity with their better-paid but less organized brothers at Stelco had failed. The fledgling uswa local 1005 in Hamilton had stayed on the job throughout the fracas. The key to management's success in repulsing Millard's offensive lay in the association of any major concession in steel wages with an irreparable breach in Ottawa's wage control program. Even King, who genuinely sympathized with labour's plight, breathed more easily after McTague's decision, noting that he had succeeded 'in making minor wage adjustments without destroying the stabilization policy or the price ceiling.'[36]

The strikes of January 1943 left a lingering sense of bitterness and suspicion between labour and management in Canadian steel. Although small and brief strikes did erupt before the peace, Ottawa succeeded in keeping the steel industry at work without major interruption. At Algoma this achievement served to sour previously harmonious labour relations. Having lost the conciliatory talents of T.F. Rahilly, the company more and more dealt with labour through its lawyers. When asked in July 1943 by works manager Louis Derrer if Sir James might address the mill crews, union official William Mahoney replied: 'No I don't think so. The men will not take very well to that.'[37] In the same month, rcmp surveillance of Sault labour reported 'very unsettled' conditions.

In the wake of its mid-war setbacks, the United Steelworkers began to reorient their strategy. Union officials increasingly recognized the necessity of an organizational assault on Stelco. Inclusion of Hamilton steelworkers in swoc would provide sufficient leverage to win an acknowledgment of national bargaining status from management and at the same time pierce the government's wage ceiling. These tensions, latent through the last years of the war, surfaced with a vengeance in 1946, jeopardizing the transition of the national economy to peacetime norms. True to labour's strategy, the fractious events of 1946 unfolded at Stelco, with Algoma being relegated to the role of 'bystander.' By 1946 uswa local 1005 in Hamilton still found itself in 'a precarious position.'[38] It had only just concluded its first labour agreement with the company in February 1945 but had failed to secure ironclad union security or a wage hike. Stelco's stubborn determination to limit the union to these initial gains precipitated the dramatic clash of 1946. Millard informed the federal deputy minister of labour, 'I wish to draw your attention also to the apparent desire of the Steel Company of Canada to have a "trial of strength" with our union. I do not think the other two companies have any such intention, but unfortunately they seem afraid to differ with Stelco.'[39]

Sir James Dunn was by 1946 temperamentally inclined to commit Algoma to a head-on confrontation with labour. 'As far as I have had an opportunity to judge the labour attitudes of today,' he lectured the *Financial Post* editor, 'it is a class attitude and not interested in the emergence of individual talent or capacity for leadership.'[40] Fortunately, saner minds prevailed in the formation of Algoma's response to labour's new post-war challenge. By the end of the war, uswa local 2251 at the Sault had solidly entrenched itself. In July 1946, 3492 of Algoma's approximately thirty-five hundred employees were union members.[41] The union's right to bargain collectively for Sault labour was reaffirmed in an April 1946 agreement with the company, in which voluntary check-off, a forty-eight-hour week, and paid vacations were conceded. Only the pay clause was left unsettled. As the federal director of industrial relations acknowledged, the 'matters of recognition, check-off, seniority and vacations have all been finally dealt with in the existing agreement' and Algoma did not 'consider them to be matters of dispute or presently open for discussion.'[42]

In view of organized labour's strength at its plant, Algoma acquiesced in the initiatives taken in 1946 by Stelco and prepared to reap whatever gains that company might make at the union's expense. The three primary steel employers carefully shunned any open semblance of a collective stance in the face of the union's demand for national bargaining. At the same time they secretly coordinated their tactics to stymie Millard's ambitions. While the strike was to take a more peaceful course at the Sault than in Hamilton, Dunn none the less felt a close sympathy for the stance of the Stelco president H.G. Hilton during the conflict, frequently praising his counterpart's 'greatest courage and resource in dealing with his end of the strike.'

Looming ominously in the background of the labour dispute was the federal government's resolve to maintain price and wage equilibrium in the post-war economy. Any upward pressure on steel production costs, Ottawa planners feared, would in turn trigger a host of inflationary increases in other sectors of the economy. While Finance Minister Ilsley preached tight control of the post-war price structure, the command post in the battle against inflation was the Wartime Prices and Trade Board, given a post-war reprieve under the tough-minded direction of Donald Gordon. Gordon argued for unflinching restraint of wages and prices, prophesying that any strike-induced shortage of steel would create 'an unbearable burden on our entire price structure.'[43] This view was shared by Reconstruction Minister C.D. Howe, whose whole economic strategy hinged on unimpeded production and rigidly controlled costs.

Ironically, a major concession in the price ceiling on steel products granted by Gordon in April 1946 precipitated the final clash with steel labour. Through the last years of the war, the primary steel industry had cited dwindling profit ratios as evidence of the need for price increases in iron, steel, and coke. Dunn adopted the tack that if government was to dictate the nature of production and its price, the company had a right to assured profits. The government responded with various subsidies to producers as an indirect means of avoiding direct price increases. Howe's department, for instance, doled out $5 million in freight subsidies during 1946 to maintain a stable price on steel. In March 1946, nevertheless, Algoma joined the other primary steel producers in requesting an upward revision of steel, iron, and coke prices. Dunn was elated to hear from Controller Hoey that the WPTB was 'inclined to be generous,' especially since his last visit to Ottawa had led him to believe that 'it was Donald Gordon's intention to delay fixing the new prices until the new labour rates had been settled.'[44] While the WPTB denied any adjustment in coke prices, it did on 1 April grant a $5 a ton hike in iron and steel prices. Gordon justified the move by citing the 'rapidly declining' profit margins of steel producers.[45]

The steel price increase sparked intense reaction. Despite the profuse assurances of Gordon and Ilsley that the hike in no way courted inflation but was 'a planned policy of adjustment to peacetime conditions,' severe criticism was levelled at the decision from both sides of the House. Concern was, for instance, expressed that higher steel prices would burden other primary producers, notably agriculture. 'I am not at all sure,' Mackenzie King noted in his diary, 'that this particular happening is not the beginning of a little breach – of a crack in the Government's position with the matter of removing controls and the position that will arise therewith. The truth is these are inevitably consequences of what was done in the war.'[46]

King's prophetic 'little breach' widened into a chasm somewhat more quickly than anyone had anticipated. In July 1945 USWA national director Charles Millard urged Labour Minister Mitchell to institute 'tripartite industry councils' to facilitate labour-management consultation in the transitional period and thereby prevent any 'return to the planless and confused conditions which existed in steel and other industries prior to the effective controllership established to meet the needs of war production.'[47] Six months later USWA national officials renewed their campaign for certification of steel as a national employer, citing the 1943 'memorandum of agreement' as a precedent. When this gambit failed, separate negotiations were initiated with each of the 'big three' producers. At Algoma, this entailed settling the wage and hours of work clauses open in the April agreement concluded by local 2251. Millard demanded an across-the-board 19½¢ hourly pay boost for steelworkers from each company and a reduction of the work week from forty-eight to forty hours. In each case management balked at these terms, refusing to submit to Millard's bid to induce it into *de facto* national bargaining. 'I regret to report,' an infuriated Millard told Ottawa in late May, 'that unless there is a decided change in the attitude of the management of the "big three" before June 8th, we will be compelled to conclude that no progress toward the realization of our wage programme can be made in direct and separate negotiations with these employers.'[48]

Desperate to avert a repetition of the calamitous US steel strike, Labour Minister Mitchell intervened in the situation, appointing W.D. Roach, a Toronto justice, to investigate the conflict as an industrial disputes inquiry commissioner. 'Very early in the course of the discharge of my duties,' Roach later reported, 'it appeared to me that it was very doubtful that I would be able to bring about an agreement between the parties by conciliatory action.'[49] At a 20 June meeting with Roach, Algoma executives J.G. Fogo and E.G. McMillan 'emphatically stated that Algoma was opposed to the idea of the steel industry being treated as a "national industry"' and claimed that their company could only sustain an 8¢ an hour hike over a forty-eight-hour week. On 4 July, all pretence of negotiation came to an abrupt halt with the disclosure that local 2251 in Sault Ste Marie had delegated the right to ratify any agreement tentatively concluded with Algoma to the National Advisory Committee of the USWA. In Hamilton, Roach was greeted by Stelco's blunt refusal to partake in any inquiry that simultaneously or seriatim delved into the labour-management relations of all the 'big three.' Despite such intransigence on Stelco's part, Roach's interim report revealed a much deeper animus toward the USWA: 'The "union" has become the master of the employees rather than their servant and in the hands of a group of men known as the National Advisory Committee of the United Steel Workers Unions rests the economic destiny of 13,000 odd employees ... This is not collective bargaining as I understand it ... In my opinion it constitutes a dictatorship.'[50] This chilling conclusion was followed by the recommendation of a 10¢ an hour increase over a forty-eight-hour week coupled to a ninety-day cooling-off period.

By early July, neither labour nor management was inclined to cool off. Neither could now contemplate any retreat or any bending of principle without fear that such concessions would irreparably jeopardize its whole strategy. Realizing this, the government braced for a strike by appointing F.B. Kilbourn as controller of the steel industry with 'custody and control of such property and assets of each of the Companies as he in his uncontrolled discretion and judgement may deem necessary in order to manage, operate and carry on the business of each.'[51] Kilbourn had little opportunity to wield his powers before the USWA labour force at the Sault, Hamilton, and Sydney brought primary steel production to a halt on 14–15 July 1946.

In Ottawa, Mackenzie King was immediately confronted by colleagues, notably Ilsley, who advocated a tough and legalistic response to the 'illegal' strikes. Premier Drew in Toronto called for the use of 'seasoned troops' to quell the strike. King thought differently. The prime minister characteristically opted 'at all costs to keep on with conciliation' and with uncharacteristic suddenness committed the whole issue to the Commons Standing Committee on Industrial Relations. This, he believed, would 'bring out the facts, and the mere fact that they are being investigated publicly will make the party in the wrong come to time.'[52] King's naive faith in publicity overlooked the deep and irreconcilable differences that divided steel labour and management. 'Much as I hate strikes,' Dunn privately noted later in July, 'since one has been forced on us I would rather that it lasted long enough to be a cure for a while even though we suffer by waiting.'[53] Sault unionist William Mahoney was equally trenchant, warning the strikers two months later: 'If we give up now and agree to the latest proposals, it means the end of the union. It is imperative that we stick together until our original demands are met.'[54]

Unlike the turbulent confrontation brought on in Hamilton by Stelco's attempts to maintain production with non-union labour, the strike at the Sault was remarkably peaceful. RCMP reports monotonously reported 'peaceful picketing' outside the Algoma gates by small groups of men.[55] Although management tried to frighten labour back to work by brandishing the government's $20 a day penalty on illegal strikers, they made it clear that non-union operation of the mills was 'entirely in the hands of the Steel Controller,' who as yet had done little to exercise his considerable authority. Except for a trickle of domestic coke, 'the chief industry of the Soo,' as Dunn noted, 'was like a cow gone dry.' Against this peaceful background, Algoma labour and management postured and negotiated, all the time keeping an eye on the decisive events at Stelco.

Algoma defended its refusal to bargain with the steelworkers' union at the July sessions of the Commons Industrial Relations Committee. Presented by corporate counsel E.G. McMillan, the brief depicted Algoma struggling to readjust and survive in the uncertainties of the post-war economy and therefore unable to meet union demands. While 'substantial earnings' had been made during the war, Algoma was now hampered by government controls, inflation, and material shortages. In short, 'the company now finds itself in a straitjacket ... unable to supply the national demands of our customers for steel.' McMillan stressed that 'even with all these advantages throughout the war we did not make enough money to justify a dividend on the common shares which were exchanged for the $14,000,000 odd of bonds formerly outstanding.' This misleading description of Dunn's parsimonious 'no dividends' policy was followed by the equally misleading assertion that Algoma was 'at present' not in receipt of any government subsidies.[56] When asked to what extent government assistance bolstered Algoma's wartime production, McMillan flatly claimed that 'the government did not give us anything' except special depreciation. Asked if Algoma faced possible financial problems, McMillan insisted that an imposed 19½¢ an hour wage increase would drive the company into 'difficulties from the drop of a hat.' The $5 price increase on steel, McMillan maintained, was merely a remedial measure, easing accumulated cost pressures. Finally, Algoma resisted any acknowledgment of national employer status for the steel industry by citing innumerable differences in production costs and working conditions among the 'big three.' Throughout the brief, McMillan echoed Dunn's firm belief that Algoma in the north should not be forced to pay wages comparable to subsidized Dosco or centrally located Stelco.

Labour's response to Algoma's 'straitjacket' arguments was to insist that the company 'had fared very well during the war,' benefiting from generous capital assistance programs that had underwritten Algoma's profitable expansion. Millard alleged that while Algoma's per capita productivity had increased 173 per cent since 1939, payroll had lagged at 133 per cent.[57] 'This company can pay,' the union brief bluntly asserted.[58] As management and labour both recited their set pieces, it became apparent that little room remained for conciliation amid the atmosphere of exaggeration and allegation. Leonard W. Brockington, appointed by the Commons committee in August to negotiate the dispute, emerged from negotiations with labour and management as frustrated as his predecessor, W.D. Roach. Brockington's proposed settlement, including a 10¢ hourly increase retroactive to April 1946, an immediate return to work, and subsequent arbitration of union security and other crucial issues, was summarily rejected by labour.[59] In mid-August, the union tempered its demands to an hourly increase of 15½¢ and a forty-four-hour week. This was rejected by management, especially at Dosco where corporate insolvency was continually cited in response to wage demands. In the Commons, CCF leader M.J. Coldwell voiced the growing mood of exasperation and suspicion surrounding the strike, alleging that 'there are certain powerful interests in this country which dislike the progress that labour made during the war and were determined ... that these new unions and even the older ones had to be broken if possible.'[60]

The existence of solid but not entirely visible opposition to union demands tended to substantiate M.J. Coldwell's allegation and explain the slow pace of negotiation. While steadfastly refusing to bargain jointly with Millard, executives of the 'big three' were coordinating their strike strategies behind the scenes. Throughout the strike, Dunn maintained frequent communication with Hilton of Stelco, praising Hilton's 'fine job at Ottawa.'[61] Furthermore, Dunn and Hilton found a sympathetic hearing in the office of Reconstruction Minister Howe, who, like the steel presidents, believed that the strike jeopardized his whole post-war steel strategy. In the face of persistent criticism from CCF stalwarts like Clarie Gillis, Howe vigorously upheld the companies' claim that varying production costs and product lines precluded national bargaining with labour and that any overgenerous wage settlement would scuttle

Ottawa's wage and price stabilization policy. 'The Gordon line may bend here and there,' argued one Liberal backbencher, 'a salient may be driven into it here and there, but we cannot allow that Gordon line to break.'[62] When the union rejected the government's next bid to conciliate a settlement, a 11¢–11½¢ wage increase proposed in mid-September, Howe urged Labour Minister Mitchell to be tough. 'Having taken the punishment for this long time, I would be inclined to wait a little longer before taking down the flag.'[63] The close and sympathetic understanding between steel management and several of the most influential Liberal ministers was a prime determinant in prolonging the steel dispute into early October and in eventually bringing labour to accept a 13¢ wage increase. The alliance of business and government, however, was ultimately not strong enough to stem the tide of union security at Stelco.

The decisive breakthrough came in late September when Steel Controller Kilbourn met with Millard in Montreal and mapped out a proposed settlement built around a 10¢ pay hike retroactive to 1 April, coupled with an additional 3¢ boost on return to work. What made the agreement palatable to labour was the assurance that all unresolved issues would be mediated by T.F. Rahilly, the former Algoma general manager and a man known for his fair-minded approach to labour problems. While the union had retreated considerably from its objective of a forty-hour week and a 19½¢ wage increase, the tacit acceptance of a uniform wage structure by the companies acknowledged that 'big steel' could no longer circumvent the authority of the USWA as a national bargaining agent. Secret ballots conducted at the three strike-bound centres gave Millard an overwhelming mandate (7169:789) to bring the strike to a conclusion. On 8 October, the steel controller ordered Algoma to reheat its furnaces. Although Kilbourn's pervasive powers were not officially rescinded until February 1947, he had done little to intevene in the internal affairs of any of the three companies during the strike.

The steel strike of 1946 left deep and festering wounds in the steel industry. For the first time, labour had effectively challenged the hegemony of management and government in setting the framework within which the steel industry would develop. The centralizing economic pressures of the war had created a dynamic national framework for steel management and now labour, not surprisingly, sought to emulate their employer's achievement. Although Stelco and local 1005 finally concluded an agreement in March 1947 ensuring some measure of union security, an atmosphere of distrust and recrimination was to permeate labour relations in Hamilton for many years. At Algoma there was a partial return to the amicable labour-management relations which had prevailed before the strike. Dunn privately continued to associate the CIO with social ills ranging from communism to working-class sloth, but by 1949 he had sufficiently mellowed to advise C.H. Millard to protect his health with vitamin E. None the less, Algoma did keep alive its hope of reestablishing a pattern of wage differentials within the steel industry and as late as 1949 still bucked against having to conform to 'the Hamilton pattern.'[64] The 1946 strike had instilled a sense of solidarity, not only in labour, but also in 'big steel' management. 'I agree with you,' Dunn told Hilton in 1948, 'that in this and in fact all matters relating to the difficult labour problems of the day we should keep each other informed and act in unison for the advantage of our industry.'[65]

The problem of determining how the general advantage of the Canadian steel industry was best pursued continued to bedevil the whole spectrum of government-industry relations in the post-war period. The task of adjusting and reconciling the varying perspectives on the post-war role of Canadian steel created tensions down to the Korean War. The catalyst in this process of accommodation was C.D. Howe, who, as reconstruction and subsequently trade and commerce minister, vigorously directed Canada's industrial strategy. Howe did so against the increasingly foreboding backdrop of the Cold War. With the fall of Czechoslovakia in 1948, the Western democracies began to calculate their ability to withstand the Communist bloc in terms of their military and economic prowess. Principal among the effects of the ringing down of the iron curtain was a new-found interest in the West's ability to make steel. 'Wars can be won or lost with steel,' *Saturday Night* warned in 1949, 'and we need to be very sure that we have adequate steel capacity for national security purposes.'[66] Despite Canada's status as the world's seventh largest steelmaker, newspaper and magazine articles cast this achievement in the light of the Soviet Union's ambitious five-year plan for steel expansion. In Ottawa, C.D. Howe was determined to keep pace with the Russians by increasing steel capacity and by opening Canada's iron ore reserves for the benefit of its principal ally, the United States. Aided by these pressures, Howe was gradually able to ease the friction between big government and big steel and replace it with a spirit of cooperation emphasizing mutually advantageous goals. Sir James Dunn not only acted as midwife at the birth of this cooperative relationship but fully exploited its possibilities to build Algoma's financial and operational performance to unprecedented limits.

Throughout the late 1940s the federal government continued to exercise its pervasive controls over national steel production. 'We are still half bound and half free in prices,' Dunn lamented in late 1946.[67] Responding to Dunn's incessant pleas for the removal of irksome price controls, export embargoes, and enforced distribution of steel output, Howe curtly informed the steel president that Canada was 'still in a period of acute shortage of primary steel.' The minister elaborated his reasoning in the Commons a year later: 'As I say, steel is today controlled, and it is being moved in an abnormal way to meet the abnormal demand which is partly the result of Canada's inability to buy steel outside its own boundaries. That is a unique situation; it does not ordinarily apply ... It is necessary for Canada to get the last ounce of production from its own facilities and to control the price, which otherwise would be a runaway price.'[68] A new steel controller, F.K. Ashbaugh, intervened in almost every aspect of steelmaking. The government, for instance, began subsidizing scrap used by the steelmakers. 'In summary,' Howe stated with some pride to the Canadian ambassador in Washington, 'both domestic and export uses of iron and steel in Canada are under effective control which is directed to the elimination of less essential uses.'[69]

The controls program had been conceived and implemented as a remedy for certain post-war industrial shortcomings. Confronted with an unrelenting demand for steel, Howe concluded that certain structural changes were necessary in the Canadian primary iron and steel industry, if, as he believed, Canada was to be set on an even keel. The imposition of post-war controls was based on the idea that the steel economy would ultimately establish a new equilibrium and the grip of controls could then be relaxed. If Canada was not to be caught off guard by overreliance on foreign steel, Ottawa reasoned, then her best defence lay in a high degree of steel sufficiency. 'Industrial preparedness' became a watchword for national security in the late 1940s and, in the planners' eyes, was best effected through a judicious expansion of primary and finishing capability. While there was general agreement between government and industry on the necessity of this expansion, the rub again lay in mutually determining the scope, size, and speed of such restructuring and, most important, how the burden of risk was to be apportioned. Unlike the crisis-filled atmosphere that had produced the forced industrial growth of the war, discussion in the late 1940s was less frenzied, with industry and government each adroitly jockeying to extract the maximum advantage at the minimum of risk.

Throughout 1947, C.D. Howe frequently pointed to the 'lack of balance' in Canadian steel capacity. Aware that subsidies and controls could only temporarily alleviate the situation, he announced that 'consideration' was being given 'to inducing our manufacturers to provide more basic steel.'[70] Unfortunately, Howe's eagerness to promote expansion coincided with the final phasing out of the industrial expansion programs developed during the war. The special depreciation program implemented in 1944 had, for instance, been wound up in November 1947, depriving Howe of one of the tools that had provided him with so much leverage in shaping wartime industrial production. Having approved $1.4 billion in depreciation concessions in three years, Ottawa was unwilling to perpetuate industrial expansion at so great a cost to government.

If the public sector was unwilling to assume the burden of the expansion, the steel industry was itself extremely hesitant to undertake additional capacity unassisted. Despite near-capacity operation at Canadian steel mills, a mood of hesitancy prevailed in the late 1940s. 'It bears emphasis,' a 1949 government report warned, 'that the post-war expectations of businessmen ... may not be realized in full. Changes in price-cost structure, a weakening of demand at home and abroad, increased domestic and foreign competition, increased foreign exchange difficulties, changes in the national and international political atmosphere ... are all factors that may well defeat or curtail plans of business to produce the capital and consumer goods if the economy is to continue to expand.'[71] Dunn reflected this mood of unease about the future. He reacted bitterly to Howe's call for expansion, complaining that the financial burden of any wholesale expansion in steelmaking 'hangs over us during good or bad times.'[72]

Howe's efforts to prod the major steel producers into voluntary expansion were consequently held in check during 1948 and early 1949 as 'big steel' resolutely refused to respond to the minister's blandishments. 'I think the "big 3" are "missing the boat" not going along with your offer,' Frank Sherman of Dofasco told the minister.[73] Dunn was quick to assure Howe that his refusal was not rooted in lack of interest but in uneasiness over the conditions of expansion. 'I hope something can be done for Algoma,' he told the minister in April 1949, 'rounding out our steel works and making us more effective and valuable in Canadian steel position for peace and war.'[74] Dunn's resistance stemmed from a fear of committing Algoma to heavy capital expenditures at a time of spiralling costs and uncertain future markets, a fear that was exacerbated by the belief that Algoma was already being 'robbed of the fruits of her labours and her wise development' by current government control policies.[75] H.G. Hilton of Stelco joined Dunn in his reluctance to initiate costly expansion projects. By 1951, he pointed out in *Industrial Canada*, construction costs for steel plants had risen 300 per cent over pre-war levels.[76]

Critics of ' big steel's' cautiousness depicted the refusal as a brake on national economic expansion by a selfish industry. As one CCF critic noted, 'I believe that the crux of the matter is that the steel companies believe this is an abnormal market. They are afraid that when the defence program is over, and the needs of war are met, they will find themselves with plants on their hands and no market for the product; that is the problem.'[77] Further fuel was added to the controversy by developments in the United States, where a cool response by the steel industry to President Truman's call for enlarged steel capacity in the 1949 State of the Union address had inflamed business-government relations. Like their American counterparts, Canadian steelmen defended their stance by pointing to generally low profit margins, which averaged 6.14 per cent for Algoma, Stelco, and Dosco over 1945–9, and to the unrelenting pressure of rising costs.[78] While Dunn and the other steelmakers maintained generally affable relations with Howe in Ottawa, it was evident by 1949, as the Cold War intensified, that a credibility gap had opened between the steel industry and government. 'I judge that you are not interested in expanding your plant at this time,' Howe laconically told Dunn in March 1949. 'Perhaps you are right.'[79]

Out of the atmosphere of hesitancy in the late 1940s, a workable relationship between government and 'big steel' reemerged in the early 1950s. This new understanding was of tremendous importance in facilitating the phenomenal growth in Canadian steelmaking capacity from 1950 into the 1960s. Whereas capacity had expanded 17.6 per cent in the five years immediately after the war, the 1950–5 period witnessed an increase of 34 per cent, followed by 28.1 per cent between 1955 and 1960 and a staggering jump of 72.6 per cent between 1960 and 1965.[80] Much of this growth was attributable to C.D. Howe's abilities in building lines of communication between business and government and engendering a consequent common outlook and purpose. No Canadian politician has ever matched Howe's ability to create business confidence, one of the crucial motivators of economic growth in a capitalist society. Drawing heavily on his wartime experience with Munitions and Supply, Howe fostered the emergence of a series of advisory bodies that promoted cooperation between Ottawa and the key sectors of the economy, notably steel. These channels of communication, accompanied by various fiscal incentives, proved strong enough to overcome the hesitancy displayed by Dunn and the steel industry.

In December 1947, an advisory committee on steel, adjunct to the minister's office, was established 'to explore the possibility of our getting or saving a maximum amount of u.s. dollars in steel imports.'[81] In January 1949 the wartime Steel Control Advisory Committee had a 'reunion' and, as Hilton of Stelco reported, its members 'were unanimous in saying that their services would be available again in that capacity if the need arises.'[82]

Further rapport between business and government was fostered by the Industrial Defence Board, a quasi-government advisory panel, and the Industrial Preparedness Association, a purely private lobby group. The IDB was founded in 1948 'to advise the Government of Canada and the Minister of National Defence on all matters pertaining to the industrial war potential of Canada.' Egged on by Defence Minister Brooke Claxton's clarion warning that the next war would be a 'tough slugging match,' the IDB warned the cabinet in late 1948 that Canada lacked sufficient steel capacity to satisfy both civilian and military demand.[83] The Industrial Preparedness Association tackled the same problems as the IDB, using subcommittees of industrialists to assess Canada's economic muscle. Dunn of Algoma and Hilton of Stelco were prominent members of the iron and steel committee. Although he acknowledged that these bodies were 'purely advisory,' H.G. Hilton was left with the impression that they were in fact intended to constitute 'a shadow Department of Munitions and Supply.'[84]

Beyond the formalized channels of interaction, the real crucible of new industrial strategies was the system of personal friendships centred around Howe himself. Harry J. Carmichael, who had served on the Production Board during the war, was again, for instance, seconded from the private sector to head the IDB. Before the Commons, Howe avowed that 'frank discussions' with the leaders of industry were the shortest route to joint confidence and cooperation.[85] The Dunn-Howe friendship again exemplified this pattern. While Howe frequently differed with Dunn on the degree of the government's obligation to business, he harboured a deep respect for the Algoma president, not only seeking his advice but at times even deputizing him to perform government functions.[86] Conversely, Dunn was quick to seek the minister's cooperation in coping with innumerable bureaucratic details, such as securing visas, tickets for the coronation, and even special preference in ordering a Vickers Viscount aircraft for his private use. When Howe purchased a home at St Andrews near Dunn's New Brunswick home, business confidences came to be frequently mingled with social niceties. Howe's whole approach to the problem of industial preparedness was to find the right men with the right ideas and trust that the desired results would inevitably follow from their actions. 'An industry,' he said in 1951, 'is built around a man with specialized skill and driving ability. Until that man comes forward to actively take charge there will never be a steel industry anywhere.'[87]

Throughout 1949 and 1950 a new *modus operandi* for business-government relations emerged. Although Howe frequently complained that it was 'impossible to create a feeling of urgency about getting on with defence production,' there were definite signs of progress. By 1949 the 'steel famine' had eased sufficiently for Ottawa to contemplate dismantling steel controls. 'The reason we have been cutting down the subsidies,' Howe announced in mid-1950, 'and plan to do away with them entirely at the end of this fiscal year, is that conditions are coming back to normal. ... We feel that we have bridged over the transitional period and allowed the steel plants to function as they did in pre-war days.'[88] Algoma and Dosco were both permitted to reenter the export trade and subsidies were limited to payments on semi-finished steel shipped from Dosco to central Canada. Reviewing the record of control, Howe vigorously defended steel control as the 'most necessary' of the transitional controls. At one point in 1949, Steel Control was subsidizing the monthly transfer of eighteen thousand tons of Algoma steel and ten thousand tons of Dosco steel to Hamilton. 'In other words,' Howe boasted, 'when conditions were abnormal we changed the geography of Canada.'[89] The relief was temporary.

The outbreak of the Korean War in mid-1950 once again strained national steel capacity to its limit and reintroduced the question of long-term expansion. Once again Howe applied his skills as an economic improviser. By late 1951 he had created a sense of common purpose between Ottawa and the steel industry and had fashioned policies and mechanisms which opened the way to a vastly expanded steel capacity in Canada. Cognizant of the strain that a forced growth of steel capacity would exert on the national economy, Ottawa opted for a more cautious, gradual approach to steel expansion. With this approach came agreement on the respective responsibilities of government and industry in the prospective expansion. After a meeting with Ottawa defence planners in January 1949, H.G. Hilton of Stelco reported that accord had been reached on an important principle: 'They also agreed that if, in the judgement of the industry, adequate capacity for peacetime needs exists and the government feels increased capacity necessary for national defence provision of such added capacity should not be the responsibility of private industry but that of the government.'[90]

Government's willingness to underwrite the risk of expansion met with Dunn's approval. Above all else, it obviated the necessity of seeking external financing by allowing Algoma to expand on the basis of ploughed-back profits and government incentives. Throughout the next few years Sir James kept Howe intimately informed of Algoma's progress towards greater capacity. In July 1950, for instance, the minister lunched in Dunn's private rail car in Ottawa and 'went over most things relating to Algoma.'[91] This frank and harmonious relationship was founded on Howe's implicit trust in 'the judgement of the industry.' 'Certainly we will have a steel industry that will be based on the requirements of this country,' he told the Commons in 1950, 'and our steel men will be delighted to put in the capacity to the full extent they are able to sell the product.'[92]

In the fall of 1950 Howe introduced the Essential Materials (Defence) Act 'to make sure that Canada's military program and Canadian international commitments with regard to preparedness and defence can be implemented without undue delay or disruption.' After outlining measures for allocation of essential materials and regulation of prices, Howe confidently predicted that steel would not need such strict controls because the primary producers were already 'working closely with the department.' The outbreak of war in Korea forced Howe to change course. In April 1951 he christened the new Defence Production Department in an attempt to centralize control over the government-assisted and -controlled portions of the economy. In November of the same year, 'end use' rationing of steel was introduced to ensure that war-related, essential industries had priority in the consumption of steel. Once again, government undertook to rationalize the shortcomings of a crucial sector of the private economy, undertaking to minimize its risks and implement a balanced industrial strategy unattainable by purely private initiative. 'Free enterprise has fallen down on the job on the production of steel,' CCF critic Clarie Gillis complained,[93] but for Dunn and Howe the new balance of responsibilities was simply a reflection of a mutually advantageous compromise between business and government.

Algoma profited handsomely from these new arrangements. Large volumes of traditional steelwares such as structural steel and shell steel were produced at the Sault to feed Canada's defence industries. At the same time, the corporation fully utilized special depreciation privileges extended by the government to facilitate a wholesale expansion in the early 1950s. Drawing on a loan from General Motors, Algoma embarked on a mammoth expansion and modernization of its coking facilities, blast furnaces, open hearths, and structural mills, and, most important, on the erection of a Morgan finishing mill. 'Today,' the shareholders were informed in 1953, 'you have an expanded capacity in coke ovens, blast furnaces, open hearths, and mills all the way down the line. Particularly outstanding is the increase in first class finishing capacity from 180,000 tons to 682,000 tons of which 120,000 tons is rail capacity.' In the 1954 production year, 80 per cent of Algoma's steel was rolled on equipment installed since 1942. Total costs of these additions by 1955 was $83 million.[94] Although Dunn had been instrumental in nurturing the atmosphere in which this expansion had occurred, it was David Holbrook who conceived and implemented the actual program in the face of his ageing president's increasing conservativism and not infrequent paranoia. Dunn's receptivity to any proposal for expansion or new product line was still coloured by the memory of the tinplate mill fiasco of the late 1930s. Sir James' relationship with even his senior executives was marked by a deep, almost irrational, fear of betrayal. This introduced a distinct dysfunctionalism into corporate planning. Algoma remained a one-man steel company subject to the whims of its irascible chief executive. To his credit, Dunn did realize that the modernization program urged on him by Howe and Holbrook represented the final step in the corporation's long campaign to rectify its lack of diversification. In doing this, Dunn knew that he was allowing his huge investment in Algoma to appreciate handsomely in value at a time when the financial burdens of expansion were defrayed by Ottawa's accelerated depreciation allowances. In late 1954, Sir James boasted to his old friend E.R. Peacock in London that of the capital already spent on Algoma expansion 'substantially more than half' had been amortized from earnings before tax.

The 1950–5 expansion program marked Algoma's coming of age as a steel producer. A combination of Dunn's frugal no-dividend policy, Holbrook's managerial competence, and the federal government's assistance finally enabled the corporation to exorcise the deficiencies that had limited and at times hobbled its productive and earning potential since the days of F.H. Clergue. In May 1954, Holbrook informed his president that Algoma was 'currently experiencing just about the lowest blast furnace cost of hot metal in the industry.' Furthermore, the cost of steel ingots was 'about the best of any mill in the Chicago, Detroit, Cleveland, Pittsburgh, or Valley Districts. Our problems are now mainly in expanding our markets and building up volume.'[95] The expansion and modernization of Algoma in the early 1950s were accompanied by similar government assistance to other Canadian steel producers, notably Stelco and Dofasco.[96]

This overall expansion fostered important technological changes in the Canadian steel industry. Continuous casting of steel ingots and oxygen steelmaking made an early appearance in Canada. Bolstered by Howe's assistance, Canadian steel was thus able to match the traditional advantages of American steelmakers and thereby maintain if not improve its continental competitiveness. By 1955, a level of productive capacity generally acceptable to both the industry and government had been attained in Canada. Howe was satisfied that the country had attained a practical level of steel sufficiency. Steel capacity, he told the Commons,

is to be 4,800,000 tons by 1955. At the present time consumption is about 5,500,000 tons. But there are certain types of steel Canada would never set out to produce. I have in mind, for instance, very heavy structural members. We have never supplied our full requirements, and I do not know if it is advisable to do so. It is just as well to have a margin of tonnage that we import in good time, and do not require in poor times – just a little cushion for our steel industry, which has a rather restricted market.[97]

By mid-decade 'big steel's' prospects for further government-assisted expansion were abruptly checked. The cessation of Korean hostilities and a post-war economic downturn allowed the relaxation of steel control regulations in 1954 and a deceleration of defence-oriented industrial expansion. 'I cannot arrange for accelerated depreciation for the next round of expansion,' Howe regretfully told Sherman of Dofasco in September 1955. Explaining that he had been pressured by the prime minister and finance minister, Howe said that he 'had to reluctantly concur with the views of the Government that special treatment must end.'[98] The national steel question continued to occupy Howe's attention. By early 1956, he concluded that further steel expansion was necessary. 'It seems to me that our steel industry must keep on building for some time to come,' he told Frank Sherman. 'Imports of steel and steel products are still about the largest items in our too large list of imports.'[99]

There was a cruel irony in the fact that the Trans-Canada pipeline project which Howe had so zealously promoted, and which largely brought about his political demise, was designed to stimulate continued steel consumption in Canada. 'I believe that we finally have won the battle of the pipeline,' he confided to Holbrook of Algoma in May 1956, 'which should mean business for all Canadian steel companies, probably enough to keep your mill reasonably full for some years.'[100] Pipeline construction did eventually open a new market for Algoma but it was to be product line built on an ignominious reversal of Howe's political fortune.

The growing resilience of Canadian steel in the years 1945–55 enabled Algoma to rectify other shortcomings that had plagued it since its insolvent early decades. Tariff and freight rates, the two contentious issues so frequently portrayed by pre-war management as prime impediments to corporate prosperity, progressively diminished in significance throughout these years. After repeated pre-war complaints about the tariff and freight rate schedules, post-war expansion and well-being finally afforded Algoma the opportunity of surmounting these two persistent barriers by less direct methods.

Algoma had emerged from the war with high hopes of utilizing its expanded capacity to exploit steel-hungry European markets. Blocked in this ambition by Ottawa's export sanctions, Dunn argued in 1947 that Canada 'should sell at least a million tons of steel abroad while she can and build up credits instead of keeping the steel at home and encouraging extravagance.'[101] Frustrated in his European ambitions, Dunn eyed the American market with equal ambition, noting in 1946 that Algoma's 'purpose is to preserve what advantage present tariffs give us unless the surrendering of any advantage is compensated by more favourable entrance to the larger American market.' While earlier Algoma presidents had ceaselessly pleaded for higher tariffs, Dunn now proclaimed that Algoma was 'not afraid of low tariffs or no tariffs at all.'[102] Algoma's road into the American market and to a more generous slice of the Canadian market lay increasingly in its ability to exploit improved productivity and the better economies of scale afforded by expansion rather than by the age-old Canadian remedy of tariff-tinkering.

Although Algoma did manage during the late 1940s to reestablish itself as a rail exporter, the decisive breakthrough into the American market for steel came in the Korean War period. Not only was Algoma able to market large quantities of its shell steel to American armament producers, but it concluded a highly advantageous, long-term supply deal with the General Motors Corporation of Detroit in May 1951. Conceived of by Holbrook, the idea of tying Algoma to a large American steel consumer at first aroused only suspicion in Dunn, ever on guard against challenges to his control of Algoma. GM's interest in Canadian steel was sparked by the American steel 'famine' – which peaked in the 1952 American steel strike – and the realization 'that Algoma was the only producer whose existing plant was susceptible to substantial expansion without going back into radical coke and blast furnace additions.'[103] This reasoning, coupled to the American corporation's offer to extend long-term financing for Algoma's expansion, gradually eroded Dunn's suspicions to the point that he actually visited GM president Charles

Wilson in Detroit. The ensuing contract, signed in May 1951, provided Algoma with a $15 million loan to be repaid with shipments of Algoma pig iron and semi-finished steel to GM and its Canadian subsidiaries down to the end of 1967. In one stroke, Algoma had penetrated the lucrative market for automotive sheet steel on both sides of the border. Dunn thereafter enthusiastically referred to GM as 'our greatest customer.' Together with Ottawa's depreciation allowances, the General Motors loan precluded any resort to external financing during the upcoming expansion program, a factor of great salience for a president unwilling to loosen his grip on corporate control at any cost.

Once it was able to compete with American steelmakers for some types of American demand, Algoma's concern for tariff restructuring waned considerably. Although Canada's four integrated steel producers petitioned Ottawa in 1954 for 'a modernization and simplification of the 1907 Customs Tariff,' they no longer employed the pretext of being an 'infant industry.' Their goal was now rationalization, rather than an intensification, of the tariff. Throughout the whole 1945–66 period the Canadian iron and steel tariff remained consistently at a 'moderate,' and at times 'low,' level of protection, indicating that improved economies of scale and increased productivity rather than heightened protection were more directly responsible for Canadian steel's post-war prosperity.[104] Further acknowledgment of Algoma's international competitiveness was won in May 1955, when Mannesmann AG, a German steel multinational, agreed to build a seamless tube works at the Sault, contracting Algoma to supply the raw steel for production. The Mannesmann deal was negotiated by Holbrook and, like the GM deal, allowed the company to capitalize on the demand by a growth sector of the Canadian economy. Algoma now had sufficient momentum to move with steel demand as it materialized. Gone were the days of 'do or die' reliance on rails.

From the perspective of the Algoma boardroom it was clear that the ability to produce steel on a continentally competitive basis had to be matched by an ability to assemble raw materials as cheaply as possible and to market its products competitively. Freight rates structured to cater to the needs of industrial Old Ontario had aroused Algoma's ire for decades. Furthermore, the steel company had always felt that its operations were completely at the mercy of the railways and shipping companies which carried its raw materials and finished products.[105] Like many of its American counterparts, Algoma began to consider the advantages of vertical integration to overcome its transportation difficulties. Thwarted in his wartime bid to gain control of the Algoma Central, Dunn concluded after the war that it was imperative for Algoma to break the monopoly of the railways and gain cheap entry to southern markets. 'From the days of Hepburn,' he reflected, 'I have wondered how we could make a similar inroad on the geographical privileges of Steel of Canada but never seem to be able to get anywhere which, perhaps, is the only reason why I have begun to feel that our only answer to the railways is Canada Steamship.'[106] As a director of the company since 1944, Dunn appreciated that the Canada Steamship fleet offered Algoma a means of assured transport for its ore and coal requirements, at the same time offering some competitive leverage on the railways. Dunn's ambition of using the CSL fleet primarily for upper-lakes traffic was repeatedly overruled by a majority of company directors whose inclination was to favour the needs of the lower-lakes customers and 'down river' traffic, a policy tailor-fit to Stelco's needs.

Infuriated by Canada Steamship's willingness to sign 'imbecile' contracts with Stelco, the Algoma president railed at the policies of the line's management, citing, among other follies, the profligacy of maintaining passenger service on the Great Lakes at a time when tourists were turning to airlines and cars.

Unable to have his way on the CSL board, Dunn struck out to seize financial control of the line. 'My present thought,' he concluded in 1948, 'is that we should take an interest big enough to swing the policy from down the river to the upper lakes as we must look ahead to people who can carry our coal and ore.'[107] This resolved, Dunn surreptitiously began buying CSL stock, a campaign for which his more than forty years of financial fast-dealing stood him in excellent stead. Dunn bought CSL stock on both his private accounts and Algoma's corporate account, a two-pronged assault that drove the selling price of CSL common from $15 to over $50 a share by 1950.[108] Only the disastrous fire on the *Noronic* (an incident which underscored Dunn's insistence that CSL abandon passenger service) reversed the stock's upward climb, albeit temporarily. Sir James' market operations were underwritten by generous lines of credit, frequently surpassing a million dollars, from the Royal Bank and the Bank of Montreal. At one point in 1951, Dunn incurred the wrath of the Royal Bank manager, W.E. McLaughlin, by overextending his credit line by $500,000 to a total of $1.5 million, in flat contradiction to the government's anti-inflationary freeze on loans to individuals for investment purposes. McLaughlin plaintively expressed a hope that Dunn would be 'quick to realize the sort of squeeze that we are in.'[109]

With assistance from Henry Gauer, a Winnipeg grain dealer also dissatisfied with CSL policies, and Montreal publisher J.W. McConnell,

Dunn worked Algoma into a position to exercise a controlling influence over the steamship company's affairs by April 1951. With control established, Dunn sold his personal holdings in CSL to Algoma at current market prices, an act of questionable financial propriety that yielded the president a handsome profit at the expense of his own company. After disposing of the old CSL board, Dunn turned to C.D. Howe for advice on the selection of a new steamship president. On the minister's advice, the presidency was given to T.R. 'Rodgie' McLagan, the wily former president of Canadian Vickers. As if to symbolize Algoma's victory, CSL's newest laker was christened the *S.S. Sir James Dunn* in late 1951. At the Port Arthur launching of the vessel, the largest yet built in Canada, Dunn claimed that the vitality of Canadian shipbuilding was 'a triumph of the man I admire most greatly,' namely the local MP, C.D. Howe.[110]

The assurance of steady deliveries of American coal and ore to the Sault by the Canada Steamship Line was reinforced by the outright acquisition of Yankcanuck Steamships Limited in April 1951. Engineered by Holbrook, the Yankcanuck deal provided Algoma with a small fleet of lakers capable of delivering finished steel to southern markets and, like the CSL deal, afforded Algoma some means of influencing Great Lakes freight rates. Dunn's determination to offset Algoma's geographical disadvantages in producing and marketing its products was further evidenced by the 1950 purchase of the Canadian Furnace Company in Port Colborne. Canadian Furnace gave Algoma additional pig iron capacity and carried the parent company's operations into the centre of industrialized Old Ontario. With control of two transportation subsidiaries and a beachhead in Canada's industrial heartland, Dunn congratulated himself that he had set the capstone in place on an Algoma 'empire,' an empire vertically integrated from iron mine to marketplace. In his more nostalgic moments, Sir James envisaged himself as the man who had brought order to the shambles of Clergue's brilliantly conceived but recklessly implemented industrial empire at the Sault. To author Alan Sullivan, Dunn confided the belief that he had unlocked Clergue's 'treasure house.' When David Holbrook suggested in 1955 that Algoma had achieved such economies of scale that it could now contemplate entering the American pipe market, Dunn revealingly replied:

This crossing of the River to the U.S. side is all in line with the original programme of that very great man Francis Hector Clergue. I think we are entitled to aim at taking and holding our place in both U.S. and Canadian markets. I can envisage a time – not too many years ahead – when we will have become, as far as necessary, equipped from the raw material to the finished product on both sides of the line. Our geographical position for this achievement is not equalled by any other Canadian steel enterprise.[111]

'Crossing the river to the U.S. side' had a much deeper significance than the fulfilment of a dream jointly held by Clergue and Dunn. It was one indication of the strong continentalist pressures that had pushed and at times engulfed the Canadian economy in the years since the war economy of the Second War had jolted North America out of the Depression. Canadian steel, stalwartly supported by the Canadian government, had met the American advance with a double response. The working consensus achieved between Howe and the leaders of Canadian steel in the years since 1940 had, in the first place, enabled Canada to build up sufficient productive capacity by the mid-1950s to reduce its previously high level of dependency on foreign steel imports. By 1955, 'big steel' in Canada was in a position to ward off the intrusion of all but the most specialized types of foreign steel by matching the costs, productivity, and economies of foreign producers and by incorporating technological advances in steelmaking at a comparatively rapid pace. As Howe had theorized before the Commons, steel imports now acted as a 'cushion,' absorbing marginal consumption in fat years and contracting in lean years. The Canadian steel industry had thus become an exemplary model of a National Policy 'infant industry' that had grown up able to displace imports, to compete abroad, and to retain a high degree of domestic control. Reaction to the pressures of continental integration at the extractive levels of the industry, on the one hand, followed a markedly different course.

Availability of high-grade American iron ore from the Superior ranges, coupled with the belief that Canada's iron ore was low-grade and inaccessible, had long precluded the development of a viable Canadian iron ore industry. Since the late 1930s low-grade Algoma sinter from the Helen mine had found its way to American blast furnaces, serving in a small way to offset Canada's heavy reliance on Mesabi ore. War and the accelerated depletion of high-grade domestic ores intensified American interest in Canada's iron ore potential. James Dunn had a formative influence on these developments. To George Humphrey of the Hanna Company he confided in 1947: 'Canada as a nation is increasingly concerned with iron ore. Our Minister [Howe] has discussed our low grade ore with me frequently lately and told me something of Labrador. I am anxious to learn as much about the latter as you can tell me. While you and I are still "young" men we must devote our energies vigorously to assuring North America of a plentitude of the raw materials from which to maintain our dominant position in the steel trade of the world.'[112]

For Dunn, the iron ore question had a deep personal importance that transcended pure economics and touched on the psychological mainsprings of his entrepreneurial motivation. The Helen mine in Dunn's mind symbolized not only the resurgence of a vital sector of Canadian mining but acted as a touchstone for a belief in his own vitality as an entrepreneur and his at times obsessive veneration of the hardy individualism he saw as central to North American society. 'Our Continent must maintain individual liberty,' he sermonized to Humphrey, 'and dominate the world to save it.'[113] Dunn's messianic fervour was intensified by his post-war realization that Britain had abandoned 'her old Imperial role,' leaving North Americans either to shoulder the burden 'or retreat and contract our vast production of trade and our own consuming powers.'[114] Unwilling to counsel retreat, Dunn advocated that North America gird itself with a strong resource base, a crucial sector of which was iron ore. 'I believe,' he told an audience in Sault, Michigan, in 1947, 'Divine Providence intended people of the two Saults to tie a knot between the two nations, so that together we will develop the vast wealth to the north of us and thus perpetuate into the distant future the dominance of North America in the industrial wealth, power and culture of the world. We North Americans should have no economic boundary lines.'[115] Often perplexed by the technical intricacies of steelmaking, Dunn could readily grasp the relatively simple act of ore extraction at the Helen and in time it came to assume an immense significance for him. 'I agree,' he told Beaverbrook in 1949, 'that the extent of the ore discoveries and of the developments gradually being made there far out-rank the importance of the Algoma Steel Company itself.'[116] Dunn's obsessive interest in Algoma's iron ore wealth frequently drove company managers to distraction. Instead of turning his attention to the business of steelmaking, the president basked in the glories of iron-mining. In 1954, he unsuccessfully plotted to change the name of Wawa to Jamestown. When the new town name was inscribed on the local post office, the citizens of Wawa pulled the letters off under cover of night. Sir James owned the Helen mine, but he did not own the town.

Dunn's predisposition for an integrated continental resource strategy was willingly reflected by fellow Canadian and American steelmen and by Ottawa politicians, although their motivations differed from that of the Algoma president. Desperate in their search for new ore sources,

American steel companies were scouring North and South America for exploitable ore bodies. In the opinion of George Humphrey, Canada's Steep Rock and Labrador iron ore projects proved alluring for more than geological reasons. American mining promoters, he explained, had great confidence in their 'friends in government in Canada and in the stability of the Canadian Government and economic condition.'[117] From Howe's perspective, a rejuvenated Canadian iron ore industry held out the prospect of diminishing Canada's long-standing dependency on American ore. Total national self-sufficiency in iron ore, he reasoned, was an impossibility, given the intricate mix of ores necessary to produce steel, many of which were unavailable in Canada. 'All ore goes into the Great Lakes pool,' Howe told the Commons in 1948. 'Our industry gets the ore it needs out of the pool and the United States industry gets the ore it needs. A steel company cannot operate on one class of ore.'[118] At other times Howe spoke of the ore trade as 'a national movement' that operates 'without trade restriction and as the economy dictates.' Echoing these sentiments, Dunn told the New York *Herald Tribune* that Americans must 'remove trade barriers between our two halves of North America; write "interchangeable" on the money of both countries.'[119] Drawn together by a common perspective on continental resources, Howe, Dunn, and Humphrey formed the nucleus of a strong transnational government-business lobby dedicated to exploiting the iron wealth of Quebec and Ontario. Joined by Jules Timmins, 'Charlie' Wilson of General Motors, Quebec premier Duplessis, and others, the group exerted a formative influence on the opening of a new Canadian mining frontier in the 1950s. Interest in mineral exploitation was intertwined with advocacy of other schemes for integrated continental development. Dunn became an outspoken proponent of the St Lawrence seaway proposal, arguing that 'all the guns, all the planes and all the gold would avail us nothing if iron ore were not available to 75% of the blast furnaces in the u.s.'[120]

Both Howe and Dunn insisted that the benefits of iron ore exploitation within this continental alliance be subject to an equitable reciprocity in which Canadian interests were well protected. Howe frequently reiterated his belief that Canadian entrepreneurs must 'do all they can to make Labrador a Canadian project.' In Dunn and the Helen mine at Wawa he found cause for considerable hope. By 1952, Algoma Ore Properties was able to market 1,232,006 tons of Algoma sinter, approximately half of which was shipped to American consumers.[121] A major expansion program, announced in late 1953, was geared to extract a further 50 million tons of ore from the Helen and its adjacent ore bodies. In the words of economist V.C. Wansbrough, iron ore held out 'the promise, power and potentiality of a giant'[122] to Canadians. By 1956, Canada mined 16.2 million tons of iron ore. In 1946, the country's mines had produced only 1.5 million tons.

If any one factor was to be singled out of the myriad of influences shaping the remarkable post-war advances of the Canadian steel industry, it would have to reflect the dynamic relationship that had developed between 'big steel' and the federal government since the outbreak of the Second War. At the centre of this business-government linkage was the relationship of Sir James Dunn and C.D. Howe. Not so much a friendship as a meeting of minds, the Dunn-Howe relationship welded the fortunes of Algoma Steel to the policies of Ottawa. In the face of this federal ascendancy, the influence of the Queen's Park government had dwindled, significant only as a factor in the securing of hydro power rights and in the simmering and inconclusive feud over the cancelled Hepburn iron ore bounty. The primacy of federal policies was the direct result of the ability of Howe and the steelmakers of Canada to agree upon mutually advantageous goals and mutually acceptable methods of achieving them.

The Dunn-Howe entente was never totally free of friction. On at least two occasions, in 1948 and 1951, Sir James clumsily intruded into the arena of federal politics, pressuring his old friend and former cabinet minister 'Chubby' Power to seek the national Liberal leadership in a bid to spite Howe. Dunn was annoyed with Howe in 1948 because 'some ruling of Howe's had caused difficulty for Algoma Steel.'[123] The tiff passed quickly. By the early 1950s minister and steel magnate shared a strong bond of trust and respect. Both came to speak of the fate of Algoma and the fate of Canada in the same sentence. For Dunn and Rodgie McLagan at Canada Steamship, Howe was 'the Great White Father' in Ottawa.[124] For Howe, Dunn amply substantiated his belief that millionaires were the artisans of national prosperity.[125] Dunn was not alone in fitting the minister's predilection for the rich and powerful. Howe's office in Ottawa and his fishing club at St Marguerite, Quebec, were frequented by North America's corporate élite. American businessmen learned to trust Howe as implicitly as their Canadian counterparts. Two of them, Charles Wilson of General Motors and George Humphrey of Hanna Mining, took up important executive positions in the Eisenhower administration. In Canada, men like R.E. 'Rip' Powell, the president of Alcan, relied on Howe for advice in shaping crucial sectors of the new Canadian economy. In a sense, these men stood apart from James Dunn. They were industrial managers, men who were paid to manage – albeit at princely salaries –

North America's corporate economy. Sir James Dunn drew a salary too, but it was a salary from his own company. This independence lent a special significance to the relationship of the two men who came to be neighbours in St Andrews.

Despite the closeness of their ties, Howe saw little conflct of interest between his role as a federal policy-maker and his status as confidant to a steel president. Throughout the early 1950s, for instance, he bought a sizeable holding of Algoma common stock in trust. He later sold these shares at a handsome profit when forced, as an executor of Sir James' estate, to surrender the investment. While Howe may have at times failed to make the subtle distinction between the good of James Dunn and the good of Algoma Steel, he by and large shared the Algoma president's view that the ends of business and government were largely synonymous. A year after Dunn's death in 1956, just before Sir James' massive Algoma holdings were parcelled out to a group of predominantly Canadian buyers, Howe reiterated his belief in this parallelism of interests to Lady Dunn: 'It seems to me that the transaction as now arranged is not only good for the Dunn estate but is also good for Canada.'[126]

Conclusion

In March 1954, an eager reporter from Beaverbrook's *Evening Standard* intercepted Sir James Dunn on his way to the boat train at the end of a visit to England. When asked his plans for the future, the seventy-nine-year-old steel magnate haughtily answered: 'I am going back to Canada to do more work.'[1] Throughout his last years, Dunn took a vainglorious pride in the success and longevity of his business career. When Ben Fairless stepped down from the presidency of US Steel in 1954, Dunn snidely cabled his best wishes: 'I send you warm greetings and every kind thought and think it all wrong that you retire at 65 while I go on in my small way at 80.'[2] This overweening self-esteem was for Dunn mingled with a growing sense of bitterness and isolation. He faced, on the one hand, what he perceived as the insidious 'slavery of bureaucracy,'[3] gnawing away at the hardy individualism he saw as the foundation of Western civilization. On the other hand, Dunn had to contend with the disheartening attrition of his old financial acquaintances. As he told 'Chubby' Power in 1950, 'The old group of merchant bankers who made London – and London made England – are all dead.'[4] Dunn combatted these dyspeptic observations by redoubling his efforts at Algoma and intensifying his vigilance over his many other business involvements. He conducted himself as if he and the values he embodied would endure forever. The Canadian public certainly perceived the ageing and eccentric mogul of Canadian steel in this heroic light. Dunn was, in the words of *Maclean's*, 'the last of the multimillionaires.'[5] After proposing a feature story on Dunn's long career, a bumptious young Canadian reporter assured the steel president in 1950 that 'it would be a nice way of putting forward a little propaganda about the merits of our economic system. The Horatio Alger story still excites.'[6] Sir James, as the *Globe and Mail* later eulogized, 'was among the last of a type once common in North America – the totally self-made man.'[7] Until within two days of his death, Sir James Dunn continued to trade heavily and frequently on the Montreal and Toronto stock exchanges. There was always money to be made. 'Sir James not only made money,' Beaverbrook noted in *The Three Keys to Success*, 'he enjoyed money. He lived usefully and he died rich.'

In many ways, Dunn was a member of a dying breed of North American capitalists. The fame that Sir James attracted during his last years at Algoma was no doubt occasioned by the knowledge that his feat of monolithic control at Algoma was unlikely ever to be duplicated. By the mid-1950s, the odds of any would-be successor's retracing Dunn's illustrious path to wealth and corporate power had been diminished by obstacles thrown up by a changed capitalist system. Dunn had himself sensed that the times were changing. Since the Ives Royal Commission of 1945 first scrutinized the structure of Canadian income taxation, the financial rights and privileges of 'closely held' corporations, such as Algoma, had come under increasing pressure for reform.[8] As one member of parliament pointed out in 1953:

I have no hesitation in mentioning in the House the great Algoma Steel Company which issues an unconsolidated balance sheet from which you cannot get any information about its subsidiaries. Whether Sir James Dunn likes it or not, there are some subsidiaries of Algoma Steel which are making as much money as Algoma Steel itself. Yet this Company has not paid any dividends to its shareholders for over 20 years. ... How can you expect people to participate in our industries unless there is a law to protect the investments of our people?[9]

The key to much of Dunn's success in revivifying Algoma had lain in his power to allocate corporate profits arbitrarily. At times, Sir James' adherence to a policy of no dividends made him the envy of other Canadian industrialists. R.S. McLaughlin of General Motors Canada, for instance, praised Dunn for his 'ability to "plough back" such a large percentage of [his] earnings.'[10] Dunn's position of control was increasingly threatened in the late 1940s and early 1950s by changes in the income tax and company laws of Canada. The federal finance minister, D.C. Abbott, noted in 1950 as he introduced new taxation regulations on undistributed income, 'It appears to me as sensible to encourage these family corporations to pay reasonable dividends while at the same time making it possible for them to retain profits essential for growth and expansion without imposing on shareholders an almost impossible potential tax burden.'[11] New taxes plugging old loopholes, the creeping incidence of personal and corporate taxes, and the ever-insistent call for dividends from Algoma's long-suffering minority shareholders all combined to make Dunn's style of financial control and management increasingly untenable.[12]

Dunn's style of business leadership was also vitally challenged by the escalating complexity of modern business enterprise. A financial manager of superlative calibre, Dunn progressively found himself out of his depth in the myriad technicalities involved in the management of a modern steel plant. In fact, Dunn's inability to grasp or act on many of the pressing demands for modernization confronting the steel industry in the 1950s frequently introduced a dysfunctional element into Algoma's corporate planning, much to the chagrin of the firm's senior executives. Decision-making at Algoma was never systematically delegated as it was in most modern corporations. All decisions, whether large or small, were routed across Sir James' desk. Algoma's managers were all motivated by a strong fear of their president's intemperate outbursts. In Dunn's mind, even an incidental matter of policy could easily take on huge significance. Only David Holbrook, Algoma's senior manager, developed the knack of working around Dunn's iron will or at least making it more malleable. Holbrook's success in this respect was a reflection of the trust invested in him by C.D. Howe. Sir James instinctively followed the minister's suit.

Construction of the corporate decision-making process was made worse by Dunn's peripatetic lifestyle. He seldom visited the Sault, and when he did, he spent much of his time at the Helen mine in Wawa rather than at the steelworks. Algoma executives were therefore obliged to seek out their president in unaccustomed places. In his late years, Dunn travelled widely, frequently flying according to a schedule of his own making in his private DC-3. At times he was at 'Dayspring,' his home in St Andrews, New Brunswick. On other occasions he might be found in England, at the Ritz-Carlton in Montreal, or in New York, socializing with artistic friends such as Salvador Dali or Ed Sullivan at his private table at Le Pavillon Restaurant. Holbrook's monthly long-distance telephone bill often totalled $1500. When the DC-3 did make an appearance in the sky over the Sault, mixed emotions of relief and trepidation spread through the company's head office. Even in the boardroom, Dunn's attention was never wholly assured. In one notorious incident, Dunn absent-mindedly left the Sault in his DC-3 before the company's annual meeting was convened. Without the voting power of the president's huge stockholding, the meeting became an absurdity and had to be postponed.

As long as Dunn lived, Algoma was fated to be managed along idiosyncratic lines. As a steel president, however, Sir James did possess certain unique advantages. His overwhelming control of the corporation allowed him to dispense with any pretence of corporate democracy. This could facilitate expeditious handling of corporate policy, provided the policies made sense. Even in his late years, Sir James retained a keen mind for financial affairs. As the General Motors loan and the federal government's special depreciation allowances illustrated, Dunn never lost the art of spreading financial risk. Dunn's one incomparable advantage lay in his friendship with C.D. Howe. Ready access to the minister's office and the consequent bestowal of the federal government's confidence on Algoma were prerequisites of the company's post-war expansion.

When Ben Fairless departed the US Steel Corporation in 1954, he grudgingly noted that 'the trouble with the old-time management was that it was just a little too individualistic.' Acknowledging that 'the lone wolf genius' had given birth to many of the giants of American steel, Fairless nevertheless insisted that the time had come for professional management: 'Some critics – *Fortune* magazine is one of them – deplore the fact that all businessmen today seem to be modest and polite duplicates of one another instead of flamboyant "characters" as in the old days. But you cannot have it both ways, and today's man in the gray flannel suit is ten times more efficient than his more colorful, more hot tempered predecessor.'[13] Such was the case at Algoma. Having boldly created the new company in 1935 in an act that bore all the marks of the classic Schumpeterian entrepreneur, Dunn was never willing to let what Alfred Chandler has described as the 'visible hand' of modern management fully intrude into Algoma's affairs. He remained a 'lone wolf' until his death. Yet the ultimate success of the whole Sault enterprise undeniably lay not with the captains of industry like Clergue and Dunn, but with the trained professional managers. While financial control would always be the ultimate seat of authority, technocratic expertise governed the day-to-day success of the investment. As J.K. Galbraith has perceptively noted: 'Thus what the entrepreneur created passed inexorably beyond the scope of his authority. He could build. And he could exert influence for a time. But his creation, were it to serve the purposes for which it was brought into being, required his replacement. What the entrepreneur created, only a group of men sharing specialized information could ultimately operate.'[14]

In December 1954, Sir James used his annual Christmas radio broadcast to the people of the Sault to announce that he had no intention of retiring from the presidency of Algoma Steel. In passing, he mentioned that David Holbrook would be his eventual successor when and if the occasion ever arose. For Holbrook the presidency must have at times seemed a very distant prospect. Throughout the early 1950s, Dunn displayed remarkable vitality, interrupted only by a hernia operation in 1952. A lifetime regimen of vitamin supplements and wholesome food, Dunn was quick to inform his admirers, gave him deep reservoirs of strength. Yet, during the autumn of 1955, there were alarming signs that the reservoirs were running dry. Just before Christmas, Sir James suffered a thrombosis and the medical specialists were called to 'Day-spring.' The holiday passed without further crisis but on the morning of New Year's Day, another thrombosis struck. Lying in bed, Dunn seemed to sense that the end was near. 'Hallo, kid,' he said to his wife, Christofor, 'Don't let me go.'[15] And then he died. Almost immediately, Lady Dunn had the body loaded onto the DC-3 and flown from St Andrews to Saint John for cremation at Fernhill Cemetery. Such was the haste of this operation that a death certificate was not obtained. The lack of a certificate and the fact that Dunn had died just before the weekend obliged Lady Dunn to have Sir James' body brought back to St Andrews. Cremation and interment eventually took place early the next week. A handful of close friends attended the private ceremony. Beaverbrook, Dunn's closest friend, was in Jamaica. He had flown to Miami to talk to his boyhood friend by telephone just before he died. 'We have lost Sir James Dunn,' Beaverbrook reported shortly thereafter to Churchill; for years to come the thought of his departed friend created a strong sense of nostalgia in him.[16] 'Sir James Dunn had tremendous faith in himself and in Canada,' the *Globe and Mail* noted in its tribute to the dead millionaire, 'and because of it left Canada a tremendous inheritance.'[17] Early in 1956, Dunn's heirs learned that their inheritance was to be just over $66 million. Dunn left nothing to charity.

In the wake of Sir James' death, Algoma's transition from 'one-man' steel company to technocratic corporation was overseen by C.D. Howe, D.S. Holbrook, and the corporate lawyers. Howe saw his status as an executor of the Dunn estate not only as an act of personal loyalty to a friend, but as a national duty. After hurriedly divesting himself of his own Algoma holdings, Howe devoted his prodigious energy to the management and disbursement of Sir James' massive controlling block of Algoma common shares. Although Dunn had bequeathed his entire estate to his widow and children, Howe speedily concluded that there could be no question of their assuming executive control at the Sault. 'I think,' he confided to David Holbrook shortly after Sir James' death, 'we can agree that none of the heirs should continue in charge of the property.'[18] The time had come for Algoma to be managed by professional steelmen alone. In Howe's opinion, David Holbrook was 'the one man able to represent the value of the property in terms acceptable to another steel man and answer the questions that a steel man would ask.'[19] Consequently, Holbrook acted as Howe's lieutenant throughout the ensuing negotiations for the sale of Dunn's controlling interest in Algoma. In May 1956 Holbrook was elevated to the Algoma presidency – an appointment that Howe was quick to describe as 'long overdue.'[20] Holbrook's only possible rival for the post was Dunn's lone son, Philip. While he inherited his father's baronetcy, Sir Philip Dunn showed little inclination to abandon the social advantages of life in England. Sir Philip thus remained an Algoma director but took little interest in his father's company.

Howe's initial actions as an executor were shaped by the pressing necessity of paying the succession duties on the estate, a payment estimated at about $35 million.[21] Only by disbursing some, if not all, of their Algoma holdings could the heirs hope to satisfy this heavy obligation imposed by the state. More important, Howe was vitally concerned that control of Algoma should devolve into responsible hands. With the news of Dunn's passing, and the sudden hopes of dividends from a profitable company, the price for Algoma leapt dramatically upwards. In the very act of dying, Dunn had unwittingly created his last 'bull' market. Howe feared that in such a volatile market, Algoma might fall victim to unscrupulous interests that could use the controlling block of shares 'to raid the finances of the company.'[22] 'I think,' he advised Holbrook, 'it would be better for Algoma to have ownership that is better able to supply the capital needs of the company for development.'[23]

Howe's search for the 'right customer,' or, as Lady Dunn called it, 'the dynamic bid,' lasted until April 1957.[24] In the interim the Dunn block of shares attracted immense interest in the business and political world. After twenty years of Dunn's careful husbanding of corporate finances, control of Algoma seemed a lucrative and enticing investment opportunity in many eyes, especially in view of the significant expansion and 'rounding out' of its facilities which had occurred during the early 1950s. Howe and the executors, aided and advised by Holbrook and various corporate lawyers, were confronted with a wide range of interested purchasers. American steel companies, notably Inland Steel and the M.A. Hanna Company, eyed the Sault works as a prospective Canadian beachhead for their operations. European firms, like the German steel multinational Mannesmann AG, similarly viewed Algoma as an entrée into the expanding Canadian market. Within Canada, financial coteries, ranging from E.P. Taylor and associates to McIntyre Porcupine Mines, plotted and schemed to seize control at Algoma. Discussions were held throughout the spring of 1957 with all these parties against a backdrop of incessant journalistic speculation. Finally, on 18 April, the executors met for the last time to preside over the breaking-up of Sir James' financial empire. In a transaction involving $60 million, a half-million Algoma common shares were sold in blocks to Mannesmann AG, A.V. Roe Canada Ltd, McIntyre Porcupine Mines, and the Royal Bank. The Dunn heirs retained a small remnant of their previous holdings. No one party held controlling interest, although Mannesmann and A.V. Roe possessed the largest blocks.[25] As if to symbolize their manumission from Dunn's rule, the Algoma directors immediately split the stock 4:1 and voted the first common share dividend since 1935.

In the Commons, Howe was much criticized for his role as an executor of the Dunn estate. Noting that Howe was occupying the trade and commerce portfolio at the same time as he was involved in determining Algoma's fate, Conservative Donald Fleming alleged that the minister was guilty of 'a fundamental moral conflict.'[26] Howe answered his critics by asserting that his ties with Algoma through the estate were only 'fiduciary' and that he had 'no financial interest in any asset of the estate.'[27] When the Opposition continued its campaign of insinuation, Howe angrily defended himself. He had never endured criticism tolerantly. 'If every little twerp – excuse me – someone who is just out of kindergarten can get up here and slander me as he likes, I do not like it.'[28] By April 1957, Howe's patience was so thin on the subject of the Dunn estate that he simply shouted 'Nuts!' across the House floor in response to his persistent critics.[29] In C.D. Howe's mind there was no conflict of interest between his obligation to the late Sir James and the affairs of state. While the Opposition searched vainly for evidence that the minister had abused his position as an executor of the estate, Howe assured himself that the only profit he had exacted was for Canada. He repeatedly talked of Algoma as 'a great Canadian asset' that could not be squandered in a fit of rashness. 'I do not want to see control of this company pass outside of Canada,' Howe proclaimed on the eve of the final sale. 'I think I have been influential in preventing any trend in that direction.'[30]

The faith that C.D. Howe placed in the Algoma enterprise throughout the transition of ownership was amply justified over the next two decades. The effects of the business-government consensus that had formatively moulded the tremendous expansion of the Canadian steelmaking in the early 1950s continued to be felt into the 1960s, well after both Dunn and Howe had gone to their graves. 'Had Sir James appeared here today,' David Holbrook declared at the hearings of the Royal Commission on Canada's Economic Prospects in January 1956, 'the Commission would have the greatest possible proof of unalterable belief in the future of the Canadian Iron and Steel Industry.'[31] The succeeding twenty years bore witness to this faith in the Canadian steel industry in terms of buoyant demand, steady profits, and high operating ratios. The vitality of Canadian steel had provided Canada with a model of competitive and domestically controlled primary industry in an economy that has all too frequently suffered from foreign ownership and low productivity.

The health of Canadian steel was readily attested to by the 1957 Report of the Royal Commission on Canada's Economic Prospects. At the extractive level of the industry, the Gordon Commission pointed with satisfaction to Canada's new-found status as an iron ore exporter and predicted that iron ore was 'likely to show the greatest increase in volume from the 1955 level over the next quarter century with a fivefold to sixfold expansion.' Steel production, the commissioners reported, had become 'a soundly-based and strong contributor to the Canadian economy' and could be 'expected to triple in the twenty-five year period.'[32] These conclusions coincided with the 'bright picture' foreseen for Canadian steel by Algoma in its brief to the commission. By Algoma's calculations, Canadian steel capacity would grow to 11 million tons by 1975, by which time it would cater to 85 per cent of domestic steel requirements.[33] The Gordon Commission's conclusions were reinforced and amplified by a wholesale investigation of the steel tariff conducted by the Tariff Board in 1957. While conceding that the ageing 1907 steel tariff was in need of some simplification, the Tariff Board praised the competitiveness of Canadian steel producers and suggested that 'in the case of not a few important lines of basic steel, the industry today practically disregards the tariff.'[34]

By the late 1960s and early 1970s the optimistic predictions of the mid-1950s had been largely realized. 'The Canadian primary iron and steel industry,' observed one economist in 1969, 'scores high both by the standards of performance of the Canadian economy and by the tests one can devise for comparing industries across international boundaries. It is an industry that has surged ahead, from its modest beginnings as a small, tariff-protected industry, to become a reasonably large giant (ranking tenth in world output of raw steel in 1966) able for the most part ... to stand on its own feet internationally.'[35] In 1974, the Steel Profits Inquiry conducted by Mr Justice Willard Estey was moved to much the same conclusion. 'This is an industry uniquely Canadian,' Estey concluded. 'It is almost entirely owned and financed by Canadians. It is an unusual phenomenon in our community in that it produces a manufactured product at prices currently below the United States, Western European and Japanese levels. There are few industries, or manufactured products, if any at all, in Canada today about which this can be said.'[36] Such evidence of the vigour of Canadian steel continues to the present day.[37] While the early 1980s have not been auspicious times for world steelmakers, the Canadian industry has weathered economic depression far better than its American and British counterparts.

Since the death of Sir James, Algoma Steel has not lagged in the steady process of Canadian steel. From 1956 to 1966 net annual earnings at the Sault climbed steadily from $15.7 million to $24.8 million, with only slight recessions in 1958 and 1960. Through the same period, net earnings as a percentage of total income averaged a very respectable 11 per cent. Such financial performance was made possible not only by the buoyant and expanding demand for steel generated by the Canadian economy but also by the solid financial patrimony bequeathed to the company by Sir James Dunn, whose conservative, if outwardly stingy, fiscal policies gave Algoma a sturdy foundation on which to expand. Although dividends were regularly paid after 1957, the company still managed to devote $195,905,000 to expanding its capacity in the years 1952 to 1962. Such spending ensured that the Sault steelworks remained at the forefront of steelmaking technology. In 1957, Algoma became the eighth major steel producer in the world to adopt the revolutionary and highly efficient oxygen steelmaking process and, a decade later, introduced the cost-saving continuous casting method to its mills. Such progress helped Algoma to overcome, finally and decisively, its long-standing problems in diversifying its product line. In 1952, Algoma was able to compete for only 25 per cent of the Canadian steel trade, but by 1963, with its new array of primary and finishing equipment, it was a keen competitor for 68 per cent of the trade. Steel rails, the old centre-piece of Algoma's market offerings, had by 1966 withered to 7 per cent of total sales. Algoma, after Dunn's death, continued to play a leading role in the reawakening Canadian iron ore industry. Relying on both its own mines and free market purchases, the company drew ore from its own Michipicoten mines, Steep Rock, and various American mines, including the Tilden mine in which it holds part ownership. When the venerable Helen mine was finally closed in 1962, its place was taken by the Sir James and George W. MacLeod mines. The progress of steel at the Sault over the last two decades has, by any yardstick, been remarkable and, while the credit to a large degree belongs to its present, competent management, few can forget, as the Sault *Daily Star* told its readers in 1956, that it is still 'The House Sir James Rebuilt.'[38]

The post-war success of the Canadian steel industry provides one of the few examples of a Canadian industrial strategy which has actually worked. This success was in large measure built on the consensus which had developed between the federal government and 'big steel' in Canada since the beginning of the Second World War. The ability of politicians, bureaucrats, and steelmen to determine the guiding principles of the industry's expansion provided steel management with the crucial advantage of a secure investment climate. While the chummy relationship of Howe and Dunn was never duplicated, the men managing Canada's three major steel companies have continued to enjoy open and generally cooperative relations with Ottawa. Given this overriding security, they were able to embark on strategies that enabled them to maximize their companies' chances of success.[39] The decline of the American steel industry in these same years provides an example of 'a failed industrial strategy.' From the time of President Truman's confrontation with the American steel industry during the Korean War, American steelmen have never enjoyed the kind of workable business-government consensus which has prevailed in the Canadian steel industry. In the words of one observer of the American steel industry, 'we simply limp from one crisis to the next, uncertain of where we are going, and how to get there. Strategy formulation, such as it is, remains firmly within the private sector. The end result is often economic chaos, confrontation and decline.'[40] As a consequence, the American steel industry was fatally slow in adopting new technologies such as oxygen steelmaking and continuous casting.[41] By the mid-1970s America found itself challenged as the world's leading steelmaker by countries like Brazil, Japan, South Korea, and Canada where greater cooperation had prevailed between government and the steelmakers.

When Sir Leonard Tilley brought down his 1879 National Policy budget, he spoke in terms of the necessity of cladding his young nation in some industrial armour: 'We find in every country, no matter what country it is – take England for instance, take France or any other country that has risen to any position of wealth and commercial greatness – and you will find the iron interest is one of the most important interests of that country. I would also instance the United States. It may safely be said that it is the basis of every other industry. It is true we have not developed it to a great extent yet.'[42] In the minds of many late-nineteenth-century Canadian nationalists, iron and steel occupied an important, symbolic position. It loomed large as a *sine qua non* in their schemes for national survival. 'In the great age of steel this was the fondest of hopes,' two historians have recently noted. 'Iron and steel production was at once the prestige symbol of industrialization and the base of any respectable industrial power.'[43]

If the vision and hopes of Macdonald, Tilley, and the National Policy have in large measure been fulfilled by the Canadian steel industry, the journey from conception to reality does not lend itself to simple explanation. The fluctuating fortunes of Algoma Steel and its parent industry have been governed by an intricate skein of influences. The relationship of steel industry and state has been, however, of overarching importance. The Canadian steel industry attained its maturity with the cooperation of the state, not in spite of it. Government at all three Canadian levels initially served to stimulate and protect the nascent industry. As early as the 1830s, the owners of the Marmora Iron Works had, for instance, petitioned the government for assistance in the form of improved transportation and prison labour. The pattern continued. F.H. Clergue turned to Ottawa for bounties, tariff changes, and grants for railway construction. Where Ottawa was constitutionally powerless, Clergue looked to Queen's Park for assistance in developing the province's natural resources. Several decades later Sir James Dunn trod the same path. Mitchell Hepburn supplied the crucial legislated sanction which allowed Dunn to clinch his 1935 takeover of the bankrupt Sault corporation. From C.D. Howe, Dunn sought and won wartime contracts, subsidies, and special depreciation allowances. If the Canadian steel industry has achieved a high level of diversified self-sufficiency, much of the credit must go to this confluence of private and public ambitions to promote its growth.

The political will underlying the establishment of the Canadian steel industry was rooted in the desire to achieve certain national and regional goals. Regional development, job creation, and the promotion of a well-rounded industrial base all weighed heavily in the balance of federal and provincial policy-making. From the economic point of view, a healthy steel industry offered inviting multiplier effects in the shape of employment, natural resource development, and import displacement. Businessmen like Clergue and Dunn were able to co-opt these public ambitions and to press them into the service of private capital. They learned to flatter politicians' ambitions with their schemes of development for private profit. When circumstances compelled them, they also mastered the art of appealing to politicians' sense of expediency and were not averse to playing one level of Canadian government off against another. Capitalists sought to enlist the assistance of the state because the state had the power to diminish their risk and to influence the external circumstances of their investment. Politicians willingly participated in such partnerships because they served national ends. Laurier tolerated Clergue's flamboyance because the Sault enterprise flattered the federal government's economic ambitions. C.D. Howe's support of Sir James Dunn was similarly predicated on the belief that Algoma could further national ends – initially winning the war and subsequently building a continentally integrated economy.

The Canadian steel industry found its origins in this meeting of government vision and business ambition. Ultimately, however, it was prescient men like Clergue and Dunn who set the course for Canadian steel, leaving government to respond to their bold and often devious entrepreneurial exploits. The cost of their achievement was often high, devastatingly high when measured in terms of jilted investors, absentee ownership, and meagre wages, but it was their actions, never as heroic as they painted them, that at root accounted for the eventual success of Canadian steel.

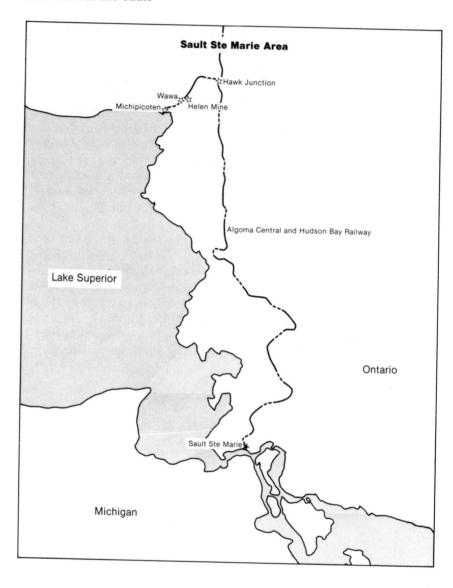

Sault Ste Marie Area

☆Hawk Junction

Wawa☆

Michipicoten ☆ Helen Mine

Algoma Central and Hudson Bay Railway

Lake Superior

Ontario

Sault Ste Marie

Michigan

The Consolidated Lake Superior Corporation, 1897-1904

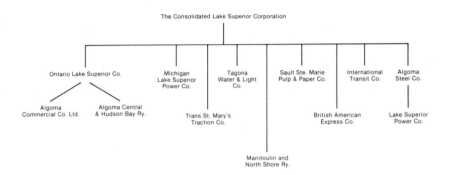

The Lake Superior Corporation and Its Related Companies: 1928

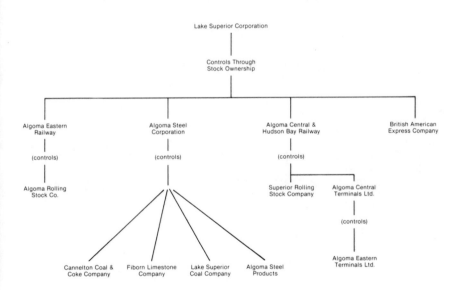

The Algoma Consolidated Corporation and Its Related Companies: 1931-4

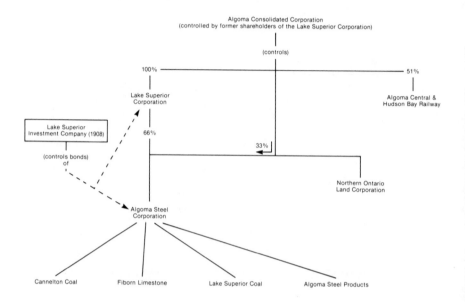

The Algoma Steel Corporation (1934): 1935-56

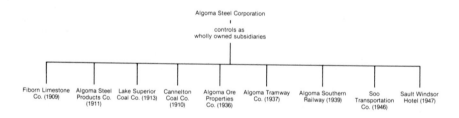

Notes on Sources

The Sir James Dunn Papers at the Public Archives of Canada served as the principal source of information for this book. A massive collection of just over four hundred volumes, the Dunn Papers afford the historian an intimate understanding of Sir James' business and private affairs from 1905, when he transferred his financial operations to London, to the day of his death in 1956. Filed with meticulous thoroughness, these volumes contain copies of all incoming and outgoing correspondence relating to Dunn's activities and interests in any given week thoughout his long career. In the period after Dunn's assumption of the Algoma presidency in 1935, the papers disclose an excellent record of how Dunn managed the last 'one-man' steel company in North America, a record ranging from the president's pedantic concern over trivial details to multi-million-dollar investment decisions.

The Dunn Papers have a significance beyond their immediate relevance for Algoma's history. They offer a unique window on the evolution of the modern Canadian economy and its business community. The collection reflects a business career that spanned more than half a century of national growth, wartime upheaval, and economic depression. Dunn's papers begin with correspondence with the great railway barons of the turn of the century, Sir William Van Horne and Sir William Mackenzie, and conclude with letters exchanged with Canadian businessmen like E.P. Taylor and J.A. 'Bud' McDougald, the mid-century wizards of corporate Canada.

F.H. Clergue's career is less easily traced. Clergue left no consolidated body of papers. His wandering entrepreneurial trail must instead be picked up in the papers of various politicians and in the press. The Laurier Papers at the Public Archives of Canada provide an especially illuminating picture of the American's activities in Ottawa. The chronicle of Clergue's activities is thus a patchwork – a documentary fate which often awaits those who fail.

Historical records retained by Algoma Steel provided a supplement to the Dunn Papers. Company files, for instance, furnished the most detailed account of the earliest years of the Sault enterprise, especially the support rendered by the local municipality and Ontario provincial government. Correspondence and directors' minute books from the Lake Superior Corporation provided a revealing picture of Algoma's original absentee owners, meeting in New York and Philadelphia hotels to discuss the fortunes of their distant and often ailing investment. Reports of Algoma general managers at the Sault eloquently testified to the operational shortcomings of the mill and the never-ending and at times desperate search for markets; as such, they provided an excellent barometer to measure the progress of a crucial primary industry against the fluctuating performance of the national economy. During the period of Dunn's presidency, 1935–56, the Algoma records provide striking testimony of the totality of Dunn's grasp on corporate affairs. Company papers also yield a record of Algoma's ongoing relations with its bankers, lawyers, and shareholders, as well as its formal dealings with Canadian governments in matters of tariff, freight rates, and resources policy, although the informal relationships cultivated by Dunn underlying these delicate issues are better revealed in the Dunn Papers.

Other collections consulted include:

MANUSCRIPT COLLECTIONS

Public Archives of Canada
R.B. Bennett Papers
R.L. Borden Papers
A.K. Cameron Papers
L.C. Christie Papers
R. Dandurand Papers
J.W. Flavelle Papers
C.D. Howe Papers
W.L.M. King Papers
W. Laurier Papers
J.A. Macdonald Papers
J. Malcolm Papers
A. Meighen Papers
W.T. White Papers

Public Archives of Ontario
E.C. Drury Papers
G.H. Ferguson Papers
W.H. Hearst Papers
G.R. Henry Papers
M.F. Hepburn Papers
J.A. McPhail Papers
G.W. Ross Papers
J.P. Whitney Papers

Queen's University Archives
T.A. Crerar Papers
C.A. Dunning Papers
J.W. Flavelle Papers
C.G. Power Papers

House of Lords Record Office
Beaverbrook Papers

PUBLIC RECORDS

Public Archives of Canada
RG 19: Department of Finance Records
RG 27: Department of Labour Records
RG 28: Department of Munitions and Supply and Department of Reconstruction Records
RG 30: Canadian Northern Railway Company Records
RG 33: Royal Commissions
RG 36: Boards, Offices and Commissions Records
RG 49: Department of Defence Production Records

Public Record Office, London
Foreign Office Files, especially FO 371 and FO 382.

Notes

ABBREVIATIONS

ABTT	Advisory Board on Tariffs and Taxation
ASC	Algoma Steel Corporation
CAR	*Canadian Annual Review*
CJEPS	*Canadian Journal of Economics and Political Science*
CLS	Consolidated Lake Superior Corporation
CSL	Canadian Steamship Line
DBS	Dominion Bureau of Statistics
DHC	*Debates of the House of Commons*
DP	Dunn Papers
FO	Foreign Office
HLRO	House of Lords Record Office
ISC	*Iron and Steel of Canada*
JHD	James Hamet Dunn
LSC	Lake Superior Corporation
MTA	*Monetary Times Annual*
PAC	Public Archives of Canada
PAO	Public Archives of Ontario
PRO	Public Record Office
RG	Record Group

INTRODUCTION

1 *Report of the Consultative Task Force on the Canadian Iron and Steel Industry,* chairman A.V. Orr (Department of Industry, Trade and Commerce, Ottawa, 1978), 1.

2 John J. Shepherd, *The Transition to Reality – Directions for Canadian Industrial Strategy* (Ottawa, 1980), 20.

CHAPTER ONE

1 E.C. Guillet, *Early Life in Upper Canada* (Toronto, 1963), and M.Q. Innis, 'The Industrial Development of Ontario, 1783–1820,' in *Papers and Records of the Ontario Historical Society*, 34 (1937), 105–13.
2 Albert Tessier, *Les Forges Saint Maurice 1729–1883* (Trois Rivières, 1952).
3 T. Ritchie, 'Joseph Van Norman, Ironmaster of Upper Canada,' *Canadian Geographical Journal*, 77:2 (Aug. 1969), 46–51; F.E. Leonard, 'The Normandale Furnace, 1829,' *Papers and Records of the Ontario Historical Society*, 20 (1923), 92–3; Senator Alex McCall, 'Normandale and the Van Normans,' ibid., 94–7; W.J. Patterson, 'The Long Point Furnace,' *Papers and Records of the Ontario Historical Society*, 41 (1944), 70–8, and A.H. Lang, 'Discovery and Benefits of the Marmora Iron Deposit,' *Canadian Mining Journal*, Aug. 1970.
4 D. Eldon, 'American Influence in the Canadian Iron and Steel Industry' (PH D thesis, Harvard University, 1952), 27.
5 Gerald Tulchinsky, *The River Barons: Montreal Businessmen and the Growth of Industry and Transport 1837–53* (Toronto, 1977), 20–6, and B.H. Scott, 'The Story of Silver Islet,' *Ontario History*, 49: 3 (1957).
6 J.H. Bartlett, *The Manufacture, Consumption and Production of Iron, Steel and Coal in the Dominion of Canada* (Montreal, 1885), 27.
7 David Landes, *The Unbound Prometheus: Technological Change and Industrial Development in Western Europe from 1750 to the Present* (London, 1970), 249–50; J.C. Carr and W. Taplin, *History of the British Steel Industry* (Cambridge, Mass., 1962).
8 See W.W. Rostow, *The Stages of Economic Growth* (London, 1960), chp. 4, and R.W. Fogel, *Railroads and American Economic Growth: Essays in Econometric History* (Baltimore, 1964), chps. 5 and 6.
9 W.T. Hogan, *Economic History of the Iron and Steel Industry in the United States* (Lexington, Mass., 1971), 1: 13, 40, and 117.
10 Alfred D. Chandler, Jr, *The Visible Hand: The Managerial Revolution in American Business* (Cambridge, Mass., 1977), 296. See also Jeanne McHugh, *Alexander Holley and the Makers of Steel* (Baltimore, 1980).
11 As quoted in Peter Temin, *Iron and Steel in Nineteenth Century America: An Economic Inquiry* (Cambridge, Mass., 1964), 23.
12 O.J. McDiarmid, *Commercial Policy in the Canadian Economy* (Cambridge, Mass., 1946), 89.
13 W.J.A. Donald, *The Canadian Iron and Steel Industry: A Study in the Economic History of a Protected Industry* (Boston, 1915), 67.

14 See, for instance, W.G. Phillips, *The Agricultural Implement Industry in Canada: A Study in Competition* (Toronto, 1956).

15 J.A. Bannister, 'The Houghton Iron Works,' *Papers and Records of the Ontario Historical Society*, 41 (1944), 79–82.

16 B.J. Harrington, *Notes on the Iron Ores of Canada and Their Development* (Montreal, 1874), 57.

17 Bartlett, *The Manufacture, Consumption and Production of Iron, Steel and Coal in the Dominion of Canada*, 1–2.

18 H.A. Innis, introduction to E.S. Moore, *American Influence in Canadian Mining* (Toronto, 1941), ix; see also H.A. Innis, 'Iron and Steel, Wheat and Finance,' in *Problems of Staple Production in Canada* (Toronto, 1933), 17–23.

19 C.D.W. Goodwin, *Canadian Economic Thought: The Political Economy of a Developing Nation 1814–1914* (Durham, NC, 1961), 70.

20 *Monetary Times Annual* (1916), 230–43, and T. Naylor, *The History of Canadian Business 1867–1914* (Toronto, 1975), 1: 52–5.

21 Harrington, *Notes on the Iron Ores of Canada*, 52–62. Titaniferous meant ore containing abnormal amounts of impurities such as phosphorus and silica.

22 DHC, 14 March 1879, p. 421.

23 R.C. Brown and R. Cook, *Canada 1896–1921: A Nation Transformed* (Toronto, 1974), 87.

24 DHC, 22 April 1879, p. 1450.

25 See 'Report of A.H. Blackeby on the State of the Manufacturing Industries of Ontario and Quebec,' *Sessional Papers* 1885, 37: 10.

26 DHC, 24 April 1879, p. 1531.

27 DHC, 19 April 1883, p. 710; domestic production of pig iron was about twenty thousand tons in 1882.

28 Donald, *The Canadian Iron and Steel Industry*, chp. 6, especially pp. 118–20.

29 William Kilbourn, *The Elements Combined: A History of the Steel Company of Canada* (Toronto, 1960), 14–18.

30 Joint petition to Sir Charles Tupper, 15 Feb. 1888, Macdonald Papers, 63277-80. The petition was signed by the Ontario Rolling Mills Co., Hamilton Iron Forgings Co., Pillow-Hersey Manufacturing Co., Montreal Rolling Mills, Nova Scotia Steel Co., and other manufacturers.

31 Ibid., 21 April 1887, 62543-4.

32 Donald, 108.

33 W.H. Merritt, 'Let Us Smelt Our Own Steel,' *Canadian Magazine*, 1: 3 (May 1893), 181–5. A graduate of the Royal School of Mines in England, Merritt at various times served as a lecturer at the Kingston School of Mining, as a member of the 1890 Royal Commission on Mineral Resources, and on the executive of the Ontario Mining Institute.

34 *Report of the Ontario Royal Commission on Mineral Resources* (Toronto, 1890),

123. The commissioners toured mines in the Eastern Ontario, Sault Ste Marie/Killarney, and Atikokan areas.

35 *Report*, 327; statistics from the Advisory Board on Tariffs and Taxation, RG 36/11, vol. 5, file 2–29, tables supplied by Minerals Division, Department of Mines, Ottawa, Jan. 1927. Ore from the Wilbur mine was, for instance, bought by Bethlehem Steel.

36 See Crowell and Murray Inc., *The Iron Ores of Lake Superior* (Cleveland, 1927), 11, and Lake Superior Iron Ores Association, *Directory of Mine Operators and Statistical Data* (Duluth, 1935), 26.

37 K. Warren, *The American Steel Industry 1850–1970: A Geographical Interpretation* (Oxford, 1973). Warren describes the 'intrinsic unsuitability of the upper lakes district' (p.73) for integrated steel production, citing such 'flash in the pan' projects for establishing mills on Superior shores as the 1903 scheme to build a mill at Sault Ste Marie, Michigan (p. 75).

38 W.H. Merritt, 'Notes on the Possibilities of Iron and Steel Production in Ontario,' *Transactions of the Canadian Institute* (1890–1), in pamphlet form, p. 3.

39 *Report*, 65–9, xvii, and 464–7.

40 Donald, *The Canadian Iron and Steel Industry*, 121–2; George Mackenzie, 'The Iron and Steel Industry of Ontario,' Ontario Bureau of Mines, *Annual Report*, 17 (1908). Mackenzie complained that lack of fossil fuels was 'our greatest drawback in Ontario' (p. 199).

41 Donald, 98.

42 Merritt, 'Let Us Smelt,' 181.

43 C. Tupper to J.A. Macdonald, 11 Nov. 1889, Macdonald Papers, 17617-23.

44 Ibid., 116460.

45 John Milne testimony before Tariff Commission, Toronto, 1 Dec.1896, RG35/8, vol. 1.

46 Donald, 68; see also E. Porritt, *Sixty Years of Protection in Canada 1846–1907* (London, 1908).

47 Merritt, 'Notes,' 15.

48 Ontario Bureau of Mines, *Annual Report*, 2 (1892), 63.

CHAPTER TWO

1 *Report of the Royal Commission on the Mineral Resources of Ontario and Measures for Their Development* (Toronto, 1890), xvi; H.V. Nelles, *The Politics of Development: Forests, Mines and Hydro-electric Power in Ontario, 1849–1941* (Toronto, 1974), chp. 3; and R.S. Lambert and P. Pross, *Renewing Nature's Wealth: A*

Centennial History of the Public Management of Lands , Forests and Wild Life in Ontario 1763–1967 (Toronto, 1967).

2 J. McDiarmid, *Commercial Policy in the Canadian Economy* (Cambridge, Mass., 1946), 206. Interpretations of the Liberals' volte-face range from Edward Porritt's allegation of 'industry leaning on the politician' in his *Sixty Years of Protection in Canada 1846–1907* (London, 1908) to W.J.A. Donald's assertion in his *The Canadian Iron and Steel Industry: A Study in the Economic History of a Protected Industry* (Boston, 1915) that Liberal policy represented 'a nice balancing of warring interests' (p. 138).

3 Fielding Tariff Commission, hearing of 20 Nov. 1896, pp. 373–4, RG 36/8, vol. 1.

4 Ibid., testimony of John Milne, 1 Dec. 1896, pp. 570–1.

5 McDiarmid, *Commercial Policy*, chp. 9.

6 *Report of the Royal Commission on the Mineral Resources*, xvi.

7 H.V. Nelles, *The Politics of Development*, 152. See also Albert Tucker, *Steam into Wilderness* (Toronto, 1978).

8 T. Naylor, *The History of Canadian Business 1867–1914* (Toronto, 1976), vol. 2, chp. 13, and J.M. Bliss, 'Canadianizing American Business: The Roots of the Branch Plant,' in Ian Lumsden, ed., *Close the 49th Parallel* (Toronto, 1970).

9 W. Kilbourn, *The Elements Combined: A History of the Steel Company of Canada* (Toronto, 1960), 48–9.

10 Ontario Bureau of Mines, *Annual Report*, 9 (1900), 102.

11 James Dunn to L.H. Derrer, 30 April 1946, Dunn Papers, vol. 328, and *Report upon the Existing Conditions at Sault Ste. Marie*, International Waterways Commission, 1913–14, found in Borden Papers, vol. 174, file 210.

12 R.G. Thwaites, *The Jesuit Relations and Allied Documents* (New York, 1959), 72 vols.; K. Punch, 'Sault Ste. Marie,' *Canadian Geographical Journal*, Dec. 1966; G.A. MacDonald, 'The Ancient Fishery at Sault Ste. Marie,' ibid., April/May 1977; and Don W. Tompson, *Men and Meridians: The History of Surveying and Mapping in Canada* (Ottawa, 1966), 1: 64.

13 W.T. Hogan, *Economic History of the Iron and Steel Industry in the United States* (Lexington, Mass., 1971), 1: 19.

14 G.M. Grant, 'The Jason of Algoma: An Account of the Wonderful Industrial Development in New Ontario,' *Canadian Magazine*, Oct. 1900, p. 485.

15 L.L. Prior, 'Sault Ste. Marie and the Algoma Steel Corporation Ltd.' (unpublished MA thesis, University of Toronto, 1956), chp. 1.

16 *Canadian Census of 1941* (Dominion Bureau of Statistics, Ottawa), 1: 590, and M. Van Avery, 'Francis H. Clergue and the Rise of Sault Ste. Marie,' *Ontario History*, 56: 3 (Sept. 1964).

17 *The Algoma District and That Part of the Nipissing District North of the Mattawan River, Lake Nipissing and the French River, Their Resources, Agriculture and Mining Capabilities* (Toronto, 1884); and *Northern Districts of Ontario, Canada, Nipissing, Temiscaming, Algoma, Thunder Bay, Wabigoon, Rainy River* (Toronto, 1899).

18 *Canadian Census of 1891*, 1: 3 and 144.

19 Evidence before *Royal Commission on the Mineral Resources of Ontario* (1890), 60–1, 62, 20, and 231.

20 Ontario Bureau of Mines, *Annual Report*, 6 (1897), 205.

21 E.H. Capp, *The Story of Baw-a-ting, Being the Annals of Sault Ste. Marie* (Sault Ste Marie, 1904).

22 M. Van Avery, 'F.H. Clergue and the Rise of Sault Ste Marie,' 192, and F.N. Speller, 'Metallurgical Industries at Sault Ste. Marie,' Ontario Bureau of Mines, *Annual Report*, 10 (1901), 61–8.

23 See Alan Sullivan, *The Rapids*, University of Toronto Press edition (Toronto, 1972). The details of Sullivan's fictionalization of the Sault's rise to industrial status cannot be taken as historical evidence per se but, because Sullivan served as an engineer in Clergue's works, his impressions provide valuable insights into the problems faced at the Sault.

24 See Donald Eldon, 'The Entrepreneurial Career of Francis H. Clergue,' *Explorations in Entrepreneurial History* (April 1951), 254–68; M. Bliss, introduction to *The Rapids*; Van Avery, 'F.H. Clergue'; W.R. Stewart, 'Francis Hector Clergue,' *The Cosmopolitan*, 36 (Dec. 1903), 179–83; *Bangor Daily Commercial*, 20 Jan. 1939; and G.M. Grant, 'The Jason.'

25 F.H. Clergue, 'Address at a Banquet Given in His Honor by the Citizens of Sault Ste. Marie,' 15 Feb. 1901, p. 5.

26 Grant, 'The Jason,' 489.

27 T. Veblen, *Absentee Ownership and Business Enterprise in Recent Times*, in *The Portable Veblen*, Viking edition (New York, 1948), 380.

28 Eldon, 'The Entrepreneurial Career,' 256.

29 T.W. Gibson, *Mining in Ontario* (Toronto, *1937*), 126–7.

30 Dunn to T. Arnold, 8 Feb. 1939, Dunn Papers, vol. 320.

31 *Ontario Statutes*, 57 Vict., sec, 23, chap. 80, and Sault Ste Marie, civic by-law 322, 1894.

32 Documents Relating to the Financial Agreements of the Consolidated Lake Superior Company, 1903–04,' Dunn Papers, vol. 386. Clergue was never actually president of the corporation. F.W. Lewis served as president nominally while Clergue as vice-president directed policy.

33 John N. Ingham, *The Iron Barons: A Social Analysis of an American Urban Elite, 1874–1965* (Westport, Conn., 1978), 8.

34 E. Digby Baltzell, *Philadelphia Gentlemen: The Making of a National Upper Class* (Glencoe, Ill., 1958).

35 The best list of Clergue's American backers may be found in PAO, Ross Papers, 'Consolidated Lake Superior Company' file, and in the Consolidated Lake Superior Company *Annual Reports*, reprinted in the *Annual Financial Review* (Toronto, various years).

36 F.H. Clergue, 'An Address by Francis H. Clergue at Sault Ste. Marie, Michigan at a Banquet Given in His Honor,' 21 Feb. 1901, p. 3.

37 See, for instance, A.P. Coleman, 'Iron Ranges of the Early Huronian,' Ontario Bureau of Mines, *Annual Report*, 10 (1901), 192–4.

38 Ibid., 3 (1894), 249–50.

39 Ibid., 9 (1900), 103–3.

40 'Geology of the Nipissing-Algoma line,' ibid., 5 (1896),167–84.

41 Ibid., 8 (1899), 18.

42 Ibid., 9 (1900), 101–2.

43 Ibid., 12 (1903), 22.

44 A.B. Willmott and A.P. Coleman, 'The Michipicoten Iron Range,' ibid., 8 (199), 254–8; 'Josephine Mine' file, Ross Papers, special series.

45 Bureau of Mines, *Annual Report*, 8 (1899), 257; A.B. Willmot, 'The Iron Ores of Ontario,' *Journal of the Canadian Mining Institute*, 11 (1908); and D.M. Le Bourdais, *Men and Metals: The Story of Canadian Mining* (Toronto, 1957), chp. 18.

46 F.H. Clergue, *An Instance of Industrial Evolution in Northern Ontario* (Toronto, 1902), 17.

47 J. Konarek, 'Algoma Central and Hudson Bay Railway: The Beginnings,' *Ontario History* (June 1970), and O.S. Nock, *Algoma Central Railway* (London, 1975).

48 Bureau of Mines, *Annual Report*, 12 (1903), 19.

49 Ibid., 11 (1902), 94.

50 C.H. Speer, 'History of the Algoma Steel Corporation' (typescript, PAC, MG 31 B3), 12–14.

51 F.N. Speller, 'Metallurgical,' 62–8.

52 Peter Temin, *Iron and Steel in Nineteenth Century America: An Economic Inquiry* (Cambridge, Mass., 1964), 196.

53 Speller, 'Metallurgical,' 63–8.

54 Clergue 'Address at a Banquet Given in His Honor by the Citizens of Sault Ste. Marie,' 15 Feb. 1901.

55 CAR, 1902, p. 298.

56 F.H. Clergue, *An Instance*, 15.

57 E. Porritt, 'Iron and Steel Bounties in Canada,' *Political Science Quarterly*, 22:

2 (June 1907), 193–223. The Hamilton Steel and Iron Company, which had collected bounties since 1898, collected $1,416,469 up to June 1906.

58 See 'Buying German Rails,' *Industrial Canada*, Dec. 1902, pp. 234–5, and 'The Duty on Rails,' ibid., Sept. 1904, p. 70.

59 Clergue to Laurier, 22 Nov. 1901, Laurier Papers, no. 60125-29.

60 Ibid. and G.G. Schroeder, *The Growth of Major Steel Companies 1900–50* (Baltimore, 1953).

61 A.E. Dyment to Laurier, 10 Aug. 1903, Laurier Papers, no. 75974-5.

62 Clergue to Laurier, 15 July 1905, Laurier Papers, no. 99726-9. Laurier had first met Clergue in the mid-1890s, when the latter had pestered Ottawa for a Franco-Canadian steamship scheme that ultimately bore no fruit.

63 CAR,1902, p. 299, and Clergue to Laurier, 18 May 1905, Laurier Papers, no. 97675-86.

64 Dandurand to Laurier, 9 April 1903, Laurier Papers, no. 72010; see also Kerr to Laurier, 16 Feb. 1902, ibid., no. 62777-83.

65 Donald, *Industry*, p. 174; Montreal *Star*, 27 April 1901.

66 DHC, 9 April 1901, pp. 2629–40, and 23 April 1901, pp. 3547–95.

67 Ibid., 2629. Although vigorously supported by A.E. Dyment, Liberal member for Algoma, Blair eventually turned his back on the opposition (ibid., 3631–4).

68 Laurier to Dandurand, 10 April 1903, Laurier Papers, no. 72011.

69 6–7Ed. VII, 1906, c. 11.

70 Assistant to Sir Thomas Shaughnessy to W.S. Fielding, 23 March 1903, RG 36/17, vol. 16.

71 Hays to Fielding, 17 April 1903, ibid.

72 Clergue to W. Paterson, minister of customs, 4 April 1902, Laurier Papers, no. 71791-2, and Algoma Steel and Drummond McColl to Fielding, 13 Feb. 1902, RG 36/17, vol. 11.

73 Clergue to Laurier, 20 March 1903, RG 36/17, vol. 16.

74 H.V. Nelles has aptly described the Clergue enterprises as the 'natural children of its [Ontario's] resource development policies,' *The Politics*, 132 and 133–8.

75 B.D. Tennyson, 'The Political Career of Sir William H. Hearst' (unpublished MA thesis, University of Toronto, 1963), 12–14; B.D. Tennyson, 'The Cruise of the *Minnie M*,' *Ontario History*, June 1967.

76 Laurier to Clergue, April 1903, Laurier Papers, no. 71794.

77 W.R. Williams, 'The Midland Blast Furnace,' *Inland Seas*, 19: 4 (1963), 308–10.

78 Clergue to Laurier, 18 May 1905, Laurier Papers, no. 97675-86.

79 Minutes of Sault Ste Marie sitting of Fielding tariff inquiry, 21 Dec. 1905, RG

36/17, vol. 5. Clergue at this point was seeking an abolition of import duties on coke.

80 F. McMath to R.F. Sutherland, MP, 11 March 1902, RG 36/17, vol. 11.

81 L. McKim Jones to Fielding, 31 March 1903, ibid., vol. 14.

82 Minutes, 21 Dec. 1905.

83 Clergue to Laurier, 31 March and 4 April 1906, Laurier Papers, nos. 103972-8 and 109178-80.

84 DHC, 23 April 1907, p. 7458.

85 CAR, 1905, p. 150.

86 'Statement in Support of Bounty on Pig Iron Submitted by all the Iron and Steel Manufacturers in Canada,' 21 Nov. 1911, Borden Papers, vol. 13.

87 CAR, 1912, p. 184.

88 'Statement.' An editorial in the *Monetary Times Annual*, 1915, p. 18, protested that 'large secondary industries are growing up whose existence may depend on the maintenance of supplies of raw material entering at low duties.'

89 Howland to Borden, 28 Nov. 1911, Borden Papers, vol. 132.

90 See, for instance, CAR, 1905, p. 159; and S.D. Clark, *The Canadian Manufacturers Association: A Study in Collective Bargaining and Political Pressure* (Toronto, 1939).

91 Clergue evidence to Fielding Tariff Inquiry, Sault Ste Marie, 21 Dec. 1905, RG 36/17, vol. 5.

92 Kilbourn, *Elements*, 83–4.

93 Dunn to Wm Lilley, 21 March 1934, Dunn Papers, vol. 311.

94 26 Sept. 1903.

95 Clergue to Laurier, 7 July 1905, Laurier Papers, no. 99468.

96 For oral evidence of this, see the reminiscences of one of the Sault workers of the period in Bill McNeil, *Voice of the Pioneer* (Toronto, 1978), 87–9.

97 Walker to J.H. Plummer, 9 Sept. 1902, Walker Papers, University of Toronto Archives, box 29.

98 CAR, 1903, p. 513; by December 1902, $99,684,400 of a total authorized capital of $117,000,000 had been issued (Dunn Papers, vol. 386).

99 CAR, 1904, p. 271; *Iron and Steel of Canada*, Aug. 1923, p. 156; and *Financial Post*, Aug. 24, 1928.

100 Sigmund Samuel to W.S. Fielding, 2 July 1903, RG 36/17, vol. 15.

101 CAR, 1903, p. 512.

102 E.H. Bronson to G.W. Ross, 2 Oct. 1903, Bronson Papers, PAC, vol. 695.

103 See Livo Ducin, 'Labour's Emergent Years and the 1903 Riots,' in *50 Years of Labour in Algoma: Essays on Aspects of Algoma's Working-Class History* (Sault Ste Marie, 1978), 1–18.

104 Clergue to Laurier, 18 May 1905, Laurier Papers, no. 97675-86.

105 CAR, 1903, pp. 511–15, and 1904, pp. 268–74. A young B.K. Sandwell was dispatched by J.S. Willison of the Toronto *News* to investigate the 'smash at the Soo.' See Sandwell's perceptive report in the Toronto *Daily News*, 26 Sept. 1903.
106 CAR, 1904, p. 269; details of reorganization in Dunn Papers, vol. 386.
107 Toronto *Daily Star*, 4 April 1904.
108 Ibid., 9 March 1904. The company promised among other things to complete the railway north to the CPR mainline, to pay off the Speyer loan, to repay its other liabilities, and to reimburse local banks for guarantees on Sault wages.
109 Speech Notes, 8 April 1904, Ross Papers, 'Consolidated Lake Superior File,' and M. Prang, *N.W. Rowell: Ontario Nationalist* (Toronto, 1976), 50.
110 Toronto *Daily News*, 14 April 1904.
111 CAR, 1904, pp. 270–4.
112 Sault *Daily Star*, 13 May 1935.
113 Ross to Laurier, 7 April 1904, and Laurier to Ross, 9 April 1904, Laurier Papers, no. 4253-6.
114 CAR, 1905, pp. 195–204.
115 Ibid., 195.
116 Lambert and Pross, *Renewing Nature's Wealth*, 258–9, and Peter Oliver, *G. Howard Ferguson: Ontario Tory* (Toronto, 1977), 28–32.
117 CAR, 1906, p. 312. Warren reported in the 1906 Lake Superior Corporation *Annual Report* the 'great development and improvement' at the steelworks, citing a record of 1004 tons of rails rolled on one day.
118 CAR, 1909, p. 364.
119 Toronto *Daily News*, 6 April 1904.
120 King Diaries, 3 Nov. 1936, King Papers, J13 series, vol. 80.
121 For details of the North Railway, see the papers of Robert Borden, Thomas White, and Lomer Gouin at the PAC. See also CAR, 1913, p. 477.
122 LSC *Annual Reports* filed in Dunn Papers, vol. 386.

CHAPTER THREE

1 Railway mileage in operation in Canada more than doubled between 1905 and 1915 from 20,487 miles to 45,833 miles. M.C. Urqhuart and K. Buckley, *Historical Statistics of Canada* (Toronto, 1965), 528–32.
2 LSC, *Annual Report*, 1906, and CAR, 1906, p. 313.
3 J. Whitney to J.H. Dunn, 18 Sept, 1908, Dunn Papers (hereafter DP), vol. 254, and Drummond to Borden, 12 March 1912, Borden Papers, vol. 132.
4 LSC, *Annual Report*, 1915.

5 CAR, 1913, p. 113, and LSC, *Annual Report*, 1913. See also W. Kilbourn, *The Elements Combined: A History of the Steel Company of Canada* (Toronto, 1960), 83.

6 LSC, *Annual Report*, 1916.

7 LSC, *Annual Report*, 1914; O.S. Nock, *Algoma Central Railway* (London, 1975), chps. 7 and 8.

8 From 1905 to 1915, Americans controlled the majority of the corporation's directorships, Canadians never holding more than five seats.

9 *Iron and Steel of Canada*, Aug. 1923, p. 156.

10 W.K. Whigham to R. Fleming, 18 Sept. 1908, and H.S. Fleming to W.K. Whigham, 18 Sept. 1908, DP 254.

11 H.S. Fleming to W.K. Whigham, 18 Sept. 1908, DP 254.

12 Ibid.

13 Dunn to Pearson, 4 Sept. 1908, ibid.

14 CAR, 1909, p. 167, reported the switch as 'the end of a long, spectacular series of financial changes and ups and downs.' The actual purchased holdings were said to be $19,000,000, while CAR, 1910, p. 79, noted that Fleming had captured 78,000 shares of LSC. The Lake Superior Investment Company had capitalization of $1 million in 10,000 shares, of which the syndicate had the controlling interest (DP 385, file 5).

15 Drummond, with his brother George, had extensive interests in the Canadian iron and steel industry and had long championed the Sault industries. See G. Drummond to Laurier, 27 Jan. 1904, Laurier Papers, no. 81629-30.

16 Dunn to Fleming, 20 June 1909, DP 256; CAR, 1909, p. 165. There were rumours that Fleming and Pearson were attempting to sponsor a giant amalgamation of Nova Scotian and Ontario steel plants; see Dunn to Fleming, 22 Feb. 1909, DP 255.

17 Laurier to G. Drummond, 18 Jan. 1904, Laurier Papers, no. 81388.

18 G.W. Ross to Laurier, 7 April 1904, Laurier Papers, no. 84253-6.

19 Both Lord Grey and Lord Northcliffe visited the Sault (CAR, 1910, p. 338).

20 CAR, 1908, p. 280.

21 B.D. Tennyson, 'The Political Career of Sir William H. Hearst' (unpublished MA thesis, University of Toronto, 1963), chp. 2.

22 Whitney to W.H. Hearst and A.J. Matheson, cables, Sept. 1908, DP 11.

23 Whigham to Fleming, 18 Sept. 1908, DP 254.

24 Dunn to Whigham, 31 Dec. 1909, DP 13. H.M. Price, a LSC director from 1909 to 1913, also served as a corporate lobbyist in Ottawa.

25 E. Haanel, *Report on the Experiments Made at Sault Ste. Marie, Ontario, in the Smelting of Canadian Iron Ores by the Electro-thermic Process* (Department of the Interior, Ottawa, 1909).

26 T.J. Drummond to R. Dandurand, cable, 22 March 1910, Laurier Papers, no. 168571.

27 'Pig Iron Industry at Port Arthur,' *Industrial Canada*, 20 Sept. 1907, pp. 28–9.

28 Ontario Bureau of Mines, *Annual Report*, 22 (1913), 28.

29 Other iron ore mines were at Atikokan, Bessemer, and Moose Mountain, but only the Helen mine yielded good hematite ore, comparable to American Superior ore; *Report of the Ontario Iron Ore Committee* (Toronto, 1923), 158–61.

30 CAR, 1910, p. 563.

31 CAR, 1907, p. 242.

32 W.H. Hearst, 'Northern Ontario: Its Wealth of Resources and Future Greatness,' CAR, 1912, Supplement p. 67; see also C.W. Humphries, 'The Political Career of Sir James P. Whitney' (unpublished PH D thesis, University of Toronto, 1966).

33 12 June 1912.

34 Frater Taylor to Thomas White, 14 Dec. 1914, White Papers, no. 7389-91.

35 White to Frater Taylor, 17 Dec. 1914, White Papers, no. 7392.

36 *Iron and Steel of Canada*, Feb. 1918, p. 28.

37 T. White to Borden, 7 Sept. 1916, Borden Papers, no. 113208; White to President, Algoma Steel, cable, 23 June 1916, White Papers, no. 9031.

38 Frater Taylor to White, cable, 23 June 1916, ibid., no. 9038.

39 Ibid., 24 June 1916, no. 9039-42.

40 J. Flavelle to Borden, 10 Oct. 1917, Borden Papers, vol. 186, file 566.

41 Borden to Sir Henry Drayton, 29 June 1917, Borden Papers, vol. 221, file 1613.

42 See, for instance, 'Making Shrapnel Shells in Canada,' *Industrial Canada*, Feb. 1915, pp. 718–21; *Iron and Steel of Canada*, Sept. 1918, p. 333; and CAR, 1917, pp. 386–7.

43 *Iron and Steel of Canada*, Feb. 1918, p. 28.

44 Flavelle to Borden, 14 March 1916, Borden Papers, no. 108996.

45 Lake Superior Corporation, *Annual Reports*, 1916–19, and memo of 4 Feb. 1916 'in respect to the booking of steel with the Algoma Steel Corporation,' Flavelle Papers, PAC, vol. 3, file 19.

46 Flavelle to Borden, 5 Jan. 1917, Borden Papers, vol. 216.

47 'Report to Hon. N.W. Rowell on steel situation,' by F.P. Jones, 17 Jan. 1918, Flavelle Papers, PAC, vol. 13; Flavelle to Rowell, 29 Jan. 1918, Borden Papers, vol. 216.

48 See David Carnegie, *The History of Munitions Supply in Canada 1914–18* (London, 1925); R.C. Brown and R. Cook, *Canada 1896–1921: A Nation Transformed* (Toronto, 1974), chps. 11 and 12; and J.M. Bliss, 'A Canadian Business-

man and War: The Case of Joseph Flavelle,' in J.L. Granatstein and R.D. Cuff, eds., *War and Society in North America* (Toronto, 1971).

49 Frater Taylor to White, 24 June 1916, White Papers, no. 9039-42.

50 'History of Algoma Steel,' unpublished manuscript by D.A. Machum and D. Johnston, n.d., Algoma Steel Historical Files, pp. 185–9.

51 'Memo: concerning Algoma Steel labour force,' 9 March 1916, Borden Papers, no. 108997-109001.

52 Flavelle to Mayor of Sault Ste Marie, cable, 5 Jan. 1917, Borden Papers, no. 121849; Department of Labour strike files, RG27, vol. 306.

53 Flavelle to Borden, 30 Jan. 1917, Borden Papers, no. 121860.

54 Flavelle to Mark Workman, 5 Jan. 1917, Flavelle Papers, PAC, vol. 10, file 97.

55 Frater Taylor to Flavelle, 22 Oct. 1917, ibid.

56 Flavelle to J. Frater Taylor, 26 Oct. 1917, ibid.

57 J. Frater Taylor to Flavelle, 30 Nov. 1917, ibid.

58 'Memorandum by Algoma Steel Corporation to the Minister of Marine,' by J. Frater Taylor, 24 Nov. 1917, ibid.

59 *Iron and Steel of Canada*, Feb. 1920, p. 39.

60 Cable, J.H. Dunn to F.P. Jones, 9 Jan. 1919, DP 80; and Hearings of Sir Henry Drayton's Tariff Commission, at Sault Ste Marie, 19 Oct. 1920, p. 1793, RG36/8, vol. 6. Franz alleged that Drayton had promised 'special legislation' to assist in building the plant. Franz to Flavelle 2 Feb. 1920, Flavelle Papers, PAC, vol. 22.

61 LSC, *Annual Report*, 1918.

62 Details of sale in J.A. McPhail Papers, PAO, box 7.

63 R.S. Sayers, *The Bank of England, 1891–1944* (Cambridge, 1976), 315–16. Years later E.R. Peacock described Frater Taylor to C.D. Howe as 'the best doctor of sick companies that I have ever met.' Peacock to Howe, 16 July 1953, Howe Papers, vol. 181.

64 J.S. Dale to Rbt. Fleming, 6 Sept. 1919, DP 76.

65 N.J. Greene to D.A. Machum, 28 July 1964, Algoma Steel Historical Files.

66 B.K. Sandwell to W.H. Moore, 22 Nov. 1928, RG 36/11, file 2-1.

67 'General Report on Algoma Steel Situation,' submitted by J. Frater Taylor to board of directors, 29 Jan. 1918, Algoma Steel Historical Files.

68 'Memo re: a Conference between the Reconstruction and Development Committee and various officials of Canadian Railway Companies, Steel Manufacturers and Car Manufacturers,' 15 Nov. 1918, White Papers, no. 11534-41. G.A. Irwin represented Algoma.

69 CAR, 1919, p. 405.

70 'Memo re: a Conference' and *Iron and Steel of Canada*, Feb. 1920, editorial, p. 1.

71 C.F. Whitton, 'The Present Position,' ISC, Feb. 1918.
72 CAR, 1919, p. 414.
73 *Monetary Times Annual*, 1916, p. 243.
74 Sept. 1919, p. 199.

CHAPTER FOUR

1 *Iron and Steel of Canada* (hereafter ISC), Sept. 1919, editorial.
2 See W.L. Edmonds, 'Production Caught Up with Demand in 1920,' *Monetary Times Annual* (herafter MTA), 1921, p. 223. See also RG 36/8, vol. 6, 18 Oct. 1920.
3 ISC, Feb. 1920, p. 1.
4 In the year ending May 1922 Algoma had rail bookings totalling 51,176 tons and by May 1923 bookings totalling 75,999 tons (MTA, 1924, p. 164).
5 *Minutes of Board of Directors' Meetings*, 1922–7, book no. 4, Algoma Steel Historical Files.
6 MTA, 1924, p. 164.
7 MTA, 1926, p. 182, and William Kilbourn, *The Elements Combined* (Toronto, 1960), 102–12. Stelco was not, however, without its difficulties in the early 1920s, but by 1921, as Kilbourn concedes, it was 'the least damaged of all the Canadian steel companies.'
8 MTA, 1922, p. 30, and LSC, *Annual Report*, 1922.
9 *Annual Reports*, 1921–3.
10 'Report on Algoma Steel,' Coverdale and Colpitts, New York, 15 Aug. 1923, McPhail Papers, box 7.
11 'Condensed Summary of Freyn, Brassert Company's Report on Algoma Steel Company,' 10 May, 1924, Ferguson Papers, 1924 general correspondence.
12 'Mooted Changes at the Soo,' ISC, Aug. 1923, p. 156.
13 W.C. Franz to J.A. McPhail, memo, Sept. 1927, McPhail Papers, box 8.
14 J.H. Dunn to H.C. Hamilton, 8 July 1948, DP 329, and F. Common to J.H. Dunn, 6 Nov. 1930, DP 387.
15 Gary to Borden, 17 Feb. 1917, and G. Foster to Gary, 26 Feb. 1917, Borden Papers, vol. 218, file 2-29.
16 C.F. Whitton, 'The Present Position and Future of the Iron and Steel Industries in Canada,' ISC, Feb. 1918, pp. 29 and 37.
17 CAR, 1920, p. 191.
18 For an analysis of the American steel industry, see Alfred Chandler, Jr, *The Visible Hand: The Managerial Revolution in American Business* (Cambridge, Mass., 1977), 359–60.
19 'Where Are the Leaders?' ISC, March 1922, p. 37.

20 Throughout the 1920s iron ore from the American shore continued to pour into the eastern industrial heartland, 56,814,500 tons being shipped between 1920 and 1930 (Lake Superior Iron Ore Association, *Directory of Mine Operations and Statistical Data* [Duluth, 1935], 25). While the extractive industry bustled, efforts to establish integrated steelworks on the Superior shore foundered. Plans for steelworks at Duluth and the American Sault failed earlier in the century. 'The projection,' notes a historian of the American industry, 'were all sadly awry, ambitions remained unfulfilled, for in each case there was a strange lack of appreciation of the economics of iron and steelmaking, and the intrinsic unsuitability of the upper lakes district' (K. Warren, *The American Steel Industry: 1850–1970: A Geographical Interpretation* [Oxford, 1975], 73).

21 Ontario Bureau of Mines, *Annual Report* (hereafter OMB *Report*), 28 (1919), 31–2.

22 Ibid., 30 (1921), 66.

23 Mineral Resources Division statistics, submitted to the Tariff Advisory Board, RG 36/11, vol. 5, file 2-29.

24 ISC, June 1920, p. 139; T.W. Gibson, *Mining in Ontario* (Toronto, 1937), 136; and MTA, 1924, p. 160.

25 Gibson, 134.

26 OMB *Report*, 34 (1925), 22.

27 ISC, Jan. 1931, p. 9.

28 'Canadian Iron Ores Can Be Used,' ISC, April 1923, p. 72.

29 ISC, Nov. 1920, p. 292.

30 DHC, 21 Feb. 1927, p. 522. For contemporary geological explanations of the formation of iron deposits on both sides of Lake Superior, see Gibson, *Mining in Ontario*, 134; E. Lindman and L.L. Bolton, *Iron Ore Occurrences in Canada* (2 vols.;Ottawa, 1917); W.A. Parks, 'The Mineral Resources of Northern Ontario,' *Journal of the Royal Society of Arts*, 73 (Aug. 1925); and Crowell and Murray, Inc., *The Iron Ores of Lake Superior* (Cleveland, 1927).

31 It was estimated that Huronian rock comprised only 12 per cent of the Shield (Parks, p. 900).

32 A.L. Parsons, 'The Productive Area of the Michipicoten Iron Ranges,' OMB *Report*, 24 (1915), 185–203; A.B. Willmott, 'The Iron Ores of Ontario,' *Journal of the Canadian Mining Institute*, 11 (1908).

33 *On the Utilization of the Low Grade Iron Ores of Canada* (Honorary Advisory Council for Scientific and Industrial Research, Ottawa, 1924), 12.

34 J.B. MacDougall, *Two Thousand Miles of Gold: From Val d'Or to Yellowknife* (Toronto, 1946), 166–7.

35 Sault Ste Marie tariff hearing, 18 Oct. 1920, RG 35/8, vol. 6, p. 1791.

36 C.P. McCormack, 'The Economics of Iron Ore Benefication,' in *Iron Ores of Lake Superior*, 118.

37 Ibid.

38 *On the Utilization*, 27, and *Report of the Iron Ore Committee of Ontario* (Toronto, 1923), 161.

39 C.K. Leith, 'Report on Helen Siderite Property,' 10 Aug. 1917, DP 320.

40 Only 26,385 tons of Moose Mountain briquettes, 63 per cent iron, were produced by 1920.

41 Parks, 'The Mineral Resources of Northern Ontario,' 909. See also W.H. Collins, T.T. Quirke, and E. Thompson, *Michipicoten Iron Ranges* (Geological Survey of Canada Memoir 147, Department of Mines, Ottawa, 1926).

42 '*On the Utilization*,' 5.

43 Ibid., 55.

44 CAR, 1914, p. 383.

45 CAR, 1920, pp. 252–4.

46 See testimony of R.J. Manion and J.J. O'Connor at tariff hearings of 16 Oct. 1920, RG 36/8, vol. 6.

47 ISC, Sept. 1920, p. 235.

48 ISC, Nov. 1920, pp. 314–15, and June 1921, p. 146; also 'The Development of New Ontario,' speech draft by W.L.M. King, n.d., King Papers, J4 series, vol. 125.

49 J.A. Hussey at Sault tariff hearing, 18 Oct. 1920, RG 36/8, vol. 6, p. 1753.

50 ISC, Feb. 1921, p. 3, and May 1921, p. 104.

51 Jones to J.A. McPhail, 7 Dec. 1922, McPhail Papers, box 4. See also J.D. Jones, 'The Development and Use of Low Grade Iron Ores,' speech to Sault branch of Canadian Mining Institute, Dec. 1922, DP 312.

52 'Uncertain Outlook in Iron and Steel,' MTA, 1920, p. 238.

53 ISC, March 1920, p. 50.

54 DHC, 30 April 1924, p. 1619.

55 ISC, July 1922, p. 113.

56 Ibid., 118. The conference also voiced the recurrent complaint that too little mining exploration was done in Ontario. The Canadian Institute of Mining and Metallurgy pointed out that less than 50,000 feet of diamond drilling had been done in Ontario as opposed to over 11,000,000 feet in Minnesota (ISC, Feb. 1922, p. 19).

57 *Report of the Iron Ore Committee of Ontario* (Toronto, 1923), 10; see H.V. Nelles, *The Politics of Development* (Toronto, 1974), 431–3, and P. Oliver, *G. Howard Ferguson: Ontario Tory* (Toronto, 1977), chp. 10.

58 ISC, March 1920, p. 50, and Dec. 1923, p. 243. In 1925 Quebec passed an Iron Ore Premium Act.

59 CAR, 1924/5, p. 274.

60 Ferguson to E. Fitzgerald, 8 June 1925, Ferguson Papers, 1924 general correspondence. Fitzgerald had wartime experience with the steel industry with Flavelle and the IMB.

61 Frater Taylor to E.R. Wood, 21 Oct. 1924, ibid.

62 Ferguson to Wood, 24 Oct. 1924, ibid.

63 J.A. McPhail to M.J. Insull, 8 Dec. 1924, McPhail Papers, box 4.

64 Fitzgerald to Ferguson, 12 April 1926, Ferguson Papers, 1926 Algoma Steel file.

65 McPhail to Cunningham, 18 Feb. 1927, McPhail Papers, box 4. The 'Provincial Government,' McPhail noted, 'is a one man concern and that one man in [sic] the Prime Minister.'

66 See C. Armstrong, *The Politics of Federalism: Ontario's Relations with the Federal Government 1896–1941* (Toronto, 1981). In his 1972 University of Toronto doctoral thesis (p. 249) Armstrong commented that 'Ontario policy-makers made their customary assumption that provincial and national goals were or ought to be identical. The fact that they were not led to interminable wrangling between Howard Ferguson and Mackenzie King.' See also Oliver, *Ferguson*, chp. 9, Richard Simeon, 'Federalism and the Politics of a National Strategy,' and Ken H. Norrie, 'Regional Economic Conflicts in Canada: Their Significance for an Industrial Strategy,' both in *The Politics of an Industrial Strategy: A Seminar* (Science Council of Canada, Ottawa, 1979).

67 DHC, 8 March 1929, pp. 788–9, and 15 March 1927, p. 1236.

68 ibid., 22 May 1928, pp. 3260–2.

69 Copy of speech, dated 15 Nov. 1927, Malcolm Papers, vol. 11.

70 DHC, 2 March 1928, p. 991.

71 Speech draft for budget debate of 1928, Malcolm Papers, vol. 11.

72 'One Step Nearer to an Iron Ore Supply,' ISC, Feb. 1931.

73 ISC, Jan. 1926, p. 4.

74 D.H. Cowan, DHC, 18 March 1929, p. 1058.

75 Ibid., 17 May 1926, p. 3424.

76 ISC, Nov. 1924, p. 207. For a detailed analysis of the steel industry's tariff concerns in the 1920s, see Tom Traves, *The State and Enterprise: Canadian Manufacturers and the Federal Government 1917–1931* (Toronto, 1979), chp. 7.

77 DHC, 3 May 1926, p. 3049. In 1928 Thomas Cantley complained to the House that there were seventy items on the free list or with 99 per cent rebate (ibid., 22 May 1928, p. 3260).

78 MTA, 1921, p. 246.

79 W.C. Franz to J.A. Robb, 3 April 1926, Advisory Board on Tariff and Taxation Papers, RG 36/11 (hereafter ABTT).

80 ISC, Sept. 1924, p. 160, and DHC, 13 Feb. 1925, p. 153–4.
81 C.C. Ballantyne to Meighen, 8 Feb. 1924, memo attached, Meighen Papers, no. 034255-60.
82 ISC, May 1924, p. 86.
83 Ibid., Sept. 1924, p. 159.
84 *Iron and Steel and Their Products* (DBS, Ottawa, 1926), table 4.
85 Frater Taylor to Ferguson, 3 Feb. 1925, Ferguson Papers, 1925 general correspondence.
86 ISC, Oct. 1925, p. 203.
87 DHC, 12 April 1929, p. 1522, and 6 May 1930, p. 1821; see also W.C. Franz, 'The Steel Industry Needs,' ISC, March 1926, p. 97.
88 DHC, 12 April 1929, p. 152.
89 Ibid., 16 March 1927, p. 1264.
90 'I had great hopes that Meighen would come in with a clear majority and we could look for better times in those industries that must have protection.' J.H. Dunn to E.R. Wood, 9 Nov. 1925, DP 295.
91 Ernest R. Forbes, *The Maritime Rights Movement 1919–1927: A Study in Canadian Regionalism* (Montreal, 1979), chp. 4.
92 CAR, 1926/7, p. 268, and 1928/9, p. 271.
93 *Iron and Steel and Their Products* (DBS, Ottawa, 1935), tables 49, 52, and 53.
94 DHC, 9 April 1929, p. 1384.
95 King to A.W. McColl, 24 Feb. 1938, King Papers, J1 series, vol. 154.
96 Moore to King, ibid., 29 Jan. 1927. The board was convened under PC 530, 7 April 1926, and was responsible to the minister of finance.
97 The Algoma application alleged, for instance, that Buffalo pig iron could be delivered to St Catharines, Ontario, for $2.30 per ton, whereas freight from the Sault was $4.90 per ton. The precariousness of tariff protection was revealed in the fact that Buffalo's freight advantage was only just covered by the $2.80 per ton tariff. ABTT, files 2-1 and 2-41, vols. 1 and 5.
98 Ibid.
99 The workers' petition estimated that Sault labour had been deprived of $17 million in wages by steel imports between 1920 and 1926. Ibid., file 2-1, exhibit 10.
100 Report of 10 Aug. 1926, file 2-16, ABTT, vol. 3.
101 'Report on the Iron and Steel Industry of Canada,' ABTT, file 2-29, vol. 4.
102 A.P. Theurerkauf, 'Report on European Steel Situation,' 18 April 1927, ABTT, file 2-34, vol. 4.
103 Report of J. Dix Fraser and D.M. McDougall, 29 Jan. 1929, ABTT, file 2-50, vol. 5.

104 Confidential report to W.H. Moore, 15 Sept. 1928, ABTT, file 3-15, vol. 9.
105 ABTT, *Record of Public Hearing*, 29–31 Jan. 1929, p. 98; Diplock to Moore, 23 Jan., 29 Jan., and 7 March 1929, ABTT, file 2-8, vol. 2; and Toronto *Mail and Empire*, 3 Jan. 1928 and 1 Feb. 1929.
106 CAR, 1928/9, pp. 274, 335; ISC, Sept. 1926, p. 240; and Kilbourn, *Elements*, 136–40.
107 ABTT *Record*, 29 Nov. 1928, pp. 112–13.
108 Dominion Foundries and Steel application, 25 June 1926, ABTT, file 2-8, vol. 2.
109 ISC, Jan. 1929, pp. 1–2; 'Claim Lack of Unanimity Weakened Steel Companies' Case,' *Hardware and Metal*, 5 June 1926.
110 'Farmers and Consumers Organizations,' Sept.–Nov. 1926, ABTT, file 2-38, vol. 5.
111 Brantford TLC to ABTT, 4 Sept. 1926, ABTT, file 2-19, vol. 3.
112 ABTT *Record*, 27–29 Nov. 1928, pp. 9–24.
113 Ibid., p. 83.
114 Lysaght Sheet Metal Corporation brief, 28 Jan. 1929, ABTT file 2-38, vol. 5.
115 ABTT, Nov. 1928, file 2-42, vol. 5.
116 ABTT, Canadian Locomotive brief, n.d., file 2-2, vol. 1, and Dominion Forge brief, 24 Nov. 1928, file 2-43, vol. 5.
117 ABTT, 24 Nov. 1928, file 2-24, vol. 3.
118 Ontario Steel Products brief, Nov. 1928, ABTT, file 2-21, vol. 3.
119 Vaughan to G. Graham, 20 May 1926, ABTT, file 2-15, vol. 3.
120 A.T. Enlow to ABTT, 2 Dec. 1928, ABTT, file 2-38, vol. 5.
121 Lysaght brief.
122 ISC, Dec. 1926, p. 287.
123 ABTT *Record*, 27–28 Nov. 1928, pp. 9–10.
124 Ibid., 29 Nov. 1928; Toronto *Mail and Empire*, 30 Nov. 1928.
125 CAR, 1930, pp. 34–45; H.B. Neatby, *William Lyon Mackenzie King: The Lonely Heights 1924–32* (Toronto, 1963), 325–6.
126 Spence to King, 3 May 1930, King Papers, J1 series, no. 155322, vol. 182. Spence was a lobbyist for Dominion Foundries.
127 ISC, May 1930, pp. 109–10.
128 DHC, 28 May 1930, p. 2732, and 15 May, p. 2140. An amendment, moved by Woodsworth, for an eight-hour day in the steel trade was defeated.
129 Franz to Dunn, 1 and 6 Aug. 1930, DP 315.
130 'The Merchant Mills of Algoma Steel,' ISC, March 1930.
131 LSC *Annual Reports*, 1928–31.
132 Dec. 1927, p. 360.

CHAPTER FIVE

1 See DP 330 for details of Alan Sullivan's 'Before the Tide.' See also Allen A. Kennedy and Terrance E. Deal, *Corporate Cultures: The Rites and Rituals of Corporate Life* (Reading, Mass., 1982).

2 JHD to J.C. Webster, 5 Sept. 1945, DP 328.

3 See Lord Beaverbrook, *Courage: The Story of Sir James Dunn* (Fredericton, 1961), and Peter C. Newman, *The Flame of Power: The Story of Canada's Greatest Businessmen* (Toronto, 1959). Dunn family biographical information: JHD to Royal College of Arms, 4 and 5 Feb. 1921, DP 282, and JHD to *Who's Who*, 4 July 1921, ibid.

4 Beaverbrook, *Courage*, p. 21.

5 'Address by Sir James Dunn to Graduates of Mount Allison on May 11, 1954,' DP 339.

6 L'Université du Sacré-Cœur newspaper, May–June 1954.

7 JHD to Beaverbrook, cable, 6 March 1923, DP 105; see also M. Barkley, 'The Loyalist Tradition in New Brunswick: The Growth and Evolution of an Historical Myth, 1825–1914,' *Acadiensis*, 4 (spring 1975).

8 JHD to Bennett, 29 July 1930, DP 308.

9 JHD to Beaverbrook, 20 Nov. 1929, DP 147.

10 28 Aug. 1928.

11 Halifax *Chronicle*, 19 Jan. 1921. See John Willis, *A History of Dalhousie Law School* (Toronto, 1979), 56.

12 See T.W. Acheson, 'The National Policy and the Industrialization of the Maritimes 1880–1910,' *Acadiensis*, 1 (spring 1972).

13 Canadian Northern Railway Company Records, RG 30, vol. 1211, p. 12.

14 Quoted in A.J.P. Taylor, *Beaverbrook* (London, 1972), 12.

15 'Political Jottings,' July–Aug. 1951, C.G. Power Papers, box 1.

16 Montreal *Gazette*, 29 Aug. 1901.

17 JHD to Dunn, Fischer and Co., London, 22 Aug. 1906, DP 1. All arbitrage communications were dispatched in code.

18 JHD to Dunn, Fischer and Co., 19 March 1907, DP 2.

19 Horne-Payne to JHD, 7 April 1907, DP 7; see D.P. Hanna, *Trains of Recollection* (Toronto, 1924).

20 W. Vaughan, *Sir William Van Horne* (Toronto, 1926), chp. 24.

21 JHD to F.C. Annesley, 24 Jan. 1923, DP 290; see T.D. Regehr, *The Canadian Northern Railway: Pioneer Road of the Northern Prairies 1895–1918* (Toronto, 1976).

22 JHD to Laurier, 7 June 1904, Laurier Papers, no. 86507-8.

23 New York *Times* 9 May 1915; entry for F.S. Pearson in *The Dictionary of American Biography* (New York, 1934), 14: 358–9.

24 See H.V. Nelles, *The Politics of Development* (Toronto, 1974), 222–3. The people's power movement did not, however, invariably triumph in Canada. See H.V. Nelles, 'Public Ownership of Electrical Utilities in Manitoba and Ontario, 1906–30,' CHR, Dec. 1976.

25 See C.A. Gauld, *The Last Titan: Percival Farquhar* (Stanford, 1964).

26 See copies of concessions, especially the lavish terms extracted by M.C. Keith for his International Railways of Central America, in DP 390. See also: Gauld, *Last Titan*; S.G. Hanson, 'The Farquhar Syndicate in South America,' *Hispanic American Review*, 17 (1937); P. Farquhar, 'South America and Investments,' *North American Review*, March 1916, pp. 397–402; R. Graham, *Britain and the Onset of Modernization in Brazil, 1850–1914* (Cambridge, 1968); and M. Wilkins, *The Emergence of Multinational Enterprise: American Business Abroad from the Colonial Era to 1914* (Cambridge, 1970).

27 See, for example, An Act Respecting the Mexican Light and Power Co. Ltd., 3 Edward VII, c. 153, and incorporation correspondence for Mexican North Western Railway Company, Incorporations Branch, Secretary of State Department, RG 95, file no. 146908.

28 Joseph Pope, secretary of state, to Blake, Lash and Cassel, 16 Nov. 1908, RG 95, file 1-1149.

29 See J.H. Dunn and Co. to JHD, 15 Sept. 1906, DP 16.

30 T. Mulvey, 'Minority Shareholders,' *Monetary Times Annual*, 1919, p. 109; see also 'Changes in Company Act,' ibid., 1918, pp. 54–8.

31 Fischer to JHD, 8 June 1908, DP 10.

32 JHD to R. Fleming, 8 July 1910, DP 258.

33 See, for instance, JHD to Hans Schuster, Berlin, 2 July 1906, DP 249.

34 CAR, 1907, p. 34. Other loans unrelated to Dunn also precipitated Stewart's fall.

35 Stewart to JHD, 14 June 1911, DP 32.

36 JHD to Jarvis, 10 Feb. 1908, DP 252. The Sovereign Bank did have to write off $700,655 in bad debts.

37 JHD to V.J. Hughes, 28 May 1912, DP 262.

38 Violet Stuart-Wortley, *Grow Old along with Me* (London, 1952), 113.

39 Augustus John, 'Fragment of an Autobiography XIV,' *Horizon*, (Dec. 1945), 428.

40 Noel Coward, *Present Indicative* (London, 1937), 214.

41 See Dora de Houghton Carrington, *Carrington: Letters and Extracts from Her Diaries* (London, 1970), 408 and 417.

42 *Time*, 16 Jan. 1956.

43 A.W. Routledge to JHD, 20 March 1912, DP 37.

44 P.H. Emden, *Money Powers of Europe in the Nineteenth and Twentieth Centuries* (New York–London, 1938), 290–6; F. Redlich, *The Molding of American Banking: Men and Ideas*, Part II, 1840–1910 (New York, 1951), chp. 21; N.S.B. Gras, *Business and Capitalism: An Introduction to Business History* (New York, 1939), chp. 6.

45 R. Kellet, *The Merchant Banking Arena* (London, 1967), p. 4; for the North American context, see F. Redlich, *The Molding*, and Hugh Bullock, *The Story of Investment Banking* (New York, 1959).

46 English Construction Co. files, 1908–39, DP 350-1.

47 Agreement between H.M. Hoskins and Dunn, Fischer and Co., 6 Feb. 1910 (for Bolivian railway concession), DP 389.

48 See W.E. Smith to JHD, 5 March 1909, DP 13, offering St Petersburg tram concession.

49 See Agreement between Dunn, Fischer and Co. and E. Stallaerts and Loewenstein, 17 July 1912, DP 390 (for exchange of Brazilian Traction shares); for Loewenstein's career see London *Times*, 6 July 1928.

50 J.M. Bello, *A History of Modern Brazil* (Stanford, 1966), 178.

51 Pearson to JHD, 9 March, 14 April, and 15 May 1906, DP 6.

52 JHD to A. Loewenstein, 18 March 1912; JHD to Pearson, same date; JHD to J.H. Horace, 8 May 1912, DP 262; and Pearson to JHD, 14 Feb. 1913, DP 42.

53 Fischer to JHD, 19 Aug. 1910, DP 27. Havana Docks was promoted by Sir William Van Horne and Sir Robert Perks.

54 JHD to Farquhar, 3 Aug. 1909, DP 256.

55 JHD to F.H. Deacon, 20 July 1909, DP 256.

56 JHD to H. Price, 22 Sept. 1910, DP 259.

57 JHD to Hayden, Stone and Co., New York, 23 May 1911, DP 261.

58 JHD to Pearson, 20 May 1913, DP 265.

59 JHD to F.D. Bryne, 13 Aug. 1909, DP 256.

60 JHD to Sir William Van Horne, 27 July 1909, DP 256.

61 JHD to M. Goran, 11 Nov. 1913, and JHD to Fischer, 19 Nov. 1913, DP 266.

62 JHD to M. Bonham Carter, 11 Feb. 1913, DP 264; Lady Cynthia Asquith, *Diaries 1915–1918* (London, 1968), 26 and 46–7.

63 Borden to Sir Thomas White, 22 Nov. 1918, White Papers, no. 11570-1.

64 Asquith to JHD, 14 July 1923, DP 108.

65 *Courage*, 18.

66 JHD to D. Hazen, 23 Sept. 1911; JHD to T. White, 5 Oct. 1911, DP 261.

67 JHD to B.F. Pearson, 16 Oct. 1911, DP 261; JHD to Fielding, 11 March 1912, DP 262; and Fielding to Dunn, 29 June 1912, DP 38.

68 JHD to C.L. Fischer, 7 Sept. 1909, DP 16.

69 JHD to R.C. Brown, 29 Jan. 1913, DP 254.

70 Beaverbrook, *Courage*, 77.

71 JHD to Hans Schuster, 19 July 1906, DP 249. Dunn's 'friends' were probably D.M. Stewart of the Sovereign Bank and E.R. Wood of National Trust.

72 Kellet, *The Merchant Banking Arena*, and W. Turrentine Jackson, *The Enterprising Scot: Investors in the American West after 1873* (Edinburgh, 1968), 21–2, 71, and 313.

73 JHD to W.K. Whigham, 2 Sept. 1908, and JHD to F.S. Pearson, 4 Sept. 1908, DP 254.

74 JHD to Pearson, 4 Sept. 1908; see also cables in DP 11. Dunn to Clergue, 24 Oct. 1908, DP 254.

75 JHD to R. Lindsey, 19 Oct. 1909, DP 256, and JHD to R. Fleming, 19 Nov. 1908, DP 254.

76 JHD to B. Mackelvie, 29 Aug. 1910, DP 259.

77 See: R. Atkin, *Revolution! Mexico 1910–1920* (London, 1969); R.E. Quirke, *The Mexican Revolution 1914–1920* (Bloomington, 1960); C.C. Cumberland, *The Struggle for Modernity* (New York, 1963); and J.C.M. Ogelsby, *Gringos from the Far North: Essays in the History of Canadian–Latin American Relations 1866–1968* (Toronto, 1976), esp. chp. 6.

78 JHD to T. Aitken, 23 March 1913, DP 264.

79 Harrsen cable from Mexico City, 22 March 1912, DP 42.

80 Anon. to Pearson, 18 Feb. 1914, DP 53.

81 Pearson to JHD, 29 Sept. 1912, DP 39.

82 JHD to Sir Arthur Nicholson, 1 Oct. 1912, DP 263; JHD to Pearson, 4 March 1913, DP 264; JHD to Greenwood, 4 March 1913, ibid.; JHD to Borden, (?) Jan. 1913, DP 42; and 'Mexico' files, FO 371, vols. 2029, 2030, and 2387, PRO.

83 Marginalia on telegram Sir L. Carden to Sir Edward Grey, 26 June 1914, FO 371, vol. 2029, no. 28758, PRO.

84 JHD to A. Ellert, 22 April 1914, DP 268; R. Quirk, *An Affair of Honour: Woodrow Wilson and the Occupation of Vera Cruz* (Lexington, 1962).

85 JHD to L. Christie, 4 March 1919, DP 277.

86 JHD to H. Wauters, 9 July 1927, DP 297; see Dunn's efforts to form a private air force to police his Mexican holdings, JHD to Sir William Wiseman, 11 Aug. 1919, DP 277.

87 JHD to W. Gow, 15 April 1937, DP 179.

88 E.R. Wood to JHD, 23 July 1913, DP 46.

89 Loewenstein to JHD, 5 Dec. 1913, DP 50.

90 Ashurst, Morris, Crisp and Co. to JHD, 27 Feb. 1915, DP 61.

91 JHD to M.C. Keith, 3 April 1914, DP 268.

92 JHD to H.H. Harrsen, 24 April 1914, ibid.

93 See E.V. Morgan and W.A. Thomas, *The Stock Exchange: Its History and Functions* (London, 1961), chp. 14.

94 JHD to Frick, 24 July 1914, DP 269.

95 JHD to F.C. Annesley, 28 Jan. 1924, DP 290.

96 JHD to Williams-Taylor, 7 April 1915, DP 271.

97 JHD to H. Greenwood, 20 Aug. 1914, DP 269.

98 JHD to R. de la Chaume, 9 July 1915, DP 272.

99 JHD to R. Fleming, 12 Feb. 1915, DP 271.

100 See, for instance, JHD to M. Bonham Carter, 24 Feb. 1915, DP 271; memo of conversation with J.H. Dunn, 9 March 1916, Flavelle Papers, PAC, vol. 6, file 58.

101 See: H.V. Nelles, *The Politics of Development* (Toronto, 1974), 352–6; O.W. Main, *The Canadian Nickel Industry: A Study in Market Control and Public Policy* (Toronto, 1955); *Royal Ontario Nickel Commission: Report and Appendix* (1917); and D.M. Le Bourdais, *Sudbury Basin: The Story of Nickel* (Toronto, 1953).

102 *Royal Ontario Nickel*, 83–90 and appendix: 'The Hybinette Process.'

103 See J.H. Dunn, 'Memorandum Concerning B.A.N.C. and K.N.R. and My Efforts to Prevent K.N.R. Nickel Going to Germany,' 10 July 1917, FO 382, vol. 1472, no. 140644, PRO.

104 Wood to JHD, 14 April 1913, DP 44. Ontario's Metal Refining Bounty Act of 1907 extended bounties to copper, silver, nickel, and cobalt.

105 Wood to JHD, 16 Jan. 1914, DP 52.

106 JHD to Pearson, 16 Oct. 1914, DP 59; see A.C. Bell, *The Blockade of Germany and the Countries Associated with Her in the Great War 1914–18* (London, 1937).

107 Pearson to JHD, 18 Oct. 1914, DP 59; see Dunn's efforts to lobby Sam Hughes in London, JHD to Pearson, 29 Oct. 1914, DP 270.

108 Pearson to Borden, 20 Nov. 1914, Borden Papers, no. 58531-39, c-282.

109 Perley to Borden, 15 Dec. 1914, ibid.; Governor General to secretary of state for colonies, 2 March 1915, FO382, vol. 300, PRO.

110 White to Borden, 3 and 27 Feb. 1915, Borden Papers, nos. 58689-92 and 58788.

111 JHD to A. Anderson, 31 March 1915, DP 271; see Foreign Office Norwegian nickel files, FO 382, vols. 300, 884, 906, 1472, and 2235.

112 JHD to Anderson, 31 March 1915, DP 271.

113 Ontario Bureau of Mines, *Annual Report*, 30 (1921), 66; Le Bourdais, *Sudbury*, 127.

114 J. Frater Taylor to JHD, 1 Dec. 1917, DP 77.

115 JHD to Wood, 5 Feb. 1921, DP 91.

116 Wood to Dunn, 20 Jan. 1921, DP 91.

117 Flavelle to JHD, 1 Jan. 1921, DP 91.
118 JHD to Kahn, 19 and 23 Feb. 1920, DP 278.
119 JHD to H. Macdougall, 2 Feb. 1921, DP 281.
120 JHD to D.M. Stewart, 13 Jan. 1921, ibid.
121 JHD to Mrs Narbord, 17 May 1929, DP 305.
122 JHD to Krassin, 9 March 1921, DP 281.
123 L. Christie to JHD, 17 May 1923, DP 107; L. Christie to R. Borden, 15 March 1926, Borden Papers, no. 148306.
124 JHD to Killam, 14 June 1920, DP 88.
125 JHD to E.R. Wood, 12 Sept. 1920, DP 88.
126 W.A. Thomas and E. Morgan, *The Stock Exchange*, chp. 13.
127 See: D. Landes, *The Unbound Prometheus* (Cambridge, 1970), 276 and 454–6; D.C. Hague, 'The Man-made Fibres Industry,' in D.L. Burn, ed., *The Structure of British Industry* (Cambridge, 1958); and R.S. Sawyer, 'Springs of Technical Progress in Britain 1919–39,' *Economic Journal*,60 (1950), 275–91.
128 JHD to Otto Kahn, 19 Feb. 1920, DP 278; A. Spitzer to JHD, 16 March 1920, DP 86.
129 JHD to McGowan, 3 June 1924, DP 291.
130 JHD to G. Hayet, 28 July 1924, DP 292.
131 6 July 1928. Loewenstein pursued the lucrative possibilities of artificial silk with his International Holding and Investment Company Ltd.
132 Loewenstein to JHD, 23 June 1926, DP 297.
133 JHD to Peacock, 8 Dec. 1922, DP 286.
134 JHD to Sir F. Williams-Taylor, 1 Feb. 1927, DP 298, and E.R. Wood to JHD, 12 Jan. 1927, DP 157.
135 JHD to Williams-Taylor, 7 Jan. 1927, DP 298.
136 Christie to JHD, 10 March 1927, DP 138, and King to Sir Henry Thornton, 6 July 1928, King Papers, J1 series, no. 134970-1.
137 6 July 1928; see Dunn's explanation, JHD to H. Stinnes, 26 July 1928, DP 145.
138 Details in DP 160.
139 F.C. Strudwick to JHD, 16 Feb. 1932, DP 163, and JHD to Fosdick, 11 May 1932, DP 184.
140 Coward, *Present Indicative*, 212.
141 JHD to W.F. Benson, 10 May 1926, DP 134.
142 JHD to Meighen, 15 Sept. 1926, and Meighen to JHD, 18 Sept. 1926, Meighen Papers, no. 87765-7.
143 JHD to W.C. Franz, 2 July 1929, DP 305.
144 JHD to Philip Dunn, 28 Nov. 1927, DP 300.
145 A. Stanley Mackenzie to JHD, 2 July 1929, DP 151. Dunn declined the honour.

146 *Courage*, inscription.

147 F. Redlich, 'The Business Leader as a "Daimonic Figure,"' in *Steeped in Two Cultures: A Selection of Essays* by Fritz Redlich (New York, 1971), 33–64. See also P.M. Sweezy, 'The Heyday of the Investment Banker' and 'The Decline of the Investment Banker,' in *The Present as History* (New York, 1953).

148 Redlich, *The Molding of American Banking*, 382.

149 R. Home Smith to JHD, 13 Sept. 1920, DP 90. Smith was describing the shareholders of the Algoma Central Railway.

150 S.G. Archibald to JHD, 8 May 1924, DP 119.

CHAPTER SIX

1 JHD to R. McColl, 17 Dec. 1910, DP 260.

2 JHD to H.C. Frick, 24 July 1914, DP 269, and JHD to E.R. Wood, 12 Sept. 1923, DP 289.

3 JHD to P.G. Dunn, 15 June 1927, DP 299.

4 Equitable Office Building file, DP 365.

5 Empire Trust files, DP 349.

6 Frater Taylor to JHD, 24 June 1924, DP 120.

7 JHD to E.R. Wood, 9 Nov. 1925, DP 295.

8 L. Christie to R.L. Borden, 22 Sept. 1924, Borden Papers, C-347, no. 148098-100; Lord Beaverbrook, *Courage* (Fredericton, 1961), 66; and Franz Newman, *Behemoth: The Structure and Practice of National Socialism 1933–34* (New York, 1966), 15.

9 See Stephen Miall, *History of the British Chemical Industry* (London, 1931), and Hector Belitho, *Alfred Mond: First Lord Melchett* (New York, 1933). Other friends of Dunn's, notably Reginald McKenna, were leading exponents of 'rationalization' in the British steel industry in the 1920s; see Lord Vaisey, *The History of British Steel* (London, 1974).

10 JHD to L. Christie, 2 Aug. 1926, DP 133, and JHD to J.A. McPhail, 12 Jan. 1934, DP 318.

11 JHD to E.R. Wood, 9 Nov. 1926, DP 295, and JHD to Meighen, 15 Sept. 1926, Meighen Papers, no. 87766-7.

12 O.S. Nock, *Algoma Central Railway* (London, 1975), chps. 7 and 8.

13 23 Aug. 1928.

14 W.H. Cunningham to W.K. Whigham, 18 May 1927, McPhail Papers, box 7.

15 Ibid.

16 Frater Taylor to JHD, 23 Jan. 1925, DP 128.

17 Wood to Ferguson, 22 Oct. 1924, Frater Taylor to Wood, 21 Oct. 1924, Ferguson Papers, 1924 general correspondence.

18 McPhail to M. Insull, 13 May 1925 and 1 Sept. 1927, McPhail Papers, box 4.

19 See, for instance, Toronto *Mail and Empire*, 29 Nov. 1928, and Winnipeg *Free Press*, 30 Nov. 1929.

20 JHD to E.R. Wood, 23 June 1927, and cable, JHD to Leroy Baldwin, 23 June 1927, DP 299.

21 JHD to E.R. Wood, 7 July 1927, ibid.

22 H.H. Prince to JHD, 5 Jan. 1923, DP 103.

23 JHD to Leroy Baldwin, 31 May 1928, DP 302.

24 JHD to W.K. Whigham, 25 Jan. 1927, DP 298.

25 JHD to Frater Taylor, 21 July 1927, DP 299.

26 JHD to W.K. Whigham, 25 Jan. 1927, DP 298.

27 JHD to W.C. Franz, 13 Dec. 1927, DP 300.

28 JHD to W.K. Whigham, 14 Dec. 1927, ibid.

29 JHD to J.S. Dale, 26 April 1928, DP 301, and London *Times*, 23 April, 1928.

30 JHD to E.R. Wood, 3 May 1928, DP 302.

31 See Nock, *Algoma Central Railway*, chp. 8.

32 See W. Kilbourn, *The Elements Combined* (Toronto, 1960), 129. For BESCO reorganization, see CAR, 1927/8, pp. 446–7 and 354–5, and David Frank, 'The Cape Breton Coal Industry and the Rise and Fall of the British Empire Steel Corporation,' *Acadiensis*, 7: 1 (autumn 1977). Dunn in mid-1929 feared that Holt et al. had designs on Algoma (JHD to Sir Frederick Williams-Taylor, 17 Aug. 1929, DP 151).

33 *Financial Post*, 24 Aug. 1928.

34 JHD to W.K. Whigham, 17 Jan. 1928, DP 301.

35 Robert F. Dodd, born at Cherry Valley, PEI, in 1883, began his financial career in 1908 in a New York trust company, subsequently moving to Montreal where he had great success in floating the Alabama Traction, Light and Power Co.

36 *Financial Post*, 24 Aug. 1928; *Monetary Times Annual Review*, 1929, pp. 208–10; and CAR, 1927/8, pp. 356–7.

37 See N.J. Greene to D.A. Machum, 28 July 1964, Algoma Steel Historical Files. Greene, a Philadelphia broker, helped Dodd buy on American markets.

38 JHD to Sir F. Williams-Taylor, cable, 10 April 1929, DP 304.

39 JHD to F. Meredith, cable, 28 May 1929, DP 305.

40 JHD to Thomas Arnold, 29 April 1929, DP 305.

41 JHD to H. Coppell, 15 Aug. 1929, DP 306, and JHD to W.C. Franz, 23 Dec. 1929, DP 307.

42 E.V. Morgan and W.A. Thomas, *The Stock Exchange: Its History and Functions* (London, 1962), chp. 14; R. Kellet, *The Merchant Banking Arena* (London, 1967); and A. Boyle, *Montagu Norman: A Biography* (London, 1968).

43 See Vincent Carosso, 'Washington and Wall Street: The New Deal and Investment Bankers 1933–40,' *Business History Review*, 44 (winter 1970).

44 Ibid., 426.

45 See Samuel Merwin, *Rise and Fight Again: The Story of a Lifelong Friend* (New York, 1935), and JHD to H. Greenwood, 20 June 1944, DP 210.

46 E.W. Beatty to JHD, 2 May 1932, DP 171.

47 See notes of private meeting between Dunn and Bennett, Ritz-Carlton Hotel, Montreal, May 1932, DP 172, and JHD to Bennett, 16 March 1932, ibid.

48 Rhodes to JHD, 24 Aug. 1933, DP 173.

49 Ferguson to JHD, 29 Dec. 1934, DP 191.

50 'Sir James Dunn Correspondence, 1933,' Bennett Papers, vol. 947, no. 598337-56.

51 Ferguson to Bennett, ibid., no. 201512.

52 Ibid., 21 June 1934, no. 201541.

53 Bennett to Ferguson, 21 June 1934, ibid., no. 201538.

54 See also W.C. Franz, 'Primary Iron and Steel Had Difficult Year,' *Monetary Times Annual*, 1932, p. 14.

55 LSC, *Annual Reports*, 1929–33, and Algoma production statistics, DP 316. Only coke for domestic use increased in output during these years.

56 JHD to Franz, 30 July 1931, DP 309.

57 Kilbourn, *Elements Combined*, chp. 9.

58 See R.H. McMaster to Bennett, 14 July 1932, Bennett Papers, no. 458326; 'Memorandum for R.W. Breadner, Commissioner of Customs, Ottawa, referring to Report of Conference between British and Canadian Iron and Steel Manufacturers, 15 July 1932, ibid., no. 458327-33; and 'Brief Prepared by the Primary Steel Producers of Canada, June 28, 1932,' ibid., no. 458356-475.

59 JHD to Frank Common, 17 May 1930, DP 308.

60 JHD to Glendyne, 13 Aug. 1930, ibid.

61 JHD to A.M. Erlinger, 19 Dec. 1933, DP 385.

62 JHD to Frater Taylor, 19 June 1930, DP 156.

63 JHD to W.C. Franz, 11 March 1931, DP 309.

64 See Vaisey, *The History of British Steel*.

65 JHD to Franz, 22 Nov. and 15 Dec. 1930, DP 315.

66 JHD to Baldwin, 28 Nov. 1939, DP 343.

67 Algoma Consolidated Corporation, *Annual Report*, 1932; see also Algoma Consolidated Corp. Ltd. File, RG 95, file 146144.

68 JHD to S.C. Norsworthy, 29 June 1932, DP 314.

69 JHD to E.R. Wood, c. Dec. 1930, DP 387.

70 Franz to JHD, 27 April 1932, DP 315.

71 J. Frater Taylor to JHD, 30 May 1932, DP 317.

72 Wickes and Neilson to N.W. Rowell, 10 May 1932, DP 319.

73 JHD to Baldwin, 30 June 1932, DP 344.

74 See file 7, DP 311.

75 *Financial Times*, 14 Oct. 1932.

76 J.A. McPhail to JHD, 12 Oct, 1933, McPhail Papers, box 5.

77 *Iron and Steel and Their Products* (DBS, Ottawa, 1935), table 19.

78 W.C. Franz to T.E. Simpson, 27 Oct. 1932, Bennett Papers, vol. 789, no. 485662.

79 W.C. Franz to JHD, 2 April 1934, DP 315, and Bennett Papers, vol. 789, no. 485663. Sault Ste Marie's population in 1932 was 23,000.

80 H.M. Jaquays, 'Canadian Steel Industry Now Shows Upward Trend,' *Monetary Times Annual*, 1934.

81 H.M. Jaquays, 'Canadian Steel Industry Continues Upward Trend,' *Monetary Times Annual*, 1935.

82 Financial report to receivers, 1933/4, DP 311.

83 McPhail to JHD, 12 July 1934, DP 318.

84 Memo by T.E. Simpson, 27 Oct. 1932, Bennett Papers, vol. 789, no. 485663.

85 Perley to Bennett, 19 June 1933, ibid., no. 316111.

86 Privy Council Order 1285, 28 June 1933; Simpson to Perley, 24 June 1933, Bennett Papers, vol. 508, no. 316118; and Perley to Hungerford, 30 June 1933, ibid., no. 316125.

87 DHC, 26 March 1934, p. 1826. Dosco received a similar rail deal.

88 Ibid., 11 April 1934, pp. 2052–3.

89 JHD to A.M. Erlinger, 9 Oct, 1933, DP 385.

90 Manion to Bennett, 4 May 1934, Bennett Papers, vol. 508, no. 316159.

91 McPhail to Simpson, 27 April 1934, DP 318.

92 JHD to Lilley, 14 June 1934, DP 311.

93 Curran to Henry, 4 Aug. 1931, Henry Papers, PAO, 'Department of Northern Development' file.

94 Franz to JHD, 12 May 1934, DP 315.

95 R.M. Alway, 'Mitchell F. Hepburn and the Liberal Party in the Province of Ontario 1937–43' (unpublished MA thesis, University of Toronto, 1965), 62.

96 Memo by Dunn, n.d. (c. 1934), DP 315.

97 Curran to JHD, 7 Oct. 1933, DP 310.

98 Curran to JHD, 4 Nov. 1933, DP 310; see also Sault *Daily Star*, 2 and 3 Oct. 1933.

99 *Report to Sir James Dunn on the Works of the Algoma Steel Corp.*, Oct. 1934, DP 310. American-born, Atha had a considerable repute in the British Steel industry. See Vaisey, *British Steel*, 73.

100 Atha to JHD, 14 Nov. 1934, DP 310.
101 W. Wright to F. Wickes, 21 Nov. 1933, DP 319.
102 Rowell to JHD, 9 June 1933, and JHD to McPhail, 22 Dec. 1934, DP 319.
103 Franz to JHD, 26 June 1934, DP 315.
104 Ibid., 9 Nov. 1934, DP 315.
105 M.F. Hepburn to Wright, 22 Nov. 1934, DP 319.
106 This is the interpretation in N. McKenty, *Mitch Hepburn* (Toronto, 1967), 101.
107 See M. Prang, *N.W. Rowell: Ontario Nationalist* (Toronto, 1975).
108 JHD to F. Wickes, 16 Oct. 1934, DP 189.
109 JHD to Wright, cable, 16 Oct. 1934, DP 319.
110 Wright to JHD, 17 Nov. 1934, ibid.
111 Nixon to Roberts, 7 Nov. 1934, ibid.
112 Wright to JHD, cable, 7 Nov. 1934, ibid.
113 JHD to Wright, 12 Nov. 1934, DP 320.
114 Wright to Hepburn, 15 Nov. 1934, DP 319.
115 'Memorandum for the Hon. Mr. Nixon from F.V. Johns,' 22 Nov. 1934, Hepburn Papers, 1934 private correspondence.
116 Confidential memo, Humphries to H.C. Nixon, 24 Nov. 1934, ibid.
117 Roebuck to Hepburn, n.d., ibid.
118 JHD to Wright, 7 Dec. 1934, DP 320.
119 Application made 29 Nov. 1934, letters patent issued 12 Dec. 1934, DP 320.
120 Agreement of 14 Dec. 1934, DP 310.
121 See London *Times*, 2 Jan. 1935.
122 Wright to JHD, 29 Nov. 1934, DP 319.
123 8 Jan. 1935, ibid.
124 'Notice of Submission of Plan of Exchange,' circulated by Philadelphia Committee, 26 Jan. 1935, DP 311.
125 What publicity there was was generally sympathetic; see 'A Prospect for the Sault,' editorial, Toronto *Globe*, 20 March 1935.
126 Wright to JHD, 8 Jan. 1935, DP 319.
127 McPhail to JHD, 6 April 1935, DP 318.
128 Toronto *Globe*, 3 April 1935.
129 McPhail to JHD, 6 April 1935, DP 318.
130 *Ontario Statutes*, George V, xv, chp. 76.
131 JHD to Philip Dunn, 7 May 1935, DP 193.
132 Dinner guest list, 10 May 1935, DP 319.
133 JHD to Wright, 18 May 1935, DP 319.
134 Costello to Bennett, 5 Dec. 1934, Bennett Papers, vol. 146, no. 96810.
135 C.H. Cahan to Costello, 10 Dec. 1934, ibid.

136 C.D. de Bosdari to Toronto General Trusts, 16 Nov. 1936, DP 318.
137 W.R. McKague, *Investment* (Toronto, 1931), 18.
138 F.W. Wegenast, *The Law of Canadian Companies* (Toronto, 1931), 315.
139 *Report of the Royal Commission into the Affairs of the Abitibi Power and Paper Company Ltd.* (Toronto, 1941), 4–6.
140 Editorial, May–June 1935.
141 Toronto *Globe*, 3 April 1935.
142 JHD to Hepburn, 13 Aug. 1941, Hepburn Papers, 'Sir James Dunn file – private, 1941.'

CHAPTER SEVEN

1 Adolf A. Berle and Gardiner C. Means, *The Modern Corporation and Private Property* (New York, 1932), preface.
2 Alfred D. Chandler, Jr, *The Visible Hand: The Managerial Revolution in American Business* (Cambridge, Mass., 1977), 381.
3 Ibid., 491.
4 The notion that the same managerial or psychological belief can explain both initial success and ultimate failure is explored in Anne Jardim, *The First Henry Ford: A Study in Personality and Business Leadership* (Cambridge, Mass., 1970). Ford's dogmatic belief that America wanted the Model T explains both his company's tremendous early success and its gradual eclipse by competitors. Success and failure are not therefore necessarily the products of autonomous factors. Dunn's obsession with control fits this pattern.
5 *Minutes of Directors' Meetings*, Algoma Steel Corporation, Book I, 4, 6, and 10 May 1935.
6 Sault *Daily Star*, 13 May 1935. Also present were T.E. Simpson, MP, A.D. Roberts, MPP, and Ward Wright, and J.W. Curran of the *Star*.
7 Algoma's New Steel Sheet Piling and Structural Shapes,' *Iron and Steel of Canada*, July–August 1935, pp. 54–7.
8 *Iron and Steel and Their Products, 1934–5* (DBS, Ottawa, 1935); H.M. Jaquays, 'Canadian Steel Industry Continues Upward Trend,' *Monetary Times Annual*, 1935, pp. 62–4, and ibid., 1936, pp. 15–18.
9 JHD to Atha, 9 April 1935, DP 310.
10 JHD to Rahilly, cable, 14 May 1935, DP 316.
11 Ibid., 3 June 1935.
12 Privy Council Orders 1462 and 1533, 7 June 1935; DHC, 28 June 1935, pp. 4106–7; and CAR, 1935/6, p. 23.
13 *First Annual Report*, Algoma Steel Corporation, 1935/6.
14 Rahilly to JHD, 2 Aug. 1935, DP 316.

15 JHD to Rahilly, 16 Aug. 1935, ibid.

16 Barber to JHD, 7 Aug. 1953, DP 224.

17 *Minutes of Directors' Meetings*, 4 June 1936; By-Law No. 8, passed 4 July 1936; Sault *Daily Star*, 6 July 1936; and 'Memo: Algoma Steel New Common shares: property of Sir James,' 1 July 1937, DP 310.

18 'Prospectus of Algoma Steel Corp., November 30, 1935,' DP 314.

19 'Memo: Lake Superior Investment Co. holders,' 30 Nov. 1936, DP 310.

20 JHD to Glendyne, 25 Oct. 1935, DP 311, and 19 Oct. 1949, DP 217.

21 Standard letter form, prepared by Dunn, May 1937, DP 201.

22 Algoma Steel Corporation, *Annual Reports*, 1935–9.

23 JHD to E. Blundell, 30 June 1937, DP 201, and JHD to A.A. Ritchie, 25 March 1938, DP 310.

24 JHD to MacPhial, 25 March 1935, DP 318, and *Minutes of Directors' Meetings*, 6 Nov. 1938.

25 O'Brien to JHD, 24 Nov. 1938, DP 376.

26 JHD to W. Lilley, 14 Dec. 1936, DP 311.

27 C.D. de Bosdari to Toronto General Trusts, 16 Nov. 1936, DP 318.

28 See 'A Man of Steel: Forty Years Ago a Struggling Lawyer, Sir James Dunn Today Nears Realization of His Dream to Create a Steel Empire,' *Financial Post*, 13 March 1937.

29 This persecution complex is one consistent theme that emerges from Lord Beaverbrook's *Courage: The Story of Sir James Dunn* (Fredericton, 1961). Dunn's whole career is depicted as one long struggle against the perfidiousness of his friends, from C.L. Fischer, his London partner, to C.D. Howe, who is said to have tried to topple Dunn in the early years of the Second War.

30 Interview with D.S. Holbrook, 4 Aug. 1977.

31 Kilbourn, *Elements*, 155–6.

32 The Algoma fiscal year ended on 30 April each year. See Algoma Steel Corporation, *Annual Reports*, 1935–7, and 'Investigation of Algoma Steel Co,' conducted by J. Adamson, McClelland and Ker Co., London, April–June 1938, DP 320.

33 Born in Michigan in 1892, Rahilly worked with the Algoma Central and Algoma Eastern railways from 1913 to 1920, then joined the steel company as assistant to the general manager J.D. Jones.

34 'Investigation of ...,' 30.

35 JHD to McPhail, 11 Jan. 1934, DP 318.

36 'Memo: suggestion for consideration, re: iron ore,' by JHD, n.d., DP 315.

37 *Report of Mineral Production of Canada* (DBS, Ottawa, 1935–9 editions).

38 See W.T. Hogan, *Economic History of the Iron and Steel Industry in the United States* (Lexington, Mass., 1971), 4: chp. 40.

39 DHC, 29 May 1936, pp. 3239–40.

40 Ibid., 8 Feb. 1937, p. 675.

41 T.A. Crerar, *The Future of Canadian Mining: A Series of Twelve Radio Addresses Delivered over the National Network of the Canadian Radio Commission* (Ottawa, 1936).

42 Crerar's failure to back up his rhetoric with positive incentives for mining may in part be due to his suspicions of the motives of some of the more prominent mining promoters, notably J.P. Bickell and Ben Smith, of whose rascality he was frequently reminded. See Crerar to A.K. Cameron, 20 April 1936, Cameron Papers, vol. 35.

43 A.D. Roberts warned Hepburn that some northern residents were discussing secession from the province. See Hepburn Papers, file 'Dr. A.D. Roberts: private, 1936.'

44 See: C.K. Keith, 'Report on Helen Siderite Property,' Aug. 1917, DP 320; S.J. Kidder and G.C. McCartney, *Mining and Geology at the Helen Mine* (American Institute of Mining and Metallurgical Engineers, Technical Publication no. 1971, March 1946).

45 C.B. Randall to W.C. Franz, 13 Oct. 1930, DP 342.

46 Memo by JHD, n.d.(c. 1935), DP 375.

47 J.D. Jones, 'Report on "Diversification" Policies to Receivers and Managers of Algoma Steel,' 1 March 1934, DP 312.

48 Rahilly to Hamilton, 23 Feb. 1937, DP 313.

49 See: JHD to Hepburn, cables 30 Aug. and 15 Oct. 1935, DP 313, and Hepburn to JHD, 21 Sept. 1935, DP 177. Dunn also cultivated several of Hepburn's associates, notably Harry Nixon and T.B. McQuesten (JHD to H.J. Allen, 8 Sept. 1935, DP 338). The political implications of Hepburn's relations with Ontario's mining magnates are perceptively discussed in R. Whitaker, *The Government Party: Organizing and Financing the Liberal Party 1930–58* (Toronto, 1977), chp. 8, esp. p. 318. See also H.A. Innis, 'The Canadian Mining Industry,' in M.Q. Innis, ed., *Essays in Canadian Economic History* (Toronto, 1956), 317–18.

50 JHD to T.R. McLagan, 12 March 1955, DP 338. Dunn had told Wright the previous November that Algoma 'can get a good bonus deal with the Government which I am under the impression Mr. Hepburn had already promised me.' JHD to Wright, 3 Nov. 1936, DP 319.

51 Hepburn to Curran, 10 Feb. 1937, Hepburn Papers, box 274, file: 'Iron Ore Industry 1937,'

52 Curran to Hepburn, 13 Feb. 1937, ibid.

53 Roberts to Hepburn, cable, 16 Feb. 1937, ibid. and file 'Dr. A.D. Roberts, M.L.A., Sault Ste. Marie – 1937.'

54 JHD to Wright, 13 Jan. 1936, and JHD to Roberts, 14 Jan. 1936, DP 310. See the accounts of the Roberts affair in Neil McKenty, *Mitch Hepburn* (Toronto, 1967), 95–7.
55 JHD to Hepburn, cable, 5 March 1937, and J.C. Shipley to Hepburn, 31 May 1937, Hepburn Papers, box 274.
56 'Report on the Proposal of the Algoma Steel Corporation Ltd. to Mine and Beneficiate Iron Ore from the New Helen–Michipicoten District,' D.H. McDougall, 3 March 1937, ibid.
57 *Ontario Statutes*, 1 George VI, c. 34; see also R.M. Alway, 'Mitchell F. Hepburn and the Liberal Party in the Province of Ontario 1937–43' (unpublished MA thesis, University of Toronto, 1965), 105–6.
58 JHD to Hon. Paul Leduc, minister of mines, 2 March 1937, DP 313.
59 E.B. Barber to Rahilly, 29 July 1937, DP 313.
60 Algoma Tramways Ltd., incorporated provincially on 29 June 1937. O.S. Nock, *Algoma Central* (London, 1975), 100–1.
61 'Agreement of Algoma Ore Properties and M.A. Hanna Co.,' 1 April 1939, Algoma Steel Historical Files. Interview with George McLeod, 17 Feb. 1977.
62 4 Nov. 1938. See also *Saturday Night*, 7 Jan. 1939. The entire issue was devoted to the Sault, which was 'marching vigorously forward.'
63 See: *Report of Mineral Production of Canada* (DBS, Ottawa, 1940); 'What's Ahead for Canada's Iron Ore?' *Financial Post*, 12 Aug. 1939; and 'Algoma Has Mineral Riches Awaiting Exploitation,' *Saturday Night*, 7 Jan. 1939.
64 JHD to Hepburn, 23 May 1945, DP 213, and Alway, 'Mitchell F. Hepburn and the Liberal Party,' 102–7.
65 Atha to JHD, 23 July 1935, DP 310.
66 Rahilly to JHD, cable, 21 July 1935, DP 316.
67 JHD to C.D. Howe, 17 March 1936, DP 311.
68 Howe to JHD, 19 March and 12 May 1936, ibid.
69 JHD to W. Wright, 30 July 1936, DP 319.
70 Rahilly to G.H. Sedgewick, chairman, Tariff Board, 27 Feb. 1936, DP 316.
71 DHC, 1 May 1936, pp. 2390–1. The 1936 budget did extend increased protection to the Canadian automotive industry, but only in the form of increased tariffs on vehicles and parts, not on raw materials imported prior to production.
72 DHC, 16 March 1936, p. 1111.
73 JHD to Rahilly, 4 July 1939, DP 317.
74 JHD to Wright, 1 may 1936, DP 319.
75 Wright to JHD, 22 Sept. 1936, DP 319.
76 JHD to Rahilly, 21 June 1937, DP 317.

77 JHD to Rahilly, 14 July 1939, DP 317.
78 JHD to Hepburn, 9 June 1938, Hepburn Papers, file: 'Sir James Dunn – private – 1938.'
79 Ibid., 12 Nov. 1938.
80 Rahilly to JHD, 21 May 1935, DP 316, and JHD to Hepburn, 26 May 1939, Hepburn Papers, file: 'Sir James Dunn – 1939 – private.'
81 See 'Hepburn's Right on Sydney's Subsidy,' Sault *Daily Star*, 17 Dec. 1938.
82 JHD to Duplessis, 19 July and 5 Nov. 1939, DP 347. See also R. Whitaker, *The Government Party*, 317.
83 W.L. Mackenzie King diary, 5 Jan. 1939, PAC, MG26 J13.
84 C.H. Charls to Rahilly, 19 Feb. 1936, DP 316.
85 C.G. Atha to JHD, 12 May 1936, DP 310.
86 'Conway Contract, 1937,' DP 320A.
87 'Notes on Continental Can contract and its advantages,' 18 Nov. 1937, and 'Memo for conversation with W. Wright,' 22 Nov. 1937, DP 320A. *Minutes of Directors' Meetings*, Algoma Steel Corp., 17 Dec. 1937 and 4 May 1938.
88 'Report on the Algoma Steel Corporation Ltd.,' Coverdale and Colpitts, New York, 10 Dec. 1943, Algoma Steel Historical Files. See article by Dunn on Algoma's new structural steel shapes in the Toronto *Globe and Mail*, 3 Jan. 1938.
89 'South African rail business, 1934,' DP 383, and JHD to Sir Andrew Duncan, 26 June 1939, DP 310.
90 JHD to Hepburn, 26 May 1939, Hepburn Papers, file: 'Sir James Dunn, private – 1939.'
91 See Glendyne, Fleischmann, Gundy, and Greenwood files in DP 311.
92 Algoma Steel, *Annual Reports*, 1935–7; for Dunn's personal finances see Lake Superior Investment Co. files, DP 385.
93 *Minutes*, 28 Feb. and 10 June 1936.
94 *Minutes*, 23 and 24 July 1937; JHD to E.H. Rawls, Guaranty Trust, 25 April 1938, DP 319. It was alleged that Beaverbrook exerted pressure on Wilson to come to Dunn's assistance.
95 *Minutes*, 28 Oct. 1938. Syndicate members were: Wood, Gundy and Co.; McLeod, Young, Weir and Co.; and Cochran, Murray and Co.
96 *Minutes*, 2 Nov. 1938.
97 DHC, 16 March 1936, p. 1107.
98 Rahilly to JHD, 31 May 1935, DP 312.
99 JHD to Rahilly, 29 March 1938, DP 317.
100 'To the Men,' 8 Jan. 1937, DP 317, and *Minutes of Executive Committee*, 12 May 1939.

101 Coverdale and Colpitts report, 174–5.
102 Rahilly to JHD, 9 Dec. 1936, DP 316. There are no entries for Algoma between 1919 and 1943 in the Department of Labour's 'strikes and lockouts' file, PAC, RG 27.
103 JHD to Rahilly, 9 Dec. 1936, DP 316.
104 JHD to W. Lilley, 30 April 1937, DP 311; Rahilly to JHD, 27 Dec. 1938, DP 317; and I.M. Abella, *Nationalism, Communism, and Canadian Labour* (Toronto, 1973), chps. 1–3.
105 JHD to Rahilly, 2 Sept. 1938, DP 316.
106 JHD to Howe, 17 March 1936, DP 311.

CHAPTER EIGHT

1 JHD to Franz, 26 March 1935, DP 315. Certain of Dunn's English friends, notably Lord Rothermere, had distinct pro-fascist sympathies. Dunn was also close to the Stinnes family, German industrialists who were early backers of Hitler.
2 JHD to W. Lilley, 18 Oct. 1935, DP 311, and memo by JHD, 24 Oct. 1935, DP 195.
3 JHD to Hepburn, 5 Nov. 1938, Hepburn Papers, file: 'Sir James Dunn – private, 1938.'
4 JHD to Duplessis, 19 July 1939, DP 347. Dunn seemed oblivious to French-Canadian anxieties about the impending conflict.
5 'Memo, for M.F.H. from JHD,' 24 April 1939, Hepburn Papers, file: 'Sir James Dunn, private – 1939.'
6 N. McLarty to JHD, 20 Dec. 1939, and JHD to McLarty, 18 Jan. 1940, Hepburn Papers, file: 'Sir James Dunn, private – 1940.' Dunn was protesting PC Order 3495, of 7 Nov. 1939.
7 'Dunn has convinced Premier Hepburn that England is in danger of imminent collapse. Dunn cites personal messages from Churchill and Beaverbrook in support of this view.' Message from 'my representative in U.S.A.,' Beaverbrook in an undated (c. late 1940) letter to 'Hay' (?), Beaverbrook Papers, HLRO, file D12.
8 JHD to Inskip, 27 Oct. 1938, DP 311.
9 Rahilly to JHD, 17 Oct. 1938, DP 311.
10 JHD to Hepburn, 26 May 1939, Hepburn Papers, file: 'Sir James Dunn, private – 1939,' and JHD to Greenwood, 18 may 1939, DP 311.
11 Contract dated 4 Dec. 1940, Department of Munitions and Supply Papers, RG 28A, vol. 172.

12 J. de N. Kennedy, *History of the Department of Munitions and Supply* (2 vols.; Ottawa, 1950); 'Report on the Activities of the Steel Control from Its Establishment by Order-in-Council of June 24, 1940 to October 1, 1943,' dated 1 Nov. 1943, RG 28A, vol. 261; and W. Kilbourn, *The Elements Combined* (Toronto, 1960), chp. 10.

13 Privy Council Order 2742, 24 June 1940.

14 Privy Council Order 8053, 9 Sept. 1942.

15 J.L. Granatstein, *Canada's War: The Politics of the Mackenzie King Government 1939–45* (Toronto, 1975); C.D. Howe, *The Industrial Front* (Ottawa, 1944); R. Warren James, *Wartime Economic Co-operation: A Study of Relations between Canada and the United States* (Toronto, 1949); K.W. Taylor, 'Canadian Wartime Price Controls, 1941–6,' CJEPS, 13 (Feb. 1947); and Kennedy, *History of the Department*.

16 JHD to Howe, 25 Nov. 1942, DP 324. For Howe's wartime role, see Robert Bothwell and William Kilbourn, *C.D. Howe: A Biography* (Toronto, 1979), chps. 9–11.

17 'Report on the Activities.'

18 Howe to Godsoe, 14 Jan. 1944, RG 28A, vol. 261.

19 DHC, 30 July 1940, p. 2119.

20 Department of Munitions and Supply news release, 13 Aug. 1941, RG 28A, vol. 261.

21 'Principles of Control,' in 'Report on the Activities,' 29.

22 Copies of all Steel Control orders are in RG 28A, vol. 258.

23 Privy Council Order 11/10066, 24 Dec. 1941.

24 'Report on the Activities,' and 'Steel Budget for Calendar Year 1942,' dated 22 Oct. 1941, RG 28A, vol. 171.

25 H.D. Scully to JHD, 14 Nov. 1940, RG 28A, vol. 206.

26 H.D. Scully to W.A. Mackintosh and Louis Rasminsky, 2 June 1941, RG 19 E3(J), vol. 3560, 'D-9.'

27 JHD to C.D. Howe, 2 June 1941, DP 395.

28 JHD to C.D. Howe, 8 July 1941, ibid.

29 JHD to C.D. Howe, 7 July 1941, ibid.

30 Department of National Revenue to Algoma Steel, 24 June 1942, Algoma Steel Historical Files.

31 Brown to Clark, n.d. (probably mid-1942), DP 328, file 5.

32 'Submission to the Steel Controller by Algoma Steel Corp. and Dominion Steel and Coal Ltd. to F.B. Kilbourn,' 3 Oct. 1941, RG 28A, vol. 307.

33 Howe to R.A.C. Henry, 22 Nov. 1941, Howe Papers, vol. 207.

34 JHD to Philip Dunn, 4 Oct. 1940, DP 207.

35 A.G. Bryant to JHD, 8 Sept. 1940, DP 348. 'I realize that I cannot visit England again unless this tax claim is settled and I also realize that it is of a political character and cannot be pursued against me in this country.' JHD to Bryant, 12 April 1945, DP 208.

36 JHD to Hugo Cunliffe-Owen, 28 Aug. 1940, DP 207, and Lord Beaverbrook, *Courage* (Fredericton, 1961).

37 *Minutes of Directors' Meetings*, 30 May 1940, held at Ross Memorial Hospital.

38 Toronto *Globe and Mail*, 16 July 1981.

39 Beaverbrook to Hay (?), mid-Oct. 1940, and Beaverbrook to Churchill, mid-Oct. 1940, Beaverbrook Papers, file D132. Beaverbrook's informant recalled an argument between Ben Smith, a close financial friend of Dunn, and Brendan Bracken, another of his friends, in which Smith had bet that England would be 'completely finished within six weeks.'

40 Howe to Beaverbrook, 10 Aug. 1943, Howe Papers, vol. 170.

41 JHD to F. Sims, 23 Dec. 1940, DP 206.

42 Interview between Brown and D.F. Forster, c. 1965. Transcript courtesy of Professor Robert Bothwell.

43 Howe to Beaverbrook, 18 Dec. 1959 and 17 Aug. 1960, Howe Papers, vol. 187. W.J. Bennett, Howe's chief executive assistant, recalled considerable 'friction' between Howe and Dunn. 'Sir James had his own ideas about what Algoma should produce and these did not always conform to the programme of the Steel Controller' (Bennett to author, 26 July 1977). F.M. Covert of the department's legal staff recollected that while there was never any overt sign that Dunn and Howe were 'at loggerheads,' Dunn 'was always difficult to deal with ... simply because he was the kind of a man who wanted to get the best deal that he could' (Covert to author, 26 July 1977).

44 E.G. McMillan to Board of Transport Commissioners, 21 Nov. 1942; memo by JHD entitled 'Clergue's Railroad,' 4 Dec. 1941, DP 327; see also O.S. Nock, *Algoma Central Railway* (London, 1975), 100–3.

45 Howe to Rahilly, 21 Nov. 1942, DP 327.

46 JHD to Howe, 25 Nov. 1942, DP 327.

47 Smith, Rae, Greer, and Cartwright to Board of Railway Commissioners, 7 Dec. 1942, DP 327.

48 JHD to Rahilly, 11 June 1943, DP 330, and *Minutes of Directors' Meeting*, 16 and 31 Aug. 1943. In 1944, Rahilly sued Algoma for wrongful dismissal and settled for $30,000 (Rahilly to E.G. McMillan, 25 March 1944, DP 330).

49 'Howe had great faith in him [Rahilly],' F.M. Covert to author, 26 July 1977. Howe later secured a consultant's job for Rahilly at Steel Control.

50 See Beaverbrook, *Courage*, chps. 9 and 10, especially the description of Dunn's 'base and wicked foes' and the 'deadly threat from Howe' (p. 148).

51 Howe to Beaverbrook, 17 Aug. 1960, Howe Papers, vol. 187.

52 JHD to J.G. Godsoe, 29 March 1944, RG 28A, vol. 261.

53 JHD to W.H. Coverdale, 22 May 1944, DP 328.

54 Howe to Beaverbrook, 10 Aug. 1943, Howe Papers, vol. 170.

55 Taylor to JHD, 16 Nov. 1942, DP 213.

56 DHC, 18 March 1941, p. 1629. See James, *Wartime Economic Cooperation*, chp. 6, especially p. 135.

57 J.L. Ilsley to Howe, 7 Sept. 1942, RG 19 E-1(d), vol. 2720.

58 *Iron and Steel and Their Products* (DBS, Ottawa, 1938–9, 1940–2, and 1943–5 editions).

59 'Estimate of Canadian Steel Requirements – 1941,' 28 Nov. 1940, revised 6 March 1941; 'Steel Budget for 1942,' 22 Oct. 1941; and 'Steel Budget for 1943,' 15 Feb. 1943, RG 28A, vol. 171.

60 DHC, 21 May 1942, p. 2659.

61 See: R.W. James, *Wartime Economic Cooperation*; J.L. Granatstein and R.D. Cuff, *Canadian-American Relations in Wartime: From the Great War to the Cold War* (Toronto, 1974); and J.L. Granatstein, *Canada's War* (Toronto, 1975), chp. 4.

62 Howe to J.L. Ralston, 20 Dec. 1941, RG 28A, vol. 67.

63 M. Hoey to Howe, 13 May 1943, RG 28A, vol. 260.

64 DHC, 21 May 1942, pp. 2655–8.

65 See Kennedy, *History of the Department*, chp. 22.

66 Ibid., 488–95.

67 See J.H. Perry, *Taxes, Tariffs and Subsidies: A History of Canadian Fiscal Development* (2 vols.; Toronto, 1955), 2: 357.

68 See C.D. Howe and J.R. MacNicol, DHC, 18 March 1941, pp. 1627–8.

69 Privy Council Order 1171, 18 Feb. 1941, confirming contract MP 432 between Algoma Steel and government.

70 Letters of T.N. Kirby, War Contracts Depreciation Board, to Algoma Steel and JHD to C.D. Howe, both 20 Feb. 1941, cited in *Minutes of Directors' Meetings*, 20 Feb. 1941.

71 'Tentative Summary of Progress in the Canadian Steel Industry from the Outbreak of the War 1939–41,' submitted to Steel Control by E.A. Taylor, 18 Oct. 1941, RG 28A, vol. 306.

72 Privy Council Order 9924, 19 Dec. 1941, copy of contract in file 196-14-1, RG 28A, vol. 258.

73 *Report on the Government-Financed Expansion of Industrial Capacity in Canada, as at Dec. 31, 1943* (Economics and Statistics Branch, Department of Munitions and Supply, Ottawa, 29 Feb. 1944) and 'Capital Assistance Projects – Steel Control,' as of 31 Dec. 1944, RG 28A, vol. 205.

74 Government auditor's composite figures for Algoma Steel Corp., 1938–45, signed by R.E. Saunders, 13 March 1946, RG 28 B-2, vol. 1.

75 Memo by Ilsley, 7 Sept. 1942, RG 19 E-1(d), vol. 2720.

76 Howe to Ilsley, 10 Sept. 1942, ibid.

77 DHC, 26 Jan. 1942, p. 53.

78 DHC, 19 May 1942, pp. 2548–9.

79 DHC, 14 June 1943, p. 3619.

80 F.H. Brown to M.A. Hoey, July 1944, RG 28A, vol. 293.

81 T.F. Rahilly to F.B. Kilbourn, 5 Sept. 1944, RG 28A, vol. 195. Rahilly believed Dosco was 'entitled' to assistance because 'acts of Government have placed it in its present position.'

82 DHC, 13 April 1945, p. 868.

83 Special Committee on War Expenditure, *First Report*, 5 May 1942.

84 Ibid., Joint Subcommittees nos. 2 and 3, *Report on the Aluminum Industry*, 26 Jan. 1944.

85 'Production: Estimated and Actual, Oct. 1941–Dec. 1943,' RG 28A, vol. 307. Post-war statistics published in *Iron and Steel and Their Products* showed higher production results of 1,975,014 tons of pig iron and 3,110,254 tons of ingots.

86 DHC, 11 June 1943, p. 3553.

87 *The Industrial Front* (Ottawa, 1944), p. 286.

88 *Iron and Steel and Their Products, 1943–5*.

89 'Report on the Activities of the Steel Control from October 1, 1943 to Its Termination on Nov. 1, 1945,' dated 1 Jan. 1946, RG 28A, vol. 22.

90 Howe to Borden, 30 Oct. 1943, RG 28A, vol. 201.

91 'Report on the Activities ... 1945,' p. 47.

92 Brown-Forster interview, 1965.

93 Contracts of 5 Feb. and 31 Dec. 1943 between Algoma Department of Munitions and Supply, RG 28A, vol. 488.

94 Brown-Forster interview, 1965.

95 PC 5752, 20 July 1943, and 'F.H. Brown correspondence, 1943,' DP 328.

96 Contract of 16 Feb. 1945, RG 28A, vol. 488.

97 'Report on the Algoma Steel Corp. Ltd.,' Coverdale and Colpitts, New York, 19 Dec. 1943, p. 146, Algoma Steel Historical Files. Coverdale and Colpitts apparently tendered a 'secret' report to C.D. Howe in which they expressed some anxiety over Dunn's age and capacity to carry on as president. It was this note of concern that coloured Howe's reaction to Rahilly's dismissal. David Holbrook interview, 4 Aug. 1977.

98 Winslow-Spragge to Algoma Steel, 13 March 1945, RG 28 B-2, vol. 1.

99 'Statement of Percentage of Increase in Costs of Principal Raw Materials Aug. 31, 1939 to Aug. 31, 1941,' presented by Algoma Steel, n.d., RG 28A, vol. 307.

100 'Algoma Steel Corp.: Comparative Profit and Loss Account for the years ended April 30, 1940, 1941 and estimated by 1942,' n.d., RG 28A, vol. 307.

101 See, for instance, F.H. Brown to W.C. Clark, n.d. (c. mid-1943), DP 328.

102 Brown-Forster interview, 1965.

103 Howe to Beaverbrook, 17 Aug. 1960, Howe Papers, vol. 187.

104 Lambert diary, 27 April 1942, Lambert Papers, Queen's University Archives, box 10. It is difficult to establish whether the federal Liberal party 'tollgated' Algoma for its munitions contracts, although this was certainly likely. Algoma contributed $10,000 to Liberal coffers in the 1940 election. R. Whitaker, *The Government Party* (Toronto, 1977), 125.

105 B.B. Berle and T.B. Jacobs, *Navigating the Rapids 1918–1971: From the Papers of A.A. Berle* (New York, 1971), 492–3.

106 J.W. Pickersgill and D.F. Forster, eds., *The Mackenzie King Record 1944–5*, vol. 2 (Toronto, 1968), entry for 9 June 1945, p. 406.

107 JHD to Beaverbrook, cable, 5 Aug. 1943, DP 208.

108 JHD to T.B. McQuesten, 19 Oct. 1944, DP 215.

109 Memo by JHD, 26 April 1944, DP 328.

110 Memo by JHD, 28 March 1944, DP 328.

111 Memo by JHD, 26 April 1944, DP 328. Drew probably saw little political advantage in subsidizing a bustling war industry and also probably realized that federal excess profits taxes would severely curtail the effect of a bounty.

112 M.A. Hoey to MacLeod, 14 Dec. 1943, ibid. Steel Control claimed that the proposed 50¢ a ton price would have an 'adverse moral effect' on wage and price controls.

113 Contract of 20 July 1944, DP 320.

114 'Summary of Estimated Capital Expenditures for Underground Mining and Development: Helen Mine,' 17 Feb. 1943, DP 327.

115 Frequent wartime interruptions in Algoma's supply of American coal had painfully illustrated this to Dunn. See, for instance, H.J. Sissons to T.M. Bryson, 25 July 1945, RG 28A, vol. 293.

116 DHC, 14 June 1941, p. 4023.

117 DHC, 3 May 1939, p. 3539.

118 Perry, *Taxes, Tariffs and Subsidies*, 2: 357; for Howe's interest in the Steep Rock project see Howe Papers, vol. 21, especially C.D. Howe to General D.M. Hogarth, 28 Nov. 1947.

119 *Minutes of Directors' Meetings*, 28 Aug. 1945 and 10 Jan. 1946. Brown subsequently quit the board after an encounter with Dunn's violent temper. Fogo's role as president of the National Liberal Foundation provided Algoma with a link with the party that was to dominate federal politics well into the 1950s.

120 JHD to Glendyne, 23 Jan. 1948, DP 217.

121 A. Aitken to JHD, 12 Aug. 1943, DP 329.
122 JHD to Hobbs, 21 April 1943, ibid.
123 JHD to Meighen, 25 Sept. 1943, DP 331.
124 *Minutes of the Directors' Meetings*, 20 Dec. 1940.
125 JHD to Glendyne, cable, 16 Dec. 1944, DP 210.
126 JHD to Hoey, 30 Aug. 1944, DP 330.

CHAPTER NINE

1 'Location and Effects of Wartime Industrial Expansion in Canada 1939–1944,' Department of Reconstruction and Supply, Directorate of Economic Research, Nov. 1945, p. 6, RG 28 A, vol. 13. See also J.D. Gibson, 'Post-war Economic Development and Policy in Canada,' CJEPS, 20 (1954).
2 Jim Gillies, *Where Business Fails: Business-Government Relations at the Federal Level in Canada* (Montreal, 1981), chps. 1 and 6.
3 JHD to H. Richards, 17 Feb. 1945, DP 233.
4 Kilbourn to J.H. Berry, acting chairman, Departmental Advisory Committee on Dominion-Provincial Conference, 31 Aug. 1944, DP 330.
5 'Location and Effects,' 10.
6 Submission of R.H. McMaster to Steel Control on the post-war steel outlook, 25 Aug. 1944, DP 330.
7 JHD to M. Hoey, 22 Aug. 1944, DP 330.
8 See, for instance, 'What Post-war Markets for Steel: Count on General Expansion to Absorb Our Doubled Capacity,' *Financial Post*, 29 July 1944.
9 JHD to editor, *Financial Post*, 21 Nov. 1945, DP328.
10 W.T. Hogan, *Economic History of the Iron and Steel Industry in the United States* (Lexington, Mass., 1971), 4: 1445. For the origins of the American 'steel crisis' of the late 1940s, see Henry W. Broude, *Steel Decisions and the National Economy* (New Haven, 1963).
11 M.A. Hoey to C.D. Howe, 14 May 1946, DP 330.
12 Howe to H.B. Hosmer, 7 May 1946, Howe Papers, vol. 171.
13 JHD to Howe, 6 May 1946, and Howe to JHD, 27 May 1946, DP 329.
14 JHD to D.S. Holbrook, 7 April 1946, DP 329.
15 M. Hoey to JHD, 28 Nov. 1946, DP 330, and DHC, 20 March 1946, p. 118.
16 'Memo. for Ottawa,' prepared by JHD, c. mid-1946, DP 329, and C.D. Howe to JHD, 20 June 1947, DP 234.
17 C.D. Howe to J.G. Fogo, 7 Dec. 1946, DP 329.
18 DHC, 17 July 1947, p. 5888.
19 JHD to J.S. Duncan, 24 Aug. 1947, DP 331.
20 Howe to JHD, 21 Dec. 1946, DP 329.

21 L.S. MacDowell, 'The Formation of the Canadian Industrial Relations System during World War Two,' *Labour*, 3 (1978), 181.

22 'Speed-up Policy in War Industries,' RG 27, vol. 80, file 401: 55.

23 See R.M. Adams, 'The Development of United Steelworkers of America in Canada, 1936–1951' (unpublished MA thesis, Queen's University, 1952), and I.M. Abella, *Nationalism, Communism and Canadian Labour* (Toronto, 1973), chp. 3.

24 C.H. Millard, *Victory Needs Steel* (published by SWOC, Canadian region, 1942), introduction.

25 *Crisis in Steel* (published by the National Office, USWA, Toronto, 1943).

26 JHD to McGowan, 2 April 1943, DP 212.

27 Millard to W.L.M. King, 21 Aug. 1942, and King to Millard, 26 Aug. 1942, King Papers, J1 series, vol. 330.

28 J.W. Pickersgill, *The Mackenzie-King Record, 1939–44*, vol. 1 (Toronto, 1960), 441. King also noted: 'What we prevent even more than what we do is what counts most in the long run.'

29 'Labour trouble at Sault Ste. Marie, Aug. 29–Sept. 3, 1942,' memo by T.F. Rahilly, DP 330; Millard, *Crisis in Steel*; and Adams, 'The Development.'

30 'Steel Workers: Algoma Steel Corporation,' strike file, statement of Hon. Humphrey Mitchell, 13 Jan. 1943, RG 27, vol. 424, and Privy Council Order 5963, 14 Sept. 1942.

31 'Majority Report,' *Report* of the Royal Commission appointed to report as to the adjustments (if any) of wage rates of employees in Algoma Steel Corp. Ltd. and Dominion Steel and Coal Corp. Ltd., RG 27, vol. 424.

32 *Crisis in Steel*, 6.

33 Pickersgill, *Record*, 1: 466–74.

34 *Record*, 1: 473.

35 *Crisis in Steel*. There is no direct evidence to substantiate Millard's charge, but Dunn and McTague soon became close friends. See JHD to McTague, 27 April 1944, DP 329.

36 Pickersgill, *Record*, 1: 475.

37 Memo from telephone call, 27 July 1943, DP 330.

38 William Kilbourn, *Elements Combined* (Toronto, 1960), 183ff.

39 Millard to A. MacNamara, 1 July 1946, RG 27, vol. 1744.

40 JHD to the *Financial Post*, 21 Nov. 1945, DP 328.

41 'Interim Report of Justice W.D. Roach,' 16 July 1946, RG 27, vol. 1744, p. 11.

42 M.M. Maclean to J.G. Fogo, 26 June 1946, RG 27, vol. 1744. Fogo agreed that there were 'fewer issues between Algoma and its local than in the case of the other steel companies' (Fogo to Maclean, 2 July 1946, RG 27, vol. 1744).

43 D. Gordon to A. MacNamara, 16 July 1946, RG 27, vol. 1744.

44 JHD to J.G. Fogo, 21 March 1946, DP 329.

45 Hearing of 26 July 1946, Commons Standing Committee on Industrial Relations, *Evidence*, (Ottawa, 1946), p. 295.

46 J.W. Pickersgill and D.F. Forster, *The Mackenzie King Record 1945–46*, vol. 3 (Toronto, 1970), 200–1.

47 C.H. Millard to H. Mitchell, 20 July 1945, RG 27, vol. 1744.

48 Millard to M.M. Maclean, 28 May 1946, RG 27, vol. 1744.

49 'Interim Report of Justice W.D. Roach on Steel Dispute,' 16 July 1946, RG 27, vol. 1744.

50 Ibid.

51 PC 2901, 10 July 1946. Kilbourn was appointed under authority of the National Emergency Transitional Powers Act of 1945.

52 DHC, 16 July 1946, pp. 3488–90, and Pickersgill and Forster, *Record*, 3: 285–6.

53 JHD to J.W. Hobbs, 25 July 1946, DP 329.

54 Toronto *Globe and Mail*, 10 Sept. 1946.

55 RCMP 'O' Division reports, RG 27, vol. 499.

56 All McMillan quotations from Commons Standing Committee on Industrial Relations, 24 July 1946 sitting. Although Algoma was receiving government freight subsidies throughout 1946, McMillan's statement was true in the strictest sense. Algoma did, however, have a guarantee from Howe's department of guaranteed profits of $500,000 a quarter which was held in abeyance during the strike.

57 Glace Bay *Gazette*, 6 Sept. 1946, and statistical information furnished by Murray Cotteril, publicity director of USWA, to Labour Minister Mitchell, n.d., RG 27, vol. 1744.

58 'Submission of U.S.W.A. to Industrial Disputes Inquiry Commissioner,' June 1946, p. 3, RG 27, vol. 1744.

59 'Brockington's proposed settlement,' 15 Aug. 1946, RG 27, vol. 1745.

60 DHC, 21 Aug. 1946, p. 5175.

61 JHD to J. Hobbs, 25 July 1946, and 'Memo of conversation between E.G. McMillan and Hilton of Stelco,' 17 Sept. 1946, DP 330.

62 L.E. Baker, DHC, 21 Aug. 1946, p. 5145.

63 Howe to Mitchell, 20 Sept. 1946, RG 27, vol. 1745, and Pickersgill and Forster, *Record*, 3: 340–1.

64 E.G. McMillan to JHD, 6 May 1949, DP 348.

65 JHD to H.G. Hilton, 26 Jan. 1948, DP 333.

66 Harriet Parsons, 'Our Growing Pains in Steel – A Challenge to Canadians,' *Saturday Night*, 1 Nov. 1949. See also John Marston, 'In Rearming, What about World Steel?' *Saturday Night*, 17 Oct. 1950.

67 JHD to J.G. Fogo, 22 Oct. 1946, DP 329.

68 DHC, 27 March 1947, p. 1814.

69 Draft notes for reply to Hume Wrong, 24 Dec. 1947, Howe Papers, vol. 86.

70 DHC, 19 Dec. 1947, p. 498, and Kilbourn, *Elements Combined*, chp. 12.

71 *Encouragement to Industrial Expansion in Canada: Operation of Special Depreciation Provisions, Apr. 10. 1944–31 March, 1949*, prepared by O.J. Firestone (Ottawa, 1949).

72 JHD to D.S. Holbrook, 7 March 1949, DP 332.

73 Sherman to Howe, 4 Feb. 1949, Howe Papers, vol. 173. For an interesting interpretation of North American business-government relations in the early Cold War, see R.D. Cuff and Granatstein, *Canadian-American Relations in Wartime – from the Great War to the Cold War* (Toronto, 1975), chp. 7: 'Looking Back at the Cold War.'

74 JHD to Howe, 4 April 1949, Howe Papers, vol. 173.

75 Memo by JHD, 12 Oct. 1948, DP 395.

76 *Industrial Canada*, Jan. 1951.

77 C. Gillis, DHC, 2 April 1951, p. 1555.

78 R.B. Elver, 'Economic Character and Change in the Canadian Steel Industry since 1945' (Mineral Information Bulletin MR94, Mineral Resources Branch, Department of Energy, Mines and Resources, Ottawa, 1969), table 4, and Algoma Steel *Annual Report*, 1948–9.

79 Howe to JHD, March 1949, Howe Papers, vol. 173.

80 Elver, 'Economic Character,' 8, and Lucy Morgan, *The Canadian Primary Iron and Steel Industry*, brief submitted to Royal Commission on Canada's Economic Prospects (Ottawa, 1956), chp. 4 and table 11.

81 *Minutes* of Minister's Advisory Committee, 15 Dec. 1947, Howe Papers, vol. 86.

82 H.G. Hilton to Major-General G.B. Howard, 31 Jan. 1949, DP 348.

83 Industial Defence Board, *Minutes* of meetings, 5 May and 6 Oct. 1948, Howe Papers, vol. 197.

84 'Memo: Defence Organization – Ottawa,' H.G. Hilton's office, 1 Feb. 1949, DP 348.

85 DHC, 8 Sept. 1950, p. 459.

86 In 1952, for instance, Howe asked Dunn to report on the European steel situation. Howe to JHD, 11 Oct. 1952, Howe Papers, vol. 179.

87 DHC, 14 June 1951, p. 4095.

88 DHC, 26 June 1950, p. 4175, and 'Have We the Key to Great Steel Famine?' *Financial Post*, 30 Oct. 1948.

89 DHC, 26 June 1950, p. 4175.

90 'Memo: Defence Organization.'

91 JHD to G.M. Humphrey, 11 July 1950, DP 334.

92 DHC, 26 June 1950, p. 4174.

93 DHC, 14 June 1951, p. 4075, and RG 49, vol. 18.

94 'Summary of Expenditures Necessary to Increase Iron and Steel Production and Produce Additional Rolled Products – Algoma Steel Corp. Ltd.,' prepared by D.S. Holbrook, 12 April 1951, Algoma Steel Historical Files and Algoma Steel *Annual Report*, 1955.

95 Holbrook to JHD, 29 May 1954, DP 339.

96 'In five years we have doubled our ingot production: 1950 – 300,000 tons; 1955 – 600,000 tons,' F.A. Sherman of Dofasco wrote Howe on 24 September 1955. 'We spent over $50,000,000 ... This, of course, would not have been possible without accelerated depreciation.' Howe Papers, vol. 195. See also Kilbourn, *Elements Combined*, chp. 12, and J.H. Dickey, DHC, 11 Dec. 1953, pp. 580–1.

97 DHC, 7 May 1953, p. 4924.

98 Howe to Sherman, 30 Sept. 1955, Howe Papers, vol. 195.

99 Howe to Sherman, 3 Jan. 1956, Howe Papers, vol. 184.

100 Howe to D.S. Holbrook, 31 May 1956, Howe Papers, vol. 185.

101 JHD to Essington Lewis, 9 May 1947, DP 331.

102 JHD to J.G. Fogo, 21 March 1946, DP 329, and JHD to J.A. McPhail, 15 Feb. 1946, DP 330.

103 D.S. Holbrook to JHD, 26 Oct. 1950, DP 334.

104 R.B. Elver, 'Economic Character.'

105 'A Brief on behalf of Algoma Steel Corp. Ltd.,' re: application of Railway Association of Canada, 5 Feb. 1947, Algoma Steel Historical Files.

106 JHD to J.G. Fogo, 28 Nov. 1949, DP 332.

107 JHD to E.G. McMillan, 25 Oct. 1948, DP 332.

108 *Minutes of Directors' Meetings*, 20 Nov. 1948.

109 McLaughlin to JHD, 4 Sept. 1951, DP 242.

110 Montreal *Star*, 6 Dec. 1951.

111 JHD to Holbrook, 25 March 1955, DP 339. Clergue had in fact incorporated a tube works in 1902, but predictably it had failed.

112 JHD to Humphrey, 18 Dec. 1947, DP 329. Dunn also corresponded with Cyrus Eaton, head of Steep Rock Iron Mines, and was rumoured at one point to have refused an offer to buy out Eaton's Steep Rock holdings.

113 JHD to Humphrey, 20 Dec. 1946, DP 329.

114 JHD to R. Adeane, 8 March 1947, DP 208.

115 *Evening News*, Sault, Michigan, 5 Aug. 1947.

116 JHD to Beaverbrook, 29 Dec. 1949, DP 216. See also JHD to M.L. Duplessis, 17 July 1952, DP 225. See Conrad Black, *Duplessis* (Toronto, 1977), chp. 18.

117 Humphrey to W.H. Durrell, 27 March 1950, Howe Papers, vol. 176.
118 DHC, 23 Feb. 1948, p. 1518.
119 4 Jan. 1949.
120 Montreal *Star*, 6 Oct. 1952.
121 Algoma Steel, *Annual Report*, 1951–2, and G.W. MacLeod to JHD, 3 April 1952, DP 336.
122 V.C. Wansbrough, 'Implications of Canadian Iron Ore Production,' CJEPS, 16 (1950), 239.
123 N. Ward, ed., *A Party Politician: The Memoirs of Chubby Power* (Toronto. 1966), 394–7. See also 'July and August 1951,' in 'Political Jottings,' Power Papers, Queen's University Archives, box 1.
124 McLagan to JHD, 23 Feb. 1954, DP 338.
125 Howe to H.R. Milner, 2 April 1955, Howe Papers, vol. 183.
126 Howe to Lady Dunn, 12 April 1957, Howe Papers, vol. 138.

CONCLUSION

1 London *Evening Standard*, 13 March 1954.
2 JHD to B. Fairless, cable, 18 May 1954, DP 340.
3 JHD to Hon. A.L. MacDonald, 17 Dec. 1945, DP 215. Reacting to Truman's presidential victory of 1948 and the proposed nationalization of the British steel industry, Dunn confided to Senator T.A. Crerar: 'All this is so contrary to your idea and mine that individualism has developed the world as it is or was before the Roosevelts and similar like people in Britain began to upset it.' JHD to T.A. Crerar, 18 Nov. 1948, Crerar Papers, Queen's University Archives, vol. 88.
4 JHD to C.G. Power, 14 June 1950, DP 222.
5 See Ian Sclanders, 'The Last of the Multimillionaires,' *Maclean's*, 14 Nov. 1950.
6 John Fisher to JHD, 14 Nov. 1950, DP 221.
7 Toronto *Globe and Mail*, 3 Jan. 1956.
8 J.H. Perry, *Taxes, Tariffs and Subsidies: A History of Canadian Fiscal Developments* (Toronto, 1955), 2: 404–7.
9 Charles Parent (Liberal–Quebec West) in DHC, 3 March 1953, p. 2591.
10 R.S. McLaughlin to JHD, 20 July 1955, DP 339.
11 DHC, 28 March 1950, p. 1217. See C.P. Keeping, 'Tax on Undistributed Income of Closely-Held Companies,' *Tax Review*, Sept. 1950, pp. 133–6.
12 See J.H. Perry, 'Development of the Corporation Income Tax in Canada,' *Report of the Proceedings of the Fourth Tax Conference* (Canadian Tax Foundation, Toronto, 1950).

13 B.F. Fairless, *It Could Happen Only in the U.S.* (New York, 1956), 37.

14 J.K. Galbraith, *The New Industrial State* (Boston, 1967), 101. See also J.A. Schumpeter, *Capitalism, Socialism and Democracy* (New York, 1975), chp. 12.

15 Lord Beaverbrook, *Courage* (Fredericton, 1961), p. 263.

16 Beaverbrook to Churchill, 9 Jan. 1956, Beaverbrook Papers, HLRO, file C90.

17 Toronto *Globe and Mail*, 3 Jan. 1956.

18 Howe to D.S. Holbrook, 19 Jan. 1956, Howe Papers, vol. 138.

19 Howe to E.G. McMillan, 26 April 1956, Howe Papers, vol. 138.

20 Howe to D.S. Holbrook, 31 May 1956, Howe Papers, vol. 185.

21 See financial details of Dunn Estate in vol. 138 of the Howe Papers. The 'windfall' revenues accruing to the federal government from the estates of Sir James Dunn and I.W. Killam were subsequently used to establish the Canada Council. J.W. Pickersgill, *My Years with Louis St. Laurent* (Toronto, 1975), 318.

22 C.D. Howe to E.G. McMillan, 14 April 1956, Howe Papers, vol. 138.

23 C.D. Howe to D.S. Holbrook, 20 Feb. 1956, Howe Papers, vol. 138.

24 Howe to E.G. McMillan, 25 April 1956, and Lady Dunn to Howe, 11 March 1957, Howe Papers, vol. 138.

25 *Financial Post*, 20 April 1957, and Toronto *Daily Star*, 20 April 1957. Mannesmann took 200,000 shares or 14 per cent of total stock; A.V. Roe, 150,000 or 10.5 per cent; McIntyre Porcupine, 100,000 or 7 per cent; and the Royal Bank, 50,000 or 3.5 per cent. In May 1957 Algoma split its 1.4 million shares 4:1, at the same time cancelling 225,030 shares held by its subsidiaries in the parent company.

26 DHC, 29 June 1956, pp. 5525–9.

27 DHC, 12 April 1957, p. 3503.

28 DHC, 29 June 1956, p. 5541.

29 DHC, 12 April 1957, p. 3503.

30 DHC, 12 April 1957, p. 3506.

31 *Royal Commission on Canada's Economic Prospects: Public Hearings*, Toronto hearing of 30 Jan. 1956, RG 33/35, p. 5437.

32 Royal Commission on Canada's Economic Prospects, *Final Report* (Ottawa, 1957), 217 and 218–29.

33 Hearing of 30 Jan. 1956.

34 *Report by the Tariff Board: Relative to the Investigation Ordered by the Minister of Finance Respecting: Basic Iron and Steel Products* (Reference no. 118, Ottawa, 1957), p. 53.

35 Jacques Singer, *Trade Liberalization and the Canadian Steel Industry* (Toronto, 1969), 3.

36 Mr Justice W.Z. Estey, *Steel Profits Inquiry Report* (Ottawa, 1974), 115.

37 See, for instance, Roderick Oram, 'Canadian Steel Industry Is Considered among the Best,' Toronto *Globe and Mail*, 12 Nov. 1977.

38 Sault *Daily Star*, 3 Jan. 1956. All Algoma performance statistics from Algoma Steel *Annual Reports*, 1954–76.

39 See A.V. Orr, chairman, *A Report by the Sector Task Force on the Canadian Primary Iron and Steel Industry* (Ottawa, 1978).

40 Paul Tiffany, 'Industrial Policy and the Decline of the American Steel Industry,' *Journal of Contemporary Business*, 11: 1 (1982), 58.

41 See Thomas O'Boyle, 'Steel's Management Has Itself to Blame,' *Wall Street Journal*, 17 May 1983.

42 DHC, 14 March 1879, p. 421.

43 R. Cook and R.C. Brown, *Canada 1896–1921: A Nation Transformed* (Toronto, 1974), 87.

Index